An
English-Spoken Khmer
= D I C T I O N A R Y =

An
English-Spoken Khmer
= D I C T I O N A R Y =

With Romanized Writing System

Usage and Idioms

and Notes on Khmer Speech and Grammar

Allen P. K. Keesee

KEGAN PAUL INTERNATIONAL
London and New York

First published in 1996 by
Kegan Paul International
UK: P.O. Box 256, London WC1B 3SW, England
Tel: (0171) 580 5511   Fax: (0171) 436 0899
E-mail: books@keganpau.demon.co.uk
Internet:http://www.demon.co.uk/keganpaul/
USA: 562 West 113th Street, New York, NY 10025, USA
Tel: (212) 666 1000   Fax: (212) 316 3100

Distributed by
John Wiley & Sons Ltd
Southern Cross Trading Estate
1 Oldlands Way, Bognor Regis
West Sussex, PO22 9SA, England
Tel: (01243) 779 777   Fax: (01243) 820 250

Columbia University Press
562 West 113th Street
New York, NY 10025, USA
Tel: (212) 666 1000 Fax: (212) 316 3100

© Allen P.K. Keesee 1996

Printed and bound in Great Britain by
T. J. Press (Padstow) Ltd.

British Library Cataloguing in Publication Data

Keesee, Allen P.K.
English-Spoken Khmer Dictionary: With
Romanized Writing System, Usage and
Idioms, and Notes on Khmer Speech and Grammar
I. Title
495.932321
ISBN 0-7103-0514-1

Library of Congress Cataloging-in-Publication Data

Keesee, Allen P.K.
An English-spoken Khmer dictionary : with romanized writing
system, usage, and idioms, and notes on Khmer speech and grammar /
Includes bibliographical refrences
Allen P.K. Keesee
ISBN 0-7103-0514-1
1. Khmer language--Dictionaries--English
PL4326.K44   1995
495.9'32321--dc20   95-8393
CIP

แด่
แคน ตา นวย
("ต้า"),
นักรบผู้กล้าหาญชาญชัย

Introduction

By 1995, Cambodia, for years a society torn by war, had become one beset by a range of new problems arising out of the relative peace brought by the suspension of the country's civil war in 1991 and United Nations-supervised elections in 1993 -- problems including how to achieve "sustainable" development in the face of rapid population growth, high unemployment and on-going environmental deterioration; how to combine social equity with a new free-market environment; how to construct something at least as difficult to build as Angkor Wat -- competent government.

With the shift in Cambodian attention from military to econo-social matters has come an increase in tourism, foreign investment, the NGO/multilateral-institution/diplomatic presence and the general level of "foreign" travel to and residence in Cambodia. Many of the non-Khmer associated with this development, whether short-term visitors or potential long-term residents, and whether or not from English-speaking countries, have either a native or a working knowledge of English. Many may also have an interest in acquiring some knowledge of Khmer. It is for such visitors to, and residents in, the Kingdom, as well as for students outside Cambodia, that this book has been prepared. It attempts to present, in a simplified Romanized form, the Khmer language as it is spoken both in Phnom Penh and in the countryside today; it focuses, that is, on the sound of the language and its working structure rather than on the grammatical rules or word spellings of the written language. Emphatically, it does not attempt "letter-for-letter" transliterations of written Khmer.

The system of transliteration used here relies to an appreciable extent on letter combinations not found in English ("hh" and "ooo", for example); requires close attention to the phonetic key provided later in this volume; and is in no sense "simple". It strives, however, to convey Khmer sounds with Roman letter combinations that spontaneously, for one familiar with English, "lead" to that Khmer sound: using, for example, "aae" to convey the Khmer sound similar to an English long A. The system used here also avoids the non-Roman sound symbols -- lambda's, theta's, backward "c"s, etc. -- , found in some language manuals, which often seem to take as long to master as the target language itself. Hopefully, these approaches will make acquisition of spoken Khmer a more rapid and pleasant process.

Every effort has been made to proof the text carefully to achieve consistency in transliteration, cull out typographical errors and render Khmer letter-sounds accurately. Inconsistencies, however, undoubtedly remain, and for this the user's indulgence is requested.

In addition to the hundreds of Cambodians I have had the pleasure of meeting over past years, both in Cambodia and the United States, all of whom have contributed to my understanding of spoken Khmer, special thanks for invaluable assistance in the preparation of this volume are due to Phalla Teng Chey, Phally Kem Teng, Chandara Chey Kem, Borasmy Ung, Marina Keo, Sokheartha Chhim, Sokhon Pheng and Samol Chuan, and for first suggesting the need for this volume, to Sok Sinan. Errors in the text are, of course, my responsibility alone.

Allen P. K. Keesee, Bangkok, June 1995

Transliteration/Pronunciation Key

The sounds of the spoken Khmer language have been transliterated into Roman script in this book according to the following system:

Vowels:

"A" sounds:

ae, ay, aae	=	long A as in "<u>a</u>viator" or "<u>a</u>ce"; used, i.e., in "sraae" (woman) and "choo'ay" (help); the "aae" sound is a bit longer than the "ay" or "ae" sounds and is usually heard as a last, rather than an early or middle, syllable.
ey, e'	=	mid-way between long A and the opening "eh" of "every"; used, i.e., in "prey" (forest) and "te'ang" (all)
ei	=	mid-way between long A "aae" and long I "eye"
aa at end of syllable, or ah, a, or o	=	short "ah" sound as in "<u>o</u>tter" or "o" as in "<u>o</u>live; used, respectively, in, i.e., "ro'bah" (thing), "to'la'ka" (court), "bot"(lost), "klaah" (some) and "baa" (if)
aa followed by any consonant except h	=	"a" as in "<u>a</u>pple" or "<u>a</u>sset"; used, i.e., in "kaan kaab" and "kaat"
aw	=	aw as in "<u>aw</u>ful"
auw	=	ow sound as in "<u>ou</u>ch" or "h<u>ou</u>r"
awh	=	aw, "<u>aw</u>ful", with aspiration
eaou	=	as in "me<u>ow</u>"; used, i.e., in "eye leaou" (now) and T'keaou (province name)

"E" sounds:

i in middle or at end of syllable; ee	=	long E as in "<u>e</u>vent"; used, i.e., in "ti" (here), "ni" (this), chia (like, as), "pieh" (part), "dow'ee" (by) and "ka'neea" (like)
e between two consonants	=	short e as in "<u>e</u>ver"; used, i.e., in "kej" (thing)
eu	=	eu as in "<u>e</u>arth"
euu	=	i'yoo as in "<u>U</u>tah" or "<u>U</u>lysses"

2

"I" sounds:

eye, y-[consonant]-e, ye, ai	=	long I as in "ivy"; used, i.e., in "sreye" (rice paddy), "chyke" (divide, distribute), "dum'bye" (for, in order to), and "tlai" (expensive)
i before "t"	=	short i as in "if"; used, i.e., in "chee'it" (national) and "k'mau'it" (ghost)
yng	=	ing

"O" sounds:

o or o' followed by "h" or nothing; oe; or o-[any consonant]-e	=	long O as in "oval"; used, i. e., in "koh" (wrong, bad), pdo (change), do (change), "to'h" (wrong), "po't" (corn), "to'tool" (receive); "ploe" (road); and "jchole" (come)
o followed by consonant other than "h"	=	short "o" as in "olive"; used, i.e., in "mwot" (mouth), "muon" (chicken), "bot" (lost) and "doll" (up to, until)
ong	=	"ong" sound of "long"
ow, au, ao, auw	=	ow sound as in "tower" or "hour"
oo, ooo, ooo'	=	long U sound as in "loot"
oi or oy	=	oi as in "ointment"
eau	=	"e" as in "else", followed by long O, as in French rd for "water" (eau); used, i.e., in "peau" (youngest) and "l'peau" (pumpkin)

"U" sounds:

u or uu at end of syllable, or oo, ooo, or ooo' in middle or at end of syllable	=	long U sound as in "loot"; used in "nu" (that), "kruu" (teacher), "loo'h" (to sell), "toook" (a small boat) and "tooo'b" (to restrain)
u at the start, or in the middle, of syllable	=	short u sound as in "under"; used in "um'bul" (salt), "kut" (to think), "la'ut" (small), etc.
uu in middle of syllable	=	oo sound as in "book"; used, i.e., "kom'puung" (boat landing), "chuum" (camp) and "chuun" (people)

Consonants:

b and p --

In Khmer the pure "b" sound is expressed by the letter "baw", with no accent mark (called a "pun'taw(k)" or "sala") above it, when "baw" occurs at the beginning of a word. When "baw" without a "sala" appears at the end of a word, it receives in spoken Khmer a pronunciation which is mid-way between "b" and "p" but slightly closer to "p". "Baw" at the end of a word with one "sala" is even closer to "p".

"Baw sala pi" -- baw with two sala's -- is used only at the beginning of words and has a distinct "p" sound; it appears at the beginning of such words as "pu'man", "pun'ha", "pun'ta'aae" and "Pali". A distinct "p" sound is also given to the letters "paw", "po", "phaw", and "pho". Because of the "p" sound associated with "baw" without sala and "baw" with one sala at the ends of words, ending "baws" in this transliteration will be rendered as "p" rather than "b".

ch and jch --

The Khmer alphabet contains four letters that represent most "j" and "ch" sounds in spoken Khmer. The Khmer names of the letters are jchaw, chhaw, jcho and cho. Their sound values may be described as follows:

1) Jchaw is often transliterated into English as "jch", as, for example, in the words "jchaan" (plate) and "jchole" (to enter). Following convention, jchaw will be generally be transliterated herein as "jch", but with the admonition that its pronunciation in many words has a sound which to English speakers may seem closer to a "ch" (as, say, in "church") than to a "j" (as, say, in "judge") and that where the "ch" bias is particularly strong, jchaw may be transliterated as "ch".

2) Chhaw is often transliterated into English as "chh" rather than simply "ch" to suggest that its "h" sound   is quite pronounced, somewhat as is the "h" in the English name "Chuck". That "chh" convention will generally be followed here. Khmer words with "chhaw" include "chh'mar (cat), "chhn'aang" (pot), "chh'nam" (year) and "chhoo'ah" (pain).

3) Jcho, despite sometimes being transliterated as "jch", has a sound closer to "ch" than to "j". It will therefore be transliterated here as "ch". Khmer words with jcho include "chuun" (people) and "chee'it" (nation).

4) Cho is pronounced close to the English sound "ch" and will be transliterated herein as "ch". Khmer words with "cho" include "choh" (to stand up) and "chamoo'h" (name).

gk -- an amalgam of "g" and "k"; a cross between the "g" of "gunk" and the "k" of Kelly".

h -- adds aspiration, as does the "h" in the American Indian name "Tecumseh" and is used to emphasize "shortness" of pronunciation of any vowel it immediately follows; in "kuhl" (stump or base of tree trunk), for example, the "h" is used to emphasize the fact that the word is pronounced like the English word "cull" rather than like "cool".

'h at end of syllable -- aspiration similar to the "h" at the end of the American Indian name "Tecumseh".

hh -- stressed aspiration.

j -- see discussion of ch and jch, above.

l and r -- At the beginning and in middle of words, the pronunciation of each of these respective letters is little different from what it would be in English. When a Khmer letter representing either of the two sounds appears at the end of a word, however, it may be difficult for a listener to be sure which sound -- that of "l" or of "r" -- he or she is hearing. Transliterations in the text are determined by which of the two sounds seems to be the most often heard. One of the words for "time", for example, is written in Khmer with an ending letter that represents the sound of "l"; in speech, however, it is arguably more often heard as ending with an "r" sound. Hence in the text the word is written not "peyl" but "peyr".

Additionally, the Khmer letter whose name is pronounced approximately "ar" when found at the end of words tends to be pronounced in a way that can be heard either as "ah" or "ar" or "a(r)" (a very faint "r" sound (similar to some Australian pronunciations of the letter "a" coming at the end of a word)) or even "ahl". In the text, words ending in this letter are trans- literated according to which -- for the Khmer word in question -- of these alternatives seems the most heard in speech. For example:

English word	written in Khmer	most commonly pronounced and so written in text as...
if	baar	baa'
to walk	dahr	dah
journey	dum'naar	dum'naar
to send, keep	p'nyar	p'nya(r)

nyh -- similar to, but not as distinctly pronounced as, sound of "ny" in Russian "nyet"); the word "banyh", (to fire, e.g., a gun), for example, is not pronounced "bani" or "bonny" but closer to "ban'yuh".

p -- see discussion of "b and p", above.

ph -- the sound of an asphirated "p", not of an "f".

th -- as in "throw" or "theory".

y -- "y" more as in "Yugoslavia" than in "yes", i. e., with a very slight "j" sound in front of it; this pronunciation would be heard, for example, in the Khmer words "yun hawh" (airplane) and "yeung" (we).

AP -- "alternate pronunciation"; this aspect of Spoken Khmer is discussed, and examples are given, in the <u>Notes on Khmer Grammar and Speech</u> section below.

NB -- ("nota bene"); introduces commentary or information related to a word or phrase being defined or used in a usage-illustrative sentence.

S -- "slang"

( ) around a consonant at the end of a word indicates that the sound of the consonant is barely heard. Prominent examples would be words ending in "ch" such as "klait(ch)" (fear) and klao'ee(ch)" (burned) in which the "ch" is almost silent.

" ' " -- referred to herein as a "separator" -- is used to separate Khmer syllables which, taken together, have a given meaning (usually single- or two-word) in English; for example, the syllables making up the cluster "a'noo'sow'ree" mean "souvenir" or "memory"; those making up "chng'anyh" mean "delicious"; those in "s'ta'ni laan ch'nool" mean "bus station"; those in "t'nam" mean "medicine", etc.

Separators have been used both when the Khmer word or phrase is given as a definition and when it appears in a usage-illustrative sentence or phrase on the theory that in both instances they are a useful aid to correct pronunciation. Their value in long words -- such, for example, as "twa'ma'chee'it" (natural) or "praw'teea'neea' tep'a'dye" (president) -- is fairly clear, and even in short words they are helpful. The word for "eye", for example, is rendered in the text is rendered "pn'aae'k". To omit the " ' " markers and render the transliterated word merely as "pnaaek" could arguably open the door to erroneous pronunciations such as "pnaa'ek" or "pna'aek".

The specific sorts of situations in which use of one or more separators might assist in proper pronunciation would include:
1) those in which certain letters which might otherwise seem to go naturally together should in fact be pronounced as parts of separate syllables, viz: the word "a'veye" in which the "a" should be pronounced separately from the other letters in the word, but which, absent the separator, might be taken as "av'eye" or "avey'e", both incorrect;

2) those in which certain vowel groups should be broken into separate syllables and not pronounced as a diphthong (examples are "choo'ay" (help) and which, as indicated, contains two separate syllables);

3) those in which it is necessary to indicate that a very slight pause should be given between two letters (for example: there is no pause in "pwa" (color) or "koh" (wrong) but there is after the "p" in "p'ka" (flower) and after the "oh" sound in "to'h" (wrong); and

4) those at the end of a syllable in which one should give a "clipped" emphasis to the last letter thereof; and

5) those where the separator is needed to indicate a certain vowel pronunciation. An example is "ro'ng" (place) which following the Transliteration/Pronunciation Key is pronounced with an English long O sound rather than the English short O sound that would be prescribed by the Key if the transliteration spelling were "rong" (i.e., without separator).

In a few short words, such as "buon", "muon" and "pieh", a separator is not used, it being left to the English speaker's natural inclination to supply the syllable break between vowels.

[   ] -- words in brackets in English illustrative sentences are the definition of the Khmer words in brackets in the matching Khmer sentence. For example, in the sentence pair "He didn't go to the [office] yesterday because he was sick." -- "Gwat mun teuh [kaar'ya'lye] musl'munyh bee'proo'a gwat ot s'bai.", the bracketing indicates that the Khmer word for "office" is "kaar'ya'lye".

The user will note that, as in the example above, many usage-illustrative sentences given in the text are not mere "He drank milk." or "The grass is green." examples but are somewhat more complex. This practice has been followed not to confuse but to further two positive objectives: first, to give the dictionary user a clear idea of how a given Khmer word being supplied as a definition is actually used in Khmer sentence structure; and, second, to stimulate the user -- hopefully -- to look up (and hence learn) words that appear in the usage-illustrative sentence but which he/she may not yet know.

Notes on Khmer Grammar and Speech:

There are three aspects of spoken Khmer that a student, in order to avoid confusion and expedite understanding of the language, should note in particular: obviously, 1) respects in which Khmer grammar differs significantly from English grammar; perhaps less obviously, 2) variations of pronunciation within the boundaries of Khmer speech itself; and 3) similarities between and among certain Khmer words which could be potentially confusing to a beginning student. Each of these areas is discussed in turn below.

1) Major English-Khmer Grammatical Differences:

All translational efforts, beyond confronting the fundamental "literalist/interpretivist" issue of how much to hew to the line of literal rendering, versus how much to seek to bring out essential meaning by using phrases that are word-for-word imprecise but collectively and ultimately correct, must deal with respects in which the grammar of the "foreign" language differs from English.

An awareness of such differences is important to a student not only as an aspect of the grammatical learning process per se but also as a means of minimizing confusion as new words are heard, seen, looked up, etc. To understand target language grammar, that is, is fundamental to being able to readily assimilate new vocabulary. To take a simple example, if one knows that certain Khmer words (such as "teuh" which can mean either "to" or "to go") may function as prepositions as well as as verbs, one will not be confused by encountering, say, "teuh' in a context in which it seems to mean "to" after having first (perhaps) encountered it in a context in which it seemed to mean "to go". If one is unaware of such verb/preposition "doubling", however, one may be momentarily confused as to whether (in the "teuh" case) one is encountering the same word being used in two different ways, or two entirely different words, each with its own meaning.

From this "vocabulary-centric" point of view, the major points to keep in mind about Khmer grammar are the following:

A) Verb Tenses:

Khmer has the following notable verb tense characteri stics:

-- a single present tense rather that the "go/am going/do go" tri-otomy found in English;

-- a single future tense sometimes denoted by a single word -- "nung" -- but often implied by context, rather than the "will go/will have gone/will be going/etc." of English;

-- a past tense frequently established by the word "howi" or "baan" and sometimes by context, but not variegated as is English through its array of "have gone/had gone/did go/went/etc." constructions;

-- identity of infinitive with gerund and declensional forms: i.e., the Khmer word "loo" can mean "to hear"   or, "hearing" or, "I hear, "you hear," etc.;

8

-- the "split verb" construction; here, an initial segment of a verb phrase precedes some intermediary information while the balance of the phrase follows it. For example, "could not find the way to go home" would commonly be expressed "[initial segment] find the way ... [intermediate information] to go home ... [following segment] could not."

Khmer verb tense rules can be summed up as follows:

To express this tense:	use:	as in:
simple past or, context	baan	I have eaten. -- Kyom nyam baan. I went yesterday. -- Kyom teuh musl'munyh.
past perfect + howi	present	I have finished drinking my coffee. -- Kyom puk nyam cafe howi.
future	nung	We will go to Takeo Tuesday. -- Yeung nung teuh T'keaou ong'keea.
	mok chia	It will be difficult to find him. -- Mok chia pi'bah rok keunyh gwat.
present continuous	kom'puung	We are eating. -- Yeung kom'puung nyam bye.
"just"	teup tai; srab tai	They just left two minutes ago. -- Pooh'gkay teup tai (or, srab tai) teuh pi nee'a'tee mok howi.
"about to"	chit jchaap p'daum	They are about to eat. -- Pooh'gkay chit jchaap p'daum nyam bye.
"would have"	jchong da'aae	I would have come, but I had to go to the market. -- Kyom jchong mok da'aae pun'ta'aae kyom tro kaa teuh psa.
"should have"	koo'a tai	He should have gone. -- Gwat koo'a tai teuh.
can, able to	adje	He can't go. -- Gwat teuh mun adje.
May (s.th. take place)	Sum; or,. sum pong; or, sum owi	May God help me. -- Sum preah choo'ay kyom pong.
passive voice	tro or baan or tro baan;	I was robbed. -- Kyom tro baan plun dow'ee.
	or kaw da'aae	Each one was destroyed. -- Moi na kaw ko'itch da'aae.

B) Negation:

Negation is commonly achieved by i) the addition to a phrase of one of several specific words ("mun", "ot" or"k'miun"), sometimes coupled with ii) the deletion from that phrase of a word which had suggested positive action:

i) addition only:

I am going.	-- Kyom teuh.
I am not going.	-- Kyom mun teuh.
There is rice.	-- Bye miun.
There is no rice.	-- Bye ot miun.

ii) addition plus deletion:

There is rice.	-- Bye miun.
There is no rice.	-- K'miun bye. ("miun" deleted)
No more rice.	-- Ot bye. ("miun" deleted)

For moderate emphasis, "tay" may be added to the end of the sentence:

There is no rice.   -- Bye ot miun tay.

For substantial emphasis, the addition can be "ni tay":

There is (absolutely) <u>no</u> rice! -- Bye ot miun ni tay.

C) Verb-Prepositions:

A few verbs in Khmer are used also as prepositions, viz.:

Teuh:

... from here <u>to</u> Kra'ko... -- ... pi ni <u>teuh</u> Kra'ko...
We must <u>go</u> now. -- Yeung tro kaa <u>teuh</u> eye leaou.

Mok:

Give it <u>to</u> me. -- Owi kyom <u>mok</u>.
They will <u>come</u> tomorrow. -- Gkay nung <u>mok</u> s'eye'd.

Praw'chang:

...<u>against</u> the Thais... -- ...<u>praw'chang</u> See'um...
...<u>oppose</u> corruption... -- ...<u>praw'chang</u> pu'ka'ra loi...

D) Singulars and Plurals:

Pluralization is not achieved in Khmer by addition of a letter (i.e., such as "s" in English or "x" in French) or standardized changes of word endings (such as, for example, in Portuguese) but generally either by i) indication of a specific number or a quantity of more-than-one of the item being pluralized, or ii) simple context, viz.:

one cow	-- gko moi k'bal (lit: cow one head)
two cows	-- gko pi k'bal
many cows	-- gko ch'raan
How many cows does he have?	-- Tau(v) gwat miun gko pu'man?

Specifically, the modes of pluralization used in Khmer include the following:

(i) use of a Khmer "number word": We bought six kilos of rice. -- Yeung tinh ung'kaw prum'moi kilo.;

(ii) use in Khmer of multiple nouns as equivalent to single English pluralized word:
I met his parents. -- Kyom choop oeuv'puk m'dye. (lit: I met his father'mother.)

(iii) use of a Khmer word implying a quantity of s. th. (how many, some, etc.):
How [many] children do you have? -- Neh miun gkon [pu'man]?;
He has [some] friends. -- Gwat miun pooh'mah [klaah klaah] (or, [av'eye av'eye]);
They own [many] companies. -- Gkay miun krun'huun [ch'raan].;

(iv) double repetition of nouns, such as using "sraae sraae" to connote "women" (where "sraae" used once can convey either "woman" or "women" depending on context);

(v) no "number" or "quantity" word or doubling used but pluralization made definite in Khmer by context:
Po'sat has good [oranges]. -- Po'sat miun [krau'itch Po'sat] chng'anyh.;

(vi) no "quantity word" used but pluralization implied by context:
Does he have any friends? -- Gwat miun po'mah tay?
Yes, he does have friends. -- Baa, gwat miun po'mah.;
There are three of us; we all need horses. -- Yeung bye neh; yeung te'ang awh tro kaa seh.; and

(vii) use of a specialized term (such as ro'up", as below) indicating pluralization:
one thousand -- moi pwan; thousands and thousands -- ro'up pwan.

E) Possessive Pronouns:

The use of possessive pronouns is more limited in Khmer than in English. "I lost my key.", for example, in Khmer would typically be stated simply as "I lost [key]." -- "Kyom bot [gkon saow]."

F) "And":

"And" connecting nouns or pronouns is generally expressed by use of the Khmer word "nung":

> you and me -- neh nung kyom

"And" connecting verbs or clauses is generally expressed by "howi nung" if the intent is to express "and then", or by context with no specific connector word:

> went and then came back -- teuh howi nung mok venyh
> go and eat -- teuh nyam

G) Multiple Counterpart Words:

As with many language pairs, comparison of English and Khmer discloses numerous instances where there many be only one word for a given concept or action in one of the languages but several "matching" words in the other. The English "uni-concepts" of "eat" and "drink", for example, are expressed in Khmer by a range of words related to (and indicative of) the condition of what is being eaten or drunk, the degrees of familiarity between the speakers'/actors' respective social ranks, etc. There are also several Khmer analogues for the single English word "rice", each expressive of different states the rice may be in: young-in-paddy, older-in-paddy, harvested-but-unmilled, milled, cooked, etc.

H) "Couples":

A distinctive construction in spoken Khmer is the use of two words one after the other (or, "back-to-back") to express a concept which can also be conveyed by one or both of the two words alone. An near-example from English of such a construction would be the terms "flip-flop" or "inner-sanctum", in which the two words together as a unified phrase and also each word individually conveys somewhat the same meaning. Whereas in English such constructions are somewhat unusual, in Khmer they are common, and may take either one of two forms:

i) Two words follow each other, each word having a similar meaning and the two together having that same meaning; examples are:

> to surround   -- huhm, or pwat, or huhm pwat
> to suspect   -- muun'thul, or song'sye, or muun'thul song'sye; or

ii) Two words follow each other, but only one of the words has the same meaning as the meaning of the two words together; examples are:

> famous   -- l'bye, or l'bye l'banyh, but not l'banyh alone
> plate   -- jchaan, or jchaan k'ban, but not k'ban alone.

As illustrated, the two-word, or "couples", construction is used to express adjectival ("l'bye l'banyh"), verbal ("huhm pwat") and noun ("jchaan k'ban") concepts.

1) Noun Markers:

There are several words in Khmer that are used to convert verbs into nouns. The two most common are:

kaa:	to protest -- thaaw'va;	a protest -- kaa thaaw'va
s'kd'eye:	to love -- sra'laanyh;	love -- s'kd'eye sra'laanyh

Three others are commonly found as parts of multi-syllable nouns:

pheap:	peace -- san'ti'pheap
kej:	economy -- set'a'kej;
kaam:	agriculture -- kaah'se'kaam

2) Variations Within Khmer Speech:

a) Overview -- Varieties of Variation:

Beyond the obvious "external" differences between English and Khmer grammar, a student of Khmer must also contend with variations internal to Khmer -- the fact, that is, that the spoken Khmer "language" is a confluence of three "languages" -- the standard, or "classroom" version; slang; and rural dialectical variations -- and that even "classroom" Khmer, when spoken at a normal conversational pace, subjects "textbook" pronunciations to substantial torque and distortion. In essence, the problem in Khmer, as in most languages, posed by such intra-lingual variation is that a large proportion of the core vocabulary can be pronounced at least two somewhat different ways, and a large handful -- perhaps forty-to-fifty -- of core words may have four or five different commonly-heard pronunciations.

A number of Khmer terms are used to refer to different elements of the modern Khmer language.

"Pee'esa A'saw" translates as "written Khmer", a version of the language that tends to include a substantial number of words that are closer to Pali forms than words in the spoken language.[1]

"Pee'esa Sa'muun" refers to the language as ordinarily spoken, a standard vernacular Khmer.

The sort of words that in English are typically referred to as "slang" -- not part of the "textbook" language nor of a rural dialect nor of technical jargon, but a sort of "lingo" on its own -- may in Khmer be called "pee'esa jchum awh", "pee'esa tee'up tauk" or "pee'esa ch'leu'ee", all of which terms connote something low-class, cheap or irregular. Particularly rough or crude slang is referred to as "pee'esa bot p'sa", or "bottom-of-the-market talk".

---

[1]An example would be the words for "meeting": spoken sa'muun would use "pra'choom", written Khmer (closer to Pali), "ong'pra'choom". A few words like "ong'pra'choom" which are basically written forms but which are used occasionally in speech are included in the text with the remark "written form".

Modern spoken Khmer is treated in this volume as consisting in "pee'esa sa'muun" plus "slang" (including a very few words of "bot p'sa"), plus a selection of commonly heard words from what may be called "Rural Dialect".[2]

Some cognizance is taken in the text of written forms when, as occasionally, the Romanization of a Khmer word given in the text differs markedly (in order to better convey the way in which the word is pronounced in Khmer) from a what a "letter-by-letter" transliteration of the way the word is written in Khmer would yield. In these situations, the "letter-by-letter" rendition is provided simply to alert the student to the fact that the written form may include letters substantially different from what the transliterated spoken form would suggest.[3]

With the exception of a few words that are principally used in written Khmer rather than in standard spoken "pee'esa sa'muun"but which nevertheless may wander into conversation from time to time (much as might "disestablishmentarianism" or the legal phrase,"now, therefore" in English), the vast bulk, in spoken Khmer, of variations (mainly in pronunciation but occassionaly even in entire words themselves) from sa'muun consist in i) "slang", ii) Rural Dialect, iii) what may be called "Accelerated Speech" (i.e., a quick or "chatty" conversational pace as opposed to the slower, more deliberate pace one might use, for example, in a business conversation or academic or governmental meeting context); and iv) idiosyncratic "personal variations" (having nothing to do with slang, rural origins or pace of speech) in the way individuals choose to pronounce sa'muun words.

To take these sources of variation one by one:

"Slang" tends to add mainly new words (i.e., words not found in sa'muun) rather than differing pronunciations of sa'muun words. Rural Dialect tends to add both a) new words and b) pronunciations of sa'muun words which vary from the generally sa'muun pronunciations one would hear in Phnom Penh. "Accelerated Speech" adds not new words but pronunciations which, because they are rapid, tend to compress the sounds of the syllables of the word being spoken ("teuh howi", for example, becomes "teh' hi"). "Personal variations", finally, tend to add only non-standard (sometimes hyper-compressed; sometimes with a consonant arbitrarily changed) pronunciations of sa'muun words.

Granting that virtually all words in Khmer, as indeed in all languages, are subject to some variation in pronunciation from region to region, and indeed, from individual to individual, where a particular Khmer word has in addition to its "standard pronunciation" an additional (i.e., Rural, Accelerated, or "personal variation") pronunciation which is especially and very widely used or commonly heard, that additional pronunciation is considered for the purposes of this volume an "Alternate Pronunciation", or "AP". When such a Khmer word is transliterated in the text as the (or as a part of the) definition of an English word, the Alternate Pronunciation is also given, preceded by the initials AP. For example: reply -- jchum'la'wee (AP: ch'la'wee).

---

[2] Not including words from separate regional dialects like "Pasa Suay" (used in parts of northeast Thailand and adjacent areas of Cambodia) and Khmer Leuh (used primarily by hill tribes in Rattanakiri and Mondolkiri).

[3] For example, the transliteration of the word for "you" or "people" -- presented throughout the text as "neh", effectively its sound as pronounced -- would, if transliterated to match the written form of the Khmer word letter-for-letter, be closer to "nia'k". "Nia'k" is mentioned in the definition of "you" and "people" to alert the user to the fact that the written form of the word is significantly different from its pronounced form.

b) New Words from "Slang":

The use of slang in Khmer is arguably less extensive than in some other languages regularly encountered by practitioners of English. "Slang" words, for example, appear to be less pervasively used in Khmer than are terms from "branche" in French.

Such "slang" (including "pee'esa bot psa") words as there are often take the form of abbreviations of sa'muun words which truncations are so extreme as to create new words rather than to represent mere "alternate pronunciations".

An example of an abbreviation forming such a "new" word is the "slang" word for "embassy" -- "'toot". In the text, "toot" is treated as being different enough from the "standard" (or, sa'muun) word for "embassy" -- "s'tahn'toot" -- to constitute not just an "Alternate Pronunciation" but a separate word altogether.

Other examples of "new words" found in "slang" would include:

English --	sa'muun	slang
watch	ni'a'li'ka	lee'li'ka
love	sra'lannyh	lang, lang
what	a'vaae	eye
yes	baat	eu'h[4]

c) New Pronunciations and New Words from Rural Dialect:

Among examples of "new words" from Rural Dialect, some of the most common Phnom Penh/countryside variations encountered are the following:

	Phnom Penh	Rural
father --	pa	oeuv'puk
week --	su'pa'da	a'tthit
five --	pay'am	praa'm
seven --	prum'pul	praa'm pi
here --	ti ni	eye'neh

---

[4]"Eu'h" is a relatively unique word. Acceptable as conveying "yes" in Khmer if used among close friends or by an older family member to a younger, it is considered uncouth, even more so than "yeah" in English, if used in addressing individuals in categories other than those. Despite its in-this-respect slightly unsavory character, however, "eu'h" is one of the extremely few words common not only to Khmer, Thai and Lao (which share many words) but also to Vietnamese. Its usage in all four languages -- acceptable among close friends/family, rude otherwise -- is the same. Among the very few other words so shared by the four languages are a set of words meaning mother, all pronounced roughly "meh".

15

"Alternate" rural pronunciations (akin to changing "you all" to "y'all" in English) would include:

to come --	mao	mok
to go --	teuh	toeh
you --	neh	nee'eh
mother --	ma	ma'dye
not --	ot	et
chillie spicy --	hull	hahl

Generally, it is the Phnom Penh pronunciation that is used in the text, both when a Khmer word is offered as a definition and when it is included in a usage-illustrative sentence. Romanization in the text of all Khmer words is based on their most common pronunciation, with Alternate Pronunciations (or, APs) supplied also in cases where they are frequently encountered.

d) "Alternate Pronunciations" from "Accelerated Speech" and Personal Variations:

"Alternate Pronunciations" can, as noted, spring (as well as from slang) from Accelerated Speech or simple individual preferences in pronunciation of sa'muun words. While these sources of variation are found in virtually all linguistic environments -- (in English, for example, there are both Accelerated Speech ("c'mere") and personal variations (occassionally pronouncing cigar as "cee-gar"; saying "cannot" instead of "can not"; emphasizing as one chooses either the first or the third syllable of the word "cigarette"; etc.)) -- , in Khmer, the degree to which APs occur is high and can present problems for a student of the language unaware of what sort of transformations he/she is hearing.

The types of pronunciation changes produced by Accelerated Speech and personal variations tend to be three:

i) the frequent non-pronunciation of ending consonants ("gwat" (he) becoming "gwa", "mok" (to come) becoming "mo'", etc.);

ii) the dropping or changing of beginning consonants ("roo" (or) becoming "oo"; mun seou" (hardly) becoming "puum seou"; the pronunciation of the ending negative marker "tay" as "day", thus changing the Khmer of "I won't go." from "Kyom mun teuh tay." to "Kyom mun teuh day."); and

iii) the compression, as a result of the language being spoken at a normal "conversational", as opposed to a "classroom", pace, of multi-syllables to fewer or shorter syllables. Ready examples from Khmer are the compression of the three-syllable "chia moi" into the two-syllable "chi'moi"; and of the single-syllable "mok" to an even shorter mono-syllabic form, "m'". Examples from English of such compression variations would be the election to pronounce t-o-d-a-y closer to "t'day" than to "too-day"; to pronounce "hurry up" as "hurr'yup"; or to pronounce "going to" as "gonna". (Compression variations appear a feature of virtually all languages, viz., the French "puis je" becoming "pui'j", the Haitian Creole "mwen" ("I, me") regularly contracting in speech to "m'", the Thai "ma ni" ("come here, or come") contracting to "ma'", the Arabic "wela" ("and", or "then") contracting to "w'", etc.).

Interesting examples of the extent and degree of the changes normal Khmer conversational modalities (i.e., the spectrum of Accelerated Speech/ personal variation phenomena -- the dropping and changing of beginning/ending consonants, and the compression of sounds) can wreak on "classroom" Khmer are found, among other places, in the dialogues in the tape cassette/ handbook sets created by the U.S. State Department's Foreign Service Institute for its basic Khmer language course. There, the letters printed in the Handbook version of a given practice sentence -- ostensibly transcriptions of the words being spoken on the tapes -- in many instances hardly correspond at all with the sounds of the spoken language as heard on the cassettes.

The tapes indeed provide good examples of actual day-to-day conversational Khmer in which "standard", or "textbook", pronunciation is generally replaced by compressed and otherwise altered word sounds on a wholesale basis. Two brief sentences (not from the tapes) may illustrate this transformational process. 1) The sentence which in "textbook" (or Handbook) form -- i.e., with all sounds of the word as written in Khmer more or less properly written out -- means "Why did I even meet you?" would be in Khmer "Hyte eye kyom keunyh neh?"; spoken in conversation, however, it would sound much more like "Hat eye 'yom keu' ne'?". 2) Similarly, the sentence which would translate as "Why are you so sad?" in textbook form would be "Mutch baan neh mok ch'ooo maleh?" but in spoken form could sound like "Mek baan mo' ch'ooo m'eh?". It is to assist the the user of this volume to follow such conversational twists and turns that Alternate Pronunciations are provided for a number of the Khmer words given as definitions..

Some of the more common of these APs are listed below; the "standard" pronunciation is given first:

all	--	tang awh, te'ang awh
already	--	howi, hi', 'eye
also	--	da'aee, dai, doi
American	--	A'maae'ri'cang, A'kaae'eng, Am'rik
answer	--	jch'la'wee, jchum'la'wee
arrive	--	dull, doll, dul
bad	--	a'krah, a'kraw
bamboo	--	russei, uh'ssei
book	--	s'po, see'a po
close to	--	chit, chet
come	--	moe'k, mok, mao, ma, m'
come here	--	mao ti ni, mok'ni, m'ne'
electricity	--	ak'ti'cen'ee, 'ti'cen'ee
every	--	rawl, roe'vul, roe'vwul, ru'vul, ruvwul
five	--	prum, pram, pay'am, 'm (as, in "eight o'clock" -- the "textbook" "mao prum'bye" becomes "mao m'bye")
foreign	--	bor'tay, baw'tay, bor'a'tay
friend	--	mit, mut, met
give	--	owi, ow, aw, a
go	--	tueh, toeh, t'
hardly	--	mun seou, puum seou
he/she	--	gwat, gwa, kuh
heart	--	jchet, jchut
help, aid (n. and v.)	--	choo'ay, choo'ee
how much, how many	--	pun'man, pu'man, p'man
I, me	--	kyom, 'yom
like that	--	doj chia nu, doj ch'nu

(a) little	--	tic tic, tek tek
(a) lot, many	--	ch'raan, ch'run, ch'rna, cha'rauw'n
man	--	proh, po
Man or woman?	--	Sraae roo proh?, S'eye oo po?
money	--	loi, low'ee
mouth	--	mwot, ma
no, not	--	mun, men, min, man
one	--	moi, m' (as, "one dish" -- "moi jchan" becomes "m'jchan")
or	--	roo, 'oo
place	--	cunlye'ng, cum'lyne, kun'lyne, ka'line, ka'lye
riel (currency)	--	riel, hiel
see, find, meet	--	keunyh, keu'
seven	--	prum pi, prum pul (as in, "seven o'clock" (mao prum'pi) which becomes mao prum'pul)
slow, late	--	yeut, yeu'
small, little	--	to'ich, tow'ch, toy'ch, to'wich, too'ch
that, which or who	--	dael, da
time	--	mao(ng), mao
watch	--	nee'a'li'ka, nee'ri'ka, lee'li'ka
Where are you going?	--	Neh teuh ti na? , Teuh na?
woman	--	sraae, s'eye
you	--	neh, nee'eh, ne'a, nay'eh

In a few cases, a compressed pronunciation arising from Accelerated Speech is so pervasively used that it cannot be termed "alternate" and is in fact standard. Two prime examples are "chi'moi" -- meaning "with" -- which, as noted above, is a compressed pronunciation of "chia moi", words which are virtually never heard as two distinct successive sounds; and "ma'neh" -- "one person" -- which is a compressed pronunciation of "moi" and "neh", which, again, are virtually never heard as separate successive sounds. Chi'moi and ma'neh are therefore treated in the text not as APs but as standard unified (spoken) words.

3) "Clusters":

A third element of spoken Khmer to which attention should be paid in the learning process is the fact that there are groups, or "clusters", of words in Khmer all of which may have similar sounds or meanings, or sometimes both, and which thereby may be readily confused with one another.

As was the case with the pronunciation variations discussed above, this is not a phenomenon unique to Khmer. Clusters in English, for example, could be seen to consist in the following groups: i) pane (window section), plain (unadorned) and plain (a broad open expanse), all of which sound alike and relate to something open, clear and unobscured; ii) flea (the insect), fly (the insect), fly (move through the air) and flew (move through air, past tense); and iii) drink, drunk, draught and drought, all of which sound somewhat alike and relate to the use of liquids. One of the best examples in English of words that sound very much alike and have similar if-not-identical meanings would be "oldest" and "eldest". Of pairs and groups of words with this degree of aural and content similarity, Khmer has an abundance. Granting that it is judgemental exercise, numerous sets of such similar-sound/ similar-meaning Khmer words can be constructed. With the thought that these very similarities may be the source of some confusion in the learning process, one possible collection of such sets or "clusters" has been set out below to serve a a reference tool to assist in differentiating among Khmer words that do sound, and often mean, alike. If, that is, one a) encounters (for example) the Khmer word "pray(k)", is b) told it means "stream", and reacts c) by thinking, "Yes, but I was sure it meant 'forest'", one may consult in the "Cluster" section below the word set that includes not only pray(k) (stream) and prey (forest) but also several other words with similar sounds to help establish which sound goes with which meaning. The "cluster" sets are as follows:

1)   a'noo   --   deputy, vice, second; to help, assist or support
                --   a'noo'pun   --   attache
                --   a'noo' sena thum   --   division
                --   a'noo' sena eyke   --   captain
                --   a'noo'sow'ree   --   memory, remembrance
                --   a'noo'naaht   --   to approve, authorize
                --   a'noo'vwut   --   to practice
                --   a'noo'mit   --   to pass (legislation)
        a'nutt   --   to pity or feel pity
        nuhk   --   to miss s. o.
                --   nuhk ptay'a   --   homesick
        op'sup   --   lonely
                --   Gwat nuek op'sup.   --   He feels lonely.
        ot'tuun   --   patient
        op'ruhm   --   discipline, training
        a'ro'um   --   to feel an emotion
          -- miun a'ro'um tha tveu koh   --   to feel guilty

2)   baah   --   to force
        -- baah saahk   --   to make hair stand on end
        -- baah bauw   --   to impose views upon
        -- neh baah bauw   --   insurgent
        bauw   --   to pop up, surge, move forward
        ba'oo   --   rice sack
        bauw'ee   --   servant
        bau'hhs   --   to sweep
        baa'baw   --   rice soup
        praw'bo mwot   --   lip
        baa   --   if, otherwise
        baat (AP: baa(t))   --   yes
        bawh   --   to toss
        -- bawh chuum'hee'an   --   to step
        -- bawh jchowl   --   to throw away, abandon
        -- bawh puum   --   to print
        -- bawh ch'nowt   --   to vote
        -- bawh tra leuh sum'buht   --   to stamp/seal a document
        bawh   --   thread

19

3)   bah(k)   --   to break or splinter s.th, esp. items made of wood such as houses, chairs, tables, etc.
    -- bah(k) to'up   --   to defeat
    -- baan bah(k) to'up   --   to be defeated
    -- spee'un bah(k)   --   the bridge collapsed
    -- bah(k) kum'lung   --   to over-work s.o.

    byke   --   to break apart, splinter, re glass, porcelain, TV, etc.
    -- t'nawl byke   --   fork in the road

    baahk   --   to open or turn on
    -- baahk baw (laan)   --   to drive (a car)
    -- baahk pleung   --   to turn on a light
    -- baahk t'veea   --   to open a door
    -- baahk loi   --   to get paid
    -- baahk pra'op   --   to uncover a box
    -- baahk pu'iy   --   to lift off a blanket
    -- baahk ko'hng   --   to open a bank account
    -- baahk owi   --   to allow or permit
    -- baahk haang   --   to open a shop or business

    buhk   --   to collide or husk
    -- tveu toook buhk m'ning   --   to cause trouble for
    -- buhk sro   --   to husk rice
    -- kaa buhk kaneea   --   collision

    bauwk   --   to wash, deceive, thresh
    -- bahwk bauwk   --   to blow hard (as, wind)
    -- bauwk sro   --   to thresh rice

    baw(k) (v-pnun: "boss")   --   to peel
    -- baw(k) chenyh   --   to peel, scrape
    -- baw(k) gkey   --   to speak badly of
    -- baw(k) pr'eye   --   to translate
    -- dawh sr'eye owi   --   to solve

    bahwk   --   to blow (as, wind), fan s.o.

    bo'k   --   to add, calculate

    bot   --   to disappear, vanish, lose s.th.
    -- bot loi   --   to lose money
    -- bot bong chi'vut   --   to lose a life
    -- bot la'meuh   --   a crime
    -- vi'bot   --   a crisis
    -- bot kloo'an   --   missing in action
    -- bot bun'to   --   to refrain

bawt	--	to fold, turn
-- bawt chwayne	--	to turn left
-- ploe bawt	--	the road winds
-- bawt cheung	--	to go to the toilet (lit: to fold one's legs)
butt	--	to turn off, close or shut
-- butt pleung	--	to turn off a light
-- butt t'veea	--	to close a door
-- butt sum'buht	--	to seal a letter
-- butt cha'pooh mwot	--	"ferme ta geule"

4) baan	--	signifies that s. th. i) can be done or ii) has happened; indicates, i.e., i) capability, or ii) past tense
-- (i) Kyom adje teuh Po'sat baan.	--	I can go to Po'sat.
-- (i) baan [tic] baan [to'ich]	--	do-able/done [a little]
-- (ii) Kyom baan nyam	--	I ate.

banyh		
-- banyh jchenyh	--	to take out forcefully, to blow out
-- banyh jchawp	--	to finish, end
-- banyh jchawp sung'kree'um	--	to end a war
-- banyh kum pleung	--	to fire a gun
-- banyh chheh laan	--	to start a car

bum		
-- bum byke	--	to destroy
-- bum plic bum planyh	--	to destroy
-- bum ploo(ss)	--	to exaggerate
-- bum penyh	--	to finish or complete s.th.

bun		
-- bun chope	--	to stop or halt s. th.
-- bun lum	--	to cheat or knock down
-- bun sron	--	to pray or hope
-- bun yul	--	to demonstrate or explain
-- bun jchoh bun jchole	--	to influence
-- bun jchenyh	--	to reveal, "let s.th. out"

bung		
-- bung howi	--	to finish
-- bung kaut	--	to create
-- bung sum'nanyh trei	--	to cast a fishnet
-- bung kaat loi/mit	--	to lose money/a friend
-- bung kaat peyr	--	to waste time
-- bung puun	--	to pay taxes
-- bung roo'inyh	--	to abbreviate
-- bung (kaat) [tro'up sum'baat]	--	to pay [the cost] (of some loss or failure)

5)	ban'tope	--		room
	ban'to'up	--		next in a sequence or series
	-- bun'to'up bun'sum	--		trivial
	bun'twa(t)	--		a line

6)	bun'chee	--		list, written record, account, document, form
	bun'chee'a	--		order or command (written or verbal, military or commercial)
	-- ti bun'chee'a kaa	--		headquarters

7)	banyh	--		(see Cluster Group 4, above)
	sahk lo'bong	--		to test
	l'bong	--		variant of form-of-address "bong" (see, Prepositions)
	l'bye	--		famous
	-- l'bye l'banyh	--		famous
	l'bye'ng	--		game, match, contest
	-- l'bye'ng see sawng	--		gambling
	-- praw'dob k'mayng leng	--		toy

8)	cha	--		fried
	-- bye cha	--		fried rice
	chaa	--		yes (form of response for women)
	chaa(v)	--		raw
	jcha(h)	--		to gouge or bore
	jchik	--		to dig
	choo'ah	--		to fix or repair
	jchao	--		judge
	-- jchao'vye	--		boss, owner
	jchaao	--		thief
	jchowl	--		throw
	gkon chao(v)	--		grandchild

9)	chheh	--		to work, function or burn
	jcheh	--		to know how to
	jchawh	--		to pierce; pierced
	jchaah	--		old, dark (of colors)
	jcho	--		over-ripe
	k'chey	--		green, unripe; to borrow
	chey			
	-- choke chey	--		success
	-- k'miun choke chey	--		failure
	-- chey yo'	--		"Viva"
	jcheyr	--		to curse
	jchayk	--		banana

10)
chh'ooh	--	pain, illness; ill
cheung	--	foot
chh'ung	--	bone
chung'ka	--	chopsticks, drumsticks
cho'un	--	floor or level in a building
ch'rung	--	face or exposed side of object
choong	--	gulf (body of water)

11)
chiang	--	more
chiang	--	one who does work or has a trade
-- chiang ptay'a	--	builder
jchian	--	fried

12)
chii	--	herbs, fertilizer
jchee	--	respectful term of address for older people
-- jchee ta	--	uncle
-- jchee doe'n	--	"grandmother"
jchi	--	to mount, ride, board or sit on
jchik	--	to dig
-- kraw'kye	--	to dig by scratching
jcha(h)	--	to gouge or bore a hole
chuh(s)	--	to scrape
-- ma'seen chuh(s)	--	bulldozer
-- chuh(s) cheu	--	a wood plane (tool)

13)
ch'looay	--	to choke on s.th. (briefly)
ch'laa(k)	--	to choke (seriously)
chuum'loo'a(s)	--	to get into a fight
ch'leu'ee	--	rude

14)
choo'ah	--	to fix or repair
cheu'a	--	to believe
cheu	--	wood
-- daum cheu	--	tree
chreu'reu'	--	to choose

15) ch'ool -- to rent or hire
ch'nool -- rented, hired, for rent
-- laan ch'nool -- taxi
-- tveu ch'nool -- labor
-- ch'nool sa'la -- school fees

16) ch'oooh(k) -- pink
choo'ah -- to fix or repair
chooo -- sour taste; bitter
-- salaw m'chooo -- sweet and sour soup
ch'roo'hk -- pickled
-- ch'roo'hk spay -- pickled cabbage
-- scngau ch'roo'hk muon -- lemon grass chicken soup
jch'roook -- pig
ch'roo'ah -- ravine

17) choop -- to magically make appear
-- choop lee'ung -- a party or feast
-- jchop lee'ung -- mixed fruit and ice drink

choo'up -- to meet

chope -- to stop, halt
-- chope tveu kaa -- to quit (a job, etc.)
-- kaa lee'a chope pi dum'nye'nyh -- resignation

cho'op -- strong, durable
-- cho'op yoo' -- long-lasting
-- cho'op ka'neea -- to stick together, connect
-- bun cho'op -- to join or link
-- cho'op cooo'k -- to be in prison
-- neh cho'op cooo'k -- prisoner

chhop (v-pnun: auto) -- fast; hurry
-- yang chhop -- early
-- chhop laung -- to hurry up

jchaap -- to catch or grab
-- jchaap frang -- to "hit the brakes"
-- jchaap a'rom -- to be interested in
-- jchaap p'daum -- to start or begin
-- jchoke jchaap -- injured
jchawp -- to finish
-- bun jchawp -- to finish
-- rian jchawp -- to graduate
jchahb -- sparrow

24

18)	choon	--	to give or present
	-- choon dum'narr	--	to accompany
	-- choon po'	--	to bless s.o.; "may you be blessed" (may be said as a toast)
	-- choon tuk	--	to give (a glass of) water to s.o. (respectful form)
	choong	--	gulf (body of water)
	chuun	--	person
	jchun	--	China; Chinese (adj.)
	jchung	--	monks
	-- jchung 'aha	--	monks' food
	plun	--	steal, rob

19)	ch'raw't	--	to lean
	-- cheu ch'raw't	--	crutch, cane
	cha'ruk	--	attitude

20)	chuum'looa(s)	--	a fight; get into a fight
	jchun'lawh	--	gap or opening
	jchum'lawh	--	skipping over
	jchum'la'wee	--	to answer; an answer
	-- jch'la'wee	--	answer (v. or n., AP)

21)	chuum'noo'ee	--	aid, help, assistance
	chuum'noo'inyh	--	business
	jchum'nenyh	--	profit
	jchuum'nee'inyh	--	skilled, proficient
	jchum'nan	--	skillful
	chuum'ngeu	--	disease
	chuum'neuu'a	--	religion
	chuum'nooh(s)	--	instead of; to replace or substitute for s.th.
	chuum'looa(s)	--	a fight; get into a fight
	tuk chuum'nuhn	--	flood
	chuum'nuuhm	--	second-hand
	chuum'nay'eh	--	victory
	chuum'nah	--	age of s.th.
	jchum'naut	--	airfield, bus station
	jchum'nowt	--	puzzle
	jchum'nut	--	slice of s.th.
	chuum'no'an	--	era, phase, time in office
	jchum'noo'an	--	amount
	jchum'now'm	--	among

22) chuum'hee'an -- a step
     jchum'ree'ung -- song
     cho'un -- floors/levels of a bldg
     -- cho'un leuh -- step on s. th.
     -- a'ret cho'un -- possessed by a spirit
     chuum ho -- rank; organizational position
     -- kohl chuum ho -- political position
     jchuum'runyh owi -- to urge, influence, advocate
     chuum'venyh -- to be (all) around s. th.

23) da'aae (written da'ee(r)) -- also
     -- aae (or eye) kaw baan da'aae -- whatever, nevertheless
     -- Tau(v) yang na da'aae noeh Po'sat? -- How are things in Po'sat?
     dow'ee -- by means of
     -- yang na kaw dow'ee -- anyhow, anyway, despite
     -- Kyom tro kaa tveu yang na kaw dow'ee -- I have to work anyway (i.e., regardless.)
     dai -- hand, arm
     daiy -- land, earth
     -- sun'dyke daiy -- peanuts
     day -- to sew
     dyke -- metal, iron, steel

24) dah -- to walk
     dah(k) -- to put
     dach -- separated from; able to
     -- pheap dach -- isolation
     -- kaat'pa'dach -- cut (adj.), cut off from

     daw -- which is, which are

     dawh -- to take off or remove
     -- dawh kow-aow -- to take off clothes
     -- adje dawh jchenyh baan -- removable
     -- dawh sr'eye -- to solve or untangle
     -- kaa dawh sr'eye -- settlement amount
     -- ruhm dawh -- to liberate

     dawh -- breast
     -- tuk'dawh'gko -- milk

     dawk -- to take away, subtract
     -- dawk loi -- to withdraw money
     -- dawk hote avwut -- to disarm
     -- dawk hote mok venyh -- to revoke
     -- dawk dung'hauwm -- to breathe, take a breath
     -- dawk praw'op -- to take out of a box

25)	daum	--	original; tree trunk, stalk
	-- daum cheu	--	tree
	-- gkon daum	--	children of first wife
	-- neh daum jchowt	--	plaintiff
	duhm	--	single, unified piece; clump; cube
	-- duhm daiy	--	piece of land
	-- looh duhm	--	to sell wholesale
	-- duhm t'kaw	--	ice cube
	dam	--	to cook; to plant; to grow s. th.
	-- dam bye	--	to boil rice
	-- dam dahm cheu	--	to grow any plant
	-- dam tum'paae'ang bai'ch'ooo	--	to grow grapes
	dos	--	to wash or scrub; to grow naturally (i.e., in nature, without human assistance)
	-- po't dos	--	corn grows
	-- dos tming	--	to brush teeth

26)	daw	--	which is, which are
	dael	--	ever, that, which
	doll	--	to arrive at or attain; for
	pdull	--	to provide or deliver
	pdo	--	to change, move or transfer
	do	--	to change, move or transfer

27)	dop	--	bottle
	dup	--	ten

28)	dum'bawng	--	a stick
	dum'bauw	--	a wound

29)	dum'bole	--	roof
	-- dum'bole miun	--	advice, moral of story
	-- dum'bole ptay'a	--	roof
	kum'pool	--	top, high-point
	dum'bong	--	beginning

30)	dam bye	--	cook rice
	dum'bye	--	to, for, in order to

31)	dum'lung	--	potato
	daum'laung	--	to raise or increase
	-- daum'laung tlaı	--	raise prices
	dum'lye	--	price
	-- owi dum'lye	--	to offer
	dum'nye'nyh	--	social/business position, rank

32)	dum'nak	--	a stop (i. e., on a journey), destination
	-- dum'nak kaa	--	phase
	dum'nall	--	to reminisce or talk about
	dum'nahng	--	to represent
	-- neh dum'nahng ree'eh	--	representative
	dum'nam	--	crops, vegetables
	dum'narr	--	a journey or process; to conduct or operate
	-- choon dum'narr	--	to accompany
	dum'nop	--	jam ("confiture")
	dum'nung	--	information
	dum'naugh sr'eye	--	to solve
	dum'naw	--	joint, knot, link

33)	dum'ro(v)	--	to require
	-- dum'ro(v) jchet	--	to accomodate
	-- sman dum'ro(v) mun tro	--	unexpected outcome
	dum'rong	--	to funnel or direct
	-- dum'rong choo'a	--	make a straight line
	-- kai dum'rong	--	to justify

34)	gkay	--	they, them
	gkay ma'ra'da	--	heritage
	-- jchyke gkay mo'ra'da(k)	--	inheritance
	gko	--	cow
	gko	--	to stir
	gko	--	mute, dumb
	daum gko	--	"cotton" tree
	gkoo(r)	--	a couple

35)	gkon	--	child
	gkun	--	movie
	kaan	--	to follow, believe, hold, grasp
	-- Gwat kaan ses'na Preah Phut.	--	He's Buddhist.
	-- Kyom kaan kang gwat.	--	I'm on his side.

36)	jchaang vaang	--	school principle, company president
	sum jchang	--	to shine
	-- chlawh banyh jchang	--	to reflect
	jchaawng	--	to tie (a rope)
	-- jchaawng dai	--	part of marriage ceremony
	-- jchaawng krong s'po	--	work on a book
	-- jchaawng s'bye'k cheung	--	tie one's shoes
	-- jchaawng cho'op	--	tie a knot

37)	jchak	--	to stab, lock, unlock or inject
	-- jchak tnam	--	inject medicine
	-- jchak taahs	--	play records
	-- jchak ka'ssett	--	play tapes
	-- jchak tuk	--	pour water
	-- jchak jchowl	--	pour (s.th.) out
	-- kreung jchak	--	molded products
	jchuhk	--	to bite (snakes) or peck
	-- jchuhk	--	(S) make love
	jchaak jchenyh	--	to leave
	-- jchaak jchowl	--	to abandon
	jch'uch	--	to push or poke
	jchawh	--	pierced
	jchawk	--	pain; stop up a hole

38)	jcham	--	to remember, wait
	-- jcham moi plet	--	wait a second
	-- jcham batch	--	necessary, important
	-- jcham'ngai	--	distance
	jchum	--	to coincide with; exact
	-- Jchum howi!	--	That's it! Exactly!
	-- ree'up jchum	--	to make, prepare,
	-- jchum'long	--	to copy
	jchum'ng'eye	--	distance
	chng'eye	--	far

39)	jchawh	--	pierced
	chaa	--	to fry; fried
	jchowl	--	to abandon
	jchak	--	to pour or inject
	jchawt	--	to stop
	-- jchawt laan	--	park a car
	jchowt	--	to blame or accuse
	chhaut	--	innocent, naive

40) jchanyh   --   to lose
     -- jcha(w) jchanyh   --   to surrender
     -- jchanyh chuum'loo'a(s)   --   to lose a fight
     -- kruun jchanyh   --   malaria
     -- p'jchanyh   --   to defeat

     ch'neh (written ch'neh(s))   --   to win
     -- yok ch'neh   --   to defeat s. o.
     bong ree'up   --   to defeat s. o.

     para   --   to lose
     para'chey   --   to be defeated; a defeat (lit: to lose victory)
     -- neh eiyne tro para'chey   --   you will lose
     -- para'muk   --   to lose face

     choke chey   --   victory
     -- Cheya'varman   --   kingly name
     -- chey yo'   --   hail, viva
     -- Baan chey howi!   --   We won! We did it!

41) jchawh   --   pierced
     jchawk   --   pain; stop up a hole
     -- jchawk ch'nawk   --   cork a bottle
     -- jchawk poo'ah   --   upset stomach
     -- jchawk dai   --   cramps
     -- jchawk t'nam   --   chew tobacco

     choke chey   --   victory
     cho chaae'k   --   to discuss casually
     -- kaa cho chaae'k   --   discussion

     jchaiyk   --   to distribute, divide up

     jchat
     -- jchat kaa   --   to expedite
     -- jchat chaiyng   --   to organize
     -- jchat owi   --   to order or direct

42) jcheh   --   to know how to, to know
     -- mun jcheh chope   --   endlessly
     chheh   --   inflammable; to turn on (an engine or machine)

     jchaah   --   old, elderly, dark (of colors)
     jcho   --   over-ripe

43)	jchet sup	--	seventy
	chit	--	near, close
	ch'yete	--	full, as in i) unable to eat more, or ii) having had enough sleep
	chut	--	to slice
	jchat owi	--	to command or order s. o.
	jchet (AP: chut)	--	feeling, emotion, heart
	jch'eye't daiy	--	tomb, stupa
	jchaiyk	--	to divide or distribute
	jch'eye	--	lice
44)	jchenyh	--	to leave
	-- jchaak jchenyh	--	to leave
	jchenyh jchum	--	to raise or maintain
	jchanyh	--	to lose
	jchong	--	to want
45)	jchoh	--	to go down; to sign (e.g., a document)
	-- jchoh krauwm	--	to go down stairs
	-- jchoh bun'chee	--	to write down
	-- jchoh tlai	--	to reduce a price
	-- lic jchoh	--	to sink (in water, etc.)
	-- jchoh gkat chi'moi	--	to get along with, fit in
	jcho(r)	--	may you... ; please...
	jcho	--	over-ripe
	-- bun jcho	--	to flatter
	jcha(r)	--	to inscribe
	-- jcha(r) jchaeng	--	to describe
	jchaw		
	-- a'kas jchaw	--	airline
	-- chh'nam jchaw	--	year of the dog
	-- tess jchaw	--	tourist
	-- jchaw jchanyh	--	to surrender
	-- jchaw jchaa	--	to discuss or negotiate
	cho chaae'k	--	to discuss casually
	-- cho chaae'k ka'neea klang	--	to talk loudly or argue
	-- kaa cho chaae'k ka'neea	--	argument
	-- cho chaae'k leng	--	to chat

46)	jchole	--	to go in
	-- jchole taam	--	according to
	-- jchole jchet	--	to like or favor
	-- jchenyh jchole jchole jchenyh, jchole jchenyh jchenyh jchole	--	to go in and out or back and forth
	-- jchole sun chee'it	--	to become a citizen
	-- jchole chuun chee'it	--	to become a citizen
	-- jchole chum'now'm	--	to fit in, or move, among
	choh	--	to stand
	cho chaae'k	--	to discuss casually
	jchaw jchaa	--	to discuss seriously, negotiate
	jchong	--	to want
47)	jchong	--	to want
	jchung	--	tip or end of s. th.
	-- jchong bom'pot	--	final
	-- jchong'ul	--	to point to s.th.
	jchong vaa(k)	--	rhythm
	jchong kran	--	oven
	jchong vaa	--	smelt (fish)
	jchong vaa	--	oar
	jchong vang	--	school principle
	chung'ka	--	chopsticks, drumsticks
	jchung'rut	--	cricket
48)	jchree'ung	--	to sing
	jchum'ree'ung	--	a song
	kaa jchree'ung	--	singing
	neh jchum'ree'ung	--	a singer
	-- Neh jchum'ree'ung jchree'ung jchum'ree'ung.	--	The singer sang a song.
49)	jchum'poo'h	--	to, about, concerning
	chuum'poo'h	--	part or portion; type
	jchum nutch	--	point (of a comment)
	jchum'noo'an	--	amount
	jchum'now'm	--	among
	jchum'nong	--	knot
	-- cho'op jchum'nong	--	to be tied up with rope
	-- cho'op ro'vull	--	to be "tied up"/busy
	-- jchum'nong cheung	--	title, as of a book

32

50)	jchum'nung	--	temptation; to want s.th.
	chuum'nole	--	to like; be interested in, fond of
	-- praak chuum'nole	--	income
	-- praak chuum'nanyh	--	profit
	-- chuum'nole jchet	--	to like
	-- kaa chuum'nole	--	interest in s. th.
	jchum'neh	--	knowledge
	jchum'nah	--	mature
	jchum'nan	--	skillful
	jchum'nye	--	to spend; expenses
	jchum'naee	--	food
	jchum'nyke	--	part, portion
	-- jchum'nyke eye	--	whereas (but)
	jchum'lyke	--	strange
51)	jchum'ree'ung	--	song
	-- neh jchum'ree'ung	--	singer
	-- chree'ung	--	to sing
	jchuum ree'up	--	to tell
	-- jchuum ree'up soo'a	--	hello
52)	chuum raan	--	to increase (grow or spread)
	jchum raan	--	progress, prosperity
	daum'laung	--	to increase (build or assemble)
	kauwn laung	--	to increase (grow)
	kaut laung	--	to happen
53)	kaa peea	--	protect
	kaa peea kum owi	--	prevent
54)	kaae'oo	--	glass
	kaow	--	glue, plastic
	-- kaow'soo	--	rubber
	-- but kaow	--	to glue s. th.
	kow	--	pants
	kaeo'eye	--	chair
	gkoo(r)	--	pair, couple
	-- sraw vaa koh gkoo(r)	--	to choose the wrong mate
	gkoo	--	to draw (a picture or design)
	koo'h	--	to strike or flick
	-- dyke koo'h	--	cigarette lighter

55)	ka'na'ta 'ma'ti'ka	--	spokesman
	ka'na'ka a'tep'a'dye	--	dignitary
	ka'nak ka'ma'ti'ka	--	committee
	ka'nak ka'ma'ti'ka praw'tay bawt	--	executive committee
	ka'ma'ka	--	commission
	ka'nak ka'ma'ka	--	commission
	sa'nong ka	--	commission
	-- a'ki'et sa'nong ka	--	commissioner

56)	kat	--	press
	-- song'kat	--	push down, squash, squeeze
	-- piht praw'kat	--	really, for sure
	kaat	--	to cut; through or across
	-- kaat'pa'dach	--	cut off, interdicted
	-- kaat howi	--	gone, finished, over
	-- kaat ti krong	--	through the town
	-- kaat stung	--	across the stream
	-- haang kaat day kow-aow	--	tailor (shop)
	-- kaa veh kaat	--	operation (medical)
	-- kaat muk chia	--	cut in front of
	-- song'kaat	--	subdivision of city ward
	-- kwah kaat	--	to lack
	kaht	--	to waste or lose
	-- kaht peyr	--	to waste time
	-- bong kaht	--	lose property, be wiped out
	kaut	--	to happen, be born
	-- Preah a'tthit kaut howi.	--	The sun is up (has risen).
	kut	--	to think
	kuut	--	exact, only
	-- moi kuut	--	only

57)	kaw(ss)	--	a subpoena
	kaa(k)	--	formerly, small coin
	kaa	--	noun marker; matter, affair
	khaw	--	neck
	kaw	--	will/may be; if... then
	-- eye kaw baan da'aae	--	whatever
	-- roo kaw	--	or else
	-- kyom kaw teuh...	--	if I go, then ...
	kaw	--	article or section of agreement
	leh kan	--	term/condition of an agreement
	kaw(k) saahk	--	to wash hair
	k'awh	--	island

34

58)	kauwn laung	--	to increase
	kaut laung	--	to happen

59)	kej kaa	--	work, job
	tek tong	--	connection, relationship
	kej sun'nyaa	--	a written contract
	kaa sun'nyaa	--	a promise or verbal contract
	peea sun'nyaa	--	verbal promise
	tek tee'inhy	--	influence s. o.
	sun'ya	--	advertising sign, sign of s. th. (evidence, indication)

60)	k'nauwi	--	pillow
	kn'yaye	--	ginger

61)	ko	--	pile s.th. up
	gko	--	cow
	gko	--	to stir
	gko	--	mute, dumb
	koh	--	wrong
	ko'itch	--	bad, broken
	kahtch	--	mean, rude
	to'h	--	punishment, abuse
	to'ahs	--	objection
	toa	--	religious verses

62)	kom'puung	--	riverside boat landing; (us- ually, as in Cambodian province names, Romanized as "Kompong"; Romanized "kom'puung" here to convey correct pronunciation.)
	-- Kom'puung Thum	--	"Kompong" Thum province
	-- kom'puung pa'aae	--	pier
	kom'puung	--	"ing" (gerund marker)
	-- kom'puung tveu kaa	--	working
	kum'pong	--	container, tin can
	kra'pong	--	large container or can
	kum'pool	--	top
	-- kum'pool ree'up	--	plateau
	kum'pee	--	compilation of Buddhist teachings

63)	khung	--	angry
	klang	--	loud, strong, extreme
	klung	--	Indian (person from India)

64)	kong	--	bike, tire, wheel
	kongtak	--	electrical switch
	kuun	--	to multiply
	gkun	--	to grind

kaan -- to hold, grasp or support
-- kaan kaab -- control, hold power
kawng -- force, unit, bracelet
-- kawng dai -- bracelet
kang (v-pnun: kangaroo) -- side
-- krum kang na -- that team
ko'hng -- bank account; curve
-- Kaw'h Koh'ng -- "curved island" (name of Cambodian province)

65) kro vwat -- to throw
kro vanyh -- cardamom

66) kro'up -- grain, seed
-- kro'up kum'pleung -- bullet
-- kro'up bai -- grenade
-- kro'up scaw -- candy
tra'up -- eggplant

kroop -- every
-- kroop kro'un -- enough
kroop krong -- to govern

67) krau -- out, outside
krowm -- below, under
krow'ee -- behind, in the rear, later

kraw -- poor
a'krah -- dirty, evil, bad

kr'mauw -- black
kro'mauw -- dark
k'mau'it -- ghost, spirit

68)	kum'hawh	--	fault, mistake, error
	k'mah	--	shy, ashamed
	a'mah	--	embarrassed, ashamed
	ahp	--	fog
	-- ahp muk	--	to be ashamed
	ko'hawk	--	a lie (or, to lie)
	ko'itch	--	wrong
	koh	--	mistake, error; morally wrong
	to'h	--	punishment, abuse; legally guilty
	to'ah(s)	--	a quarrel
69)	kum'rut	--	limit(s)
	kum'nut	--	idea
	kum'naut	--	birth
	kum'nauwt	--	requirement or condition
	kum'not	--	data, information; date of s.th.
	kra'no't	--	sam pan
	kra'dah	--	paper
	kum'nenyh	--	selfish
	kum'noh	--	a pile of (certain nouns)
	poom'noo(k)	--	a pile of (certain other nouns)
	kum'naup	--	treasure, wealth
	kum'naahp	--	poem, poetry
	kum'nap	--	piece (of wood)
70)	kum'raw	--	rarely
	kum'rong	--	a plan
	kum'roo	--	pattern, sample
	kum'noo	--	pattern, design
	kum'rooh	--	sleazy
	kum'reehh	--	greedy
	kum'ranyh	--	thrifty
	kum'nenyh	--	selfish
71)	k'tee'up	--	short
	tee'up	--	low

72) k'too'ee   --   homosexual (n. and adj.)
     cun'toi   --   tail

73) kwah   --   shortage; to stop
     -- hahw kwah   --   prohibit
     kwahk   --   blind
     kraw' kwah   --   dirty

74) la'bot   --   (roughly) intimidating, strong, formidable
     -- prey la'bot   --   forest; deep forest
     -- ngyee'um la'bot   --   guard, servant, retainer
     -- neh la'bot   --   ranger
     daiy la'bub   --   clay or clay-y mud
     bot bong   --   to lose
     -- bot la'meuh   --   a crime
     -- vi'bot   --   a crisis

75) leh kan   --   condition of a contract
     -- leh kan taae'kah   --   function, responsibility, order
     leh ka'nak   --   aspect of character, characteristic, physical condition
     -- leh ka'nak ploe   --   condition of the road
     -- leh ka'nak ney neh chuum'ngeu --   the patient's condition
     sa'ta'na'pheap   --   social conditions

76) leng   --   to play or joke
     lay'ng   --   to release
     -- lay'ng ka'neea   --   to get divorced
     leh   --   to give up s. th.
     -- leh bong chook b'r'eye   --   to give up smoking

77) looh   --   to sell
     -- looh duhm   --   sell wholesale
     looh   --   deeply, completely
     -- looh geyng howi   --   already sound asleep
     loo'ich   --   to steal

     loo   --   to hear
     loo'ah   --   to redeem (property); to lose s.th.; wire (fence,
                                                 telegraph, etc.); (three different Khmer words
                                                   with same sound but different spellings)

     -- loo'ah aae'van   --   to redeem property
     -- loo'ah pro'lung   --   to lose one's soul
     -- k'sye loo'ah   --   a cable gram

38

78)	maan'eh	--	really?; really.
	ma'neh	--	one person
	ma'neh eiyne	--	alone

79)	maan'tan	--	really
	maan (AP: men)	--	true
	-- Mun maan tay.	--	Not true
	mun (AP: min)	--	no, not
	muun	--	last, most recent
	-- leuk muun	--	last time
	-- a'tthit muun	--	last week
	-- ch'nam muun	--	last year
	-- yoop muun	--	(any previous night)
	munyh	--	suffix for "yesterday"
	-- musl'munyh	--	yesterday
	-- yoop munyh	--	last night

80)	mao	--	hour
	mok (most common AP: mao;		
	also: moe'k; mawk)	--	to come
	muk (AP: muk)	--	face
	meuk	--	squid
	a'meuk	--	squid/chicken pate

| 81) | ma'teh(k) | -- | idea |
| | ma'taae'(s) | -- | hot pepper (red or green) |

| 82) | maw'ool | -- | to twist |
| | mool | -- | to roll up |

83)	maw(t) jchawt	--	serious, dedicated, hard working
	mwot	--	mouth
	mutt	--	serious
	muuht	--	sharp
	mung mutt	--	strict

84)	nah	--	very
	na	--	what
	nehh	--	here
	neh	--	people; you
	ney	--	of
	nay	--	meaning

85)	ni'yaye	--	to speak
	-- ni'yaye srool	--	easy to say
	ngi'yaye	--	easy
	-- ngi'yaye srool	--	very easy (lit: easy, easy)

86)	nung	--	will
	nung	--	and; with

87)	ot	--	not, no
	awh	--	no more; completely
	-- awh bye	--	no more rice
	-- awh kum'lung	--	no more strength
	-- te'ang awh ka'neea	--	all together
	et	--	northern and western Cambodian AP of "ot"
	ahws	--	firewood
	ahp	--	fog
	-- ahp muk	--	to lose face, be ashamed
	owi	--	to give, allow or cause

88)	oeuv'puk	--	father
	aow	--	shirt

89)	pa'choo baan na pheap	--	current events
	pa'choom	--	to come together
	-- pa'choom ban	--	holiday of remembrance of ancestors
	-- moi pa'choom	--	average, standard
	-- kaa yul choom to'ahs	--	disagreement

90)	pa'di'seyt	--	refusal; to deny or refuse
	pa'da'sye	--	influenza
	pa'ti'kaam	--	strike, demonstration
	pa'ti'vwut	--	revolution
	pra'ti'kaam	--	reaction
	pra'ti'kaa	--	development; s. th. that happens

91)	paeng	--	cup
	penyh	--	full

92)	p'daum	--	to start or begin; to promote or advocate an idea
	p'dum	--	to tell or inform
	-- pnya(r) p'dum	--	to leave a message (lit: to send-tell)
	p'dom	--	to gather
	p'dung	--	to report
	pa'dung	--	to sue
	p'dum	--	vicinity, area
93)	peh (AP: pe'ch)		
	-- slee'a peh	--	to dress or put on
	-- chuum peh	--	to owe
	pieh (AP: pee'h(k), peh)	--	part, portion
	-- pieh ch'raan	--	most
	-- pieh kan'dal	--	half
	poo'ah (written poo'ah(s))	--	stomach, snake, tube
94)	pn'aae'k	--	eye
	pnya(r)	--	to send, deliver or keep
	-- p'dum pnya(r)	--	leave a message
	pn'yeh	--	to wake up or shock; a physical reflex
	p'nyke	--	section, sector, or part
	pieh	--	part, portion
	p'nehk	--	agent
	pyke	--	direction, region
	p'eye'k	--	to lean
	p'k'eye	--	star
	ps'eye'n	--	smoke
	p'eye'm	--	sweet
	ps'eye	--	to spread
	-- ps'eye taam vichu	--	radio broadcast
	p'sa	--	market
	p'saa	--	to weld
95)	kum'pooh	--	height
	k'poo'h	--	high
	p'shoo'a	--	to hang or suspend (delay)
	p'tooh(s)	--	to explode
	p'chooh	--	to toss from the ground
	-- k'shaal p'chooh	--	hurricane
	-- k'shaal koo'itch	--	tornado

96)	plum	--	to blow
	peup powm	--	balloon
	beuwt	--	to suck
	-- um'peung beuwt	--	drinking straw
	k'seuht	--	to sniff or inhale

97)	pooh	--	group, bunch, people
	poo'h	--	to boil
	-- tuk poo'h	--	boiling water
	-- por poo'h	--	bubble
	poo'h	--	to chop
	-- poo'h awh	--	chop firewood
	phoo'(a)	--	mud

	pha(w)k	--	AP for mud
	phuk	--	to drink
	pooo	--	uncle
	poo'a	--	fan, admirer

	pieh (AP: pee'h(k), peh)	--	part, portion
	-- pieh ch'raan	--	most
	-- pieh kan'dal	--	half
	poo'ah (written poo'ah(s))	--	stomach, snake, tube

98)	pra	--	to use
	prap	--	to tell
	praa(k)	--	money

	prey	--	forest or jungle
	pray(k)	--	a stream
	pruhk	--	morning

99)	praw'chang	--	against; to oppose
	praw'kaan	--	to dislike
	praw'sar chiang	--	better
	praw'sun baa	--	if
	praw'saa tha	--	(s.o.) says/said that

100)	praw'chia a'tep'a'tai	--	democracy
	praw'teea'neea a'tep'a'dye	--	president
	-- a'tep'a'dye	--	chairman
	-- a'tep'a'dye pheap	--	sovereignty
	-- a'tep'a'dye s'day'tee	--	acting chairman
	-- ka'na'ka a'tep'a'dye	--	dignitary

101)	praw'long	--	test s.o.; exam
	pro'lung	--	spirit, soul
	praw'lye	--	irrigation ditch

102)	pra'ngya	--	intelligent, witty
	poo'k'eye	--	good at s. th.
	praw'nyab	--	fast
	-- praw'nyab laung	--	hurry up

103)	preah (AP: preh)	--	(a) god
	preh	--	cracked
	prey	--	forest
	pray(k)	--	stream
	pruhk	--	morning

| 104) | p'toi | -- | opposite |
| | taw'i | -- | to back up or go backwards |

105)	ptay'a	--	house, home
	p'tay	--	area, space
	-- miun p'tay poo'ah	--	pregnant
	p'taay	--	to change, switch

106)	pooht	--	to bend
	puuht	--	to pretend; fake
	-- tveu puuht	--	to pretend or falsify
	-- ma'nooh leh puuht	--	hypocrite
	-- choo'ah puuht	--	fake illness
	-- puuht roob jchum'lak	--	fake statues
	-- miun puuht	--	dishonest
	t'ngai put	--	Wednesday
	Preah Phut	--	Buddha
	piht	--	true, real, really, truly
	-- kaa piht	--	a fact
	-- piht praw'kaat	--	for sure
	-- piht man	--	really, truly
	-- mun piht	--	not true, false, fake
	pooo'k	--	mattress

| 107) | pun'lut | -- | turn off (as, a light); put out (as, a fire) |
| | puun'leuh | -- | sunlight, moonlight, bright light |

108)	pwan	--	thousand
	pwa	--	color

109)	ree'up jchuum	--		prepare
	jchuum ree'up	--		tell
	-- jchuum ree'up soo'a	--		hello

110)	ree'ech	--		royal; holy; dynastic
	-- ree'ech bahl'lang	--		throne
	-- lok preah ree'ech	--		high-ranking monk
	ree'ech chia	--		royal
	-- ree'ech'chia ni'yuum	--		royalist
	-- ree'ech'chia na'jcha	--		kingdom
	-- ree'ech'chia kaal	--		reign
	-- ro'yeht peyr (+ monarch name)	--		reign (of that monarch)
	tuk ree'ech	--		flood
	ree'eh	--		citizens, people
	-- dum'nahng ree'eh	--		a representative of the people
	ree'k	--		to increase, get bigger; progress
	-- ree'k jchum raan	--		to increase, make progress
	ree'uhk	--		diarrhoea

111)	ro'k	--		to look for
	rohk	--		disease, illness
	-- may rohk	--		germs

112)	ro'vull	--	busy
	rawl (AP: ro'al)	--	every; all, completely

113)	reu'	--		to pull out or open
	-- jchreu' reu'	--		choose
	-- sa'reu'	--		inventory
	reuh jchole	--		to move in
	reuh jchenyh	--		to move out
	roo'h	--		stay, live, be alive

114)	roo'itch	--		finished, released, escaped
	rut	--		to run
	-- rut jchenyh	--		run away, escape, after being trapped
	-- rut jchowl	--		run away leaving s.th. behind
	-- rut roo'itch	--		escape before being trapped, avoid trap
	-- rut puun	--		to smuggle

115) ruhm   --   to wrap

    -- ruhm chuum veng   --   to wrap around
    -- chuum ruhm   --   a camp
    -- ruhm dum'naek   --   to make love
    -- jchenyh jchum op'ruhm gkon   --   to raise a child

    -- kaa op'ruhm   --   reform
    -- ruhm kaan   --   to bother
    -- ruhm keuh   --   to quake or shake
    -- ruhm kuhl   --   to move slightly, budge

    -- ruhm luk   --   to remind, or to refresh one's memory
    -- kaa ruhm luk   --   reminder
    -- ruhm leung   --   to uproot
    -- ruhm long   --   to skip or pass over
    -- ruhm lope   --   to demand, break or rape

    -- moi ruhm pech   --   suddenly
    -- ruhm pech nu   --   instantly
    -- ruhm pheup   --   to excite
    -- op'ruhm   --   education, training, discipline
    -- pheap ruhm tuum   --   modesty
    -- sum'ruhm   --   honest, logical, proper
    -- ruhm vuung   --   circle

ru'um   --   to come together; together
    -- ru'um dum'naek   --   to make love
    -- jchole ru'um   --   to join, get involved in, involve, participate, take part in, move in

    -- ru'um layke   --   to share; to sympathize with
    -- chuun ru'um chee'it   --   compatriot
    -- ru'um ka'neea   --   to rally together

roh'ul   --   to slide
luhm pong   --   to echo

116) ru'ung   --   story
roong   --   tunnel, (animal's) den
ro'am   --   dance
    -- ro'am vuung   --   circle dance

ree'ung   --   shape (esp. human body)
ro'ng   --   place
    -- ro'ng gkun   --   movie theatre
rung   --   hard, obstinate; iron
ruhm tooo'k   --   prepare in advance (lit: wrap and keep)
rong tooo'k   --   sorrow

117)	sa'ha'kuum	--	community
	sung'kuum	--	society
	sa'ma'kuum	--	committee
	sa'ha'chuun	--	corporation
	ka'nak ka'ma'ti'ka	--	committee
	ka'nak ka'ma'ti'ka praw'tay bawt	--	executive committee
	ka'ma'ka	--	commission
	ka'nak ka'ma'ka	--	commission
	sa'nong ka	--	commission
	-- a'ki'et sa'nong ka	--	commissioner

118)	saah	--	people
	saah	--	to heal
	-- saah (sa'bauw'ee)	--	(hope you) get better
	-- dum'bow saah howi	--	the wound healed
	sahk	--	to test or try out; a sample of s.th.
	suk sah	--	to study
	saa	--	message, information
	-- no'um saa	--	send a message
	-- saa por'da'mee'an	--	newspaper
	-- dah(k) bun'dah saa	--	put a curse on
	-- praw'saa	--	to say
	-- eyke'a'saa	--	document
	-- chi'vut'sahs	--	biology
	-- phum'i'sahs	--	geography
	-- ak'saw'sahs	--	literature
	saa'	--	to get, take, collect
	-- Teuh saa' kow-aow.	--	Go get your clothes (from line, closet, etc.).

119)	saah	--	people
	saat	--	animal
	-- saat slaab	--	birds
	sat(ch)	--	meat
	saahk	--	hair
	saak	--	tattoo, stripes, mark
	-- laung saak	--	to promote (raise in rank)
	sahl(t)	--	remaining, left-over
	salm	--	humid
	-- sun salm	--	dew
	sawh	--	aroused sexually
	-- k'sawh	--	exhausted
	sang	--	tame (re animals)

120)	smaa	--	shoulder
	sm'au	--	grass
	sm'auu	--	even, equal, still
	-- sm'auu ni howi	--	still, even now
	sm'oh	--	sincere, faithful
	-- sm'oh nung gkoo(r) swaa'mye		-- faithful to her husband

121)	sngoo'it	--	dry
	sng'at (AP: sngy'aat)	--	quiet
	sngyee'im	--	still, not moving or talking, quiet
	sngyee'im sng'at	--	silent, not moving or talking (sng'at is somewhat stronger than sngyee'im)

122)	sohk	--	peace, security; safe
	suk	--	military, martial
	sok	--	to insert
	-- sok loi	--	to bribe

123)	sraae (AP: sr'ei)	--	woman
	sr'eye	--	rice paddy
	sr'eye (jchum'nong)	--	to untie
	-- baw(k) sr'eye owi	--	to solve or explain
	sreyk	--	thirst
	ser'ei	--	free (adj)
	sa'trei (AP: sa'tr'eye)	--	woman (formal)

124)	sra'laanyh	--	to love or like
	sra'laang	--	AP for sra'laanyh
	saa'laang	--	ferry (boat)

125)	seou	--	"loco", "spacey"
	mun steu	--	hardly, barely
	-- steu tai	--	almost
	-- steu	--	insufficient
	-- vwah loi steu	--	not enough money

126)	sum'baat	--	property, wealth
	sum'but	--	oath
	sum'buht	--	letter, ticket, document
	jchum butch	--	necessary, important
	sum'bul	--	skin color

127)	sum'rach	--	decision, accomplishment
	-- sum'rach jchet	--	to decide
	sum'raak	--	a rest, siesta, break from work
	sum'rut	--	bronze
128)	sung'khum	--	to hope; a hope
	sung'kuum	--	society
	sa'ha'kuum	--	community
	sum'nang	--	luck
	sum'narr	--	a request or proposal
	sum'nawl	--	extra; to put aside or made ahead of time
129)	sun'ya	--	clue, sign, signal
	-- sun'ya bot	--	diploma
	sun'nyaa	--	to promise
	kaa sun'nyaa	--	a promise
	kej sun'nyaa	--	a contract
130)	sv'eye	--	mango
	sveye	--	to look for or at
	swaa'mye; koo swaa'mye	--	husband (formal term)
131)	tau(v)	--	question marker
	-- Tau(v) neh teuh?	--	Are you going?
	tha	--	that
	taa	--	say
	-- Taa mutch?	--	What did (he/you/etc.) say?
	ta	--	elderly man, grandfather
	taw'hh	--	let's
132)	tek tong	--	relationship, connection
	kej kaa	--	work, job
	kaa tveu	--	work, job

133)	to'ich	--	small	
	toe	--	"two" in B'laae counting system	
	to'h	--	punishment, abuse (n), bad, corrupt (adj)	
	-- dah(k) tooo'k to'h	--		to abuse
	-- a ma'nooh to'h	--		inhumane
	to'	--	small vase or jar	
	-- to' p'ka	--		flower vase
	to'ahs	--	quarrel, obstacle	
	-- yul to'ahs	--		object to s.th.
	toa	--	religious verses, mantra	
	-- leng toa k'dau	--		"read the riot act to"
	-- yoo'teh'toa	--		justice
	-- a'yoo'teh toa	--		injustice
	tohk	--	table	
	-- tohk bye	--		dining table
	too'	--	cabinet (furniture piece)	
134)	tooo'k	--	to put, place, keep	
	-- tooo'k jchet	--		trust
	-- ree'up tooo'k	--		prepare in advance
	-- yok jchet tooo'k dah(k)	--		care about
	-- rong tooo'k	--		sorrow
	-- dawh tooo'k to'h	--		to cause trouble
	thuk	--	bad condition, trouble	
	-- miun thuk thum	--		be in serious trouble
	-- dah(k) thuk to'h	--		to abuse
	-- Kum no'um thuk owi kyom	--		Don't give me trouble.
	-- tveu owi miun thuk	--		make trouble for s.o.
	toook	--	small boat	
	tuk	--	water	
	p'toooh(s)	--	to explode	
	tooh(b)	--	incense	
	tooo'b	--	to restrain	
	-- tooo'b jchet	--		to restrain oneself emotionally
	-- s'kd'eye tooo'b	--		restraint
	-- kaa tooo'b	--		repression
	tooo'ng	--	to transplant	

135)	traw'cheh(k)	--	cold
	traw'chi'eh(k)	--	ear
	traw'chheh	--	stubborn
	traw'chaek leng		
	(AP for cho chaek leng)	--	to chat

136)	tra'paeng	--	pond
	traa'paae'ang	--	bamboo shoot (edible)
	tum'paae'ang bai'choo	--	grapes
	tuum'paae'ang	--	bamboo shoot (AP)

137)	tro (written tro(v))	--	necessary; to undergo
	-- trum tro	--	correct, accurate
	troh	--	to support or prop up

138)	tul	--	across
	-- tul muk	--	facing, across from
	-- tul'dyne	--	border
	twal (AP: to'al)	--	block, stop, obstruct
	-- Ploe' ni twal.	--	This road is blocked.

139)	tuuyh tro'an	--	bored; sick and tired
	tuun	--	soft, weak
	thoun	--	long-lasting
	thuun	--	type of s.th.
	tuung	--	bucket, container, water tank
	tooo'ng	--	to transplant
	tuum	--	ripe; over-ripe
	-- sv'eye tuum	--	ripe mangoes
	-- pheap ruhm tuum	--	modesty
	-- tuum nong	--	likely to
	-- tuum lee'aae	--	perforate
	-- tuum loo'h	--	perforate
	thuum	--	to sit or stay
	thum	--	big, large
	-- Kom'puung Thum	--	province name

140)	tlung	--	to weigh s. th.
	tuum'nguun	--	weight of s. th.
	-- ro'bah tuum'nguun	--	a load (i.e., cargo)
	t'nguun	--	heavy

141)	um'bawh	--	twine for tying rice sack
	-- bawh	--	thread
	um'bau'hhs	--	broom
	-- bau'hhs ptay'a	--	to sweep (e.g., a house or floor)
	um'bul	--	salt
	um'pil	--	tamarind
	alm'pul	--	trouble
	-- alm'pul tooo'k	--	to make trouble for
	-- tveu alm'pul	--	to make trouble for
	am'peau	--	cane
	-- scaaw am'peau	--	sugar cane
	um'peuh	--	magic spell; action; act
	-- tveu um'peuh	--	put a spell on s. o.
	um'peung	--	drinking straw
142)	un'cheunyh	--	please
	an'chung	--	in that way (casual, familiar)
	aae'chung	--	that way (stronger than an'chung)
143)	un'dah	--	tongue
	un'dauk	--	turtle
144)	ung'kaw	--	milled but not-yet-cooked rice
	Ang'kor	--	Angkor Wat
	ung'koi	--	to sit
	ong'kah	--	organization
145)	veng	--	wide, broad, big
	venyh	--	"re-"; back, return
	-- mok venyh	--	to come back
	vehng	--	to lose
	-- vuung vehng	--	to confuse s.o.
	-- bung vehng	--	to get rid of s.o.
	vee'ung	--	a detour or curve
	vaae'eng	--	palace
	vee'in	--	intestine
	-- poo'ah vee'in kong	--	inner-tube
	ving	--	to braid or twist
	-- ving k'sye	--	to twist rope

146)	vit'naae	--	discipline
	vit'neea	--	disaster, hard times
	vi'tı	--	action, activity
	-- kaam vi'ti	--	act, action
	vee'neea(s)	--	destroyed
	vit'na'ti	--	an instant, second

147)	yeung	--	we
	yun	--	machine
	-- yun hawh	--	airplane

148)	yeut	--	slow, late, stretch
	-- Un'dauk nu yeut nah	--	That turtle is very slow.
	-- aow yeut	--	T-shirt
	yoo	--	long (re time)
	-- Eye kaw yoo ma'leh?	--	What took you so long?
	-- mun yoo mun chhop	--	sooner or later
	yoop	--	night
	-- yoop ch'row	--	late at night (lit: deep night)

| 149) | yuum | -- | to cry |
| | ngyim or ngyo' ngyim | -- | to smile |

Lists

Set out below are sets of related terms which may be usefully defined in combined lists as well as in sequential dictionary format.

Pronouns:

I, me (generally, male or female speaker)	-- kyom
-- to show respect/affection (particularly used by female or younger-than-person-addressed speaker)	-- own
-- used by person older or of higher social status than person addressed	-- bong
("Own" and "bong" are commonly used among family members and girl-friends/boy-friends)	
-- female speaker, used to show respect	-- nee'eng kyom
you (singular and plural)	-- neh (written "ni'ak"; AP: nee'eh)
-- to show particular respect:	
-- to man	-- lok
-- to woman	-- lok sraae
-- to close friend or family member, younger or of lower social standing	-- own
-- to close friend or family member, older or of higher social standing	-- bong
he, she (general term)usually means "he"	-- gwat
-- that guy (for children, generally, and used re an adult)	-- gwat nu
-- meaning only "she"	-- nee'eng
-- derogatory name pre-fix if used before male name	-- a'
-- complimentary name prefix if used before female name	-- a' (e.g. a' Dani, a' Bora, a' Chantha)
him, her (used as above)	-- gwat, nee'eng
-- him (derogatory)	-- a' nu
-- her (derogatory)	-- neh nu
it (also means he, she, him and her but only re. a child or among close friends, otherwise disrespectful/derogatory	-- veea
we, us	-- yeung
you (singular)	-- see "you (plural)", below
they, them	-- pooh'gkay ; gkay

Times of Day:

morning (sunrise to noon)	-- peyr pruhk
noon (12 a.m.)	-- peyr t'ngai trong
afternoon (12 a.m. to 4 p.m.)	-- ro'seel
evening (4 p.m. to sunset)	-- long'aae't
night (sunset to 10-11 p.m.)	-- yoop
midnight	-- kan'dal yoop (lit: middle of the night)
late night (11 pm to sunrise)	-- yoop ch'ro (lit: deep night)
one o'clock	-- mao moi
seven o'clock	-- mao prum'pul
eleven o;clock	-- mao dop moi
six thirty	-- mao prum'moi kan'lah
eight fifteen	-- mao prum'bye dop prum
quarter of nine	-- kwah dap pram mao prum buon
ten past midnight	-- mao dop pi dop na'tee*
in ten minutes	-- krow'ee dop na'tee*
five minutes ago	-- pram nee'a'tee muun
What time is it?	-- Mao pu'man aee?

*["nee'a'tee" -- minute -- in this construction is almost invariably pronounced "na'tee" -- which pronunciation is given as an "AP" as a part of the definition of the word "minute".]

Selected Prepositions:

about	-- om'pee, pi, jchum'poo'h
according to	-- taam
across	-- kaat
at	-- noeh
below	-- krowm
beside	-- krow pi
between	-- ro'vieng
by (close to)	-- chit
by (by means of)	-- dow'ee, dow'ee sa
down	-- jchoh
from	-- pi
in	-- k'nong
in, inside of	-- noeh k'nong
of	-- ney, ney k'nong
on	-- leuh
out	-- krau
over, on top of, on	-- noeh leuh
to	-- teuh, mok
under	-- noeh krowm
up	-- laung
with	-- chi'moi, nung

Provinces:

Northeast of Phnom Penh:
  Mun'dol'ki'ri
  Ra'ta'na'ki'ri
  Kra'tchie
  Stung Treng
  Kom'puung Cham

The north between Highway 6 and the Dongrek Range-Thai border:
  Kom'puung Thum
  Preah Vi'he'ar
  Si'em Ri'ep
  Od'dar Me'an'chea
  Ban'tea Me'an'chea

The far west, abutting Thailand along the Wattana Plain-Malai-Pailin-Kaw'h Ko'hng line:
  Bat'tam'bong
  Po'sat
  Kaw'h Ko'hng

Due west of Phnom Penh, South of Tun'lay Sap, and south and southwest of Phnom Penh east and west of Highways 3 and 4 to Sihanoukville:
  Kom'puung Chhn'aang
  Kom'puung Speu
  Kam'pot
  T'keaou
  Kan'dal

East of Phnom Penh on Highway 1 leading to An Loc (Vietnam):
  Sveye Ri'eng
  Prey Veng

River and Stream Terms .... As Used in Prominent Khmer Place Names:

tun'lay -- river

    Tun'lay Sap -- central lake/river system

stung -- small river

    Stung Treng -- northeastern province

prayk -- stream or canal

    Prayk K'dam -- locale south of Phnom Penh

o -- small stream, brook

    O Bawk, O Trau -- pre-1994 Khmer Rouge bases in northern Cambodia

Months:

January	-- Mak'ka'ra	mid December -mid January	-- B'o
February	-- Koom'peh	mid January -mid February	-- Mee'a
March	-- Mih'nee'a	mid February -mid March	-- Pa'kun
April	-- Me'sa	mid March -mid April	-- Chai'yt
May	-- Oo'sa'phea	mid April-mid May	-- Pit'sak
June	-- Mi'too'na	mid May-mid June	-- Jchey
July	-- Ka'ka'da	mid June-mid July	-- A'saht
August	-- Say'ha	mid July mid August	-- S'rop
September	-- Ken'ya	mid August mid September	-- Put'a'bot
October	-- Tho'la	mid September mid October	-- A'syte ka'duck
November	-- Vi'chi'kaa	mid October -mid November	-- Meh'ka'say
December	-- T'noo	mid November -mid December	-- Mi'di'cit

Directions on the Compass:

north	-- kang jcheun (colloquially also, kang leuh);	pyke oo'daw
south	-- kang t'bong;	pyke te'ak'sen
east	-- kang kaut;	pyke bo'pheap (or, bo)
west	-- kang lic;	pyke pa'chim

north-east
-- kang jcheun chiang kang kaut
-- kang kaut chiang kang leuh
-- pyke ee'sahn

north-west
-- kang jcheun chiang kang lic
-- kang lic chiang kang leuh
-- pyke pee'a yoo'up

south-east
-- kang kaut chiang kang t'bong
-- kang t'bong chiang kang kaut
-- pyke a'ka'nee

south-west
-- kang t'bong chiang kang lic
-- kang lic chiang kang t'bong
-- pyke neea ruh'dye

Military Organizations:

Armed forces	-- kawng thwaap
Army	-- thwaap cheung daiy; tee'hee'an cheung daiy (or kok);
-- soldier	-- tee'hee'an; cheung daiy; yo'tee'a
Navy	-- thwaap cheung tuk
-- sailor	-- tee'hee'an cheung tuk
Air Force	-- thwaap a'kas
-- airman	-- tee'hee'an a'kas
militia	-- kawng sveye tran; kawng chee'veea pul
plantation guards	-- sveye kaa'pee'a
guerrillas	-- kawng ch'lope
Khmer Rouge term for its military forces	-- kawng thwaap chee'it

Ranks within Armed Forces:

(Insignia are stripes, "saak," and stars, "pk'eye." The Khmer words "trei," "toe" and "eyke" signify "third-class", "second-class" and "first-class", respectively.):

English title	Khmer title	Usual Insignia
lance corporal	-- pul'la'boh trei	
sergeant	-- pul'la'boh toe	
1st sergeant	-- pul'la'boh eyke	
2nd lieutenant	-- a'noo' sena trei	-- saak moi ("one stripe)
lieutenant	-- a'noo' sena toe	-- saak pi ("two stripes")
captain	-- a'noo' sena eyke	-- saak bye (etc., etc.)
major	-- va'ret sena trei	-- saak buon
lieutenant commander	-- va'ret sena toe	-- saak buon kan'la
lieutenant colonel	-- va'ret sena toe	-- saak buon kan'la
colonel	-- va'ret sena eyke	-- saak prum
brigadier general	-- o'dum'sena trei	-- pk'eye moi("one star")
lieutenant general	-- o'dum'sena toe	-- pk'eye pi (etc.)
major general	-- o'dum'sena eyke	-- pk'eye bye

Units (with typical 1990 manning levels):

brigade	-- kawng pul or kawng pul thum	2000
division	-- kawng pul to'ich	1000
regiment	-- kawng va'ret sena thum	300
battalion	-- kawng va'ret sena to'ich	100
company	-- a'noo' sena thum	30
platoon	-- a'noo' sena to'ich	10
squad	-- krum	3

Common Food and Restaurant Terms:

milk	-- tuk dawh gko
-- (common AP (compressed form)	-- t'd'gko)
iced coffee (with milk)	-- cafe (t'd'gko) t'kaw
tea	-- ta'aae
hot tea	-- ta'aae k'dau
hot tea with milk	-- ta'aae t'd'gko; t'd'gko tuk ta'aae
cola	-- s'cola
cola with ice	-- s'cola t'kaw
rice soup	-- baa' baw
chicken soup with lemon	-- scng'au ch'roo'hk muon
boiled rice	-- bye saw
fried rice	-- bye chaa
sticky rice	-- dum'now'p
traditional Khmer fish spread or pate, eaten with rice	-- pro'hoke ba'raang
eggs	-- pong muon
omelet (lit: fried eggs) with pork	-- pong muon jchian chi'moi sat(ch) jch'roook
beef chunks over salad	-- lok'lak chi'moi sa'lat
sliced beef over salad	-- gko dah(k) leuh sa'lat
chive and egg white with soy sauce and lime	-- num kroo
noodles with curried chicken and bean sprouts	-- num bun chawk
french fries	-- dum'lung jchian
yogurt	-- m'sang gko
rice powder	-- m'sauw ung'kaw

Vegetables:

cucumber	-- traw sawk
white, Chinese radish	-- cha'law
scallions	-- chee ch'eye
green onions with pork	-- k'tum sat(ch) ch'roook
chinese water cress	-- traw koo'un; traw'koo'un spay
pickled (vegetables)	-- ch'roo'hk
mustard greens	-- spay kec'o
mustard greens with beef over rice	-- spay kec'o sat(ch) gko

Desserts/pastries:

pyramid-shaped palm-leaf wrapped pastry	-- num pahng bung'oo
square-shaped palm-leaf wrapped pastry	-- num pahng knaut
coconut milk pastry	-- num hal
chopped ice and fruit	-- tuk kraw'lawk

Telephone ("To'ra'sap") Terms:

I want to call...	-- Jchong to'ra'sap tcuh...
I need "Information." (lit: I need their telephone number.)	-- Tro kaa lek to'ra'sap gkay.
Please get me the number of...	-- Sum owi lek to'ra'sap ..... mok kyom baan tay?
The line was busy	-- To'ra'sap cho'op. (lit: occupied)
No answer	-- Ot miun neh na jchum'la'wee.
To answer the phone	-- Leuk to'ra'sap.
To hang up	-- Dah(k) jchoh (to'ra'sap)
I want to leave a message for Mr. [ ]	-- Kyom jchong p'nya(r) p'daam teuh Lok [ ].
I want to tell Mr. [ ] that...	-- Kyom jchong p'daam teuh Lok [ ] tha....
Please tell that him Mr.[ ] called.	-- Sum prap gwat tha Lok [ ] baan to'ra'sap mok.
I will call back at [ ] o'clock.	-- Kyom nung to'ra'sap tcuh venyh mao [ ].
We were cut off	-- To'ra'sap kaat bot howi.
Please try again.	-- Sum sahk (to'ra'sap) m'dong tee'it.
That was a wrong number.	-- Layke nu chia layke koh.

Proverbs:

Tro'up kung proo sraae Jcheh sum chai tok.	If wealth is preserved it is because women Know how to keep it.
Ptay'a thum sra'nuh Proo'eh leh sraae chia.	A home is as large and comfortable as The spirit of the woman of the house.
Tuk ho mun'dael hawt, Proh bot, mun'dael cheu'a.	As water flows and never tires, so Men swear but should never be believed.
Jchet mun dach Tveu s'dach mun baan.	He who has a soft heart Will never be king.

59

<u>DEFINITIONS</u>

A

a, an art. moi (lit.: one): a plate of fish -- trei moi jchaan; ("moi" in everyday speech is often compressed to the sound "m'" as: a plate of fish -- trei m'jchaan); [understood; not explicitly stated]: I'd like to have [a] new house. -- Kyom jchole jchet [ ] ptay'a t'maee.; act like [a] soldier -- tveu chia [ ] tee'hee'an

abalone n. a'ba'lawn; k'chawng sa'mut (lit: sea snail)

abandon v. leave behind -- tooo'k jchowl: He abandoned his car. -- Gwat tooo'k jchowl laan.; run away from -- rut jchowl; jchak jchowl: They abandoned the village. -- Gkay rut jchowl phum.; give up -- leh bong: abandon all hope of love -- leh bong kaa sung'khum sra'laanyh; abandon s. o. (lit: stop loving s. o.) -- chope sra'laanyh

abandoned adj. gkay roo'it jchowl; k'miun m'chah (lit: without owner)

abbreviate v. bung roo'inyh; compress -- song kype

abbreviation n. kaa bung proo'ing; (if of a word) peea saw'say kaat

abdicate v. dawk ree'ech (lit.: give (up) reign)

abdication n. kaa dawk ree'ech

abdomen n. poo'ah

abduct v. jchaab bung kum; jchaab puun roo'it; (both, lit.: "Grab (and) run"); jchaab yok teuh dow'ee kum'lung (lit: grab and take by force)

abduction n. kaa puun roo'it; kaa no'um jchenyh

ability n. sa'ma'ta'pheap

able v. free to, not physically unable to -- adje: Are you able to go? -- Tau(v) neh lok adje teuh tay?; have the skill to -- miun leh'ta'pheap: Are you able to play the piano? -- Tau(v) neh miun leh'ta'pheap leng piano?

abnormal adj. mun (AP: min, mun) twa'ma'da; (lit.: "not normal")

aboard adv. laung chi; aboard the plane -- laung chi ka'pal hawh; aboard the boat -- laung chi toook

abolish v. loup bum'bot; destroy -- bum plaang jchowl

abortion n. kaa praw'loot

about prp. concerning -- om'pee; jchum'poo'h: What is he talking about? -- Gwat ni'yaye om'pee a'veye?; about s. th. -- om'pee kaa: about the lost luggage -- om'pee kaa bot aye'von; approximately -- praw'heil: We have about [ten customers]. -- Yeung mium [p'nee'oo] praw'heil [dop neh].; chit (AP: chut, chee'ut); We have about [ten customers]. -- Chit miun [dop p'nee'oo].

about to v. chit jchaap p'dam

above prp. kang leuh: He lives above the shop. -- Gwat noeh kang leuh haang.; the sky above -- mey'k noeh kang leuh; re prices -- tlai: Rice went above 1000 riels [per kilo]. -- Ung'kaw laung tlai moi pwan riel [nung moi kilo].; above all -- yang jchum'batch bom'pot ·

abroad prp. bor'tay; noeh praw'tet krau

absent adj. choop; dael mun muk; bot muk (lit.: "face (muk) missing")

absent-minded adj. plic plee'eng

absolute adj. total, complete -- ch'bah; che'h le'h; pure -- sut'satt

absolutely adv. yang praw'kut; yang ch'bah: Absolutely wrong! -- Koh yang praw'kut! or, Koh yang ch'bah!

absolutely not adv. ot baan; mun kaa tay

absorb v. sro'b jchole

abstain v. chee'h vee'ung; fast (abstain from eating) -- thaawm

abstract adj. a'roo'pye: abstract idea -- a'roo'pye kum'nut; vague, not clear -- chia mun adj meuhl keunyh

abuse n. kaa tveu tooo'k to'h; kaa chi cho'an: human rights abuse -- kaa chi cho'an se'rei ma'nooh

abuse v. tveu tooo'k to'h; dah(k) tooo'k to'h; chi cho'an

academy n. sa'la bun'dut'sat: military academy -- sa'la bun'dut'sat tee'hee'an

accent n. sum'leng (lit: "voice"), or kshaw sum'leng: He speaks Khmer [with a Vietnamese] accent. -- Gwat ni'yaye pee'esa Khmei (kshaw) sum'leng [doj yuen].; He speaks with a Po'sat accent. -- Sum'leng gwat doj ni'yaye Po'sat.

accept v. to'tool (AP: to'too'al); yul'prome

accessory n. kreung

accident n. kroo'ti'nak: auto accident -- kroo'ti'nak laan; airplane crash -- kroo'ti'nak yun hawh

accomodate v. dum'row jchet

accompany v. choon dum'narr; teuh chi'moi

accomplish v. sum'rach

according to prp. taam tai; jchole taam; yang teuh taam

account n. bank account -- ko'hng; business account -- bun' chee; on account of -- bi'proo'ah; on (my) account -- dow'ee sa (kyom); take into account -- kut... owi mutch chuk: Please take this into account before deciding. -- Jcho(r) kut ru'ung ni owi mutch chuk muun peyr sum'rach.

accountant n. keh'neh'naae

accurate adj. correct -- trum tro: His story is not accurate. -- Ru'ung gwat ot trum tro.; clear -- ch'bah; good, correct -- la'aw

accusation n. kaa cho'up jchowt

accuse (of) v. jchowt; jchowt praw'kaan

accustomed to adj. so'um k'nong; They are not accustomed to eating snake. -- Gkay ot so'um k'nong kaa nyam poo'ah.

ache n. chh'ooh

achieve v. baan sum'rach; choke chey

across prp. kaat: across the stream -- kaat stung

across from prp. tul muk; The house is (located) across from [the hospital]. -- Ptay'a noeh tul muk [mun'ti'peh].

act n. s.th. done, an action -- um'peuh; pretense -- tveu peuh: It was all an act! -- Veea tveu peuh ma'leh!

act v. perform an action -- tveu; perform [on stage] -- leng [leuh chaa(k)]; pretend, deceive -- puuht: That guy is just acting. -- Moi nu puuht doll howi.

acting adj. temporary -- s'day'tee; acting chairman -- praw'teea'neea s'day'tee

action n. um'peuh

active adj. sa'kaam

activity n. sa'kaam'a'pheap

actor, actress n. actor -- too'a proh; chia dal too'a; actress -- too'a sraae; or, su'la'pa kar'nee; a famous actress -- su'la'pa kar'nee l'bye l'banyh

actual adj. piht praw'kat; men'tan

actually adv. taam piht; taam piht teuh: Actually I came at two o'clock. -- Taam put teuh kyom mok mao pi.

add v. total up numbers, calculate -- bo'(k) layke; add to, increase the quantity of -- tyme; add a small amount more to -- owi tyme tee'it teuh

addict n. ma'nooh ni ngyee'un

addicted adj. ngyee'un

addictive adj. ngyec'un; narcotics -- kreung ngyee'un (lit: addictive things)

address n. physical residence -- ti luum noeh; street number, etc. -- a'sigh'a'tan

address v. an envelope -- kaa k'nawng sum'buht

adjust v. to a condition -- kye sum roo(l); or, kye sum rawp; equipment -- mool: Please adjust [the radio (lit: the station frequency)] to make it (a little) clearer [,OK?]. -- Un'cheunyh mool [pawh raad'yo] owi ch'bah baan tek [meuhl].

administration n. governmental -- ratt'a'bal; conceptually -- ratt'a'ka

administer v. govern -- kroop krong; control -- kaan kaab

admiral n. op'dum neea'vee

admire v. kaut'sor'sa(rl)

admit v. acknowledge -- to'tool (AP: to'too'al) sum srawp; to'tool sa'ra'pheap; sa'ra'pheap (NB: all three foregoing terms very similar in usage.): He admitted that [it was his brother's fault.] -- Gwat to'tool sa'ra'pheap tha [ni veea chia kum'hawh p'twal kloo'an bong proh ro'bah gwat]; or, that it was his own fault -- chia kum'hawh p'twal kloo'an ro'bah gwat.

adopt v. a child -- sum yok teuh jchenyh chum; He is an adopted child. -- Gwat chia gkon jchenyh chum.

adult n. penyh vay: Kids are $1, adults $2. -- Gkon k'mayng keuh moi do'lla, penyh vay keuh pi do'lla.

adultery n. pet ko'bot; yok pra'pun gkay (lit.: "take the wife of someone")

advance v. move forward physically -- teuh muk; make progress -- tveu owi ree'k jchum'raan; advance rapidly -- tveu owi cheuan'leu'an; in advance -- chia muun

advanced adj. jchong k'poo'h

advantage n. a'thaa'praw'yow'it; phal praw'yow'it: [The other side] has the advantage because they [are used to] fighting at night. -- [Krum ma'kang tee'it] miun phal praw'yow'it bee'proo'a gkay [so'um k'nong] kaa banyh peyr yoop.

adventure n. kaa p'son preng

advertise v. jchoh psigh loo'a

advertisement n. commercial -- kaa jchoh ps'eye; political -- kos'na (lit: propaganda)

advice n. kaa nye'noo'um; kaa too'miun; dum'bole miun

advise v. too'mee'un: advise someone -- too'mee'un nye noo'um gkay

advisor n. tee'pruk'sa; neh owi yo'bal

advocate v. jchum runyh owi

a few adv. tek to'ich: a few things/items/of them -- jchum'noo'an tek to'ich; baan tek baan to'ich: a few things -- ro'bah baan tek baan to'ich; pi-bye (lit: "two-three"); a few (two or three) books -- s'po pi-bye

afford v. adje miun loi kroop (lit: "can have enough money"): I can't afford [don't have enough money] to buy this car. -- Kyom [mun adje miun loi kroop] nung tinh laan ni.

afraid adj. to be in fear of -- klait(ch): They are not afraid of the Khmer Rouge. -- Pooh'gkay mun klait(ch) Khmei Kra'hom.; not to dare to -- ngyo'ngyeut mun hee'an: I'm afraid to go. -- Kyom ngyo'ngyeut mun hee'an teuh tay.

after adv. in time -- krow'ee; in sequence -- bun'to'up: the next person -- neh bun'to'up; time/sequence combination -- taam: Please repeat after me. -- Sum taa taam kyom.; I will go after you. -- Kyom nung teuh taam neh.; in sense of if, or when, s. th. occurs -- ot pi: after he goes... -- ot pi gwat teuh...

after that adv. in time -- krow'ee nung or krow'ee peyr nung; in sequence -- bun'to'up nung

afternoon n. generally -- peyr ra'seel; late afternoon (approx. 4 p.m. to 8 p.m.) -- long'aae't (AP: lon'gnyee'et); also, although usually used in writing, esp. re early and mid-afternoon -- peyr t'ngai ch'ray

again adv. m'dong tee'it; chia t'maee

again and again adv. m'dong howi

against prp. praw'chang: against the law -- praw'chang ch'bop

age n. a'yoo: What is your age? (lit: How old are you?) -- Tau(v) neh a'yoo pu'man? [or] A'yoo neh pu'man? [or] A'yoo pu'man howi? [or] A'yoo aae??

agency n. of government -- p'nyke (lit: section): What agency do you work for? -- Neh tveu kaa noeh p'nyke na?; commercial agency -- ti p'nyke'ngyeea krum'huun (lit: company office/branch) or kaar'ya'lye (lit: office):

insurance agency -- ti p'nyke'ngyeea insurance; travel agency -- kaar'ya'lye looh sum'buht a'kas (lit: office that sells airline tickets)

agenda n. conceptually -- ro'bah dael tro tveu; in written form -- bun'chee ro'bah tro tveu

agent n. generally (sales, real estate, business, etc.) -- p'neh'ngyeea; spy, secret agent -- p'neh'ngyeea sum'ngut

ago adv. muun: He called just [a minute] ago. -- Gwat tuep tye telephone kyom [moi nee'a'tee] muun.; kun'lung howi; kun'lung mok howi; kun'lung mok ni; or, kun'lung teuh: It happened three years ago. -- Veea kaut laung bye chh'nam kun'lung howi [or, kun'lung mok howi, or, kun'lung mok ni, or kun'lung teuh].

agony n. kaa chh'ooh jchaab yang klang: the agony of the KR years... -- kaa chh'ooh jchaab yang klang k'nong ro'bab KR...

agree v. yul'prome: I agree!, or, Agreed! -- Yul'prome!; sohk jchet: agree subject to the approval of -- sohk jchet noeh k'nong kaa run'eye yul pro'me

agreement n. generally -- kej yul'prome; kaa yul'prome; contract -- kej sun'nyaa

agressor n. neh ruhm lope; neh chlee'un pee'un

aggression n. kaa ru'um'lop; kaa chlee'un pee'un

agriculture n. kaah'se'kaam (APs: kaak'se'kaam; kaat'se'kaam; NB: the suffix "kaam" generally denotes an activity)

ahead (of) prp. miun pree'up chiang; The Po'sat team is ahead of Kandal. -- Krum Po'sat miun pree'up chiang kang Kan'dal.; in the sense of "in front of" -- kaa muk; in advance, ahead of time -- chia muun

aid n. help or assistance, generally -- choo'ay; financial assistance -- choom'noo'ee; loi choo'ay; financial aid for students -- loi choom'noo'ee teuh gkon'sa

aide n. neh choom'noo'ee

air n. k'shaal a'kas

air conditioner n. ma'cheen traw'cheh(k)

air field n. jchum'nawt yun hawh

air force n. p'nyke a'kas; kawng thwaap a'kas

Air Cambodia n. A'kas Jchaw Kampuchea

airline n. a'kas jchaw

airmail v. taam yun hawh; send (via) airmail -- p'nya(r) taam yun hawh

airman n. air force enlisted man or officer -- tee'hee'an yun a'kas

airplane n. yun hawh; ka'pal hawh

airplane ticket n. sum'buht yun hawh

airport n. jchum'naut yun hawh

alarm n. (loosely) ma'seen ro (ro = to ring or clang); hence alram clock may be expressed "ni'a'li'ka ro"

alcohol n. medical or industrial -- a'coll; for drinking -- sra (AP: so'ra); kreung sro'vung (AP:sro'vaang)

alike adj. doj; doj ka'neea

alive adj. noeh rooh; or rooh noeh; or miun chi'vut (AP: chee'vit, chee'vut): Are (you) still alive? -- (Neh) Rooh noeh tay?; rooh rian miun chi'vut: He's still alive. -- Gwat rooh rian miun chi'vut.

all adv. te'ang (AP: tan, tang, tee'eng) awh (written awh(s)): all of Cambodia -- te'ang awh Kampuchea; all of (you, us, them, etc.) -- te'ang awh ka'neea; all of us -- yeung te'ang awh ka'neea; All you men are [the same]! -- Neh ma'nooh proh te'ang awh [doj doj tai] ka'neea.; in sense of all of it -- te'ang duhm: Bring all of it. -- Yok mok te'ang duhm.; in sense of every -- kroop: all kinds of things -- kroop bye yang; in sense of full, complete -- penyh: I worked all day. -- Kyom tveu kaa penyh moi t'ngai.; all the time -- kroop peyr; almost all -- steu tai te'ang awh; He ate almost all that food. -- Gwat nyam steu tai te'ang awh ma'hope nung.; not at all -- a tay; All right (OK) -- baat (response for men) or chan (response for women); all finished (e.g., food) -- awh row'lin howi; they're all gone (i. e., all of those people are gone) -- pooh'gkay teuh awh howi

all over adv. in all parts of -- kroop ti cunlye'ng: all over the world -- kroop ti cunlye'ng ney pope'lok; or, kroop ti cunlye'ng k'nong pi pope'lok; covering -- pieh penyh noeh leuh: There are books all over the table. -- Miun s'po pieh penyh noeh leuh tohk.

alley n. ploe ch'raw

alliance n. sum'poan'na mit (lit: relationship of friendship)

allow v. owi or baahk owi: They do not allow you to go. -- Gkay mun owi neh teuh.; They do not allow you to go alone. -- Gkay mun baahk owi neh teuh tai eiyne.; to be allowed to do s. th. -- tro baan a'noo'naaht: You are not allowed to go alone. -- Neh mun tro baan a'noo'naaht ma'neh eiyne.; approve legally -- a'noo'naaht

ally n. sum'poan'na mit nung: Vietnam used to be Cambodia's ally against the Khmer Rouge. -- Sruk Vietnam tra'laawp keuh chia sum'po'an'na mit nung Kampuchea praw'chang Khmei Kra'hom.

almost adv. steu: almost equal -- steu sm'auu ka'neea; chit: almost finished -- chit jchob howi; pra'heil; almost the same as -- pra'heil ka'neea nung; almost equal to -- pra'heil pun ka'neea

alone adj. by onesself -- tai eiyne; eiyne; ma'neh eiyne; He went alone. -- Gwat teuh tai eiyne.; You're not allowed to go alone. -- Neh mun owi dull teuh eiyne.; tai m'yang; ...with [promises] alone... -- chi'moi [kaa sun'nyaa] tai m'yang...

along prp. taam mun'do'wi; along with -- teuh chi'moi, or teuh pong

a long time n. peyr dull yoot (AP: yoo(t)); a long time ago -- peyr dull yoo' kun'lung mok (howi)

a lot adv. ch'raan; [AP: cha'ran, ch'rown]

already adv. roo'it howi; I've already ordered. -- Haow roo'it howi.

alright adj. ot aae tay: Don't worry, it's alright. -- Kum ba'rum, vee'a ot aae tay.

Alright! interj. Baat, baan!

also adv. along with -- chi'moi; I will go too. -- Kyom nung teuh chi'moi.; as well -- da'aae; Thai people also eat a lot of rice. -- Saah see'um nyam bye ch'raan da'aae.; in addition -- pong

alternative n. other approach -- ploe p'sayng tee'it; choice -- kaa jchreu'reu': I have no alternative. -- Kyom k'miun kaa jchreu'reu'.

although conj. twye't'butt'tha'ee: Although I am sick... -- Twye't'butt'tha'ee kyom chh'ooh....

always adv. generally -- tyne tai... chia'nik [NB: accent in "chia'nik" is heavily on last syllable]; in short sentences only, either tyne tai or chia'nik can be used alone: He is always happy. -- Gwat s'bai ree'ree'aae chia'nik.; in longer sentences, tyne tai and chia'nik should be used together: The KR are always saying that Vietnam is a threat to Thailand. -- Khmei Kra'hom tyne tai ni'yaye chia'nik tha sruk Vietnam cum'ree'um cum'hyne sruk See'um.; thus, depending on the length and organization of the sentence, "always" can be expressed by any of "tyne tai... chia'nik", "chia'nik chia kaal" or "tyne tai" alone, viz.: I always eat "baa' bawh" (rice soup) in the morning" can be expressed as:

  1) Kyom tyne tai nyam baa' bawh noeh peyr pruhk chia'nik.; or
  2) Chia'nik chia kaal kyom nyam baa' bawh noeh peyr pruhk.; or
  3) Kyom tyne tai nyam baa' bawh noeh peyr pruhk.;

"always" in sense of "every day" -- rwal t'ngai; or yang tee'ung twa(t): He always comes to school [on time]. -- Gwat mok sa'la yang tee'ung twa(t) [peyr va'lee'a].

am v. keuh chia: I am a student. -- Kyom keuh chia gkon'sa.; [unexpressed, understood]: I (am) ill. -- Kyom ( ) chh'ooh.; I'm sick and tired of eating french fries. -- Kyom ( ) tunh tro'an nung nyam dum'lung jchian.

a. m. n. t'gnai: ten a. m. -- mao dap t'ngai

amazed adj. pn'yeh p'aal (lit: wake up (pn'yeh) shocked (p'aal)): I was amazed that he was still alive. -- Kyom miun kaa pn'yeh p'aal dael gwat noeh miun chi'vut.

amazing xcl. or adj. Bah(k) saahk! (lit: makes hair stand on end); unbelievable: -- Mun cheu'a!; or, Mun koo'a owi cheu'a.; wonderful: -- awh jcha; never seen anything like it before, unusual, different -- pl'eye'k p'nyke (lit: eye opening); great, wonderful -- la'aw chat'chai

ambassador n. neh kaa 'toot; eyke'a'keea ratt toot

ambulance n. laan peyt

ambush n. and v. lom'po'ut

amen! xcl. sa'tooo'k!

America n. sruk Am'rik; Americaa

American adj. Am'rik (APs: A'kaae'eng; A'mer'i'cang; A'kee'un); re nationality -- chuun chee'it Am'rik

ammunition n. kro'up (AP: kro'op)

amnesty n. kaa leuk laung to'h; give amnesty -- leuk laung to'h owi: I will give you all amnesty. -- Kyom nung leuk laung to'h owi neh te'ang awh ka'neea.

among prp. k'nong jchum'now'm: among friends... -- k'nong jchum'now'm mit...

amount n. jchum'noo'an

amusing adj. rik ree'aae; cum'plyne; s'bai; amusing story -- ru'ung s'bai

ancient adj. bora(n)

and conj. nung: you and me -- neh nung kyom; howi nung; pepper and salt -- ma'ric howi nung um'bul; and also -- prome te'ang... pong da'aae: The road was muddy and also [slippery]. -- Ploe paw pet paw pat(ch) prome te'ang [ro'ul] pong da'aae.); [implied]: Wait [and] say (it) after me. -- Jcham [ ] tha taam kyom.; re numbers -- ro'up: "thousands and thousands of people..." -- pra'chee'chuun ro'up pwan; millions and millions of riels -- riel ro'up lee'en

and not conj. howi mun men: for them and not for you -- sum'rap gkay howi men mun sum'rap neh

angel n. generally -- tay'va'da; angels depicted at Anghor Wat, Angkor Thum and other temples -- ap'sa'ra

angelic adj. slote; slote bote

angle n. mum; corner -- ch'rum

angry adj. generally -- khung; very upset at s. th. -- mua mao kaaw ru'ung

animal n. saat (NB: "race" or "people" = saah; "meat" = sat(ch)); domestic animal -- saat sruk; wild animal -- saat prey; dangerous, man-eating animals (lion, tiger, bear, etc.) -- saat sa'how

ankle n. kaw cheung

announce v. praw'kas; ps'eye

announcer n. (including master of ceremonies) -- neh praw'kas

annoy v. ruhm'kahn

annually adv. praw'chum chh'nam

another adj. moi tee'it; moi p'sayng tee'it: I have another teacher. -- Kyom miun kruu moi p'sayng tee'it.; the other -- daw tay tee'it: Go to the other [house]. -- Teuh [ptay'a] daw tay tee'it.

answer n. jchum'la'wee; (APs: ch'la'wee; chum'lye); kaa jchum'la'wee

answer v. jchum'la'wee

answering machine n. ma'seen tooo'k p'nya(r)

ant n. s'raw ma'mee'ch; flying ant -- ma'mee'ch

any adv. [implied]: We don't have any (uncooked) rice. -- Yeung ot miun [ ] ung'kaw tay.; moi na... da'aae: Any house will be expensive. -- Ptay'a moi na kaw tlai da'aae.; any minute -- peyr chop chop ni

anyhow adv. yang na kaw dow'ee: There are many problems but we will try to study anyhow. -- Miun pun'ha ch'raan, pun'ta'aae yeung pyee'a yee'im rian yang na kaw dow'ee. (NB: see, also, discussion of respective usages of "yang na kaw dow'ee" and "da'aae" under definition of "anyway".)

any more adv. tee'it: We can't come here any more. -- Yeung mun adj mok ti ni tee'it tay.

anyone, anybody adv. no na; no na moi: Anyone you want. -- No na moi kaw baan da'aae.

anything adv. a'veye: anything you want... -- a'veye dael neh jchong baan...; aae tee'it (AP: eye tee'it): Do you want anything else? -- Tro kaa aae tee'it?; Is there anything else? -- Miun eye tee'it?; [implied]: I don't want to buy [anything]. -- Kyom ot jchong tinh [ ].

any time adv. kroop peyr

any way adv. in any fashion possible, by whatever means, by any means possible -- yang na dow'ee; an'chung dow'ee

anyway adv. regardless, nevertheless, whatever the circumstances -- yang na kaw dow'ee: Tomorrow is a holiday; I'm going to work anyway. -- S'eye'd t'ngai choop; kyom nung tveu kaa yang na kaw dow'ee.; da'aae -- Even though it is raining, I have to go back again (anyway). -- Plee'eng yang na kaw dow'ee, kaw kyom teuh venyh da'aae.;

NB: Expression of "anyhow", "anyway", "despite", "even though", "nevertheless", "regardless" and "still" is usually achieved by use of "yang na kaw dow'ee" placed at or near the beginning of a sentence. It is also, however, conveyed by the use of "da'aae" at the end of a sentence where the speaker wishes to i) emphasize especially the person he is referring to or ii) emphasize especially the concept of "also", or iii) impart added emphasis to the "regardless" or "despite the circumstances" connotation of "yang na kaw dow'ee".

Examples of these respective usages would be as follows:

i) Da'aae would be used to convey "anyway" would be: What do you think (of s.th. or s.o.) (anyway)? -- Kut yang na da'aae? Here there is no concern with "circumstances" and the emphasis is on finding out what the "you" thinks of the point is question; hence, da'aae.

i and ii) Are you going to work tomorrow anyway? (emphasis on "despite the circumstances" and/or on comparison of what "I" am going to do with what "you" are going to do) -- Neh eiyne nung tveu kaa s'eye'd yang na kaw dow'ee?.; BUT: Are you going to work tomorrow anyway (too)? (emphasis on what "you" are going to do and hence on "too", whether or not spoken) -- Neh eiyne nung tveu kaa s'eye'd da'aae?.

iii) To add emphasis to the "despite the circumstances" connotation already supplied by "yang na kaw dow'ee": Even though he was hungry, he still could not eat. -- Too'a chia gwat klee'un, yang na kaw dow'ee gwat mun adje nyam bye da'aae.

anywhere adv. kroop ti cun'lye'ng

apart prep. p'sayng pi: The child lives apart from its parents. -- Gkon rooh noeh p'sayng pi oeuv'puk m'dye.; into separate pieces -- chia p'nyke

apartment n. individual flat -- ptay'a l'veng; apartment building -- a'keea

apologize v. sum to'h: He should apologize. -- Gwat koo'a sum to'h.

appeal v. om'pee'oo vnee'oo: They appealed to [the government] to stay in the US. -- Pooh'gkay om'pee'oo vnee'oo teuh [ratt'a'pi'bal] sum'rap snak noeh sruk Am'ric.

appear v. seem to be -- doj; or, meuhl doj teuh; or, hyte doj chia; come into view -- bung hanyh; lik laung: He appeared yesterday. -- Gwat bung hanyh kloo'an musl' munyh.; He appeared suddenly. -- Gwat s'rop tai lic laung.

appearance n. way one looks -- thut'ta'pheap

apple n. plai pomme

application n. peea'sum: job application -- peea'sum tveu kaa; legal or travel application; petition -- sum'num ru'ung; visa application -- peea sum'rap sum vi'za

apply v. dah(k) peea'sum: He applied for a job. -- Gwat dah(k) peea'sum tveu kaa.

appoint v. tha'ing'tung

appointed adj. ploe'kaa; an appointed officer -- mun'trei ploe'kaa

appointment n. kaa na(th) choop; pra'choom

approach v. mok chit

approval n. yul'prome; kaa yul'prome; subject to the approval of... -- noeh k'nong kaa run'eye yul'prome ney [or, pi]... ; receive aproval of -- to'tool yul'prome: They did not receive approval of your application. -- Pooh'gkay mun to'tool yul'prome sum'num ru'ung lok.

approve (of) v. yul'prome: They did not approve your visa (application). -- Gkay mun yul'prome peea sum'rap sum vee'za lok.; authorize -- a'noo'naaht

approximately adv. pra'heil; pra'man pra'man; chit; chit doj ka'neea

April n. Me'sa

arbitrate n. psahs'psah

arbitration n. kaa sum'rach ney a'nya kan'dal

arch n. architectural feature -- plong t'veea

architect n. neh tek tong nung (or chi'moi) som'nong; or
neh tek tong nung (or chi'moi) kaa song; (construction = som'nong or kaa song; hence these phrases are literally, "person involved with [tek tong nung, or chi'moi] construction [som'nong or kaa song])

are v. baan chia: Why are you so lazy? -- Mutch baan chia neh peyk k'chill?; chia or keuh chia: They are members. -- Gkay keuh chia sa'ma'chik. or, Gkay chia sa'ma'chik.; in sense of "are they that" -- dael: [What books] are you looking for? (lit: What books are they that you are looking for?) -- [S'po aae] dael neh sveye ro'k?

area n. vicinity -- cunlye'ng; ti; amount of land -- dum'bun: The soldiers control a large area [lit.: The area the soldiers control is large.] -- Dum'bun dael tee'hee'an kaan'kaab (or troo'it tra) thum.

argue v. praw'kye ka'neea; ch'loo ka'neea; ch'loo praw'kye

argument n. kaa jchaw jchehk ka'neea; kaa ch'loo'a

arithmetic n. lake'no'poon

arm n. dai; (NB: same word as that for "hand")

armed forces n. kawng thwaap (AP: tho'up)

army n. yo'tee'a (AP: yoo'tee'a); thwaap: National Army (nomme-de-guerre used by Khmer Rouge to refer to its military forces) -- Thwaap Chee'it; as differentiated from navy and air force -- thwaap cheung daiy (lit: land armed force)

around prp. surrounding -- chuum'venyh: The para's were all around the village. -- Para noeh po'at chuum'venyh phum.; in the neighborhood of -- chit: The para's were around (near) the village. -- Para noeh chit phum.; present, available, can be found -- mao nyut nyoo'up: He's never around. -- Gwat mun'dael mok nyut nyoo'up tay.

arrest v. jchap kuum kay'eng: He was arrested yesterday. -- Gwat tro baan jchap kuum kay'eng pi musl' munyh.

arrive v. at a near place (direction of movement towards speaker's location) -- mok dull [or] mok howi: The teacher has arrived (here). -- Neh kruu mok howi [or, in accelerated speech, Neh koo ma 'oi] ti'ni.; at a distant place (direction of movement away from speaker's location) -- teuh dull [or] teuh howi: After leaving here last week, he arrived in Battambong yesterday. -- Krow'ee peyr jchenyh pi ti ni pi a'ttith muun, gwat teuh dull Bat'tam'bong musl'munyh.

arrogant adj. (see "insolent")

arrow n. proo'ing

art n. seh'la'pah

article n. section of a document -- kaw; kaw praw'kaah; story in a publication -- a'ta'bawt; thing, item, as "articles to declare" -- ro'bah

artist n. su'la'pa' koo

artillery n. kum pleung thum

as conj. as being -- chia: Think of me as a friend. -- Kut kyom chia mit paya.; at the time that -- noeh peyr dael: As he was speaking... -- Noeh peyr dael gwat kom'puung ni'yaye...

as if adv. hyte doj chia; teuh: It looks as if we cannot eat here. -- Meulh teuh yeung mun adj nyam bye ti ni tay.

as soon as adv. dull: As soon as you learn a little, you want to go too fast! -- Dull jcheh, leu'an hoo'a! [lit: As soon as learn, go too fast.]; peyr na... plee'em: As soon as he arrives, please tell him about this. -- Peyr na gwat mok dull plee'em, jcho(r) prap gwat ru'ung ni.

as soon as possible adv. yang ro'has: Please call me as soon as possible. -- Jcho(r) telephone kyom yang ro'has.; I want to learn Khmer as soon as possible. -- Jchong rien Khmei yang ro'has.

as usual adv. taam twa'ma'da; chia twa'ma'da

As you like. xcl. Taam neh jchole jchet.; Srech tai eiyne.

ashamed (of, or to) adj. koo'a tai k'mah (jchum'poo'h); The government [should be] ashamed of all [the corruption]. -- Ratt'a'pi'bal koo'a tai k'mah jchum'poo'h [um'peuh pu'ka'ra loi] te'ang awh nu.; koo'a owi k'mah: You should be ashamed. -- Veea koo'a owi k'mah.; somehwat stronger -- a'mah muk

Asia n. Asie; Southeast Asia -- Asie pyke a'ka'nee

ask v. soo'a

asleep adj. dayke loo(k); geyng loo(k)

aspirin n. t'nam aspirin

ass n. derriere -- koo'it; fool -- plei pleuh; ma'nooh ch'koo'it

assassinate v. tveu kiet; sum'lop

assassination n. kiet'a'kaam

assault n. kaa vi'yaye thwaap; kaa vi'yaye lok

assault v. vi'yaye lop

assemble v. build, put together -- daum laung

assembly n. su'phea: National Assembly -- Su'phea Chee'it; kaa pra'choom: general assembly -- Kaa pra'choom chia too' teuh;

asset n. tro'up sum'baat; tro'up ro'bah

assert v. praw'kas

assign v. award a position to -- tai'ny tung; command to do s. th. -- chut owi: I assign you (order you to go to) Po'sat. -- Kyom chut owi neh Po'sat.

assist v. choo'ay (AP: choo'i)

assistant n. neh choo'ay; neh chuum'noo'ee

associate v. jchole ruum; sype'koop: I do not want to associate with you anymore. -- Kyom mun jchong sype'koop nung neh tee'it tay.

associate n. neh tveu kaa chi'moi

association n. group -- sa'ma'kuum; relationship -- toom neh, toom nong; kaa tek tong

assortment n. sap'peea: an assortment of weapons -- sap'peea a'vwut

assume v. sa'ni'tan; I assume it is ready. -- Kyom sa'ni'tan taa roo'it howi.

assure (that) v. ti'neea (tha); I assure you it is ready. -- Kyom ti'neea tha roo'it howi.

at prp. a place -- noeh: He lives at Po'sat -- Gwat noch Po'sat; The regiment is based at Po'sat. -- Kawng varet sena thum te'ang mool'than noeh Po'sat.; a time -- noeh, or peyr, or noeh peyr: The bus leaves at 7 p. m. -- Laan ch'nool jchenyh pi noeh mao prum'pul yoop.; at night -- peyr yoop; at that time -- noeh peyr nu; at the same time -- noeh peyr chi'moi; at once -- yang jchaap, yang ro'has; at first -- chia dum'bo'ng; at last -- jchong krow'ee; at least -- yang howi bom'pot; at your convenience -- taam neh jchole jchet; srech tai neh eiyne

athlete n. a'ta'pu'la'kam

atmosphere n. setting, conditions, circumstances -- pak'rik'ya'kaa: talks in a friendly atmosphere... -- kaa ni'yaye noeh k'nong pak'rik'ya'kaa mi'ta'pheap...

attache n. a'noo'pun

attack n. kaa vye; kaa praw'yoot; Last rainy season there were many attacks. -- Noeh ro'doe t'leh plee'eng kun laung mok ni miun kaa praw'yoot ka'neea chia ch'raan.

attack v. vye; vye'lop; praw'yoot; attack and kill -- praw'ha

attack v. praw'yoot

attempt n. if already taken place -- kaa l'bong meuhl; if in future -- kaa pun'pong

attend v. jchole roo'um

71

Attention! xcl.   Prong praw'yaat!

attitude n.   aae'ree'ya'but: The attitude of the French Government was [to favor] Sihanouk. --   Aae'ree'ya'but ro'bah ratt'a'pi'bal ba'raang keuh [to'tunh teuh kang] s'dach Sihanouk.; He had a bad attitude. --   Gwat miun aae'ree'ya'but a'krah.; cha'ruk: He has a bad attitude. --   Gwat miun cha'ruk a'krah.

attorney n.   may'tia'vi; attorney general --   aa'kehk may'tia'vi

audience n.   generally --   neh too'sna; viewing --   neh meulh; listening --   neh s'dap

August n.   Say'ha

aunt n.   younger than parent to which related --   m'dye ming; older than parent to which related --   m'dye thum; m'dye om

author n.   neh ni'puu'n; neh saw ru'ung

authority n.   power, generally --   ah'nya'thoa; specific authorization --   um'nach

authorize v.   a'noo'naaht; baahk owi

automatic adj.   s'eye praw'vwut

automatically adv.   dow'ee s'eye praw'vwut

automobile n.   laan; auto accident --   kroo'ti'nak laan

available adj.   in supply, in stock, extant --   miun; Is there any tea available? Yes, it is available.   --   Ta'aae miun tay? Miun.; not busy --   miun leh'ta'pheap: Mr. Smith is not available (e.g., to come to the phone). --   Mr. Smith ot [or, mun] miun leh'ta'pheap tay.

average adj.   so-so; not good, not bad --   mut s'yom: ...an average harvest --   ... po't a p'auwl mut s'yom; average income --   praa(k) chum'nole mut s'yom; typical --   twa'ma'da: The average five-year-old has lost some teeth.   --   Twa'ma'da k'mayng a'yoo pram chh'nam tro doll t'ming.; Today was an average day.   --   T'ngai ni twa'ma'da.; average age --   a'yoo twa'ma'da; moi pa'choom: average people --   pra'chee'chuun moi pa'choom

average n.   pin'tooo'k: His average in school...   --   Pin'tooo'k gwat noeh sa'la...

avoid v.   chee'a vee'ung; chee'a jchenyh: avoid him --   chee'a vee'ung pi gwat; In order to avoid [more bloodshed]... --   Dum'bye chee'a vee'ung [kaa kap sum'lop chia t'maee]...; kej jchenyh: to avoid an accident --   dum'bye kej jchenyh pi kaa kroo'ti'nak...

awake adj.   pn'yeh: He is awake now.   --   Gwat pn'yeh dung kloo'an howi.

away adv.   ch'ng'eye (AP: ch'nai); to go away --   teuh chng'eye; far away --   chng'eye chng'eye; Go away! (Go, go ! or Get out!) --   Teuh, teuh!

awe n.   s'kd'eye ch'ngau'itch

awful adj.   a'krah krye leng

a while adv.   moi plet

awkward adj.   ungainly --   ch'king, ch'kong; difficult --   mun sroul (lit: "not easy"); an awkward situation --   s'tan'kaa mun sroul

ax n.   poo'tauw; [to split] firewood with an ax --   [poo'h] awhs nung poo'tauw

B

baby n. generally -- gkon ngaa'; tee'a roo'a(k); small child -- gkon to'ich; gkon k'chaiy; have a baby -- **ch'long tunlay** (lit.: "cross the river", e. g., into life)

bachelor n. neh kum'lawh; kum'lawh; neh noeh liv (NB: liv = unmarried); Is he a bachelor? -- Tau(v) ma'neh nu noeh liv?

back n. of the human body -- knawng; behind your back -- kang krow'ee knawng neh; back of a vehicle -- koot: back of the car -- koot laan (lit: trunk); back and forth -- teuh venyh, teuh mok; teuh mok, teuh mok; or [_____] teuh, [_____] mok: The rockets flew back and forth. -- Ro'kit plong teuh, plong mok.; in back of -- kang krow'ee; to be back -- tra'laawp mok venyh; coming back -- tra'laawp mok venyh; to talk behind the back of -- ni'yaye daum

back and forth, to go v. jchenyh jchole jchole jchenyh, jchole jchenyh jchenyh jchole (single, unified phrase, usually used with humorous connotation/intent)

background n. life history -- chi'vut pro'wat; prior experience -- but pi'sowt

backtalk n. pee'a thum thum (lit: arrogant talk); ni'yaye thaawp mwot

backward adv. directional -- bun ch'ra: Crocodiles can swim backward. -- Kaw'per adje hahl bun ch'ra tuk.; not modern -- mun tuum'neup

back up v. back up a vehicle -- toi: back a car up -- toi laan

bad adj. generally -- a'krah (written: akra(k)): bad luck -- sum'nang a'krah; too bad -- a'krah nah; mun la'aw (lit: not good); morally bad, corrupt -- to'h: All politicians are bad/corrupt. -- Neh na'yo'bye te'ang awh choop'up to'h.; morally bad -- koh; evil -- chung'rai; crude -- ch'leu'ee (as. "bad language"); rude, rough, (as "bad manners") -- kahtch

bag n. small bag -- tung; ka'pow; handbag -- kaa'bok; rice bag or sack -- kaa rong ung'kaw; ba'oo; bag(s), suitcase(s) -- va'leez

bake v. dut num

balcony n. yo: a room with a balcony -- ban'tope chi'moi yo; ree'en haa'l: from the balcony of the hotel -- pi ree'en haa'l ney o'tyle

bald adj. trung 'our

ball n. toy -- balle (pronounced like French "balle")

ballet n. ro'ban ballet

balloon n. peut'pown

ballot n. sum'lup ch'naut

ballpoint pen n. bic

bamboo n. bamboo shoots -- traa'paae'ang (AP: tuum'paae'eng, ta'paeng); full-grown bamboo -- a'ssei (written: russei); (Khmer riddle: What is "ta" when young but "a" when old? (the reverse of usual where "ta" means "old man" and "a" can be use to signify a child): answer: bamboo, which grows from "ta'peang" to "a'ssei".)

banana n. jchayk; short-variety banana -- jchayk um'va

band n. krum plaeng

bandage v. tnal bong smong; rum ro'booh

bandage n. bong si'mon

bandit n. jchaao

bank n. financial institution -- enna'te'an; banque; bahng (fr. Fr.); river bank -- ch'raae'ung tun'lay; (NB: "kom'puung" as in "Kompuung Cham" and other Khmer province names, sometimes seen translated "river bank," means a point on a river bank where boats stop, i. e., to off-load/pick up passengers/cargo to/from villages or individual houses and hence translates more accurately as "landing" than "bank".)

bank account n. kohng; open a bank account -- baahk kohng

bank note n. praa(k)

bar n. for drinks -- baaa'; for doors/windows -- chum rung

barber n. chee'ung kaat saahk; neh kaat saahk

bare adj. taw'tay

barefoot adj. cheung taw'tay

barely adv. mun steu (AP: mun soeu) tay; The crocodile could barely lift its tail. -- Kaw'per leuk cun'toi mun steu tay.; mun roo'it

bargain n. good deal (usual spoken form; used to refer in speech to a bargin price) -- tauk tlai; good deal (written form used, for example, in advertising signs with meaning "low price") -- tlai tauk

bargain v. tauk tlai; Don't bargain too much. -- Kum tauk tlai peyk.; bargain for -- thaw'va

barren adj. k'sawh

bartender n. neh lee'aae sra

base n. location -- mul'a'tan: military base -- mul'a'tan kawng thwaap (lit: location of a force); army base -- pu'tee'aae tee'hee'an

based at prp. sun'tach noeh; noeh chuum'ruhm (lit: stay at camp (in) Po'sat) ... based at Po'sat -- neoh chuum' ruhm

based on prp. ru'ung mok pi; sm'oh taam

basic adj. pi daum kum'naut; the basic problem -- pun'ha pi daum kum'naut

basil n. basil-like spice -- chii nee'ung vong

basket n. kun'traw; take a basket to market -- yok kun'traw teuh p'sa; flat woven basket or tray used to husk rice by tossing it in air -- chung'aae

bath n. moi tuk (AP: ngoy tuk)

bathe v. ones'self -- moi tuk or ngoy tuk; s.o. else -- moi tuk, or ngoy tuk, owi s.o.

bathing suit n. aow-kow mooch tuk

bathroom n. ban'tope tuk

battalion n. loosely -- kawng va'ret (AP: kawng varee'a); to differentiate from "regiment" -- kawng va'ret'sena to'ich

battery n. for [flashlight] -- ta'mau [pul]; for car -- a'koy; ba'trec

battle n. sa'mau'ra'phum

battlefield n. ti lien praw'yoot; veal praw'yoot; sa'mau'ra'phum

bay n. chaaw

bayonet n. bayonet

bazaar n. p'sa

bazooka n. kum pleung bazooka

be v. physically -- noeh: I won't be here. -- Kyom ot noeh ni tay.; situationally -- keuh chia; or, for future conditions, pr'eye chia: One day you will be rich. -- T'ngai na moi neh nung pr'eye chia neh miun.

Be careful ! -- Praw'yaat!

beach n. ch'ney k'suj (lit: sand coast)

beam n. of light -- ras'mye; of building, e.g., rafter -- p'tong

bean n. generally -- sun'dyke (AP: s'dye); soy beans -- sun'dyke siang; mung, or green, beans -- sun'dyke bye or sun'dyke kee'oo; mung bean sprouts -- sun'dyke baan dos; bean curd -- t'auw'hoo; bean thread (noodles) -- mee soo'a; powdered bean drink -- tuk sun'dyke; (peanuts -- sun'dyke daiy; black eyed peas -- sun'dyke saw)

bear n. kla ka'mum

beard n. puk jchung'kaa (lit: "hair (at) chin"; moustache = puk mwot, or "hair (at) mouth")

beat n. rhythm -- kun'dong; to have a fast beat -- miun kun'dong leu'an

beat v. defeat s. o. (lit: win against) -- ch'neh: We beat the enemy. -- Yeung ch'neh sa'tro.; hit, generally -- vye; vi'yaye: beat drums -- vye sco; hit, with hands only -- thaawp

beat up (s.o.) v. thaawp

beaten (by) adj. pa'ra'chey (dow'ee sa): The enemy was beaten by our troops. -- Sa'tro tro baan pa'ra'chey dow'ee sa tee'hee'an ro'bah yeung.

beautification n. kaa tyng loom'aw

beautiful adj. sa'aat

beautify v. fix up, up-grade -- tyng loom'aw: I beautified my house. -- Kyom tyng loom'aw ptay'a kyom.

beauty n. sym'pwah

because conj. bee'proo'a; because of -- mawk pi

become v. pr'eye teuh chia: He became a monk. -- Gwat pr'eye teuh chia neh lok.; pr'eye chia: He thinks he will become king again. -- Gwat kut tha nung pr'eye chia s'dach m'dong tee'it.; t'lch: They have all become sick. -- Pooh'gkay t'leh kloo'an chh'ooh.

bed n. gkrey; to go to bed -- teuh geyng; or, (more colloquial) teuh dayke

bee n. k'muum

beef n. sat(ch) gko

beer n. bee'a

beetle n large, black common Cambodian variety -- kun'chai

before prp. muun: Before I met her... -- Muun choop vee'a... ; before that -- muun nung; earlier, at an earlier time -- chia muun: Before, I would have agreed. -- Chia muun, kyom yul prome.

beg v. sum: beg for money/beg for food -- sum loi/sum ma'hope; I beg your pardon (for error). -- Sum to'h.; I beg your pardon? (What did you say?) -- Sum to'h, ni'yaye m'dong tee'it mok? (lit.: "speak again, please"); Ta mutch? (lit.: "say what?"); beg for mercy -- sum kaa an'kroo'a; sum may'daa

begin v. jchaap p'daum (AP: jchaap p'dam); pra'rup... laung: The ceremony begins at ten o'clock. -- Pi'ti buun pra'rub laung noeh mao dup.

beginning n. kaa jchaap p'dam; dum'bong; kaa jchaap dum'bong: the beginning of the book -- kaa jchaap p'dam chia s'po; kaa jchaap p'dam dum'bong ney s'po; from the beginning -- jchaap p'dam om'pee dum'bong; at the beginning (or, "to begin"; often said at start of meetings) -- chia dum'bong; chia ba'tum

behind prp. in back of -- kang krow'ee; pi krow'ee; losing, not leading -- kom'puung jchanyh

behind-the-scenes adj. leh bum poo'un: behind-the-scenes foreign business interests -- leh bum poo'un ney chum'noo'inyh bor'tay

believe v. cheu'a (AP: cheu'): I don't believe it. -- Mun cheu'a.; Believe me! -- Cheu'a kyom teuh!; believe in (as in politics, religion, ideology); favor -- ni'yuum

bell n. kind that can be struck -- joo'ung; kind that is rung by pushing switch, button, etc., like door bell -- kun'dung

belong (to) v. be the possession of, be mine/his/hers/etc. -- ro'bah [or] chia ro'bah (written or formal spoken style: ka'ma'sit ro'bah); This car belongs to me. -- Laan ni ro'bah kyom.; This wristwatch is mine/belongs to me. -- Ni'a'li'ka ni chia ro'bah kyom.; belongs to, re non-material things -- tow kai; That business belonged to Chinese people. -- Muk chuum'noo'inyh tow kai saah jchun.; is a member of -- chia sa'ma'chik: He used to belong to the CPP [Cambodian Peoples' Party]. -- Gwat tra'laawp chia sa'ma'chik CPP.

below prp. kang krowm

belt n. k'sye kro'vat

bend v. one's body -- ouwn; wood, metal, etc. -- pooht owi kouwng; bend the rules -- pdo ch'bop: [If] they give the police [1000] riels, they will bend the rules. -- [Praw'sun'baa] gkay owi dam'roo'it [m'pwan] riel, gwat nung pdo ch'bop.; (NB: "m'pwan" is a common AP compression of "moi pwan"); He won't bend. -- Ma'nooh nu rung k'bal nah. (lit: That man (has a) very "iron" mind.)

beneath prp. kang krowm

benefit n. advantage accruing from s. th.; reason; motive -- p'auwl praw'yow'it: for the benefit of the Cambodian people -- dum'bye bung p'auwl praw'yow'it sum'rap pra'chee'chuun Kampuchea; profit -- jchum'nenyh

beside prp. k'bye

besides prp. in addition to -- krow pi: Besides working, I like to watch tennis. -- Krow pi tveu kaa, kyom jchole jchet meuhl gkay leng tennit.

best adj. la'aw awh jchaa; la'aw bom'pot

bet n. kaa p'noo'al

bet v. p'noo'al

betel nut n. m'loo; white paste spread on leaf with which betel nut often eaten -- k'bauw

betray v. k'but; k'but jchet

better adj. re quality -- la'aw chiang; krawn baar chiang; praw'sar chiang: This room is better than that room. -- Ban'tope ni la'aw chiang ban'tope nu.; better hygene -- a'na'mye praw'sar chiang; re advisability -- praw'sar chiang: It is better [to wait] than to go. -- [Kaa rong jcham] praw'sar chiang teuh muun.; better than nothing -- la'aw chiang ot; better [i.e., healthier] -- saah sa'bauw'ee; or krawn baar: I hope you get better. -- Kyom sung'kum tha neh chia saah sa'bauw'ee.; I feel better. -- Kyom chia krawn baar howi.; re food -- chng'anyh: The food here is better than at the hotel. -- Ma'hope ti ni chng'anyh chiang ti o'tyle.

between prp. chan lawh; noeh chan lawh; ro'vieng

beyond prp. just past -- hoo'a: The UNTAC office is just beyond the Ambassador Hotel. -- Kaa'ri'a'lye UNTAC hoo'a O'tyle Ambassador.; farther away than -- hoo'a pi: The enemy is beyond the range of these (artillery) guns. -- Sa'tro noeh hoo'a pi kum'lung banyh ro'bah kum pleung thum ni.

biased adj. praw'kaan; luum'ee'eng

bible n. Christian Bible -- Bible; comparably authoritative Buddhist work -- kum'pee

bicycle n. kong: I [used to] ride a bicycle to school. -- Kyom [tra'laawp] chi kong teuh sa'la.; (NB: kong also = wheel or tire; hence, motorbike tire = kong moto and bicycle tire = kong kong, or kong sum'rap kong)

big adj. generally -- thum; spacious -- too'lee'ay; broad, wide, as rice paddy -- l'vung, l'veng

bigger adj. thum chiang

biggest adj. thum bom'pot: the biggest thief -- jchaao thum bom'pot

big-shot n. neh thum; ma'nooh dael kut gwat/nee'eng sum'kahn (lit: person who thinks he/she is important.)

bill n. restaurant check -- kit loi: Check, please! -- Sum kit loi!; invoice for goods or services -- sum'buht kit loi; invoice for gasoline -- sum'buht, or bun'chee, sum'rap praeng; bill, invoice; written form, often printed at top of bill or invoice forms -- vi'k'eye ya'but

binoculars n. ka'eoo yeut

biology n. bi'o'lo'ji (fr. Fr.); chi'vut'sahs

bird n. saat slaa'b (lit: feathered, or winged, animal); baak'saiy

birth n. kum'naut

birth certificate n. bun'chee chi'vut (or, (AP) chee'it); sum'buht kum'naut

birth control n. t'nam kaa pee'a kum'naut (lit.: medicine for protection against birth)

birthday n. t'ngai kum'naut

birth place n. sruk kum'naut

bite v. animals (except snakes and birds) and people -- kam: People do not bite snakes. -- Ma'nooh ot kam poo'ah tay.; snakes and birds -- jchuhk: The snake bit the child. -- Poo'ah jchuhk gkon k'mayng.

bitter adj.   taste -- lo'ving; emotionally -- chooo jchaw(t)

bitterness n.   kuu'm

black adj.   k'mau; pwa k'màu; blacked out, unconscious -- ot dung kloo'an; ot cheu'a kloo'an; black market -- psa ngo ngut (lit.: "dark market")

black-out n.   of an area -- kaa pun'lut pleung; (more commonly expressed as verb, viz.: There will be a black-out at ten o'clock. -- Yeung tro pun'lut pleung noeh peyr mao dop. (lit: We must black-out from ten o'clock.)

blame n.   kaa bun'to'h; kaa s'day owi

blame v.   bun'to'h; jchowt

blanket n.   pu'iy (AP: poi'ya)

bleed v.   jchenyh chee'um [AP: chim]: The soldier is bleeding. -- Tee'hee'an kom'puung jchenyh chee'um.

bless v.   choon po': Bless you! (blessing as given by monk, as in temple) -- Preah choon po' neh.; Bless you! (as said after sneeze) -- Sa'bauw'ee! [or] Sa'bauw'ee teuh!

blessing n.   po': She received a blessing from her parents. -- Nee'eng to'tool po' om'pee oeuv'puk m'dye.

blind adj.   k'vah; blind person -- ma'nooh k'vah

block n.   city street length -- l'veng; or ploe: Go two or three blocks more. -- Teuh pi-bye l'veng tee'it (or, ploe tee'it).

block v.   obstruct -- k'hae'ng: The guerrillas were blocking the road. -- Kawng chlope kom'puung k'haeng ploe.

blocked adj.   twal (AP: to'al): This road is blocked; you can't go on. -- Ploe ni twal; mun adje teuh roo'it.

blood n.   chee'um (AP: chim)

bloodshed n.   kaa kap sum'lap

blossom n.   p'ka pee'k

blouse n.   aow; short-sleeved -- aow dai klai; long sleeved -- aow dai veng

blow n.   negative event, "heavy blow" -- sum'nang a'krah

blow v.   bahwk: the wind blows -- K'shaal bahwk; force air into s. th. -- plum: blow a whistle -- plum kun'chai

blow up v.   inflate with air -- plum; blow up a balloon -- plum peut'pown; destroy -- p'tooh(s) bum'byke: blow up a bridge -- p'tooh(s) bum'byke spee'un

blowout n.   of a tire -- kaa p'tooh(s) byke

blue adj.   kee'oo

blush v.   laung kra'hom; kra'hom priung priung: Why are you blushing? -- Hyte aae baan chia t'poiel neh kra'hom priung priung?

boa constrictor n.   poo'ah thlaang

board n.   wood -- k'daa

board v.   get aboard s. th. -- laung chi: What time will you board the plane? -- Peyr na laung chi yun hawh?

boat n.   small, like row-boat or skiff -- toook; small, with motor -- kra'not; sam pan -- sum peuh; ship -- ka'pal (AP: ka'pow)

body n.   live -- kloo'an; cadaver -- k'mau'it

boil v.   dam: boil water -- dam tuk; boil (cook) rice -- dam bye: Is the water boiled (yet). -- Tuk dam howi roo noeh?; poo'h

boiled water n.   tuk dam poo'h: Is this boiled water? -- Tau(v) ni tuk dam poo'h?

bomb n.   kro'up bai (AP: kraw bai): smoke bomb -- kro'up bai ps'eye'n; bomb dropped from plane -- kro'up bai tun t'leh; (grenade = kro'up bai chowl (lit: thrown bomb))

bomber n.   airplane -- yun hawh t'leh kro'up bai

Bon appetit! xcl.   'Cheunyh!; or, Un'cheunyh!; or, (formal) Sum un'cheunyh chng'anyh.; (NB: the phrase "Un'cheunyh pee'sa." -- lit: please eat -- is often used as a polite way of declining to join s.o. in a meal, conveying, (you) please eat (but I won't; but I have already eaten, etc.))

bone n. cha'ung

book n. s'po (AP: see'a po): This country needs books. -- Sruk ni tro kaa s'po.

bookstore n. hawng looh s'po (lit.: store selling books): There is only one bookstore in Phnom Penh. -- Miun tai haang looh s'po moi kaat noeh Phnom Penh.

boot n. s'bye'k cheung kaa veng

boot-licker n. baw'ri'va; ma'nooh ruh'naup

border n. of country, province, etc. -- tul'dyne; prum'dyne; prum'praw'tul; chee'dyne: He crossed the border from the Thai side. -- Gwat ch'long tul'dyne pi kang See'um.

bore v. make a hole in s. th. solid (wall, paper, ground, etc.) -- jchaw

bored adj. op'sup; tunyh tro'um: They get bored [if there's no] music. -- Pooh'gkay tunyh tro'um [baa ot miun] plaeng.

boring adj. ot la'aw: a boring movie -- gkun ot la'aw

born adj. kaut: Where were you born? -- Neh kaut noeh ti na?

borrow v. k'chey (also means "young" or "unripe"): Can I borrow your pen? -- Kyom sum kch'eye bic neh?

boss n. jchao'vye

both adv. te'ang pi (AP: tang, tay'ung): both Samol and Li -- te'ang pi neh Samol nung Li; both of you -- neh eiyne te'ang pi; both sides -- song kang; te'ang song kang

bother v. ruhm'kaan: Please [don't] bother me [right now]. -- Sum [kum] ruhm'kaan kyom [eye leaou].

bottle n. dop

bottom n. directional -- kang krowm; or, bot: the bottom of s. o.'s feet -- bot cheung; qualitatively (as, "the bottom of the barrel") -- bot: "like the bottom of/worst in the market -- doj bot p'sa

boulevard n. ma'ha'vi'tay

boundary n. (see "border")

bow n. for shooting arrows -- t'noo

bow v. generally -- ouwn lum tone; with hands together (respectful Khmer and Thai greeting) -- sum'paya

bowl n. jchaan (can also mean "plate") or (to specify bowl shape, as soup bowl) jchaan kraw'lome

box n. generally -- praw'op; small box, pack -- kun'chop; large box, truck, chest -- hopp

boxing n. praw'dall

boy n. k'mayng proh

boy friend n. song sa

bra n. troh noo'up

bracelet n. ks'eye' dai; kawng dai; kawng: Golden Bracelet (a well-known Mekong River trading village (and sruk) in southern Kom'puung Cham) -- Kawng Mee'ch

brag v. oo'it; inflate one's importance -- un'koi leuh chung'aae leuk kloo'an eiyne (lit: sit down on a rice basket (or tray) and lift one's self up (i.e., by one's self))

braid v. krong; ving

brain(s) n. anatomical term -- koo'a k'bal; intelligence (critical) -- koo'a or pun'nya; to have no brain, i. e., not be smart -- ot miun pun'nya; or, ot koo'a k'bal: Have you got any brains?!? -- Pun'nya neh tra'laawp mok venyh tay?!?; intellect or intelligence (complimentary) -- prat'nya: That student has brains. -- Gkon'sa nu miun prat'nya.

brakes n. frang: "hit", or put on, the brakes -- jchaab frang

branch n. of a company -- sa'ka; of a tree -- may(k) thi'ung

brand n. yee'haow; marque

brass adj. or n. spo'an; spo'an tuk mee'ch

brassiere n. aow tro neup

brave adj. hee'an; kra'han

bravery n. kaa kra'han, s'kd'eye kra'han

brawl n. or v. chloos vye thaawp; wrestle -- vye chum'bop

bread n. num; num pahng: fried puffy bread -- num chaa kwai

break n. relief from work -- sum'raak; Give me a break! -- Kum ruhm kaan peyk! (lit: Don't bother me so much!)

break v. bum'byke; break a window -- bum'byke kun'chaw; destroy -- kum'tic; break apart -- dawk jchenyh pi ka'neea; break up, knock down -- bah(k): The strom knocked down a lot of trees.; K'shaal p'chooh baan tveu owi bahk daum cheu chia ch'raan.; break a leg or an arm -- bahk cheung roo dai; break down (as, a car or machine) -- ko'ich: The car broke down in the road. -- Laan ko'ich leuh noeh [or taam] ploe.; break even -- aroo'it kloo'an: His business broke even. -- Chum'noo'nyh gwat aroo'it kloo'an.; break off or pull away (s. th. from s. th.) -- thee'eng jchenyh; break out (as, disease, war) -- kaut laung taam; break up (e.g., of an alliance) -- byke ka'neea; break the law -- tveu koh ch'bop: He broke the law. -- Veea tveu koh ch'bop.; break an agreement, contract, treaty -- mun koo'a roop; mun reh'sa: Thailand broke [the terms of] the treaty. -- Thailand mun reh'sa [kaa kaah] sun'nyaa. (lit: did not adhere to the terms...)

breakfast n. aha' peyr pruhk

breast n. dawh

breath n. dung'hauuwm

breathe v. dawk dung'hauuwm

breeze n. k'shaal l'howi; a nice breeze -- k'shaal l'howi la'aw nah

bribe n. sum'noek; kaa sok

bribe v. sok; sok'pahn

brick n. utt

bride n. gkon kra'mum

bridegroom n. gkon kum'lawh

bridge n. spee'un

brief adj. sung'khybe; yang klye: a brief conversation -- kaa sun'tance'a yang klye; yang ro'has

briefcase n. ka'top

briefing n. to impart information -- kaa prap; to impart information and instructions -- kaa prap owi tveu

brigade n. kawng pul to'ich

brigadier general n. o'dum sena trei (insignia: one-star [p'k'eye moi]; ranks next above colonel [va'ret sena eyke; insignia: five stripes [saak pram] and next below lieutenant general [o'dum sena to'; insignia: two-stars [p'k'eye pi])

bright adj. smart -- ch'laat; intensely lit -- ploo: a bright light - pleung ploo; jchang: a bright light -- pleung jchang; bright sun -- t'ngai jchang

bring v. transport -- yok... mok (AP: mao); Bring a book (with you). -- Yok s'po mok chi'moi.; bring s. o. to a place, accompany -- no'um... mok: Bring the child home. -- No'um gkon k'mayng mok ptay'a.; bring as help or assistance to s. o. -- choon... mok; bring... over here -- no'um mok; causes to happen -- no'um mok... noeh: She brings me (good) luck. -- Nee'eng no'um mok kyom noeh sum'nang.

bring back v. yok mok venyh

Britain n. sruk An'glaae

British adj. An'glaae

broad adj. too'lim, too'lee'aae; thum

broadcast n. kaa ps'eye taam vi'chu: I [heard] the broadcast [last night]. -- Kyom [loo] kaa ps'eye taam vi'chu [yoop munyh].

broadcast v. ps'eye; broadcast by radio -- ps'eye taam vi'chu

broccoli n. p'ka spay kio

broke adj. out of money -- awh loi; lacking funds, perhaps never had any -- ot loi; He's broke. -- Gwat ot loi.

broken adj. not functioning -- ko'ich; in pieces -- bahk: a broken chair -- kaeo'eye bahk; breached, as treaty, agreement, contract, promise, etc. -- bahk bong: a broken promise -- kaa p'dach peea sun'nyaa; broken-hearted -- ko'ich jchet

broken-hearted adj. ko'ich jchet; "defeated on the road of love" -- pa'ra'chey kang ploe snai'ha

bronze adj. or n. long'hun; sum'rut

broom n. um'bau'hhs

brother n. older brother -- bong proh; younger brother -- pa'own proh

brother-in-law n. older br. in law -- bong kl'eye proh; younger br. in law -- pa'own kl'eye proh

brown adj. pwa t'naut

bruise n. chjoo'um; pau(k)

brush n. for cleaning in general -- jch'ras; toothbrush -- ch'ra(ss) dos tming; for clothes -- jcha'ras dawh kow-aow; for hair -- jch'ras suk saahk; (western Cambodia (Battambong) term = snut); vegetation, bushes -- prey kum'pote: The guerrillas [hid] in the brush. -- Kawng chlope [leh kloo'an] k'nong prey kum'pote.

brush v. dos; brush teeth -- dos t'ming; brush clothes -- dos kow-aow

B. S. n. a' gko

bubbles n. foam -- por pooh tuk

bucket n. tuung; bucket of water -- tuung tuk

buckle n. k'bal k'sye kra'vat

Buddha n. Preah'Phut

Buddhism n. Phut'teh se'sna; Phut se'sna; se'sna Preah'Phut

Buddhist adj. preah'puht: This is a Buddhist prayer. -- Ni toa Preah'Phut.; chia ro'bah Preah'Phut: This is a Buddist temple. -- Wat ni chia ro'bah Preah'Phut.

Buddhist n. gkon se'sna Preah'Phut

buddy n. klaa(r)

budget n. thak vi'cah

buffalo (caribau) n. kraw'bye

build v. song: build a house -- song ptay'a; build up, develop -- bung kaut: build up a business -- bung kaut krum'huun

builder n. contractor, one who builds houses, buildings, etc. -- chiang ptay'a

building n. a'keea (large, generally of stone or brick) or ptay'a (lit: house); made of wood -- a'keea or ptay'a cheu; made of palm leaves -- ptay'a sluk

built of adj. song pi: a house built of stone -- ptay'a song pi t'mawh

bulldozer n. ma'seen chuh(s) daiy

bullet n. kro'up kum pleung

bulletin n. praw'tek'bot

bullshit n. a' gko

bump n. bruise -- pau(k)

bumpy adj. ro'leh(k); pot-holed -- kra'heang kra'hoeng

bunch n. of objects -- batch: a bunch of flowers -- p'ka moi batch; of people -- krum: a bunch students -- gkon'sa moi krum

burglar n. jchaao

Burma n. sruk poom'ea

burn v. burn down, destroy s.th. -- dut; kum'tic chowl: They burned the village. -- Pooh'gkay kum'tic phum jchowl. (jchowl, lit. = throw or throw away); singe, partially burn s.th. -- klow'eet(ch): She burned the food. -- Veea tveu owi ma'hope klow'eet(ch).; become consumed by flame -- chheh: The paper burned. -- Kra'dah chheh.

burned adj. klow'eet(ch)

bus n. laan ch'nool; rot'yun ch'nool; bus

bus station n. chum'nawt laan ch'nool; s'ta'nee laan ch'nool

bush n. kum'pote; kum'cheu

business n. in general -- rawk'see: I want to start a business. -- Kyom jchong jchaap p'daum rawk'see.; a specific company -- chum'noo'inyh; muk ro'bawr; muk chum'noo'inyh: a foreign business -- chum'noo'inyh bor'tay; personal affairs -- ru'ung: That's my business. -- Nu ru'ung kyom!

businessman n. neh chum'noo'inyh

busy adj. cho'op dai; cho'op ro'vull; ro'vull (AP: ro'vwul): not so busy today -- mun seou ro'vull t'ngai tay; have s. th. to do -- miun kaa

but conj. and prp. in sense of however -- pun'ta'aae: I wanted to go but [I couldn't]! -- Kyom jchong teuh pun'ta'aae [mun adje ni tay]!; except -- kaw pun'ta'aae: He did [all] but page seven. -- Gwat tveu [kroop muk] kaw pun'ta'aae tum'poa prum'pul.; except -- tai: Mun was [nothing] but trouble. -- Mun [k'miun dung eye no'um] tai ru'ung.

butter n. beure

butterfly n. may um'bauw

buy v. tinh (AP: ting)

by prp. by means of -- dow'ee; dow'ee sa; taam: by car -- dow'ee sa laan; taam laan; call by telephone -- haow dow'ee to'ra'sap; by ones'self alone -- kloo'an eiyne: Go and eat by yourself. -- Teuh nyam kloo'an eiyne teuh.; by himself (his own means) -- dow'ee sa kloo'an gwat; by (near) the bank -- noeh k'byke banque; by that time -- noeh peyr nu; by the way -- "aaaw... " ; together with -- nung: The dimensions of this book are [12] by 8. -- Tuum huum s'po ni [pi tun dop] nung pram bye.

C

cabbage n. common, round whitish cabbage -- spay saw; purple or green cabbage; a;so, round lettuce -- spay k'dau(p); purplish cabbage -- spay k'mau; "water" cabbage (large, heavy leafde variety that grows on pond vines) -- tra'ku'un spay

cabinet n. governmental -- kuna ratt'mun'trei; chest, piece of furniture -- too'

cable n. metal cable for hauling -- poo'a; electric or light cable -- k'sye pleung; cable-gram -- k'sye loo'eh

cable v. send a cable -- vi'yaye k'sye loo'eh; vi'yaye telegram; vi'yaye too'ra'laek; p'nya(r) k'sye

cache n. cunlye'ng leh aye'von (lit: place to hide things)

cadre n. ka'ma'pi'bal

cage n. trung

cake n. num (can also mean "bread"); num p'eye'm (lit: "sweet cake"); num dutt (lit: "baked cake")

calculate v. kut'lake

calculator n. ma'seen kut lek

calendar n. calendree'ay

caliber adj. of weapon -- p'see'us

call n. telephone call -- telephone; haow telephone; haow to'ra'sap; to receive a telephone call: to'tool telephone; to'tool to'ra'sap: I received two telephone calls (i.e., calls [from two people]) yesterday. -- Pi musl'munyh kyom baan to'tool telephone [pi neh].; I received two telephone calls (i.e., two calls, whether or not from two different people) yesterday. -- Pi musl'munyh kyom to'tool telephone [pi dong] (lit., [two times]).

call, call up v. call by telephone -- telephone; haow dow'ee to'ra'sap; haow dow'ee telephone: I [just] called yesterday morning. -- Kyom [tuep tye] haow telephone pruhk munyh; call and find out -- telephone soo'a. (lit.: "call and ask."); call back -- haow venyh; telephone tra'laawp venyh: I will call you back. -- Kyom nung telephone neh venyh.; call a wrong number -- telephone (or, haow) koh layke (or, layke koh)

call v. shout -- haow; contact -- haow: I'll call my friend to go with us. -- Kyom haow mit teuh chi'moi.

call for v. demand -- praw'kas: They called for new elections. -- Pooh'gkay praw'kas baw'ch'naut t'maee.; They called for [one thing after another]. -- Gkay praw'kas ru'ung ni'moi ni'moi.

call off v. bun choop; loob jchowl

call on v. jchole

call s.o. or s.th. v. taa + pronoun or haow + pronoun: He called him a dishonest snake. -- Gwat taa a' nu [him] poo'ah ot sm'oh trong.; He called him a dog. -- Gwat haow a' nu sh'kye.

called, to be v. tro baan haow

calm adj. jchet traw'cheh'(k); (lit: cool-hearted)

Calm down! xcl. Sum s'ngohp jchet!

Cambodia n. Kam'pu'chea; sruk Khmei; praw'tet Khmei; Kampuchea yeung (lit: "our Cambodia"); under Sihanouk -- Sung'kuum Ree'ech Chia Ni'yuum; under Lon Nol -- [Sa'teea'raw'nak ratt] Khmei (i.e., Khmer [Republic]); under Hun Sen -- Sa'teea'raw'nak ratt [pra'chee'a'ree'a mit] Kampuchea (i.e., [People's] Republic of Kampuchea)

Cambodian adj. of nationality, and generally -- Khmei: He's Cambodian. -- Gwat Khmei.; Cambodian food -- ma'hope Khmei; "in the Khmer style" -- chia Khmei: This temple looks Cambodian. -- Wat ni doj chia Khmei.

camera n. a'pa'r'eye (fr. Fr.)

camouflage n. bun'lum; bom'bang bun'lum

camp n. general -- chuum'ruhm; military camp -- chuum'ruhm tee'hee'an

can n. generally -- kum'pong; large can -- kra'pong; canned food -- ma'hope kum'pong; can opener -- praw'dop baahk kum'pong (lit.: "tool to open can")

can v. be able to -- adje: I can't see. -- Kyom mun adje keunyh.; baan: I can eat. -- Kyom nyam baan.; adje baan: The rubber can be delivered only if... -- Kaow'soo adje baan jchenyh teuh loo'a tra tai...

can't I, you, etc.? xcl. tau(v)... adje owi... baan tay?: Can't you leave me alone? -- Tau(v) neh adje owi kyom noeh tai eiyne, baan tay?

canal n. pre(k)

cancel v. cancel [a meeting] -- leu(b) jchowl [pra'choom]; cancel [a purchase order] -- pa'di'say't jchowl [bun'chee'a tinh]

candidate n. pye'ka'chuun

candle n. tee'un

candy n. sc'aaw kro'up or kro'up sc'aaw; ("kro'up" also means "seed", "sc'aaw" means sugar)

cannon n. kum pleung thum

cannot v. mun adje; I cannot go. -- Kyom mun adje teuh.

canvas n. kraw'nut sam'rup tveu ten'; (lit: cloth to make tent)

capital n. national capital city -- thi krong; provincial capital -- thi krong kyte; funds -- daum thuun; praa(k); praa(k) daum

captain n. a'noo'sena eyke; (insignia: saak bye -- three stripes; ranks between lieutenant (anuk sena toe) and major (ve'ret sena trei))

capture v. jchaap

captured adj. seized -- rup'oh': They captured some of his property. -- Gkay rup'oh' tro'up sum'baat ro'bah gwat.; fall into the hands of -- t'leh teuh k'nong kun'dap dai: That village fell into [the hands] of the enemy. -- Phum nu t'leh teuh k'nong kun'dap [dai] ro'bah sa'tro.

car n. laan; rot yun; ma'seen

carbine n. kum pleung car'been

carbon paper n. kra'dah kal'kay'a

card n. playing cards -- bee'a; I. D. card, ration card, etc. -- kaat: Let's see your I.D. card. -- Sum kaat meulh.

cardamom n. kro'vanyh

care n. tai'tho'um

care v. in sympathetic way -- yok jchet tooo'k dah(k): People should care about their parents. -- Ma'nooh yeung koo'a tai yok jchet tooo'k dah(k) om'pee ocuv'puk m'dye.; be concerned with -- kwal: He didn't care about anything. -- Gwat mun kwal om'pee a'veye tay.; care for -- p'chia bal: They were caring for him at Calmet. -- Gkay p'chia bal gwat noeh Cal'met.; (NB: Calmet Hospital was one of only two above-clinic-level medical facilities in operation in Phnom Penh pre-1992.); care for, take care of (property) -- tai reh'sa: For many years no one cared for the statues at Angkor Wat. -- Ch'raan chh'nam kun'lung mok howi k'miun neh na tai reh'sa roob jchum'lak noeh Angkor Wat.

career n. mok ro'bawr praw'cham: One error can ruin his career. -- Kum'hawh moi adje bum'planyh mok ro'bawr praw'cham gwat.; (mok ro'bawr by itself means "occupation")

careful adj. praw'yaat (NB: praw'yoot = fight)

carefully adv. prong praw'yaat

careless adj. k'chee k'chee'a; k'chaya k'cheea

carelessness n. kaa ch'veh praw'heh

caress v. ong'eye'l

carpet n. pruhm

carry v. hold, (generally) carry by hand -- kaan: It's difficult to carry this box. -- Pi'bah kaan praw'op ni.; carry away -- yok teuh; carry s. th. if done by several people on shoulders -- sye'ng; carry by holding the bottom of s. th. is sometimes expressed by use of "troh" (lit: to support) or "leuk" (lit: to lift); carry holding close to chest -- kaan tra'kang; carry in belt (as, a knife) -- see'ut; carry in both hands -- bye (used to describe mode of carrying [baby]: bye gkon ngaa'); carry on shoulder -- li; carry on one end of "dong'rek" pole -- puuhn; carry suspended from hands -- yoo'a; carry on hip -- kun'dee'ut or paw (used, inter alia, to refer to mode of carrying [child older than baby]: paw [gkon k'mayng]); carry on head -- tooo'l

carry a disease v. no'um: Mosquitoes carry malaria. -- Moo(ss) no'um chuum'ngeu kruun'jchanyh.; (chuum'ngeu = disease, kruun'jchanyh = malaria)

cart n. ro'teh; ox cart -- ro'teh gko

cartridge n. kro'up kum pleung

case n. kaa ra'nye; sum'num ru'ung; in case -- k'nong kaa ra'nye; in that case -- k'nong kaa ra'nye nu; legal case -- kaa ra'nye sraw(b) ch'bop; k'dye

cash n. loi; cash a check -- bauwk loi

cassette player n. muun'yaye; ka'ssett

casualty n. kaa ko'ich kaat; fatal casualty, fatality -- kaa bot'bong chi'vut

cat n. ch'maa

catastrophe n. mo'hun'na'rye

catch n. jchaap: catch a chicken -- jchaap muon; catch fish -- jchaap trei; catch a thief -- jchaap jchaao; children's [game] "catch a baby chick" -- [l'bye'ng] jchaap gkon muon; tay'eh (used only re elephant trapping): catch an elephant -- tay'eh dum'rei

catch up with v. teuh owi too'an: I will catch up with you. -- Kyom nung teuh owi too'an neh.

category n. chum poo(k); praw'peyt

catsup n. tuk peyng'paw (lit: tomato sauce), tuk pwa kra'hom (lit: red-colored sauce)

caught pp. jchaap baan; He was caught yesterday. -- Gwat jchaap baan musl'munyh.

cauliflower n. p'ka spay saw

cause n. chia daum'hyte; The Khmer Rouge are not the cause of all the problems. -- Khmei Kra'hom mun keuh chia daum'hyte kroop pun'ha.

cause v. nyang owi... kaut: A weak [economy] can cause higher unemployment. -- [Set'a'kej] tuun k'sow'ee adje nyang owi kaut kaa'ngyeea mun kroop kron.; owi miun; bung'dull owi: Mosquitoes cause malaria. -- Moo bung'dull owi miun chuum'ngeu kruun'jchanyh.; Poverty causes [corruption]. -- S'kd'eye kraw bun'dull [pu'ka'ra loi].; create, cause to occur -- bung kaut: Corruption causes revolution. -- Pu'ka'ra loi bung kaut pa'ti'vwut.; cause trouble [for] -- tveu toook buhk m'ning [sam'rap]

cautious adj. praw'yaat

cave n. roo'ng

cease v. bun chope; stop temporarily -- pa'aa'kh

ceasefire n. kaa pa'aa'kh sung'kree'um

ceiling n. pee'dahn

celebrate v. tveu bun

celebration n. kaa tveu buun; kaa choop; party -- choop lee'ung; holiday -- buun: September holiday honoring ancestors -- p'choom' buun

cement n. see'mon

cemetary n. veal p'no k'mau'it (lit.: field (of) graves (of the) dead)

center n. kan'dal (same as province name, "Kandal"): in the center -- noeh kan'dal; middle -- pieh kan'dal; the middle of the pen -- pieh kan'dal noeh bic.

centimeter n. song'tee'met

Central Committee n. organ of People's Republic of Kampuchea Government -- ma'chum'pac

century n. sat'ta'vwut

ceremony n. vi'ti'buun; buun; ceremony investing novice monks -- bum'booh lok

certain adj. unquestionable, not subject to doubt -- praw'kat (AP: praw'kawd); piht praw'kat: It's certain I'm going. -- Kyom teuh, piht praw'kat.; unambiguous, easy to make out or understand -- ch'bah: It's not certain what he meant. -- Dael gwat miun ney mun ch'bah tay.; specific, particular -- tai... moi kut: I want to work in a certain bank. -- Kyom jchong tveu kaa noeh tai banque nung moi kut.; I (only) want a certain car. -- Kyom jchong baan tai laan nung moi kut.

certainly adv. piht praw'kat; piht howi

certificate n. bun'chee

chain n. chraw'vah

chair n. kaeo'eye

chairman n. praw'tee'an

challenge n. test -- sah lo'bong

champion n. cheung a'ek

chance n. opportunity -- oh'ka(ss); sum'nang; luck, fortune -- sum'nang

change n. "small money", coins -- loi do (do = exchange); alteration -- kaa pdo; change for a bill -- loi op

change v. plas pdo: change into s. th. different, become s. th. different -- plas pdo teuh chia; change one's mind -- plas pdo jchet, or plas pdo kum'nut, or, plas pdo jchet kum'nut (jchet = heart, kum'nut = mind or idea); do: Don't change! -- Kum 'do!; pdo (less used as verb than plas pdo or do; more frequently found as part of the noun "change" i. e., "kaa pdo"); change in sense of provide a new (hence, different) one -- p'tay: Please change this glass of water. -- Sum p'tay tuk kaae'oo ni.; changing his mind -- kye pr'eye kum'nut gwat

character n. leh ka'nak; or, (more formal), a'tak'cha'a'rut: good character -- leh ka'nak la'aw; a person's character or personality -- leh ka'nak ma'nooh; in a book or film -- too'a: leading character -- too'a eyke gkun

charade n. children's game -- l'bye'ng pror'sna; creation of false appearance -- kaa lob'leh: [The development effort] was just a charade. -- [Kaa kaut kaam a'pi'vwut] kroan tai chia kaa lob leh pun'noh.

charcol n. k'choong

charge n. accusation -- kaa cho'up jchowt

charge v. a price -- dah(k) tlai; This store charges too much. -- Haang ni dah(k) tlai ch'raan.; with a crime -- dah(k) to'h: He was charged [with murder; lit: as a murderer; or, with killing s. o.] yesterday. -- Gwat tro baan dah(k) to'h [chia kee'et ta'kahw; or, dow'ee sum'lap gkay] musl'munyh.

charge d'affaires n. pooh'choo'ay toot

charming adj. miun sum'poa(s); s'raaw

chart n. ta'rang

chase v. denyh; rut denyh: chase a rabbit -- rut denyh tun'sye

chat n. kaa cho chaae'k leng

chat v. cho chaae'k; cho chaae'k leng

chauffeur n. chauffer, driver, neh baat laan (owi gkay)

cheap adj. tauk; ot tlai (lit: not expensive); a cheap, low or reduced price -- t'lai tauk

cheat v. deceive -- bun'luhm; cheat out of (lit: clean out) money -- bauw(k) praa(k)

cheating n. kaa bun'luhm; kaa bauw(k)

check v. examine -- pee'nut; ch'eye ch'aae

check n. for payment of funds -- check

Check, please! xcl. Sum kit loi!; Kit loi!

check-in n. kaa ch'eye ch'aae jchole k'nong

cheeks n. t'poiel

cheese n. fro'maa (fr. the Fr. "fromage")

chemistry n. kee'mee

cherry n. plai che'ree

chest n. of body -- daum troong; furniture -- taawt too'

chew v. jchawk: chew tobacco -- jchawk t'nam

chewing gum n. scaaw kaow'soo (lit.: rubber candy)

chicken n. animal -- muon (AP: mo'an); chicken meat -- sat(ch) muon

chicken soup with lemon n. scng'au ch'roo'hk muon (lit: sour chicken soup)

chief n. may: village chief -- may phum; praw'tee'an; praw'tee'an ket'na'matee'ka: Chief of Po'sat Province -- praw'tee'an ket'na'matee'ka kyte Po'sat; may duk no'um; chief of staff -- may lun chia kaa thum

child n. gkon: young child -- gkon k'mayng; adopted child -- gkon jchenyh chem; youngest child -- gkon peau; gkon chau(v) -- grandchild

childish adj. a'laae a'lah

chills n. kruun rong'ee'a

China n. sruk jchun

Chinese adj. jchun

chocolate n. sok'ko'la

choice n. kaa jchreu'reu'; jchreu'reu': They [have no] choice. -- Pooh'gkay [k'miun, or ot miun] kaa jchreu'reu'.; or, Pooh'gkay [k'miun, or, ot miun] jchreu'reu'.; to have no choice -- twal jchreu' (lit: dead end): Because he had no choice, he stole. -- Bee'proo'a gwat twal jchreu', baan chia gwat loo'ich.

choke v. suffocate s. o. -- ch'rawh batch kaw; choke on s. th. slightly or briefly -- ch'loo'a(k); choke on s. th. seriously -- ch'looh

cholera n. a'sun'na rohk

choose v. reu'; jchreu' reu'

chop v. kap; chen' ch'raam; poo'h

chopsticks n. chung'ka

chubby adj. tw'aot; ka'mop

church n. preea'vi'heea ka'to'lik; aac'gleez (fr. Fr.)

cigarette n. ba'r'eye

cinema n. film -- gkun; movie theatre -- ro'ng gkun

circle n. vuung mool: Please draw a circle. -- Cheunyh gkoo vuung mool.; ruhm vuung

cistern n. ahng trong tuk

citizen n. pra'chee'chuun; ree'h; pra'chee pul'rawt; become a citizen -- jchole sun chee'it

citizenship n. chuun chee'it

city n. krong

civil servant n. neh meuhn; neh tveu kaa ratt'a'pi'bal (lit: person who works for the government)

civil service n. ratt'a'kaa

civilian adj. cee'vil: civilian aircraft -- yun hawh cee'vil

civilian n. chuun sa'muun; chuun cee'vil: They are civilians. -- Pooh'gkay chia chuun cee'vil.

claim n. kaa thee'um thee'a; kaa thaw'va

claim v. allege without proof -- thee'um thee'a: Vietnam claimed Cambodian land. -- Sruk Vietnam thee'um thee'a dai Khmei.; state, announce [that] -- ni'yaye [tha]; praw'kas [tha]: The Thais claimed that... -- Neh See'um praw'kas tha...

class n. social category -- t'nak: lower class -- t'nak krowm; middle class -- t'nak kan'dal; upper class -- t'nak leuh; ruling class -- va'nak (derivative of "t'nak"); school subject -- t'nak: What classes are you taking? -- Neh yok t'nak s'eye?; academic level -- t'nak: What class are you in? -- Neh t'nak pu'man?; "class" as rank or size, esp. in military usage: first class -- eyke; second class -- toe; third class -- trei (NB: eyke, toe and trei are words drawn from the B'lye numbering system)

classroom n. t'nak sa'la'rin

clay n.   daiy la'bub

clean adj.   sa'aat (AP: sum'aat)

clean v.   dos: clean clothes -- dos kow-aow; or, bauwk kow-aow; lee'ung: clean dishes -- lee'ung jchaan

clean up v.   wash up, clean up, brush hair, for women put on make-up, etc. -- sum ut sum ang kloo'an

clear adj.   easily understood -- ch'bah; unclouded -- sraw'lah: a clear sky -- mey'k sraw'lah

clearing n.   open area between tree- or brush-lines -- chraw'lah

clerk n.   smee'un; secretary -- buh'kuh'lut

clever adj.   ch'laat (AP: chal'aat); poo'k'eye; praw'ngya

client n.   common, general term -- p'nee'oo (lit: customer); more specific/formal terms -- a'ti'ni'chuun; or, a'deh ti chuun

climate n.   tee'ut a'kas

climb v.   laung

clinic n.   mun'ti chia'bal rohk

clique n.   pah'pooh

clock n.   wristwatch -- ni'a'li'ka dai (PS: lee'la'ka; or, lee'a'li'ka); wall clock -- ni'a'li'ka pow

close prp.   in distance, i.e., nearby -- chit; chit chit; closer and closer -- chit laung chit laung; emotionally -- ng'ee'it: a close friend -- ng'ee'it mit

close v.   butt: Close (your) books. -- Butt s'po.; Close the door. -- Butt t'veea.; close a hole in s. th. -- jchawk: cork a bottle -- jchawk ch'nawk

closet n.   thhoo kow-aow; ban'tope dah(k) kow-aow

cloth n.   kraw'not

clothes, clothing n.   kow-aow (lit: "shirt-pants"); sum'lee'a; bum'pay'eh

cloud n.   paul'pauk

cloudy adj.   miun paul'pauk

club n.   social organization -- sa'ma'kuum

clue n.   evidence, sign -- yoo'bal; sun'ya: The police have no clues at all. -- Dum'roo'it ot miun sun'ya tek to'ich sah.; hint -- pee'a'praw lo'ee; any idea -- scwaal kum'nut: He had no clue about her. -- Gwat k'miun scwaal kum'nut ro'bah veea.

coach n.   neh bung haht

coalition n.   sa'ma'sa'pheap

coals n.   in a fire -- ngaw ngeuk; (charcol = k'choong)

coast n.   ch'ney sa'mut

coat n.   aow raw'ngee'a

cobra n.   poo'ah vwe'(k) (AP: vway)

cock fighting n.   l'bye'ng ch'loo'a muon

cockroach n.   gka'laat

coconut n.   do'hng

coconut milk n.   k'tee(k) do'hng; tuk do'hng

coconut palm n.   tree -- daum do'hng

coconut pastry n.   num hal

coffee n.   ka'fae (fr. Fr. "cafe")

cognac n.   sra cogn'ieh (fr. Fr. "cognac")

coins n.   kaa(k); sayn; Give me some coins. -- Kyom sum kaa(k) klaah. or, Sum owi loi sayn mok.

cola n.   's'cola

cold adj.   chilly, re water, food, weather, etc. -- traw'cheh(k)'; chilly, re self or s.o. else -- raw'ngee'a: Are you cold? -- Tau(v) neh raw'ngee'a tay?; (NB: "traw'cheh(k)" can be translated as "cold" or "cool", and "traw'cheh(k) klang" and "raw'ngee'a" as "cold"); insensitive, unfeeling -- jchet ot la'aw

cold n. "the cold" (weather condition) -- pheap traw'cheh(k); illness, flu -- pad'i'sye: Do you have a cold? -- Neh pad'i'sye roo?

collaborate with v. work on mutually (non-perjorative) -- tveu sa'kaa chi'moi ka'neea: They collaborated on the study. -- Pooh'gkay tveu sah(k) nu sa'kaa chi'moi ka'neea.; cooperate with (perjorative or non-, depending on context) -- jchole dai: They say [he] used to collaborate with the Khmer Rouge. -- Pooh'gkay taa [veea] tra'laawp jchole dai chi'moi Khmei Kra'hom.

collapse v. person -- dool; structures -- raw'lum; or bah(k): The bridge collapsed. -- Spee'un bah(k); The house collapsed. -- Ptay'a raw'lum.

collect v. assemble together -- pra'mole; collect [stamps] -- sun'sum [t'eye'mbr]; ask for donations -- ong'kee'a; collect s. th. due or claimed owed -- thee'a

collide v. buhk ka'neea

collision n. kaa buhk ka'neea

colonel n. va'ret sena eyke; (insignia: five stripes ["saak prum"]; rank above lt. commander ["ve'ret sena toe"] and below brigadier general ["o'dum sena trei"])

colonial, colonialist adj. chia a'na'ni kuum; ney a'na'ni'kuum

colonialism n. a'na'ni'kuum ni'yuum

colony n. a'na'ni'kuum; praw'tet ru'nawt

color n. pwa (AP: po'a); re human skin -- sum'bul

comb n. snut

comb v. set saahk; (NB: also means "to brush")

combine v. p'sum

come v. mok (AP's: mao, mo'k, mowk, ma', m'; basic pronunciations mok, mo'k and mao are frequently compressed in spoken Khmer to "ma" and "m'''; for example, "mok nee" ["Come here!"] becomes "ma ni" and even "m'neh'", somewhat as the English "come here" may become "c'mere"): I will come on time. -- Kyom nung mok owi twon peyr.; come with me! -- mok chi'moi kyom; come in sense of arrive here -- dull mok or mok dull: Many foreigners who come here [have moustaches]. -- Chuun bor'tay ch'raan dael mok ti ni miun puk mwot.; come in -- jchole; come in! -- cheunyh jchole! or, cheunyh mao!; come through s. th. -- jchole taam: The thief came through the window. -- Jchaao jchole taam bung'oo'it.; come to the end of -- bun jchawb: come to the end of the road -- bun jchawb ploe; He came to the end of his money -- Gwat bun jchawb loi.

come back v. mok venyh (AP: ma venyh); tra'laawp mok; tra'laawp venyh; jchole ...dael: It comes (back) to this problem (again) ..." -- Jchole pun'ha ni dael.

comfortable adj. sra'nok; sroo(l)

command n. any context, (military, commercial, etc.), written or verbal -- kaa bun chee'a; high command -- a'kieh may bun' chee'a kaa

command v. jchat owi; bun chee'a; give a command -- owi bun chee'a

commandeer v. rubh yok

commander n. may bun chee'a kaa (NB: "may" (chief) in rapid conversation is Khmer usually pronounced "mee"; hence, "commander of a troop" could be "mee thwaap" rather than "may thwaap".)

commando n. ko'man'do

commerce n. pia'ni'chi'kaam

commission n. administrative body -- ka'ma'ka; ka'nak ka'ma'ka; sa'nong ka: International Control Commission -- Ka'nak Ka'ma'ka [commission] Un'ta'ra'chee'it [international] Kaan Bot Troo'it Tra [control]; payment -- kum'r'eye

commissioner n. a'kiet sa'nong ka

commit v. perpetrate -- praw'prit; commit a crime -- praw'prit ok'krut'a'kaam; guarantee to do -- tee'nee'a nung: Can you commit to this assignment? -- Tau(v) neh adje tec'nec'a nung tveu kek'kaa ni, baan roo tay?

committee n. sa'ma'kuum; ka'nak ka'ma'ti'ka; executive committee -- ka'nak ka'ma'ti'ka praw'tay bawt

common adj. general, commonplace -- too'h'teuh miun: [Malaria] is common in western Cambodia. -- [Kruun' jchanyh] too'h teuh miun noch dum'bun kang lic ney Kampuchea.

commune n. sub-division into which Cambodian districts (or, "sruks") are divided -- kuum

communication n. infrastructural, connoting roads, RRs, telephone service, etc. -- kaa tek tong; between/among individuals -- ni'yaye ka'neea: There must be communication within families. (lit: Families must talk together.) -- Kroo'e'sa neh tro ni'yaye ka'neea.

communism n. leh'ti co'moo'neest (NB: leh'ti = idea or philosophy)

communist n. chuun co'moo'neest

community n. sa'ha'kuum

community development n. a'pi'vwut sa'ha'kuum

company n. business enterprise -- kruum'huun: a printing company -- kruum'huun bawh puum; chum'noo'nyh; bo'ri'sat; military unit -- a'noo' sena thum

compatriot n. chuun ru'um chee'it

compare v. pree'up tee'up; praw'doj: Don't compare me to him. -- Kum praw doj kyom nung gwat.

comparison n. kaa pree'up tee'up: You can't make a comparison between this problem and that one. -- Mun adje tveu kaa pree'up tee'up ro'vieng pun'ha ni nung pun'ha nu tay.

compass n. trey'vi'sigh

compete v. pro'koo'ut; praw'chang; praw'nang

complain v. la'oo (written ra'oo); What are you complaining about? -- La'oo ru'ung 'aae?; whine -- la'oo ro'too'am; pa'dung pdo: Why are you whining to me? -- Neh pa'dung pdo kyom hyte aae?

complaint n. kaa la'oo ro'too'am

complete adj. roo'it rawl: Are your [preparations] complete? -- Tau(v) [kaa ree'up jchum] ro'bah neh roo'it rawl roo noeh?

complete v. bunyh jchob: I will complete my book next year. -- Kyom bunyh jchob s'po chh'nam krow'ee.; miun... howi: Did you complete your work? -- Miun tveu howi roo noeh?; bum penyh: Did you complete the application? -- Tau(v) neh bum penyh sum'num ru'ung howi roo noeh?

completely adv. te'ang awh: It is completely out of the question. -- Ot miun sum'noo'a a'veye tee'it te'ang awh.; sah: He is completely broke. -- Gwat ot miun loi sah.; Absolutely! Completely! -- Penyh!

complicated v. sa'nyh munyh

complication n. kaa ru'ung sa'nyh munyh; kaa ru'ung pi'bah

comply with v. sraawb nung; sraawb taam

compromise v. sum'rawh sum'rool

computer n. ma'cheen (AP: ma'seen) cum'puu'teuh: (for methods of data entry, type, punch, etc., see listings under "enter")

concering prp. om'pee; jchum'poo'h

conclusion n. judgement or ending -- kaa bun jchawb

concrete n. t'maw; bay'to(ng) (fr. Fr. "beton")

concubine n. sa'hai

condition n. social conditions, situation -- s'ta'na'pheap: Conditions in Phnom Penh are not good. -- S'ta'na'pheap noeh Phnom Penh ot la'aw; physical condition, i. e., state of health or state of repair -- leh ka'nak: The patient's condition worsened. -- Leh ka'nak neh chuum'ngeu t'nguu'ng t'ngaw laung.; His car [was] in bad condition. -- Laan gwat [tut] noeh k'nong leh ka'nak ot la'aw.; (NB: tut = is or was; word used re vehicles and machinery); term of an agreement -- leh kan: A condition [of the contract] was that she go far away. -- Leh kan [ney kej sun'nyaa] keuh baan veea teuh chng'eye.; There are two conditions in the contract. -- Miun [leh kan pi kaw)] noeh k'nong kej sun'nyaa. (lit: [conditions, two articles] or,[two articles of conditions]); requirement -- kum'nauwt

cone n. shape -- sa'chee

confer v. pee'kruu'h; The leaders conferred about conditions in the countryside. -- Neh duk no'um pee'kruu'h om'pee s'ta'na'pheap noeh cheu'na'bot.

conference n. pra'choom

confess v. sa'ra'pheap; sum sa'ra'pheap

confession n. kaa sa'ra'pheap; He has two prisoners and three confessions. -- Gwat mium neh choop'knawh [or, neh choop cooo'k] pi howi nung kaa sa'ra'pheap bye.

confident adj. kaw'k'dau; tooo'k jchet

confidential adj. secret -- sum'ngut: confidential information -- por'da'mee'an sum'ngut; or dum'nung sum'ngut

confirm v. bun chi'eh

confiscate v. roop yok

conflict n. kaa to'tay'ng

confuse v. bum po'an; vuung vehng: don't confuse me -- Kum vuung vehng kyom.

confused adj. po'an jchraw lum

confusion n. kaa jchraw lum

Congratulations! xcl. mild exclamation conveying "Good for you!" -- Keuh chia kaa praw'sar nah.; slightly stronger expression conveying "Congratulations on your success.", used on occassion of military victory or other important achievement -- Awp'awh'sa'tho jchum'poo'h cho'k chey.; expression for wedding or other family event -- Choon po' neh! (lit: Bless you.)

congress n. ratt'sa'pheap

congressman n. dum'nang ree'eh (lit.: "representative of the citizens [ree'eh]")

connect v. thaw p'choo'up

connected adj. attached, as electrical wire -- thaw p'choo'up; linked together -- p'choo'up ka'neea; associated with -- miun kaa tek tong: He has been connected to the US Mission. -- Gwat miun kaa tek tong chi'moi 'toot A'kaae'eng.; to be well connected --pooh'gkay miun tek tong; or, ngyaye sroul k'nong kaa tek tong

connections n. links, ties -- kaa taw p'choo'a; kaa tek tong: "really close" connections -- tek tong chit snut

conscious n. adj. awake, not unconscious -- dung kloo'an; knowledgible of s. th. -- dung

conservatism n. kaa son'sum sum'chai

conservative adj. frugal, prudent -- son'sum sum'chai

consider v. pi'cha'ra'na

consist of v. miun: It consists of three parts. -- Veea miun p'nyke bye.

conspire v. p'som kum'nut

constitution n. ratta'thum'nenyh

construct v. song; saang song; They will construct a temple. -- Gkay nung song wat.; They will construct a bridge and a road. -- Gkay nung song spec'un nung ploe.

construction n. of house or building -- kaa song; som'nong; kaa saang; or, kaa kaw saang; of s. th. abstract (peace, a relationship, etc.) -- saang

consult v. som yo'ball

consultant n. ti'pruk'saa

consume v. pra'pras

consumer n. neh pra'pras

contact v. tek tong

container n. small -- kum'pong: tin can -- kom'pung; small jar of pills or medecine -- kum'pong t'nam; small-to-medium size box -- praw'op; suitcase, foot-locker or packing chest size -- tuung; very large, as urban trash container size -- tuung thum

contingency n. yeh'taa'pheap; contingency plan -- pyne'kaa bum rong tooo'k chia muun

continue v. bun taw

contract n. kej sun'nyaa; verbal contract or promise -- pee'a sun'nyaa; either contract or promise -- kaa sun'nyaa

contract v. sign a contract for s.th. -- jchoh kej sun'nyaa

contrary, on the prp. p'toy teuh venyh

contribute v. pdull owi; choo'ay: Please contribute for the temple. -- Jchoh pdull owi jchum'poo'h wat.; or, Jchoh pdull owi teuh kang wat.

contribution n. kaa tveu vi pieh; kaa thien; kaa owi thien; kaa owi um'now'ee -- Please give us a contribution for the temple. -- Sum choo'ay pdull um'now'ee owi yeung dull wat.; I gave them a contribution. -- Kyom owi thien teuh gkay.

control n. kaa pee'nut; kaa troo'it tra; kaa troo'it pee'nut; lose control of. s. th. politically or militarily, or of a car -- bat bong; lose control of one's temper (lit: to become angry) -- khung: He really lost control. -- Gwat khung yang klang.

control v. pee'nut; troo'it; troo'it pee'nut; kaan kaab: control [a business] -- kaan kaab [chuum'noo'inyh]

convenient adj. srool; la'aw: Is this a convenient time for you to come? -- Tau(v) veea chia peyr la'aw sum'rap neh mok?

conversation n. san'ta'nee'a; kaa ni'yaye ka'neea

convict v. find guilty -- kaat to'h

convince v. tveu owi cheu'a (lit: make to believe)

convoke v. haow pra'choom

convoy n. chia ka'buon: We will go in convoy from the Sokhalay to the Monorum! -- Yung teuh chia ka'buon pi So'kha'l'eye teuh Mo'no'rom! (The Sokhalay and Monorom are the two Phnom Penh hotels which, along with the Samaki, were the three leading hostelries in the city (and the HQ of a number of NGO's that had operated in Phnom Penh through the 80s) prior to the 1992 UNTAC hotel boom.)

cook v. generally -- dam slaw; jchum'un a'ha; cook [rice] -- dam [bye]

cook n. jchong peau; neh jchong peau; neh dam s'law; or, neh jchum'un:: The cook at that restaurant doesn't make good food. -- Jchong peau noeh poch'ni'tan nu tveu ma'hope ot chng'anyh.

cool adj. temperature -- traw'cheh(k); (NB: "traw'cheh(k) can mean "cool" or cold"; "very cold" can be expressed as "traw'cheh(k) klang"); Cool! (great, terrific, neat, etc.) -- 'Chung hi! ("hi" is commn AP of "howi")

cooperate v. sa'ha'ka; work together -- sraaw ka'neea

cooperation n. kaa sa'ha'ka

cooperative n. chia sa'ha'ka; sa'ha'ka

coordinate v. organize (others to work well together) -- sum'rawb, sum roo'l; work in harmony with -- tveu owi see ka'neea

coordinates n. convergence of, on a map -- ti pra'choom

copper n. spo'an; spo'an kra'hom

copy n. reproduction (made by hand) -- kaa jchum long; reproduction (made by machine) -- co'pee: When will my (photo)copies be ready? -- Co'pee owi kyom howi peyr na?; versions, editions -- I need three copies of that newspaper. -- Kyom tro kaa ka'ssett bye ch'bop.; I need three copies of that book. -- Kyom tro kaa s'po ni bye k'bal.

copy v. by hand -- jchum'long; or jchum'long dow'ee dai; by machine -- co'pee; or, jchum'long dow'ee ma'seen; in sense of print, puum or bawh puum; follow, watch, pay attention to -- taam tveu: Don't copy everything he does. -- Kum taam tveu te'ang awh dael gwat tveu.

cork n. in bottle -- ch'nawk

corn n. po't; plai po't

corner n. ch'ruu'ng

corporal n. nee'aae toe; cap'a'ral

correct adj. tro; Correct! -- Trum tro!; Tro howi!; Baat, tro howi!

correct v. correct [an error] -- kaa'aae kum'hawh

correspondent n. journalist -- neh ka'ssett

corroborate v. bung chi'eh ch'bah law

corrupt adj. mun trum tro; dael pu'ka'ra loi

corruption n. om'peuh pu'ka'ra loi; kaa pu'ka'ra loi; pu'ka'ra loi

cost n. tlai: This costs too much. -- Tlai ni ch'raan.; kaa chum'nye: the cost of living -- kaa chum'nye sum'rap rooh noeh; dum'lye: the cost of a car -- dum'lye laan; The cost of one bowl of num'bun'chawk... -- Num'bun'chawk jchaan moi dum'lye... ; in sense of price -- dum'lye: Can you reduce the cost/price? -- Jchoh dum'lye (or tlai), baan tay?

cost v. in sense of price -- tlai; How much does this cost? -- Tlai pu'man? or A ni [this] tlai pu'man? (casual, familiar forms); or Tau(v) tlai pu'man?, or Tau(v) a ni tlai pu'man? (more respectful); What does [this book] cost? -- Tau(v) [s'po ni] tlai pu'man?

cot n. gkrey; (also means bed)

cotton n. the plant in the field -- daum cham'bah (AP: kaa(m)'bah); as cloth -- kraw'not; puffy cotton as used for swabs -- sum'lie; "cotton" tree -- daum gko

cough n. ka'aah(k): He has a bad cough. -- Gwat ka'aah(k) klang.; sore throat -- chh'ooh khaw

could v. have the ability to -- adje chia: You could be a good soldier. -- Neh eiyne adje chia tee'hee'an la'aw.; be possible -- da'aae: I [pray] it could be so. -- Kyom [buun srun] da'aae.

council n. krum pruk'sa: Council of Ministers -- Krum Pruk'sa Ratt'mun'trei; [Supreme] National Council -- Krum Pruk'sa Chee'it [national] Choo'an [K'pooh]; Security Council -- Krum Pruk'sa San'tek'sok

counsellor n. ti'pruk'sa

count v. compile numbers -- bo'k lek; ro'up

count on v. pung pa'eye

counterfeit adj. kl'eye'ng klai

country n. nation, fatherland -- sruk; praw'tet; tuk'daiy

countryside n. cheu'na'bot

coup d'etat n. ratt praw'haa; (lit: "killing of the government")

couple n. two associated people -- gkoo(r): Pia and Aae are a nice couple. -- Pia howi nung Aae chia gkoo(r) dael la'aw.; any two people -- pi neh: two farmers -- neh sr'eye pi neh; a few (people) -- pi-bye (lit: two-three): We saw a couple of militia [guarding] the headquarters. -- Yung keunyh kawng svaay tran pi-bye [kom'puung gyee'um la'bat] ti bun'chee'a kaa.; a few (things other than people) -- We saw a couple of [tanks] guarding the bank. -- Yeung keunyh [ro't troe] pi-bye kom'puung gyec'um la'bat bahng.

courage n. s'kd'eye kra'han

course, in the -- of prp. kum'lung peyr; noeh peyr dael

court n. of law -- to'la'ka: Who is [the judge] in that court? -- Neh na [chia chao krum] noeh k'nong to'la'ka nu?; tennis court -- cunlye'ng leng te'nnit

court v. pursue -- jchai'jchong

courtyard n. ti klee'a

cousin n. in general -- jchee doe'n moi (NB: jchee doe'n = respectful term for grandmother); first cousin -- jchee doe'n moi; first cousin on mother's side/on father's side -- jchee doe'n moi kang m'dye/kang oeuv'puk; (NB: for second, third, etc., cousins, and cousins "removed", the relationship is expressed by explication of the lineage rather than by a three- or four-word phrase.)

cover n. for container -- kum'rop; for bed -- kum'raal

cover v. in order to preserve or shelter -- kro'p; cover up, hide -- leh; cover (with a blanket) -- dun'dob (poi'y); cover a news story -- baan dum'nong pi: Many reporters covered the trial. -- Neh ka'ssett ch'raan baan dum'nung pi kaa vi'ni'ch'eye.; cover, in sense of follow, a story -- tham daan sat(ch) ru'ung (lit: follow the "meat" of a story)

cow n. gko

coward n. ma'nooh kum sahk

crab n. k'daam; soft-shell crab -- k'daam sawh

cradle v. cuddle -- tnauwm

crack n. kaa snaam preh; kaa preh snaam; kaa bah(k) byke

crack v. preh; snaam preh; bum byke; to "crack" s.o.'s head -- bum byke k'bal

cracked adj. preh

cramps n. stomach cramps -- chh'ooh jcho'k jchaab k'nong poo'ah; leg cramp -- k'daam katch (lit: "crab breaking"); to get arm or leg cramps -- jchawk dai; muscle twist or pull -- l'mool kaw'per (lit: crocodile twist)

crane n. ma'cheen stoo'eet

crate n. laa'ng

crawl v. for infant -- vee'a: the baby crawls -- gkon veea; for snake, insect, etc. -- veea or loon: the snake crawls -- poo'ah loon (or veea)

crazy adj. ch'koo'it: crazy with love -- ch'koo'it snai ha!; really crazy -- ch'koo'it jch'roook (lit: crazy as a pig); "spacey", "loco" -- seuh

cream n. crem (AP: kryme)

create v. build, develop -- bong kaut: create a business -- bong kaut krum'huun; make, cause -- tveu: create problems for... -- tveu pun'ha sam'rap...

credentials n. sa'taang

credit n. opposite of blame -- p'auwl: get the credit for -- to'tool p'auwl; buy on credit -- tinh cheu'a (lit: buy on belief, on faith)

cricket n. jchung'rut

crime n. generally -- bot ok'krut; um'peuh ok'krut; ok'krut'a'kaam (both, lit: wrong act); bot la'meuh; tuht'jchak'rut

criminal adj. ok'krut

criminal n. ma'nooh (or, neh) to'h; ma'nooh (or, neh) bot ok'krut; chee'a'chuun ok'krut

crippled adj. pi'kaa

crisis n. vee'bot; economic crisis -- vee'bot set'a'kej; political crisis -- vee'bot na'yo'bye

critical adj. important -- song'kahn; judgemental -- tung tyme; dun dop

criticism n. tic'tee'an; svey tic'tee'an

criticize v. rih'kun

crocodile n. kaw'per

crop(s) n. dum'nam; po't p'auwl; grow crops -- tveu jchum'kar; tveu dum'nam

cross v. place in crossed position -- kwaeng: Cross your arms! -- Kwaeng dai teuh!; go across -- ch'long: They crossed the Kompuung Thum/Kompuung Cham border into Cham Kalor District near Barei. -- Pooh'gkay ch'long tul'dyne Kp. Thum/Kp. Cham teuh sruk Cham Kalor noeh chit Ba'rei.

crossroads n. ploe kwaeng; choop ka'ncea ploe

crow n. k'eye't

crowd n. fo'ng: a crowd of students -- fo'ng gkon'sa; a big crowd -- ma'nooh paw peh paw poon: There was a big crowd in front of the station. -- Miun ma'nooh paw peh paw poon noeh muk s'ta'nee.

crowded adj. kaaw'kunyh; jchung ee'it; crowded/noisy -- ooo'aw

cruel adj. jchet yeh (lit.: heart of a monster); sa'how

crush n. sralaanyh (lit: love); to have a crush in s. o. -- baan sralaanyh

crush v. k'en; ngyee

crutch n. cheu ch'raw't (lit: wooden support)

cry v. weep -- yuum; sob noisily -- yuum law'uk; shed tears quietly, whimper -- k'suk k'sup; cry out, shout -- sr'eye't

cube n. duhm; ice cube -- duhm t'kaw

cube v. tveu owi trei kun

cubic adj. kuu'beek (fr. the Fr.)

cucumber n. traw'sawk (AP: tra'sa)

cultural adj. chia wa'pa'toa

culture n. in general -- wa'pa'toa (APs: wa'pa'ta, wa'pa'to): Cambodian culture -- wa'pa'toa Khmei

cup n. with or without handle -- paeng; rarely used word for cup specifically with handle -- kaa; (NB: "kaa" is reference to Buddha's ear (called "kaa") shape of which cup handle is suggested as resembling.)

cure n. p'chia bal; kaa meuhl chuum'ngeu: Protection [is better than] cure. -- Kaa pee'a [praw'sar chiang] p'chia bal.

cure v. meulh chuum'ngeu; to treat an illness -- p'chia bal chuum'ngeu: or, p'chia bal: The doctor was curing/treating him. -- Neh kruu p'chia bal gwat.

cured adj. chia: He was cured. -- Gwat baan chia howi.; saah s'bai; or, saah (lit: healed): ...will never be cured of... -- ... mun'dael chia saah sa'bauw'ee om'pee....

curfew n. bum raam ko chaw

currency n. roo'pye'o'baan

current adj. not late, as payments that are "current" -- k'nong peyr: contemporary, not old-fashioned -- peyr t'maee t'maee (lit: "new new time"); on-going -- k'nong peyr ni; k'nong eye leaou ni: a current problem... -- pun'ha k'nong eye leaou ni...; current events -- pa'choo baan na pheap

current n. in water -- k'sye tuk; electrical -- chu'ran

curry n. kaa'ree; popular curry-with-noodles dish -- num bun chawk

curse v. daum ni'yaye; bun da sa; jcheyr; bun chao

curve n. ko'hng: curve in wood -- cheu ko'hng; bot: curve in the road -- ploe bot

curved adj. ko'hng; "curved [island]" -- kaw'h ko'hng"

custom n. tradition -- tum nee'a tum lot

custom-made adj. kaat... dum'ro(v)... : Where can I get a custom made shirt? -- Kyom adje kaat aow dum'ro(v) kyom ti cunlye'ng na? ; or, kaat.. : Kyon adje kaat aow noeh cunlye'ng na?

customer n. p'nee'oo

customs n. import-export monotoring authority -- kaw'ee; mores and traditions -- tum nee'm, tum lo'ab

cut pp. severed as with knife -- kaat; cut the cake into three pieces -- kaat num chia bye jchum'nyke; interdicted, as by flood, military action, etc. -- kaat'pa'dach

cute adj. sa'aat; la'aw; cute like a baby -- kraw'mutch kraw'mum

cyclo driver n. neh teh' cyclo (NB: "teh" means "pedal")

cylindar n. see'lung

cymbal n. musical instrument -- chaa'b

D

daily adv. moi t'ngai teuh moi t'ngai

daily adj. rawl t'ngai

dam n. thum'noop

damage n. kaa ko'ich kot

damage v. ko'ich kot; byke bah(k)

dance, dancing n. in general -- ro'um; classical or traditional dancing -- ro'bahm: classical/traditional Khmer dancing -- ro'bahm Khmei; or, ro'um ro'bahm Khmei (NB: two of most common forms of classical Khmer dance are 1) ro'um'vuung, or "circle dance" (two steps forward, one step back, with hand movement) and, "kh'ba(ch)" (two steps forward with turn/bend to right, two steps forward with turn/bend to left, again, hand movements); classical Thai dancing -- ro'bahm Sec'um

dance v. traditional Khmer -- ro'bahm; any other -- ro'um

dance hall n. rung kuh sa'la

dancer n. neh ro'um

danger n. kroo'ti'nak

dangerous adj. kroo'ti'nak

dark adj. color -- jchaah; k'mau: dark blue -- kee'oo k'mau; kee'oo jchaah (lit: old blue); lacking light -- ngo'ngut: a dark room -- ban'tope ngo'ngut

dark n. the dark -- t'ngai lic (lit: end of day); before dark -- muun t'ngai lic

darling adj. term of address, romantic -- baan doll jchet; or, pro'lung (lit: "soul"); term of address, more casual -- puun'lok; peau (lit: "youngest"); peau puun'lok; mee'ch (lit: "gold")

data n. por'da'mee'an; kum'not

date n. of calendar -- t'ngai ti: The date [today] is the 4th. -- [T'ngai ni] t'gnai ti buon.; What date did he get here? -- Gwat mok doll ti ni t'ngai ti pu'man?; What's the date today? -- T'ngai ni ti pu'man?; (NB: What <u>day</u> (e.g., of the week) is it today? -- T'ngai ni chia t'ngai a'veye?); appointed time -- kaa choop chi'moi: I set a date for the meeting. -- Kyom kum'not t'ngai pra'choom.; or, Kyom kum'not t'ngai kaa choop chi'moi.; social outing -- bun'dah leng: He wants a date with Nayana. -- Gwat jchong bun'dah leng nung Nayana.; I have a date with her. -- Kyom not choop ka'neea. or, Kyom not choop nee'eng. or, Kyom not peyr choop veea.; palm fruit -- plai t'naut

[this is sentence definitely OKd at Herndon Oct 30] We need to set a date for the meeting. -- Yung tro kaa kum'not tngai choop ka'neea.

daughter n. gkon sraae

daughter-in-law n. gkon pra'sa sraae

dawdle v. walk slowly -- dah meuhk meuhk

dawn n. praw'lum

day n. generally -- t'ngai: days of the week -- t'ngai ney a'tthit; one day (whether in sense of "a one-day vacation", "one day we will go there", or "one day last year") -- moi t'ngai; all day long -- penyh moi t'ngai; day before yesterday -- musl'm'ngai; day after tomorrow -- kan s'eye'd; pay day -- t'ngai bot loi; day and night -- te'ang yoop te'ang t'ngai [lit: night and day]; day off -- t'ngai chope; holiday -- t'ngai chope buun; day(time) (as contrasted to night(time) - peyr t'ngai: it happened during the day. -- Veea kaut laung peyr t'ngai.; in those days... -- noeh ro'ycht peyh nu...

dead adj. slop; for crops -- nwop; humorous, as "dead tired" -- slop howi; humorous, as "I'm going to go and die (if you don't do this or that)" -- "Kyom teuh slop." or, "Kyom teuh mwop."

dead end n. ploe t'wal

deaf adj. t'laahng

deal n. arrangement -- tek tong: Sihanouk and Hun Sen had tried to make a deal. -- Sihanoo' howi nung Hun Seyn pyee'a yee'um tek tong ka'neea.; a bargain (cheap price) -- tauk; tlai tauk

deal with v. pra srei tek tong; teuh p'nawl ka'neea

deal in v. choo'inyh: They deal in firewood. -- Gkay choo'inyh nung awh.

Dear... adj. form of salutation -- Choon jchum'poo'h...; teuh doll; or mok doll: Dear Nayana,... -- Mok doll Nayana,... ; close -- jchet snut: a dear friend -- po'mah jchet snut

dearest adj. most loved -- bun doll jchet; somewhat casual -- peau puun'lok

death n. kaa bot bong chi'vut; of a monk -- mo'ra'na

debate n. conversation among small group -- jchaw jchaa; public discussion -- sun'ni'baat; kaa cho chaae'k; kaa pee'pee'a(k) sa

debris n. kum'tic

debt n. bum'nawl (AP: bum'nol)

debtor n. neh chuum'pe'eh bum'nawl

deceive v. kaa jcheyr; bong jchet

December n. T'noo

decide v. sum'rach jchet; tang jchet

decision n. kaa sum'rach jchet

declare v. chaeng; praw'kas; The minister declared a new law. -- Ratt'mun'trei chaeng (or, praw'kas) ch'bop t'maee.

decline n. bun'toi: decline in sales -- bun'toi noch kaa looh

decorate v. ta'tayng

decrease v. reduce speed -- ban'toi la'beu'an; decease the price of s. th. -- jchoh dum'lye: That is too expensive; can you decrease the price? -- Nu tlai nah; jchoh dum'lye, baan tay?

decree n. ch'bop

deep adj. ch'ro: deep water -- tuk ch'ro

deer n. branch-horned deer -- pre(s); bi-horned antelope -- ka'don; non-horned antelope -- ch'loo(s)

defeat n. kaa pa'ra'chey

defeat v. yok ch'neh: If he is able to defeat [the German player], the US will win the Davis Cup. -- Baa'sun chia gwat adje yok ch'neh [neh leng A'la'maan], US nung baan to'tool Davis Cup.; defeat an enemy -- bong ree'up; or, p'jchanyh: If we can defeat them in Siem Reap, we can win (the war). -- Baa'sun yeung adje bong ree'up pooh'veea noeh Siem Reap, yeung nung baan choke chey.

defeated adj. bahk to'up

defector n. neh rut jchowl sruk

defend v. kaa pee'a; barricade or stop -- toop tole

defendant n. neh jchong jchowt

definite adj. chia s'taa po; mwa muon

definitely adv. piht praw'kat; chia dach kat

degree n. academic -- sun'ya bot; of temperature -- ong'sa

delay v. tok'yoo

delegate n. praw'ti'phum

delegate v. bun choon owi tveu chum noo'a; pra'kul um'natch

delegation n. kieh nat praw'teh'poo'

delicious adj. chng'anyh (APs: chng'ang, chng'angyh)

deliver v. jchenyh teuh owi: The rubber can be delivered only if the army provides an escort. -- Kaow'soo adje baan jchenyh teuh owi luke tra tai yo'tee'a pdull kawng kaa'pee'a.; pdull: deliver a package -- pdull praw'op ; sell -- looh

delta n. of river -- mwot tun'lay.

demand n. for a product -- s'kd'eye tro kaa; insistence upon s. th. -- kaa thee'um thee'a; ruhm lope

demand v. generally -- praw'kas; demand that s. th. be done, order -- bun'chee'a; demand in argument or bargaining, negotiate, bargain for -- thaw'va; express strong preference for s. th. -- thee'um thee'a; sum'lut thee'a

democracy n. praw'chia a'tep'a'tai

democratic adj. chia praw'chia a'tep'a'tai

demolish v. ruuh: demolish a house -- ruuh ptay'a

demonstrate v. for social or political cause -- tveu pa'ti'kaam; show how to -- bun'yul

demonstration n. political, to some extent violentl -- pa'ti'kaam; political, peaceful -- pa'ti'kaam dow'ee pheap scngo'p scngee'um; of how to do s. th. -- kaa bun'yul bung hanyh; kaa sum'rey bum pleu(s); kaa bung hanyh; (NB: bun'yul alone conveys concept of explanation while bung hanyh alone conveys concept of showing how s.th. is done)

demonstrator n. neh tveu pa'ti'kaam

dengue fever n. kruun chee'im (lit: blood fever)

denial n. kaa pa'di'seyt

dentist n. peyt t'ming

deny v. pa'di'seyt; praw'kayt: He denied that he knew her. -- Gwat praw'kayt tha scwaal veea.

deodorant n. deo'daw'rong (fr. Fr.)

depart v. go out, leave -- jchenyh; teuh jchenyh; [The convoy] will depart at 4 o'clock. -- [Ka'buon] nung jchenyh noeh mao buon.; go and do s. th. -- jchenyh tveu: We have to go [fix] the car. -- Yeung tro jchenyh tveu [choo'ah chul] laan.

department n. ministry -- kra'soo'ung: Ministry of Foreign Affairs -- Kra'soo'ung Kaa Bor'tay

depend on v. rely on -- ruhm'pung leuh: Children depend on their parents -- Gkon ruhm'pung leuh oeuv'puk m'dye.; is a function of -- dow'ee sa; yul teuh leuh: That depends on the price. -- Veca yul teuh leuh (or, dow'ee sa) dum'lye.; will be decided by -- srech noeh leuh; srech tai: Whether we go or not depends on whether the Ministry approves the trip. -- Praw'sun' baa yeung teuh roo ot srech noeh leuh kra'soo'ung a'noo'naaht roo ot.; (It) depends on you. -- Srech tai neh eiyne.

deposit n. down payment on s. th. -- kaa bong loi muun

deposit v. dah(k); deposit money -- dah(k) loi: deposit money in a bank -- dah(k) loi k'nong bahng

depot n. storage yard or area -- kum'no

depressed adj. downcast -- sawh'ka'krah

depth n. ch'ro: What is the depth? -- Ch'ro pu'man?

deputy adj. a'noo: deputy director -- a'noo praw'tee'an; pooh'choo'ay

deputy n. in sense of assistant -- pooh'choo'ay; in sense of assemblyman or representative -- dum'nahng

descend v. go down, as in, stairs -- jchoh

describe v. ree'up roo'up; jcha(r) jchaeng; por'neea

desert n. veal k'suj (lit. field, or plain, of sand)

desert v. run away -- rut jchenyh; rut jchowl

deserve v. sum; or, tro tai baan: He deserves more money. -- Gwat sum loi ch'raan chiang. or, Gwat tro tai baan loi ch'raan chiang.

design n. ka'bat ka'bo: graphic design or picture -- kum'noo

desire v. jchong; tro kaa; prat'na

desk n. tohk

despite prp. yang na kaw dow'ee: Despite the rain, we will go. -- Plee'eng yang na kaw dow'ee, yeung nung teuh.; despite the fact that... -- too'a... yang na kaw dow'ee: Despite the fact that they say he is bad, he is a good man. -- Too'a neh na tha gwat a'krah, yang na kaw dow'ee, gwat ma'nooh la'aw.

dessert n. bung eye'm; fruit and chopped ice dessert -- tuk kraw'lawk

destination n. cunlye'ng (AP: kunlyne, cum'lyne, ka'lyne) teuh; ti doll

destroy v. blow up, knock down, etc. -- kum'tic

destroyed pp. kum'tic; bum plynyh: Seven houses in that village were destroyed by APC gunfire. -- Ptay'a prum'pul neoh k'nong phum nu tro baan bum'plynyh dow'ee sa kaa banyh ka'neea APC.; in sense of broken, damaged -- ko'ich: Each one was destroyed (damaged). -- Moi na kaw ko'ich da'aae.; in sense of smashed into small pieces -- rawl lut, rawl lee'aae: absolutely smashed -- rawl lut, rawl lee'aae awh howi; re ships, sunk -- lic jchoh: The ship was destroyed (sunk). -- Toook lic jchoh k'nong tuk.; beaten, defeated -- jchanyh; or, vee'neea(s): The enemy was destroyed by our troops. -- Sa'tro tro baan jchanyh dow'ee sa tee'hee'an yeung.; destroyed emotionally, heart-broken -- jchet rawl lut, rawl lee'aae

details n. ka'bah ka'bye: Just give me the details. -- Ni'yaye owi chia ka'bah ka'bye.

detective n. with national police -- ki'nyh; p'nehk nich sum ngut; chief detective -- may ki'nyh; with local police -- p'nehk nich dum'roo'it

deteriorate v. kan'ta'ee laung: The factory has deteriorated. -- Ro'ng jcha kan'ta'ee laung.; kan'ta'ee jchaap jchenyh laung: His health had deteriorated. -- Sok'a'pheap gwat kan'ta'ee jchaap jchenyh laung.

determined adj. jchet rung; p'day'nyaa

detour v. ploe vee'ung: Where does the detour go to? -- Ploe vee'ung jchenyh teuh ti na?

devastation n. vee'nia'sa'kaam

develop v. generally improve -- jchum raan; bung kaun; pung ree(k); develop business or trade -- kaan laung chia laung dop; build up -- kaut; film -- pa'dut, or lee'eng: Go develop the film. -- Teuh pa'dut roob'tawt teuh.; or, Teuh lee'eng svil teuh.

developed adj. processed -- pa'dut howi: developed film -- svil pa'dut howi; matured, advanced -- choo'un leu'an: a developed economy -- set'a'kej choo'un leu'an

development n. economic progress -- a'pi'vwut; event, s. th. that happens -- pra'ti'kaa; new happening -- kaa (lit. thing): a strange development -- kaa ply'ke ply'ke; s. th. built up -- kaw saang: housing development -- kaw saang ptay'a

devil n. bye'sak

dew n. sun salm

dial v. a phone number -- ro'vaae'ng layke torasap; or, on a touch-tone phone -- jchuch layke (lit. "push" the number)

dialect n. pee'esa ta'ana sruk; pee'esa ro'bah gkay (lit: "someone's language")

diamond n. pi'(ch); t'bong pi(ch)

diarrhea n. ree'uhk; rohk choh ree'ukh; a particularly serious case of diarrhea -- ree'uhk mool

dice n. a'pawng; to play dice -- leng a'pawng; or, jchch a'pawng

dictator n. neh pa'doch'kaa

dictionary n. vi'cha'na'no'um krom; s'po bauw'pr'eye (lit: book of translations)

die v. slop; n'wop (AP: mwop)

die, to go and v. PS phrase which can convey either i) "(You) Get out of here!" -- "Teuh slop!"; or, "Teuh nwop!"; or ii) "I've had it, I'm `going off to die'!" -- "Kyom teuh slop!"; or, "Kyom teuh mwop!"

diesel adj. ma'zoot: The truck uses diesel gas. -- Laan trung (or laan ca'mion) pra praeng ma'zoot.

different adj. p'sayng tee'it; ot doj (lit: not the same); p'sayng: It means something different. -- Vee'a miun ney p'sayng.; different from -- p'sayng p'sayng ka'neea

difficult adj. pi'bah

difficulty n. pun'ha (written: pun(y)'ha; AP: pun'i'ha)

dig v. generally, in ground -- jchi(k); dig by scratching, as chickens or dogs -- kaw'kye (refers primarily to animals); dig a hole in a wall, bore -- jchaw

dignitary n. ka'na'ka a'tep'a'dye

dim adj. ot seou pluu: a dim light -- pleung ot seou pluu

dim v. bun toi

dim sum n. num pahng (lit: bread); ma'hope runyh (lit: cart food)

dimension(s) n. tuum'huung (NB: as with English word "dimensions", "tuum huung" can also mean "size"): The dimensions of this book are 12 [by] 8. -- Tuum huum s'po ni pi tun dop nung pram bye.

diminish v. bun toi

dining room n. ban'tope to'tool tee'ung bye; ban'tope nyam bye

dinner n. bye long'aae't; a'ha long'aae't (lit: evening meal)

diploma n. sun'ya bot

diplomacy n. kaa toot

diplomat n. neh kaa toot

diplomatic adj. om'pee (or, pi) kaa toot; sum'rup kaa toot

diplomatic corps n. ung toot (lit: body of diplomats)

direct adj. trong

direct v. troo'it meuhl; bong hang; prap

direction n. kang: They went in that direction. -- Pooh'gkay teuh kang nu.; (NB: "kang" can also express the direction in which something lies of or from a given point of reference, viz.: "The stream is [south of] this village." -- "Stung noeh [kang t'bong] phum ni."); tuhs: They went in different directions. -- Pooh'gkay teuh taam tuhs p'sayng ka'neca.; re any distant point that cannot be reached by road from the point at which the speaker is located -- teuh taam tuhs: Which direction is [the Morning Star]? -- [P'k'eye pruhk] teuh taam tuhs na moi?; re a destination that can be reached by road from where the speaker is located -- teuh taam ploe: What direction is that village from here? -- Phum nu teuh taam ploe na moi?

directions n. instructions, guidance -- tuhs da'oo

director n. jchang vang; lok nee'a yoo'k

dirty adj. kra'kwah; ot at'a'na'mye; smoe'kro'; mun sa'aat

disabled person n. ma'nooh pee'ka

disadvantage n. kaa jchanyh pree'ub; kaa k'miun pree'ub

disagree v. praw'kayt; yul to'ahs

disagreement n. kaa yul choom to'ahs; kaa kaut toook mun sohk jchet

disappear v. bot; bot mok; bot roob riun

disappointed adj. kaw(k) jchet; sraw'nga jchet

disapprove v. choom to'ahs

disarm v. by one's own action, i.e., give up one's arms -- owi a'vwut: They are supposed to disarm. -- Pooh'gkay koo'a tai owi a'vwut.; disarm s. o. else -- dawk hote a'vwut: UNTAC did not disarm the KR. -- UNTAC mun dawk hote a'vwut Khmei Kra'hom.

disarmament n. kaa dawk hote a'vwut: Before peace, there must be disarmament. -- Krow'ee peyr miun san'ti'pheap, tro baan miun kaa dawk hote a'vwut.

disaster n. un'ta'rye; vaae't'neea (AP: vit'neea): "everything gone wrong" -- rawl chan; "everything lost" -- rawl lee'aae

discipline n. military -- praw'dow; or, vit'naae; for students, children -- vit'naae; op'ruhm

discontent (with) n. kaa to'ahs main'uh (jchum'poo'h); to be discontented (with): miun kaa to'ahs main'uh (jchum'poo'h)

discover v. ro'k keunyh

discovery n. kaa ro'k keunyh

discuss v. have a conversation about -- san'ta'neea om'pee; discuss seriously, negotiate (about) -- jchaw jchaa (om'pee); discuss casually -- cho chaae'k ka'neea pi: We discussed politics. -- Yeung cho chaae'k ka'neea pi na'yo'bye.; discuss seriously (e.g., to find a solution) -- pi'kroo'a: discuss with you -- pi'kroo'a chi'moi neh; discuss with one another -- pi'kroo'a ka'neea

discussion n. kaa cho chaae'k; kaa pee'pee'a(k) sa

disease n. chuum'ngeu; rohk

disgraceful adj. a'krah; lazy, drunken, of bad character, no good, etc. -- tauwp thee'up

dish n. jchaan

dishes n. cups, saucers, plates, etc., colectively -- jchaan k'ban

dishonest adj. tuuch cha'ret; a'krah; ot sm'oh trong

disinfect v. ruhm ngwob may'rohk; (may'rohk = germs)

dislike v. mun jchole jchet; mun jchong

disobey v. mun ko'rup taam la'aw tay; mun s'dap bong kwap; mun tveu taam

dispatch v. send -- bun'chuun: despatch reenforcements -- bun'chuun thwaap chum'noo'ee

dispensary n. clinic, i.e., facility that provides medical care -- mun'ti chia'bal rohk; shop that sells medicine -- oo'ta'lye; haang looh tnam peyt

displaced adj. forced to move -- bun chee'a owi jchenyh; bun'kum owi jchenyh: There were 10,000 displaced persons there last year. -- Miun chum'noo'an dap pwan neh dael tro baan bun'kum owi jchenyh noeh chh'nam teuh.; picked up and moved -- ruum'kul; pdo: The [border markers] have been displaced -- Ruum'kul (or, pdo) [sun'ya prum'pra'tul].

disrespectful adj. ch'leu'ee

distance n. jchum'ngai

distilled water n. tuk sok

distract v. with harmful intent, as, mislead -- bum po'an; with helpful intent, as, take one's mind off s. th. -- choo'ay bum plic

distribute v. jchaiyk; p'sye

distribution n. kaa pdull owi chia um'nowi

distributor n. chum'noo'inyh looh duhm; (NB: looh duhm = wholesale; duhm alone = all together, all at once, as: Bring it all together. -- Yok veea mok duhm.)

district n. political subdivision of Cambodian province similar to US county -- sruk; district chief -- may sruk; area -- dum'bun

distrust v. mun tuk jchet: Ranariddh and Chea Sim distrusted [each other]. -- Ranariddh howi nung Chea Sim mun tuk jchet [ka'neea teuh venyh teuh mok].

disturb v. ruhm'kaan

ditch n. un'dow; or, run'dow; or, t'naam ploo'a; (NB: t'naam ploo'a also means small canal; large canal = prayk (NB: also means "stream"); praw'lye

divert v. bung vee'eng ploe

divide v. in order to share -- bayng jchaiyk; split in order to take one by one or weaken (divide a class; divide the enemy) -- bum byke

division n. military unit -- kum pul, or kum pul thum; splitting, rendering, disgreement -- kaa bayng jchaiyk; or, jchaiyk yo'bal: There was a division of opinion between OXFAM and ICRC about the aid. -- Miun kaa bayng jchaiyk kum'nut (or, jchaiyk yo'bal) ro'vieng OXFAM howi nung ICRC om'pee kaa choo'ay.; mathematical division -- layke jchaiyk

divorce n. one partner -- layng lee'a: She divorced him. -- Nee'eng layng lee'a gwat.; each other -- layng ka'neea

divorced pp. layng ka'neea; layng lee'a; They are divorced. -- Gkay layng ka'neea.

dizzy adj. ngo ngut muk; veul muk (lit: head turning)

do v. t'veu: Do whatever you want. -- Jchong tveu 'aae, tveu teuh.; do s. th. in a hurry -- tveu av'eye chhop chhop; something to do -- miun kaa: I wanted to go shopping but I couldn't because I had something to do at home. -- Kyom jchong teuh psa pun'ta'aae mun adje bee'proo'a miun kaa noeh ptay'a.

do away with v. daeng... jchole teuh: She wanted to do away with Ung Mang. -- Gwat jchong daeng Ung Mang jchole teuh.

dock n. wharf, quay -- dai ka'pal (AP:ka'pow) (lit: arm for ship)

doctor n. kruu; kruu'peyt; neh tai chuum'ngeu; way'chia'bun'det; doctor: go see a doctor -- jchole teuh kruu; or, jchole teuh doctor

document n. bun'chee (NB: bun'chee translates as document, certificate, etc., i. e., a physical piece of paper; bun'chee'a translates as the conceptual order, information or other substance that the paper may be conveying); eyke'a'saa (AP: eyke'a'zaan)

dog n. sh'kye

doll n. gkon kra'mum

dollar n. loi chai

domestic adj. nationally indigenous -- noch sruk; noch k'nong sruk: domestic beer -- bee'a paw'let noeh k'nong sruk; or, bee'a tveu noch sruk; intra-familial -- k'nong ptay'a: a domestic quarrel -- kaa chum'loo' ka'neea k'nong ptay'a

dominate v. politically -- kroop krong

don't v. imperative -- kum; Don't worry too much. -- Kum proo'i peyk; negation -- ot: don't have -- ot miun; don't know -- ot dung; (NB: ot can also mean "haven't" as in "(I) haven't seen (him' her, it, etc.)." -- "Ot keunyh.")

door n. t'veea

double adj. tvay'teea pi; doop: ride a moto "double" -- moto doop; ride a bike double -- doop kong

double-cross v. k'but: Don't double-cross them. -- Kum k'but nung pooh'gkay.; dah k's'eye leuh (lit: walk the high wire): I don't want to do business with him because I'm sure he will try to double-cross me. -- Kyom ot jchong tveu chuum'noo'inyh nung gwat bee'proo'a kyom dung tha gwat nung dah k's'eye leuh.

doubt v. sung sai; without a doubt -- chia mun kaan; chia ruhm kaan; or mun kaan: You will come back without a doubt. -- Neh mao venyh mun kaan.

down prp. krowm: The child fell down. -- Gkon k'mayng t'leh jchoh krowm.; tauk: Prices went down last week. -- A'tthit muun tlai jchoh tauk.

downstairs adv. kang krowm

dozen n. lo'; one dozen -- moi lo' (AP: m'lo')

draft animal n. saat pee'a'hawt'na

drag v. bung oh; sun downg; oh: She had to drag the kid to school. -- Nec'eng tro kaa oh gkon teuh sa'la'rin.

dragon n. nee'ehk; pwih'chung nee'ehk; dragon-snake -- poo'ah nee'chk ka'ree'ych

drama n. play -- lu'kauwn

draw v. draw a picture -- gkoo kum'noo; draw up a plan -- ree'up jchum kum rong kaa, or kro'ng kaa, or pyne'kaa; draw water -- bo'm tuk

drawing n. kum'noo

dream n. kaa yul'sob; a bad dream -- kaa yul'sob a'krah

dream v. dream about -- geyng yul'sob pi: Last night I dreamed about her. -- Yoop munyh kyom geyng yul'sob pi veea.; dream that -- yul'sob keunyh; or, geyng'sob tha: Last night I dreamed that my mother was sick. -- Yoop muun kyom geyng'sob keunyh m'dye kyom chh'ooh.; Last night I dreamed that she had come. -- Yoop muun kyom yul'sob tha veea mok.; Don't even dream about it. -- Kum p'dayke yul'sob.

dress n. specifically -- aow'rope; female clothing -- sum'lee's bum'pay'a sraae; conceptually, as "Proper dress is important." -- kow-aow

dress v.   slee'a peh (AP: slee'peh; slee'a pay'a); She still has to dress. -- Veea kom'puung slee'a peh noeh low'ee.; Hurry up and get dressed. -- Prawn'yab slee'a peh laung teuh.

drink v.   nyam tuk; puk (AP: putt): I just finished drinking my coffee. -- Kyom teup tai puk cafe howi.; formal -- **pee'sa** (can, depending on context, also mean "eat"): What would you like to drink? -- Lok jchong pee'sa a'veye?

drinks n.   p'es'cheeh'

drive v.   baahk (most common; also used = baahk baw and baw): drive a car -- baahk laan; or, baahk baw laan; or, baw laan; (NB: turn = bawt; hence: Drive straight ahead, then turn right. -- Baahk teuh trong, howi nung bawt s'dam.)

driver n.   neh baahk; neh baahk baw laan

drop v.   drop by itself -- ch'roo: the fruit dropped -- plai cheu ch'roo; to drop s. th. -- t'leh: I dropped my book. -- Kyom t'leh s'po.; a bomber (lit: airplane that drops bombs) -- yun hawh t'leh kraw'bai

drought n.   ray'ang

drug n.   medicine -- t'nam peyt; narcotics, generally -- kreung ngyee'un; opium -- a'pee'en; ganja -- gun'jcha; k'chaa

drum n.   sco

drummer n.   neh leng sco

drunk adj.   sro'vung (AP: sco'vung); very drunk -- sro'vung choke

drunkard n.   ma'nooh sro'vung; neh praw'muk

dry adj.   not wet -- sngoo'it: a dry road -- ploe sngoo'it; re ground only (NB: in appropriate context, may may connote "parched") -- ko'k: on dry land -- noeh daiy ko'k; dehydrated -- kree'um: dry food, as for soldiers -- ma'hope kree'um; sun-dried -- kree'um: rice, cooked, dried 2-3 days in sun, then edible as is, or re-boil-able, or fry-able into popped-rice -- bye kree'um

dry season n.   ro'doe (written ro'do(v)) k'dau (lit: hot season)

duck n.   tee'a; duck meat -- sat(ch) teea; roast duck -- teea ka'v'eye

due adj.   expected to arrive -- nung mok doll (AP: dul): When is the plane due? -- Yun hawh nung mok doll peyr na?; It is due any minute. -- Veea nung mok dull k'nong peyr chhop chhop ni.; to be supplied at particular time -- baan kum'not: [The report] was due last week. -- [Ro'bye'kaa] baan kum'not a'tthit muun.; re money -- tro bong (lit: must be paid): The rent was due at the end of the month. -- Tlai ptay'a (or, ch'nool ptay'a) tro bong noeh dach kye (or jchong kye).

dumb adj.   not intelligent -- plee pleuh; unable to speak -- ko'hh

durian n.   plai krem

during adv.   while s. th. was going on -- noeh peyr: during the movie -- noeh peyr gkun leng; They [stole] my bike during the night. -- Noeh peyr yoop gkay [loo'ich] kong kyom.; in the course of -- noeh k'nong; The student [fell asleep] during [class]. -- Gkon'sa [ngaw ngoi geyng] noeh k'nong [t'nak].; in the course of -- roy'yet peyr...moi: during this week -- roy'yet peyr moi a'tthit ni; k'nong: during this week -- k'nong a'tthit ni; over the course of -- kum'lung peyr: during the war -- kum'lung peyr sung'kree'um

dusk n.   pro'lup

dust n.   too'lee: He should be as dust under the feet of the people. -- Gwat koo'a tai chia too'lee krowm bot cheung pra'chee'chuun.; dust swirl -- k'shaal koo'it

dusty adj.   inside the house -- too'lee; outside -- hoiyh: This road is very dusty. -- Ploe ni hoiyh nah.

duty n.   pee'reh'keut; mok'ka

dysentery n.   rohk mool

E

each adj.   moi moi; Each house is different. -- Ptay'a moi moi p'sayng ka'neea; each other -- ka'neea; They will met each other next week. -- Gkay nung choop ka'neea a'tthit krow'ee.; each other -- ka'neea... teuh venyh teuh mok: They told each other lies. -- Gkay ni'yaye ko'hawk ka'neea teuh venyh teuh mok.; each one -- moi na: Each one was destroyed. -- Moi na kaw ko'ich da'aae.

ear n.   traw'chi'eh(k); (NB: "cold" = traw'cheh(k))

earlier adv.   muun nung: I saw him earlier (in the day). -- Kyom keunyh gwat muun nung.; earlier than s.o. or s.th. else -- muun nung... baan: Please come earlier than seven o'clock. -- Sum mok muun mao pram'pul baan tay.

earliest adv.   yang chhop bom pot

early adv.   quickly, ahead of time -- chhop; yang chhop; muun; early in the morning -- pi pro'lum: wake up early -- krau pi geyng pi pro'lum; or, pn'yeh pro'lum; early in the evening or at night -- pi pro'lup: go to sleep early -- teuh geyng pi pro'lup

earn v.   ro'k loi

earring n.   kro'vull; (AP: ka'ball)

earth n.   ground, soil, land -- daiy; the planet Earth -- pan daiy; preah tor'ni

east n.   kang kaut

easy adv.   srool (compressed in speech to "sool" and "soo"): Khmer is easy. -- Pee'esa Khmei srool nah.; ngi'yaye: This work is easy for me. -- Kej kaa ni veea ngi'yaye sum'rap kyom.

eat v.   if done by humans -- n'yam, n'yam bye; if by animals -- see; The cow ate grass. -- Gko see sm'au.; (formal: pitsa (AP: pee'sa))

echo n.   kaa luhm pong

echo v.   luhm pong

eclair n.   suuu

economic adj.   chia set'a'kej

economics n.   set'a'kej vich'ea

economist n.   set'a'sa'vitoo

economy n.   set'a'kej

-ed past tense indicator.   howi: I wanted it then but not now. -- Kyom jchong veea teuh howi pun'ta'aae mun eye leaou.; baan: He received the money yesterday. -- Gwat to'tool baan loi pi musl'munyh.; baan... howi: He had already started. -- Gwat jchap p'dam baan howi.

edge n.   gkem: edge of the table -- gkem tohk

editor n.   neh ree'up ree'um; neh bun tyme bun toi; re-write editor -- neh kye

educate v.   train -- op'roum; take care of -- tai'reh'sa

educated adj.   jcheh dung; He is an educated man. -- Gwat chia neh jcheh dung.

education n.   kaa suk'sah; kaa rian sah: Ministry of Education -- Krasoo'ung Op'roum; elementary education -- ba'tum suk'saah; secondary education -- ma'choom suk'saah, or vich'eea'lye; higher education: -- maha'vich'eea'lye

effect n.   a'ti'p'auwl: She has a bad effect on me. -- Gwat miun a'ti'p'auwl a'krah mok leuh kyom.; pul: The dry [weather] [had] a bad effect [on] the crops. -- [Tee'ut a'kas] sngoo'it [ho'ich] p'auwl a'krah [teuh leuh] dum'nam.

effective adj.   gkut chia kaa; sak'sut

efficient adj.   tveu kaa la'aw

egg n. pong; chicken egg -- pong muon; duck egg -- pong tee'a

eggplant n. tra'up

eight adj. prum'bye (AP: in accelerated spoken Khmer, "'m'bye"); eight p. m. -- mao prum'bye (AP: mao m'bye)

eighteen adj. dop'prum'bye

eighth adj. ti'prum'bye

eighty adj. pad'sup

either adj. one or the other -- roo... moi na kaw baan: Please give me either coffee or tea. -- Sum owi kyom cafe roo ta'aae moi na kaw baan.; also -- pong da'aae: Don't hit me and don't hit her either. -- Kum vye kyom nung howi kum vye nee'eng pong da'aae.; either one -- moi na: Either one is OK. -- Moi na kaw baan da'aae.

elaborate adj. ruh'chi'na; ch'nye: elaborate design -- kum'roo ch'nye; praw'duht: elaborate story -- ru'ung praw'duht; ch'nye praw'duht

elaborate v. owi ru'ung ka'bah ka'bye

elder n. elderly woman, grandmother -- ee'yaye; more polite, respectful term -- jchee doe'n; elderly man, grandfather -- ta

elderly adj. jchaah

elect v. jchreu'reu'; baw ch'naut owi: The people voted for FUNCINPEC and elected Ranariddh. -- Pra'chee'chuun baw ch'naut owi FUNCINPEC howi jchreu'reu' yok Ran'riddh.

election n. bawh ch'naut; kaa jchreu'reu'

electric adj. a'ki'ce'nee; electric lights: -- pleung a'ki'ce'nee; electric power -- kum'lung a'ki'ce'nee; chu'ran (fr. Fr. "currant") a'ki'ce'nee

electricity n. generally -- pleung; ("pleung" lit. = fire or light, as: pleung jchong kee'ung = kerosene lamp, pleung a'ki'cenee = electric light, but is also loosely and widely used to mean domestic electricity generally); electricity (specifically, not only re light as with "pleung) -- pleung a'ki'cenee: Electricity in Phnom Penh is cheaper than in Po'sat. -- Pleung a'ki'cenee noeh Phnom Penh tauk chiang noeh Po'sat.; electricity as electric power or current -- chu'ran a'ki'cenee; electric power -- kum'lung a'ki'cenee

elementary school n. sa'la ba'tum

element n. aspect of s. th. -- kat'tha: one element of [the situation] -- kat'tha moi ney [s'ta'na'pheap]; part -- p'nyke: one element -- p'nyke moi; something needed to accomplish s. th., component -- kreung: component/element of a computer -- kreung cum'puu'teuh

elephant n. dum'rei

elevator n. chun'dow yun (lit: stair machine)

eleven adj. dup'moi

eliminate v. bom but: We should eliminate corruption. -- Yeung tro kaa bom but om'peuh pu'ka'ra loi.

elite adj. vo'ret; special -- pi'sch

elite n. vo'ret'chuun

elope v. bung rut ("rut" means "to run")

else adj. something in addition -- aae tee'it: Anything else? -- Tro kaa aae tee'it? or, Miun aae tee'it? or, Aae tee'it?; nothing else -- ot miun aae tee'it; as alternative -- roo kaw: Leave, or else I will hit you. -- Neh koo'a jchaak jchenyh, roo

kaw kyom nung vee'aye neh.

embarrass v. tveu owi k'mah muk: The teacher embarrassed the student. -- Kruu tveu owi k'mah muk gkon'sa.; somewhat stronger, i.e., to "shame" s.o., embarrass badly -- tveu owi a'mah muk

embarrassed (by) adj. para'muk (bee'proo'a); a'mah muk; k'mah muk: He was embarrassed by [his mistake]. -- Gwat k'mah muk bee'proo'a [kum'hawh gwat].; miun k'mah (lit: be ashamed; k'mah also means "shy" and "shame")

embassy n. s'tahn'toot; PS -- 'toot: the Chinese Embassy -- 'toot Jchun

emerald n. t'bong mo'ra'kut (AP: mor'kawht)

emergency n. a'sun; pee'up'a'sun

employee n. neh tveu kaa; manual laborer -- ka'ma'kaaw

employer n. jchao'vye

employment n. kaa'ngyeea; mok'ngyeea; the employment problem... -- pun'ha mok'ngyeea...

empty adj. taw'tay; empty-handed -- dai taw'tay

enchant v. romantically -- tveu owi sra'laanyh klang

encircle v. po'at chuum'venyh

end n. jchung: end of the week -- jchung a'tthit; jchung krow'ee: end of the book -- jchung krow'ee ney s'po; end of the movie -- jchung krow'ee ru'ung; He was strong [at the beginning] but at the end he was weak. -- [Noeh peyr dum'bong] gwat klang, pun'ta'aae noeh peyr jchung krow'ee, gwat k'sow'ee.; at the end of -- jchung krow'ee bom'pot; noeh jchung bun jchawp: I left at the end of the movie. -- Kyom jchenyh noeh jchung bun jchawp ru'ung.

end v. bun jchawp; How did it end? -- Tau(v) bun jchawp dow'ee ro'bee'up mutch?; How can we end this (thing, matter)? -- Tau(v) yeung bun jchawp (   ) dow'ee ro'bee'up na?

endlessly adv. mun jcheh awh; mun jcheh howi; mun jcheh chope

endure v. traum: I cannot endure this pain. -- Kyom traum chh'ooh ni mun baan.; miun kaa ot t'mut: They still endure the pain of those memories. -- Gkay noeh miun kaa ot t'mut a'noo'sow'ree nu.

enemy adj. sa'tro

enemy n. generally -- sa'tro; enemy particularly in battle or politics (used, for example, by Khmer Rouge to refer to political opponents) -- ka'mung

energy n. kum'lung

enforce v. dum'ro(v); enforce the law -- dum'ro(v) ch'bop

engaged adj. to be married -- p'choo'o(b) pee'a; engaged in s. th., busy -- ro'vull

engagement n. military -- choop banyh; choop praw'yoot ka'neea; pre-marriage -- kaa pchoo'o(b) peea'a(k)

engine n. ma'seen (AP: ma'sheen); yun

engineer n. vi'swa(k)'ka; chee'um

engineering n. vi'swa(k)'kaam

England n. praw'tet Aw'nglay

English n. language -- pee'esa Aw'nglay

English adj. Aw'nglay; English tea -- ta'aae Aw'nglay

enjoy v. generally relating to s. th. either in the past or ongoing -- s'bai: Did you enjoy the movie? -- Gkun s'bai tay?; Are you enjoying yourself? -- S'bai tay?; or, jchole jchet (lit: like) -- I enjoyed (i.e., liked) the movie [a lot]. -- Kyom jchole jchet gkun nu [nah].; generally relating to s. th. in future; connotation of looking forward to s. th. -- kum saam: Kyom jchong [teuh dah'leng] kum saan jchet. -- I want [to go out] and enjoy myself.

enough adv. adequate quantity -- kroop; kroop kro'un (AP: krup kro'an); l'maw'm; l'maw'm howi: Enough, enough, no more! -- Baan howi (AP: baan'ai); pa'nung baan howi; Slow enough? -- Yoot l'maw'm tay?

enter v. come inside -- jchole mok k'nong (common AP: jchole mao k'nong); go inside -- jchole teuh k'nong; put [data] in computer -- dah(k) [por'da'mee'an] noeh k'nong cum'puu'teuh; "punch" data in -- wai bun jchole k'nong cum'puu'teuh; type data in -- tap jchole teuh k'nong cum'puu'teuh

entertain v. to show hospitality to -- kum'san leng: How will we entertain them? -- Tau(v) yeung koo'a tai kum'san pooh'gkay yang mutch?

entrance n. t'veea jchole

envelope n. generally -- sr'auwm; (AP: traum); envelope for a letter -- sr'auwm sum'boht

envious adj. ch'raw nye'n

environment n. generally -- pa'ri'taan: Ministry of Environment -- Krasoo'ung Pa'ri'taan; nature -- twa'ma'chee'it; atmosphere, circumstances -- pa'ri'kya'kaa; surroundings, home environment -- kaa op'ruhm

environmental adj. chia pa'ri'taan

equal adj. sm'auu ka'neea: Those two people are equal. -- Pi neh nung sm'auu ka'neea.; The two forces were equal. -- Kum'lung pi sm'auu ka'neea.; trum ka'neea; pun ka'neea: Those two men are the same (i. e., of equal) [size]. -- [Mee'ut] gwat pun ka'neea.

equal rights n. su'tee sm'auu ka'neea

equality n. pheap sm'aau ka'neea; sa'ma'pheap

equip v. owi sum'pee'a'ree'a: The government must equip its soldiers. -- Ratt'a'pi'bal tro owi (or, tro pdull) sum'phea'ree'a teuh tee'hee'an.

equipped (with) adj. praw'dop (dow'ee): Thay are [only] equipped with rifles. -- Pooh'gkay praw'dop dow'ee kum pleung [pun'noh].

equipment n. generally -- sum'pee'a'ree'h; military -- oh'pa'kaaw; kreung sum'pee'a'ree'h; office equipment -- praw'dop, praw'daw

era n. sa'mye; choom'no'un; in Lon Nol's era -- noeh choom' no'un Lon Nol; Reagans' era -- sa'mye praw'teea'neea a'tep'a'dye Reagan; ro'yeht peyr: in Sihanouk's era -- noeh ro'yeht peyr Si'ha'nou'; reign -- ree'ech'ia kaal

erosion n. sum'not

error n. kum'hawh

escape v. roo'it; rot roo'it (lit: run [and] escape): He escaped from the jail. -- Gwat rot roo'it pi cooo'k.:

escort n. kawng kaa'pee'a (lit: protective force); You can't go to An Long Veng without a [military] escort. -- Neh mun adje teuh An Long Veng dow'ee k'miun kawng kaa'pee'a tay [pi tee'hee'an].

escort v. protect -- kaa'peea; guard, confine -- bun'darr: [The prisoner] was escorted to jail. -- [Neh cho'up to'h] tro baan bun'darr teuh kang cooo'k.; accompany as courtesy -- hye'hawm; show the way, lead -- no'um mok (NB: "no'um" = "take"): [The soldiers] will escort us [through/across] the mountains. -- [Tee'hee'an] nung no'um mok yeung [ch'long] phnom.

especially adv. chia pi'seh

espionage n. cha'ra'kaam

essential adj. jcham'batch

establish v. p'daum; tang: I want to establish my own [business]. -- Kyom jchong tang [kaa looh do] ro'bah kyom.

estimate n. kaa pree'up tee'up

estimate v. pree'up tee'up; st'wong; smann; pa'n

et cetera, et cetera n. ...nung tek taa p'sayng p'sayng tee'it

even adv. also -- pong: He even has money. -- Veea miun loi pong.; even if -- som bai: Even if you have money, I don't. -- Som bai neh miun loi, kyom ot.; even more -- taw teuh tee'it: I want to study even more. -- Kyom jchong rian taw teuh tee'it.; even now, even then, etc., i.e., in sense of still "at this/that time" -- pro'me te'ang: Even [today] they still cannot decide. -- Pro'me te'ang [t'ngai ni] pooh'gkay mun adje sum'rach; even so, still -- An'chung kaw dow'ee... kaw... : Even so, I (still) don't like it. -- An'chung kaw dow'ee, kaw kyom mun jchole jchet veea.; even though -- too'a chia: Even though he was hungry, he [still] could not eat. -- Too'a chia gwat klee'un, [yang na kaw dow'ee] gwat mun adje nyam baan [da'aae*].; even though -- kaw dow'ee: Even though there are important things still to do, I cannot stay. -- Miun kaa sum'kahn kaw dow'ee, mun adje noeh baan tee'it tay.; even though -- thoop bye chia: Even though he is a good student, he is still abused. -- Thoop bye chia gwat gkon'sa la'aw, gwat noeh tai to'tool tooo'k to'h.; even though... still -- yang na kaw dow'ee... da'aae: Even though it is raining, (still) I have to go back again. -- Plee'eng yang na kaw dow'ee, kaw kyom teuh venyh da'aae*.; tvai but tai: Even while he was working... -- Tvai but tai gwat kom'puung tveu kaa...

　　　　{*NB: da'aae in these sentences repeats the connotation of "even so" already conveyed by "yang na kaw dow'ee". The word "pong" ("too") is also used in similar "repetitious" fashion. (See discussion at definition of "too".) While such phrasing would be termed a redundancy in English, it is grammatically correct in Khmer.}

even adj. flat -- ri'ep; equal -- sm'auu ka'neea: The sleeves are not even. -- Dai aow ot sm'auu ka'neea.; get even -- tveu owi sm'auu ka'neea; even-tempered -- mun kum'raal; even-handed -- sm'oh

evening n. long'aae't; peyr long'aae't

ever adv. dael: Have you ever been to Siem Riep? -- Tau(v) neh dael teuh Siem Riep tay?; (NB: dael also means "that", "who" or "which": viz., "the man that you saw..." -- "ma'nooh dael neh keunyh..."

every adj. kroop (AP: kro'up); rawl (AP: ro'vwul); rec'eng rawl: every week -- rawl a'tthit; every day -- kroop t'ngai; rwal t'ngai

everybody prn. kroop ka'neea; rawl ka'neea; te'ang (AP: tang) awh ka'neea: Everyone looked scared. -- Neh te'ang awh ka'neea doj chia pay klait(ch) nah.

every kind adv. kroop muk: every kind of wood -- daum cheu kroop muk; We [use/put it] all kinds of ingredients. -- Yeung [psawlm] kreung kroop muk.; kroop yang: every kind (or, every sort) of vegetable -- bun'lye kroop yang

every night adv. rawl yoop; kroop yoop

everyone prn. (see "everybody")

everything adv. te'ang awh; a'veye a'veye; sop kroop: We have everything we need. -- Yeung miun praw'dop praw'daw sop kroop (lit: "all kinds of stuff").

every time adv. kroop peyr

everywhere adv. pieh penyh: Everywhere I go, [the people] are kind. -- Pieh penyh te'ang awh dael kyom teuh, [ma'nooh saah] tai la'aw.

evidence n. pwah' taang

evil adj. chung'rai: That country's military is as evil as the Khmer Rouge. -- Kawng thwaap praw'tet nu keuh chia ma'nooh chung'rai doj chia Khmei Kra'hom.; He is a devil (lit: he is very evil). -- Gwat keuh chung'rai nah.

exact adj. praw'kat; tee'ung ta(t); trum tro

exactly adv. chia praw'kat

Exactly! interj. Jchum howi! Piht praw'kat!

exaggerate v. bun jchenyh, bun jchole; bum ploo(ss); bum leuh; You exaggerate [constantly]. -- Neh ni'yaye bun jchenyh bun jchole [chia nik chia kaal].

examination n. academic test and/or medical exam -- kaa praw'long: Yesterday the students took the examination [to move up to] the next grade. -- Pi musl'munyh gkon'sa teuh praw'long [laung] t'nak.

example n. oo'teea'haw: Give me an example of how he has done something wrong. -- Owi oo'teea'haw a'veye kyom moi dael gwat t'veu a'veye koh.; moral model -- kum'roo: a bad example -- kum'roo a'krah; to be a bad example -- tveu kum'roo a'krah

Excellency, your n. A'yoo'dop

excellent adj. poo'k'eye: He's an excellent student. -- Gwat gkon'sa nu poo'k'eye nah.; excellent food -- mahope pi'seh; Oh, excellent! -- Praw'sar nah!

except prp. mun tray kaa;

exchange v. pdo; do: exchange money -- do loi

exchange rate n. kaa plas p'do

excite v. ruhm pheup

excited adj. miun jchet ruhm pheup: Everyone was excited to meet her. -- Neh te'ang awh ka'neea miun jchet ruhm'pheup cho'op nee'eng.

exciting adj. interesting -- chia a'ro'um; koo'a jchaap a'ro'um: an exciting discovery -- kaa ro'k keunyh jchaap a'ro'um; thrilling or dangerous -- chia ruhm'pheup

excitement n. s'kd'eye ruhm'pheup

excuse me xcl. sum to'h: Excuse me for being late. -- Sum to'h kyom mok yeut.; in slightly casual sense of, "Sorry about that." -- Ot to'h kum praw'kaan.

exercise n. haht prang; practice -- kaa a'noo'vat; kaa haht

exhausted adj. physically -- awh kum'lung: You look like you're exhausted. -- Neh meuhl teuh doj chia ahw kum'lung nah.; used, used up -- awh mium tee'it tay; awh ro'ling: The supply of rice is exhausted. -- Jchum'noo'an ung'kaw awh ro'ling. [or] Kaa pdull owi ung'kaw awh ro'ling.; barren, unproductive -- k'sawh

exile n. neh ra'tay

exit n. ploe jchenyh

expand v. puhng ree; vee'it: He expanded his land holdings. -- Gwat vee'it daiy.

expatriate n. neh re'tay

expect v. believe -- tun tung; anticipate -- tun tung jcham: I am expecting him tommorow. -- Kyom tun tung jcham gwat mok doll s'eye'd.; kut ruhn peyr: I expect it will rain. -- Kyom kut ruhm peyr tha nung plee'eng.

expedite v. jchat; jchat kaa; jchat vi'ti kaa

expedition n. dum'narr yap yeun; dum'narr chng'eye; dum'narr yap yeun chng'eye

expensive adj. tlai

experience n. knowledge gained in a job; skill -- kej kaa pi'sowt; event or "happening" -- kaa but; kaa pi'sowt; kaa but pi'sowt: The plane crash was a frightening experience. -- Kroo'ti'nak yun hawh keuh chia but pi'saut dawh koo'a owi klait(ch) moi (or, dawh a'kraw moi).

experienced adj. t'nuk; an experienced pilot -- pee'lut t'nuk

expert n. choom'nee'eng' kaa

explain v. bun'yul; dawh sr'eye... owi: Can you explain this problem to me? -- Tau(v) neh adje dawh sr'eye pun'ha ni owi kyom baan tay?

explanantion n. kaa bun'yul: The profits of the store are down; you have to give me an explanation. -- Praa(k) chuum'nenyh haang jchoh; kyom tro kaa kaa bun'yul.; milder, in sense of an answer -- kaa jchum'la'wee

explode v. p'tooh(s)

exploit v. resources -- jchun choo'a(k) p'auwl praw'yow'it; exploit people -- jchun choo'a(k) chee'im (NB:

exploitation n. kaa chuun choo'a(k) praw'yow'it

explore v. sau(v) 'chree'oo(v)

explosion n. kro'up p'tooh

export v. looh jchenyh; no'um jchenyh; looh jchenyh teuh bor'tay

exports n. kaa no'um jchenyh; kaa looh jchenyh: Cambodia's main exports were [rubber], [timber] and rice. -- Kaa looh jchenyh sum'kahn ro'bah praw'tet Kampuchea keuh [kaow'soo], [cheu hope] nung ung'kaw.

expose v. lee't traw dong: The newspaper exposed the corruption of the armed forces. -- Ka'ssett lee't traw dong om'peuh pu'ka'ra loi ro'bah kawng thwaap.

express adj. exact -- yang ch'bah; rapid -- leu'an: express train -- ro'teh pleung leu'an

expropriate v. rubh yok

extra adj. luuh: They need to have extra money. -- Pooh'gkay jchong baan loi luuh.; bun tyme: an extra ten thousand [tons] of rice -- ung'kaw dop lee'en [tauwn] bun'tyme; prepared in advance, put aside -- sum'nawl: They made extra food. -- Gkay tveu ma'hope sum'nawl.

extremely adv. kr'eye leng: [The minefields] around that village are extremely dangerous. -- [Veal meen] chit phum nu kroo'ti'nak kr'eye leng.; sum bon: That flight was extremely dangerous. -- Dum'narr yun hawh nu kroo'ti'nak sum bon.

eye n. pn'aae'k (NB: star = p'k'eye; part or portion = p'nyke)

eye-glasses n. ven'taa

eye witness n. saah saey

F

face n.   muk: face to face -- tul muk; facing, opposite -- tul muk; His office was facing the palace. -- Kaa'ree'a'lye gwat noeh tul muk vae'ang.; to lose face -- k'mah muk; a'mah muk; or a'hp muk: They lost face because of you. -- Gkay k'mah muk dow'ee sa neh eiyne.; ah'p muk; Srei Peau lost face when she ran away to Vietnam. -- Srei Peau ah'p muk peyr veea rot teuh Vietnam.

fact n.   kaa'piht; in fact -- taam piht

faction n.   pi'eh ki: Which faction does he belong to (lit: come from)? -- Gwat mok pi pieh ki na moi?; in sense of organized political party -- ka'na'pac; if not necessarily organized -- pac: In Cambodian politics there are still four factions. -- K'nong na'yo'bye Kampuchea, noeh miun tai buon pac.; in sense simply of group -- pooh (lit: people)

factor n.   chia kaa tha: [The election] was an important factor. -- [Kaa bawh ch'naut] keuh chia kaa tha daw sum'kahn.; in sense of reason for s. th. -- hyte

factory n.   large -- ro'ng jcha: This factory makes fish oil. -- Ro'ng jcha ni tveu praeng trei.; small, workshop -- ro'ng a'chee'va'kaam

fail v.   generally -- [to be] k'miun choke chey (lit: to be without success); do poorly on/in -- t'leh: fail a test -- praw'long t'leh; not accomplish -- mun baan: He failed to convince the voters [that his party was good]. -- Gwat mun baan tveu owi cheu'a neh baw ch'naut [tha ka'na'pac gwat trum tro].; fail in business -- duel (lit: fall); without fail -- chia mun kaan: Without fail I will come here. -- Kyom nung mok ti ni chia mun kaan.

faint v.   sun lauwb

fair adj.   reasonable -- koo'a sum; Fair enough! -- Koo'a sum l'mawm howi!; honest -- sum'ruhm: That [official] is fair. -- [P'nch nu ratt'a'ka] nu keuh chia ma'nooh sum'ruhm.

fake adj.   klaeng bum'lum; klaeng klai: He [sold] them fake [statues]. -- Gwat [looh] owi pooh'gkay nu [roob jchum'lak] klaeng klai tay.; puuht

fake v.   klaeng bum'lum: He faked his diploma. -- Gwat klaeng bum'lum sun'ya bot.

fall v.   from a short distance -- t'leh: The picture fell down. -- Roop'tawt t'leh.; The fruit fell from the table. -- Plai cheu t'leh.; from a substantial height -- ch'rooh(ss): The [ripe] mangos fell from the tree. -- Plai sv'eye chr'rooh(ss) [penyh] krowm daum.; fall over -- ro'luum: That tree fell this morning. -- Daum nu ro'luum pruhk ni.; [trip] and [fall] -- [jchum'pope cheung] [duel]: He tripped and fell down. -- Gwat jchum'pope cheung duel.; fall for, come to like a lot -- jchole jchet klang; n'uub... klang: [How could you] fall for her[??] -- Hyte'eye n'uub nung veea [klang ma'leh??] ; fall for, be taken in or tricked by -- cheu'a (lit: believe); fall from power -- t'leh pi um'natch

false adj.   klaeng klai; puuht; a false illness -- chh'ooh puuht

falsely accuse v.   mool bung kaat(ch)

family n.   kroo'e'sa; head of a family -- at'pi'bal kroo'e'sa

famine n.   kaa ot bye (lit.: condition of no rice)

famous adj.   l'bye l'banyh; l'bye chamoo'h

fan n.   admirer -- poo'a; electric -- dung'hal; hand -- ple(t)

fan v.   bahwk; (same word as "blows", as "the wind blows" -- k'shaal bahwk)

fancy adj.   chat'chai

far adv.   chng'eye (AP: jchum'ngai): How far is it from here to Battambong? -- Tau(v) pi ni teuh Battambong miun chng'eye pu'man?

Far East n.   jchong bo'phea'

fare n.   cost of ticket -- dum'lye; food -- ma'hope

farm n. generally, for vegetable products -- jcham'kar (APs: jchun'caa, jchun'cal): rice farm or paddy -- sr'eye jcham'kar; rubber plantation -- jcham'kar kaow'soo; vegetable farm or garden -- jcham'kar bun'lye; for animal products -- cunlye'ng jchenyh jcham: chicken farm -- cunlye'ng jchenyh jcham muon; crocodile farm -- cunlye'ng jchenyh jcham kaw'per

farm v. tveu jcham'kar

farmer n. kaah'se'ko (APs: kaat'se'ko, kaak'se'ko); neh jchum'kar; rice farmer -- neh sr'eye

farming n. generally -- kaa tveu sr'eye; kaa tveu sr'eye jcham'kar

farther adv. chng'eye chiang: Moung is farther from Phnom Penh than Po'sat (is). -- Moung chng'eye pi Phnom Penh chiang Po'sat.

fast adv. ro'has: eat fast -- nyam ro'has; praw'nyab; plee'um plee'um; leu'an: This motorcycle can go fast. -- Moto ni adje teuh leu'an.; chhop

faster adv. leu'an laung; leu'an chiang: Faster, faster! -- N'yab, n'yab!; Chhop chhop!

fat adj. thwat (AP: thu'at)

fatality n. kaa bot'bong chi'vut

fate n. vee'sna (NB: common Cambodian given name for both girls and boys)

father n. country term -- oeuv'puk; Phnom Penh term -- pa

father-in-law n. oeuv'puk kh'mayt; pa kh'mayt

fault n. kum'hawh; It's not my fault. -- Mun men kum'hawh kyom.; (NB: lie = ko'hawk)

favor n. choo'ay; Please do me a favor. -- Sum owi choo'ay kyom.

favor v. like -- jchole jchet; or, sra'laanyh; favor a policy, ideology, political party, etc. -- ni'yuum; favor and take steps to assist -- luum ee'eng: The French Government favored Sihanouk. -- Ratt'a'pi'bal ba'raang luum ee'eng Sihanou'.; to'tunh teuh kang

favorite n. and adj. jchole jchet: This is my favorite book. -- Ni chia s'po dael kyom jchole jchet.

fear n. s'kd'eye klait(ch); kaa pay klait(ch): the smell of fear -- klen ney kaa pay klait(ch)

fear v. klait(ch): She fears deep water. -- Nee'eng klait(ch) tuk ch'ro.

feast n. buun; party -- lee'ung; choop lee'ung; kaa choop lee'ung

feather n. slaa'b (also means "wing"); ro'm slaa'b (may connote either "feather" or "down")

feeble adj. weak -- k'sow'ee; slow moving -- pem peuhm

February n. Koom'pheh

feel v. have an emotion -- jchet; (NB: same word as "heart"; AP: chut): Do they feel happy? -- Gkay s'bai jchet tay?; feel stressed out, under pressure -- pi'bah jchet; have an emotion -- dai: How do you feel today? -- Yang mutch dai t'ngai ni?; have an emotion -- miun a'ro'um (AP: a'rum): I feel guilty. -- Kyom miun a'ro'um tha tveu koh.; feel sorry for or feel pity for -- a'nutt: I don't feel sorry for (or, pity) them. -- Kyom ot a'nutt pooh'gkay tay.; should feel -- koo'a owi: You should feel (or, be) ashamed. -- Neh koo'a owi k'mah.; You should feel happy. -- Neh koo'a owi s'bai.; believe, think -- kut: I feel he is wrong. -- Kyom kut tha gwat koh.; believe, have a feeling (that) -- miun a'rom: I feel that he is coming. -- Kyom miun a'rom gwat nung mao.; sense physically -- [implied]: I [feel] cold. -- Kyom [ ] traw'chieh(k).; How do you [feel] today (anyway)? -- Yang mutch [ ] (da'aae) t'ngai ni?; I [feel] a little (better) now. -- Kyom [ ] (krawn baar) baan tic howi.; I [feel] OK. -- Kyom [ ] chia howi.; touch s. th. -- kaan: Don't touch the book.

feeling n. emotion -- a'nutt; have a feeling that -- kut; miun a'rom; hurt s. o.'s feelings -- tveu owi on jchet (lit: to give s. o. an unhappy heart); sensation of s. th. -- rooh chee'it: The feeling during the Pol Pot time was... -- Rooh chee'it k'nong ro'bab Pol Pot keuh chia...

fees n. tlai ch'nool: school fees -- tlai ch'nool sa'la

feet n. ch'eung

fellow n. gwat: Who is that fellow? -- Gwat nu nch na? (common AP: Gwat nu no na?); somewhat rude term -- ma'see'a

female adj. ma'nooh sraae; on printed forms, as in "male/ female" questions -- payt sraae

fence n. ro'bong

ferry n. saa'laang: ... the famous ferry at Neak Loung... -- saa'laang l'bye l'bong ti Neak Loung...; (NB: Other well-known ferry crossing points are Preah Ka'dam, north of Phnom Penh, and Tuk K'mau to the city's south.)

fertilizer n. chii

fever n. kreun k'dau

few adv. tek to'ich; baan tek baan to'ich: Few Khmer people have cars. -- Chuum'noo'an tek to'ich ney Khmei miun laan.; Cambodia has few hospitals. -- Sruk Khmei miun mun'ti'peyt baan tek baan to'ich.; tek nah: We have few choices. -- Yeung mium jchreu'reu' tek nah.; a few (lit: two-three) -- pi-bye

fiance n. (m. or f.) coo'dung'dung

fiction n. ru'ung praw'dutt (lit: created (i.e., made-up) story)

fickle adj. pdo jchet ro'has; unfaithful -- jchet chow'eet

field n. veal; open, or empty, field or paddy -- veal raw nee'um; rice field or paddy -- veal sr'eye; occupation -- mok ngyeea; What field are you in? -- Neh miun mok'ngyeea a'veye?

fifteen adj. dap'prum

fifth adj. ti'prum

fifty adj. ha'sup; "fifty/fifty" (NB: common way of expressing idea of "comme ci, comme ca" or "so-so") -- ha'sup, ha'sup

fight n. kaa praw'yoot; chuum'looh

fight v. praw'yoot; chuum'looh

fighter n. neh praw'yoot

fighting n. kaa praw'yoot; an attack -- kaa vye

file n. office files, records, documents -- bun'chee; sum'num ru'ung (same as word for "case" as in "legal case"); sum'num eyke'a'saa; file cabinet -- too' dah(k) bun'chee

fill v. s. th. up -- bum penyh: I want to fill that glass with water. -- Kyom jchong cha tuk owi penyh kaae'oo. or, Kyom jchong bum penyh kaae'oo ni chi'moi nung tuk.

film n. motion picture -- gkun; film in sense of its story -- ru'ung gkun: It was an interesting film. -- Veea keuh ru'ung gkun la'aw.; movie theater -- ro'ng gkun; photographic film -- svil: Go develop the film. -- Teuh lee'eng svil teuh.

final adj. jchong krow'ee; jchong bom'pot; krow'ee bom awh

finally adv. jchong bunyh chope; ti bom'pot; noch ti bom'pot

finance n. heh'ranya'vuh'to: Ministry of Finance -- Kra'soo'ung Heh'ranya'vuh'to

find v. s. th. lost -- ro'k; keunyh ro'k; ro'k keunyh; sveye ro'k; sveye ro'k keunyh: Did [you] find it? -- [Lok] ro'k keunyh veea tay?; s. th. not lost but needed -- miun praw'tay keunyh: Did you find a new hotel? -- Tau(v) neh miun praw'tay keunyh o'tyle p'sayng tay?; s. th. not lost but needed -- ro'k baan howi

fine n. for an offense -- peeh'naae; ticket (parking ticket or other such police citation) -- poli' pa(ks)

finger n. ma'ri'um dai

fingerprint n. daan dai

finish v. bung'howi: We want to finish the work as soon as possible. -- Yeung jchong bung'howi tveu kaa yang ro'has.; banyh jchawp: When will they finish? -- Peyr na pooh'gkay nung banyh jchawp?; roo'it sratch: When will they finish? -- Peyr na gkay nung roo'it sratch?

finished adj. jchawp howi: Nyam bye jchawb howi? or, Hope bye jchawb howi?; roo'it howi: Have you finished eating? -- Nyam bye roo'it howi? or, Hope bye roo'it howi?; Yes, I have finished. -- Baa, roo'it howi.; I have finished eating. -- Kyom nyam roo'it howi.

fire n. generally, anything burning -- pleung; or, kaa pleung: Let's make a fire (can refer to small cooking fire or, generally, any fire). -- Ta' bung kaut pleung.; large fire (for example, for warmth or warning) -- pleung kob; Let's make a fire and cook some food. -- Ta' dut pleung cham'un sat(ch).; on fire -- t'aee chheh; or, t'aae chheh pleung: The house is on fire. -- Ptay'a kom'puung t'aee chheh pleung.; put out a fire -- lut pleung; or, pun'lut

pleung; set on fire -- dut pleung: He set that house on fire. -- Gwat dut pleung ptay'a nu.; (gun)fire -- kaa banyh; fire engine -- laan tuk (lit: water truck)

fire v. a gun -- banyh; terminate s. o. from a job -- denyh vec'a jchowl: I had to fire him. -- Kyom tro kaa denyh veea jchowl.

firewood n. ahws: There is no more firewood near that village. -- Ot miun ahws noeh chit phum nu.

fireworks n. banyh kum chroo'ik: Tomorrow night they will have fireworks. -- S'eye'd yoop gkay nung miun banyh kum chroo'ik.

first adj. ordinal number -- ti moi: first, second, third.... -- ti moi, ti pi, ti bye....; the first floor -- cho'un ti moi; The first time... -- Leuk ti moi...; first in a sequence -- dum'bong: the first time (in a series) -- leuk dum'bong; first in a series -- muun: Who is first? -- Neh na muun?; Take a shower first! -- Moiy tuk muun!; earliest, first chronologically -- dum'bong; or, dum'bong bung awh: I met my first Cambodian (person) in 1980. -- Kyom choop Khmei chia dum'bong noch chh'nam 1980. or, Kyom choop Khmei dum'bong bung awh noeh chh'nam 1980.

first aid n. t'nam p'chia bal

first class, first quality adj. layke moi (lit: number one)

first of all adv. muun kay bung awh; dum'bong; muun awh

fish n. trei: fish sauce -- tuk trei; to go fishing -- too'ch trei; to catch fish -- jchaab trei; dried fish -- trei ngee'ut haal; fish oil -- klang trei

fish v. too'ch trei

fish-hook n. plai sun'to'ich

fish pate n. pro'hoke (traditional Khmer cuisine consisting of 2-to-3-day-aged minced fish mixed with salt; eaten with rice)

fit v. l'mawm: Do these shoes fit you? -- Tau(v) s'bye'k cheung ni l'mawm neh tay?

fit in (with) v. jchoh gkay (chi'moi)

five adj. prum (AP: pay'am); (NB: the pronunciation of the word for "five" varies slightly with its place in a phrase; alone or at end of phrase, it is pronounced "pram", as in "dop pram" ("fifteen"); when follows by other number words in a phrase, however, it is pronounced closer to "prum", as in "prum'pul" ("seven") or "dop prum buon" ("nineteen").)

fix v. choo'ah: fix the road(s) -- choo'ah ploe

flag n. generally, any flag -- tung (AP: tu'ong) chaye; national flag -- tung chee'it; flag of Cambodia -- tung chee'it Khmei; (NB: "tung" signifies cloth hung in the wind; a "tung k'mau'it", for example, (with "k'mau'it" meaning "ghost" or "dead person") is a cloth effigy or figure similar to a scarecrow hung from a pole outside the home of someone recently decreased)

flakey adj. wierd, somewhat dumb -- plee pleuh; scuh scuh

flammable adj. chheh

flank n. military term -- chim chum hee'ung

flash n. illumination device on camera -- pleung a'ppa'rei

flashlight n. pul; pleung pul

flat adj. ri'ep; (NB: "riep" can also mean "flattened" in the sense of "crushed and defeated"; hence, "riep" in the Cambodian province name "Siem Riep" is said to refer to the fact of a major defeat in the area of troops from Siam ("Siem") by Khmer forces.)

flat tire n. byke kong, or kong byke; (NB: "kong" is the same word as that for "bicycle")

flatter v. yok jchet: leuk cheung (lit: carry s.o.'s feet); bun'jcho(r)

flattery n. jchor(r); kaa bun jcho(r): She doesn't want flattery; she wants true friendship. -- Gwat ot see (lit: eat) jcho(r) tay; gwat jchole jchet mit'a'pheap putt putt.

flavor n. rooh chee'it

flee v. pee'h kloo'an; rut jchenyh (see,also, "escape")

flesh n. satch

flick one's finger v. ap'toe'ut dai

flight n. dum'narr yun hawh

flirt v. nyee'et nyuum, nyee'et nyuum (lit: peek and smile, peek and smile)

float v. un'day't

flood n. flood that inundates but recedes without causing major destruction -- tuk'lic; major destructive flood -- tuk jchoom nuhn; flood season -- ro'doe jchoon nuhn

floor n. general -- k'ral; tile floor -- att k'ral; floor of wood boards -- ka'dah k'ral; bamboo slat floor as in houses in countryside -- rongnee'ap k'ral; story, level in a building -- cho'un: He lives on the second floor. -- Gwat rooh noeh (or snak noeh) cho'un ti pi.

floor show n. classical dance -- ro'bahm or, ro'bahm Khmei; naked dancing -- rohm sraat

flour n. m'sauw (AP: m'sa'oo); lit: powder

flower n. pka

flu n. pa'da'sye

fly n. insect -- rr'oy

fly v. for birds -- haa or hawh haa: birds fly -- saat haa; (NB: haa is written "haar" but the "r" is completely silent in speech); for planes -- hawh; the plane flew -- yun hawh hawh; for rockets, missles, etc. -- plong: The rockets flew back and forth. -- Ro'kit plong teuh plong mok.; for people -- teuh (lit: go) or jchi k'pal hawh (lit: take/board a plane): What day are you flying to HCM (Ho Chi Minh City)? -- Neh teuh Ho Chi Minh t'ngai na?

foam n. por pooh tuk

fog n. ahp; to get foggy -- jchoh ahp

fold v. bawt

folding adj. bawt: folding-stock AK-47 -- Ah-Kah s'eye bawt (s'eye praw'vwut, or s'eye, = automatic)

follow v. go with or go behind -- taam: Why are you following me? -- Hyte eye (baan) neh taam kyom?; accept orders or directions -- s'dop taam: She never follows my instructions. -- Nee'eng mun dael s'dop taam kaa bung hanyh kyom.; listen to -- s'dop: She never listens to me. -- Nee'eng mun dael s'dop kyom.; copy -- tveu taam: Don't follow bad examples. -- Kum tveu taam kum'rooh a'krah.

follower n. neh krowm um'natch

food n. ma'hope; jchum'naee; a'ha; for monks -- a'ha lok

fool n. ma'nooh ch'koo'it

fool v. bauwk; cheat out of money -- bauwk praa(k)

fool around v. go to flirt with s.o. -- teuh po't stee'up; lit: "go caress the corn"; derivation: Phnom Penh men are said to sometimes suggest to friends they meet (after work, et.) at a certain market or other location to "get some roast corn", a trip allegedly sometimes intended to facilitate fraternization with the female corn vendors rather than the purchase of food; hence the phrase, "going to caress the corn".)

foot n. cheung (also means "leg")

footprint n. daan cheung

for prp. generally -- dum'bye or sum'rap (AP: sam'rap, sam'rup):

for the sake of, in order to do s. th. -- dum'bye: We work for money. -- Yeung tveu kaa dum'bye loi.

with respect to -- sum'rap: This food is for four days. -- Ma'hope ni sum'rap buon t'ngai.; This job is easy for me. -- Kej kaa ni veea ngi'yaye sum'rap kyom.; We must make a schedule for the meeting. -- Yeung tro tai tveu kam'vi'tee sum'rap pra'choom.

for a certain time -- sum'rap: We must schedule the meeting for tomorrow. -- Yeung tro tai tveu kam'vi'tee pra'choom sum'rap s'eye'd.;

for the benefit of -- choon: Shall I pour some coffee for you? -- Tau(v) kyom adje cha choon lok, baan tay?; used for -- pra sum'rap

for sure -- piht praw'kat

for example -- oo'tee'haw

for rent -- sum'rap ch'ool

for sale -- looh, sum'rap looh

for (from beginning to end) a length of time -- awh ro'yeht peyr... howi: The meeting lasted for two days. -- Kaa pra'choom awh ro'yeht peyr pi t'ngai howi.

for (over a continuing span) a length of time -- kum'lung mok howi: He had known Nayana for four months. -- Gwat baan scwall Nayana buon kye kum'lung mok howi.

[the reason] for -- [mool'hyte] ney

For sure? -- Ch'bah howi rooh?

forbid v. hahm... mun owi: Gkay hahm yeung mun owi teuh Battambong tay. -- They forbade us to go to Battambong.; hahm kaht... mun owi; The government forbade us to go there. -- Ratt'a'pi'bal hahm kaht yeung mun owi teuh ti nu.; The government forbade any more hunting. -- Ratt'a'pi'bal hahm kaht mun owi baw banyh tee'it.

forbidden adj. hahm

force n. in the abstract -- kaa bung'kum: They [say] Pol Pot thinks force is a good thing. -- Gkay [taa] Pol Pot kut tha kaa bung'kum chia ru'ung la'aw.; kum'lung: military forces -- kum'lung; kawng thwaap; special (mil.) forces -- kawng thaawp pi'sch; power -- a'ti'pul: The President has great power. -- Praw'teea'neea tep'a'dye miun a'ti'pul ch'raan.; by force -- dow'ee bung'kum

force (to) v. bung'kum.... (owi): Why do you force yourself [to write]? -- Hyte a'veye neh bung'kum kloo'an einye [owi saw say]?

forecast v. tee'aae

forehead n. tang'ah

foreign adj. bor'tay (AP: baw'tay, bo'ra'tay, bor'a'tch): foreign aid -- chum'noo'ee bor'tay; foreign affairs -- kaa bor'tay; Foreign Ministry -- Kra'soo'ung Kaa Bor'tay

foreigner n. chuun bor'tay

foreman n. kaa p'raahl

forest n. prey; (NB: Also frequently translated as "jungle", "prey" (and, among English speakers, the words "the forest") is employed in Cambodian usage to express two somewhat different concepts. First, "prey" (or "the forest") may be used to refer to truly scrub or scrub-and-tree covered areas, such as in Cambodia the Dong'rek, Dom'rei and Cardamom mountain ranges, and northern Kom'puung Cham, Stung Treng, Preah Vihear, etc. Alternatively, the two terms may be invoked in reference to remote rural areas not because they are heavily vegetated but to contra-distinguish them, in a way suggesting wildness and inaccesibility, from more settled and accessible (including urban) areas. Eastern Kom'puung Speu, southern and central Siem Riep, parts of Po'sat more than 10-15 kms off Highway 5 but not yet in the Cardamoms, eastern Battambang, most of Bantea Meanchey, and sparsely populated portions of Kan'dal and Svey Rieng are examples of areas that are not particularly heavily forested but may still be referred to as "prey".)

forestry n. ro'ka bra'munyh

forever adv. k'miun t'ngai banyh jchawb; This war will go on forever. -- Sung'kree'um ni k'miun t'ngai banyh jchawb tay.; chia daw raab: I will love you forever. -- Own sra'laanyh bong chia daw raab.; chia'nik; chia'nik chia'kaal; chia ree'ing ra'hote; baan ro'hote

forward adv. teuh muk; teuh muun: Please walk forward. -- Cheunyh dah teuh muk (or muun).

forget v. plic: I forgot it all. -- Kyom plic te'ang awh veea.; bum plic: Forget it! -- Bum plic! or, Bum plic chau! or, Bum plic teuh.; I want to forget all the bad [memories]. -- Kyom jchong bum plic noeh [a'noo'sow'ree] dael a'krah.

forgive v. praw'nay; leuk to'h owi; or, ot to'h owi: Please forgive me. -- Sum neh leuk toh owi kyom teuh.; or, Sum neh ot to'h owi kyom pong.; briefer, less formal phrase: Excuse me. -- Ot pay to'h.

forgiveness n. may'daa

fork n. for food -- psalm; in the road -- ploe bye; ploe bum bye; We came to a fork in the road. -- Yeung teuh doll ploe bum bye.

form n. printed -- bun: for currency exchange -- roo'paya bun

former adj. muun; at'taye'tah: He is the former [coach]. -- Gwat at'taye'ta [neh bung haht].; (somewhat "flowery" or poetic) a'dut: ... a former girl friend -- ... a'dut song sa

formula n. chemical or mathematical -- roo'pa'mun; in sense of solution -- k'boo'an: formula for success -- k'boo'an sum'rap cho'ke chey

fort, fortress n. bun tee'aye

fortune n. property, wealth -- trawp sum'baat; good fortune -- so'pay'mung kwal; future fate -- thee'aae: Can you tell (lit: see) my fortune? -- Neh too'tee'aae kyom meuhl?; fortune teller -- how'ra; kruu tee'aae (lit: one who sees)

forty adj. s'eye sup; forty-one -- s'eye sup moi

found v. establish -- bung kaut

found pp. discovered, recovered -- ro'k; or, ro'k keunyh: I found it. -- Kyom ro'k baan.; The teacher found her watch at her home. -- Neh kruu ro'k keunyh ni'a'li'ka nee'eng noeh ptay'a nee'eng.

foundation n. of a building -- kruuh; organization -- ong'kah: Lung Disease Foundation -- Ong'kah Chuum'ngeu Soo'it; basis -- pwah'taang (lit: evidence): [The charges] were without foundation. -- [Kaa cho'up jchowt] keuh k'miun pwah'taang.

fountain n. ma'cheen tuk

four adj. buon

fourteen adj. dap buon

fox n. kun'ch'ro'ng

foxhole n. soldiers' shelter -- un'loo'ung: We dug many foxholes. -- Yeung chi un'loo'ung owi ch'raan.; (NB: to dig a foxhole or "entrench" is "trang'say", derived from the French word for "entrench"); burough for an animal -- pra'hou'ng; roong

fourth adj. ti buon

France n. sruk Ba'raang

free adj. not occupied, not busy, available -- tum'nay: Are you free? -- Neh tum'nay tay?; free time -- peyr tum'nay; free of charge -- tum'nay; taw taae; possessing freedom -- se'rei: the free world -- lok se'rei; the Free Khmer (1950's-60's anti-Sihanouk insurgent movement) -- Khmei Se'rei; (NB: A second "Free Khmer" were the guerrilla forces formed along the Thai-Cambodian border, principally 1979-83, and used (principally 1982-90) by Thailand, Mainland China and a number of Western powers including the United States as an instrument of harrassment against the People's Republic of Kampuchea administration established at Phnom Penh in 1979. These forces, whose formal name was the Khmer People's National Liberation Army and which ultimately melted away after the signing of the October 1991 Peace Accords, came during the 80s to be called "Se'rei Ka" in reference to the associations of some of their early leaders with the Khmer Se'rei bands of the 50s and 60s or with the descendants of those bands in the 1975-78 period.)

freedom n. se'rei'pheap; freedom of speech -- se'rei'pheap nung kaa ni'yaye

French language n. pee'esa Ba'raang

frequency n. broadcasting -- "faye kong" (adaptation of Fr. "fraye'quence"); radio station -- pawh; rate of occurrence -- pee'up nyek nyoo'ub: the frequency of the attacks -- pee'up ny'ek nyoo'ub ney kaa praw'yoot

fresh adj. not stale -- s'raw: fresh vegetables -- bun'lye s'raw

Friday n. t'ngai sok

fried adj. with liberal oil, "deep fried" -- jchian: fried fish -- trei jchian; french fried potatoes -- dum'lung jchian; with little oil, "stir-fried" -- cha: fried rice -- bye cha; grilled (i.e., without pan) -- ang: fried chicken -- muon ang

friend n. mit (APs: met, mut); mit pay'a; mit sum'lanyh; rope'an (AP: ro'it'an)' pooh'mah (AP: po'mah, poo'a'mah); two friends -- mit pi neh (or, pi nec'eh; see note under "people"); close or best friend -- pooh'mah jchet dut

friendly adv. koo'a owi rope'an: She's friendly. -- Nee'eng koo'a owi rope'an.; koo'a jchole jchet rope'an: She is friendly. -- Gwat koo'a jchole jchet owi rope'an.; (NB: koo'a = to feel like doing s. th); jchole jchet rope'an: Why are you friendly with those bad people? -- Hyte 'eye neh jchole jchet rope'an pooh a'krah nu, ma'leh?

friendship n. mit'a'pheap

frighten v. bum'pheut, bum'pay; tveu owi klait(ch); bun lye(k): Don't frighten me. -- Kum bun lye(k) kyom.

frightened adj. tro tveu owi klait(ch); The children were frightened by the thunder. -- K'mayng tro tveu owi klait(ch) [or pay klait(ch)] dow'ee sa p'kaw lo'an.

frightening adj. scary -- dael tveu owi klait(ch): a scary movie -- gkun dael tveu owi klait(ch)

frog n. kong kype

from prp. pi: I come from Phnom Penh. -- Kyom mok pi Phnom Penh.; from here to Battambong -- pi ti ni teuh Battambong; om'pee: to hide from -- leh kloo'an om'pee; kang: ...KR from Takeo (province)... -- ...KR kang (kyte) T'keaou...

from now on adv. pi peyr ni

frond n. i.e., of leafy plant such as banana tree -- ti'ng(t)

front adv. the front side of s. th. -- kang muk; in front of -- noch kang muk; or, noeh muk: My car is in front of the house. -- Laan ro'boh kyom chawt noch kang muk ptay'a.

front n. front side of s. th. -- kang muk: The front of the house needs painting. -- Kang muk ptay'a tro kaa lee'up.; military position, frontline -- choo'mak; political front -- raw'na say; put up a good front -- pun peeh(k) kang krow; false front -- leh bum bang: That restaurant was a front for drug (trafficking). -- Poch'ni'tan nu chia cunlye'ng leh bum bang kreung ngee'in.; in front of your friends -- jchum'poo'a muk [or noeh muk] mit neh

frown n. kaa jchong (raise) jchim'jchowm (eyebrows)

frown v. jchong jchim'jchowm

fruit n. plai: "grenade fruit" -- thee'p; mango -- sveye; banana -- jchay; coconut -- do'hng; guava -- traw bye; jack fruit -- plai ka'nau; green fruit like orange -- plai krau'itch; apple -- plai pomme; The fruit that is sour this season is sweet the next. -- Plai dael ch'ooo noch k'nong ro'doc ni nung p'eye'm noch ro'doe krow'ee.

fruit smash n. sidewalk drink -- tuk kraw'lu(k)

fruit and ice chips dessert n. t'kaw lee'aae plai cheu

frustrated adj. mua moa; very frustrated -- mua moa klang

fry v. deep fry foods that "puff up" -- um'pong: mee um'pong -- fried noodles; fry with substantial oil, but without connotation of "puffing up" -- jchian: french fried potatoes -- dum'lung jchian; fry with little oil -- cha; fry with no oil, roast -- lee'eng: lee'ng po't -- fried/roast corn; lee'eng ung'kaw -- fried/roasted rice; grill without pan -- ang

fuel n. generally -- praeng: for vehicles and planes -- praeng'sa(ng); kerosene -- praeng'kat

full adj. penyh: a full day -- penyh moi t'ngai; not full, partly empty -- penyh kan'lah (lit: half full); I'm full. -- Ch'eyte howi.; full of holes, bumpy -- kra'haeng kra'hoeng

fully adv. men'tan: He was not fully [awake]. -- Gwat mun baan [pn'yeh dung kloo'an] nen'teyn tay.; ka'bawh ka'bai sah: He did not fully [explain] it. -- Gwat mun baan [dawh sr'eye owi] baan ka'bawh ka'bai sah.

fun n. s'kd'eye s'bai; kaa s'bai; s'bai: to have fun -- miun kaa s'bai; Yesterday we had lots of fun. -- Pi musl'munyh yeung miun kaa s'bai ch'raan.; It will be fun. -- Veea nung s'bai.; make fun of (s. o.) -- jcham ahw

function n. mok'ngyeea (same word as "job"): His function is train the teachers. -- Mok'ngyeea ro'bah gwat chia kruu bung rian.; What is the function of this machine? -- Ma'cheen ni miun mok'ngyeea sumrup tveu a'veye?; purpose -- kohl bum nong: What is the function/purpose of this training? -- Kaa a'veye chia kohl bum nong ney kaa haht rian ni?; leh kan'taae'kah: [The Khmer Women's Association] has three [main] functions. -- [Sa'ma'kuum Nee'ree Kampuchea] miun leh kan taae'kah bye [chum bong].

function v.   run, work, operate properly -- chheh

fundamental adj.   pi daum kum'nut

funnel n.   sa'chi

funds n.   loi; praa(k)

funeral n.   bun k'mau'it

funny adj.   cum'plyne; oo'owi'sow'it; (NB: sow'it = to laugh; nyo nyim = to smile)

furniture n.   kreung tohk kaeo'eye (lit: things, table-chair); or, kreung tohk too' kaeo'eye (lit: things, table-cabinet-chair)

further adv.   thaw teuh tee'it

fuse n.   of a bomb -- kup'cha'noo'un: light a fuse -- bun chheh (or aw'ch) kup'cha'noo'un; in electric circuit -- foo'zi

future n.   ah'na'kuut; t'ngai mok; in the future -- peyr ah'na'kuut; or, noch t'ngai mok (lit: in days to come...)

G

gain v. generally -- laung: I want to gain a little weight. -- Kyom jchong laung kilo.; or, Kyom jchong laung twuat baan tek.; gain power, profit fr. s. th., etc., -- jchum'nenyh

galanga n. mut'daeng; (NB: mut'daeng is a spice widely used in Khmer cooking; it is also used in Thai cuisine (its Thai name is "kaah") in such dishes as the popular soup Tom Kai Kaah.)

gamble v. leng l'bye'ng: He likes to gamble. -- Gwat jchole jchet leng l'bye'ng.

gambling n. l'bye'ng see song; (NB: see = "eat" or consume", i.e., win; "song" = "pay back", i.e., "lose")

game n. casual, children's, non-contact, etc. -- l'bye'ng; serious, contact, match as, football, soccer, etc. -- kaa praw'koo'it; sport -- kye'laah

gang n. krum ma'nooh ko'ich

gangster n. jchaao; pooh dah plun (lit: pooh = people; dah = walk or go about; plun = rob; hence, people who go about and rob)

gap (between) n. jchun'lawh (kaa kvee'ung ka'neea ro'vieng): There is a gap between [income and] expenses. -- Miun jchun'lawh kaa kvee'ung ka'neea ro'vieng [jchum'nole nung] jchum'nye.; There is a gap between the (two) mountains. -- Miun jchun'lawh noeh ro'vieng phnom te'ang pi.

garage n. gah'rajh (fr. Fr.)

garbage n. sum'rahm

garden n. generally -- soo'un; flower garden -- soo'un ch'ba; vegetable garden -- soo'un ch'ba bun'lye

garlic n. k'tum saw

garnet n. t'bong kun'tim

gas n. for cooking -- gaz; praeng kaat; for vehicles -- 'sang (fr. Fr. "essence"); praeng; praeng 'sang

gasoline n. praeng; praeng 'sang

gate n. tvee'a ro'bong (lit: door of fence)

gather v. meet, get together -- choop; collect, bring together -- praw'mole

gauche adj. ch'kong

gay adj. cheerful -- s'bai; homosexual -- tu'eey; ngye ngyo

gear n. in a machine -- leep'kreung; equipment -- aye'von; kreung aye'von; praw'dop, praw'dah

gekko (lizard) n. ma'chul (lit: needle); chin'chaw

gem n. t'bong

general adj. too'teuh: a general amnesty -- kaa leuk leng to'h too'teuh

general n. military rank -- o'dum'sena

generally adv. chia too'teuh: Generally I go to bed early. -- Chia too'teuh kyom jchole geyng ro'has.; Generally I get up early. -- Chia too'teuh kyom ro'has pn'yeh [or, pn'yeh chop].

generator n. ma'cheen pleung

generous adj. jchet la'aw

gentle adj. slote

genuine adj. piht praw'kat; men'tan

geography n. phum'i'sahs

German adj. A'la'maan

germ(s) n. may rohk

gesture n. kai vee'ka

get v. acquire physically, get one's hands on -- yok: I got [the last one] in the store. -- Kyom yok baan [a sahl(t) moi] noeh haang.; obtain/find -- [unstated]: I need to get two people [to sign contracts]. -- Kyom tro kaa [ ] ma'nooh pi neh [dum'bye sin'y'aae kej sun'nyaa].; get s. th. for s. o. -- yok... owi mok choon : I'll get [a new one] for you. -- Kyom nung yok owi [t'maee moi] mok choon lok.; find in order to acquire -- ro'k tinh: Where can I get one of these? -- Tau(v) kyom adje ro'k tinh veea noeh cunlye'ng na?; find in order to acquire -- ro'k keunyh: We can't get it anywhere. -- Yung mun adje ro'k veea keunyh noeh kroop ti cunlye'ng.; find in order to acquire -- ro'k: We can get it somewhere. -- Yeung adje ro'k veea noeh cunlye'ng klaah.

get along with -- jchoh chi'moi: I get along with him. -- Kyom jchoh chi'moi gwat.; jchole jchum'now'm.... jchoh: get along [with] them -- jchole [jchum'now'm] gkay jchoh

get back at -- (see "get revenge")

get better -- (i.e., in health, in a sport, etc.) -- krawn baar howi

get ...-er and ...-er -- ...teuh ...teuh: get hotter and hotter -- k'dau teuh k'dau teuh

get farther from -- teuh kaan tai chng'eye pi: The farther they get from the border, the harder it gets. -- Pooh'gkay teuh kaan tai chng'eye pi tul'dyne, kaan tai pi'bah.

get in touch with -- tek tong chi'moi

get into -- jchole k'nong

get into/onto a car/bus/train/plane -- laung chi: [One] got into [a bus] and [the other] onto a train. -- Ma'neh laung chi [laan ch'nool] howi miun [ma'neh tee'it] laung chi ro'tch pleung.

get it (understand) -- jchawb yok baan: "Got it?" (i.e., Understand???) -- Jchawb yok baan tay??; "Yes, I got it!" -- Jchawb yok baan howi!"; (NB: In speech, in exclamations like this, "howi" is invariably compressed to "hi".)

get it (be punished) -- "[tro eye leaou nung]...". (lit: (implied: If you don't stop what you're doing) stated: [right now] (implied: you're gonna get it!)

get a job -- baan kaa tveu

get married -- teuh riap kaa

Get out! -- Jchenyh krau!; or, Teuh krau!; or, Jchenyh teuh!

get out of -- jchenyh krau: They got out of the car. -- Pooh'gkay jchenyh krau laan.

get out of hand -- leng toop tul baan howi: The students got out of hand. -- Gkon'sa leng toop tul baan howi.

get revenge -- jchong pee'a... venyh; jchong song suk... venyh; I will get back at/get revenge on you. -- Kyom nung jchong pee'a neh venyh.; or, Kyom jchong song suk neh venyh.

get rid of -- daeng jchole... teuh

get sick -- t'leh kloo'an chh'ooh (lit: fall sick)

get stuck -- cho'up; cho'up po'ng: My car got stuck. -- Laan kyon cho'up po'ng;

get together -- chuum ru'um ka'neea; mool ka'neea: get together with friends -- mool ka'neea chi'moi mit'paya

get tough with s. o. -- leng to'a k'dau (lit: read a "hot prayer" to s. o.): (You) have to get tough with that guy. -- Ma'nooh ni baan tai leng to'a k'dau tay.

get up -- krau(k) pi geyng; krau(k) laung; pn'yeh laung; (wake up = pn'yeh pi geyng or pn'yeh pi dayke)

get used up -- pra te'ang awh: All the sugar got used up. -- Yeung pra sc'aaw te'ang awh.

get worse -- nung klai chia a'krah chiang

ghost n. k'mau'it

giant n. yeh

gift n. um'now'ee

ginger n. kn'yaye (AP: kin'y'eye, k'nyaae)

girl n. sraae; k'mayng sraae

girlfriend n. song sa; mit sraae; lover -- snai ha

give v. generally -- owi (AP: ow'): Give me a sentence with [the word] "mok'ngyeea." -- Owi klia moi chi'moi [peea] "mok'ngyeea."; What help do you need me to give you? -- Neh tro kaa kyom owi choo'ay a'veye?; give

to me -- owi mok: Give it to me. -- Owi veea mok kyom.; give to s. o. else. -- owi tueh: Give it to them. -- Owi teuh veea teuh.; give helpfully, or as favor or service -- choon: I'll give you some medicine. -- Kyom nung choon t'nam teuh lok.; make available to -- pdull owi ... teuh; give an interview to the press -- pdull kaa sum'pee'a owi teuh neh ka'ssett; give, hand in, submit -- pdull owi noch

give a ride to v. dow'ee sa teuh: Please give me a ride to Kuk Mong. -- Kyom sum dow'ee sa teuh Kuk Mong.

give away -- owi; give away in shares, "divvy up" -- jchaiyk: He gave away all his money. -- Gwat jchaiyk loi gwat te'ang awh.

give in return -- mok owi venyh: I have nothing to give you in return. -- Ot miun mok owi venyh.

Give me a break! exp. Owi kyom sum'raak teuh!; Kum ruhm kaan peyk!

give up -- surrender -- jchaw jchanyh; luek tung ch'eye saw (lit: raise a white flag); give up (i. e., cease) doing/using s. th. -- leh bong: You should give up smoking. -- Neh koo'a tai leh bong kaa choohk ba'r'eye.; sacrifice, forfeit -- pdo... chi'moi: I will happily give up my life for you. -- Kyom sohk jchet slop rooh pdo chi'vut chi'moi neh.

glad adj. s'bai; trey'aw

glass n. for drinking -- kaae'oo (AP: kae'ow); for windows, etc. -- kun'chaw

glasses n. eyeglasses -- ven'taa; for drinking -- kaae'oo

glove n. sr'auwm dai

glue n. jchoa kaow

glue v. but kaow

gnat n. moh'mung

go v. move from one place to another -- teuh: We will go tomorrow. -- Yeung nung teuh s'eye'd.; What time did he go? -- Gwat teuh peyr na?.; Go cook the soup! -- Teuh dam sa'law tueh! (NB: one way that the imperative can be formed in Khmer is [action-descriptive verb (with or without object noun), followed by "teuh"]; in the "soup" example, the first "teuh" expresses "Go", the second "teuh" signals the imperatve. Thus, "Cook the soup!" would be just "Dam sa'law teuh!")

go against v. praw'chang (NB: praw'chang can also be usd as preposition: against Vietnam... -- praw'chang sruk Vietnam...)

go ahead imp. Go ahead! -- Teuh mok!; go ahead and do s. th. -- [action-descriptive verb (with or without object noun), followed by "teuh"]: Go ahead and [eat]! -- [Nyam] teuh!; or, Go ahead and eat the [bananas]. -- Nyam [jchay] teuh.

Go away (and die)! -- Teuh slop jchoh!

go back -- teuh venyh

go back and forth -- jchenyh jchole, jchole jchenyh, jchole jchenyh, jchenyh jchole

go by -- The time went by fast. -- Peyr teuh mok ro'has nah.

go far away -- teuh chng'eye

go get (call) a friend -- haow mit

go off and die -- (e. g., out of sadness, anger, etc.) -- teuh slop; or, teuh mwop

go off to (in sense of "disappear to") -- (vulgar) teuh tai haow: Where the hell did he get to?/Where the hell did he go off to?/Where the hell did he disappear to? -- Teuh tai haow ti na?; (NB: for lit. meaning of "tai haow", see definition of "go to hell", below)

go down (stairs, a hill, etc.) -- jchoh

go down (in price) -- jchoh krowm; jchoh tauk; Prices went down. -- Tlai jchoh krowm (or, jchoh tauk).

go look for -- dah ro'k

go out (i. e., for fun; walk around; sight-see; have a date) -- dah'leng

go out to eat -- teuh nyam bye haang

go out together -- no'um ka'neea dah'leng: They went out together. -- Gkay no'um ka'neea dah'leng.

Go out(side). (command) -- Teuh krau.! (Get out! -- Jchenyh krau!)

go out -- cease working, quit -- ro'luut: The lights went out. -- Pleung ro'luut.

Go quickly! -- Teuh leuan lang!

Go safely! -- Teuh owi baan sohk s'bai.

go see a movie -- jchole meuhl gkun

go shopping -- teuh p'sa

go to bed (to sleep) -- teuh dayke (generally means to sleep alone); teuh geyng (may mean to sleep alone or with s.o. else.)

go to bed with s. o. (sexual connotation) -- teuh geyng, plus context

go to hell excl. (loose equivalent: Teuh tai haow! (lit: go and become like the spirit of one who has killed himself; i.e., (since suicide is considered sinful), go become an eternally damned spirit)

go toward -- teuh kang

go up the steps, or stairs, of a house -- laung chan'dal

go with (match) -- scawb ka'neea chi'moi nung: This color goes with that color. -- Pwa ni scawb ka'neea chi'moi nung pwa nu.

goal n. vuh'to'bum'nong: The goal of the government is to give the people enough food. -- Vuh'to'bum'nong ratt'a'pi'bal keuh pdull owi pra'chee'chuun noch ma'hope jchum'nace.

goat n. po'pay

god n. preah (AP: preh)

godfather n. oeuv'puk to'a

godmother n. m'dye to'a

gold adj. and/or n. generally -- mee'eh; 24 karat -- mee'eh teuk dawp; 14 karat -- mee'eh ba'raang

gone pp. used up -- awh; awh hiwi; missing, lost -- bot; re animals or people, ij sense of missing -- teuh bot awh (lit: gone missing)

gonorrhea n. rokh sv'eye

good adj. decent, competent, or generally "OK" morally, physically or intellectually -- la'aw: He is a good man. -- Gwat chia ma'nooh la'aw.; They have a good house. -- Pooh'gkay miun ptay'a la'aw.; ... a good student... -- gkon'sa la'aw... ; specifically physically decent or adequate -- sam'rum: The people need good housing. -- Pra'chee'chuun tro'kaa kaa ch'ro'k noch sam'rum.; specifically morally good -- trum tro: She is a good woman. -- Veea chia sraae trum tro.; skilled at s. th. -- poo'k'eye; chuum'nee'inyh: He is good at swimming. -- Gwat poo'k'eye hahl tuk.; advantageous -- praw'sah: a good thing -- chia kaa praw'sah; It is good/a good thing to have [some secrets]. -- Veea keuh chia kaa praw'sah dael miun [kaa sum'ngut klaah].; no good, useless -- mun baan kaa; ot praw'yow'it

Good bye! xcl. relatively informal -- lee'a howi (NB: invariably compressed n speech to "lee'a hi"); to get attention of one in gathering of several -- lee'a sun howi; (NB: again, "howi" in these phrases is generally compressed to "hi", viz.: lee'a sun hi); formal, to show respect -- jchuum ree'up lee'a; formal -- Kyom jchuum ree'up lee'a.; Go safely -- Teuh owi baan s'bai.; or, Teuh owi baan sohk s'bai.; Have a good time! -- Owi baan s'bai!; Good bye (to you), madame. -- Jchuum ree'up lee'a howi, lok sraae.

good luck n. sum'nang la'aw; Good luck! -- Sum'nang la'aw!

Good morning! xcl. A'roon soo'si dye!

goods n. ro'bah ro'baw; tum'neng; aye'von

goose n. ka'ngan

gossip n. kaa sup kaa see'oo

govern v. kroop krong (NB: "enough" = kroop kro'un); troo'it tra

government adj. ratt (AP: rawt): a government minister -- ratt' mun'trei; ro'bah ratt: The Monorom is a government hotel. -- O'tyle Monorom ro'bah ratt.

government n. ratt'a'pi'bal (AP: ratt'pi'ban, ratt'a'pi'baan, rat'ta'pi'barr, etc.)

government official n. mun'trei ratt'a'kaa; mun'trei ploe'kaa; mun'trei tveu kaa; high official -- ka'ma'pi'bal

governor n. jchao'vye (AP: cha'oo'vye): provincial governor -- jchao'vye kyte; (NB: jchao'vye also means "boss")

grab v. jchaab

grade n. level, rank -- t'nak; in school -- t'nak

graduate v. rian jchawp: What school did you graduate from? -- Tau(v) nch rian jchawp pi sa'la na?

grain n. kro'up (AP: kroop; same as word for seed and bullet)

grandchild n. gkon chau(v)

grandfather n. jchee ta

grandmother n. yaye; (AP: jchee); jchee doe'n

grape n. plai tum'paae'ang bai'choo; kro'up tum'paae'ang bai'choo

grapefruit n. krau'itch t'long

grass n. sm'au

grateful adj. dung kun

grave n. p'no

gravel n. t'maah l'ut l'ut (lit: stone small small); pebbles -- k'rooh

grease n. for cooking or for lubrication -- klanyh; for lubrication -- klanyh (or praeng) gko

great adj. accomplished, successful -- ma'het'meea; awh jcha; He is a very great man. -- Gwat chia ma'nooh ow'cha nah.; Great! Good news! -- Praw'sar nah!; serious, extreme -- daw ch'raan; There is a great need for medicine. -- Tro kaa tnam peyt daw ch'raan.; ma'ha: the Great Leap Forward -- Ma'ha Lote Plong

greatest adj. maha: the greatest treasure... -- chia maha kum' nawp; chia thum bom'pot: this is the greatest mistake... -- ni keuh chia kum'hawh daw thum bom'pot ...

greed n. lope'lun

greedy adj. lope'lun: [Most] politicians are greedy. -- [Pich ch'raan ney] neh na'yo'bye lope'lun.; kum'nunyh

green adj. the color -- bye tong; unripe -- k'chey

greet v. sva'kum: We must greet the guests. -- Yeung tro sva'kum p'nee'oo.; make palms-together sign of greeting/respect -- sum'paya; bless, as sometimes when guests leave a celebration -- choon po'

grenade, bomb, explosive n. kro'up bai (AP: kroop bai, krup bai)

grenade launcher n. kum pleung banyh kro'up bai

grey adj. pwa praw'peh ("peh" = "ashes")

grilled adj. ang: grilled chicken -- sat(ch) muon ang; (NB: pan fried with little oil = cha, pan or pot fried with substantial oil = jchian)

grind v. gkun: grind corn -- gkun po't

grip n. kun'dap dai

grope around for v. ree'oo ro'k; jchraaw vaa ree'oo

gross adj. bad -- kra' kwah: So gross! -- Kra' kwah ma'lch!

ground n. earth -- daiy

group n. krum; faction -- pooh; political party -- ka'na'pac; that group (over there) -- pooh nu; jchum'mauwm

grow v. get bigger, as children, crops, etc. -- loot law; raise, by human effort, plants or crops -- baan dam (lit.: "make sprout"); dam: They grew corn. -- Gkay dam po't.; grow naturally (without human intervention) -- dos: The trees grew. -- Daum cheu dos.; increase in size -- kauwn laung: The population increased quickly. -- Jchum'noo'an pra'chee'chuun kauwn laung yang ro'has.; increase in size, strength, prosperity, etc. -- ree'k jchum raan; become -- teuh... chia: They grew [tired] of waiting. -- Gkay teuh jcham chia [kaa tuun ka'sow'ee].

guarantee v. ti'nee'a: I guarantee that there is no problem. -- Kyom ti'nee'a tha ot miun pun'ha a'veye tay.

guaranty n. kaa ti'nee'a

guard n. neh gyhee'um; neh sveye kaa'pee'a; plural form, i.e., group performing guard function -- kawng sveye kaa pee'a

guard v. tveu pee'a; dah gyee'um (lit: walk guard); gyec'um la'bat; We must guard the bank day and night. -- Yeung tro tai gyee'um la'bat banque te'ang yoop te'ang t'ngai.

guava n. traw'bye

guerrilla(s) adj. or n. kawng ch'lope; kawng chh'muk

guess v. generally -- sman: Don't just guess. -- Kum jcheh tai sman.; estimate (i.e, when person guessing has some idea of answer ("educated guess")) -- pahn; pahn meuhl; I would guess it's another twenty kilometers. -- Kyom pahn meuhl tha praw'heil chia m'pye ki'lo'met teuh tee'it.; when person guessing has no idea of answer ("wild guess") -- tee'aae... lo' meuhl: Guess my age. -- Tee'aae a'yoo kyom lo meuhl.; think or believe -- hah(k) doj chia: I guess it's OK. -- Hah(k) doj chia mun aae tay.; feel that one will do s. th.; should -- koo'a tai: I guess I'll (i.e., I really should) go. -- Kyom koo'a tai teuh.

guest n. p'nee'oo

guide n. one who shows the way -- neh no'um ploe; one who gives instructions or information, as instructor or tour guide -- neh no'um bong hanyh

guide v. nye no'um; bong hanyh ploe

guilty adj. in legal sense -- to'h: The gcourt found him guilty. -- To'la'ka ni'yaye tha gwat to'h.; in moral sense -- koh: All politicians are guilty of something. -- Neh na'yo'bye te'ang awh choo'up koh kaa a'veye a'veye.; I [feel] guilty. -- Kyom [miun a'rom] tha tveu koh.

gulf n. body of water -- choong sa'mut; Gulf of Thailand -- Choong sa'mut Thai (or See'um)

gum (chewing) n. sc'aaw kaow'soo (lit: sugar rubber)

gun n. rifle -- kum pleung; artillery -- kum pleung thum

guy n. gwat; that guy -- gwat nu; bora: some guy -- bora ma'nch

H

habit n. tum'lawp: He has many bad habits. -- Gwat muin tum'lawp a'krah ch'raan.

hack n. cut through (as, bushes) -- vay't ploe; cut up (as, hunk of meat) -- chin ch'rum

hail n. t'leh t'kaw (lit: falling ice)

hail v. acknowledge as great -- ku'roop; call (as, hail a taxi) -- haow

hair n. saahk

hairdresser n. chee'ung oat saahk

half n. pi'eh (AP: peh) kan'dal: Do you want half my rice? -- Neh jchong baan bye kyom pieh kan'dal tay?; We have gone half way now. -- Yeung baan teuh doll pieh kan'dal ploe.; We have done half of it. -- Yeung tveu baan pieh kan'dal howi.; Give me half. -- Owi kyom pieh kan'dal mok.; kan'lah' (AP: kan'lah(k)): one half -- moi kan'lah'; one and a half -- moi nung kan'lah; 1:30 [p.m.] -- mao moi kan'lah' [nung peyr kan'dal]; three thirty a. m. or p. m. -- mao bye kan'lah'; half a glass of water -- tuk kan'lah' kaae'oo; "half dead" -- awh kum'lung (lit: no more strength); or, jchong slop teuh howi (lit: wanting to die); half-Chinese, half-Khmer -- chemie jchun, chemie Khmei; half-Khmer, half-western child -- metisse, kone'can; fifty percent -- ha'sup pi roi; "fifty-fifty" -- ha'sup, ha'sup

hall n. sa'la: city hall -- sa'la krong; or, ti s'day kaa a'pi'bal krong; dance hall -- ro'ng kuh sa'la

hallucination n. specter, mirage -- k'mau'it laung (lit: ghost appearing)

Halt! xcl. Chope! (AP: Choop!; NB: finished = jchawp, grab = jchaap; meet = choop)

ham sandwich n. Phnom Penh term -- pan'sock

hamlet n. phum

hammer n. nyow ngyoo'a; a'nyuu'a

hand n. dai (same as word for arm): made by hand -- tveu dow'ee dai; (NB: fingers -- ma'ree'um dai; toes -- ma'ree'um cheung); in sense of grip, fist -- kun'dap dai; on the one hand... on the other hand -- m'yang... m'yang venyh tee'it: On the one hand, he is smart, but on the other hand, he is [sometimes] naive. -- M'yang gwat' ch'laat, punta'aae m'yang venyh tee'it [chu'on kaal] gwat keuh chia chowt nah!; get out of hand -- leng toop tul baan howi

hand v. ho'ich: Please hand me that book. -- Sum ho'ich kyom s'po nu.

hand over v. pruh'kul: Hand your money over to me! -- Pruh'kul loi owi kyom!

handicraft n. su'pa'kaam

handle n. do'ng; pump with hande -- an'do'ng

handle v. deal with, manage -- dawh sr'eye: Can you handle this problem [alone]? -- Tau(v) neh adje dawh sr'eye pun'ha ni [ma'neh eiyne] baan tay?

handsome adj. song ha; sa'aat

hang v. p'shoo'a: The calender must be hung on [the wall] -- Ca'len'dree'ay tro baan p'shoo'a noeh leuh [chuun chee'ung].; The flag was hanging on the wall. -- Tung ch'aye p'shoo'a noeh leuh chuun' chee'ung.; clothes hanging on a line -- kow-aow p'shoo'a leuh k'sye; hang to execute -- jchaawng khaw; p'shoo'a khaw: We'll hang him at dawn. -- Yeung nung p'shoo'a khaw gwat peyr pro'lum.; sticking out (of) -- euut (jchenyh): The dog was hanging out the window of the car. -- Sh'kye euut jchenyh taam bung'oo'it laan.

hang out with v. sype'koop ka'neea

hang up v. p'shoo'a: hang up clothes -- p'shoo'a kow-aow; dah(k): hang up the phone -- dah(k) to'ra'sap jchoh (lit: put telephone down);

hanky-panky n. suum kro luu'm

happen v. baan: How did that accident happen? -- Yang na baan kroo'ti'nak?; kaut laung: It happened three years ago. -- Veea kaut laung bye chh'nam kun'lung howi [or, kun'lung mok howi].; It happened [to] him yesterday. -- Veea kaut laung [jchum'poo'h] gwat pi musl'munyh.; veea baan chia: He drove so slowly that it happened that we [arrived late]. -- Gwat baahk baw yeut peyk veea baan chia yeung [mok doll mun twon peyr].

happy adj. s'bai; s'bai jchet: Greeting "How are you?" -- Neh sohk s'bai tay? -- is literally Are you healthy and happy?"; very happy -- s'bai reek'ree'aae; Happy [Birthday]! -- S'bai reek'ree'aae [t'ngai kum'naut]!; tray'awh: I am happy to be living in Po'sat. -- Kyom tray'awh dael baan roo' noeh Po'sat.

hard adj. not soft -- rung; hard bread -- nom rung; hard cheese -- froma' rung; difficult to do physically -- pi'bah; Khmer is hard to write. -- Pee'sa Khmei pi'bah saw'say.; full of problems -- lum'bah: hard life -- chi'vut lum'bah; a difficult situation -- s'tana'pheap lum'bah; hard times -- peyr vaae'ten'eea; intensely -- klang: try hard -- kom yang klang

hardly adv. mun steu: I hardly had time [to unpack]. -- Kyom mun steu miun peyr [reuh kow-aow jchenyh pi va'leez].

hardship n. kaa vaae'te'neea

hard-wood n. cheu nee'eng'nuun (generally used in reference to a seris of smooth, dense tropical woods such as mahogany, teak, kuring, albercia and yospero.)

harrass v. tveu lum'bah om'pee

harrassing fire n. (mil. term) harcelement (fr. Fr.)

harvest n. kaa chroht kaat

harvest v. chroht kaat

hassle n. ru'ung hoo'hyte: Too much hassle! -- Ru'ung ch'raan hoo'hyte!

hat n. moo'a (AP: mooh)

hatchet n. poo'tauw

hate n. s'awp; kaa s'awp

hate v. s'awp

have v. have available -- mi'un: I have only four books with me. -- Kyom miun tai buon s'po kaat chi'moi kyom.; experience -- miun; or, kaut laung: Tornadoes? In what provinces do you have them? -- K'shaal p'chooh? Veea miun noeh k'nong kyte na? or, Tau(v) veea kaut laung noeh k'nong kyte na?; own -- miun: I have only one car. -- Kyom miun tai moi laan kut.; want, will have, as in restaurant -- yok, or jchole jchet, or jchong baan: I will have rice soup. -- Kyom yok baa' baw.; past tense auxiliary verb -- [implied from context]: Have you seen him? -- Tau(v) [ ] neh keunyh gwat?; I have never been there before. -- Kyom [ ] mun'dael teuh ti nu tay.; baan... howi: I have seen that already. -- Kyom baan keunyh veea howi.

Have a good time! -- Owi baan s'bai!

have an effect (on) v. ho'itch p'auwl (teuh leuh): The hot weather had a bad effect on the crops. -- Tee'ut a'kas k'dau ho'ich p'auwl a'krah teuh leuh po't p'auwl.

"have no brain" v. ot miun praw'ngya

have to v. mandatory, non-optional -- tro tai: I have to pay taxes. -- Kyom tro tai bong tax.; I have to buy gas (or else I'll be stuck here). -- Kyom tro tai tinh gaz...; optional, a matter of preference rather than absolute necessity -- tro; or tro kaa: (It was so good) I have to see that movie again! -- Kyom tro meuhl gkun nu m'dong tee'it!.; I have to have one more cup of coffee. -- Kyom tro kaa cafe moi paeng tee'it.

hay n. chum'bal(ng) (AP: chum'b'ow)

hazard n. obstacle -- aw'pa'sa

he prn. polite, for person of any age -- gwat (AP: gwa, kut, kuh); vee'a (familiar; acceptable for child, young person, younger family member or close friend or family member, but used re older person suggests disrespect; may be used re criminal or other person in disrepute to intentionally avoid showing respect.)

head n. part of the body -- koo'k'bal; brain -- praw'ngya: He has no brain [i. e., is dumb]. -- Gwat ot miun praw'ngya.; head of an organization -- may: head of a family -- may kroo'e'sa; head of a village -- may phum; (but "head" (i.e., governor or chief minister) of a province or ministry -- at'pi'bal)

headache n. chh'ooh k'bal

headman (of a village) n. may phum; praw'tee'un phum

headquarters n. ti bun'chee'a kaa; ti snak kaa

health n. sok'a'pheap

hear v. loo: I hear that... -- Kyom loo tha...; loo so (lit: to hear the sound of): I hear [them talking] together. -- Kyom loo so [gkay ni'yaye] ka'neea.; I hear the music. -- Kyom loo so sum'leng plaeng.; understand -- s'dap baan: I hear that he's already gone. -- Kyom s'dap baan tha gwat teuh howi.

heart n. anatomical feature -- be'dong; seat of emotion -- jchet; sentimentally -- doo'ung jchet: My heart is with you. -- Doo'ung jchet kyom noeh jchum'poo'h neh.

heartbroken adj. ko'ich jchet

heat n. and v. kum'da'oo

heavy adj. t'nguun (AP: t'ng'alm): This is very heavy. -- Ro'bah ni t'nguun nah.

hectare n. hec'taa

hedge n. ro'bong (same as word for "fence")

height n. kum poo'h

helicopter n. 'eh'le'kop'tayr; aw'thum'pi'ch'ka'cha

hell n. n'roo(k): Go to hell! -- Jchoh n'roo(k) teuh!

Hello! xcl. Soo'si'dye!; or, Jchuum ree'up soo'a!

help n. assistance -- choo'ay (AP: choo'i); or, choom'noo'ee: Can I help you? [i. e., "What help do you need?"] -- Neh tro kaa choo'ay a'veye?;

help v. choo'ay (AP: choo'i): Can I help you? [i. e., Do you need me to help?] -- Neh tro kaa kyom choo'ay tay?

Help! xcl. Choo'ay, choo'ay! or, Choo'ay pong, choo'ay pong!

hen n. may muon (NB: "may" (lit: mother) used before the name of any animal denotes the female of the species)

hepatitis n. chuum'ngeu kaut leu'ung (lit: illness of becoming yellow)

her possessive generally -- nee'eng; or, ro'bah nee'eng: Her car. -- Laan nee'eng.; also, although generaly used to mean "him", gwat: Her car. -- Laan gwat.; familiar (disrespectful if not used re close friend or younger family member) -- veea: Her (that little girl's, that kid's) toys -- praw'dop leng veea

her prn. generally -- nee'eng: I asked her to dance. -- Kyom sum nee'eng ro'am.; casual -- gwat; very familiar (as, close friend or younger relative) -- vec'a; respectful -- sraae

herb(s) n. chii

here adv. ni: Come here! -- Mok ni!; ti ni: It's near here. -- Veea noch chit ti ni.; eye ni; (AP: outside Phnom Penh "ni" may be pronounced "neh")

heritage n. gkay ma'ra'da

hero n. vorak'chuun

hesitate v. s'teh's'teu: They hesitated too long. -- Pooh'gkay s'teh steu yeut nah.

hex v. tveu um'peuh

hide v. hide oneself -- poo'un: They hid in the forest. -- Pooh'gkay poo'un k'nong prey.; hide oneself -- leh kloo'an: They hid from the Khmer Rouge in the forest. -- Pooh'gkay leh kloo'an noeh k'nong prey om'pee Khmei Kra'hom.; hide s. th. -- leh; hide money for savings -- leh loi tooo'k; hide/keep/save up money for fun -- leh loi jchole

high adj. (also, tall, large or supreme) -- k'pooh; in sense of superior or supreme -- leuh: Ong'kah Leuh (term used by Khmer Rouge cadre and "ka'ma'pi'bal" to refer to the upper levls of their organization.)

high school n. vi'chi ro'ng

highway n. t'nawl (APs:tha'nol, tha'non)

hi-jack v. generally -- bung'ruut: hi-jack a plane -- bung ruut ka'pal hawh; plun: hi-jack a car -- plun laan (lit: steal a car)

hi-jacker n. neh bong'ruut (also means "kidnapper" or "abducter")

hill n. gkon phnom; ti too'ul

him prn. generally -- gwat (AP: gwa'); re young boy -- nee'eng; to younger person, close friend, (otherwise disrespectful) -- veea; respectful -- lok; lok nu: I gave it to him. -- Kyom owi teuh lok nu.

Hinduism n. pro'munyh'tus'na; se'sna'pree'um

hint n. pee'a praw'lowee (also means "clue"): Give me a hint. -- Sum owi pee'a praw'lowee.

hips n. jchung keh

hire v. ch'ool: I want to hire a cyclo to take me to the office. -- Kyom jchong ch'ool cyclo chi teuh kaar'ya'lye.; (NB: while the verb "to hire" is "ch'ool", the adjectival phrase "for hire", "hired" and "rented" is ch'nool, viz.: taxi ("car for hire" or "rented car") is laan ch'nool, employee(s) ("hired labor") is tveu ch'nool, etc.

his adj. gwat; ro'bah gwat

history n. pro'wa'ti'sa

hit v. vi'yaye; kaow: hit s. o. on the head -- kaow k'bal; to hit with a fist -- koo'uh; hit the dirt -- kraap: The soldiers hit the dirt when [the firing] started. -- Tee'hee'an kraap peyr kaa banyh jchaap p'dam.; beat hard -- thuung; hit a drum (loudly, as by monks in a temple celebration) -- thuung sco

hoe n. choe'up kohp

hoist v. lift up -- stoo'ich

hold v. grasp -- kaan: hold a glass -- kaan kaae'oo; keep temporarily -- tooo'k: Please hold this money for me -- Tooo'k loi ni owi kyom pong.; keep, take care of -- tai ret'sa; accomodate as passengers -- chi: This [boat] can hold four people. -- [Toook] ni chi baan buon nch.; accomodate as contents -- dah(k): This box can hold three telephones. -- Praw'op ni dah(k) baan to'ra'sap bye.; hold on to s. th. -- taow'ng: hold onto the boat -- taow'ng toook; hold back, retard -- ohn'toi; to be held back by -- onh'toi dow'ee sa

hold back v. prevent from falling -- tooo'b tul; block, obstruct or handicap s. o. -- bung ot

Hold on! xcl. Jcham moi plet! (lit: Wait one instant.); Choop sun!

hole n. perforation, generally, as through wall or roof or cloth -- praw'hoeng; holes with bottoms: small hole in ground or wall -- ruun; large hole in ground, burough -- roong; full of holes, bumpy -- kra'haeng kra'hoeng; make a hole in s. th., bore into -- jchaw

holiday n. t'ngai buun; t'ngai chope buun; t'ngai chope sum'raak (lit.: "day to stop (and) rest"); vee'sma'kaal

holy adj. sat'set: holy water -- tuk sat'set

home n. ptay'a: Where is your home? -- Ptay'a neh noeh aae na?; Is he at home? -- Tau(v) gwat noeh ptay'a tay?; ti'luum'noeh: You have a good home. -- Nch miun ti'luum'noeh la'aw.

homeland n. praw'tet kum'naut

homeless adj. a'na'tah: homeless people -- a'na'tah chuun

homesick adj. nuhk ptay'a (lit: to miss home)

hometown n. mee'a'to phum

homosexual adj. ngye ngyo

homosexual n. neh ngye ngyo; k'teu'y

honest adj. sm'oh trong; sek char'ut; trum tro

honesty n. kej tic sek char'ut

honestly adv. without deception -- sm'oh trong: Answer honestly. -- Jchum'la'wee yang sm'oh trong.; actually, really -- taam piht

honey n. tuk k'mum

honor n. ki'ta'yoo

hope n. s'kd'eye sung'khum; sung'khum: Don't lose hope [yet]. -- Kum [twon] awh sung'khum.

hope v. sung'khum (AP: sum'kum, som'kum): I hope I can. -- Kyom sung'khum tha adje.; I hope so. -- Kyom sung'khum tha an'chung. or, Kyom sung'khum tha an'chung dai.; in sense of wish -- bun s'rung: I hope so (i.e., I wish it could be so.) -- Kyom bun s'rung dai.; or, Kyom bun s'rung dai owi baan dai chit.

hopeless adj. (from the outset) ot sung'khum; no more hope -- awh sung'khum

horn n. of vehicle -- siff'lay; The horn is broken. -- Siff'lay laan ko'ich.; of animal -- sn'eye'ng

horse n. seh: horse cart -- ro'tch seh

hospital n. mun'ti peyt

hospitality n. kaa reh teh

hostage n. neh too(s)

hot adj. re temperature -- k'dau: a hot day -- t'ngai k'dau; spicy -- huhl: spicy food -- ma'hope huhl; aroused sexually -- sawh; miun kaa sawh

hot season n. ro'doe k'dau

hotel n. o'tyle

hour n. mao (written maong); Five dollars per hour. -- Mao moi prum dolla'.

house n. ptay'a; ti luum noeh

housing n. kaa ch'ro'k: The people need good housing. -- Pra'chee'chuun tro kaa kaa ch'ro'k noeh sam'rum.

housewife n. may ptay'a

how adv. in what manner -- yang na; yang mutch: How did that accident happen? -- Yang na baan kroo'ti'nak nu?; doj ma'dek: They don't understand how [things] are in Cambodia. -- Gkay ot yul [ro'bah] doj ma'dek k'nong Kampuchea.; yang doj ma'dek: How did that happen? -- Yang doj ma'dek baan chia kaut laung?

How are you? -- Sohk s'bai tay? (lit: (are you) healthy and happy?)

how long, how much time? xcl. -- Pu'man mao?

how much, how many adv. when seeking specific number as answer -- pu'man (AP: p'man, pah'man; usually followed by noun such as kilo, kilomet, riel, etc.); when answer may be less specific response such as "a lot", "many", "a few", etc., pronunciation may be -- pun'na (not necessarily followed by noun), as: How much does it hurt? -- Chh'ooh pun'na teuh?

How much? (lit: "how expensive is it?") -- Tau(v) t'lai pu'man?

How old are you? -- A'yoo pu'man?

however adv. on the other hand, but nevertheless -- yang na kaw dow'ee; pun'ta'aae: That place was very dangerous; however, he still wanted to go there. -- Cunlyc'ng nu kroo'ti'nak nah, yang na kaw dow'ee gwat noeh tai jchong teuh.; in whatever manner -- yang na kaw dow'ee: However you do it, it will [(still)] be expensive. -- Yang na kaw dow'ee aae neh tveu veea, veea [noeh tai] tlai.

huge adj. thum

human being n. ma'nooh: They are not animals, they are human beings. -- Pooh'gkay mun men saat tay; pooh'gkay chia ma'nooh.

humid adj. salm

humidity n. salm nauwm

humiliate v. tveu owi k'mah; tveu owi a'mah muk

humiliated adj. humiliated (by) -- on jchet (dow'ee); or (less serious) to'ich jchet (dow'ee); humiliated (because of) -- on jchet (bee'proo'a); or (less serious) to'ich jchet (bee'proo'a)

humorous adj. cum'plyne; gkun ri'eng

hundred adj. roi: one hundred -- m'roi (AP: mua roi, ma' roi); a hundred and two -- m'roi pi; A hundred percent! -- M'roi pi' roi!

hundreds n. ro'up roi: hundreds of people -- ma'nooh ro'up roi; (NB: ro'up = to count)

hunger n. kaa ot'bye

hungry adj.   klee'un ; (S) ro'mool pec'ah klee'un: My [stomach's turning over] I'm so hungry! -- Kyom [ro'mool poo'ah] klee'un!

hunt v.   seek for -- ro'k; find and shoot s. th. -- baw(r) banyh; hunt (lit: shoot) animals -- baw(r) banyh saat or banyh saat: hunt a tiger -- baw(r) banyh saat kla; for s. th. lost -- sveye ro'k: I hunted for my watch all day. -- Kyom sveye ro'k ni'a'li'ka kyom penyh moi t'ngai.

hunter n.   neh baw(r) banyh; prian prey

hunting n.   baw(r) banyh

hurricane n.   p'chooh song'gria; storm less strong than hurricane -- k'shaal p'chooh

Hurry, hurry! xcl.   praw'nyab; chhop chhop; leu'an leu'an

Hurry up and ... xcl.   Leu'an laung [or Chhop laung] + verb: Hurry up and eat! -- Leu'an laung nyam!; praw'nyab laung; sro't laung

hurt adj.   injured -- chh'ooh: Are you hurt? -- Tau(v) neh chh'ooh tay? emotionally -- chh'ooh jchaab; jcho'k jchaab

hurt v.   do injury to -- banyh chh'ooh; or, tveu owi chh'ooh jchaab: Did I (physically) hurt you? -- Tau(v) kyom tveu owi neh chh'ooh roo?; make upset -- chh'ooh jchaab: It hurt my feelings. -- Veea tveu owi kyom chh'ooh jchaab.

husband n.   generally -- p'dye; formal term -- gkoo(r) swaa'mye

husk n.   sum bawh; kun too'a

husk v.   buhk: to husk rice -- buhk sro

hut n.   k'tome; ro'ng (same word -- meaning place -- as in "ro'ng gkun," "ro'ng jcha", etc.)

hygiene n.   a'na'mye: We must have [better] hygene so that people will not die so easily. -- Yeung tro tai miun a'na'mye daw [praw'sar] dum'bye kum owi ma'nooh slop sroul.

hypocrisy n.   kaa puuht

hypocrite n.   ma'nooh miun puuht; ma'nooh leh puuht

I

I prn. general non-familiar, for m. or f. -- kyom; (AP: kin'yom, knyom, kyum, and condensed in rapid speech to 'yom); very respectful, used by f. only (so respectful, sometimes used jokingly with friends) -- nee'eng kyom; "familiar relationship" terms -- own and bong; both of these words are used in "familiar" relationships (family, love, to some extent employment situations); in such contexts, they can mean either "I" or "you" (with context indicating the meaning), and are usually used in tandem with each other. "Own" whether meaning "I" or "you" is used by a speaker in a dialogue to convey particular respect for the person to whom he/she is speaking, while "bong" is used by or in reference to a person in the dialogue who may be of slightly higher social stature (generally a male, or the older of the two in the dialogue, or both). Example: [I] love you (wife to husband). -- [Own] sra'laanyh bong.; [I] will call you tonight. (older brother to younger sister) -- [Bong] nung to'ra'sap own yoop ni.; term used only when speaking with close friends (otherwise disrespectful) -- angyh; (NB: the analogous "among-close-friends" word for "you" is "eingy"; hence, familiarly, "you and I" would be "eingy nung angyh")

ice n. t'kaw: I would like some ice in my drink. -- Kyom jchong t'kaw tic tic k'nong p'es'cheeh' ro'bah kyom.

ice box n. toooh t'kaw

ice cube n. duhm

iced coffee n. cafe t'kaw; with milk -- cafe ta'gko' t'kaw (NB: milk = tuk dawh gko, in rapid speech, "ta'dawh'gko"; ice = ta'kaw'; "ta'gko' t'kaw" is thus an accelerated-speech pronunciation of "cafe tuk dawh gko t'kaw")

iced tea n. ta'ee t'kaw

I. D. card n. a'tak'sa'nyeean'na'bun

idea n. kut; kum'nut; ma'teh(k)'; (NB: red pepper = ma'taae(s)); yo bawl: Good idea! -- Yo bawl la'aw!; Do you have any ideas? -- Tau(v) neh miun yo bawl aye tay?; It's my idea (lit: it came from my head). -- Veea mok pi pra'nya kyom.

identification n. sen'ya sum'pwal

ideology n. leh'tee: communist ideology -- leh'tee co'muu'neeste

idiotic adj. plee pleuh; pleu'o pleu'o

if conj. baa (pronounced with slight "r" sound at end of word): If you're hungry, eat. -- Baa klee'un, nyam teuh.; praw'sun; praw'sun baa: If they are politicians, they are bad. -- Praw'sun baa pooh'gkay chia neh na'yo'bye, pooh'gkay tro tai a'krah; If they are bad, they are guilty. -- Praw'sun baa a'krah, pooh'gkay tro tai chia ma'nooh choo'up koh.; If you want to learn, [just] copy what he's doing. -- Praw'sun baa neh jchong rian, [kron tai] tveu taam a'veye dael gwat tveu.; praw'sun chia; k'awl baa; twal'tai... teup: If the enemy attacks, we will do it. -- Twal'tai sa'tro vi'yaye sum'rot, teup yeung tveu veea.; as if -- teuh: It look as if... -- Meuhl teuh...; as if -- doj chia: It seems as if we will not be able to get to Siem Riep on time. -- Yeung hyte doj chia mun baan teuh [lit: "We seem not able to get to..."] Siem Riep twon peyr va'leea.; only if -- luke tra tai; in sense of after, or when, s. th., which is probably going to occur, does occur -- ot pi: If he goes, they will be safe. -- Ot pi gwat teuh, pooh'gkay nung keuh chia sok.

ignore v. tveu praw'ngeui; tveu peuh mun dung

ill adj. chh'ooh

illegal adj. koh ch'bop

illiterate adj. mun jcheh an

illness n. chh'ooh; chuum'ngeu; rohk: What's wrong with him? -- Gwat kaut rohk eye? (lit: he got what illness?)

illusion n. optical illusion -- kaa chhpih pn'aae'k; ro'veu ro'vee'aae; false appearance -- sraw pich sraw pul; optimistic but false belief -- kaa sa'mye; yul chra'lom: He had no illusions about that girl. -- Gwat k'mium yul chra'lom om'pee sraae nu tay.

imagine v. sruh'mao, sr'm'eye: He imagines that he will be king again. -- Gwat sruh'mao, sr'm'eye tha nung klai chia s'dot m'dong tee'it.

imitate v. traahp taam; tveu taam

immature adj. chia k'mayng

immediately adv. chia bun twon; eye laeou ni

immigrant n. prachee'chuun mok pi...: American immigrants in Australia -- prachee'chuun mok pi Americaa teuh Australie; (formal term -- chuun un'tauw'praw'veh(s)); refugee -- chuun pieh kloo'an

immigration n. kaa chuun un'tauw praw'veh(s)

impartial adj. mun reu' muk; (lit: "does not choose by face")

impatient adj. mun ot'tuun; mun ot'tro'um; tro'um mun baan: I cannot be patient anymore. -- Kyom mun adje ot'tro'um tee'it baan tay.

imperialism n. cheh'ka'po'a(t)'ni'yum

imperialist n. neh cheh'ka'po'a(t)

important adj. sum'kahn; in sense of necessary --   jcham'batch

impose v. inconvenience -- bun kum: I hate to impose on you, but would you have this paper copied? -- Kyom mun jchong bun kum neh tay, pun'ta'aae neh adje copee kra'dah ni, baan tay?; force to -- bum kum; or, dah(k): The government imposed [a new tax] on the people. -- Ratt'a'pi'bal dah(k) [pwun tmaee] noeh leuh pra'chee'chuun.; impose views, seek to have its own way -- baah bauw; The minority wanted to impose its views. -- Chuun pieh tic jchong baah bauw.

Impossible! xcl. Absolutely not -- Mun kaa tay!

imprison v. baan jchaap... k'nong pwun ta'neea keea; dah(k) cooo'k

improve v. kron'ba(r) chiang ni: The economy should improve next year. -- Set'a'kej koo'a tai kron'ba(r) chiang ni chh'nam krow'ee.; to make s. th. better -- tveu owi praw'sar laung ("praw'sar chiang" = "better"): The government [should] improve the roads. -- Ratt'a'pi'bal [koo'a tai] tveu ploe owi praw'sar laung.

in- prefix of negation -- a': justice -- yoo'teh'toa/ injustice -- a'yoo'teh'toa

in prp. located in -- k'nong; noeh k'nong: Khmer people (living) in Phnom Penh... -- Pra'chee'chuun Khmei noeh k'nong Phnom Penh...; in the provinces -- k'nong kyte; ice in my drink -- t'kaw k'nong p'es'cheeh' ro'bah kyom; by means of -- k'nong: Speak to me in Khmer. -- Niyaye chi'moi kyom k'nong pee'esa Khmei.; in a certain manner -- chia: He did it in secret. -- Gwat tveu veea chia ngo ngut.; Speak to me in English. -- Ni'yaye chi'moi kyom chia pee'esa Aw'nglay.; in one way or another -- noeh k'nong ploe moi; in which -- dael

in a hurry adv. tai'n'tai; praw'nyab

in a moment adv. k'nong baan tic tee'it

in order prp. taam ro'bee'up: Please put the files in order. -- Sum dah(k) sum'num ru'ung taam ro'bee'up.

in order to (do s. th.) prp. sum'rap (AP: sam'rap, sum'rup)

in order to (get s. th.) prp. dum'bye

incense n. tooh(b)

including adv. rop bun jchole te'ang: Everyone, including me, has to learn Khmer. -- Kroop ka'neea, rop bun jchole te'ang kyom, tro tai rian pee'esa Khmei.

income n. earnings -- praa(k) jchum'nole; praa(k) ro'k baan; kum'r'eye: income distribution -- kum'r'eye noeh k'nong praw'tet

increase v. daum laung; ree'k jchum raan

independence n. eyke ree'ech pheap

Independence Monument (in Phnom Penh) n.   Vik'mee'en Eyke Ree'ech

independent adj. i'ssa'ra(k)

Indian n. person form India klung; member of native or aboriginal group -- pnong

industry n. oo'sa'ha'kaam

inexpensive adj. tauk

infantry n.   thwap t'mal cheung; (NB: t'mal cheung = walk); tee'hee'an cheung kok; (NB: kok = daiy = land, earth)

infatuated adj.   baan sra'laanyh

infect v. tveu owi kla'ee

infection n.   chuum'ngeu: [The cause of] the infection [was] drinking dirty water.   -- [Mool'hyte ney] chuum'ngeu [baan dael mok pi] nyam tuk kraw'kwa.; kla'ee: ring-worm infection -- dum'bow kla'ee; malaria infection -- kruun jchanyh: Mosquitoes carry malaria. (lit: Mosquitoes give and have the illness of malaria) -- Moo baan dael owi miun chuum'ngeu kruun jchanyh.

infiltrate v. jchole ch'ree'it ch'rey't: infiltrate a village -- jchole ch'ree'it ch'rey't phum

inflammable adj.   simply burnable -- chheh: Trees are inflammable. -- daum cheu chheh.; particularly inflammable -- chhop chheh: Paper is inflammable. -- Kra'dah chhop chheh; highly inflammable, combustible -- chhop chheh ngi'yaye sroul: Gasoline is highly inflammable. -- Praeng'sang chhop chheh ngi'yaye sroul.

inflation n. kaa laung tlai; dum'lye tlai

influence n. a'ti'pul: He [got his job] through influence. -- Gwat [baan kej kaa tveu] dowee sa a'ti'pul.; kaa bun jchih bun jchile; kaa tek tee'eng; to have influence -- miun tuk mwot pr'eye (lit: to have salty saliva)

influence v. bun jchoh bun jchole; tek tieng: China cannot influence the Khmer Rouge very much. -- Chun mun adje bun jchoh bun jchole Khmei Kra'hom baan ch'raan.; use influence -- banyh jchenyh mok mwot (lit: let one's mouth loose); jchum runyh owi

influenza n.   pa'da'sye

informal adj. twa'ma'da

information n. generally -- dum'nung; saa; news -- por'da'mee'an; data -- kum'not

inform v. prap (lit: tell)

informer n. chia raw noo'k: He was an [inside] informer for the government. -- Gwat keuh chia raw noo'k [k'nong] ro'bah ratt'a'pi'bal.

-ing gerund. kom'puung: I am eating. -- Kyom nyam kom'puung tai.; (NB: kom'puung is <u>not</u> used with "baan" to make a past continuous; thus, "I was eating" is "Kyom baan nyam."); kaa: Singing is fun. -- Kaa jchum'ree'ung keuh s'bai.

ingenious adj. pra(ch); (NB: genius -- neh pra(ch))

ingenuity n. kaa praw'ngya

ingredient n. kreung

inhabit v. rooh noeh

inhabitant n. neh rooh noeh

inhale v. k'seuwt

inherit v. to'tool mo'ra'da(k); inherit a position -- to'tool dum'nye'nyh

inheritance n. gkay mo'ra'da(k); or gkay: an inheritance (from my) mother -- gkay m'dye kyom

inhumane adj. a' ma'nooh to'h (lit: a person not good)

inhumanity n. a' ma'nooh to'h

initiate v. p'dam

inject v. jchak t'nam

injection n. kaa jchak...: of medicine -- kaa jchak t'nam

injure v. tveu owi ro'booh

injured pp. tro ro'booh; ro'booh; chh'ooh

injury n.   ro'booh: head injury -- ro'booh pah pwoil doll koo'k'bal

injustice n.   a'yoo'teh'toa; pheap a'yoo'teh'toa

ink n.   tuk k'mau; (lit: black liquid)

in-law n.   saah tlai: older brother-in-law -- bong tlai proh; younger brother-in law -- pa'own tlai proh

inmate n.   neh cho'up cooo'k

inner-tube n.   poo'ah vee'in kong

inoculate v.   jchak t'nam

in order to prp.   dum'bye; sum'rap

innocent adj.   literally, as in legal or moral sense -- sek'cha'rut; re frame of mind (lit: without bad [intentions]) -- k'miun [bum'nong] a'krah; specifically legally not guilty -- ot koh; or, mun baan praw'pret doj peea gkay jchowt: The judge found him innocent. (lit: that he did not [commit] what he was accused of). -- jchao krum rok keunyh tha gwat mun baan [praw'pret] doj pee'a gkay jchowt [accused].; naive -- chhaut: innocent girl -- k'mayng sraae chhaut; (NB: accuse = jchowt, naive = chhaut; different Khmer spelling, similar pronunciation)

inquire v.   soo'a

inquiry n.   sum'nom pau

insane adj.   ch'koo'it

inscribe v.   jcha(r)

inscription n.   a'saw jcha(r)'ruk; (a'saw = writing)

insect n.   saat la'utt (lit: small animal); (NB: Examples of oft-encountered Cambodian insects are a) the small, large-winged type that swarms around light bulbs and other light sources after rains (the "mo'mee'ech") and b) a larger type that appears before rains and so is regarded as something of a predictor (the "may plee'eng" or, "rainmaster".)

insecticide n.   t'nam bun plyng saat la'utt

insecurity n.   a' sun'tek'sok

insert v.   saw'see'it

inside prp.   kang k'nong; k'nong; noeh k'nong

insignia n.   kreung a'sara yoo'h

insignificant adj.   to'ich ta(ch)

insincere adj.   puuht; ot sm'oh; mun piht

insinuate v.   dah(k) pl'eye; ni'yaye bun chee'ung; dee'um daum; saw see'it sum dai

insinuation n.   pl'eye p'kaa; kaa saaw see'it sum da'aee; kaa ni'yaye bun chee'ung; kaa dee'um daum

insist v.   to'too'ich; ruhm lope

insistent adj.   to'too'ich

insistently adv.   ch'rum dael ch'rum dael

insolent adj.   praw'heun; tl'aamh ree'(k) (lit: enlarged liver); jchet thum (lit: big heart)

insomnia n.   kaa daeyk mun looh

inspect v.   chai'ch chaye; pee'nit chai'ch chaye; tru'ut pee'nit: They will inspect [the luggage] at the airport. -- Pooh'gkay nung pee'nit chai'ch chaye [va'leez] noeh airport.; They will inspect the luggage at the border. -- Pooh'gkay nung pee'nit chai'ch chaye [aye'von ney dum'narr] noeh tul'dyne [or, noeh chee dyne].; meulh kaa kaw tro

inspector (police) n.   a'ti'kaa

instal v.   put in place, as equipment -- dah(k); or, ree'up dah(k)); instal wiring -- dah(k) k'sye; put in power -- bun taup: Some people [claim that] the Heng Samrin government was installed by the government of Vietnam. -- Ma'nooh klaah [praw'kas tha] ratt'a'pi'bal Heng Samrin tro baan bun taup dow'ee ratt'a'pi'bal praw'tet Vietnam.

instalation n.   of a machine or appliance -- kaa dah(k); kaa tang noeh; of an officer or official -- kaa praw'kul dum'nye'nyh; military facility -- ti tang; mool'a'tan kawng thaawp

instance n. dong; leuk: There have been many instances in which [the ceasefire] was broken. -- Miun ch'raan dong (or leuk) dael [kaa bun choop banyh ka'neea] tro baan pa'ra'chey.; for instance -- oo'tee'a'haw

instant n. pech (lit: blink of an eye)

instantly adv. ruhm pech nu

instead of prp. chuum'noo(s): You go instead of me. -- Neh teuh chuum'noo(s) kyom.; beer instead of Coke -- beer chuum'noo(s) Coke; venyh: I don't [want] Coke; I want [beer] instead. -- Kyom mun [jchong baan] Coke tay; kyom jchong baan [bee'a] venyh.

instigate v. nyeu'h nyeuu (AP: nyooh nyoo)

institute n. vi'chee'a taan

instruct v. bung rian; bung haht; bung haht bung hanyh

instruction n. kaa bung haht; kaa bung hanyh; kaa nye no'um s'kd'eye bung hanyh; s'kd'eye nye no'um

instruments n. musical -- krueng plaeng; medical/scientific -- sum pee'reh'peyt

insubordinate adj. rung taw'tung

insufficient adj. steu; mun kroop kroo'un

insult v. tveu owi... k'mah: He insulted me. -- Gwat tveu owi kyom k'mah.; curse -- jcheyr; bun jchao

insurance n. kaa tee'nee'a rap'rong; ("tee'nee'a" and "rap'rong" each means "to take responsibility")

insurgent n. neh baah b'ow; oo'tee'em; neh bong kaut jcha'la'jchaw (lit: s. o. who creates chaos)

intellectual adj. che'he'dung: an intellectual society -- sung'kuum che'he'dung

intellectual n. pun'ya'vwun: He is an intellectual. -- Gwat pun'ya'vwun.; ma'nooh ch'laat; or ma'nooh ch'laat vaae; He is an intellectual but I still think he's silly. -- Gwat chia ma'nooh miun pun'ya'vwun pun'ta'aae kyon noeh tai kut tha gwat plee pleu.

intelligence n. intellectual capability -- praw'ngya; confidential information -- kaa sum'ngyut

intelligent adj. ch'laat; poo'k'eye

intend v. pun pong; miun kohl bum'nong

intention n. kaa pun pong; kohl bum' nong; or, bum'nong: I have only bad intentions! -- Kyom miun tai bum'nong a'krah pun'noh.

intentional adj. dow'ee chaye'tun'a

inter- prefix. un'ta'ra (AP: un'tra')

intercept v. scutt ploe

intercourse n. generally -- say'veh'na'tik; sexual intercourse (more used in writing than speech) -- say ma' may'tuun

interest n. concern with s. th. -- kaa jchum'nole jchet: One of my interests is tennis. -- Moi ney kaa jchum'nole jchet ro'bah kyom keuh te'nnit.; kaa jchole jchet: The French have an interest in [restoring] Angkor Wat. -- Saah ba'raang miun kaa jchole jchet [choo'ah chul] Angkor Wat.; jchole jchet (verb form) -- I have no interest in going. -- Kyom mun jchole jchet teuh. (lit: I don't want to go.); on a deposit -- jchong kaa; praa(k) kaa

interest v. teh tee'eny jchet: This picture interests me a lot. -- Roob'pheap ni teh tee'eny jchet kyom yang klang.; teh jchet: It doesn't interest me. -- Veea mun teh jchet kyom tay.; tveu owi jchole jchet: It doesn't interest me. -- Veea ot tveu owi kyom jchole jchet tay.

interested (in) adj. jchaap a'ro'um ( ): I am very interested in it. -- Kyom jchaap a'ro'um veea yang klang.; jchaap a'ro'um (teuh leuh): I am interested in education. -- Kyom jchaap a'ru'om teuh leuh kaa suk'saa.; jchaap a'ro'um (jchum'poo'h): I am interested in the question of [population growth] in Cambodia. -- Kyom jchaap a'ro'um jchum'poo'h [kaa ree'k jchum'raan ney jchum'noo'an prachee'chuun] Khmei.; miun kaa jchaap a'ro'um (jchum'poo'h; or, noeh k'nong; or k'nong): I am interested in [the case, or story, of] Cambodia. -- Kyom miun kaa jchaap a'ro'um jchum'poo'h [ru'ung] sruk Khmei.; jchaap jchet (noeh k'nong): I am interested in [helping refugees] in Cambodia. -- Kyom jchaap jchet noeh k'nong [kaa choo'ay chuun pieh kloo'an] noeh k'nong Kampuchea.

interesting adj. koo'a owi jchaap a'rom (lit: to be, seem or feel interesting): an interesting [experience] -- [kaa pi'sowt] koo'a owi jchaap a'rom; to be interesting -- tveu owi miun kaa teh jchet: Angkor Wat is interesting to many foreigners. -- Angkor Wat tveu owi miun kaa teh jchet pi chuun bor'tay pleh ch'raan.

interfere v. ruhm kaan; cha'ree'it cha'raek

interference n. kaa bok lok; kaa ch'ree'it chr'aek

integrity n. bor'na'pheap

inter-marry v. kaa ka'neea einye

intermediary n. an'yah kan'dal

intermediate adj. mut'syo'm

intermission n. kaa sum'raak; kaa p'a(k)

intermittent adj. da(ch) da(ch); yeut yeut m'dong

intermittently adv. [ ] chope [ ] chope: fire intermittently -- banyh chope banyh chope

internal adj. kang k'nong; generally only with reference to human body -- p'tay k'nong

international adj. un'tra'chee'it: international airport -- chuum'naut yun hawh untracheeit

interpret v. baw(k) pr'eye

interpreter n. neah baw(k) pr'eye

interrogate v. soo'a jchum'la'wee

interrupt v. ni'yaye kat

intersection n. ploe' choop ka'neea; ploe' k'vyne; cunlye'ng kaat ka'neea

intertwined adj. ro'mool

interval n. ro'yee't; ro'vieng; jchun'lawh; specifically of time -- peyr va'leea; or, ree'yeh peyr

intervene v. tveu an'ta'ra'kuum; owi... chia an'yah kan'dal: They [want] [the U. N.] to intervene in Cambodia. -- Pooh'gkay [sum owi or jchong baan] [Ong'kha Sa'ha Praw'cheea'chee'it] chia an'yah kan'dal Kampuchea. (NB: owi...chia an'yah kan'dal can also mean to be "in the middle of s. th.", as "get caught in the middle")

intervention n. un'tra'kuum

interview v. sum'pee'a

interview n. kaa sum'pee'a: Sihanouk gave an interview to the reporters. -- Sihanouk pdull kaa sum'pee'a owi teuh neh ka'ssett.

intestine n. poo'ah vee'in

intimate adj. snut snaal; jchet snut

intimidate v. kum'ny'ow'inyh; kum'haeng; kum'ree'em

into prp. teuh k'nong: He went into the house. -- Gwat teuh k'nong ptay'a.; He went into the army. -- Gwat jchole ru'um chi'moi kawng thwaap.; chia: Please [translate] this into English. -- Sum [baw(k) pr'eye] ni chia pee'esa Aw'nglay.; He has [turned] into a "nut". -- Gwat [pr'eye] chia plee pleu.

intrigue n. a plan against s. o. -- pyne'kaa praw'chang; or, l'batch kal praw'chang; (mystery -- chia kaa a'kro'bong: It is a mystery how he died. -- Hyte dael gwat slop chia kaa a'kro'bong.)

intrigue (against) v. tveu l'batch kal (praw'chang)

intriguing adj. kooa jchaap a'rom

introduce v. noo'um owi scwal

invade v. ree'ut ta'baa(t)

invalid adj. not true -- mun piht; mun tro; not (duely) authorized -- mun a'noo'naaht

inventory n. ro'bah k'nong bun'chee

inventory v. sa'reu'

invest v. in a business -- tveu vi'ni'yok; invest in the future -- krayp jchin'jchoo'a jchum'poo'h ah'na'kuut

investigate v. ong'kay't; seup ong'kay't

investment n. vi'ni'yok

invitation n. sum'buht un'cheunyh

invite v. un'cheunyh: call -- haow

invoice n. vik'eye ja'bot; bung'kaan dai

involve v. jchole ru'um

involved pp. praw'loke; get involved -- praw'loke praw'la(k)

in which adv. dael: ...the way in which the ceasefire was broken... -- ...ploe dael chope banyh tro baan bum pee'an...

iris n. of eye -- praw sr'eye pn'aae'k

iron n. for smoothing clothes -- chanang oot; the mineral -- dyke; (NB: steel = dyke taiyp)

iron v. clothes -- oot kow-aow

ironic adj. paep'che'ree'aae; koo'a owi chum'lyke nah; koo'a owi a'ka'sawl

irrigation n. kaa bun jchole tuk: rice field irrigation -- kaa bun jchole tuk k'nong sr'eye

irrigate v. bun jchole tuk

irritate v. tveu owi jchaap khung; tveu owi khung

is v. commonly expressed via five following constructions:

Gwat [keuh chia] ma'nooh la'aw.　　　-- He [is] a good man.
Gwat [keuh] ma'nooh la'aw.　　　-- He [is] a good man.
Gwat [chia] ma'nooh la'aw.　　　-- He [is] a good man.
Gwat [　] la'aw.　　　-- He [is] good.
[　] La'aw.　　　-- (How is he?) [He is] good.

Other examples: keuh: She is a member. -- Nee'eng keuh sa'ma'chit.; keuh chia: He is a teacher. -- Gwat keuh chia neh kruu.; is (in sense of location) -- noeh: It is in Po'sat. -- Veea noeh Po'sat.; Angkor Wat is in Siem Riep. -- Angkor Wat noeh k'nong Siem Riep.; in sense of, is it that -- dael: What book is it that you want? -- S'po aae dael neh jchong?; Is it? -- Man' tay?; Isn't it? -- Man tay? or, Baan tay?; Is that so? -- Man roo aae?; remains in, continues to be in, esp. re machinery -- tut: That car is in bad [condition]. -- Laan nu tut [leh ka'nak] a'krah.

Islam n. I'sa'laam

island n. kawh

isolate v. separate fr. s. th. or s. o. else -- bum byke

isolation n. condition of being far from other things/ people -- noeh chng'eye dach tai eiyne; condition of being separated from other things/people, whether far away or not -- kaa bum byke; alone, by onesself -- noeh ma'neh eiyne

issue n. chuum nutch ru'ung; kaam va'toh; make an issue of -- yok tveu chia thum

issue v. jchenyh owi: The Foreign Ministry issued [a statement] about [the negotiations] in Bangkok. -- Kra'soo'ung Kaa Bor'tay jchenyh owi noeh [kaa ta'lye'ng] om'pee [kaa jchaw jchaa(r)] noeh ti krong Bangkok.

it prn. vee'a: I regret very much that it is not clear. -- Kyom sauk'dye na' dow'ee veea mun ch'bah.; I think it will rain. -- Kyom kut tha veea nung plee'eng.; a': Say it faster. -- Taa a' nyope chiang.; [unstated]: It's up to you. -- Taam neh jchole jchet. (lit: according to (what) you like); [unstated]: I found it. -- Kyom rok keunyh [　] baan howi.

it's prn. + v. veea keuh: It's a nice day. -- Veea keuh t'ngai la'aw.; vee'a keuh chia: It's no good. -- Veea keuh a'krah.; or, Veea keuh chia kaa a'krah.; [unstated]: It's time now. -- Doll mok howi. (lit: the hour has arrived); It's noisy. -- Veea [　] oo'aa nah.; It's too bad that... -- Veea [　] ot la'aw tha... tay.

itch v. ro'mwah: My leg itches. -- Cheung kyom ro'mwah.

itchy adj. ro'mwah

ivory n. pluu'k: ivory bracelet -- kawng pluu'k

-ization suffix. 'u'pa'naya'kaam: liberalization -- se'rei'pheap u'pa'naya'kaam; Vietnamization -- Vietnam 'u'pa'naya'kaam

J

jack n. for car -- dai kree'k

jack fruit n. plai k'nau

jacket n. aow yah'ket; aow thum

jade n. t'maa(r) joo(k)

jail n. cooo'k: T-3 Jail in Phnom Pehn -- Cooo'k Tay-Bye noeh k'nong Phnom Penh; go to jail -- tueh cooo'k

jail v. put (or, "throw") in jail -- dah(k) k'nong cooo'k: Put him in jail. -- Dah cooo'k veea teuh.

jailed adj. imprisoned -- baan jchaap: The French imprisoned Lok Achar Swaa. -- Ba'raang baan jchaap Lok Achar Svaa dah(k) k'nong pwun ta'neea keea.; (NB: Lok Achar Swaa was a hero of World-War-II-era Khmer anti-French resistance.)

jam n. dum'nop

January n. Mak'ka'ra

Japan n. Yi'p'pun

Japanese adj. chia Yi'p'pun; Yi'p'pun: Japanese Embassy -- S'tahn'toot Yi'p'pun

Japanese n. pee'esa Yi'p'pun

jar n. small clay jar -- k'raw tun; large clay jar -- pee'ung; glass jar -- kaae'oo [also means "drinking glass"]

jasmine n. p'ka ma'lee

jaundice n. chuum'ngeu kaut leu'ung (lit: illness of becoming yellow)

jaw n. tkee'im

jealous adj. ch'rawn'nyne

jerk v. kun'tra(k); kraw'vwot

jerry can n. tuung

Jesus Christ n. preah Yaye'soo

jet (plane) n. yun hawh jet

jewelry n. kreung a' lung'kaa; (NB: gem or stone = t'bong (AP: t'bo'ng))

job n. kaa'ngyeea; tveu kaa ngyeaa; mok'ngyeea: What's your job? (or, What do you do?) -- Miun mok'ngyeea chia a'veye?; kej kaa tveu; kej kaa: Cambodia needs businesses [that create] jobs. -- Kampuchea tro kaa chuum'noo'inyh [dael adje bung kaut owi miun] kej kaa.; There are no jobs available. -- Ot miun kej kaa ni tay.

join v. an organization, group, etc. -- jchole ru'um chi'moi: He joined Sihanouk's [party]. -- Gwat jchole ru'um chi'moi [krum or pooh or ka'na'pac] Sihanoo'.; get together with -- jchole ru'um chi'moi: I joined them in the dining room. -- Kyom jchole ru'um chi'moi pooh'gkay neoh ban'tope nyam bye.; meet -- choop (AP: choo'up): Join you later! -- Choop ka'neea peyr krow'ee.; join together, join one to another -- bun jchole ka'neea; become a part of -- jchole ru'um: I want to join that club. -- Kyom jchole jchet jchole ru'um chi'moi club nu.; be connected -- p'choop: The towns of Po'sat and Moung are joined by National Highway Number Five. -- Krong Po'sat nung krong Moung p'choop ka'neea dow'ee Ploe Chee'it layke prum.; join in, be involved in -- praw'lok; be involved in a fight -- praw'lok chi'moi jchum'looh; poo'ut ka'neea: join in an effort to... -- poo'ut ka'neea dum'bye...

joint n. dum'naw

joist n. ro' noot

joke n. kaa cum'plyng; cum'plyng: I like jokes. -- Kyom jchole jchet cum'plyng. or, Kyom jchole jchet kaa cum'plyng.; kaa ni'yaye leng; corny joke -- cum'plyng saa'b

joke v. ni'yaye leng

journalist n. neh ka'sett

journey n. kaa tveu dum'narr; make a journey, travel -- tveu dum'narr

judge n. jchao krum: Who is the judge in this [court]? -- Neh na chia jchao krum noeh k'nong [to'la'ka] ni?; neh kaat kd'eye

judge v. make a decision -- vi'ni'ch'eye:

judgement n. informal, non-official, possibly uninformed -- kaa kaat kd'eye; of court -- kaat s'kd'eye; decision -- kaa vi'ni'ch'eye

judiciary n. ni'teh praw'ni'bot

juice n. tuk: apple juice -- tuk plai pomme; orange juice -- tuk krau'itch Po'sat

July n. Ka'ka'da

jump v. lote: The frog jumped into the net. -- Kum kype lote jchole sum'nanyh.; jump over -- plong: jump over a ditch -- plong praw'lye; cross over or skip -- ruhm long

June n. Mit'to'na

jungle n. prey; "the bush" -- prey la'bot; or, prey ro'nee'um

junior adj. a'noo' (also means "deputy" or "second"); saah to'ich

junior high school n. a'nook vichia'lye

jurisprudence n. ni'teh'saa

jury n. ong vi'ni'ch'eye; neh vi'ni'ch'eye

just v. teup tai: I just came from Phnom Penh. -- Kyom teup tai mok pi Phnom Penh.; They just came back. -- Pooh'gkay teup tai mok venyh.; I just finished [drinking] my coffee. -- Kyom teup tai [puk] cafe howi.

just adv. only -- kron tai (AP: kro'an tai): Just copy what he's doing. -- Kron tai tveu taam a'veye dael gwat tveu.; I just made a joke. -- Kyom kron tai ni'yaye leng tay tha.; just at that time -- noeh peyr nu; just for -- sum'rap tai... pun'noh: This information is just for you. -- Por'da'mee'an ni sum'rap tai neh pun'noh.; This price is just for you. -- Dum'lye ni sum'rap tai neh pun'noh.; just for -- trum tai... pun'noh: This price is just for [six days]. -- Dum'lye ni trum tai [pra'moi t'ngai] pun'noh.; just for -- pun'noh: I'll do it just for you. -- Kyom nung tveu veea sum'rap neh pun'noh.

Just a minute. xcl. Jcham moi plet.; Jcham moi nee'a'tee.

justice n. yoo'teh'toa: Ministry of Justice -- Kra'soo'ung Yoo'teh'toa

justify v. tveu owi trum tro noeh; kai dum'rong noeh: How do you justify his [behavior]? -- Tau(v) neh kai dum'rong noeh [a'kup'a'kay'ree'ya] ro'bah gwat dow'ee ro'bee'up na?

jut v. peuh'ng

juvenile adj. k'mayng ko'ma; (ko'ma = young)

K

kale n. kat'nah

karma n. kaam

karate n. ka'ra'tay

keep v. prevent from doing/being s. th. -- kum owi: We must keep them from becoming afraid. -- Yeung tro tveu kum owi pooh'gkay klait(ch).; prevent from doing/being s. th. -- ke'ang... kum owi: Keep them from coming in. -- Ke'ang pooh'gkay kum owi jchole k'nong.; confine -- kum'kro'ng: keep in jail -- kum kro'ng k'nong cooo'k; retain, hold temporarily -- tooo'k: Would you keep this for me until next week? -- Sum neh tooo'k ro'bah ni owi kyom ro'hote a'tthit krow'ee?; keep temporarily -- p'nya(r): Can you keep this watch for me (temporarily)? -- Tau(v) neh adje p'nyah nee'a'li'ka ni, baan tay?; take/retain permanently -- yok teuh: I want you to keep this (i.e., for your own, for ever). -- Sum yok teuh. (lit: take this); continue to do s. th. -- noeh tai: IMF and UNDP keep ignoring the population problem. -- IMF howi nung World Bank noeh tai tveu praw'ngeui pun'ha chuum'noo'an pra'chee'chuun.

keep on v. noeh tai

Keep out! excl. Kum jchole! (lit: Do not enter!)

keep out of sight v. bot pi muk pi mwot; tooo'k owi ch'ng'eye pi pn'eye'k; leh tooo'k

keep out of trouble v. kum owi miun pun'ha

keep quiet (about) v. owi sngy'at: We better keep quiet about that. -- Yeung tro owi sngy'at ru'ung nu.; leh tooo'k kaa sum'ngut

keep a promise v. toook kaa sun'nyaa

keep a secret v. kum prap neh na

keep up with v. komk prung owi twon

kerosene n. praeng kaat

kettle n. kum'see'oo

key adj. som'kahn bom'pot

key n. gkon sauw; key hole -- rawn sauw; (NB: lock (n.) = sauw or may sauw; lock (v.) = jchak sauw; seal (i.e., to close a ballot or safe deposit box) = sauw)

Khmer adj. khmei

Khmerization n. Khmei ru'pa'naya'kaam

Khmer dancing n. rohm Khmei or ro'bahm Khmei

kick v. kick with toe or instep, as in kicking a ball -- to'at: kick out -- to'at jchowl; or, denyh jchenyh; play soccer -- to'at bal (the game of soccer -- bal to'at); kick with the bottom or ball of the foot, as in tae'kwon do -- tae'h

kid n. child, polite -- pa'own; child, typical -- gkon k'mayng; form of address for child: gkon: Kid, c'mere! -- Gkon, gkon, mok ni!

kidnap v. puung'ruht

kidneys n. dum'rong no'me

kill v. sum'lap; tveu kee'it; praw'haa; praw'lie

killing n. kaa sum'lap, kaa tveu kee'it

kiln n. laaw

kilogram n. kee'lo'gram

kilometer n. kee'lo'met

kind adj. jchet la'aw: You are kind to Raj but not to me! -- Lok sraae jchet la'aw jchum'poo'h Raj pun'ta'aae ot jchet la'aw jchum'poo'h kyom tay.

kind n. praw'pet: What kind [of thing] is this? -- Ni chia praw'pet a'veye?; What kind of food do they have here? -- Ma'hope praw'pet na dael miun noeh ti ni?; klaah: Buy me some kind of beer. -- Tinh beer owi kyom klaah.; what kind -- aae klaah (AP: eye klaah): What kind of [work do you do]? -- [Tveu] eye klaah?; what kind -- na [ ] (lit: what; "kind" is implied only): What kind of books do you read? -- S'po na [ ] dael neh an?; re people specifically -- jchum'poo'h: What kind of people do you like? -- Ma'nooh jchum'poo'h na dael neh jchole jchet?; all kinds -- kroop bai kroop yang

kindness n. twa'sub'rahw

king n. s'dach

kingdom n. ree'ech sumbaat; ree'ech chia na'jcha

kinky adj. kun'dye'ngyh; kraw'ngyh

kiss v. tope: She wants to kiss you. -- Ne'eng jchole jchet tope own.

kitchen n. cunlye'ng (AP: kalyne, kunlye) ree'up ma'hope (lit: place to prepare food); cunlye'ng tveu ma'hope; ban'tope tveu ma'hope

kitten n. gkon ch'maa

knee n. k'bal cheung kong

kneel v. bawt cheung kong

knife n. kum'but: stab with a knife -- jchak chi'moi kum'but; penknife -- kum'but bawt (NB: bawt = "folding")

knock v. kuuh: knock on a door -- kuuh t'veea; kowk: knock s. o. on the head -- kowk k'bal

knock down v. ruuh: knock down a wall -- ruuh chuun chee'ung; bun luum; kum'tic: knock down an old house -- kum'tic ptay'a jchaah

knock over v. kraw'puub

knot n. jchum'nong; dum'naw (same word as for "joint")

know v. how to do s. th. -- jcheh: I don't know Khmei very well. -- Kyom mun seou jcheh Khmei.; have knowledge of, know s. th. -- dung: Q(: Where did he go? A:) (I) don't know. -- (Kyom) ot dung tay.; Kyom ot dung.; or Ot dung!; be acquainted with, be familiar with, have met -- scwaal

knowledge n. chum'neh; vi'chi'a

knowledgible adj. jcheh

kow-tow v. tv'eye bung kum

L

labor adj. labor union -- ka'ma'ka sa'ha'chee'it; labor problems -- pun'ha ch'nool tveu

labor n. work -- kaa'ngyeea; hard labor -- kaa t'ngun; Ministry of Labor -- Kra'soo'ung Kaa'Ngyeea; the labor force, people who work -- ch'nool tveu; capital and labor -- praa(k) nung ch'nool tveu

laboratory n. mun'ti pi'sowt

laborer n. in a factory -- kama'koh

lack v. kwah kaat: We lack food. -- Yeung kwah kaat ma'hope jchum'naee.

ladder n. chun daar

ladies n. neh sraae; lok sraae

Ladies and gentlemen... intro. Usual Khmer introduction is not a direct translation of "Ladies and Gentlemen" but rather is "Lok, lok sraae, [nee'eng ken'yaa]", meaning "gentlemen, ladies, [young ladies]...".; Even though "nee'eng" can refer to boys ten-or-so and under, in this introductory phrase, "nee'eng ken'yaa" is a single, unified term meaning "young lady."

ladle n. vay(k)

lady n. sraae (AP: "srei", mid-way between long-A sound of "sraae" and long-I sound of "sreye"); see, also, discussion of terms for "Miss" and Mrs." under those two headings.

lady of the night n. street-wise, liberated girl; slightly derogatory -- sraae neh leng; (NB: leng = play; hence, lit: play girl); bar girl -- sraae p'es'cheeh' (NB: drinks = p'es'cheeh' or, AP:, put'sra); neri ree'a'trei chaahw (lit: woman who walks at night); nee'eng raw'see yoop (lit: woman who does business at night)

laity n. kro' haw

lake n. tun'lay (also means "river")

lamb n. chee'um

lamb meat n. sat(ch) chee'um

lame adj. k'chowee(ch) cheung

lamp n. chung kee'ung

lance n. lum'aeng

land n. daiy: dry land -- daiy ko'k; barren land -- daiy k'sawh; or daiy ot chee chee'it; plateau -- daiy tool; (written form: praw'tet'pee); low lands -- daiy tuum nee'up

landlady n. me'cha ptay'a sraae

landing (riverbank/riverside, for boats) n. kom'puung; (term used in Cambodian provincial names Kom'puung Thom, Kom'puung Cham, Kom'puung Chhn'ang and Kom'puung Speu, usually rendered in Roman script, for example on maps, as "kompong"; the term is rendered here as "kom'puung" to make clear the difference in pronunciation between it and "kum'pong", the word for container or tin can).

landing field n. veal chuum'naut

landlord n. me'cha ptay'a

landscape n. teh'sa'peap

language n. pee'esa (AP: pee'sa): foreign language -- pee'esa bor'tay; the Khmer language -- pee'esa Khmei; written Khmer language -- pee'esa a'saw Khmei; modern language -- chi'vut pee'esa; slang -- (referring to a single word) -- ch'leu'ee; slang referring to the body of slang words collectively) -- pee'esa ch'leu'ee (lit: slang language)

language study n. suk'sah pee'esa

Lao adj. Lee'u

Laos n. sruk Lee'u; praw'tet Lee'u

Laotian (person) n. saah Lee'u

Laotian adj. of Laotian nationality -- chuun'chee'lt Lee'u; Laotian style -- chia Lee'u

lap n. ploe (same word as for thigh and road); sit on s. o.'s lap -- ung'koi leuh ploe; (for lap (not for road), the formal term is k'ploe; most commonly used is ploe)

large adj. thum

larger adj. thum chiang: My house is bigger than your house. -- Ptay'a kyom thum chiang ptay'a neh.; treus chiang (used primarily re fruits): These oranges are bigger than [those]. -- Krau'itch ni treus chiang [a'nu].

last adj. most recently past -- muun: last year -- chh'nam muun; last week -- a'ttith muun; most recently past, only in phrase "last night" -- munyh: last night -- yoop munyh; most recently past -- teuh: last year -- chh'nam teuh; most recently past -- kun laung mok ni; or, jchong krow'ee ni: during the last rainy season -- noeh ro'doe t'leh plee'eng kun'lung mok ni; or, noeh ro'doe t'leh plee'eng jchong krow'ee ni; final, occuring after all others -- krow'ee gkay bung'awh; or, jchong krow'ee; or, jchong bun jchawp; last remaining -- a sahl(t) moi: I got the last one int h estore. -- Kyom yok baan a sahl(t) moi noeh haang.; at last -- jchong krow'ee bom'pot: At last we meet! -- Jchong krow'ee bom'pot yeung choop!

last name n. family name -- ko't ta'nee'um; nee'um tro kohl

lasting adj. chia yeut: The smell of [her perfume] had a lasting effect. -- Klen [tuk op nee'eng] miun prut'ti'bat chia yeut.; cho'op: long lasting -- cho'op baan yeut

latch n. kun'luuh

late adv. not on time -- yeut (AP: yeu'): Don't come late. -- Kum owi yeut.; The band was playing too late [i. e., after curfew]. -- Krum plaeng leng yeut.; yeut peyr: Don't come late. -- Kum mok yeut peyr.; deceased -- k'mau'it: my late father -- k'mau'it oeuv'puk kyom; late at [night] -- [yoop] cha'ro (lit: deep night); don't be late - kum owi yeut; too late -- yeut nah; too late, "missed the boat", missed a chance -- kaat howi

lately adv. k'nong peyr t'maee t'maee ni: We have studied a lot lately. -- Yung rian yang ch'raan k'nong peyr t'maee t'maee ni.

later adv. yeut chiang: He was later than me. -- Gwat yeut chiang kyom.; peyr krow'ee: See you later. -- Choop ka'neea peyr krow'ee.; krow'ee mok: Later, he died. -- Krow'ee mok, gwat kaw slop teuh.; krow'ee: Later that day... -- Krow'ee t'ngai nu... ; sooner or later -- mun yeut mun chhop

latest adv. yeut bom'pot: The latest [we can leave] is four o'clock. -- Yeut bom'pot mao buon [yeung nung jchenyh]. **lathe** n. praw'dop kraw'lung

Latin America n. Am'rik La'tang

latitude n. raw'yeh taw'tung

laugh v. sow'eet (AP: sow'it, sow't(ch))

laugh at v. in amusement -- sow'eet; make fun of -- sow'eet jchum awh

laughter n. sun'mow'ich

launch v. rockets -- bum plong; ships -- dah(k) k'nong tuk; start, as with business, political campaign, etc. -- jchaap p'daum (lit: start)

laundry n. kaa bauwk kow-aow

laundry, to do v. bauwk kow-aow

law n. ch'bop; martial law -- un'yaa suk

lawsuit n. kd'eye; file a lawsuit -- laung to'la'ka (lit: go to court)

lawyer n. neh ch'bop; viti'vee; may tia'vee

lax adj. too'; bun too' bun toy

laxative n. tnam bun jchoh

layer n. chw'un: three layers of clothes -- aow bye chw'un; sraw b'auw; sraw to'up

layman n. o'ba'sawk

lazy adj. at this moment, or sometimes (often used in jest) -- k'chill; k'chill ch'raw'oh; always, chronically (harsher than "k'chill") -- kum'chul'peh

lead n. metal -- sum'naw

lead v. duk'no'um; advise -- nyne no'um; lead by the nose -- duk ch'raw muk; lead the way -- no'um muk

leader n. neah duk no'um; may duk no'um; may klawng; political official -- ka'ma'pi'bal

leadership n. kaa duk no'um; a'tuh'pa'dye'a'pheap

leading actor/actress n. too'a eyke

leaf n. sluk (AP: 'luhk)

leaflet n. trac: drop (throw) leaflets from a plane -- bawh trac taam yun hawh

leak n. praw'howng (lit: hole)

leak v. lic; This bucket leaks. -- Tuung ni lic.

lean adj. sco'me

lean v. lean on one's arm or elbow -- ch'raw't; p'eye'k teuh: lean back -- p'eye'k teuh krow'ee; lean against the wall -- p'eye'k teuh chuun chee'ung; lean towards -- p'eye'k teuh mok

leaning adj. tay

leap v. plong; lo'te

learn v. rian; I learned a lot in that class. -- Kyom rian chia (or baan) ch'raan noeh t'nak nu.; to have learned -- rian howi (or) jcheh; You learn fast! -- Chhop jcheh!; learn one's lesson -- ree'ung ro'a: He played with fire, and he learned his lesson. -- Veea leng pleung; veea ree'ung ro'a.

lease n. kej sun'ya ch'ool: car lease -- kej sun'ya ch'ool laan; kra'dah sun'ya ch'ool

lease v. ch'ool; dah(k) ch'ool

least adv. tic bom'pot (AP: mum'pot)

at least prp. yang tic na kaw; yang howi na; baa tic na kaw: If we are not going, at least we should telephone and let them know. -- Praw'sun chia yeung mun teuh, yang howi na yeung tro to'ra'sap prap gkay.

leather adj. s'bye'k

leather n. s'bye'k

leave v.

depart, go out -- jchenyh; jchenyh pi; jcha(k) jchenyh; jchenyh baan; or, jchenyh roo'it: It leaves Phnom Penh at 7 a.m. -- Gwat jcha(k) jchenyh pi Phnom Penh noeh mao prum'pul.; Leave! (Go away!) -- Jchenyh krau!;

leave in sense of "put", as "leave it on the table", or "leave a space between the lines" -- dah(k) or tooo'k: leave a space between letters in typing -- dah(k) klia; leave a space (of a number of lines, inches, feet, etc.) on a surface being written or worked on -- tooo'k chun lawh;

leave behind -- tooo'k taam krow'ee;

leave it to me -- tooo'k owi kyom;

Leave me alone. -- Tooo'k owi kyom noeh tai einye. (lit: Leave me by myself.); or, Kum ruhm kaan kyom. (lit: Don't bother me.);

leave a message -- tooo'k pdaam (lit: leave/tell); p'nya(r) pdaam (lit: send/tell); miun pdaam (lit: have (s.th.) to tell); pdaam prap (lit: tell/tell); miun ni'yaye (lit: have a statement): Did he leave (lit: have) a message? -- Tau(v) gwat miun pdaam a'veye tay? or, Tau(v) gwat miun ni'yaye aae tay?; I want to leave a message. -- Kyom jchong pdaam p'nya(r) klaah.;

break up with, abandon -- rut jchowl: Why [did] he leave her? -- Hyte aae gwat [baan] rut jchowl nee'eng?

lecher n. cha'preull; ma'nooh koh

lecture n. kaa tveu a'ta'ti'bye

lecture v. a'ti'bye

leech n. ch'leuung

left adj. remaining -- noeh sahl(t): There is no food left. -- Ot miun ma'hope noeh sahl(t).

left prp. opp. of "right" -- ch'wayne: left side, left hand side -- kang ch'wayne

left pp. of "leave" tooo'k.... jchowl: I left my hat in the bus. -- Kyom tooo'k mooh kyom jchowl k'nong laan bus.

left behind prp. baan tooo'k noeh taam krow'ee: Three kids were left behind. -- Gkon k'mayng bye neh baan tooo'k noeh taam krow'ee.

left out p.p. noeh sahl(t)

left-over p.p. sahl(t): left-over food -- ma'hope sahl(t)

leg n. cheung (same word as "foot"); leg above the knee, i. e., thigh -- ploe; leg below the knee -- kom poo'an cheung; ankle -- khaw cheung (lit: neck of the foot)

legal adj. penyh ch'bop; sraw'p ch'bop

legally adv. penyh tee; dow'ee sa ch'bop

legend n. ru'ung praeng

legislation n. ni'te'kaam; ratta'tum'nunyh; sum'narr

legislative adj. ni'te'pun'yal

legislature n. sa'phea; ratt'sa'phea; ong'ni'te'pun

legislator n. ni'te'baw'kul

legitimate adj. dow'ee ch'bop; penyh ch'bop: the legitimate government of... -- ratt'a'pi'bal penyh ch'bop ney...

lemon n. krau'itch ch'mah; (also means "lime")

lemon grass n. in general, or to refer specifically to entire plant (stalks and leaves together) -- sluk gkray ("kuhl" = stalk, "sluk" = leaf); referring to stalk only -- kuhl sluk gkray; refering to leaves only -- sluk sluk gkray

lemon grass soup n. scng'au ch'roo'hk (AP: scng'au; lit: sour soup; even though this name does not contain the words for "lemon grass", this "sour" soup is always prepared with lemon grass; hence, the translation); lemon grass soup with chicken -- scng'au ch'roo'hk muon; lemon grass soup with fish -- scng'au ch'roo'hk trei

lend v. owi k'ch'eye (lit.: "give a loan")

length n. of physical object -- bun dow'ee; praw'veng; of time -- ro'yeea peyr

lengthen v. tveu owi veng

leprosy n. chuum'ngeu klung

less adj. tic (AP: tek): less food -- ma'hope tic; less than -- tic chiang: He [still] has less money than he wants. -- Gwat miun loi tic chiang [noeh low'ee] gwat jchole jchet.; no less than -- mun tic chiang

less adv. tic: the less dangerous road -- ploe kroo'ti'nak tic

less n. tic to'ich; tic chiang: They have less than ever. -- Pooh'gkay miun tic chiang twa'ma'da.

less prp. without -- dawk: Three less two is one. -- Bye dawk pi, moi.

lesser adj. tic chiang; to'ich chiang

lesson n. may'rien (AP: mirian)

lest conj. krye'ng lo: Lock the door lest the thieves get in. -- Jchak saow t'veea krye'ng lo miun chao.

let v. bun dow'ee owi: They will let us go to Sam'roang. -- Gkay bun dow'ee owi yeung teuh Sam'roang.; a'noo'naa't owi: They will let us go to Cham Ka'lor. -- Gkay owi a'noo'naa't teuh Cham Ka'lor.; owi: But they will not let us go to O'Kaki. -- Pun'ta'aae gkay mun owi yeung teuh O'Kaki.

let go of v. lay'ng: let go of my hand -- lay'ng dai kyom

let go out v. bun dunyh

let up n. chope: without let-up -- dow'ee k'miun chope

let up v. allow to get up -- ree'a ray'ng

let's v. ta'(AP: tawh); Let's eat. -- Ta' nyam.; Let's go -- Ta' teuh.; Let's go to sleep. -- Ta' dayke.; Let's hurry up. -- Ta' leuan laung. (NB: this is not same word as "teuh" which placed at the end (or beginning and end) of a sentence creates an imperative: Eat! -- Nyam teuh!; or, Go ahead and eat! -- Teuh nyam teuh!)

lethal adj. adje owi slop

letter n. written communication -- sum'buht; letters of alphabet, as a group -- a'saw; individual letter of the alphabet -- a'kraa'; official letter -- ngy'at

lettuce n. sa'lat; large lettuce from Cambodian northeast -- salat bo'gko; (NB: the translation for both "lettuce" and "salad" is "sa'lat"; viz., a typical Khmer salad, lettuce with beef slices on top, is "sa'lat sat(ch) gko")

level adj. ri'ep

level n. cho'un; t'nak; lum'dob; (highest level -- tee bom'pot)

level v. bong ri'ep; pung ri'ep

liberalism n. is'ra(k)'pheap; (conservatism -- sun sum som chai)

liberalization n. is'ra(k)'pheap vu'pa'naya'kaam

liberate v. bun dawh; ruhm'dawh

liberation n. ruhm'dawh: Liberation Khmer (party) -- Khmer Ruhm'dawh (NB: usually Romanized, "Khmer Rumdo"; grouping formed after Sihanouk ouster, March 1970, to promote his restoration; progressively liquidated by Khmer Rouge, 1971-1973.)

library n. bun'd'lye: Let's go to the library! -- Teuh bun'd'lye, eh!

lice n. jch'eye

license n. bun; (also, fr. Fr., lye'cen; or, pear'mee): driver's license -- bun baahk laan; or, pear'mee baahk laan; license plate -- bun tay'eh laek laan

lichi n. ko'len; mee'un

lick v. luh'

lie n. ko'hawk

lie v. tell a falsehood -- ko'hawk; recline -- dum'ray'k kloo'an (noun = dum'nay'k): They lay under the trees. -- Pooh'gkay dum'ray'k kloo'an krowm daum cheu.; lie on s. th. -- dum'ray'k kloo'an leuh; lie down to sleep -- geyng; or dayke

lien n. put a lien on s. th. -- reup o'ss yok: I will lien your house if you don't give (me) the money. -- Reup o'ss yok ptay'a neh baa neh mun song loi.

lieutenant n. a'noo sena toe; 2nd lieutenant -- a'noo sena trei; (NB: a lieutenant wears two stripes, or "saa(k) pi," on his sleeve, a 2nd lieutetant, one stripe or, "saa(k) moi")

lieutenant colonel n. va'ret sena toe (may wear four-and a-half stripes, (saak buon kan'lah))

lieutenant commander n. a'noo va'ret sena toe; (may wear four-and-a-half stripes (saak buon kan'lah))

lieutenant general n. odum sena t'ow'ich (may wear two stars (p'k'eye pi))

lieutentant governor (provincial) n. pooh'choo'ay (kyte)

life n. chi'vut (AP: chee'vit, ch'vut, chee'wit); Life is a struggle. -- Chi'vut keuh chia kaa taw'soo.; formal term -- chee'va'pheap: way of life -- chee'va'pheap chum'lye; also:

life and death -- rooh nung slop

life expectancy -- chee'vut dum'ro(v): What is the life expectancy of women there? -- Ma'nooh srei ti nan chee'vut dum'ro(v) a'yoo pun'man?

give one's life -- pdull chi'vut

life time -- chi'vut; peyr ney chi'vut

life style -- ro'bee'up rooh noeh: Different countries have different life styles. -- Praw'tct p'sayng p'sayng miun ro'bee'up rooh noeh p'sayng p'sayng ka'neea.

lift v. yong: lift water from a well -- yong tuk; leuk: lift the table -- leuk tohk; lift with a rope or crane, as cargo from a ship -- toooch

light adj. in weight -- sra'll; in color -- pwa k'chey; sra'll: light green -- pw'a bye'tong k'chey

light n. electric light -- pleung; (NB: pleung also has the meanings, depending on context, of "electricity in general", "flame" and "fire"; the word for "electricity" with no connotation of "light" is "chu'ran a'ti'ce'nee" (lit: electric current); "pleung" despite its multiple meanings is commonly used to indicate "light".): The lights are out. -- Pleung ro'luht.; Turn on the light. -- Baahk pleung.; Turn off the lights -- Butt pleung.; specifically light to see by, or radiant, but no connotation of electricity -- puun'leuh: I have electricity but no light. -- Miun chu'ran a'ti'ce'nee pun'ta'aae k'miun puun'leuh.; I need more light (e.g., to read by). -- Tro kaa puun'leuh tyme tee'it.; bright, shining ray of light, sometimes with connotation of "heavenly" light -- rch'smyc

light v. a fire or stove -- dop pleung; light a room, or turn on the light -- baahk pleung; light with match or flame -- autch: light a fuse -- autch bun chheh foo'zi; light a candle -- autch tee'en

lighter n. for cigarettes -- dyke koo'h (lit: flic steel)

lightning n. run t'ay'h; (thunder = p'kaw lo'an)

like v. jchole jchet: I like baseball. -- Kyom jchole jchet baseball.; like each other -- jchole jchet ka'neea teuh venyh teuh mok: Srei Peai and Noi like each other. -- Srei Peai nung Noi jchole jchet ka'neea teuh venyh teuh mok.; as you like -- taam jchet neh; admire -- saw'sarl

like adv. similar to -- doj: like a farmer -- doj neh sr'eye; (He doesn't speak much, but when he does,) he sounds like an American. -- (Veea mun seou ni'yaye tay, pun'ta'aae baa veea ni'yaye laung,) sum laeng doj Americang.; to be like this -- doj ch'neh; look like, seem like -- doj meulh; like (similar to) each other -- doj ka'neea: "Russia and the United States are alike; they both talk about helping [Third World peoples]." -- Sovietique nung Amerique doj ka'neea; te'ang pi neh ni'yaye om'pee choo'ay [prachee'chuun Praw'tet Ti Bye].; just like -- doj tai; like that -- doj nu; similar to -- chia ka'neea: He talks like an American. -- Veea ni'yaye Americang chia ka'neea.; like that -- aae'chung; and the like -- howi a'veye a'veye

likely adv. tuum'nong; praw'heil: It is likely to rain tomorrow. -- Veea tuum'nong nung plee'eng s'eye'd.

limb n. of a tree -- me(t); of a human body -- dai cheung (lit: arm leg)

lime n. krau'itch ch'mah (also means "lemon")

limit, limits n. kum'nauwt; kum rut; kum vi'ti'sas

limit v. set a limit -- kum rut; kum hut

limp adj. tuun; k'sow'ee

limp n. from one leg shorter than other, and generally -- ki'now'ich: He has a limp. -- Gwat ki'now'ich.; a tip'toe'ing gait -- chow'ee(ch): He walks with a limp. -- Gwat dah dow'ee chowee(ch).

limp v. dah pang'pee'it; dah kun'yow'it: He limps. -- Gwat dah kynow'ich or Dah dow'ee chowee(ch).; to wobble or walk unsteadily -- dah kleeng kloung

line n. straight line, generally -- bun'twa(t); a on a page -- bun'twa(t); parallel lines -- bun'twa(t) srawb; telephone line (referring to either actual pole-strung wire or facilities in general, as in "How many lines do you have here?") -- ks'eye telephone; telephone line/connection -- telephone: The line is busy. -- Telephone ro'vull.; the space between two lines -- chee'a raw; "out of line", off-base -- koh

line by line adv. bun'twa(t) taam bun'twa(t))

line up v. teuh dum ree'up choo'a; form a line -- dum'ree'up choo'a; make a straight line -- dum'rong choo'a; be in line -- noeh k'nong dum'ree'up choo'a

lining n. tro noo'up

link n. dum'naw

link v. taw; bun cho'op

lion n. saat sungh; saat t'ou

lip n. praw'bo mwot

lipstick n. crem (AP: kryme) lee'up mwot

liquid n. vuh'taw'ree'oo; tuk

liquidate v. ru'um lee'aae

liquor n. sra; tuk sro'vung; (a drink, drinks -- p'es'cheeh')

list n. bun'chee; (a list with columns and rows, i. e., a table -- ta'rang)

list v. make a list -- tveu bun'chee

listen v. listen to a sound -- loo: listen to a voice or music -- loo sum'leng; listen/comprehend -- s'dap baan; follow the advice of -- tveu taam: listen to (what) the parents (said) -- tveu taam oeuv-puk m'dye; follow the advice of -- s'dap: She never listens to me. -- Veea mun'dael s'dap kyom.

liter n. "lit"

literate adj. jcheh an

literature n. information; literature, as literature about a product -- por'da'mee'an; great writing -- ak'saw'sahs: French literature -- ak'saw'sahs Ba'raang

litter n. trash -- sum'ram; for carrying wounded -- praw'dap syng neh ro'booh

little adj. small in size -- to'ich (AP: too'ich, too'ch, taa'wich, to'wich): a small house -- ptay'a to'ich; small in amount -- baan tic (AP: baan tec); or, baan tic baan to'ich: a little tea -- ta'aae baan tic; a little (whether small-sized or young) boy -- k'mayng proh to'ich; young -- to'ich: little girl -- k'mayng sraae to'ich; young -- pa'own (AP: frequently condensed in speech to 'own): little brother -- pa'own proh; little sister -- 'own sraae; young -- peau: littlest sister -- sraae peaou

a little adv. baan tic (AP: baan tec): Please speak a little slower. -- Sum ni'yaye yeut yeut baan tic.; a little later -- teuh krow'ee baan tic; teuh yeut baan tic

a little n. tic; tic: Give me just a little. -- Owi kyom tic mok baan.

little by little adv. tic m'dong tic m'dong; chia loom daap

live adj. alive -- rooh noeh

live v. have life -- rooh; reside -- rooh noeh: He has been living abroad for ten years. -- Gwat baan rooh noeh bor'tay dap chh'nam howi.; live at, stay at, some sense of temporarily -- snak noeh: I lived there only four or five days. -- Kyom snak noeh ti nu buon pram t'ngai pun'noh.; noeh: What village do you live in? -- Neah noeh phum na?; a'srye noeh: Dani lives in Po'sat. -- Dani a'srye noeh Po'sat.

liver n. tl'aamh

living adj. still alive -- miun chi'vut; rooh noeh: living conditions -- chi'vut'pheap rooh noeh; standard of living -- ro'bee'up rooh noeh

living, a n. ro'ba ro'ksi: I want to make a good living. -- Kyom jchong bung kaut ro'bah ro'ksi owi baan la'aw.; a'chee'vi'kaam; make a living -- jchenyh chum chi'vut

living room n. cunlye'ng to'tool p'nee'oo; or, bantope to'tool p'nee'oo (lit: place to receive guests)

lizard n. small gekko -- chin chaw; larger, black species -- toh kye

load n. ro'bah tuum'nguun: How big a load can you carry in the jungle? -- Tau(v) ro'bah tuum'nguun pu'man dael neh adje li noeh k'nong prey?

load v. p'too(k): load s. th. into a truck -- p'too(k) noeh k'nong laan trung

loan n. k'ch'eye: loan of money -- k'ch'eye loi; He took many loans from his friends. -- Gwat baan k'ch'eye loi chia'ch'raan om'pee pooh'mah gwat.; or, Gwat baan jchong kaa chia'ch'raan om'pee pooh'mah gwat.; apply for a loan -- dah(k) pieh sum k'ch'eye loi

loan v. make a loan, lend to -- owi... k'ch'eye: He lent me his car. -- Gwat owi kyom k'ch'eye laan ro'bah gwat.

lobster n. bung'kong

locate v. sveye rok

located adj. noeh; tet noeh; tang noeh

location n. cunlye'ng (AP: kunlyne, kun'lie, kal'eyc)

lock n. may sauw or sauw: That lock is no good. -- Sauw nu ot la'aw.

lock v. jchak; jchak sauw; (NB: jchak jchak sauw usually means "lock" but can mean "unlock" if so indicated by context, viz.: Close the door and lock it. -- Butt t'veea howi jchak sauw.; but: Unlock the door and come in. -- Jchak sauw jchole.)

locked p.p. jchak sauw: a locked door -- tvee'a jchaw sauw

locomotive n. k'bal ro'teh pleung

lodging n. tee sum'nak

log n. cheu hope; connoting particularly the unsawn condition of a log -- boo'rawh

logical adj. sum'ruhum

loneliness n. pheap tyle towl

lonely adj. op'sup: He feels lonely. -- Gwat a'nuhk op'sup.

long adj. in length -- veng: a long snake -- poo'ah veng; in time -- yoo': a long trip -- dum'narr yoo'; We waited a long time. -- Yeung ro'ng cham yoo' nah.; It took a long time. -- Veea yok peyr yoo'.; a type of long banana -- jchai um'bong

long adv. how long a distance -- praw'veng pu'man: How long is [that bridge]? -- [Spee'un nu] praw'veng pu'man?; how long a time -- ro'yeht pu'man, or ro'yeht peyr pu'man: How long have you lived here? -- Tau(v) neh rooh noeh ti ni ro'yeht pu'man howi?; too long -- yoo' nah: I have been waiting too long. -- Kyom baan ro'ng jcham yoo' mok howi.; as long as, given that -- da'rap'na: As long as we have a car, we will drive. -- Da'rap'na yeung miun laan, yeung nung baahk.

long-distance adj. pi chng'eye: long distance telephone call -- call [or, haow] pi chng'eye

long-lasting adj. enduring, durable -- thuun

longer adj. veng chiang; any longer, no longer -- ot... tee'it tay: I don't want it any longer. -- Kyom ot jchong baan veea tee'it tay.; That problem is no longer important. -- Pun'ha nu ot miun jcham batch tee'it tay.

longitude n. ro'yet mun dow'ee

look v. meuhl

look after v. maintain -- tai ret'sa; supervise, keep an eye on -- meuhl owi: He is looking after that lady's child. -- Gwat meuhl gkon to'ich owi sraae nu.

look at v. meuhl

look down on v. meulh ngi'yaye

look for v. rok; go look for -- dah rok; sveye rok; look for for s. o. -- meuhl rok: He wants to look for a wife. -- Gwat jchong meuhl rok pra'pun.

look like v. doj chia: That thing looks like I saw it before. -- Ro'bah nu doj chia kyom tra'laawp keunyh.; meuhl doj; doj: He looks like a farmer. -- Gwat doj neh sr'eye.

loom n. dum'banyh

loom v. jchenyh stung mok: In 1979, [famine] loomed in Cambodia. -- Noeh chh'nam 1979, [kaa ot bye] jchenyh stung mok leuh [or, jchum'poo'h] Kampuchea yeung.

loophole n. bong vee'eng; loophole in the law -- bong vee'eng ch'bop; nutch leh

loose adj. tooo; ro'lung

loot v. kaw'kye

lorry n. laan trung; laan caa'mi'on

lose v. misplace, not be able to find -- bot (AP: bat, but): She's lost her glasses. -- Nee'eng bot ven'taa.; lose control of militarily or politically, abandon -- bot bong; lose, or waste, time -- teuh bot: Another day lost. -- Moi t'ngai tee'it teuh bot howi.; bung kaat; lose money -- bung kaat loi; lose a friend -- bot bawng mit pa'ya; lose face -- k'mah mok; bot mok; lose [a fight] -- jchanyh [chuum'looh]; lose hope -- ot sung'khum: Don't lose hope (yet). -- Kum (twon) awh sung'khum.;

lost adj. bot; (AP: bat, but): All the money is gone or lost -- bot loi; It's lost. -- Veea bot.; lost directionally/geographically -- vehng: to get lost -- vehng ruung; lost at sea (o.e., sunk) -- t'leh k'nong sa'mut; Get lost! -- Teuh slop!

lots of --, a lot adv. ch'raan (AP: ch'run, cha'rown, and condensed in PS to "cheun")

lotus n. p'ka chook

loud adj. klang; kong luhm'pong; too loud! -- loo' nah!

loudly adv. klang; kong luhm'pong

love n. sra'laanyh (AP: sa'lang, sra'law, 'lang, sraw)

love v. romantically -- sra'laanyh; to love s.o. a lot -- sra'laanyh pun phnom (lit: love like (as much as) mountains); crazy with love -- ch'koo'it snai'ha; [I] love you, [I] love you! -- 'Lang, 'lang!; snai'ha; love (appelation of endearment) -- snai'ha; love-sick -- Para'chey kang ploe snai'ha. (lit: defeated on the path or way of love.); be in love with -- sra'laanyh; to make love with, relatively polite -- ru'um sum veea; or, ru'um dum'nae'k; to make love with, vulgar, equivalent to English f--k -- jcho'nyh ka'neea; greatly like -- jchum noe'l: I love ice cream. -- Kyom jchum noe'l ice cream.

lover n. snai'ha

low adj. tee'up: This is a very low chair. -- Kow'aae ni tee'up nah.; low water -- tuk tee'up (or, tuk raae'eh); low water season -- ro'doe tuk sraw (lit: season (of) water ebbing)

lower adj. krowm: the lower plantations -- jcham'kar krowm

loyal adj. peh'k'd'eye pheap; smah trong

lubricate v. dah(k) klanyh; dah(k) praeng (NB: praeng can mean, depending on context, gas, grease or oil; see specific terms listed under "oil")

lucious adj. chng'anyh

luck n. sum'nang (AP: sam'nung): Good luck! -- Sum'nang la'aw!

lucky adj. miun sum'nang; miun lee'up; miun po'up; haeyng: I'm really lucky today. -- Kyom haeyng nah t'ngai ni.; unlucky -- soi

luggage n. individual bag -- va'leez; bags, collectively -- va'leez; aye'von neh dum'narr; aye'von

lumber n. cheu aee'yaye

lumpy adj. kruum kruum: lumpy bean meal -- m'sauw sun'dyke kruum kruum

lunch n. a'ha' t'ngai trong; bye t'ngai trong

lung n. soo'it

lurch v. of a person walking -- dah kaa'traae'a; of a vehicle -- baawk laan kaa'traae'a

lure v. tay'eh jchet; loo'ung jchet; bun chowt; loo'ung lo'me

lurk v. ch'lope: Tigers lurk in the jungle. -- Kla ch'lope k'nong prey.

lust n. kaam tun'ha: He lusts for her (lit: has lust for her). -- Gwat miun kaam tun'ha teuh leuh nee'eng.

M

ma'am, madame n. neh sraae

machine n. ma'cheen (AP: ma'seen); yun; (NB: truck -- ro't yun; airplane -- yun hawh); answering machine -- ma'cheen jchum'la'wee telephone; recording machine -- ma'cheen tawt sum laeng

machine gun n. kum pleung yun

mad adj. angry -- khung; k'dau jchet; crazy -- ch'koo'it

magazine n. for reading -- too'a'su'na'va'dye; of a weapon -- lawt

magic n. tu'p

magnet n. may dyke; dyke jchawk

magnetic adj. chawk

magnificent adj. awh jchaa

maid n. b'ow pree'oo; neh bum rahl; ch'nool

mail n. sum'buht (AP: sawnbot)

mail v. dah(k) po'; p'nya(r) sum'buht; deliver mail -- rut sum'buht; jchaiyk sum'buht; mailman -- neh rut sum'buht **mailbox** n. praw'op sum'buht

main adj. daum; may; kohl

mainstream n. kohl kum'nut pra'chec'chuun pieh ch'raan: His ideas are not in the mainstream (lit: [are outside] the main ideas of most people). -- Kum'nut gwat [jchenyh krau om'pee] kohl kum'nut pra'chee'chuun pieh ch'raan.

maintain v. tai ret'sa; maintain a car, a truck, the roads -- tai reh'sa laan... tai reh'sa laan trung... tai reh'sa ploe; support, underwrite -- jchenyh jchum: The US used to maintain the Se'rei Ka to [use against] Sihanouk. -- US tra'laawp jchenyh jchum Serei Ka dum'bye [yok muk praw'praa praw'chang] Sihanoo'.

maintenance n. kaa tai'reh'sa

maize n. po't

major adj. important -- ch'bong; chum'na; sum'kahn

major n. military rank -- va'ret sena trei; "saa(k) buon" (lit: four stripes, insignia usually indicative of rank of major in Khmer armed forces)

major general n. o'dum sena eyke

majority n. pieh ch'raan (NB: pieh = part, portion, percentage)

make v.

prepare, formulate, organize -- ree'up jchum: make a plan -- ree'up jchum pyne kaa;

create -- bung kaut: make trouble or problems -- bung kaut pun'ha; bung kaat kaa lum'bah; tveu: make bronze
      statues -- tveu roob jchum'lak sum'rut

bring about -- tveu; tveu owi: make [progress] -- tveu owi loot' lo'ah; or, tveu owi [ree'k jchum'row'm]; or
      (formal, official), tveu owi miun kaa vee'vwut: We want to make progress in agriculture. -- Yeung
      jchong tveu owi miun kaa vee vwot p'nyke kaah'se'kaam.;

fabricate -- tveu: I like to make [furniture]. -- Kyom jchole jchet tveu [kreung tohk kaeo'eye].

manufacture -- praw'lutt (AP: paa'lutt); see, also, "manufacture"

make or force s.o. to do s. th. -- tveu owi: I made him do it. -- Kyom tveu owi gwat tveu veea.

make friends with -- tveu pooh'mah chi'moi; or, jchong mi'ta'pheap chi'moi: I want to make friends with them.
      -- Kyom jchong jchaawng mi'ta'pheap chi'moi pooh'gkay. (lit: want to tie (or secure) friendship with...)

make fun of -- jchum awh lawh leui; jchum awh: Don't make fun of me. -- Kum jchum awh kyom.; or, Kum sa'wit jchum awh owi kyom.

make it impossible [for me] to... -- tveu owi [kyom] ot...

make a long story short -- tveu ru'ung veng owi klai

make love -- ru'um dum'naek

make money -- rok loi baan: Last year I made lots of money. -- chh'nam muun kyom rok loi baan ch'raan.

make a phone call -- telephone; or, haow to'ra'sap; or, haow telephone

make a report -- tveu s'kd'eye ri'yaye kaa

make up, apply cosmetics -- mak'ree'aae; top'tye'ng

make up, invent, create -- bung kaat: make up a story -- bung kaut ru'ung (NB: this phrase can also be translated/ understood to mean "make trouble for", make problems for" or even "pick a fight with"); to make clear no hostile intent, "make up a story" can be rendered "praw'dut ru'ung", viz.: make up a funny story -- praw'dut ru'ung cum'plyne)

make up with -- sum rawp sum roo'an ka'neea

make-up n. cosmetics -- kreung mak'ree'aae; mak'ree'aae

malaria n. kruun'jchanyh

Malaya n. praw'tet Ma'lay

male adj. re humans -- payt proh; re animals -- ch'mole

man n. a man -- ma'nooh proh ma'neh; ten men -- ma'nooh proh dap neh; mankind -- ma'nooh sa'chee'it

manage v. ree'up jchong; lay lo; troo'ut tra: He did a good job managing my [business]. -- Gwat tveu baan la'aw troo'it tra [kaa raw'see] kyom.

manager n. of a store, in "hands-on" sense -- neh troo'it tra; neh kaan kaab; in sense of "director" -- jchang vang haang

man-eater n. saat see ma'nooh: man-eating tiger -- saat kla see ma'nooh

mandate n. kaa bun chee'a

mandate v. jchat; commang (fr. Fr.); bun chee'a

mandatory adj. chia tro tai: In Cambodia it is mandatory to [serve] in the army. -- Noeh Kampuchea keuh chia tro tai [tveu chia] tee'hee'an.

mango n. sv'eye

mangosteen n. ma'kuut

manifest n. shipping document, bill of lading -- sum'buht ree'aae kaa (lit: list of goods)

manifest v. bun jchenyh owi keunyh

manifestation n. kaa bun jchenyh a'kas owi keunyh

manifesto n. s'kd'eye praw'kas; th'eye'ng na'yo'bye

mankind n. ma'nooh lok

manner n. mode of doing s. th. -- ro'bee'up ro'bawb; bye'b bot; mee'a yee'a; or, chia: in an orderly manner -- chia ho' hye

manners n. behavior -- sun'dop tno'op; or, mee'a yee'a; or, aae'ree'ya bawt; or, ro'bee'up ro'baw: He has no manners. -- Gwat ot miun sun'dop tno'op. or, Gwat ot dung ro'bee'up ro'baw. (lit: He doesn't know manners.); teach manners to -- praw'da'oo: Mothers teach (their) children manners. -- M'dye praw'da'oo gkon.

manoeuver v. tveu tac'tic

manoeuvers n. tac'tic; kaa la'bat(ch)

mantra n. toa; chant mantras -- sote toa

manual adj. dow'ee dai; nung dai; manual labor -- kaa haht'ha' kaam

manual n. s'po meuhl

manufacture v. fabricate and assemble -- stab'pa'na: manufacture cars -- stab'pa'na laan; manufacture trucks -- stab'pa'na laan trung; manufacture electrical components -- stab'pa'na kreung a'ti'cen'ee; manufacture various items made of metal -- stab'pa'na kreung jcha(k) (lit: molded objects); produce or make -- praw'lutt (AP: paa'lutt): That [factory] manufactures [125 pounds of sugar] per day. -- [Rong jcha] nu praw'lutt [scaw saw m'roi m'pay pram pound] k'nong moi t'ngai.(NB: "m'roi" is contraction of "moi" (one) and "roi" (hundred)); produce or make without extensive fabrication or assembly -- tveu: There is a factory in Battambong that manufactures [rice sacks]. -- Noeh k'nong Battambong miun ro'ng jcha tveu [bauw] moi.; create -- bung kaut

manufacturing n. kaa tveu; kaa stab'pa'na

many adv. ch'raan (AP: ch'ran, cha'ran cha'rown, chr'eun): many times -- ch'raan dong; chia ch'raan: many friends -- po'mah chia ch'raan; how many -- pu'man (AP: pun'man, p'man); so many that -- ch'raan dael; So many! -- Ch'raan nah!; have so many [books] -- miun [s'po'] ch'raan doj ch'ney.: He has so many books that he cannot count them. -- Gwat miun s'po ch'raan nah dael mun adje ro'up baan.; too many -- ch'raan nah (lit: very many); as many as -- dael teuh jchum'noo'an; pu'man kaw baan da'aae: You can have as many as you want. -- Neh jchong baan pu'man kaw baan da'aae.; as many as (S) -- pu'man: Take as many as you want! -- Yok teuh, yok pu'man, yok teuh!

map n. pan'tee

marble n. t'maw t'lauwm

march n. kaa dah; protest march -- pa'ti'kaam (also translates as "strike")

march v. dah; hye

March n. Mih'nee'a

marijuana n. gun'jcha

marinate v. praw'la(k); marinate beef or fish -- praw'la(k) sat(ch) gko roo trei

marine adj. om'pee tuk; om'pee sa'mut; marine life -- chi'vut noeh k'nong sa'mut

Marines n. tee'hee'an Marine; tee'hee'an cheung tuk

mark n. scar, spot, blemish -- sn'aam; score on test or exam -- pun'tooh; mark in sense of designation -- kooh chum nam; beauty mark -- pra'ch'roi; trade-mark -- yee haow (lit: business name); tattoo, scar or stripe -- saak

mark v. grade a test -- k'eye; owi pun'tooh: I already graded the students' [exercises]. -- Kyom k'eye [lu'um'ha] gkonsa howi.; mark or designate s. th. or s. o. -- kooh or kooh dow, viz. (pencilled note found on voting booth in Kom'puung Cham during May 1993 elections): [Whichever one] you like, mark [that one]. -- Sra'laanyh [moi na], kooh [moi nung].

market n. psa: I have been to both the big Phnom Penh markets: P'sa T'maee and P'sa O Russ'aae. -- Kyom baan teuh psa thum te'ang pi noeh Phnom Penh, P'sa T'maee howi nung Psa O'Ru'ssei.; black market -- p'sa ngo'ngut (lit: dark market)

marriage n. ree'up kaa

married adj. miun pra'pun (lit: have a wife); miun kroo'esa (lit: have a family); already married -- ree'up kaa howi

marry v. ree'up kaa

marshall n. field marshall (military leader) -- Say'na praw'mok: Marshall Lon Nol -- Say'na praw'mok Lon Nol

martial adj. suk: court martial -- to'la'ka suk; martial law -- a'nya suk; ch'bop suk

marvelous adj. la'aw praw'nut: The Khmer classical dancing was marvelous. -- Ro'bohm (or, ro'bohm Khmei) la'aw praw'nut.; awh jchaa la'aw: Ankor Wat was marvelous. -- Angkor Wat keuh chia awh jchaa la'aw.

mason n. meh tveu ut; neh tveu tmaw utt

massacre n. kaa sum'lop ru'um

massage n. kaa saw sye; kaa ch'raw batch

massage v. tveu saw sye; ch'raw batch

masses, the n. pra'chee'chuun moi pa'chuum (lit: avergae people): The masses need help. -- Pra'chee'chuun moi pa'chuum tro kaa choo'ay.

massive adj. thum

master n. in sense of employer -- jchao'vye; in sense of teacher or person knowledgeable in s. th. -- kruu; elder or teacher, not necessarily living in wat, with knowledge of social ceremonies -- a'char

master mind v. tveu chia may kum'nut

masterpiece n. tv'eye dye; sn'a dye

mat n. kun tale

match v. find equal or similar to, as match clothes, etc. -- see ka'neea; tro ka'neea; bring together socially -- p'sum kuu'm; p'sum: to match Sam Ol with Srei Peaou -- p'sum Sam Ol chi'moi Srei Peaou

match, matches n. for lighting cigarette, fire, etc. -- cheu'koo(ss) (AP: chuh'koo)

material(s) n. vuh'to: raw material -- vuh'to tee'it daum; raw materials [for making metals (iron, steel, etc.) -- vuh'to tee'it daum sum'rap slaw dyke]; sum'pee'a'ree'h: labor and material -- ch'nool tveu howi nung sum'pee'a'ree'h; writing materials -- sum'pee'a'ree'h saw say; cloth or fabric -- kraw'not

materiel n. (military supplies) -- paa'ri'kaa

materialist n. neh vuh'to ni'yuum

materialistic adj. vuh'to ni'yuum

material adj. physically measurable, not ethereal, -- chia roo'p ree'ung: material things -- ro'bah dael miun chia roo'p ree'ung

maternal adj. chia m'dye; chia daum

mathematics n. kenit' ta'sa; chuum'nowt (PS; lit: puzzle)

matter n. issue, problem -- ru'ung; ru'ung hyte; ke(ch) kaa: What's the matter? -- Ru'ung aae? or, Miun aae? or, Miun ru'ung aae? or, Miun kaut aae?; mind over matter -- r'oop'pa'ti't; printed matter -- a'veye a'veye dael boh'pum; as a matter of fact -- taam kaa'putt

matter v. be important -- jcham'batch; sum'kahn: It matters to all Cambodians [whether] the Thais and Singaporeans [control] their economy. -- Veea sum'kahn sum'rap chuun'chee'it Khmei te'ang praw'sun baa saah See'um nung saah Singapor [kaan kaab] set'a'kej ro'bah pooh'gkay.

mattress n. pooo'k

mature adj. generally, i. e., for crops, people, animals, etc. -- penyh jchum'nah; fruit or crops -- tum: ripe mangoes/ripe corn -- sv'eye tuum/po't tuum; people only -- dung koh dung tro (lit: knowing wrong (from) right)

maximum adj. a'teh'pah'ruu'ma; dael ch'raan bom'pot: the maximum number -- jchum'noo'an a'teh'pah'ree'ma; or, jchum'noo'an dael ch'raan bom'pot; We want the maximum number [of business] to be run by Cambodian people. -- Yeung jchong baan jchum'noo'an dael ch'raan bom'pot [ney muk chum'noo'inyh] dum'bye kaan kaab dow'ee pra'chee'chuun Kampuchea.

May n. Oo'sa'phea

may (s. one do s. th. or s. th. occur) v. sum: May I drink some water? -- Kyom sum tuk nyam, baan tay?; pong: May God help me. -- Preah owi choo'ay kyom pong.; tau(v)... adje... baan tay: May I know it or not? -- Tau(v) kyom adje dung veea baan tay, roo kaw ot?

maybe adv. praw'heil (AP: pra'heil): Maybe he is sick. -- Gwat praw'heil cheuh.; kreyn lo; praw'ha praw'heil: Maybe I saw you somewhere else. -- Kyom praw'ha praw'heil keunyh neh noeh aae na.

mayor n. chao'vye krong; may kuum

me prn. generally -- kyom (AP: kin'yom, knyom, kin'yoe'm, 'yom); familiar, among friends -- angyh; used by socially lower ranking person to refer to self when addressing socially higher ranking person -- own; used by socially higher ranking to refer to self when speaking to socially lower ranking person -- bong; "own" and "bong" are also used to mean "me" between men (bong) and women (own) in an affectionate relationship. For example, a wife might ask her husband to give her, e.g., a book by saying, "Bong, sum owi own s'po nu." ("Dear, please give me that book."); (familiar (lit: we) -- yeung: Give me (lit: us) a little. -- Owi yeung baan tic mok.; familiar -- ka'neea: [Hand] me that, give me a little! -- [Ho'ich] a'nee; owi ka'neea baan tic mo'! ("mo'" = contraction of mok)

158

meal n. food -- ma'hope; bye tuk; ma'hope jchum'naee; [soy bean] meal -- ma'sow [sun'dyke siang] (lit: soy bean powder)

mealtime n. peyr bye

mean adj. rough, wild, uncivilized -- kahtch ; unpleasant, nasty -- tl'aamh k'mau (lit: black [k'mau] liver [tl'aamh]); cruel -- koh keuv: The Takeo Khmer Rouge were very mean. -- Krum Khmei Kra'hom kang kyte T'keaou (or, dael mok pi T'keaou) keuh koh keuv nah.

mean v. miun nay: That means something different. -- Veea miun nay p'sayng.; This means that they will... -- Ni miun nay tha pooh'gkay nung... ; Do the words "roo ot" always mean "or not", or not? -- Tau(v) peea "roo ot" tyne tai miun nay "or not," roo ot?

meaning n. nay (NB: "ney" = "of"): He does not know [the meaning] [of] the word "honest." -- Gwat ot dung [nay] [ney] peea "sm'oh trong" tay!

meaningless adj. ot nay; k'miun nay

means n. ability, wherewithal, capability -- ma'cho'bye; wi'ti'sa: We [no longer] have the means to defend ourselves. -- Yeung [ot] miun ma'cho'bye dum'bye kaa pee'a kloo'an yeung [tee'it tay].

measles n. kun ch'reuhl

measure n. vi'ti'un aka; kaa vwah'vwull: [The fact that] he took money from his own mother was one measure [of how bad his attitude/behavior/character was]. -- [Kaa putt dael] gwat loo'ich loi pi m'dye ro'bah gwat keuh chia kaa vwah vwull moi [ney a'ka'pa'keh'ree'ya a'krah ro'bah gwat.]; beyond measure -- pun pra'man

measure v. length -- vwah (AP: wah); volume -- vwull; generally -- vwah vwull: I need to measure the picture so I can buy [a frame]. -- Kyom tro kaa vwah roob'pheap dum'bye kyom adje tinh [suhm roob'tawt.]; for clothing -- vwah kow-aow

measurement n. ruu'm vwa ruu'm vwull

meat n. sat(ch)

mechanic n. in general -- chee'eng ma'seen; auto mechanic -- chee'eng tveu laan

medal n. me'dye (fr. Fr.)

media n. news distribution -- kreung p'sye por'da'mee'an; member of the media -- neh p'sye por'da'mee'an; neh ka'ssett (lit: journalist)

mediate v. sum rawh sum roo'an; mediate and resolve -- psahs'psah; (psahs'psah = to weld or join)

mediator n. neh kan'dal; a'nya kan'dal

medical adj. peyt

medicine n. t'nam peyt

medium adj. average -- mut s'yom; medium sized -- toom'huum kan'dal

meet v. make the acquaintance of -- choo'up: They want to meet Hun Sen. -- Gkay jchong choo'up Hun Sen.; get together, rendezvous -- choo'up ka'neea; See you later! -- Choo'up ka'neea peyr krow'ee!; meet by accident, "run into" -- praw'tay'h keunyh: I [just] met him in the street. -- Kyom [teup tai] praw'tay'h keunyh veea noeh aae ploe.; get to know -- scwall: [He was not sorry] he met Ta'. -- [Gwat mun sawk s'd'eye] gwat baan scwall Ta'.

meeting n. conference -- pra'choom (AP: p'choom); slightly more formal -- ong'pra'choom: He had to leave the meeting. -- Gwat tro kaa jcha(k) jchenyh pi ong'pra'choom.

Mekong n. tun'lay May'kong

melody n. sum leng pee'roo'h

melon n. tra'saw

melt v. rawl lee'aae: ice melts -- t'kaw rawl lee'aae; ruhm lee'aae: The ice melted. -- T'kaw ruhm'lee'aae howi.

member n. sa'ma'chik: He is a member of the Party. -- Gwat keuh chia sa'ma'chik ka'na'pac (AP: k'nak'pa).; full member -- sa'ma'chik penyh leng; provisional or candidate member -- sa'ma'chik tree'm; members of my family -- sa'ma'chik kroo'e'sa kyom

memoirs n.   kum'naut praw'vwut (NB: praw'vwut = biography)

memorable adj.   dael jcham cho'up chia'nik

memorandum n.   sa'ra'chaw

memorial n.   pi'ti'ruum'lut

memorize v.   tun teng; jcham

memory n.   capacity to remember -- sah'teh; or, sa'mar'dye; or, jcham: He has a good memory -- Gwat miun sa'mar'dye la'aw.; from memory -- taam jcham; He lost his memory. -- Gwat pwan (or pe'ang) sa'mar'dye.; recollection -- a'noo'sow'ree (AP: sa'va'ree): She has pleasant memories of Takeo. -- Nee'eng miun a'noo'sow'ree la'aw noeh (or jchum'poo'h) T'keaou.; in memory of -- chia a'noo'sow'ree jchum'poo'h

men n.   ma'nooh proh

menace n.   a'veye dael kuum ree'um kuum haeng

menace v.   kuum ree'um kuum haeng

mend n.   repair -- paah: mend clothes -- paah kow-aow; reform -- praw'preut owi trum tro laung: He should mend his ways. -- Gwat koo'a praw'preut owi trum tro laung.

mental adj.   kang koo'k'bal; kum'nut praw'ngya: He has a mental problem. -- Gwat miun chuum'ngeu kum'nut praw'ngya.

mentality n.   tuk jchet; kum'nut

mention v.   ni'yaye om'pee; cho chaae'k om'pee

menu n.   ta'rang ma'hope; bun chee muk ma'hope

merchandise n.   tuum nenyh; aye'von; ro'bah looh do: aye'von looh do

merchantile adj.   chuum'noo'inyh

merchant n.   neh chuum'noo'inyh

merciful n.   praw'kaap dow'ee; kaa a'nutt; miun may'daa

merciless n.   k'miun may'daa; ot praw'nye

mercy n.   may'daa; kaa praa'pra'nye; show mercy -- bung hyne kaa praa'pra'nye; or, bung hyne may'taa; at the mercy of -- sre(ch) tai leuh

mere adj.   kron tai chia... pun'noh: He is a mere boy. -- Veea kron tai chia gkon k'mayng pun'noh.

merely adv.   kron tai (AP: kro'un tai)

merge v.   jchole ka'neea (or, jchole ka'neea [tai moi]; lit: merge together [into one]): The two roads merge near Po'sat. -- Ploe pi jchole ka'neea noeh chit Po'sat.

merger n.   kaa roo'up ru'um jchole ka'neea

merit n.   secular -- kuun sum'baat; promotion on the basis of merit -- laung saak dow'ee kuun sum'baat; spiritual -- bun ko' sol: Buddhist people [believe that] the accumulation of merit is important. -- Neh kaan put sa'sna [miun chuum'neuu'a tha] kaa pru'mole bun ko'sol chia kaa cham'batch.

to make merit v.   pru'mole bun; pru'mole bun ko'sol

message n.   saa (lit: information); send a message -- p'nya(r) saa (lit: send information); pdum pnya(r) (lit: inform or tell/send); leave a message -- miun pdum (lot: have (s.th.) to tell); pdum prap (lit: tell/tell); miun ni'yaye (lit: have a statement): Did he leave (lit: have) a message? -- Tau(v) gwat miun pdum a'veye tay? or, Tau(v) gwat miun ni'yaye aae tay?; I want to leave a message. -- Kyom jchong pdum p'nya(r) klaah.

messenger n.   neh no'um saa

metal adj.   dyke: not a plastic spoon, a metal spoon -- ot slap'preea cho'a, slap'preea dyke; (formal, written term, little used in spoken Khmer: lo'ha'tee'it)

metal n.   dyke: Cars are made of metal. -- Laan tveu pi dyke.

meter n.   100 centimeters -- met; measuring device -- kreung vwah; electric meter -- kreung vwah pleung; water meter -- kreung vwah tuk

method n.   viti; ma'cho'bye; ro'bee'up

methodology n.   vi'ti'sa

metric adj. pra met chia mool'tan (lit: using the meter as a base)

mice n. kun'dull

microfilm n. mee'cro'fil

middle n. of a line -- pieh kan'dal: That [point] is in the middle of the line. -- [Jchum nutch] ni pieh kan'dal ban'twa(t).; of a circle -- noeh kan'dal: That point is in the middle of [the circle]. -- Jchum nutch nu noeh kan'dal [ruhm'vuung].

Middle East n. Me'chum Bo'pheap

midnight n. kan'dal yoop; yoop ch'ro; (formal/literary/ poetic term -- kan'dal ree'a trei'; midnight (watch time) -- moa dap pieh yoop (lit: twelve o'clock at night)

midwife n. ch'maw

might n. kum'lung

might v. pra'heil: It might rain. -- Veea pra'heil plee'eng.; (Will he go?) (He) might. -- Pra'heil.; adje nung (lit: could; connotes more than 50/50 chance): It might rain (i.e., it very well could rain). -- Veea adje nung plee'eng.

mild adj. flavor -- mun klang; weather (lit: not cold or too hot) -- tee'ut a'kas mun traw'cheh(k) roo k'dau peyk; re a penalty -- mun t'nguun; or, bong kaad

mild-mannered adj. slote; jchong jchanyh

mile n. mile; milage -- jchum'ngai; cost, or price, per mile -- dum'lye k'nong moi mile; miles, in sense of far -- chng'eye: It's miles from here. -- Veea pi ni chng'eye nah!

militant n. neh taw'soo (lit: one who struggles)

military adj. tee'hee'an; military equipment -- praw'dop praw'dow tee'heean; yoo'tee'a: military police -- dum'roo'it yoo'tee'a; or, Paye Aam (fr. Fr. "Police Militaire", or P.M.); military radio station -- pawh yoo'tee'a yo'teh'pheap: military district -- dum'bun yo'tch'pheap; suk: military court -- to'la'ka suk

militia n. kawng svaay tran; kawng chee'veea pul (AP: chee' va pul)

milk n. tuk dawh gko (lit: liquid [of] breast [of] cow): sweet milk -- tuk dawh gko p'eye'm; (AP: usually condensed in speech to ta'ko' and dawh gko and tud'gko): [iced] coffee with milk -- cafe ta'gko [t'kaw]

mill n. ro'ng gkun; rice mill -- k'bal gkun sro; (gkun = to grind, sro = just-harvested rice (i.e., still on stalk))

million n. lee'en: ten million -- dop lee'en; a hundred million -- roi lee'en; moi kow(d)

millionaire n. maha'sa'tay

mind n. brain -- koo'k'bal: intelligence, intellect -- praw'ngya; make up one's mind -- sum'rach jchet; change one's mind -- pdo kum'nut

mind v. object to -- praw'kaan; praw'kye praw'kaan: Do you mind [if I eat now]? -- Tau(v) neh praw'kaan tay [baa kyom nyam eye leaou ni]?; I don't mind! -- Kyom ot praw'kye praw'kaan tay!; Never mind. -- Mun kut tay; or, Mun aae tay.

mine prn. ro'bah: That car is mine. -- Laan nu ro'bah kyom.

mine n. explosive device -- meen: set mines -- dah(k) meen; plant mines -- kawp meen; source of gems, minerals, etc. -- an'do'ng rye

minefield n. veal meen

mineral n. lo'hot'tee'it

mineshaft n. an'do'ng rye

mingle v. praw lok

minister n. ratt'mun'trei (AP: rawt'mun'trei, rup'mun'trei); cabinet minister -- krum'pruk'sa ratt'mun'trei; prime minister -- nee'aae'yok ratt'mun'trei

ministry n. kra'soo'ung (AP: kra'soo'um)

Ministry of [Agriculture], [Forestry] and [Fisheries] -- Kra'soo'ung [Kaah'se'kaam], [Ro'ka Bra'munyh] nung [A'neh'saat]

Ministry of Defense -- Kra'soo'ung Kaa Pee'a Praw'tet

Ministry of Education -- Kra'soo'ung Op'ruhm; or, Krasoo'ung Op'ruhm Chee'it
Ministry of Environment -- Kra'soo'ung Pa'ri'taan
Ministry of Finance -- Kra'soo'ung Heh'ranya'vuh'to
Ministry of Foreign Affairs -- Kra'soo'ung Kaa Bor'tay
Ministry of Health -- Kra'soo'ung Sok'a'pi'bal
Ministry of Interior -- Kra'soo'ung Ma'ha Praw'tet
Ministry of Justice -- Kra'soo'ung Yoo'teh'toa
Ministry of Planning -- Kra'soo'ung Pyne'kaa
Ministry of Public Works -- Kra'soo'ung Sa'tee'run'a Kaa
Ministry of Transportation -- Kra'soo'ung Kej Ma'nee'a'kaam
minor adj. to'ich; k'mayng
minor wife n. pra'pun jchong
minority n. pieh tic (lit: small part); chuun pieh tic (lit: minority people)
minute n. nee'a'tee (AP: na'tee)
mint n. chii un'kam
miracle n. baa'to'poo(t); (AP: paa'to'poo(t))
mirror n. kun ch'uhh(k): see one'sself in the mirror -- ch'lo kun ch'uhh(k)
miscarriage n. kaa ro'lut; ro'lut gkon
mischievous adj. ro'peuss; k'ull
miser n. ma'nooh kum'nunyh choo'a chee'it; (thrifty person -- ma'nooh kum'nunyh)
miserable adj. vaae'te'neea; ro'haem ro'haam; ro'ng toook: [The refugees] have a miserable life. -- [Chuun pieh kloo'an] rooh dow'ee vaae'te'neea.; to be miserable -- miun kaa ro'ng toook. (NB: ro'ng = to receive)
misery n. s'kd'eye vaae'te'neea
misfortune n. soi; a'ko'sul
misinform v. bong vee'ung ploe (lit: set on the wrong road)
mislead v. bong vee'ung daan
Miss n. most common terms:

nee'eng (casual; used by older person to address one younger; may be affectionate; viz, Good morning, Miss Bora! -- Sooa' s'dye nee'eng Bora!);

neh nee'eng (somewhat formal and so polite that if said to a woman younger than the speaker may be taken as a joke or cause some good natured embarrassment, as might calling someone "Madame" in English;

ken'yaa (term of formal address for students; also used to address woman in late teens or early 20s if speaker does not know definitely that she is married; if speaker knows woman is married, he/she would address her as lok sraae);

nee'eng ken'yaa (used to address woman in late teens or early 20s not known to be married);

bo'vaw ken'yaa (used to express "Miss" in contest and similar titles, as, Miss World -- bo'vaw ken'yaa Sa'ka'lok; Miss Cambodia -- bo'vaw ken'yaa Kampuchea; Miss Po'sat -- bo'vaw ken'yaa Po'sat);

also used:

neh bong and neh ming (used to refer to woman married or unmarried if addressee is of some but not substantially greater age or status than speaker);

lok sraae (usually refers to woman known to be married but can also be used by one younger or of lower social status than addressee a) if addressee at least in late 20s b) to indicate respect if addressee's marital status is unknown or even if addressee is known to be unmarried);

neh sraae (addressed to woman of unknown marital status and usually at least in 30s);

lok yaye or umm (respectively, grandmother (lok yaye) and auntie (umm); can refer to older/elderly woman married or unmarried);

(NB: It is not necessary to use any of the foregoing terms of address when speaking to someone familiar to speaker and not (i.e., by reason of being particularly advanced in years, or career or social status) normally spoken to with unusual formality; for example, expressing "Good morning, Miss Bora" by saying "Sooa'si'dye, lok sraae Bora" is quite formal; unless the woman addressed is hardly known to the speaker or is, by virtue of age or otherwise, entitled to special deference beyond normal social respect, "lok sraae" would not be used and the sentence in the example above would simply be, "Sooa'si'dye, Bora." with "Miss" merely implied).

miss v. be lonely for -- nuhk: miss a friend -- nuhk mit; miss a chance -- kaw kaan mun; kaw kaan ot: I missed my chance to go to Battambong. -- Kyom kaw kaan ot baan teuh Battambong.; not be/arrive on time at s. th. -- ot twon: I missed the bus. -- Kyom teuh ot twon laan bus.; or, Laan teuh howi. (lit: The bus already left.); miss a target with s. th. shot (bullet, arrow, etc.) -- soot koh; banyh ot tro; miss with a ball throw or hit into or through a hole (i.e., golf ball or basketball) -- bawh ot jchole (lit: thrown (but) not go in)

missing adj. bot howi: My watch is missing. -- Ni'a'li'ka (or lee'le'kaa) kyom bot howi.

mission n. task, assignment -- pae'ss suk'ka'kam: The soldiers had an important mission to carry out. -- Tee'hee'an miun pae'ss suk'ka'kam sum'kahn tro tveu.; diplomatic facility, embassy -- s'tahn'toot; (S: 'toot)

missle n. kam chroo'it

missionary n. neh ps'eye se'sna (lit: one who spreads religion)

mistake n. kum'hawh: It was your mistake. -- Veea keuh kum'hawh ro'bah neh.; admit a mistake -- to'tool kum'hawh; to'h: admit a mistake -- to'tool to'h; catch a mistake -- jchaab to'h; koh: make a mistake -- tveu koh; or, plo'ut snee'it;

mistreat v. tveu baap: He mistreats that kid a lot. -- Gwat tveu baap gkon k'mayng nung nah.

mistreatment n. kaa tveu baap: suffer much mistreatment -- ro'ng toook kaa tveu baap ch'raan

mistress n. kum'nun jchet

misunderstand v. yul koh; yul ch'raw luum

misunderstanding n. kaa yul koh; kaa yul ch'raw luum

mix v. lee'aae: mix drinks -- lee'aae sra; mix Thais and Khmers -- lee'aae bun'jchole ka'neea saah See'um howi nung saah Khmei; mix together -- p'sum: mix ingredients for the soup -- p'sum kreung sam'lop s'law; mix up, confuse -- ch'raw luum; or, ch'raw bo'k; or, ch'raw baal

mixed up adj. ch'raw bo'k; ch'raw baal; pwon ch'raw luum

mixed with adv. lee'aae chi'moi: sugar mixed with coconut milk -- sc'aaw lee'aae chi'moi tuk dohng

moan n. kaa t'ngo

moan v. t'ngo

moat n. snaam pleuh

mobilization n. kum'nyne

mobilize v. generally -- roo'up roo'um ka'neea laung: [To defend] the town [against] the KR (Khmer Rouge) we must mobilize the people. -- [Dumbye kaa'pee'a] ti'krong praw'chang Khmei Kra'hom, tro kaa roo'up roo'um ka'neea laung pra'chee'chuun.; mobilize an existing force -- leuk thwaap: mobilize the militia -- leuk thwaap kawng svaay tran

mock adj. klaeng klai: a mock tank -- ro't troe klaeng klai

mock v. payb mwot; jchum awh

model n. either fashion model or model of s. th. -- kum roo; dum rap

modern adj. tuum neuup; t'maee (lit: new)

modest adj. opposite of boastful -- dah ploo'un; simple -- twa'ma'da: a modest home -- ptay'a twamada; modest quantitatively (as, a modest income) -- mun seou ch'raan

modesty n. pheap ruhm tuum

modify v. ga'aae: amend someone's instructions -- ga'aae kaa bung haat bung hyne ro'bah gkay; reuh rooh; rooh reuh

molar n. t'ming tkee'im (NB: tkee'im = jaw)

molasses n. sc'aaw ru'ngoo

mold n. organic growth -- p'sutt (also means "mushroom"); become moldy -- dawh psutt; (NB: algae, water slime = s'l'eye); casing used to form s. th. -- puhm

mom n. Phnom Penh term, generally -- ma; provincial terms, generally -- mye, m'dye or neh m'dye; term used in parts of provinces along Mekong and Bassac (Kom'puung Cham, Kandal, etc.) -- neh

moment n. ruum pec; plet: Wait a moment. -- Jcham moi plet.; a little while -- sun'too' to'ich or, sun'too: The doctor will be back [in a moment]. -- Neh kruu peyt (or, lok vi'chet bun'dut) nung mok venyh [moi sun'too tee'it].

momentum n. penyh tuum huung; kum'lung (lit: force, power)

monarch n. s'dach (AP: sa'dak); preah ree'ech' chia; preah jchao

monarchist n. ree'ech'chia ni'yuum

monarchist adj. preah ree'ech'chia (AP: condensed in speech to "pre'h ree'chia"): a monarchist plan -- pyne'kaa preah ree'ech'chia; ree'ch'chia: Royal Communal Administration (literal translation of term once used to describe Sihanouk regime) -- Ro'bab Ree'ech'chia Ni'yuum; s'dach: Funcinpec is the monarchist party. -- Funcinpec keuh chia ka'na'pac s'dach.

Monday n. t'ngai chun

monetary adj. ruu'paya'vuh'to; International Monetary Fund -- Mul'niti Ruu'paya'vuh'to Un'tara'chee'it

money n. loi; praa(k); make money -- rok loi; rok praa(k); rok loi kaa(k) (lit: make a few coins); (NB: change = loi op; Do you have change? -- Miun loi op, tay?)

money-changer n. neh do loi

money-lender n. may bum null; (borrower = gkon bum null or, neh chuum'paya loi; lit: one who owes money)

monk n. lok; lok sung; chief monk -- preah jchao a'ti'kaa; (NB: Individuals to be able to use the foregoing titles must, inter alia, live in a wat; another commonly heard title, "a'char", is used with reference to an individual who may or may not live in a wat and who typically functions as a teacher and presides at various social ceremonies.)

monkey n. swaa'

monopolize v. p'dach'muk

monopoly n. set'dach'muk

monsoon n. rainy season -- ro'doe plee'eng; particular storm -- k'shaal moo'song

monster n. ma'nooh jchum'lyke

Montagnard n. Khmei leou

month n. kye: the month of May -- kye Oo'sa'pee'a; beginning of the month -- daum kye; end of the month -- jchong kye; last month, i. e., the month just past -- kye muun; last month, i. e., final -- ... the last month before the rains start... -- kye jchong krow'ee muun peyr t'lch plee'eng...; next month, i. e., the month after this one -- kye krow'ee; the next month, i. e., in a series -- kye bun'to'up

monthly adv. ree'eng ro'vull kye

monument n. praw'sat: Angkor Wat -- praw'sat Angkor Wat; vik'mee'en: [Independence] Monument (Phnom Penh) -- Vik'mee'en [Eye Kri'a]

mood n. a'rom: be in a... mood -- tut noeh k'nong a'rom...; He is in a good mood today. -- Gwat tut noeh k'nong a'rom la'aw t'gnai ni.; be in a strange mood -- tut noeh k'nong a'rom jchum'lyke; bad mood -- a'rom mun la'aw; also: be in a good mood -- sroul jchet; be in a bad mood -- mua mao mua mong

moon n. lok k'eye: a beautiful moon -- lok k'eye la'aw; full moon -- lok k'eye penyh vong; or, (romantic) lok k'eye penyh bauw'ra'mye; a clear, beautiful moon -- lok k'eye ploo la'aw; moon (somewhat "flowery" term) -- doo'ung chan or, preah chan; literary term -- doo'ung chan tree'a

moonlight n. puun'leuh lok k'eye

moral adj. ney sa'la'toa

moral n. value -- sa'la'toa; moral of the story -- dum'bole miun

morale n. tuk jchet

morality n. toa; sull toa

more adv. tee'it: I want more. -- Kyom sum/jchong baan tee'it.; one more -- moi tee'it: I want one more. -- Kyom sum moi tee'it.; some more -- tyme tee'it: I want some more. -- Kyom sum tyme tee'it.; I have to study (some) more. -- Kyom tro rian tyme tee'it.; a little more -- baan tic tee'it: I want a little more. -- Kyom sum baan tic tee'it.; no more -- twal: I have no more ideas. -- Kyom twal kum'nut howi.; no more -- awh: I have no more time. -- Kyom awh peyr howi.; no more rice -- awh bye; no more strength -- awh kum'lung; no more (expressed as "do [not] have more") -- [ot] miun... tee'it tay: I have no more time. -- Kyom ot miun peyr tee'it tay.; more or less -- praw'heil

more --- than adv. when in the English phrase "more" is followed by a noun -- ch'raan chiang: There are more KR than Se'rei Ka. -- Miun KR ch'raan chiang Se'rei Ka.; when in the English phrase, "more" is followed by an adjective -- chiang: This car is more expensive than that car. -- Laan ni tlai chiang laan nu.; no more than -- mun... chiang: I will pay no more than 100 riels. -- Kyom mun jchum'nye chiang m'roi riel tay.

more n. (the) more -- rut tai ch'raan

morning n. pruhk: this morning, right now or later on -- pruhk ni: We will go to the market this morning. -- Yeung nung teuh p'sa pruhk ni.; this morning, earlier -- pruhk muun: She has already gone to the market this morning. -- Nee'eng teuh p'sa pruhk muun howi.; in the morning -- peyr pruhk; tomorrow morning -- pruhk s'eyed; pra'lum: early in the morning -- pi praw'lum; I have to get up early in the morning. -- Kyom tro pn'yeh pi praw'lum.; or, very early morning -- pruhk praw'hee'em: We must go to work very early in the morning. -- Yeung tro jchenyh teuh tveu kaa pi pruhk praw'heem.

moron n. a'chey (lit: name of character in Cambodian fable whose girlfriend, also portrayed as not brilliant, is named Mi'k'rawt)

mortar n. weapon -- kum pleung ta'baal; kum pleung mor'tee'aae; material used with bricks -- bye'aw

mosque n. Cham (Cambodian Muslim minority group) religious building -- vi'hear Cham (lit: Cham temple)

mosquito n. moo

mosquito net n. moung

most adv. bom'pot (NB: spelled "bom'pot" but pronounced closer to "mom pot"): most important -- som'kahn bom'pot; the most -- yang ch'raan bom'pot: (We wanted five but) the most, we could buy was two. -- (...) Yeung adje tinh veea yang ch'raan bom'pot pi.

most of adv. pieh ch'raan: most of the people -- prachee'chuun pieh ch'raan;

at most, at the most adv. yang ch'raan; yang ch'raan bom'pot: I will pay at (the) most 100 riels. -- Kyom jchum'nye yang ch'raan m'roi riel.

(the) most ever adv. sum'bahm bom pot

most of all adv. ch'raan bom'pot: I like this one most of all. -- Kyom jchole jchet a'ni ch'raan bom'pot.; chee'eng gkay: I like Srei Peau most of all. -- Kyom jchole jchet Srei Peau chee'eng gkay.

mostly adv. ch'raan tai

mother n. Phnom Penh -- ma; provinces, generally -- mye or, neh m'dye; riverine provinces (Kompong Cham, Kandal, etc.) -- neh; birth mother -- m'dye bung kaut; step mother -- m'dye jchong; mother-in-law -- m'dye k'mayke; re animals -- may (AP: mye)

motherland n. mee'a'to praw'tet

motion n. kaa kum rauw(k)

motionless adj. sngee'um; men kum rauw(k)

motive n. hyte

motor n. ma'seen

motorbike n. mo'to

motorboat n. kra'note

motorcycle n. mo'to

mount v. get onto -- laung jchi: mount a horse -- laung jchi seh; mount an attack [against] (with connotation of striking first) -- vi'yaye praw'ha [praw'chang]; mount an attack against (with connotation of fighting back or defending against) -- vi'yaye praw'chang

mountain n. phnom; group of hills or mountains -- pra'choom phnom

mourn v. kaan toook

mouse n. kun'dull

moustache n. puk mwot (AP: pu'mwot, pu'mu'ot); to shave -- gkhao puk mwot: Go shave! -- Gkhao puk mwot jchenyh teuh!

mouth n. mwot (AP: mu'ot)

mouthfuls n. mwot: Eat [two or three] mouthfuls! -- Nyam bye [pi-bye] mwot teuh!

mouthpiece n. neh no'um pee'a

movable adj. capable of being moved -- dael adje baan reuh; portable -- to'ich (lit: small); movable property (legal term) -- cha'la'na vuh'to need real legal terms

move n. change of location -- kaa pdo

move v. move s. th. -- do cunlye'ng; pdo cunlye'ng; (NB: do and pdo are both derived from the written form "pdo(r)" and are essentially inter-changeable in usage, although pdo is generally used as part of the noun construction "kaa pdo"); Please move the TV. -- Sum pdo (or, do) cunlye'ng TV.; They moved the files from this office to that one. -- Gkay pdo cunlye'ng bun'chee pi ban'tope ni teuh ban'tope nu.;

 move s. th. away -- yok; or, yok... jchenyh: Please move this book (away from me). -- Sum yok s'po ni jchenyh.;

 move s. th., often pourable, from one container to another rather than from one location to another -- p'tay: Move it (from that box) to this box. -- P'tay veea (   ) teuh praw'op ni.;

 move of or by persons -- pdo or plas: He moved the people to a safe place. -- Gwat pdo cunlye'ng pooh'gkay teuh cunlye'ng sok.; He was moved to Thhmar Puok. -- Gwat baan plas teuh Thhmar Puok.;

 move self to a new location -- plas: He moved from one place to another. -- Gwat plas pi cunlye'ng ni teuh cunlye'ng tee'it.; pdo cunlye'ng: I'm going to move to Po'sat. -- Kyom nung pdo teuh Po'sat.;

move little by little -- ruhm kuhl... ban tic m'dong baan tic m'dong; kum'rauwk: Can you move a little? -- Sum kum'rowk baan tic?

 Don't move! -- Kum reuh!; or, Noeh owi sngee'um!;

 move in -- reuh jchole; move out -- reuh jchenyh

moved (emotionally) adj. ruhm pheup; ruhm chool; ruhm choo'ay jchet

movement n. motion -- s'eye ung'keuh; s'eye kum'rauwk: I saw a movement in the [bushes]. -- Kyom keunyh s'eye ung'keuh (or kum'rauwk) k'nong [kum'cheu].; political -- chaw'la'na: Many farmers joined that movement. -- Neh sr'eye ch'raan ch'raan jchole ruum chaw'la'na nu.

movie n. gkun; pheap yun (lit: motion picture); movie theater -- ro'ng gkun; go see a movie -- jchole meuhl gkun; teuh meuhl gkun

movie star n. da'ra pheap yun

Mr. n. term of address -- lok: I'd [like to introduce] Mr. Sok An. -- Kyom [sum nye noo'um ni keuh] Lok Sok An.; re young men -- nee'eng; (NB: at public functions, typical form of address by moderator to audience is "Lok, Lok Sraae, Nee'eng Ken'yaa" -- Gentlemen, Ladies, Young ladies")

Mrs. n. term of address -- Neh sraae: I met Mrs. Dap Chuon. -- Kyom baan choop neh sraae Dap Chuon. (see, also, under "Miss" for discussion of use of terms for Miss, Mrs., lady, etc.)

much adv. ch'raan: They need much more [seed]. -- Pooh'gkay tro kaa [kro'up poo'ch] ch'raan tyme tee'it.; I don't need much. -- Kyom ot tro kaa ch'raan tay.; how much -- pu'man (AP: pu'man, p'man, pun'na); not much

-- mun seou; or, mun pu'man; too much -- ch'raan peyk; chru'l peyk; very much -- pieh ch'raan; or, krye leng: I like it very much. -- Kyom jchole jchet veea krye leng.

mud n.   phoo'(a); la'bub

muddy adj.   byke phoo'(a); paw pet(ch) paw put(ch): The road was muddy. -- Ploe paw pet(ch) paw put(ch).

muggy adj.   humid -- sa'ott; salm

multiply v.   in mathematics -- kuun; grow in number -- kaut ch'raan laung: Last year our problems multiplied. -- chh'nam teuh pun'ha yeung kaut ch'raan laung.

murder n.   kee'it ta'kahw; kaa sum'lap

murder v.   sum'lap; tveu kee'it; pee kee'it

murderer n.   neh tveu kee'it; kee'it ta'kaw; ma'nooh sum'lap gkay

muscle n.   sak'dum

museum n.   sa'ra'mun'ti

mushroom n.   p'sutt

music n.   plaeng (AP: pleng); don'trei; wedding music -- plaeng kaa; to play music -- leng plaeng

musical instrument n.   praw'dop plaeng; praw'dop leng plaeng

musician n.   neh plaeng

must v.   optional, should, would like to, but not critical or mandatory -- tro or tro kaa: I really must (i.e., ought to) finish this work today. -- Kyom tro jchawb tveu nu t'ngai ni.; optional (i.e., want) -- tro kaa: I must have more cake! -- Kyom tro kaa num tee'it.; optional (i.e., want) -- jchong: I must have some more of that delicious fish! -- Kyom jchong trei nu chng'anyh tee'it.; not optional, non-discretionary, legally, physically, militarily, etc. mandatory -- tro tai: I must leave before my visa [expires]. -- Kyom tro tai jchenyh muun vee'za kyom [puuht kum'naut].; We must [escape] before the road is cut. -- Yeung tro tai [pee'es kloo'an] muun ploe kaat'pa'dach.; necessary to avoid seriously undesirable consequence -- tro tai: We must leave Battambong by 3 p. m.; [otherwise] we will be late getting to Phnom Penh. -- Yeung tro tai jchenyh Battambong noeh mao bye; [baa mun doj cha'neh tay], yeung mok doll Phnom Penh mun twon peyr.; We must (not just ought to but for survival have to) protect [the environmment]. -- Yeung tro tai kaa pee'a [twa'ma'chee'it].

mustard n.   mo'tar (fr. Fr.)

mustard greens n.   sp'aae

mute adj.   ko'; mute person -- ma'nooh ko'hh

mutton n.   sat(ch) chee'im

my prn.   ro'bah kyom; kyom: my house -- ptay'a ro'bah kyom; or, ptay'a kyom; ro'bah own; ro'bah bong (re own and bong see discussion under "I" and "me", and in "Prepositions" section under "Notes on Khmer Grammar and Speech")

myself prn.   tai'eiyne; kloo'an kyom

mysterious adj.   a'kum'bang: a mysterious past -- praw'vwut a'kum'bang

N

nail n. for hammering -- dyke; or dyke kohl; fingernail -- kra'jchawk dai; toenail -- kraw jchawk cheung

naive adj. chhaut

naked adj. kloo'an to' tay; sraat

name n. chamoo'h (AP: cha'mooh): What's your name? -- Chamoo'h aae? company name -- yee haow; chamoo'h krum'hun; chamoo'h chuum' noo'inyh; in the name of... -- k'nong nee'um...

name v. dah(k) chamoo'h; to be named -- miun chamoo'h

name-card n. carte chamoo'h

nap n. kaa daeyk t'ngai

nap v. daeyk t'ngai

napkin n. kon'syne; kon'syne nyam bye

narcotics n. kreung ngyee'an (lit: addictive things)

narrow adj. jchung'eet; narrow-minded -- jchet jchung'eet jchung' ol

nasty adj. a'krah; in a nasty mood -- mua mao

nation n. sruk; praw'tet; chee'it

national adj. chee'it; national flag -- tung chee'it

national n. i.e., citizen of a country -- praw'chee'a chee'it;

nationalism n. chee'it nee'uum

nationalist n. neh chee'it nee'uum

nationalistic adj. chia chee'it nee'uum

nationality n. chuun chee'it; What is your nationality? (I.e., Where are you from (lit: Your nationality is what?)) -- Lok chuun chee'it a'veye?

natural adj. twa'ma'chee'it; twa'ma'da; kwa'mon chee'it; natural disaster -- kroo'ti'nak kwa'mon chee'it

nature n. the non-man-made environment, forces of nature -- twa'ma'chee'it; person's character -- leh ka'nak; or, leh ka'nak kum'naut: her gentle nature -- leh ka'nak kum'naut slote nee'eng; person's character -- twa'ma'chee'it: That's just his nature -- Twam'chee'it ro'bah gwat tai pun'noh teuh howi.

naughty adj. ruh'peuh ruh po'ich; kull: Veesna, you are very naughty; you just like to look at girls. -- Veesna, neh eiyne kull nah, jchole jchet meuhl tai sraae sraae.

nauseous, nauseated adj. ro'mool poo'ah jchong ka'oo'it (lit: stomach upset, want to throw up)

navel n. p'sutt (same word as for mushroom)

navigation n. nee'a'vee'a chaw

navy n. thwaap cheung tuk; tee'hee'an cheung tuk; (NB: "teeheean" alone means "soldier" or "soldiers" and if followed by "cheung tuk" (loosely, "seagoing") means "sailor" or "sailors"; understood as "sailors", "teeheean cheung tuk" also expresses "navy".)

near prp. chit: It's near Ba'rei. -- Veea noeh chit (or, chit noeh) Ba'rei.; chit bun ka'wee: near the store -- chit bun ka'wee hawng; bee'it -- near the school -- noeh bee'it sala; k'bye

nearby adv. k'bye; chit; chit kang

nearly adv. chit; steu tai

necessarily adv. jchum'batch

necessary adj. jchum'batch: Is this trip nesessary? -- Tau(v) dum'narr ni jchum'batch tay?; not necessary -- mun batch tay; mun jcham'batch

neck n. khaw: hang s. o. by the neck -- p'shoo'a khaw

necklace n. k'sye khaw

necktie n. kro'vat khaw

nectar n. tuk k'muum; tuk dahm

need n. kaa tro kaa; s'kd'eye tro kaa

need v. discretionary, not mandatory -- tro; tro kaa: (To really see the country), I need to go to Battambong. -- ( ), kyom tro teuh Battambong.; (To have a really good time), I need more money. -- ( ), kyom tro kaa loi ch'raan chiang.; (It's late;) I need to go. -- ( ); kyom tro teuh.; They need to think. -- Gkay tro kut.; We need sleep. -- Yeung tro teuh geyng; legally, physically, militarily, etc., non-discretionary -- tro tai: I need [am legally obliged] to leave Friday. -- Kyom tro tai jchenyh teuh t'ngai suk.; I need a new visa; [otherwise] they may arrest me. -- Kyom tro tai miun vee'za t'maee; [praw'sun chia k'miun], pooh'gkay nung adje jchaap kyom.; He needs blood if he is to live. -- Gwat tro tai miun chec'im dum'bye rooh ree'en.

needed adj. batch: not needed -- mun batch tay

needle n. m'chul

neglect v. mun yok jchet toook dah(k): The step-mother neglected [the children of the former wife]. -- M'dye jchong mun yok jchet tooo'k dah(k) nung [gkon dahm].; mun ahl peu jchum'poo'h; neglect your [duties] -- mun ahl peu jchum'poo'h [pee'a'reh'tek] ro'bah neh

negligence n. k'chee k'chee'a; ch'weh pro'heh; kaa mun yok jchet tooo'k dah(k); kaa mun ahl peu

negligent adj. dael k'chee k'chee'a; dael ch'weh pro'heh

negotiate v. jchaw jchaa; sum ro', sum ru'ul

negotiation(s) n. kaa jchaw'jchaa(r); kej jchaw jchaa(r)

neighbor n. neh chit kang

neighborhood n. chit kang

neighboring country n. praw'tet chit kang

neither adj. te'ang pi mun: neither shoe fits -- s'bye'k cheung te'ang pi mun jchoh; Neither of them showed up. -- Neh te'ang pi mun keunyh. (or, Mun keunyh neh te'ang pi.); neither of -- k'miun neh na: Neither of us went. -- K'miun neh na teuh tay.; neither... nor -- te'ang... howi... ot: Neither you nor I are stupid, [just crazy]! -- Te'ang neh howi kyom ot plee pleuh tay, [kron tai longee long'euh]!; neither... nor -- mun... prome te'ang: We will see neither Angkor Wat nor Battambong. -- Yang nung mun toos'na Angkor Wat prome te'ang Battambong.; neither... nor -- mun... prome te'ang mun: He will neither study nor sleep; [he wants to go drinking]. -- Gwat nung mun rian prome te'ang mun geyng; [gwat jchong pokh].

nephew n. ka'mooi proh

nepotism n. kaa yul ngyee'it (lit: understand relatives): practice nepotism -- yul ngyee'it; Practising nepotism (is) breaking the law. -- Yul ngyee'it ( ) klee'it ch'bop.

nerve n. saw sye praw'sat

nervous adj. nyaw p'ahl; pay: scared -- pay klait(ch); to make s. o. nervous -- tveu owi vull

nest n. sum'bohk

net n. sum nanyh

network n. radio -- bun danyh vi'chi'yoo; of spies, etc. -- bun danyh ney neh seup kaa

neutral adj. aps'yeea'kret: The UN is neutral in Cambodia. -- Noch k'nong Kampuchea UN chia neh aps'yeea'kret.

neutrality n. aps'yeea'kret'a'pheap

never adv. mun'dael: He's never around. -- Gwat mun'dael mok tay.; never too late -- mun'dael yeut tay

Never mind xcl. Mun aae tay!; Ot aae tay!

nevertheless adv. yang na kaw dow'ee; tooo'k chia yang na kaw dow'ee; I hate it; nevertheless I will [still] do it. -- Tooo'k chia kyom sa'op veea, yang na kaw dow'ee kyom [noeh tai] tveu [da'aae].

new adj. t'maee: New Market in Phnom Penh -- Psa T'maee noeh k'nong Phnom Penh; a new singer -- neh jchum'ree'eng t'maee; new-born -- teup kaut; a new baby -- gkon teup kaut

New Year's Day n.   T'ngai bun jchole chh'nam

news n. por'da'mee'an

newspaper n. saa: Saa Por'da'mec'an Kampuchea (lit: Newspaper of the News of Cambodia; Phnom Penh government news-daily commonly referred to as "SPK" or, in Khmer pronunciation, "Ess'Pay'Kaa"); ka'sset

newspaperman/woman n.   journalist -- neh ka'sset

next adj. next chronologically -- krow'ee: Next year we will go to France. -- chh'nam krow'ee yeung nung teuh sruk Ba'raang.; next in order, line or sequence -- bun'to'up; In 1979 there were few crops, but the next year was better. -- chh'nam 1979 mun seou baan p'auwl tay, pun'ta'aae chh'nam bun'to'op mok baan krawn baar chiang.; the next person -- neh bun'to'op; Next, we will... -- Chia bun'to'up, yeung nung...

nice adj. la'aw

Nice to see you! xcl.   S'bai dow'ee baan choop neh!

nickname n.   chamoo'h haow krau; (examples of Khmer nick-names are Kun'teuu'a ("shorty"), Kraw'mop ("fatty"), Tun'sye ("rabbit"), Kum'chul'pch ("lazy"), and Mee'eh ("gold/precious".)

niece n. ka'mooi sraae

night n. yoop: Tuesday night -- yoop t'ngai ongkeea;

at night -- peyr yoop; night time -- pcyr yoop; night club -- ro'ng (k)sauw(l); last night -- yoop munyh; late at night or middle of the night -- yoop ch'ro

ninety adj. kow sup

no intrjctn.   a'tay; tay: Do you want to go? No! -- Jchong teuh, eh? A'tay!

no adj. connoting "not" -- mun, or ot miun: no [good] -- mun [la'aw]; no way (or means) -- ot miun ploe; denoting simple lack of s. th. -- ot (AP: utt, ett, a') miun: no answer -- ot miun jchum'la'wee; no candles -- ot miun tee'un; in sense of no more of s. th. that has run out or been exhausted -- awh: no (more) strength -- awh kum'lung; no more time -- awh peyr; no more rice -- awh bye (but, famine -- kaa ot bye); connoting "no more, all gone" -- awh howi

nobody, no one prn. ot miun... nch na (AP: no na): No one wants [to be partners with them]. -- Ot miun neh na jchong [tveu chia koo'kong chi'moi pooh'gkay].; k'miun... neh na: No one will come and frighten you in this village. -- K'miun neh na mok bum'put bum'pay noeh k'nong phum ni tay.

no good adj. useless, to no avail -- mun baan kaa: It is no good going. -- Teuh mun baan kaa.; useless, not functional -- ot la'aw: That car is no good. -- Laan nu ot la'aw.

no longer adv. ot baan... tee'it tay: It is no longer safe in Samroang. -- Veea ot baan sohk tee'it noeh Sam'roang tay.

no more -- ot miun tee'it tay: There is no more water. -- Tuk ot miun tee'it tay.; explicitly -- awh: no more money (it has run out) -- loi awh howi; impliedly -- ot: no (more) money -- ot miun loi.

no one -- see "nobody"

No smoking! Haam choo'h!; No talking! -- Haam ni'yaye!

No, thank you. aw'kuun ch'raan (same as affirmative "thank you" but when accompanied by appropriate hand gestures and other actions, conveys "no thank you"); casual -- a'tay (lit: no)

No thanks to you... -- Tay aw'kuun neh...

no way -- ot miun ploe; ot miun vi'ti: There is no way to solve this problem. -- Ot miun vi'ti daw sr'eye pun'ha nu tay.

No way! -- Mun baan tay! or, Jcham chi'vut krow'ee teuh. (lit: Wait till your/my/our next life!)

noise n. so; sum'leng; oo'aah

noisy adj. oo'aah; a noisy restaurant -- poch'ni'tan oo'aah; It's noisy here. -- Oo'aah nah ti ni.

none adv. k'miun; awh: None are [left]. -- Awh miun a'veye [noeh sahl(t)] tay.

nonetheless adv. yang na kaw dow'ee

nonsense n. ot praw'yow'it; ot nay; to talk nonsense -- ni'yaye ot praw'yow'it; or, ni'yaye ot dung a'veye; or, ni'yaye ot baan kaa

noodle shop n.   haang kwai tio (AP: koi' tio)

noodles n.   mee; banyh kun; kwai tio; noodles, fried w/ chicken -- mee chaa sat(ch) muon

noon n.   mao pi tun'dap t'ngai, t'ngai trong

normal adj.   twa'ma'da; moi pa'choom; mut s'yom

normally adv.   taam twa'ma'da; chia twa'ma'da; yang twa'ma'da

north n.   kang jcheun; pyke oo'daw(r); colloquial ("upper side or way or direction") -- kang leuh

northeast n.   kang jcheun chiang kang kaut; kang kaut chiang kang jcheun; pyke aae'sahn

northwest n.   kang jcheun chiang kang lic; kang lic chiang kang jcheun; pyke pee'a yoo'up

nose n.   ch'raw muk

nosy adj.   jchong dung ru'ung

not adv.

mun -- used to negate adjectives, adverbs and verbs:
> negated adjective (mun): not smart -- mun ch'laat
> negated adverb (mun): not quickly -- mun leu'ung
> negated verb (mun):I don't believe it! -- Mun cheuh!

mun.... tay -- (addition of tay provides emphasis)
> negated verb (mun... tay): I <u>do not</u> want any. --
> Mun jchong tay.

ot (AP: ut, et), and ot... tay -- used to modify verbs and adjectives:
> negated adjective (ot): not good -- ot la'aw
> negated verb (ot... tay): My older brother is not at
> > home. -- Bong ot noch pong tay.; He did not
> > go. -- Gwat ot teuh tay.

puhm -- their relations were not good. -- Tek tong gkay
> puhm seou la'aw tay.

Phrases with "not":

not at all ("pas de tout") -- ot miun kaa a'veye tay; or, ot miun a'veye tay; or, ot aae tay

not available (not in stock) -- most common, simply "ot"; also, ot miun

not available (busy) -- ot leh'ta'pheap; mun miun leh'ta'pheap

not around (can't be found (person)) -- ot miun noeh ti ni tay

not bad (OK) -- (As in, Question: How're you doing'? -- Mutch da'aae aae leuh? ; Mutch howi?; Answer: OK, not bad. -- Koo'a sum!, or, Ot aae tay, twamada. (lit: nothing wrong, (all) normal)

not only -- mun trum tai: They are not only poor [but hungry] as well. -- Pooh'gkay mun trum tai kraw [pun'ta'aae klee'un] tee'it.

not possible -- ot baan

not quite --   mun seou: Your answer is not quite correct. --   Jchum'la'wee neh mun seou tro.; mun twon... sroul bool tay: not quite finished -- mun twon roo'it sroul bool tay; mun ... sroul bool: I do not quite have [enough (money)] [to buy the ticket]. -- Kyom mun miun [kroop kron] sroul bool tay [dumbye tinh sum'buht].

not really -- mun seou: He does not really play guitar well. -- Gwat mun seou jcheh leng gi'ta.

not so (i.e., not to that extent) -- mun seou: not so busy -- mun seou ro'vwul tay

not so, not true -- mun putt tay; mun man putt tay (AP: mun putt tay)

not too [s.th.] -- [s.th.] baan tek; not too big -- thum baan tek

not well, not healthy -- mun la'aw; mun miun sok'a'pheap la'aw

not very + adjective -- mun seou; not very happy -- mun seou s'bai jchet

not yet -- mun twon: not yet dead -- slop

note n.   notation; data -- kum'nawt; (NB: idea = kum'nut; birth = kum'naut)

make/take notes v.   miun kawt traa: Did you make/take notes yesterday? -- Tau(v) neh miun kawt traa tay musl'munyh?

nothing prn.   k'miun aae (AP: k'miun eye): Nothing happened. -- K'miun aae (or, eye) kaut laung tay.; There's nothing new. -- K'miun aae (or, eye) plyke kaut laung tay.; ot... a'veye: Before we were rich, now we have nothing. -- Pi muun yeung miun, eye leaou yeung ot miun a'veye tay.; ot aae (or, eye) tay: It's nothing -- Ot aae (or, eye) tay. or, Mun aae (or, eye) tay.

notice n.   sign -- pla; sun'ya

notice v.   kaut sum kwaal; chap pleut: Did you notice which way they went? -- Tau(v) neh baan (or miun) kaut sum kwaal ploe na dael pooh'gkay teuh?

notify v.   prap owi dung

notification n.   kaa prap owi dung

noun n.   nee'om; (lit: name); (NB: among the syllables contained in Khmer nouns, the following identify the word they are part of as in fact being a noun: kaa, kej, kaam, pheap and s'kd'eye)

novel n.   praw'laum'lope; ru'ung: write a novel -- tye'ng ru'ung

November n.   Vi'chi'kaa

novice monk n.   nyne

now adv.   eye leaou (AP: aae leaou, eye lo): Where are you now? -- Neh noeh aae na eye leaou?; howi: What time is it now? -- Mao pu'man howi?; this instant, not in future -- peyr ni; k'nong peyr ni: The Khmer people need a plan now [, not next year]. -- Prachee'chuun Khmei tro kaa pyne'kaa k'nong peyr ni.; sm'auu (AP: s'maw) ni howi: Even now he has [still] not come (e.g., home). -- Sm'aw ni howi [noeh] gwat mun mok tee'it.; by now -- aae leaou nung: He should be here by now. -- Gwat tro mok doll aae leaou nung.

nowadays adv.   eye leaou ni; sm'aw ni

nowhere --   ot miun cunlye'ng; k'miun cunlye'ng: nowhere to hide -- k'miun cunlye'ng poo'un tay

nude adj.   sraat

numb adj.   spu'k

number n.   digit, integer, numeral -- lay'ke: Number One! -- layke Moi!; highway number five -- ploe layke prum; house number -- layke ptay'a; telephone number -- layke to'ra'sap; wrong number -- layke koh; serial number -- layke sum'kwal; number or amount of s. th. -- jchum'noo'an: the number of people -- jchum'noo'an pra'chee'chuun

nun n.   generally -- yaye jchee

nurse n.   keh'lee'an'nup'taa'yi'kaa; ung'fayr'm'yaye (fr. Fr.)

nursery n.   for children -- cunlye'ng meuhl k'mayng; for trees, flowers, etc. -- bun daw nung loo'a daum cheu

nut n.   edible -- kro'up plai cheu; for bolt -- k'bal lauw see; ("lauw see" = "bolt"); odd person -- ma'nooh chum'koo'it, cha'koo'it; fanatic, someone "nuts" about s. th. -- ma'nooh cha'koo'it nung a'veye moi

nutrition n.   jchum'naee aha'

Nuts! xcl.   Jchong rye!; or, Jchong rye man!!; Jchong rye yo!

nutty adj.   cha'koo'it (AP: chum'koo'it): a nutty idea -- kum'nut cha'koo'it

nuzzle v.   yok ch'mawh teuh nyul

nylon n.   nee'lohng

nylons n.   sr'auwm cheung nee'lohng

nymph n.   of the woods -- a'reh'tay'vee; beautious --   sraae miun roob chat'chai

nymphomaniac n.   (sraae dael) jchole jchet twun na'hah

O

oar n. jchong vaa

oath n. non-legal; in sense of promise -- sum'but; legal, formal oath -- s'bot; take an oath -- sawk jchet s'bot: take an oath in court -- teuh s'bot noeh to'la'ka; or (formal), seh cha praw'ni tee'un

obey v. tveu taam; ko'ruup

object n. thing -- ro'bah; s. th. to which attention is directed, "object" of attention or interest -- vuh'to

object v. yul to'ahs; to'ahs; praw'kyte; jchum to'ahs; praw'kyke (NB: agree -- yul pro'me)

objection n. kaa jchum to'ahs

objective n. kaa vuh'to; tee dow; vuh'to bum nong

obligation n. kaa to'pa'tek

obnoxious adj. arrogant, haughty -- seuhng: Don't be so obnoxious. -- Kum seuhng peyk.

obscene adj. jchum'awh: obscene talk -- pee'a jchum'awh; (NB: jchum'awh also translates as "make fun of", although this is more clearly expressed as "jchum awh lawk leui").

observe v. watch -- song'kaet; meuhl; pee'nut; observe [local customs] -- tveu taam [tuum nee'um tuum lo'ob]

observer n. neh song'kaet'kaa

obstacle n. o'pa'sak: Cambodia has to overcome many obstacles. -- Kampuchea yeung tro kaa ch'long kaat o'pa'sak chia ch'raan.

obstinate adj. rung to'tung

obstruct v. ree'ree'ung

obstruction n. kaa ree'ree'ung

obtain v. baan: It is difficult to obtain gas now. -- Veea pi'bah nung baan praeng eye leaou ni.; miun: I must obtain a new passport. -- Kyom tro kaa miun pas'a'port t'maee.

occasion n. ow'kaa

occasionally adv. yeut yeut m'dong

occupation n. mok'ngyeea

occupy v. live in -- rooh noeh: Who occupies that house? -- Neh na rooh noeh ptay'a nu?; invade, take possession of -- troo'it tra; or, kaan kaab: Soldiers occupied that village yesterday. -- Tee'hee'an troo'it tra (or, kaan kaab) phum nu musl'munyh.; spend time -- jchum'nyc peyr: How do you occupy yourself? -- Tau(v) neh jchum'nye peyr yang doj ma'dek?

ocean n. sa'mut

o'clock n. mao: two o'clock -- mao pi

October n. Tho'la

of prp. ney: a sample of fabric -- kum rooh ney kraw'not; the first of March -- t'ngai ti moi ney kye Mih'nee'a; ro'bah: a friend of mine -- mit'paya ro'bah kyom; k'nong; freedom of speech -- se'rei'pheap k'nong kaa ni'yaye; [implied]: the governor of Po'sat -- chao'vye [ ] Po'sat;

of course conj. taam piht keuh: [I like to study Khmer but] of course I can't [do it] every day. -- [Kyom jchole jchet rian pee'esa Khmei;] taam piht teuh, kyom mun adje [tveu kaut] ree'eng rawl t'ngai.

Of course! xcl. Piht, howi!; (NB: other words/phrases expressing of agreement are: yes (for male speakers) -- baat; yes (for female speakers) -- chaa; OK -- tro howi; Right! -- Sa'took.)

off prp. extinguished -- butt: The light is off. -- Pleung butt.; away from -- pi: turn off the road -- bawt jchenyh pi ploe (or, jchenyh pi t'nawl); get off of (lit: down from) -- jchoh: Where do you get off (i. e., the bus, the train, etc.)? -- Cunlye'ng na dael neh nung jchoh?; off and on (intermittently) -- [   ] chope, [   ] chope: He studies on and off. -- Gwat rian chope, rian chope. (lit: studies and stops, studies and stops)

off-shore adj. off-shore account -- kohng krau praw'tet (lit: outside the country); pi ch'raae'ung (lit: from shore): The boat sank [two miles] off-shore. -- Toook lic [pi mile] pi ch'raae'ung.

offend v. tveu owi a'on'jchet: You offended me [again]! -- Neh tveu owi a'on'jchet kyom [m'dong tee'it]!

offense n. s. th. against the law -- koh ch'bop; That gang committed many offenses. -- Krum nu baan tveu koh ch'bop ch'raan.; crime -- o'kret'ta'kaam.;

offensive n. take the offensive -- p'dam pro'ha

offensive adj. dael tveu owi a-on-jchet

offer n. owi tlai: What was his offer? -- Gwat owi tlai pu'man?; owi dum'lye: He made a high offer. -- Gwat owi dum'lye k'pooh.; dael... pdull... owi: What was his offer? -- Dael gwat pdull a'veye owi?

offer v. owi dum'lye; pdull; pdull noeh: He offered the minister money. -- Gwat pdull loi owi muntrei. or, Gwat pdull noeh loi owi muntrei.; dael... pdull... owi: What will he offer us? -- Tau(v) a'veye dael gwat nung pdull owi yeung?

office n. place of work -- kaar'ya'lye; particularly governmental or institutional -- mun'ti; position or post -- dum'nye'nyh; rank -- bun'sack

office clerk n. s'mee'un kaar'ya'lye

office worker -- neh kaar'ya'lye

officer n. military -- nee'aae tee'heean or may tee'heean; of a business -- mun'trei

official n. government official -- mun'trei; in Cambodian politics, political party official -- pa'ka'chuun; administrative (not party) official -- ka'ma'pi'bal; agent of business or government -- p'nehk; p'nehk nee'a

official adj. mun'trei: official car -- la'an mun'trei

officially adv. legally required, prescribed or sanctioned; according to law -- chia ploe kaa: The permit was officially, e.g., legally) [cancelled]. -- Pear'mee tro baan [loob jchowl] chia ploe kaa.

often adv. chia ngye nyoi; nye nyoo'op

Oh, God! xcl. Preah euoi!; Piht to'!; or, Slop howi! (lit: "I'm dead!")

oil n. generally, for non-cooking use -- praeng: motor oil -- praeng ma'zuut; (gasoline = sang or praeng sang); lamp oil -- praeng kat (jching'kee'an praeng kat = oil lamp); peanut oil -- praeng sun'dyke; change the oil -- pdo' praeng; oil s. th. -- dah(k) praeng; drill [in the ground] for oil -- chee(k) yok praeng kat [noeh k'nong daiy]; generally, for cooking use -- klanyh (can also refer to cooking fat): pork oil -- klanyh ch'roook; "cow oil" (also grease used for lubrication) -- klanyh gko; fish oil, used for wick lamps -- klanyh trei

oil well n. an'do'ng praeng; an'do'ng praeng kat;

oily adj. doj praeng

OK! stated xcl. Baat! or, Nung howi! (compressed in speech to, Nung eye!, not the "eye" meaning "what" but the last syllable of "howi"); or, Yaa'ha!; or, Sa took!

OK? query xcl. in sense of, Right? or Isn't it? -- Baan tay?; or, Nung aae? (AP: Nung eh?); or, meuhl?: Give me a little, OK? -- Choon kyom baan tek, meuhl?; in sense of, "You agree? Right? You got it now?" -- Loo'eh'?; or (very common) Nung'eh?: He's coming with us, OK? -- Gwat mok chi'moi, nung'eh?? (AP: Nung aae?)

OK adj., adv. Is that OK? -- Ot aye tay roo?; not OK (not alright) -- mun baan tay; ot baan tay; not OK (not feeling well) -- ot sroul tay.; Yes, if it's OK with you. (lit: if you have no objection) -- Baat, baa lok mun yul to'ahs; [unstated] -- Do you want more coffee? No thanks[, this is OK]. -- Jchole jchet cafe? A'tay, aw'kuun ch'raan [   ].; It's OK with me. -- Kyom ot chuum to'ahs tay. (lit: I have no objection.)

OK n. approval, authorization -- s'kd'eye yul'prome; kaa yul'prome: We need to get his OK. -- Yung tro kaa, kaa yul'prome ro'bah (or pi) gwat.

old adj. elderly -- jchaah: an old man -- ma'nooh jchaah; long-standing, not recent -- jchaah; an old friend -- mit jchaah; old-timer -- neh chuum'no'an jchaah (lit: one from an older era); old-hand -- cheung jchaah; How old are you? -- Neh a'yoo pu'man aae?; (gotten) old/stale -- awh roo chee'it; (is) old/stale -- ot roo chee'it; old-fashioned -- pi sak'mye muun (lit: from former, or past, times); chum'nah: My house is three years old. -- Ptay'a kyom chum'nah bye chh'nam.

old man n. casual -- ta (lit: grandfather); formal. polite -- jchee ta

old woman n. casual -- yaye; respectful, polite, formal -- jchee doe'n

older or younger adj. jchaeh chiang roo k'mayng chiang; bong roo pa'own

oligarchy n. a'pah'chi'neea tep'a'dye

olive n. o'leeve

omelette n. o'ma'let; pong muon jchian (lit: fried egg)

omit v. intentionally -- chowl; unintentionally -- plic

omitted pp. baan chowl

omnipotent adj. praw kowp dow'ee sa'pheap'nu'pheap

omniscience n. sop'nyoo'pheap

omniscient adj. praw'kowp dow'ee sop'nyoo'pheap

omnivorous adj. dael baw'ree pope ana kroop yang

on prp. generally -- leuh: The book is on the table. -- S'po leuh tohk.; on top of -- noch leuh: I left the pen on top of the book. -- Kyon tooo'k bic noch leuh s'po.;
Also:
(a house) on (the pond) -- (ptay'a) chit (bung)
Come on! -- Mao, na! (NB: "mao" is AP of mok.)
further on -- chng'eye tee'it
get on with -- tveu teuh
have an effect on -- teuh leuh: The rain had a bad effect on the crops. -- Plee'eng ho'ich p'auwl a'krah teuh leuh dum'nam.; mok leuh: Ta' had a bad effect on them. -- Ta' miun p'auwl a'krah mok leuh gkay.
hold on (tight) -- kaan owi (cho'ub); (cho'ub = "stick to", stay close to)
[It's] on [the 20th]. -- [Veea] noch t'ngai [ti ma'paye].
later on -- krow'ee mok
lights or equipment on -- baahk: The lights are on. --   Pleung baahk howi.
look on passively -- meuhl nung pn'aae'k
on the one hand... on the other hand -- m'yang... m'yang venyh tee'it
on time -- twon (AP: ti'ung) peyr; twon mao; twon to'at: He comes on time. -- Gwat mok yang twon to'at.; I will come on time. -- Kyom mok owi twon peyr.; twon mok; tro mok; twon peyr va'leea
one book on top of another -- s'po moi noch pi leuh s'po tee'it
on the way -- noch taam ploe
opinion on -- kum'nut jcham'poo'h
put on (shoes) -- peh (s'bye'k cheung)
working on -- kom'puung tveu

once adv. one time -- m'dong: Try it once [and] you will like it. -- Sah(k) m'dong neh nung jchole jchet.; at one time -- pi muun; a once-powerful nation -- um'natch chee'it pi muun; (if) once -- kaal baa: Once you speak, don't change the sentence. -- Kaal baa neh ni'yaye, kum pdo klia.; all at once -- peyr nu srup tai

once again adv. m'dong tee'it

once and for all adv. chia s'taa peau

once in a while adv. m'dong moi yee'um

once upon a time adv. kaal pi praeng nee'aae

one adj. moi: one car -- laan moi; one person -- moi neh (AP: moi nee'eh); one half -- moi kan'lah' (AP of kan'lak); one more time -- moi m'dong tee'it; one after the other, sequentially -- chia loom'dap; one of (people only) -- ma'neh; one of them -- ma'neh ney pooh'gkay; one of the men -- ma'nooh ma'neh or miun ma'neh:

[There is one of you/one among you] who is not honest. -- [Ma'nooh ma'neh (or miun ma'neh)] dael ot sm'oh trong.; one among them (lit: one among [the number of] them) -- ma'neh k'nong [jchum'noo'an] pooh'gkay; one of the politicians -- neh na'yo'bye ma'neh; one at a time (lit: "one , one time") -- ma'neh m'dong

one's-self prn. kloo'an eiyne

one-sided adj. luum ee'ung teuh moi kang

one-way adj. eyke teuh; one-way ticket -- sum'buht teuh pun'noh; or: sum'but teuh ot tra'laawp mok venyh (common AP: mow venyh); one-way street -- tai ploe teuh; or, tai ploe mok

onion n. k'tum ba'raang; scallion -- sluk k'tum

only adv. tai... tay: I have only two riels. -- Kyom miun tai pi riel tay.; tai... kuut: I have only two riels. -- Kyom miun tai pi riel kuut.; I have only one wife. -- Kyom miun pra'pun tai moi kuut.; I want only one cola. -- Kyom tro kaa s'cola tai moi kuut.; trum tai: only two men -- trum tai pi ma'nooh; tic tic (AP: tek tek)... tay: only a little smart -- ch'laat tic tic tay: tai... pun'noh: I want only one cola. -- Kyom tro kaa s'cola tai moi pun'noh.; pun'noh (AP: pun'nawh): They are only equipped with rifles. -- Gkay praw'dob dow'ee kum pleung pun'noh.; not only -- mun trum tai: They are not only poor but hungry as well. -- Pooh'gkay mun trum tai kraw punt'a'aae klee'un tee'it.

only if -- luke tra tai: The rubber [can be delivered] only if the army provides an escort. -- Kaow'soo [mun adje baan jchenyh teuh] luke tra tai yo'tee'a pdull kawng kaa pee'a.

onto prp. leuh

onward prp. teuh mok

open, opened adj. open fields -- veal ruum hawh: There are many open fields in Prey Veng. -- Miun veal ruum hawh ch'raan noeh k'nong Prey Veng.; open-minded -- kum'nut mun sunyh; non-restricted -- jchum'ho

open v. baahk: open the door -- baahk tvee'a; open the package -- baahk pra'op; He opened the meeting with a speech. -- Gwat baahk pra'choom chi'moi nung kaa ni'yaye.; open (lit: start) a business -- jchaap p'dam chuum'noo'inyh

operate v. machinery -- bun chee'a; or, pra (lit: use): Do you know how to operate this machine? -- Tau(v) neh jcheh bun chee'a maseen ni tay?; medically -- veh kaat; conduct oneself or conduct business -- dum'narr: That dance hall operates illegally. -- ro'ng k'sall nu dum'narr kaa koh ch'bop.; function properly -- chheh

operation n. medical -- kaa veh kaat; military -- kej praw'tay'baat kaa suk; of equipment -- kaa pra

opinion n. kum'nut; mutt'tayh; yo'ball; public opinion -- kum'nut saah tee'a'ra'nak; or, prachee'a mutt'tayh; or, mutt'tayh ro'bah prachee'chuun; have an opinion that -- mye tha; have an opinion about -- mye om'pee

opium n. a'pee'un

opponent n. neh praw'chang

opportunity n. awh'kaa: have an opportunity -- miun awh'kaa; sieze an opportunity -- ch'lee'it awh'kaa

oppose v. jchum to'ahs; p'toi

opposition n. kaa praw'chang; kaa chuum to'ahs; opposition group -- neh praw'chang; opposition party -- krum (or pooh) praw'chang

opposite prp. p'toi: Good is the opposite [of] bad. -- La'aw p'toi [nung] a'krah.; He said the opposite of what he told us before. -- Gwat ni'yaye p'toi ney a'veye dael gwat baan prap yeung pi muun.; across from -- tul muk: The Ministry of Defense building [that is opposite] the old Chinese Embassy.... -- A'keea Kra'soo'ung Kaa Pee'a Praw'tet [dael noeh tul muk] 'Toot Jchun jchaah.

oppress v. sung kaat sung kun; chi cho'un (lit: step on)

or conj. roo: him or me -- gwat roo kyom

or not conj. roo kaw ot: to go or not -- teuh roo kaw ot; roo ot: Do you want to go or not? -- Jchong teuh roo ot?; roo tay: May I have it or not? -- Tau(v) kyom adje miun veea baan roo tay?; (NB: "roo tay" can be literally translated as "or not" or left untranslated and treated simply as a question indicator; hence the foregoing sentence could also be translated simply "May I have it?"; similarly, "Neh jchong teuh, roo tay?" can mean "Do you want to go?", or (literally) "Do you want to go or not?"); in sense of "yet?" -- roo noeh: Are the photos ready yet [or not yet(ready)]? -- Roob howi [roo noeh]? (lit: Are the pictures ready or still unready?); Are you [ready] to go or not? -- Tau(v) neh [roo'it rawl] howi roo noeh? (again, the literal meaning is "Are you ready to go yet?")

oral adj. twal mwot: oral report -- ro'bye'kaa ni'yaye twal mwot; oral examination -- kaa praw'long dow'ee soo'a twal mwot

orange n. fruit -- krau'itch Po'sat; (lemon = krau'itch ch'maa'; grapefruit = krau'itch t'long); color -- pwa ta' krau'itch

orange juice n. tuk krau'itch Po'sat

orchard n. ch'ba

orchestra n. krum plaeng; (also means "band" or any musical group)

orchid n. p'ka or'ki'day

order n.

directive, generally (military, commercial, administartive, written or oral) -- bun'chee'a; court or governmental order, written or oral -- leh kan'taae'kah; a written commercial, or purchase, order, written, may be referred to as a "bun'chee" (as opposed to "bun'chec'a") in that bun'chee translates as record, document, file, etc., and as such, could refer to a written "purchase order" since such an order could also be characterized as a record or document; a purchase order could also be called a "bun'chee'a tinh" or "order to buy"; also: commerical, parental or other non-governmental order, verbal -- commang (fr. Fr. "command");

stability, opposite of "disorder", tranquility, calm -- ro'bee'up rec'p roi; (NB: disorder = ot ro'bee'up ree'p roi); put in order -- dah(k) ... taam ro'bee'up: Put them in order. -- Dah(k) veea taam ro'bee'up.; put in order -- dah(k) taam luum dap; alphabetical order -- luum dap a'saw; in order to -- dum'bye; sum'rap

order v. order on command s.o. to do s. th. -- jchat owi; owi bun'chee'a; bung ko'up; ca'mong (fr. Fr.): order food (e.g., in a restaurant) -- ca'mong ma'hope; or, haow ma'hope: (You) go to the restaurant first and order. -- Teuh poch'ni'tan muun howi nung haow ma'hope.; jchong nyam: What do you want to/what will you/ order? -- Neh jchong nyam aae?; order s. th. commercially -- dah(k) bun chee'a tinh; or, commang: order a dress -- ca'mong aow'rope

ordinary adj. twa'ma'da; too'to': ordinary people -- pra'chee'chuun too'to'; praw'pra'dye: I am an ordinary person. -- Kyom chia ma'nooh praw'pra'dye.; just (or nothing more than) ordinary... -- kron tai chia... pun'noh: IMF claims its development plan for Cambodia is special but [in fact] it's just ordinary "structural adjustment". -- IMF praw'kas tha pyne'kaa a'ti'vwut sum'rap Kampuchea keuh chia pi'sch, pun'ta'aae [taam piht teuh] veea kron tai chia "structural adjustment" pun'noh.; sa'muun: "ordinary" (everyday) language -- pee'esa sa'muun

ordinarily adv. taam twa'ma'da

ordinance n. law -- pun'yaat; ch'bop

ordnance n. ammunition -- yoo'teh pwon

ore n. ra'ee; lo'ha'tee'it

organization n. ong'kah

organize v. a political party -- jchat chaiyng ka'na'pac; jchat chaiyng krum; generally put in order, straighten out -- ree'up jchum; organize the files -- ree'up jchum bun'chee; organize alphabetically, by topic, etc. -- dah(k) taam ro'bee'up; tooo'k dahk bun'chee

original adj. daum: an original idea -- kum'nut daum; ori'jeen (fr. Fr.): an original picture -- roob o'ri'jeen

originally adv. kaa pi daum; pi dum'bong

orphan n. k'mayng kum pree'a (lit: child without care); girls without families -- nee'ree'a kum pree'a

other adj. different -- p'sayng tee'it: He isn't here; he is staying at the other hotel. -- Gwat a noeh ti ni; gwat noeh o'tyle p'sayng tee'it.; tee'it: in other words -- m'yang tee'it; the other side/team -- krum m'kang tee'it; daw tay: other people -- neh daw tay: Please use the other phone. -- Sum pra to'ra'sap daw tay.; daw tay tee'it: He has other plans. -- Gwat miun pyne'kaa daw tay tee'it.; p'sayng daw tay tee'it: Do you have any other colors? -- Tau(v) neh miun pwa p'sayng daw tay tee'it tay?

other n. a nu: (I don't want this one), I want the other. -- Kyom jchong baan a nu (lit: that one).

otherwise adv. praw' mun doj cha'neh: We should stop, otherwise we will be very tired. -- Yeung koo'a tai chope, praw' mun doj cha'neh, yeung nung awh kum'lung klang.; or: praw' mun doj cha'neh tay: ... (We must leave now;) otherwise the road will be cut. -- ... praw' mun doj cha'neh tay ploe nung kaat'pa'dach; praw'sun chia k'miun: ...otherwise he will die... -- ... praw'sun chia k'miun, gwat nung slop...

ought, ought to v. koo'a; koo'a tai

ounce and a half n. approx. weight of Cambodian unit of measurement -- dum'lung; (NB: one dum'lung = ten chee)

our, ours prp. ro'bah yeung; chia ro'bah yeung

out prp. outside -- krau: He went out. -- Gwat teuh krau.; not having s. th. because has been consumed -- awh: The truck is out of gas. -- Laan trung awh sang; I am out of patience with him. -- Kyom awh kaa ot'tuun chi'moi gwat howi.; not having s. th. because unavailable -- ot: Too many people are out of work. -- Ma'nooh chia ch'raan dael ot kaa tveu.; out of order -- ko'ich: The phone is out of order. -- To'ra'sap ko'ich.; The TV is out of order. -- TV ko'ich.; How long has it been out of order? -- Tau(v) ra'yawt peyr pu'man dael veea ko'ich?; extinguished -- ro'lut: The fire is out. -- Pleung ro'lut.

outburst n. jchow'laow

outcome n. sman: an unexpected outcome -- sman dum'ro(v) mun tro

outdated adj. no longer popular -- hoo'a kaa ni'yuum; old-fashioned (of olden times, but not necessarily unpopular) -- chum'noo'an jchaah; or, bo'raan: an old-fashioned idea -- kum'nut chum'noo'an jchaah; or, kum'nut bo'raan

outlaw n. man'ooh la'meuh ch'bop

outlaw v. tveu.... koh ch'bop: The National Assembly voted in 1995 to outlaw the Khmer Rouge. -- Ratt Su'phea tveu Khmei Kra'hom koh ch'bop noch chh'nam 1995.

outpost n. chuum'ruhm la'utt (lit: small camp)

outrun v. leu'an chiang: Population (growth) in Cambodia is outrunning employment (growth). -- Jchum'noo'an pra'chee'chuun noeh Kampuchea leu'an chiang kaa'ngyeea.

outside prp. kang krau: The KR live outside the village. -- KR rooh noeh kang krau phum.

outsmart v. p'chanyh pra'ngya leuh

outwit v. praw'ngya leuh

oval adj. pong kraw'peu (lit: (shape of) crocodile's egg)

oven n. jchong'kran

over adj. finished -- jchawb howi; ot howi: The game is over. -- L'byc'ng jchawb howi.

over and over adv. ch'raan leuk ch'raan dong

over-cast adj. mey'k ngo ngut (NB: mey'k = sky)

over-come v. ch'long: overcome obstacles -- ch'long kat o'pa'sak; defeat -- yok ch'ney; p'chanyh (NB: chanyh = lose)

over-do v. tveu ch'raan peyk

over-done adj. re food -- ch'aan hoo'a; re actions -- ch'rul hoo'a: His complaint was overdone. -- Gwat ra'oo ruh twam ch'rul hoo'a.

over-flow v. the glass over-flowed -- tuk kaac'oo penyh hoo'a; [the stream] overflowed -- [tuk stung] ch'un

over-grown with branches adj. sa'ka

over-loaded adj. pee'up

over-look v. not notice -- meuhl ch'rul; meuhl hoo'a; plic kut

over-ripe adj. tuum (also means "ripe")

over-sleep v. dayke kawk (NB: kawk = miss, as in "miss a train")

over there adv. ti nu

over-throw v. tuum leh; ruum luum

over-time n.   leuk peyr

over-turned adj.   kraw'lop

over-whelm v.   with awe -- ch'ngau'itch

over-whelmingly adv.   yang mo'how'la'ru'k

over-work v.   bum bah(k) kum'lung (lit: break the strength of s.o.)

owe v.   chuum peh (AP: pe'ch): He owes me $5. -- Gwat chuum peh loi kyom pram dolla'.; You owe them a lot. -- Neh nung chuum peh bum'nawl gkay.

owl n.   to toi; sat mee'um

own adj.   p'twal kloo'an: He [admitted] it had been his own fault]. -- Gwat [saa'ra'pheap tha] veea chia kum'hawh p'twal kloo'an.; ... with his own gun. -- dow'ee sa kum pleun p'twal kloo'an; [unstated]: I saw it with my own eyes -- Kyom baan keunyh p'twal nung pn'aae'k [   ].; ro'bah: It is my own car. -- Veea laan ro'bah kyom.; They said it was their own fault. -- Pooh'gkay taa veea kum'hawh ro'bah gkay.... But: They said it was their [implicitly, not of the "they" speaking but of some other "they"] fault. -- Pooh'gkay taa veea kum'hawh gkay.; i. e., use of "ro'bah" makes clear the concept of "their OWN" while omission of "ro'bah" leaves the sentence ambiguous.; own way, seek to have -- jchong baah bauw

own v.   miun; miun kama'sut

owner n.   m'chah (AP: meh'cha); boss -- jchao'vye

ownership n.   ka'ma'sut

ox n.   gko

oxcart n.   ro'teh gko

oxygen n.   ok'cee'zen

oyster n.   k'chong smit; nee'oo

P

pacification n. san'ti'pheap vu'pah'naya'kaam; san'ti'pheap va'kaam

pacify v. tveu owi m'lun

pack n. small box, generally -- kun'chob: pack of cigarettes -- kun'chob ba'r'eye; re playing cards only -- ma'hoo: pack of cards -- bee'a ma'hoo

pack v. ree'up dah(k): pack a suitcase -- ree'up dah(k) va'leez; pack a wooden box or crate (common rural Khmer goods container) -- ree'up dah(k) hopp; ree'up jchum: pack clothes -- ree'up jchum kow-aow; pack things for a trip -- ree'up jchum dum'narr; pack or wrap a gift -- k'jchowp

package n. praw'op; pack, small package -- kun'chob

pact n. kaa yul'prome; kej sun'nyaa

pad n. under s. th. -- tru' n'wuab; notepad -- dum kum'nauk; lotus pad -- sluk chook (lit: lotus leaf); rented place to live, apartment -- ptay'a l'veng

paddle n. for rowboat, canoe, etc. -- jchong vaa

paddle v. um: We paddle the boat. -- Yeung um toook.

paddy n. paddy land -- sr'eye: irrigate paddy land -- bun jchole tuk k'nong sr'eye; "paddy" (unhusked) rice -- sro; five kilos of unhusked rice -- sro pram 'lo

padlock n. saow tra'dauwk; may saow

pagan n. non-Christian -- neh mun cheu'a kruu ses'na; non-Buddhist -- neh mun cheu'a Phut' ses'na

page n. tum'poa

pagoda n. wat

paid pp. jchum'nye; get paid -- baahk loi: When do you get paid? -- Baahk loi noeh peyr na?

pail n. tuung

pain n. chh'ooh: sharp pain -- jchawk: sharp stomach pain -- jchawk poo'ah

painful adj. cheuh: painful experience -- bowt (or kaa) pee'sowt cheuh: Every battle was a painful experience. -- Kroop sa'mau'ra'phum keuh chia bowt pee'sowt ney kaa chh'oop jchaap.; It was a painful [decision]. -- Veea keuh chia [kaa sum'rach jchet] dael bun dael owi miun kaa chh'ooh jchaap.

paint n. tnam lee'up

paint v. lee'up po'wa; paint a picture -- koo' roob

painter n. of houses, etc. -- neh lee'up tnal ptay'a; artist -- chee'un kum koo; or, vi'che'ta'kaw

painting n. kum'noo lee'up pwa: famous painting -- kum'noo lee'up p'wa dael l'bye l'bong

pair n. koo: a pair of shoes -- s'bye'k cheung moi koo

pak chii n. chii van'soi

pal n. mit; mit'paya; rop'an; mit'paya chit s'nut

palace n. vaae'eng (AP: vaae'ng): royal palace -- vaac'eng s'dach

pale adj. pree'ul pree'ul; pale- or ashen-faced, as with malaria -- muk sl'aang

Pali adj. or n. B'lye; or, B'laae (AP: B'lee); the Pali language -- pec'csa B'lye (or, B'laae)

palm n. coconut palm -- daum do'hng; sugar palm -- daum t'naut; areca palm -- daum slaa; palm leaf -- sluk t'naut; palm of hand -- bot dai; read a palm -- tee'aae bot dai

pamphlet n. lee'kut klai klai

pan n. k'taae'eh; (pot = chn'aang)

pancake n. sweet -- nom jchak chul; filled with bean sprout, meat and coconut, and folded -- bun chae'ow (NB: bun chae'ow is a Vietnamese term adopted by Khmer.)

pane n. kun'chuh bung'oo'ıt

panel n. board of review, etc. -- krum; committee -- sa'ma'kuum

panic n. pay'ee slun slough

panic v. slun slough: Some civilians panicked at Kompong Thom [at the time of the attacks in July]. -- Chuun cee'vil klaah pay'ee slun slough noeh k'nong Kom'puung Thum [noeh peyr vye (or praw'yoot) k'nong kye July].

panicked adj. ch'rool cha'rob baal: They panicked because of the attacks. -- Pooh'gkay ch'rool cha'rob baal bee'proo'a miun kaa praw'yoot.

panties n. kow; kow noo'waup

pants n. kow

papaya n. la'hong

paper n. kra'dah (written kra'dahs)

paperwork n. tveu kraw'dah snam

parachute n. chatt yo'ng

parachute v. lo chatt

parade n. dong hye; hye ka'boo'an

paragraph n. vehh

parallel adj. sraw(b)

paralyzed adj. ngw'op: paralyzed totally (lit: hand and foot) -- ngw'op dai ngw'op chueng; arms -- ngw'op dai; legs -- ngw'op cheung

paranoid adj. ro'esse kloo'an

parasite n. insects -- jchai (lit: lice); people -- ma'nooh jchai gkay; ma'nooh sum nawl; or, ma'nooh rooh dow'ee sa gkay (lit: one who lives off someone)

paratroop n. tee'hee'an chatt yo'ng

pardon me xcl. leuk to'h; sum to'h; ot to'h

parentheses n. vung kraw chawk

parents n. oeuv'puk m'dye; m'dye oeuv'puk; rural term -- myc'ocuv

park n. soo'un; off'chee'an

park v. jchawt: park a car -- jchawt laan

parliament n. ratt'sa'phea

parrot n. saat sayk

parsley n. bun soo'ee ba'raang; chee bun soo'ee

part n. of something, generally, section or portion -- p'nyke; part of the government -- p'nyke ratt'a'pi'bal; some parts, sections, portions -- p'nyke klaah; jchum'nyke: part of the money -- jchum'nyke ney loi; amount, quantity, portion -- jchum'noo'an; one quantity or portion -- moi jchum'noo'an: Part of the people like Hun Sen, part like Sihanouk. -- P'nyke klaah prachee'chuun jchole jchet Hun Sen, moi jchum'noo'an jchole jchet Sihanouk.; some portions, some amount -- jchum'noo'un klaah; element -- chuum'poo'h: part of speech -- chuum'poo'h ney sap; pieh (AP: peh): part of the money -- pieh ney loi; for the most part -- pieh ch'raan; machinery part -- kreung; replacement part -- plah kreung k'chow; some -- klaah: Just give me part (i.e., some). -- Owi kyom klaah.; take part in -- jchole ru'um k'nong; part of a conspiracy -- kaa jchole dai; play a part -- too'a; dramatic role -- dal too'a: a good part -- dal too'a la'aw; The part was no good. -- Dal too'a chia too'a ot la'aw.

part v. ngyaek: part the trees (to clear the way) -- ngyaek daum cheu; part one's hair -- ngyaek saahk; vaeyk: part the crowd -- vyaek ploe; or, vaeyk: They parted the crowd so Sihanouk could pass. -- Gkay vaeyk ma'nooh jchenyh bawk ploe owi Sihanouk dah.

partial adj. not complete -- pieh klaah ney; partial [victory] -- pieh klaah ney [chey chuum'nay'eh]; biased, partial to one side or group -- l'ee'eng; or, dael kaan cheung moi kang (lit: hold the feet of s.o.)

participate v. jchole ru'um

particular adj. pi'seh (written pi'seh(ss)); in particular -- chia pi'seh; to be particular about -- praw'kaan

particularly adv. chia pi'seh

partisan n. eyke'a'taae

partition n. kaa bay'ng jchaiyk: partition of the country -- kaa bay'ng jchaiyk ney praw'tet

partition v. bay'ng; ro'bay'ng

partly adv. dow'ee un'leuh; pieh klaah

partner n. koo'kang; dai koo

partnership n. chia koo'kawn

part-time adj. bun tic bun to'ich

party n. political group, faction -- ka'na'pac (AP: k'na(k) pa'h, ka'na'pa); social gathering -- choop lee'eng (AP: choop lee'eng); give a party (for) -- tveu choop lee'eng (owi); give or have a party -- miun choop lee'eng: Angkor Association ("AA") will give a party next week. -- AA miun choop lee'eng a'tthit krow'ee.

party line n. political dicta -- sek cha nuuk mutch; or, kohl na'yo'bye ney ka'na'pac moi; shared phone line -- k'sye to'ra'sap jchaiyk ka'neea pra

pass n. in mountains -- ch'rawk phnom; make a pass at -- dee'd; ngy'eye; He made a pass at her. -- Gwat dee'd nee'eng.

pass v. go past s. th. -- teuh hoo'a; bung hoo'a; s. th. on the road -- teuh muk; or, teuh bung hoo'a; vaa: Pass that car! -- Vaa laan nung teuh!; pass in sense of exceed -- hoo'a pi: (The rate of population growth) has passed the levels of the 1960s. -- (   ) hoo'a pi chh'nam 1960s.; to pass the other one -- hoo'a ma'neh tee'it; pass out food, pamphlets, exam books, etc. -- ho'ich owi; or, jchaiyk: Pass the food. -- Ho'ich owi ma'hope.; Please pass out the books. -- Sum jchaiyk s'po.; a test -- praw'long cho'op; be approved, authorized -- a'noo'naaht; be approved, allowed -- a'noo'mit: The [legislation] will pass. -- [Sum'narr] tro baan a'noo'mit.

pass out v. faint -- pluu'ck; or, sun'lubb

pass over v. go across -- ch'long; skip -- plong; or, ruhm'long

pass the time v. kun'long teuh: Time passes so quickly -- Peyr kun'long teuh yang ro'has peyk.

pass through v. ch'long; or, ch'long kaat: We will pass through the village this afternoon. -- Yeung nung ch'long phum long'aee't ni.

pass up a chance v. mun ch'lee'ot yok praw'yow'it

passage n. from a book -- vaae'ek ney s'po; secret passage -- ch'raw'k; of legislation -- kaa a'noo'naaht

passenger n. neh dum'narr

passion n. twun'na'ha

passive adj. ot praw'kye'k (NB: praw'kye'k, or praw'kye'k ka'neea, = argue, kaa praw'kye'k = argument); ot praw'chang: The militia are too passive at night. -- Kawng chee'va pul ot jchong praw'chang noeh peyr yoop.

passport n. lee'kut ch'long dyne (lit: writing (re) crossing borders)

password n. peea sum'ngut

past adj. teuh: this past year -- chh'nam teuh ni; kumlung teuh howi: The time is past [when] the people [could be deceived]. -- Peyr va'leea kun'lung teuh howi [noeh peyr dael] ma'nooh [tro baan bauk bun jchong].

past n. the past -- a'tay'ta; a'tay'ta kaal; or, a'yeh'ta'kaal: live in the past -- rooh k'nong a'yeh'ta'kaal; the past, or life to date, of a person -- praw'vwut: He has a [mysterious] past. -- Gwat miun praw'vwut [a'kum'bang].

past pp. go past s. th. -- bung hoo'a

pastry n. num (AP: nom; lit: cake); French pastry -- num ba'raang; small cakes -- num to'ich; sweet pyramid pastry wrapped in banana leaf -- num pahng bung'oo; sweet square pastry wrapped in banana leaf -- num pahng knaut; (NB:num pahng = bread or pastry)

patch v. pah; patch a tire -- pah kong; patch clothes -- pah kow-aow

paternal side, on the n. choo'a kang oeuv'pook

path n. ploe luum; ploe cheung (lit: foot path); ploe (lit: a way): We have to clear a path through these trees. -- Yeung tro kaa trei ploe kaat dam cheu.; forest or jungle path -- ploe prayk

patlence n. um'naut; kaa ot'ta'mut

patient adj. ot tro'um, ot tuun; Be patient. -- Ot tro'um teuh.; ot'ta'mut: She's a patient teacher. -- Nee'eng kruu ot'ta'mut.

patient n. medical -- neh chuum'ngeu

patriot n. neh (or ma'nooh) snai ha chee'it: She is a patriot. -- Ne'eng keuh chia ma'nooh snai ha chee'it.

patriotism n. snai ha chee'it (lit: love of country)

patrol n. organized surveillance force -- chlop (term used, e.g., by Khmer Rouge to refer to their village and district surveillance groups; act of conducting or maintaining surveillance -- kaa yee'um; to'up la'batch; kaa la'batch

patrol v. yee'im la'batch; dah yee'im

patronage, power of n. um'natch ney kaa u'pa'tuum

pattern n. sketched outline, as for clothes -- kum'roo; pictoral, as a design -- kum'noo; pattern [of events] -- dum'nong [ney pra'ti'kaa]

paunchy adj. miun k'bal poo'ah pown (lit: to have a belly like a balloon)

pay n. praa(k) bun'nach; kaa chum nye; monthly salary -- praa(k) kye

pay v. jchenyh loi... owi: Please pay that cyclo driver 200 riels. -- Sum jchenyh loi [pi roi riels] owi neh cyclo nu.; or, Sum jchenyh loi owi neh cee'clo nu pi roi.; song; song loi; (spend = jchum'nye)

Pay attention! -- Yok jchet tooo'k da(ch)!

pay back v. song... venyh: Pay him back his money. -- Song loi gwat venyh.

pay for v. suffer the consequences of s. th. -- bung kaat tro'up sum'baat

peace n. san'ti'pheap; s'kd'eye sohk; (NB: particularly in written Khmer, peace is expressed by the words sohk, sann and sohk sann; see discussion under "secure" re differentiation between peace/peaceful and security/secure. "Sohk [e.g., Sohk] Sann" ("peace") was the name given by several hundred former Lon Nol soldiers lead by an officer named Prum Vith to a military enclave they established on the Thai border east of Chantaburi in late 1976 to resist first the Khmer Rouge and later, to some extent, the State of Cambodia administration. Despite its precarious position in the heart of what was otherwise Khmer Rouge territory, Sohk Sann survived to become one of the last seven border camps still in existence when Khmer refugee repatriation began under the UNHCR in 1992.)

peaceful adj. san'ti'pheap: Everyone wants a peaceful world. -- Kroop ka'neea jchong baan san'ti'pheap pi pope'lok.

Peace Corps n. lit: Krum Santi'pheap; (NB: A domestic Cambodian forerunner of the Peace Corps could be said to be the "A'pi'vwut Saha'kuum", or "Development", or "Progress", Corps organized by Sihanouk in the 1960s to promote rural development.)

peacock n. k'ngauw'k

peak n. kom'pool

peanut n. sun'dyke daiy

pearl n. k'uhch

peasants n. neh sruk'krau (AP: so'krau; lit: country people, people who live outside the cities and towns); neh sr'eye; farmers -- kaah'se'ko; neh jcham'kar

peck v. jchuhk

pedal v. a bicycle or cyclo -- teh kong; teh cee'clo

peddle v. sell on the street -- looh taam ploe

peel v. chut (AP: chet): peel a potato -- chut sum'baugh dum'lung (lit: peel potato skin); baw(k)

peeling adj. ro'baugh

pen n. ballpoint -- bic; enclosure -- trung; pig pen -- trung ch'roook

penal adj. prum'a'tun: penal code -- krom prum'a'tun

penalize v. impose sanction on (student, sports team, etc.) -- tro to'tool to'h: legally -- paak: If we break the law we will be penalized. -- Praw'sun chia yeung tveu l'meuh ch'bop gkay nung paak yeung.

penalty n. paak; pee'naae; punishment -- to'h; or, twun'a'kum

pencil n. t'mao dye

pendant n. bun tow'ng

pendulum n. pow'l

peninsula n. o'pa'tweeb

penis n. at'k'daw

penny n. i.e., smallest Cambodia coin -- sayn; (10 sayn = 1 kaeh; 10 kaeh = 1 riel)

pension n. praa(k) a'treiyt (lit: retirement money)

people n.

saah: emphasis on common racial origin or geographic   location: Cambodian people -- saah Khmei; American people -- saah Am'rik; concept of people of particular country is also expressed by name of country used alone, as: Thai people [think that]... -- Thai [kut tha]... ;

pra'chee'chuun: emphasis on citizenry, political   commonality, as in "We, the people," or "People's Party": The people of Cambodia say... -- Pra'chee'chuun Kampuchea ni'yaye ... ; also used for this concept of "people", or citizens, citizenry, the national population of a certain country, etc., are the terms bun'da chuun, bun'da ree'eh, pra'chee'a ree'eh, pra'chee'chiun, prachee'a pul   rawt, and pul'ratt;

chuun: foreign people -- chuun bor'tay; poor people -- chuun kr'eye kraw;

lok: important people -- awh lok thum thum

ma'nooh: lots of people -- ma'nooh ch'raan; men --   ma'nooh proh; women -- ma'nooh sraae; important people -- ma'nooh sum'kahn

neh: people of a region -- neh sruk; people who stay in... -- neh noeh...

pooh (written poo'ich): people in general -- pooh; Chinese people -- pooh jchun; those people -- pooh nung

ree'eh: national population -- The Khmer people -- Ree'eh Khmei

k'mayng k'mayng -- young people, generally; male youth -- yoo'veh chuun; female youth -- yoo'veh neh'ree

pepper n. black -- ma'ric; small red or green, very hot pepper -- ma'taae(s) (NB: because very piquant, nick-named ma'taae(s) ka'mung ("enemy")); bell pepper, red or green -- ma'taae(s) plauwk

percent n. pi roi: 90% -- kow sup pi roi

percentage, house n. to'ng

perch v. tuung: Animals sit, birds perch. -- Sat(ch) ung'koi, sut tuung.

perfect adj. ot k'chaw: [His work] is usually perfect. -- [Kaa'ngyeea ro'bah gwat] chia twa'ma'da keuh ot k'chaw.

perfect v. bung howi la'aw; bung chope la'aw

perfection n. pheap ot k'chaw

perforate v. punch holes, generally -- tuum loo'h; punch holes to point of destroying object being perforated -- tuum lee'aae

perform v. tveu: That child does not perform well in class. -- Gkon nu tveu ot la'aw noeh k'nong t'nak.; tveu kaa: Those soldiers performed well at Sam'roang. -- Tee'hee'an nu tveu kaa la'aw noeh k'nong Sam'roang.; rut: This machine does not perform well. -- Ma'seen ni rut ot la'aw.; sum'dye'ng: The band performed last night. -- Krum plaeng sum'dye'ng yoop munyh.

perfume n. tuk op

perhaps adv. praw'heil: Perhaps he is sick. -- Praw'heil gwat cheuh.; Do you want some? Perhaps. -- Tau(v) neh jchong klaah tay? Praw'heil.; meuhl teuh: Perhaps it will not rain. -- Meuhl teuh ot plee'eng.; Perhaps he will not come. -- Meuhl teuh gwat mun mok tay.; tuum nong chia: Perhaps it is better this way. -- Veea tuum nong chia praw'sar chiang doj cha'neh.

period n. punctuation mark -- ('The closest analogue to a period in Khmer writing is an end-of-sentence marker called a "kan"; in that a "kan" looks nothing like a "period", it is advisable to refer to a period by the English word "period".); period of time -- peyr va'leea; fixed period -- kum'naut; peyr; time span characterized by particular political or cultural phenomenon, era -- jchum'no'an; or, ree'ech'chia kaal; or, peyr ney sah'mye: the Sihanouk period -- peyr ney sah'mye Sihanoo'; the Ankgor period -- ree'ech chia kaal Angkor; reign, specifically -- ree'ech'chia kaal; Period! -- Jchawp!; I'm not going, period! -- Kyom mun teuh, jchawp!

periodical n. too'a's'nava'dye

perimeter n. pah'ree'venyh; pa'ri'met (fr. Fr.)

permanent adj. a'chen'trei; s'taa'po'

permanently adv. chia s'taa'po

permeable adj. adje baan chree'up

permeate v. chree'up

permeated adj. chree'up; ch'roo'it chrec'up

permission n. kaa a'noo'naaht; ask permission -- sum ch'bot; give permission -- a'noo'naaht owi; owi ch'bot; a'noo'naaht; owi: I will not give [permission to, let you] go. -- Kyom mun owi teuh.; get permission to -- miun kaa a'noo'naaht owi... baan: I cannot get permission to go. -- Kyom mun miun kaa a'noo'naaht owi teuh baan.

permit n. kaa a'noo'naaht: business permit -- kaa a'noo'naaht owi baahk haang chuum'noo'inyh; exit permit -- kaa a'noo'naaht jchenyh krau praw'tet; driver's permit -- pear'mee (fr. Fr.); permit to cut trees, logging permit -- pear'mee kaat cheu; permit to transport logs -- pear'mee dahk daum cheu

permit v. a'noo'naaht owi: We will permit him to go. -- Yeung nung a'noo'naaht owi gwat teuh.; They [should not] permit these [violations] to [continue]. -- Pooh'gkay [mun koo'a] a'noo'naaht owi miun [kaa ruum lok bum pee'an] [bun taw tee'it] tay.; baahk owi: We permit them to do all kinds of work. -- Yeung baahk owi pooh'gkay tveu tej kaa p'sayng p'sayng.; permit, without caring, s. o. to do s.th. harmful or dangerous -- bun dyke bun dow'ee

pernicious adj. jchong rye; p'deh p'dah: He is a pernicious influence. -- Gwat chia neh bun jchoh bun jchole jchong rye.

perpetual adj. baan ro'hote

persimmon n. plai tun'lawp

persistent adj. soo; k'choo'ib k'choo'un; be persistent -- p'syee'a yee'um (lit: to try)

person n. ma'nooh: a, or one, person -- ma'nooh ma'neh (NB: ma'neh = compression of moi neh); She's a good person.. -- Nee'eng ma'nooh la'aw.; chuun: That's the person who stole my car! -- Chuun nu howi dael baan loo'ich laan kyom.; (more colloquial) -- a gwat: That's the person who stole my car! -- A gwat nu howi dael loo'ich laan kyom.; neh: sick person -- neh chuum'ngeu; old person, mature person -- neh jchaah tuum; (NB: neh is also used as classifier {see under definition of "piece" for discussion of classifiers} for people or persons: two friends (lit: "friends two persons") -- mit pi neh); that (particular) person -- ma'neh nu (lit: that one); in person -- p'twal; p'twal kloo'an; tul muk ka'neea: I need to talk to him in person. -- Kyom tro kaa ni'yaye chi'moi gwat tul muk ka'neea.; (unstated): [young] (person) -- [k'mayng] ( )

personal adj. p'twal kloo'an

personally adv. dow'ee p'twal: I will repair your television personally. -- Kyom nung choo'ah chul too'ra'too neh dow'ee p'twal.; Personally, I don't like fish. -- P'twal kloo'an kyom ot (or, mun) jchole jchet trei.

personality n. ruk pee'a: She has a good personality. -- Nee'eng miun ruk peea la'aw.; quality of character -- leh ka'nak: a wife with every quality -- pra'pun miun kroop leh ka'nak; She has a good personality for this job. -- Nee'eng miun leh ka'nak la'aw sum'rap tveu kej kaa ni.; internal character -- mee'a yee'it; attitude -- aae'ri'ya'but: He has a bad attitude. -- Gwat miun aae'ri'ya'but a'krah.; or, ruk'peea: She has a good attitude. -- Nee'eng miun ruk'peea la'aw.

personnel n. buk'lut

perspiration n. nyeuss

perspire v. byke nyeuss

persuade v. bun jchoh bun jchole

persuasive adj. miun t'vye mwot

pervade v. yee'a yee

perversion n. vee'pa'lass

petal n. traw baw

petition n. sum'num po

petroleum n. praeng bun to'an slaw (lit: crude oil)

pharmacist n. o'suh'ta'ko

pharmacy n. haang looh tnam; ptay'a looh tnam; o'suh'taan

phase n. dum'na(k) kaa : the first phase of the election -- dum'na(k) ti moi ney bawh ch'nowt; or, dum'na(k) ti moi ney bawh ch'nowt; in sense of step -- chuum'hee'an: the first phase of the recovery of the economy... -- chuum'hee'an ti moi ney kaa sraw'srong set'a'kej...

Ph. D. n. bun'dut: I want to become a Ph. D. -- Kyom jchong klai teuh chia neh bun'dut.

phenomenon n. pa'tuk'phoot

Philippines n. praw'tet Philippines

philosopher n. too'sna nee'too

philosophy n. too'sna nee chee'a

phonograph n. ma'seen jch'ree'eng

phonograph record n. tass jchuum'ree'eng

phosphate n. phos'faat

photo-copy v. tveu co'pee; tawt sum'buht

photograph n. roob tawt; roob

photograph v. tawt roob

photographer n. neh roob tawt

phrase n. kloa; vaae'eh

physician n. kruu peyt

physics n. roo'pa'sahs

piano n. pya'no

pick v. choose -- reu'; jch'reu'; jch'reu' reu'; (NB: choice = kaa jch'reu reu'): Pick one student. -- Jch'reu reu' gkon'sa ma'neh.;

Also:

pick fruit -- beh plai cheu; pick herbs -- beh chii

pick on -- taa owi; (also: criticize -- tek tee'un; laugh at and make fun of -- sow'eet jchuum awh

pick out of s. where, extract -- s'rung; The helicopter went to pick the pilot out of the water. -- 'Eh'le'kop'tayr teuh s'rung pee'lut laung pi tùk.

pick up (from the ground, off the floor, etc.) -- huh(k)

pick up (a friend) from the airport -- to'tool mit pi airport;

pick up and bring s. where -- to'tool mok

pick up luggage at the airport -- yok aye'von pi airport

find, meet -- reu'yok: He always wants to go pick up girls. -- Gwat tyne tai jchong teuh reu' yok sraae.

pick up speed -- stooh

pickle n. ch'roo'hk

pickle v. traahm

pickpocket n. neh jchak

picture n. photograph -- roob tawt; roob pheap; [painted] picture -- [lee'ab] kum noo; mental picture -- roob pheap noeh k'nong kum'nut; moving picture -- gkun; or, pheap yun; take a picture -- tawt roob

piece n.

a piece of s. th. -- The choice of the Khmer word to use to translate the English word "piece" depends on what thing, substance or item the "piece" is of. Khmer divides nouns into groups each of whose members may to some extent have a common characteristic, such as being flat, being long and thin, having a head (like cattle) etc. Associated with each such grouping will be a Khmer word called a "classifier". (Classifiers are also found in English, examples being words like "piles" of leaves, or "head" of cattle.)

        It is the Khmer "classifier" that would be used to translate the English word "piece" with respect to any noun in that classifier's group. For example, the classifier for things that are flat is "sun'luk"; hence a "piece" of [wood] would be "[kada] moi sun'luk" and a "piece of [paper]" would be "[kra'dah] moi sun'luk". "Please give me a piece of (i. e., a sheet of) paper." would be "Sum owi kra'dah kyom moi sun'luck."

        Some other common classifiers are: (1) bun taae'a: a piece of bread -- num pahng moi bun taae'a; (2) duhm: a piece of land -- daiy moi duhm; a piece of stone -- duhm t'maw; piece of cake -- num moi duhm; and (3) kum'nup: a piece of wood -- cheu moi kum'nup.

        Among the classifers that do not translate as "piece" are "neh" -- people (as in, "two girls" -- "sraae pi neh") -- and "k'nong" (literally, rooves, and also a word for counting houses in a village.);

a small piece (of anything) -- kum'tic: a piece of [shrapnel] -- kum'tic [kraw] moi; break into small pieces -- byke tic: The glass broke into small pieces. -- Kaae'oo byke tic.;

piece (lit: section) of a machine -- p'nyke ney ma'seen

literary piece -- at'ta'bawt

musical piece -- plaeng moi bawt

pier n. pa'aae; cun'lye'ng jchawt ka'pal

pierce v. jchawh; poke -- jchak (same as jchak t'nam)

pierced adj. jchawh: pierced ears -- traw'chi'eh(k) jchawh

pig n. jch'roook

pigeon n. pree'up

pile n. poon noo(k): pile of rice -- poon noo(k) sro; pile of rock -- poon noo(k) t'maw; pile of leaves -- poon noo(k) sluk cheu; pile of firewood -- poon noo(k) awhs; kum'noh: pile of dishes -- jchaan moi kum'noh

pile v. ko': pile baggage -- ko aye'von; pile one on top of the other -- bun taup leuh ka'neea

pill n. kro'up: Take one pill each hour. -- Laae'p tnam moi kro'up moi mao m'dong.

pillow n. k'nau'wi: standard bed pillow -- k'nau'wi geyng; elongated "hugging" pillow -- k'nau'wi auwp; pillow case -- srauwm k'nau'wi

pillar n. saw

pilot n. pee'lut; aka'nee'a vuk

pin n. m'chul ba'rang; saftey pin -- m'chul k'toa; sewing needle -- m'chul day; medical needle -- m'chul jchak t'nam **pincers** n. dong kaab; dong kee'up

pinch v. kee'up; k'duk

pineapple n. munu'wa(ss) (AP: moo'nuu'aa(s))

ping pong n. ping pong

pink adj. pwa p'ka gu'lab; pwa p'ka chook

pinky n. gkon dai

pinpoint v. identify clearly -- jchong'ul owi cheh'leh: We have to pinpoint the problem. -- Yeung tro tai jchong'ul owi cheh'leh noeh pun'ha.; site carefully, aim -- dum'rong: They have to pinpoint the site carefully before shooting (or, before dropping the bombs. -- Pooh'gkay tro tai dum'rong muun nung banyh.; (NB: dum'rong lit. = aim, as in: Dum'rong kum pleung banyh saat. -- Aim the gun and shoot the animal.)

pioneer n.   neh rok rok; neh srauw chree'oo: He was a pioneer in medicine. -- Gwat chia neh srauw chree'oo tnam'peyt.

pipe n.   water, gas, etc. -- bum oung; for smoking -- k'see'a

pistol n.   kum pleung dai

pit n.   ruu'n dow

pitch v.   throw -- bawh; chowl; pitch camp -- bawh chuum ruum; pitch a tent -- bawh tenh

pitiable adj.   kum'sutt; a'nutt

pity n.   praw'nye; may'daa; a'nutt

pity v.   sum'vaeyk; a'nutt: I pity [the refugees] very much. -- Kyon a'nutt [chuun pieh kloo'an] nah.

place n.   cunlye'ng; (AP: cum'lyne, kun'lyne, kalyne, ka'lye): The place I went... -- Cunlye'ng kyom teuh...; Please mark the place on the map for me. -- Sum kooh cunlye'ng noeh leuh pan'tee tooo'k owi kyom.; ti: Wait for me at that place. -- Jcham kyom ti nu.; starting place -- daum ti; place of origin, birthplace -- sruk kum'naut; sruk tae(ss); in the first place -- chia va'tuum; work place -- ti snak kaa; cunlye'ng tveu kaa

place v.   dah(k); dum'kawl

plain adj.   lee'ut

plain n.   veal; "Wide Plain" (major Khmer Rouge staging base nad recupment area in southwestern Po'sat) -- Veal Veng;

plaintiff n.   neh daum jchowt

plait v.   braid -- krong; plait hair -- krong saahk

plan n.   design, layout, blue print -- kum'ro'ng kaa; (S) kro'ng; idea for action -- pyne'kaa: His plan sounds OK. -- Pyne'kaa gwat doj chia la'aw.; vi'ti'ya'na'ka; baep pyne

plan v.   kut; miun kum ro'ng kaa; (S) kro'ng; plan to -- pro'ng nung: I plan to go soon. -- Kyom pro'ng nung teuh yang ro'has.; prepare -- ree'up jcham

plane n.   wood-shaving tool -- chuh(s) cheu

planet n.   pope; the planet Earth -- pan daiy; (world = pik'pope lok; moon -- lok'k'eye; preah chan)

planner n.   neh ree'up pyne'kaa: economic planner -- neh ree'up pyne'kaa set'a'kej; military planner -- neh ree'up pyne'kaa tee'hee'an

plank n.   ka'dah

plant n.   generally -- daum: bean plant -- daum sun dyke; plants, crops -- dam'nam; plants and animals -- roo'ka chee'it howi nung sat(ch); trees -- daum cheu; agriculture or vegetables -- daum nam; manufacturing facility -- ro'ng jcha

plant v.   dahm

plantation n.   jcham'kar: rubber plantation -- jcham'kar kaow'soo; district in northern Kompong Cham, site of several large rubber plantations -- Jcham'kar Leuh (lit: northern, or "upper", plantations)

planting n.   i. e., of seeds -- kaa dahm

plaster n.   kum'bauw bye'awk

plastic adj.   plastique; cho'a

plate n.   jchan

plateau n.   daiy k'pung ree'up; daiy tool

platform n.   vay'ti'kaa

platoon n.   kong a'noo' sena'to'ich; artillery platoon/unit -- krum kum pleung thum

platter n.   taa'h

play v.   a game or musical instrument -- leng: play cards -- leng bee'a; play guitar -- leng gi'ta'; play a trick -- leng la'batch; play music -- leng plaeng; plaeng leng; or, praw'kum don'trei; playing too loud -- plaeng leng so klang na; play a stringed instrument -- denyh: play guitar -- denyh cha'pye; or, denyh gi'ta'; play a role -- dah too'a; play the drums -- vye sco; dum sco; play records -- jchak taahs; play tapes -- jchak k'assett (AP: k'sye't); play for time, delay -- puun'yeea peyr

play n. a drama -- ru'kauwn: modern play -- ru'kauwn sak mye; patriotic play -- ru'kauwn chee'it

player n. neh leng

playful adj. ro'leh ro'lawh

playground n. cunlye'ng leng; ti klee'a

plaza n. ti lee'en

plead v. ung'vo' kaw; ung'vo': plead for one's life -- ung'vo dum'bye chi'vut

pleasant adj. reh' teh'; s'bai; reehk ree'aae; (unpleasant -- ot reh' teh'; ot s'bai); peaceful and pleasant -- rung ru'ung

please adv. un'cheunyh; cheunyh: Please come in -- Cheunyh jchole; sum: Please give me that book. -- Sum owi kyom s'po nu.; sum un'cheunyh : Please come in. -- Sum un'cheunyh jchole.; formal, more used in writing than in speech -- jcho(r): Please submit your resignation. -- Jcho(r) pdull owi noeh kaa lee'aae chope pi dum'nye'nyh.;

pong: May [God (i.e., Buddha)] please help me. -- [Preah] owi choo'ay kyom pong.; Please tell me. -- Prap kyom pong.

please v. bum penyh jchet; p'kwap jchet: They [just] want to please [the observers]. -- Pooh'gkay [tro'un tai] jchong yok jchet [neh song'kaet'kaa].

pleased adj. penyh jchet; tro jchet; s'bai baan: Pleased to meet you! --   S'bai baan choop neh (or, ka'neea).

pleasure n. kaa s'bao; kaa penyh jchet: She takes pleasure in helping others. -- Nee'eng penyh jchet nung choo'ay gkay.; It was a pleasure [to leave Cherating camp]. -- Veea chia kaa s'bai na [dael baan jchaak jchenyh pi chuum'ruhm Cherating].; kaa kooa owi penyh jchet: It will be a great pleasure [if] we don't meet him again! -- Veea chia kaa koo'a owi penyh jchet nah [praw'sun] yeung mun choop gwat tee'it.

pleat n. plee; p'not

pledge n. sum'bot

pledge v. sum'bot

plenipotentiary adj. penyh bun toook

plentiful adj. suh'bo; kroop kron

plenty adj. baw'ri bo; ho'hee'a; po'penyh; ch'raan ho'hee'a

pliers n. dong kaap

plight n. leh ka'nak a'krah; s'ta'na'pheap a'krah: I worry about the plight of the refugees in the camps. -- Kyom proo'i om'pee s'ta'na'pheap a'krah chuun pieh kloo'an k'nong chuum'ruhm.

plot n. sinister plan -- vaae'a tuum s'naa: a plot [against] the government -- tveu vaae'a tuum s'naa praw'chang ratt'a'pi'baal; of a story -- dum'nall ru'ung; a plot of ground -- daiy moi duhm

plot against someone v. plot -- lope tveu om'peuh a'krah; lope tveu vaae'a tuum s'naa; against someone -- teuh leuh no na ma'neh; or, praw'chang gkay: Why do you plot against me? -- Hyte aae' baan chia neh lope tveu om'peuh a'krah praw'chang kyom? or, Hyte aae baan chia neh lope tveu vaae'a tuum s'naa teuh leuh kyom?

plow n. nong kw'ul

plow v. p'yoo'a; (AP: shoo'a)

pluck v. beh: pluck fruit -- beh plai cheu; dawk: pluck eyebrows -- dawk jcheng jchouwm; keh: pluck a guitar -- keh guitar

plug n. ch'nawk: plug to stop up a sink -- ch'nawk sum'rap cho'k basin tuk

plumb adj. chaw trong: Make it plumb. -- Tveu veea owi chaw trong.

plump adj. toat; re babies -- miun praw'lung (lit: having spirit, spirited; (a polite way of saying a child is plump))

plunder v. jchun: They plundered the houses during the fighting. -- Pooh'gkay jchun ptay'a noeh peyr vye ka'neea.

plus adj. bo'k: Five plus three is how much? -- Pram bo'k bye smauw nung pu'man?; fifty-plus men -- ma'nooh ha'sup chiang

plywood n. ka'da bun tay'eh

p. m. mao... yoop: ten p. m. -- mao dop yoop

pneumonia n. rokh ro'leea(k) soo'it

pocket n. kow pow

pocket v. dah(k)... k'nong kow pow: She pocketed [the money] and left. -- Nee'eng dah(k) [loi] k'nong kow pow howi jchenyh teuh.

poem n. kum'naahp

poet n. kaa nye

poetry n. kum'naahp

point n. in a discussion or story -- jchum nutch: a point -- jchum nutch moi; an interesting point -- jchum nutch chia jchaap a'rom; or, jchum nutch koo'a owi jchaap a'rom; or, jchum nutch moi chia jchaap a'rom; main point -- jchum nutch sum'kahn; to the point -- owi jchum nutch; point in a [circle] -- jchum nutch noeh [ruhm'vuung]; point on a line -- jcham nutch peh bun'twa(t); point on a map -- jchum nutch noeh leuh pan'tee; highest point on the mountain -- kum'pool noeh leuh phnom; high point of the trip -- sa'rach sum'kahn ney kaa tveu dum'nall; point of view -- kohl kum'nut; from my point of view -- kohl kum'nut ro'bah kyom

point v. jchong'ul: Please point to the north. -- Sum jchong'ul teuh kang jcheun.; point a gun at close range -- p'chuung

pointed adj. sroo'it

poison n. t'nam bun plyng; t'nam pul; pul

poison v. bum pul

poisoned pp. bum pul: He was poisoned by the French fries! -- Gwat tro baan bum pul dow'ee sa dum'lung jchian!

poisonous adj. miun puhh

poke v. in sense of push -- jch'uch; in sense of jab -- jcha(k): poke in the ribs -- jcha(k) chh'ung keh (lit: in the waist); poke s. th. into s. th. -- ruok: poke the potatoes into [the coals] -- ruok dum'lung jchole teuh k'nong [ngaw ngeuk]

pole n. dong: straight carrying pole balanced on shoulder with baskets hanging from either end -- dong'rek; (NB: because it runs in a relatively straight east-west line, the mountain range that lies along the northern Cambodia border with Thailand, the Dongrek's, was named after this sort of pole.); fishing pole -- dong sung too'ch; telephone pole -- bun kohl to'ra'sap; electric power pole -- bun kohl k's'eye pleung

police n. in Sihanouk era -- po'leez; under Lon Nol -- dum'roo'it and "paye aam" (French pronunciation of acronym "P. M." of "police militaire"); under Heng Samrin -- na'ko'bal; dum'roo'it; generally, and most common post-UNTAC -- dum'roo'it; military police -- kawng a'vut'ha'ee'it; generally: town police -- na'ko'bal krong; provincial police -- na'ko'bal kyte

policy n. foreign or state -- na'yo'bye: internal, departmental -- ch'bop; or, ko'le'ka; policy in general -- meea' keea: bad policies -- meea'keea ot la'aw

polish v. kaat; ch'n'eye; dawh: Polish my shoes really shiny. -- Kaat s'bai cheung ro'bah kyom owi ro'lung.

polished adj. pleuu ro'lung; polished car -- laan pleuu ro'lung; polished table -- tohk pleuu ro'lung

politburo n. Ka'ma'pi'bal

polite adj. koo'a sawm

political adj. na'yo'bye

politician n. neh na'yo'bye

politics n. na'yo'bye; get involved in politics, do political work -- tveu na'yo'bye

pollen n. luum ong; luum ong p'ka

poly- adv. paya'hoo'a (lit: many)

polygon n. pa'hoo'a kown (Kh. pronun of Fr. wd. po'li'gaun)

polysyllabic adj. pa'hoo'a p'shyee'ung

pond n. tra'paeng; tlawh; large pond/small lake -- bung; (large pond/small lake in central Phnom Penh -- Bung Kaak)

ponder v. ru'ung pung kut; kut ru'ung; kut ru'ung pay

poor adj. opp. of rich -- kraw; kr'eye kraw; ot miun: poor girl -- k'mayng sraae kraw; poor people -- neh ti twaal kraw; not rich -- mun... miun: He is not a rich man. -- Gwat mun man chia neh miun.; unskilled -- mun poo'k'eye; or, mun jchum'nan: He is a poor tennis player. -- Gwat leng te'nnit mun poo'k'eye; in poor condition -- raw'yee ro'y'eye; clothes in poor condition -- kow-aow raw'yee' ro'y'eye; inadequate -- baan tic: a poor harvest -- praw'mole p'auwl baan tic; pitiable, unfortunate -- ot sum'nang; kum'sot; Oh, poor Cambodia! Whew! -- Ah, Kampuchea, ot sum'nang, uuecoo!; Oh, poor Cambodia. -- Ah, Kampuchea, kum'sot!; Oh, poor Srei Peau! -- Owee, Srei Peau daw kum'sot, uuecoo!

poor, the n. i.e., poor people -- neh kraw dun'dap; chuun kr'eye kraw

pop v. explode, burst -- toook; k'toook; cause to pop -- ling: to pop some corn -- ling po't; popcorn -- po't ling; pop up, surge -- bauw

populace n. pracheea'pul rawt; bun'da chuun; (NB: see definitions of "people" for other terms for "populace")

popular adj. gkay ni'yuum ch'raan: This restaurant is popular. -- Haang'bye ni gkay ni'yuum ch'raan. (lit: this restaurant they like a lot.); praw'chia prey: He is popular [even though] he isn't rich. -- Gwat praw'chia prey [thoop bye] gwat mun man chia neh miun.; popular singer -- neh jchum'ree'ung dael gkay ni'yuum; in sense of famous -- neh jchum'ree'ung la'bye la bong; or, la'bye chamoo'h.

popularity n. praw'chia prey'a'pheap: Funcinpec won because of Sihanouk's popularity. -- Funcinpec ch'neh bee'proo'a (or dow'ee sa) Sihanoo' miun praw'chia prey'a'pheap.; Popularity is not important. -- Praw'chia prey'a'pheap ot jcham'batch.; kaa ni'yuum: I don't need popularity. -- Kyon ot tro kaa kaa ni'yuum.

population n. jchum'noo'an pra'chee'chuun: The population is increasing too fast. -- Jchum'noo'an pra'chee'chuun kaut laung ro'has nah.; pra'choom chuun: population center -- ti pra'choom chuun

pork n. sat(ch) ch'roook

port n. for shipping -- pye; kum'puung pye; pye ka'pal

portable adj. to'ich (lit: small)

porter n. generally, at railroad station, airport, etc. -- neh chuun choon aye'von; for military force, carrier of rice, ammunition, etc. -- neh chuun choon sa'bee'un

portion n. jchum'nyke... pieh; I want a bigger portion. -- Kyon jchong baan jchum'nyke ch'raan pieh.; pieh: What portion of the people are poor? -- Tau(v) pu'man pich pra'chee'chuun dael a'krah?; pn'eye'k (see examples under "part")

portray v. portray visually (in pictures, etc.) -- koo (lit: draw); portray in words -- ree'ub ro'ab (lit: detail); describe -- pee'por'neea; portray with exaggeration -- bum pleuh

pose v. for a picture -- [cho roo ung'koi owi] gkay tawt roob; (lit: [stand or sit for] s. o. to take a picture); pretend to be so. o. or s. th. -- tveu peuh; leuk tang kloo'an chia

position n. job title -- mok'ngyeea; office or relatively high position -- chuum'ho; position or office in sense of "rank" -- bun'sak; social position -- t'nak; or, dum nye'ng(y); bodily position -- bye'p but; sitting position -- bye'p but ung'koi; position on an issue -- kohl chuum'ho; political position -- kolh chuum'ho na'yo'bye: What is his position on income distribution? -- Gwat miun kohl chuum'ho aae om'pee chuum'noo'ee kum'r'eye noeh k'nong praw'tet?; a socialist position -- kohl chuum'ho na'yo'bye so'cial'eeste; difficult position -- s'ta'na'pheap lum'bah; get into position -- rok tuum no'ng; ree'up jchong srach; [the troops'] position -- kaa dap [kawng thwaap]; fortified position -- ti taang; take a [public] position on s. th. -- ni'yaye om'pee kohl chuum'ho [sa'teea'rena(ch)]

possess v. miun

possessed pp. He was possessed by a ghost -- K'mau'it jchole gwat. (lit: A ghost entered him.); He was possessed by a spirit. -- Gwat a'ret cho'un. (lit: He was stepped on/held by a spirit.)

possessive adj.   generally, in sense of greedy, -- kum'reehh; selfish -- kum'nenyh; thrifty   --   kum'ranyh

possible adj.   adje tveu baan; kaut tveu baan; leh'ta'pheap: It's possible he will win. -- Gwat miun leh'ta'pheap nung ch'neh.; adje: It's possible. -- Adje tveu kaut.

possibility n.   ratt'a'pheap

possibly adv.   praw'heil

post n.   bung kohl: fence post -- bung kohl ro'bawh(ng)

post card n.   poste kaah't

post office n.   poh; prai's'nee

postage stamps n.   t'eye'mb(r) (fr. Fr., "timbre")

poster n.   p'aakh

postpone v.   p'aakh: They postponed [the appointment] again. -- Pooh'gkay p'aakh [kaa nut'choop] m'dong tee'it howi.; leuk... teuh peyr krow'ee: They postponed [the meeting]. -- Gkay leuk [kaa pra'choom] teuh peyr krow'ee.

posture n.   ro'bee'up cho roo ung'koi (lit: manner of standing or sitting)

pot n.   chhn'aang; large pot, generally -- chhn'aang thum; for planting flowers, etc. -- pa'hl'ng; pot calling the kettle black -- dung chia neh na tha owi neh na tay

pot-holed adj.   kra'haeng kra'hoeng

potato n.   dum'lung ba'raang; potato chips -- chips; french fried potatoes -- dum'lung jchian; sweet potato -- dum'lung ch'vee'a; boiled potato -- dum'lung scnauw

pouch n.   plow

poultry n.   muon tee'a (lit: chickens [and] ducks)

pound v.   buhk: pound rice -- buhk sro'; pound corn -- buhk po't; pound meat -- dum sat(ch); koo'ah: He pounded the table with his [fist]. -- Gwat koo'ah tohk chi'moi kun'dap dai gwat.

pour v.   generally -- jchak: verify conforms to cluster): pour water -- jchak tuk; pour out -- jchak jchowl; pour (polite, formal term) -- cha; Shall I pour some coffee [for you]? -- Tau(v) kyom adje cha cafe [choon lok] baan tay?

poverty n.   kr'eye kraw; s'kd'eye kraw; poverty stricken -- tauk yaa

powder n.   m'sauw

powdered milk n.   tuk'dawh'gko m'sauw

power n.   authority -- um'natch: have power -- miun um'natch; be in power -- kaan um'natch (lit: hold power); still in power -- noeh miun um'natch d'dael; a great power (nation) -- maha um'natch; authority plus ability -- um'natch: the power to help... -- um'natch nung choo'ay...; ability -- buun: Sihanouk has the power [to help bring rain]! -- Sihanoo' miun buun [choo'ay tveu owi miun plee'eng]!; ruh'tee; physical ability -- a'ti'pul: the power to destroy the village -- a'ti'pul sum'rap bum planyh phum; electric power -- a'ti'pul nay ch'raan a'ti'ce'nee; physical capability -- kum'lung: This car has [no] power [at all]. -- Laan ni [ot] miun kum'lung [ni tay].

power plant (electric) n.   may pleung

powerful adj.   klang klaa

practical adj.   mun sum nyum; practical person -- ma'nooh mun sum nyum; practical application -- praw'tay'but

practically adv.   almost -- chit; practically speaking -- baa' ni'yaye pi kaa sroul; or, baan kaa venyh

practice n.   kaa a'noo'vwut; kaa haht; kaa hutt rian: You need practice. -- Neh tro kaa haht rian.

practice v.   a'noo'vwut: I practice it every day. -- Kyom a'noo'vwut veea rawl t'ngai.; bong haht; re s. th. physical -- haht: practice tennis -- haht leng te'nnit; re s. th. that must be studied, such as a language -- haht rian; engage in a profession -- tveu chia: She wants to practice medecine in Phnom Penh. -- Nee'eng jchong tveu chia kruu peyt noeh Phnom Penh.

praise n.   kaa saw saah

praise v.   saw saah; ni'yaye leuk; praise falsely -- bun chow'it bun chaal

praiseworthy adj.   koo'a owi saw saah

prawn n.   bung kaw

pray v.   read or chant [prayers] audibly -- sote [toa]; read or say prayers to oneself (also, meditate) -- pee'a vi'neea toa; pray [for] s. th. -- pee'a venee'a [sum]: pray for tea -- pee'a vi'neea sum ta'aae; also, oot teu'ss sum or, boo'ung soo'ung sum: On temple day the people pray for peace. -- Noeh t'ngai suhl pra'chee'chuun boo'ung soo'ung sum san'ti'pheap.; pray for rain -- boo'ung soo'ung sum plee'eng.; bun srun sum'rap: He prays for her health. -- Gwat bun srun sum'rap sok'a'pheap nee'eng.

prayer n.   toa; sum no'm po': Please answer my prayer. -- Sum ch'lye tawp sum no'm po' kyom.; prayer or blessing -- kaa tra thiun po'

preach v.   tae'ss'na

precarious adj.   kroo'ti'nak: precarious condition -- s'ta'na'pheap kroo'ti'nak; unpredictable -- mun tee'ung

precept n.   ch'bop

precious adj.   tlai; tlai tlaa; miun dum'lye; a precious [stone] -- [t'bong] dael miun dum'lye (lit: a gem that has value)

pre-condition n.   kum'nauwt

predict v.   tee'aae; tee'aae a'na'kut

prediction n.   kaa tee'aae

preface n.   buh'pey'a'kuh'ta; a'rum'kah'tha

prefer v.   jchole jchet: I'd prefer to die [rather than sell out my country]. -- Kyom jchole jchet slop [praw'sar chiang looh sruk.]; ni'yuum; sra'laanyh: Do you prefer the Sum'leng Vich'oo Khmei newspaper to SPK? -- Tau(v) neh sra'laanyh ka'ssett Sum'leng Vich'oo Khmei ch'raan chiang SPK?; miun kang... chiang: They prefer that minister to the usual politicians. -- Gkay miun kang mun'trei nu chiang nch na'yo'bye twa'ma'da.

preference n.   s'k'dye sra'laanyh chiang; s'kd'eye jchole jchet chiang; s'kd'eye lo'me ee'un

prefix n.   pee'a daum; (suffix = pee'a jchong); (formal term: bo'p jcheh bawt p'tay)

pregnant adj.   miun ptay'a poo'ah

prejudice n.   kaa luum'ee'eng

prejudice v.   luum'ee'eng; tveu owi ko'ich kaat

prejudicial adj.   owi ko'ich praw'yow'it

prejudiced adj.   praw'kaan; luum'ee'eng

premier n.   ni'aae'yok ratt'mun'trei (NB: ni'aae'yok = leading or guiding)

pre-occupy v.   ro'vull; tveu owi om'pul

pre-occupied (with) adj.   miun kaa kwawl kv'eye (k'nong): [Even while] he was working, he was pre-occupied with his [personal] problems. -- [Tvai but tai] gwat kom'puung tveu kaa, gwat miun kaa kwawl kv'eye k'nong pun'ha [twal kloo'an].

prepare v.   ree'up jchum: prepare food -- ree'up jchum bye; prepare a plan -- rec'up jchum pyne'kaa; prepare a lesson -- ree'up jchum may rian; tveu; prepare in advance -- krong tooo'k (can also mean "put aside" as, "put aside as advance provision"): They prepared the plans two years earlier. -- Pooh'gkay baan krong tooo'k pyne'kaa pi chh'nam chia muun.; prong pree'up: prepare for bad news -- prong pree'up kloo'an sum'rap dum'nung a'krah

prerequisite n.   kum'nauwt

presage v.   prawp p'no'le

prescribe v.   sum'but jchenyh tinh t'nam

prescription n.   for medecine -- sum'buht tinh t'nam; general -- kaa dah(k) penyh yaa

presence n.   vwut da'mee'an: His presence surprised me. -- Vwut da'mee'an ro'bah gwat tveu owi kyom pn'yeh p'auwl.; presence of mind -- pheap nung nahw; in the presence of -- jchum'poo'h muk

present n. eye leaou; eye leaou ni; pa'chu'bawn; at present -- sawp t'ngai; the present time -- pa'chu'bawn na kaal

presently adv. at the current time -- sawp tgai ni; in a short time, soon -- noeh peyr klai; (NB: "klai" in Khmer can mean "short" or "close"; in Thai, it is also with one intonation the word for "close" and with another, the word for "far".)

preserve n. jam -- dum'nop; refuge, reserve -- dum'bun kwat kaeng

preserve v. ka'pee'a; preserve wildlife -- ka'pee'a sat(ch) prey; preserve food -- tveu owi too'k baan yeut

preservation n. kaa ka'pee'a: The preservation of the Cambodian [forests] is very important. -- Kaa ka'pee'a [prey] sruk Kampuchea keuh jcham'batch nah.

preside v. tveu chia praw'teea'neea

president n. of a country -- praw'teea'neea tep'a'dye; of an organization -- praw'teea'neea

press n. the print media -- kaa saw'say ka'sset: freedom of the press -- se'rei'pheap k'nong kaa saw'say k'syte; printing press -- puum; ma'seen bawh puum

press v. press down on -- sung kawh(t); press a button -- ch'uch kun dung; press a coat -- uut kow; press an orange -- cha'rawp batch krau'itch

pressed for time adj. paw pet paw powee

pressure n. kaa kee'up

pressure v. s.o or s. th. politically or financially -- kee'up; kee'up song'kaat

prestige n. keh'chee'a'noo'pheap

pretence n. pheap mun piht (lit: s. th. not true): The government [hides behind] the pretence that Kampuchea is OK. -- Ratt'a'pi'bal [leh bung kawp noeh] pheap mun piht dael tha praw'tet Kampuchea yeung keuh la'aw.

pretend v. for fun or in play -- tveu peuh: Pretend to die! -- Tveu peuh chia slop!; pretend deceptively -- tveu puuht: pretend to be ill -- tveu puuht chia cheu; tveu chia: pretend not to know -- tveu chia mun dung puuht

pretension n. two-faced-ness, hypocrisy -- puuht; (NB: truth = piht): I don't like people with pretensions. -- Kyom ot jchole jchet ma'nooh miun puuht.

pretext n. les: ...use the pretext that... -- ...yok les tha...: He uses the pretext of being busy [because he doesn't want to come on time]. -- Gwat yok les tha ro'vul [bec'proo ot jchong mok owi twon peyr].

prettiness n. sum'rawh

pretty adj. re people -- sa'aat: a pretty girl -- sraae sa'aat; (polite term) -- sum'rawh; applicable to things (i.e., flowers, vegetables, etc.) as well as people -- sr'awh; re images -- la'aw: a pretty view -- teh'sa'pheap la'aw; re sounds -- peeh rooh: pretty music -- plaeng peeh rooh

prevent v. bung kaa: [Injections (of medecine)] prevent cholera. -- [Kaa jchak tnam] bung kaa chuum'ngeu a'sun'na rohk.; kaa peea: We need to prevent [crime]. -- (Yeung) tro ka'pee'a [but ok'krut].; prevent from -- ka'pee'a... kum owi: We have to prevent the enemy [from coming back]. -- Yeung tro tai ka'pee'a sa'tro kum owi [jchole mok venyh].

previously adv. chia muun; kaal muun; pi muun; pi t'ngai muun

price n. dum'lye: the price of the movie ticket -- dum'lye sum'buht gkun; cost (or costly) -- tlai: What's the price (cost) of those rubber boots? -- [Kaow'soo nu] tlai pu'man?; high price (lit: very costly) -- tlai nah; (NB: "tlai" alone also sometimes translates as "expensive" as in: This car is more expensive than that one. -- Laan ni tlai chiang laan nu.); [implied] -- tauk (lit: reasonable): a reasonable (price) -- tauk la'mawm (lit: reasonable enough); (NB: tauk can also tranlate as "cheap, inexpensive", as: That's very cheap! -- A nu tauk nah!; to express "cheap price" or "low cost", one may say "tlai tauk" or "Tlai ni tauk nah" or "tauk la'mawm" (lit: low , or reasonable, enough).

priest n. bo'peh'chit; lok sang

primary adj. dum'bong: primary stages -- dum'nall kaa dum'bong; primary election -- kaa bauw ch'nowt dum'bong; thum chiang gkay: primary reason -- mool'a'hyte thum chiang gkay; primary education -- suk'sa p'daum; primary sources -- pra'pulip daum

prime minister n. ni'aae'yok ratt'mun'trei

prince n. s'dach proh

princess n. neh mu'nee'eng: Princess Monique -- Neh mu'nee'eng Monique; loosely, also: m'chah sa'trei

principal adj. sum'kahn bom'pot

principal of a school n. ni'aae'yok sa'la; jchaang vaang

principle n. chia kohl kaa: It is an [important] principle that the economy of Cambodia [is not controlled] by the Thais. -- Veea keuh chia kohl kaa [daw sum'kahn] dael set'a'kej Khmei [mun tro baan kaan kaab] dow'ee Tha'ee.; (unprincipled = tuh'chuh'ruht)

print v. reproduce by machine -- bawh puum: Where do they print "Ess Paye Kaa"?? -- Tau(v) gkay bawh puum "Ess Paye Kaa" noeh aae na?; print (i.e., write) by hand -- saw say a'ksaw puum; print in sense of copy (by hand or machine) -- jchum'long; explicitly by hand -- jchum'long dow'ee dai; explicitly by machine -- jchum'long dow'ee ma'seen; p'dut: print pictures from photo negatives -- p'dut roob tawt

printed adj. bawh puum; puum: a printed (by machine) letter (of the alphablet) -- a'saw puum; printed [by hand] -- saw say [dow'ee dai] (lit: written): a hand-lettered [invitation] -- [sum'buht un'cheunyh] saw'say dow'ee dai; [a document] printed/copied [by machine] -- [sum'buht] jchum'long [dow'ee ma'seen]

printer n. as for computer -- ma'seen co'pee cum'puu'teuh

printing press n. puum; ma'seen bawh puum

prison n. cooo'k; po'ong teh'nee'a kee'a; be in prison or be imprisoned -- noeh cho'op cooo'k

prisoner n. neh cho'op knawh; cho'op knawh (NB: knawh = bound, handcuffed); neh cho'op koh (lit: guilty person); neh to'h (lit: criminal type); neh cho'op cooo'k (lit: person in jail); prisoner of war -- ch'loy sung'kree'um; [political] prisoner -- neh to'h [na'yo'bye]

privacy n. re both information and living conditions -- pheap eyke'a'chuun twal kloo'an: I want my privacy. -- Kyom jchong baan pheap eyke'a'chuun twal kloo'an.; isolation -- pheap'dach: isolation from people -- pheap'dach pi gkay

private adj. eyke'a'chuun: private office -- kaar'ya'lye eyke'a'chuun; private school -- sa'la eyke'a'chuun; or, sa'la ch'nool (lit: paid school); private property -- sum'baat eyke'a'chuun; private residence -- ti'luum'noeh eyke'a'chuun; p'twal kloo'an: private property -- sum'baat p'twal kloo'an; Excuse me, we are having a private conversation. -- Sum toh, yeung miun kaa ni'yaye p'twal kloo'an.; a [confidential] conversation -- kaa ni'yaye [sum'ngut]

private n. military rank -- gkon tee'hee'an; enlisted personnel generally -- pul toe; (NB: Khmer for "army enlisted" (equivalent to American term, "G.I.") is "pul toe tee'hee'an", which when spoken quickly comes out "pul't tee'eea'". A Khmer pun on the term is made by changing the pronunciation slightly to "pul'thee'a", which means literally, "a duck ("thee'a") in the army".)

priviledges n. pree'up: [The rich] have more priviledges than the poor. -- [Neh mium] miun pree'up chiang neh kraw.; the right to do s. th. -- miun sutt or, miun suh'tee

prize adj. daaw pi'seh: a prize buffalo -- kraw'bye daaw pi'seh

prize n. award given to s.o. -- ruum vwun: win a prize -- to'tool ruum vwun; spoils -- ro'baugh: a prize captured from the enemy -- ro'baugh rup'o baan pi sa'tro

prize v. owi dum'lye teuh leuh

pro's and con's n. srawb howi nung praw'chang: We should discuss the pro's and con's [before making (a decision)]. -- Yeung koo'a tai kut om'pee kaa srawb howi nung praw'chang [muun peyr tveu kaa sum'rach].

pro adj. professional -- chuum'nee'inyh: Samol is a pro soccer player. -- Lok Sam'ol neh chuum'nee'inyh kang bal toat.

pro- prp. kaan cheung: pro-Chinese -- kaan [cheung] jchun (lit: holds [the feet] of the Chinese)

probability n. pee'up adje nung miun laung

probable adj. muk chia: It's probable that I will go. -- Kyom muk chia nung teuh.

probably adv. praw'heil chia;. muk chia: I probably will go. -- Kyom muk chia nung teuh.

probe v. stoong (NB: town in southern Kom'puung Thum province -- Sto'ng)

problem n. pun'ha (AP: pun'y'ha, pun(i)'ha, pun'ha): medical problem -- pun'ha kang sok'a'pheap; financial problem -- pun'ha kang loi; political problem -- pun'ha kang na'yo'bye; economic problem -- pun'ha kang set'a'kej; no problem -- ot miun pun'ha tay; ot aae tay; cause/make problems for s. o. -- bun doll owi miun pun'ha doll: Why do you make problems for me? -- Hyte'eye neh bun doll owi miun pun'ha doll kyom?; puzzle or math problem -- jchum'nowt

procedure n. tuum ro'ng kaa

process n. ro'bee'up: the process for making fish oil -- ro'bee'up sum'rap tveu praeng trei; viti; process of -- dum'narr ney: The [loan] process (i.e., process of borrowing) is difficult. -- Dum'narr ney [kaa ree'up jcham k'chey loi] pi'bah.; be in the process of doing s. th. -- kom'puung tai tveu teuh chia: We are in the process of [setting up] our office. -- Yeung kom'puung tai [ree'up jchum] kaar'ya'lye ro'bah yeung.

process v. tveu; I have to process this application. -- Kyom tro kaa tveu da'pee'a'sum ni.; to process [logs] into timber -- tveu [boo'rawh] pr'eye chia [k'daa]

processed adj. cha'nai praw'dut howi

procession n. ka'boo'un hye

proclaim v. praw'kas

prod v. jchak owi lote (lit: poke and make jump)

produce n. p'auwl dam num; paa'lut a p'auwl

produce v. paa'lut: This farm produces vegetables. -- Jcham'kar nu paa'lut bun'lye.; And that farm produces rice. -- Howi nung veal sr'eye nu paa'lut sro.; That factory produces gunpowder and fish oil. -- Ro'ng jcha nu paa'lut kro'up ruhm sae'eoo howi nung praeng trei.; bung kaut noeh: Our meeting produced a lot of good ideas. -- Kaa pra'choom ro'bah yeung bung kaut noeh kum'nut la'aw la'aw chia ch'raan.

producer n. paa'lut'a'kaw

product n. p'auwl; paa'lut'a'kaam; paa'lut'a'p'auwl

production n. paa'lut'a'kaam; paa'lut'a'p'auwl

productive adj. baan kaa: a productive meeting -- pra'choom baan kaa; These workers are very productive. -- Neh tveu kaa ni baan kaa nah.; sum'raan: This class is not productive. -- T'nak ni mun sum'raan tay.

productivity n. paa'lut'a'pheap

profession n. vi'chia chi'vut: teaching profession -- vi'chia chi'vut kang kaa bung rian; ngee'a chee'a: teaching profession -- ngee'a chee'a neh kruu; have a profession -- praw'kawb ro'bah

professional adj. praw'sawp; poo'k'eye; professional study -- vi'chea ko'song

professor n. sas'tra'cha; kruu

proficient (at) adj. sto'ot; poo'k'eye (kang); chuum'nee'inyh (kang): She is proficient at laughing and smiling! -- Nee'eng chuum'nee'inyh kang kaa sow'it howi nung nyo'nyim!; jchum'nut (kang)

profit n. chuum'nenyh; We did not [make] any profit. -- Yeung [rok] ot baan chuum'nenyh tay.; p'auwl: There is no profit in lying. -- Ot miun p'auwl a'veye tay k'nong kaa ni'yaye ko'hawk.; loosely, in sense of income -- kum'r'eye

profit (from) v. ot baan p'auwl om'pee; or, ot to'tool p'auwl om'pee: The Khmer people will not profit from [a bad peace settlement]. -- Pra'chee'chuun Khmei ot baan p'auwl om'pee [kaa yul'prome san'ti'pheap a'krah tay].; make a profit from, generally -- bung kaat p'auwl om'pee: make a profit from business -- to'tool kaa chum'nenyh om'pee chum'noo'inyh

profound adj. ch'ro (lit: deep)

profusely adv.   yang klang; yang ch'raan: thank s. o. profusely -- aw'kuun gkay yang ch'raan

program n.   TV or radio show -- kaam vi'ti: news program -- kaam vi'ti por'da'mee'an; governmental -- kaam vi'ti or, pyne'kaa (lit: plan): development program -- kaam vi'ti ree'k jchum'raan

progress n. kaa ree'k jchum'raan; kaa luut lawh; kaa cheu'an leu'an: the illusion of progress -- kaa sa'mye ney kaa cheu'an leu'an

progress v. progress or make progress -- ree'k jchum'raan; luut lawh; cheu'an leu'an; dum'narr teuh mok

progression n. dum'narr ree'k thum; arithmetic progression -- jchum'noo'an laek'keh'nuht

progressive adj. cheu'an leu'an

prohibit v. haam kwat

prohibition n. kaa haam kwat

project n. work to do -- kej kaa; or, kaa ng'yee'a; school project -- kaa'ngyeea pi sa'la; construction, etc. -- kaa'ngyeea; developmental project -- kaa'ngyeea ree'k jchum'raan

project v. extend chronologically (i. e., into future) -- praw'man; extend physically (stick out) -- pun'toook chia mun tha; or, tveu owi law'i jchenyh

promise n. verbal -- peea sun'nyaa (AP: su'nee'ya): He broke his promise. -- Gwat ot koo'ruup peea sun'nyaa ro'bah gwat.; verbal or written, meaning either promise or contract -- kaa sun'nyaa: ...with promises alone... -- chi'moi (or, jchum'poo'h) kaa sun'nyaa tai m'yang; Promises, promises! (the same old story) -- Ni'yaye d'dael d'dael!; an empty promise -- kaa ni'yaye mwot to'tay; or, kaa ni'yaye ot baan kaa

promise v. sun'nyaa (AP: su'nee'ya): I promise to telephone you tonight. -- Kyom sun'nyaa tha to'ra'sap neh yoop ni.; He promised to marry her. -- Gwat sun'nyaa ree'up kaa nung nee'eng.; make a promise -- ni'yaye (or bung kaut) sun'nyaa: The government makes many promises. -- Ratt'a'pi'bal bung kaut sun'nyaa chia ch'raan.; break one's promise -- bum plic pee'a sun'nyaa: or mun ko'rop peea sun'nyaa; keep one's promise -- ko'rop peea sun'nyaa; sum'bot: Tuk ho', mun'dael hawt, proh bot, kum owi cheu'a. -- (As) water flows but never tires, so men swear but should never be believed. (Khmer proverb)

promote v. give advancement to -- dum laung saak; laung bon; advocate an idea, cause, etc. -- p'daum

promotion n. kaa laung saak

prone adj. reclining -- dael sraw paab; prone to, inclined to, quick to, say -- ro' peu(ss) mwot; prone to do s. th. -- tuum no'ng; prone to exaggerate -- tuum no'ng bum pleuss; prone to an emotion -- jchaap; or, ro'has; prone to anger -- jchaap khung; or, ro'has khung (lit: quick to anger)

pronoun n. sah'pa'nee'um

pronounce v. banyh'jchenyh sum'leng: It is [difficult to] pronounce (anything) clearly [with your mouth full of hamburger]! -- Veea pi'bah nung banyh'jchenyh sum'leng owi baan ch'bah ['proo'h hamburger noeh k'nong mwot]!

pronunciation n. kaa banyh'jchenyh sum'leng

proof n. pwah'taang: demand proof that/of -- thee'um thee'a pwah'taang dael; or, sum'lut thee'a pwah taang dael: They demanded proof that the KR [had broken (the ceasefire)]. -- Pooh'gkay sum'lut thee'a pwah'taang dael Khmei Kra'hom [baan ruhm lope bum pee'an (kaa baan chope sung'kree'um)].; find proof that/of -- sveye rok pwah'taang; This is the proof. -- Ni chia pwah'taang.; accept proof that/of -- to'tool yul'prome dael

prop up v. dum kawl; t'kawl

propaganda n. kaa kos'na; kaa p's'eye

propagandize v. tveu kos'na

proper adj. sum'ruhm; trum tro; koo'a sum

property n. sum'baat; tro'up sum'baat; (tro'up = s. th. that belongs to s. o.); poke'ka'tro'up; real property (e.g., real estate) -- a'cha'la'na vuh'to; in sense of wealth in general -- tun'tee'en

prophecy n. tuum ni'yaye

proponent n. neh snaa'

propose v. snaa'

prosecution n. so'phea; so'phea cha'rut'bo'rah; ratt an'yah

prosper v.   jchum'raan; loot law'h

prosperity n.   s'kd'eye jchum'raan; kaa jchum'raan; s'kd'eye loot lawh

prosperous adj.   thk'om thk'aln; rung ru'ung; cheu'an leu'an

prostitute n.   sraae p'es'cheeh; sraac ko'ich

prostrate adj.   kraab; prostrate onesself -- kraab kloo'an

protagonist n.   too'a eyke (lit: leading role)

protect v.   ka'pee'a: They must protect that village. -- Gkay tro kaa ka'pee'a phum nu.; protect against -- ka'pee'a kum owi; or ka'pee'a om'pee: ... protect the people against [losing] their freedom -- ... ka'pee'a pra'chee'chuun om'pee [kaa bot bong] se'rei'pheap; protect s.th./s.o. against the heat, cold, the enemy, etc. -- ka'peea (same word as that meaning "preserve"); or, bang kaa; against sun or light only -- bang

protection n.   kej ka'pee'a; ka'pee'a (lit. to protect): Protection is [better than] cure. -- Ka'pee'a [praw'sar chiang] p'chia'baal.

pro tem adj.   s'day'tee

protest n.   kaa thaaw'va

protest v.   thaaw'va: protest against -- thaaw'va jchum'poo'h; We must protest against [the theft of the Cambodian forest] by the Thais. -- Yeung tro tai thaaw'va jchum'poo'h [kaa loo'ich prey cheu Cambodia] dow'ee sa saah See'um.

protestant n.   pro'tes'tang

protocol n.   pi'ti'kaa

protrude v.   lee'em; lee'em cheng

proud adj.   penyh jchet: I am proud of my son. -- Kyom penyh jchet nung gkon proh kyom.; miun mo'ta'nak om'pee (or, jchum'poo'h); be proud of onesself, cocky, arrogant -- kraw euut kraw o'wng: Don't be so proud. -- Kum kraw euut kraw o'wng peyk.; be [too] proud of s. th. -- baan jchet [peyk]

prove v.   bun hanyh pwah'taang; bun chee'eh owi keunyh... owi: Can you prove you are not lying [to me]? -- Tau(v) neh adje bun chee'eh owi keunyh tha neh ot ko'hawk [kyom tay]?

proverb n.   so'phea'sut

provide v.   pdull

provided that pp.   looo'k tra'tai

providing that conj.   looo'k tra'tai: We can go providing that they agree. -- Yeung adje teuh looo'k tra'tai pooh'gkay yul'prome.

province n.   kyte: the province of Po'sat -- kyte Po'sat; (NB: Under the Khmer Rouge, the principal jurisdictional subdivision of Cambodia was referred to not as a "kyte" but as a "dum'bon", generally translated as "zone".)

provincial adj.   kyte: provincial capital city -- ti pra'choom kyte; provincial chief -- a'pi'bal kyte

provision n.   provisions, food, etc. -- s'bee'ung; term of an agreement -- leh kan; written article or section of a document -- kaah: There were seven provisions [set out, written, set forth, stated, etc.] in the contract. -- Miun kaah prum'pul [dael miun ch'eye'ng] noeh k'nong kej sun'nyaa.

provisional adj.   tree'm: provisional member -- sa'ma'chik tree'm; bun dawa'a'sun: provisional government -- ratt'a'pi'bal bun dawa'a'sun; ana'kru'ah: provisional (tendered) ballot -- sun'luck ana'kru'ah

prowler n.   jchaao

proximity n.   pheap chit'chit

proxy n.   person acting as -- neh dum'nahng (lit: representative); by proxy -- dow'ee sa'tee praw'tee'an

pry v.   physically open -- gwa(ss): pry open a wooden box -- gwa(ss) praw'op cheu; "dig" for information -- soo'a jchik roos jchik kulh. (i.e. "dig for, root and branch"): He's always prying into my business. -- Gwat tyne tai soo'a jchik roos jchik kulh om'pee ru'ung kyom.

psychiatrist n.   kruu peyt ch'coo'it; kruu peyt vee'kaw'cha'rut

psychological adj.   jchet tuh'sa; ploe jchet

psychology n. jchet tuh'sa

public adj. saah'teea'rnah'; public health -- sok'a'pee'bah saah'teea'rnah'; a public [political position] -- [kohl chuum'ho] saah'teea'rnah'

public, the n. bun'da chuun; bun'da ree'eh

public opinion n. kum'nut sa'peea'na; sung'kuum a'tej

publicity n. kos'na (also means propaganda and advertising)

publicize v. tveu kos'na

pudding n. song k'sha

puddle n. tl'ock (AP: tluk): Mosquitoes come from puddles (lit: water in puddles.). -- Mooh kaut mok pi tuk tl'ock.

pull v. generally -- tee'enyh : We need the cable to pull the truck [out of the mud]. -- Tro kaa tee'eny laa trung [jchenyh pi phoo'(a)].; yo'ng: pull water from the well -- yo'ng tuk pi undo'ng; pull away from, out of -- praw'tee'enyh: He pulled the money out of her hands. -- Gwat praw'tee'enyh loi jchenyh pi dai nee'eng.; pull back and forth -- praw'tee'enyh teuh venyh teuh mok: Look at the kids pulling each other back and forth. -- Meuhl pi k'mayng praw'tee'enyh ka'neea teuh venyh teuh mok.; pull behind, drag -- oh: Oxen pull carts. -- Gko oh ro'teh.; pull away forcefully -- kun'chaw(k): He pulled [the pistol] away from the thief. -- Gwat kun'chaw(k) [kum pleung dai] pi jchaao.; pull s. th. back fr. s. st. else -- tee'enyh mok krow'ee; pull s. th. from or to the side -- tee'enyh teuh kang; pull down -- tee'enyh ch'uhss; pull out -- dawh hote; pull over (as, a car) -- baahk... teuh kang; Pull the car over to the side of the road. -- Baahk laan teuh kang t'nawl.; pull up, lift -- leuh; pull up, hoist -- bung hote; pull back, retreat -- dawh toi

pump n. sap dye

pump v. bo'me; saw'b; pump up a tire -- saw'b kong la'an

pumpkin n. la'peau

pun n. kaa leng pee'a

punch v. top; dall: (I) saw him punch [the driver]. -- Keunyh gwat dall [neh baahk laan].; punch each other -- dall ka'neea; (NB: fist = kun'dap dai); punch a hole in -- jchak praw'howng: punch holes in paper -- jchak praw'howng k'nong kra'dah

punctual adj. tee'eng to'at

punctuation n. a'na'yuut

punish v. dah(k) twun'a'kaam; dah(k) to'h; pdaw teea to'h; to'h: Don't punish me. -- Ot to'h howi kyom pong.; Please punish me. -- Dah(k) to'h kyom jcho(r).; to be punished -- miun to'h: He was punished for being late. -- Gwat miun to'h jcham'poo'h kaa mok yeut.

punishment n. to'h (written tohs); kaa dah(k) to'h; accept or receive punishment -- to'tool to'h

pupil n. gkon'sa

puppet n. a'yong: The Thai army is the puppet of China. -- Yo'thee'a See'um chia a'yong sruk jchun.

puppy n. gkon sh'kye (AP: shi'kye)

purchase v. tinh

pure adj. bori'sutt; sutt: pure gold -- mee'eh sutt

purely adv. sutt tai: This is purely an internal matter. -- Ni sutt tai pun'ha praw'cham k'nong sruk.

purge v. bun satt bong

purification n. vi'sutt'a'kaam

purple adj. pwa sw'eye; dark purple -- pwa priung tuum

purpose n. kohl kaa; kohl bum nong: What is the purpose of [having so many telephones here]? -- Tau(v) k'nong kohl bum nong a'veye dael [miun ti ni telephone ch'raan doj ch'neh]?; What is the purpose of this meeting? -- Tau(v) a'veye chia kohl bum nong ney kaa pra'choom ni?; function -- mok'ngyeea: What purpose does it serve? -- A ni miun mok'ngyeea a'veye?; for the purpose of -- sum'rap kohl bum'nong; on purpose -- dow'ee bum'nong; or, dow'ee jchet'ta'na

purse n. ka'bo'p sa'trei

pursuant adv. srawb teuh taam; a'noo'lawm; teuh taam; mok taam: Pursuant to our telephone conversation... -- Srawb teuh taam kaa ni'yaye to'ra'sap yeung...

pursue v. denyh; taam denyh; praw denyh

pus n. k'too

push v. with moderate force -- cha'raan: push people away from the door -- cha'raan ma'nooh jchenyh pi t'veea; shove -- runyh cha'raan; push with great effort -- runyh: Aah!... please... Help me push my car out of the mud. -- Ow, bong, ow; sum choo'ay runyh laan kyom jchenyh pi poo'a pong.; push aside -- cha'raan; push away -- paat; push with a finger, generally -- jch'uch: push a buttom -- jch'uch boo'tohn; push a numbered button as on a telephone -- jch'uch lek; push a car lock button -- jch'uch kun leuh; push a button to make electric contact -- jch'uch contac'; torture or kill by pushing s. o.'s head under water -- ch'ruum mu(ch); promote, advocate -- d'daum; chuum runyh: push [progressive] ideas -- chuum runyh kum'nut [cheu'an leu'an]

put v. generally -- dah(k): Please put the book on the table. -- Sum dah(k) s'po noeh leuh tohk.
Also:

put away -- ree'up toook dah(k)

put a curse on (s.o.) -- dah(k) bun'dah'saa (gkay)

put aside -- kro'ng tooo'k

put down, set down -- dah(k) jchoh: put down a cup of coffee -- dah(k) paeng coffee jchoh

put down, quell -- bung kraab: put down an uprising -- bung kraab pa'ta'kaam; or, bung kraab kaa baah bauw

put down roots -- jchak roos

put in -- bong; chr'aeyk; dah(k)

put in a box -- dah(k) noeh k'nong pra'op

put it back -- tooo'k owi venyh

put off -- tooo'k yoo; pa'aa

put on, apply -- lee'ab: put on perfume -- lee'ab tuk op

put on, wear -- peh: put on clothes -- peh kow-aow

put on, turn on -- jchak: put on some music -- jchak pleang

put on airs -- kaat rieng

put oneself out -- ka'nah nyne

put out a fire -- puhn lut; or, praw lut

put out the light -- butt pleung

put stamps on s. th. -- butt tymb(re)

stay put -- noeh owi nung

put together, assemble -- p'kuuum; p'chuu'up

put up with -- tro'ong

put s. th. under s. th. -- dah(k) krowm

puzzle n. ngoo'ung cha'ngawl: I am puzzled by what he said. -- Kyon ngoo'ung cha'ngawl nung peea dael gwat ni'yaye.

puzzle v. tveu owi cha'ngawl

python n. poo'ah t'laan

Q

quadrilateral adj. buon cheung

quadruped n. saat cheung buon

quake v. ruhm keuh; earthquake -- ruhm choo'ay byne'daiy

qualified adj. kroop leh ka'nak: qualified for that job -- kroop leh ka'nak sum'rap kej kaa nu; fully qualified -- penyh leh ka'nak; penyh muk

quality (of) n. ka'na'pheap (ney); koo sum'baat (ney); quality of character -- leh ka'nak: a wife with every quality -- pra'pun miun kroop leh ka'nak

quantity (of) n. jchum'noo'an (ney)

quarrel n. kaa chuum'loo'h; (AP: ch'loo'h)

quarrel, have a quarrel v. chuum'looa(s); chuum'looa(s) ka'neea; (AP: ch'loo'h): They have never quarreled before. -- Pooh'gkay mun'dael chum'looa(s) ka'neea pi muun tay.; to'ah(s) ka'neea; to'ah(s) te'ang; quarrel over s. th. -- dun daum; vee'vee'at;

quarter n. one-fourth (of) -- moi pieh buon (ney); (pieh = portion or part of): a quarter of the people -- moi pieh buon ney pra'chee'chuun; quarter of an hour -- dop'pram nee'a'tee; a quarter after [   ] -- mao [   ] prum'dop (NB: prum'dop = fifteen); quarter after eleven -- mao dop'moi prum'dop (lit: hour eleven fifteen); a quarter of [   ] -- the hour preceding [   ] plus "sye'sup 'prum" (forty-five): quarter to eleven -- mao dop sye'sup'prum (lit: hour ten forty-five); a fiscal or business quarter (three months) -- tr'eye mieh: in the first quarter... -- noeh k'nong tr'eye mieh ti moi...

quartz n. kwaat

queen n. s'dach sraae: Cambodia has a queen. -- Kampuchea miun s'dach sraae.; sarcastic, slang -- s'dach sa'trei: The queen of Po'sat -- S'dach sa'trei ney Po'sat; queen, the title -- ma'ha'sa'trei: Queen Ko'ma'saak -- Ma'ha'sa'trei Ko'ma'saak

question n. sum'noo'a: a political question -- sum'noo'a na'yo'bye

question v. soo'a; soo'a sum'noo'a

question mark n. pu'tcha'na se'na

question marker words n. tau(v) .... tay?: Is it hot? -- Tau(v) k'dau tay?; tay? (alone): Do you have any? -- Miun tay?; eh?: Did you hear it? -- Luh' loo, eh?; aae?; day? (AP for tay): Do you have change? -- Miun loi op, day?

quick adj. yang ro'has; leu'an leu'an

Quick! interj. Yang ro'has!; Chhop chhop!; Leu'an leu'an!

quickly adv. yang leu'an; yang ro'has; chhop chhop; praw'nyab

quiet adj. sngy'at; not moving, still -- sngee'im

quietly adv. sng'ot sng'ot (AP: sng'ot sgn'ut): speak or talk quietly -- ni'yaye sng'ot sng'ut

quinine n. ki'neen

quit v. re things, stop working, go out of commission -- ro'luuht; stop doing s.th. generally -- leh bong: quit smoking -- leh bong kaa chook ba'r'eye; He quit his job to write books. -- Gwat leh bong kaa'ngyeea howi nung kian s'po.; give up, relinguish -- lee'a lang; chope: quit a job -- lee'a lang tveu kaa chope tveu kaa: He quit his government job yesterday. -- Gwat chope tveu kaa ratt musl'munyh.

quite adv. ch'raan (AP: cha'ran, cha'rauwn); quite expensive -- tlai ch'raan; men'tan: quite easy -- sroul men'tan; yang krah krye'l: I gave him quite a few things. -- Kyom owi ro'bah teuh gwat yang krah krye'l.

quiz n. kaa praw'long tic to'ich; quiz subject -- praw'yok

R

rabbit n. tun'sye

race n. of people -- saah; um'bo'; pooh; human race -- ma'nooh saah chee'it; foot-race -- kaa praw'nung; horse-race -- praw'nung seh

race (with or against) v. praw'nung (chi'moi); praw hoo'it (chi'moi); race an engine -- ro' ma'seen

racial adj. kang saah; lei saah

racist n. praw'kaan [pwa sum'baugh] (lit: prejudiced about [color]); praw'kaan [chee'it saah] (lit: prejudiced about [nationality])

racket n. illegal enterprise -- ro'bah tou'cha'rut

racketeer n. jchao thum; (formal term: neh praw'kaab ro'bah tou'cha'rut (lit: one whose occupation is committing crimes))

racy adj. mun som ruhm; racy story -- ru'ung mun som ruhm

radar n. raae'da

radiator n. tuung tuk; ra'de'a'tuh

radical adj. mool vee'vwut ni'yuum

radical n. neh mool vee'vwut ni'yuum

radio n. receiving set (table radio, portable radio, car radio, etc.) -- vi'choo (APs: wi'choo, vit'yoo); kreung rad'yo; two-way radio -- mo'ta'ro'la; broadcasting medium -- vi'choo (NB: television = too'ra'too'h)

radio band n. bong; pawh

radio station n. office/transmitter -- s'ta'nee vi'choo; frequency on dial -- pawh; pawh vi'choo

radius n. as in math, geometry, etc. -- kaam; radius of a circle -- kaam ruum'vuung; within a 50 kilometer radius of Po'sat -- jchum'ngai noeh k'nong ha'sup kilo pi Po'sat

raft n. k'bo'ne

rafter n. bong kong; p'to'ng

raffle n. ch'nowt vuh'to

rag n. kun'tope; in rags -- raw'yee raw'y'eye

rage n. kun hum daw klang; in a rage -- noeh kun hum daw klang

rage v. [battles] rage [fiercely] -- [sa'mau'ra'phum] chheh chool [yang klang]; [the storm] raged -- [k'shaal p'choo] bahwk bauwk

ragged adj. raw hyte raw yee raw y'eye

raid n. police raid -- kaa ch'maw' jchole looo'k; air raid -- kaa praw ha taam akas

raid v. ch'maw' jchole looo'k

rail n. hand rail -- bung kun dye; railroad track rail -- ploe dyke; go by rail -- teuh dow'ee ro'teh pleung; (PS: teuh dowee ro' pleung)

railroad n. ro'teh pleung (PS: ro'pleung); ploe ro'teh pleung; term used mainly in writing -- ploe dyke

railroad station n. s'tanee ro'teh pleung; 'raah ro'teh pleung

rain n. plee'eng; sa'ta'fa; raining cats and dogs -- plee'eng klang; plee'eng doj gkay hyke meyk

rain v. plee'eng: It will rain tomorrow. -- S'eye'd nung plee'eng.; miun plee'eng: It rained yesterday. -- Musl'munyh miun plee'eng.

rainbow n. un'ta'noo

raincoat n. aow plee'eng

raindrop n. kro'up plee'eng; dum'nop plee'eng

rainfall n. ro'bab tuk plee'eng

rain shower n. plee'eng srec srec

rainy adj. plee'eng: rainy season -- ro'doe t'leh plee'eng

raise n. kaa laung: She got a raise yesterday. -- Nee'eng baan laung praw'kye musl'munyh.

raise v. grow -- jchenyh jchum: raise chickens -- jchenyh jchum muon; increase generally -- dum'laung: raise a price -- dum'laung tlai; dum'laung dum'lye; raise the ante -- dah(k) loi tyme: He raised the ante in [the cockfight]. -- Gwat dah(k) loi tyme k'nong [kaa p'noo'ul la'bye'ng praw'chuum'looh muon].; lift -- leuk: The crocodile could hardly raise his tail. -- Kaw'per leuk cun'toi mun steu tay.; leuk laung: He raised his glass to his friends. -- Gwat leuk kaae'oo laung sum'rap mit'paya.; also:

raise a question -- jchowt soo'a

raise a [rebellion] -- bung kaut [pa'ti'vwut]

raise one's voice -- dum'laung sum'leng: Hey, don't raise your voice. -- Eh! Kum dum'laung sum'leng.

raise corn -- dam po't

raise cattle -- jchum jchenyh gko

raisin n. tum paae'ang bai'choo kree'um

rake n. roo' nwa'h

rake v. kaab: rake leaves -- kaab sluk cheu

rally n. kaa pra'mole pdom: There were five rallies in Kom'puung Cham. -- Mium kaa pra'mole pdom pram noeh k'nong Kom'puung Cham.

rally v. proo'it ka'neea; ru'um ka'neea

ram n. male sheep -- chee'm ch'mole; battering ram -- praw'dop bah(k) tuum t'veea (lit: hit, break)

rampart n. pra'saat

ramble v. in speaking -- ni'yaye ot jchong ot daum; or, ni'yaye pi ni baan tic, pi nu baan tic; ramble around -- jchaw jch'rub

rambutan n. sau'mau

ramification n. hyte p'auwl: They didn't [care about] the ramifications [of] their policy. -- Pooh'gkay ot [yok jchet tooo'k dah(k) om'pee hyte p'auwl [ney] na'yo'bye ro'bah gkay.; or: ... the ramifications of their policy ... -- hyte p'auwl [dael kaut laung pi] na'yo'bye gkay...

ramp n. incline on land -- ch'raw ch'm'reel; onto a boat -- spee'un ch'um'law

rancorous adj. kum koo'un; chaw pec'a

random adj. pree'oo: at random -- pree'oo prec'oo; random selection -- jchreu'reu' dow'ee pree'oo

range n. jchum'ngai: of a gun -- jchum'ngai dael adje baan banyh (or, banyh baan): What is the range of this gun? -- Kum pleung ni jchum'ngai pu'man dael adje banyh baan?; beyond the range of... -- hoo'a pi kaa dael banyh baan...; range of vision -- jchum'ngai dael teuh doll meuhl doll; mountain range -- choo'a phnom; electric range -- jchong kran

range v. vary -- miun dum'lye pi... teuh: The prices ranged from 500 to 1000 riels. -- Tlai miun dum'lye pi pram roi riel teuh m'pwan riel. (NB: "m'pwan" is AP compression of "moi pwan")

ranger n. military -- neh la'bat; forest -- ruk kaa reht

rank n. military -- bun'saak; ta'non'ta'rah'sat; saak: What is your rank? -- Lok peh saak pu'man? (lit: What rank do you wear?); exalted rank -- aae'sraa'yoo; rank in a line or series -- t'nak

ransom n. loi looh; dum'lye looh; pay ransom -- looh

rape n. kaa ruhm lope

rape v. ruhm lope; jchaap ruhm lope

rapid adj. nyo'wb; ro'has; leu'an

rapidly adv. yang nyo'wb; yang ro'has; leu'an leu'an

rapids n. cunlye'ng tuk ho' yang klang howi nung dael miun t'mawl pong; (waterfall = tuk ch'reuhl)

rapist n. neh ruhm lope

rare adj. scarce -- kum raw; little cooked -- mun seu ch'un; (well-done = ch'un la'aw; medium = ch'un la'mawm la'mawm)

rarely adv. kum'raw

rash adj. ill-advised -- mun baan kut owi sroul boul: a rash idea -- kum'nut mun baan kut owi sroul boul; (rarely used) moi vheng

rash n. measles -- kun ch'reuhl; skin irritation, itchy ro'mwah; skin irritation, bumpy, red -- kun too'ul: have a rash -- miun kun too'ul; abundance -- ch'raan: a rash of false reports -- ru'ung puuht ch'raan

rat n. kun'dull prye'ng ; (mouse -- kun'dull or kun'dull praw'meh)

rate n. a'tra: rate of interest -- a'tra ney kaa praa(k); rate of speed -- l'boo'un a'tra; cut rate price -- dum'lye ot tlai; dum'lye tauk

rate v. evaluate or assign ranking to -- owi layke

rather adv. jchong: I'd rather not study. -- Kyom mun jchong rian tay.; jchong... chiang: I'd rather have Coke than orange juice. -- Kyom jchong baan Coke chiang tuk krau'itch.; sok jchet: I'd rather stop studying. -- Kyom sok jchet chope rian.; rather [   ].... than [   ]: sok jchet... soo chia chiang: Rather [expend some lives] than to lose the whole country. -- Sok jchet [jchum'nye chi'vut klaah] soo chia chiang bat bong tuk'daiy te'ang mool.; better [   ]... rather than [   ]: soo... praw'sowee chiang or, soo.... praw'chia chiang: It is better to give them [what they want] rather than to fight about this. -- Soo pdull owi pooh veea [noch a'veye dael veea jchong baan] praw'sow'ee chiang (or praw'chia chiang) vye ka'neea om'pee ru'ung ni.

rather adv. baan tic; rather hot -- k'dau baan tic; rather expensive -- tlai baan tic

ratify v. owi kaa ah'ni'yaht; yul'prome

ratification n. kaa ah'ni'yaht

rating n. kum rut ka'na'pheap

ratio n. ah'nooh'baat

ration n. daily allotment -- kaa jchaiyk; kaa jchaiyk ro'bab; jchum'nyke [praw'chum] t'ngai (lit: portion [scheduled for] a day); a'ha' vi'pheap

ration v. jchaiyk; jchaiyk taam chum noo'an kum'rut (NB: kum'rut means "limit", in sense of "amount available")

rational adj. sum hyte

rationale n. moo'la'hyte

rationalize n. tveu owi keunyh tha sum (or tha sum'ruum)

rattan n. p'dauw

rattle v. make jumpy, slightly nervous -- : A few [demonstrations] would rattle the journalists. -- [Pa'ti'kaam bung hanyh] klaah klaah nung tveu owi neh ka'ssett pay klait(ch).; make very nervous -- tveu owi vull k'bong; make a rattling sound -- ruhm'dum: Something [in the back of the car] is rattling. -- Ro'bah dael [noeh k'nong koot laan] ruhm'dum ka'neea.; make a noise -- leuh so; shake s. th. or be shaken -- ruhm'keuh

ravage v. bum plek bum planyh; ree'uk ta'bot

ravine n. ch'roo'ah

raw adj. chaa(v): raw milk -- tuk dawh gko chaa(v); raw material -- vuh'to ti daum

ray n. puun'leuh; ray of light -- rch'smye

razor n. kum'but gkhao; razor blade -- kum'but gkhao; lahm

reach v.

arrive at -- doll: reach the end of [the book] -- doll jchong bun chope ney [s'po]; reach a place to which one or
    s.th. is going -- teuh doll: We wanted at least to reach Po'sat. -- Yeung jchong baa tic na kaw teuh doll
    Po'sat.; reach a place to which one or s.th. is coming -- mok doll: We hope he will reach here [before
    dark]. -- Yeung sung'khum tha gwat mok doll ti ni muun t'ngai lic.; contact face to face, meet, lit: find
    -- ro'k keunyh; contact by telephone, by radio, etc. -- tek tong: We can't reach [the headquarters] by
    phone. -- Yeung mun adje tek tong [ti bun'chee'a kaa] taam to'ra'sap.;

extend one's grasp -- looo'k; reach for and get -- looo'k yok; or, looo'k yok baan; reach for and not get -- looo'k yok num baan; or, looo'k yok mun doll: She couldn't reach it. -- Nee'eng looo'k mun doll tay.; reach for -- (not including the concept of actually grasping or getting the item reached for) -- looo'k doll teuh + object: He reached for a glass but couldn't get it. -- Gwat looo'k doll teuh kaae'oo pun'ta'aae mun adje yok veea.

reach in -- looo'k jchole;

reach out of s. th. -- looo'k jchenyh krau: He reached out of the car. -- Gwar looo'k jchenyh krau laan.

be out of reach -- hoo'a mee'at

react v. praw'ti'kaam; miun praw'ti'kaam; thawb: The government must react to this development. -- Ratt'a'pi'bal tro tai tawb (or, tro tai miun pra'ti'kaam) jchum'poo'h hyte'kaa ni (or pra'ti'kaa ni).; (NB: pra'ti'kaam = react; pra'ti'kaa = development, situation)

reaction n. pra'ti'kaam

reactionary adj. pra'ti'keh'ree'ya

reactionary n. neh praw'ti'keh'ree'ya; reactionaries, reactionary people -- pooh praw'ti'keh'ree'ya

read v. an: Can you read Khmer? -- Neh adje an Khmei baan tay?; meuhl: This (paper) is in Khmer; can you read it for me? -- Kra'dah ni khmei; tau(v) neh adje meuhl veea owi kyom?; say, convey -- meuhl: How does that line read? -- Bun'tawt nu meuhl taa mutch?; (literate -- jcheh ak'saw; illiterate -- mun jcheh ak'saw); read the riot act to -- leng to'a k'dau

readable adj. adje meuhl dach; unreadable -- mun adje meuhl dach

reader n. neh an; neh meuhl

ready adj. available for s. th. -- roo'it howi or, roo'it rawl: Are you ready (or not)? -- Neh roo'it howi roo ot?; Are you ready to go? -- Tau(v) neh roo'it rawl nung teuh?; finished -- howi: Are [the pictures] ready yet? -- Tau(v) [roob tawt] howi roo noeh?; (food) ready to eat -- chuum'un roo'it... howi: The food has been ready for an hour. -- Ma'hope chuum'un roo'it moi mao teuh howi.; (person) ready (to) -- roo'it rawl (nung): I'm ready to eat. -- Kyom roo'it rawl nung nyam.; ready as in a game -- roo'it howi: Ready, (set), go! -- Roo'it howi... Teuh!; close to, on the verge of -- chit: ready to collapse -- chit ro'lum; get ready to do d. th., re a person -- ree'up kloo'an; get ready to do s. th., re things -- ree'up jchum: get ready to move (change lodgings) -- ree'up jchum pdo ptay'a; ready-made, generally -- roo'it s'rap; s'rap; ready-made clothes -- kow-aow kat s'rap

real adj. actual -- men'tan: real life -- chi'vut men'tan; genuine -- sutt: real gold -- mee'eh sutt; real cotton -- kum'bah sutt; in sense of actual, true, not ficticious or facetious -- putt: a real (an actual, true) problem (not a facetious one) -- pun'ha putt putt; in sense (not only of actual but also) of serious or important -- sum'kahn: a real (i.e., important, not minor) problem -- pun'ha sum'kahn

real estate n. immovable objects in general -- a'cha'la'na vuh'to; house and land -- ptay'a sum'bye'ng

realism n. praw'kawt ni'yuum

realist n. neh praw'kawt ni'yuum

reality n. kaa piht: taam kaa piht; chia ro'bah piht; in reality -- taam piht; make [their dream] a reality -- tveu owi [kaa yul sob ro'bah pooh'gkay] chia ro'bah piht; hyte kaa maan'tan: [ignore] reality -- [tveu peuh mun dung] noeh hyte kaa maan'tan

realization n. sa'mi'tee

realize v. know -- dung kloo'an: I didn't realize that you were coming tomorrow. -- Kyon ot dung kloo'an tha neh nung mok s'eye'd.; remember -- yul dung: She [just] realized that she had to go. -- Nee'eng [srab tai] yul dung tha nee'eng tro teuh.; earn -- ro'k... baan: realize a profit -- ro'k chuum'nenyh baan; or, ro'k kumr'eye baan

really adv. maan; maan'tan: really delicious -- maan'tan chng'anyh; really expensive -- tlai maan'tan; praw'kat chia: I really don't want to go. -- Kyom praw'kat chia ot jchong teuh tay.; Is he really coming? -- Tau(v) gwat praw'kat chia mok tay?; not really -- mun maan... piht praw'kat: I'm not really a journalist. -- Kyom mun maan chia neh ka'ssett piht praw'kat tay.; very -- nah (AP: na'): really cold -- traw'cheh(k) nah; not really -- mun...

nah naa tay: This is not really good. -- Veea mun la'aw mun nah naa tay.; (NB: "really" can be expressed by either "nah" or "nah naa", but not by "naa" alone)

Really? (and) Really! adv. most common for "Really?" are: Maan'eh??; Maan tay?? Maan howi?? (AP: Maan hi!) and Maan roo aae?; Also used are Piht aae?; Piht aae mun roo?; and, May na?; most common for Really! are APs Maan'eh! and Maa'ne!: examples: Samol: This is [really] great soup. -- Sa'law ni chng'anyh [nah]. Chantha: Really? -- Maan'eh? Samol: Really! -- Maan'howi!

realm n. n'ko: powerful realm or kingdom (phrase used, for example, to refer to Cambodia in the Ankorian period) -- ma'ha n'ko (lit: Great Realm); ana'chuh(k) (used in Sihanouk period, as in "Ree'ch ana'chuh(k) Kampuchea")

reap v. ch'rote kaat

rear n. p'nyke kang krow'ee: rear of the truck -- p'nyke kang krow'ee ney laan trung'; The soldiers moved from the frontlines to the rear. -- Tee'hee'an teuh pi choo'a muk teuh p'nyke kang krow'ee.; kang krow'ee: They live in the rear. -- Gkay noeh kang krow'ee.

rear v. bring up [a child] -- jchenyh jchum op'ruhm [gkon]; raise any sort of animal -- jchenyh

reason n. hyte p'auwl: Give me one good reason why... -- Prap kyom noeh hyte p'auwl moi hyte eye baan....; **chia mool'hyte daum**: What was the reason for [the argument]? -- A'veye dael chia mool'hyte daum sum'rap [kaa jchaw jchehk ka'neea]?; mool'hyte: the reason that... -- mool'hyte dael..., or hyte p'auwl dael: the reason she left... -- mool'hyte dael nee'eng jchaak jchenyh ...; basic reason -- daum hyte p'auwl; by reason of -- dow'ee hyte tai; beyond reason -- hoo'a hyte; for this (or that) reason -- a'sr'eye hyte ni (or nung); howi baan chia: That's the reason I stayed. -- Nung howi baan chia kyom noeh.

reasonable adj. dow'ee sum hyte p'auwl: reasonable [conclusion] -- [kaa bun jchawb] dow'ee sum hyte p'auwl; sum hyte sum p'auwl: a reasonable [judge] -- [jchao krum kaat k'dye] sum hyte sum p'auwl; re prices -- koo'a sum; or, koo'a sum'ruum (lit: appears fair): reasonable price -- dum'lye tauk sum'ruum; or dum'lye tauk koo'a sum; or, tlai tauk la'mawm (lit: cost cheap enough)

reasonably adv. pieh ch'raan: [We are reasonably sure] we will go to Po'sat [in December]. -- [Pieh ch'raan] yeung nung teuh Po'sat [noeh kye T'noo].; [The election] was reasonably fair. -- [Bawh ch'nowt] pieh ch'raan keuh chia sum hyte sum p'auwl.

reassure v. tveu owi miun kaa tooo'k jchet; tee'a nee'a chia ta'm'eye

rebel n. krum oo'tee'im; neh baah bauw

rebel (against) v. baah bauw (praw'chang)

rebellion n. kaa baah bauw; pa'ti'vwut

rebellious adj. dael kom'puung baah'bauw; mun s'dap bung kwob: a rebellious child -- gkon mun s'dap bung kwob (lit: child who doesn't listen)

rebuke v. bun tee'up bun tauk (lit: make s.o. look cheap)

rebuttal n. kaa jchum'la'wee (AP: kaa jcha'lowee); towp; kaa jcha'lowee pah'deh'site

recall v. remember -- nuhk keunyh; jcham: recall some advice -- jcham bun dum; nuk keunyh laung venyh: recall an event -- nuk keunyh laung venyh noeh pra'ti'kaa; order back -- how mok venyh: recall [an ambassador] -- haow muk venyh [neh kaa toot]

recapture v. jchaap baan venyh; baan mok venyh

recede v. sraw(k)

receipt n. bung kun dai: Please give me the receipt. -- Sum owi bung kun dai mok kyom.; Where's the receipt? -- A' na' bung kun dai?; bung: I need a receipt for the tax payment (lit: a tax receipt). -- Kyom tro kaa bung tac'.

receive v. to'tool (AP: to'too'al): receive a gift -- to'tool um'now'ee; to'tool ru'un wan; receive a guest -- to'tool p'nee'oo; receive a degree -- to'tool baan; or, baan to'tool; receive injuries (lit: become injured) -- tro ro'booh; receive TV channel, radio station or other transmission -- jchaab pawh

receiver, radio n. vi'choo to'tool sum leng

recent adj. t'maee (lit: new)

recently adv. (k'nong) peyr t'maee t'maee ni

reception n. social event -- kaa choop lec'eng; hold a reception -- pee'tee to'tool; of a transmission -- kaa jchaap vi'choo

receptionist n. neh to'tool p'nee'oo

recess n. during school day -- peyr sum'raak; school, legislative, etc., vacation -- va'konh; t'ngai chope

recession n. economic downturn -- kaa mun jchum'raan (teuh muk): The economy was in a recession. -- Set'a'kej keuh noeh k'nong kaa mun jchum'raan (or mun jchum'raan teuh muk).; Last year there was a recession in Battambong. -- Chh'nam teuh miun kaa mun jchum'raan noeh k'nong kyte Battambong.

recipe n. ro'bee'up; kaa boo'un: Do you have a good recipe for num bun chawk? -- Tau(v) neh miun ro'bee'up la'aw sum'rap tveu num bun chawk? (NB: num bun chawk is a popular Khmer noodle curry.)

recite v. sote: recite scripture -- sote toa; (NB: because in normal use "sote toa" refers to the mantric chantings of temple monks, chanting non-intelligible to perhaps 90% of the congregation, the term is also used quasi-humourously to refer to someone who babbles on saying little of substance, as in, "Aaiiee, sote toa nah!!" -- "Aaiiee, he's going on and on!!")

reciprocal adj. teuh venyh teuh mok; reciprocal agreement -- kaa yul'prome teuh venyh teuh mok; ka'neea: reciprocal labor arrangement -- kaa praw'va(ss) ka'neea (used by Cambodian farmers for joint cultivation of tracts belonging to several or many owners)

reciprocate v. tveu thawb venyh

reciprocity n. pheap miun teuh miun mok

reckless adj. mun praw'yat praw'y'eye

reclaim v. reclaim [land] -- ree'un [daiy]; reclaim [salt from water] -- tee'nyh yok [am'bul om'pee tuk]; reclaim property -- thee'um thee'a yok mok venyh: Once peasants sell their land, they [can rarely] reclaim it. -- Peyr dael neh sr'eye looh dai gkay nu, pooh'gkay [kum'raw adje] thee'um thee'a yok mok venyh.

reclamation n. kaa ree'un

recognition n. kaa to'tool scwal: give recognition to -- owi kaa to'tool scwal noeh

recognize v. to'tool scwal: Do you recognize that man? -- Tau(v) neh to'tool scwal ma'nooh proh nung tay?

reconnaissance n. kaa yok kaa: reconnaissance platoon -- kawng yok kaa sum'ngut

reconvene v. jchole venyh; tra'laawp venyh

recoil n. kaa teh toi; of a gun -- kaa teh toi kum pleung (or, ney kum pleung)

recollect v. nuk keunyh; jcham

recollection n. kaa jcham

recommend v. owi s'kd'eye yul'prome

recommendation n. kaa owi s'kd'eye yul'prome

reconcile v. bring [opponents] together -- p'sahs p'sah (lit: healing, joining) [neh praw'chang]; reconcile conflicting facts, opinions, bank statement, etc. -- tveu owi keunyh tha sec ka'neea venyh

reconciliation n. kaa tveu owi keunyh tha sec ka'neea venyh; kaa sum'rup sum roo'ul

recondition v. fix, restore -- kye'kun... venyh; chul chun; recondition "as good as new" -- kye'kun owi baan la'aw doj t'maee venyh

record n. written record -- bun'chee'; kum'not; sum'num ru'ung: government records -- sum'num ru'ung ratt'a'pi'bal; in sense of record providing proof -- pwah'taang: No record of it existed. --- Ot miun pwah'taang veea.; historical record -- eyke'a'saa; bun'na saa; phonograph record -- taah(s); record with songs -- taah(s) jchum ree'eng

record v. a sound -- tawt: SPK recorded Hun Sen's speech. -- SPK tawt sum'leng Hun Sen ni'yaye (or kaa ni'yaye).; record a song -- tawt jchum ree'eng; s. th. in writing -- kawht; kawht tra; jchoh: record a birth -- jchoh bun'chee chee'it

recount v. ree'up rawb m'dong tee'it

recover v. from sickness -- chia pi chuum'ngeu; s. th. lost or stolen -- baan... mok venyh: I recovered my money by playing (lit: winning at) cards. -- Kyom baan loi kyom mok venyh dow'ee ch'neh bee'a.

rectangular adj. buon ch'ruung tro venyh

recur v. miun laung venyh

recurrance n. kaa miun laung venyh

recurrent adj. dael tra'laawp mok venyh; dael miun laung chia ru'ee ru'ee

red adj. kra'hom ; dark red -- kra'hom kra'mau; kra'hom cho'um; a person who is "red" politically -- neh na'yo'bye kra'hom; in the red -- kaat; a business in the red -- chuum'noo'inyh kaat; or, jchum'nye leuk jchum'nole (lit: expenses above income)

Red Cross n. Ka'ka'baat Kra'hom

red-handed adj. kom'puung praw'pret (or tveu) butt la'meuh; (lit: committing (kom'puung praw'pret; or, kom'puung tveu) a crime (butt la'meuh))

red-hot adj. rung'euh pleung

red-neck n. country person -- ma'nooh cheu'na'bot; neh sr'eye; (NB: the perjorative implicit in the English term "red-neck" is not per se conveyed by either "ma'nooh cheu'na'bot" or "neh sr'eye". Whether, for example, "Gway doj neh sr'eye." -- He looks like a farmer. -- was intended as an unfavorable judgemental comment or simply as a factual observation would depend on context and the speaker's tone of voice.)

red pepper n. generally -- ma'tteh(s): large red pepper -- ma'ttch(s) plauwk; small red pepper -- ma'tteh(s) k'mung (lit., because of its fieryness, "enemy" pepper)

red tape n. ch'bop kum pec kum pok

redeem v. get back property -- loo'ah; restore "face" -- sang kum'hawh venyh (lit: rebuild after an error)

reduce v. baan toi; baan jchoh: reduce a price -- baan jchoh t'lai; reduce a budget -- baan toi ta'vi'kaa; reduce, change the size or strength of s. th., make s. th. become s. th. -- tveu owi... teuh chia... : reduce a glass to powder -- tveu owi kaae'ooo teuh chia ma'sauw

reduction n. kaa baan toi; kaa baan jchoh

redundant adj. p'too'un

reference n. tee sum kwaal; neh scwaal; in reference to -- yang teuh taam

referendum n. praw'chee'a ma'tay

refine v. ru'ngu'ah; jchum'ranyh

reflect v. reflect light -- ch'yeh puun'lueh tra'laawp mok venyh; indicate -- bung hanyh owi keunyh; or, ch'lawh banyh' jchang: [Good grades] reflect hard study. -- [Pun'too la'aw] ch'lawh banyh jchang owi keunyh rian ch'rown.; have an affect on the image of s. o. -- ch'yeh noeh pheap... mok leuh.... : The State Department's [position] reflected badly on the Secretary. -- [Kohl chuum'ho] Krasuu'ung Kaa Bor'tay ch'yeh noeh pheap a'krah mok leuh Mun'trei.; think about -- chung nung kut

reflection n. kaa chia tra'laawp mok venyh

reflected adj. chaang

reflex n. physical -- p'nyeh; kaa tveu teuh dowee mun dung kloo'an; mental -- [   ] plee'im plee'im: a reflex answer -- jchum'la'wee plee'im plee'im

reform n. kaa op'ruhm

reform v. op'ruhm; ka'aae

refrain n. bot bun'to

refrain v. tooo'b: Please refrain from smoking. -- Sum tooo'b om'pee kaa choo'k.

refresh v. one's memory -- ruhm luk; one's self -- tveu owi traw'chch(k)

refreshing adj. tveu owi ruhm howi

refreshed adj. ruhm howi

refreshment n. p'es'cheeh (lit: drinks)

refrigerator n. too' t'kaw (lit: ice cabinet)

refuge n. chuum'rok; take refuge -- pieh kloo'an

refugee n. chuun pieh kloo'an; neh pieh kloo'an; political refugee -- chuun pieh kloo'an na'yo'bye

refund n. kaa song venyh; kaa owl praa(k) mok venyh

refund v. song venyh; owi praa(k) mok venyh

refusal n. kaa pa'di'seyt

refuse n. sum'rahm

refuse v. pa'di'seyt; praw'kyte; mun prome

refute v. counter -- jchum'la'wee pa'di'seyt; jchum'la'wee praw'kyte: It is difficult to refute that argument. -- Veea lum'bah nah k'nong kaa jchum'la'wee pa'di'seyt ma'tay (or kum'nut) nu.

regain v. regain possession of s.th. -- baan mok venyh; regain [consciousness] -- [dung kloo'an] venyh

regalia n. kreung eh'sara'jyoo

regard n. s'kd'eye nuhk; kaa yok jchet tooo'k dah(k); in regard to -- jchum'poo'h

regard as v. meuhl... doj chia: The people regard him as a great man. -- Pra'chee'chuun meuhl gwat doj chia ma'nooh awh' jcha.; tooo'k... chia: I regard him as a friend. -- Kyom tooo'k gwat chia mit pay'a.

regarding prp. jchum'poo'h

regardless adv. dow'ee k'miun kut doll: Regardless of the danger, we will go. -- Dow'ee k'miun kut doll kroo'ti'nak, yeung nung teuh.

regime n. generally -- leh'tee: socialist regime -- leh'tee sung'kuum ni'yuum; republican regime -- leh'tee sa'tia'ru'nak'ratt; communist regime -- leh'tee co'muu'neest; in sense of rule -- ro'bab: Under the KR regime... -- Noeh krauwm ro'bawb Khmei Kra'hom... ; sung'kuum; (usually translated as "society" or "community" (in national sense) but under Lon Nol took on connotation of "regime," as in "sung'kuum Lon Nol" -- "the Lon Nol regime"); formal term usually used in writing -- lok'bit

regiment n. kawng va'ret sena thum

regiment v. organize as a military unit -- ree'up chia kawng; tightly organize, non-military context -- dah(k) vi'naae daw tung tyne

region n. dum'bun; phum pee'ehk: The eastern region of Cambodia... -- Dum'bun kang kaut ney Kampuchea...; pyke: the Battambong region -- pyke kang Battambong

register n. any written register, generally -- bun'chee; register of names -- bun'chee chamoo'h; cash register -- ma'seen kut loi

register v. jchoh: register a personal name -- jchoh chamoo'h; register a business name -- jchoh yee haow; jchoh bun'chee (lit: register document): register a birth -- jchoh bun'chee kum'naut; register to vote -- jchoh bun'chee bawh ch'naut; register a (new) business -- jchoh bun'chee sum ch'bop tveu; register [a letter] -- recomman'day [ ]; register [a complaint] -- dah(k) [pee'a bun'dung]

registration n. kaa jchoh ch'moo'h; car registration -- sum'buht laan

regret n. kaa sawk s'dye; s'kd'eye sawk s'dye: They have no regrets. -- Gkat k'miun kaa sawk s'dye.

regret v. s'dye: I regret that I came late. -- Kyom s'dye dael kyom mok yeut.; sawk s'dye: I regret that it is not clear. -- Kyom sawk s'dye dael veea mun ch'bah.; come to regret later not having done s. th. -- s'dye krow'ee: I regret it very much that I did not help my older brother. -- Kyom s'dye krow'ee yang klang dael kyom mun baan choo'ay bong proh ro'bah kyom.

regular adj. chia ru'ee ru'ee; regular [intervals] -- tee'ung twot peyr va'lee'a; regular [customer] -- [p'nee'oo dael mok] chia ru'ee ru'ee

regularly adv. chia ru'ee ru'ee; tee'ung twot peyr; ny'uuk ny'o'up

regulation n. ch'bop tuum lo'op; bot bun'chee'a; rules and regulations -- praw'kaa

reign n. period of rule -- ree'ech chia kaal: Sihanouk's reign (or Sihanouk's time) -- ree'ech chia kaal Sihanouk

reign v. sow'ee ree'ch (AP: re'ach, ree'ech)

reimburse v. song; song venyh

reimbursement n. sum'nong

reincarnation n. kaa jchaap pa'deh'san'tee chia t'maee; (NB: "pah'deh'san'tee" means existence); a reincarnation of... -- ma'nooh boh ngeea vo'ta...

reinforce v. a wall -- tveu owi mo'ohm laung; an army -- bun'tyme kum'lung; one's determination -- pung rung

reinforcement n. kaa bun'tyme kum'lung; thwaap chuum'noo'ee: [send in] reinforcements -- [bun chuun] thwaap chuum'noo'ee

reinstate v. re-instal in office -- dah(k)... mok cunlye'ng... daum venyh: They reinstated [the general] last week. -- Pooh'gkay dah(k) [o'dum sena eyke] mok cunlye'ng daum venyh pi a'tthit muun.

relapse n. dum'narr lo'ab chuum'ngeu

relapse v. became ill again -- lo'ab chuum'ngeu; lo'ab laung venyh; go back to -- prye klai teuh chia... venyh: He relapsed into a life of crime (lit: to being a thief). -- Gwat prye klai teuh chia jchaao venyh.

relate v. be relevant to -- tek tong: His answer relates to my problem. -- Jchum'la'wee gwat tek tong pun'ha kyom.; tro baan tek tong: His answer does not relate to my problem. -- Jchum'la'wee gwat ot tro baan tek tong pun'ha kyom tay.; recount, tell -- ni'tee'en; dum'nall

related to adj. miun tuum neh tuum nong chi'moi: Are you related to her? -- Tau(v) neh miun tuum neh tuum nong chi'moi nee'eng?; chia sat(ch) ngee'it: Is she related to you? -- Tau(v) nee'eng chia sat(ch) ngee'it neh roo?; How is she related to you? -- Dael nee'eng tro chia a'veye nung neh?; tek tong chi'moi: Is your [work] related to [my research]? -- Tau(v) [kej kaa] ro'bah neh tek tong chi'moi [kaa srow'chree' ro'bah kyom] roo tay?

relations n. generally -- kaa tek tong: We have no relations [with them] any more. -- Yeung k'miun kaa tek tong [nung pooh'gkay] tee'it tay.; family relations -- cho'op sat(ch) ngee'it ("sat(ch) ngee'it" lit. is "close flesh", equiv. to Eng. "blood relative"); foreign relations -- kaa bor'tay; political relations -- kaa tek tong; relations between Cambodia and Thailand -- kaa tek tong ro'vieng sruk Kampuchea howi nung sruk See'um; public relations man -- neh tek tong; tuum neh tuum nong: [Their] relations [with one another] are not very good. -- Tuum neh tuum nong [ro'bah pooh'gkay] mun seou la'aw tay.

relationship n. kaa tek tong: have a relationship -- miun tek tong; miun tuum neh tuum nong

relative adj. tek tong teuh leuh: [Value] is relative to [demand]. -- [Kaa miun dum'lye] keuh tek tong teuh leuh [kaa tee'm tee'a].; ephemeral -- k'miun a'veye chee' chia'leh (NB: "chee' chia'leh" means real): [Happiness] is relative. -- [Kaa sohk s'bai] k'miun a'veye chee' chia'leh.

relative n. ngyee'it mit; blood relative -- ngee'it sat(ch) lo'hut; all one's relatives -- krum ngee'it sat(ch) lo'hut; bong pa'own: close relative -- bong pa'own chit: Is he a close relative? -- Tau(v) gwat chia bong pa'own chit ro'bah neh roo?; relatives-in-law -- sat(ch) tlai

relax v. sum'raak; lum'hye

relay v. bun choon... taw; or, bun taw: Please relay the message. -- Sum bun choon saa bun taw.; The spy had to relay the information from one person to another. -- Neh yok kaa tro tai bun choon por'da'mee'an dow'ee bun da(ch) ka'neea pi ma'nch teuh ma'neh.

relay n. kaa bun choon taw

release v. [a prisoner] -- dawh lay'ng [cho'op knauw]; [my hands] -- lay'ng [dai kyom]; [information] -- p'saw p'sye [por'da'mee'an]; [water] -- banyh'jchenyh [tuk]

relevant (to) adj. tek tong (chi'moi): They will not admit the population problem is relevant to their work. -- Gkay mun to'tool sa'ra'pheap tha pun'ha kauwn laung chum'noo'an praw'chee'chuun miun tek tong chi'moi kej kaa gkay tay.

relevance n. kaa tek tong

relentless adj. bun'thaw: a relentless attack -- vye bun'thaw choop ka'neea

reliable adj. pung baan; trustworthy -- tooo'k jchet baan

reliance n. s'kd'eye sung'khum leuh; kaa pung p'eh

relief n. relief [from pain] -- dum'narr too' sa'bauw'ee [om'pee kaa chee'chup]; of the guard -- kaa plas venyh yee'um; send relief -- bun chuun chuum'noo'ee

relieve v. tveu owi tooo' sa'bauw'ee

religion n. se'sna; chuum'neuu'a; believe in, have, or practice a religion -- kaan se'sna

religious adj. referring to things -- ney se'sna: a religious problem -- pun'ha ney se'sna; referring to people -- dael cheu'a se'sna: a religious man -- ma'nooh dael cheu'a se'sna

relinquish v. lay'ng bong

reluctant (to) adj. steh steu (dum'bye): They were reluctant to [admit] their mistake. -- Pooh'gkay steh steu dum'bye [sa'ra'pheap noeh] kum'hawh ro'bah gkay.; klait jchet (lit: fearing (i. e., feeling concern) to): reluctant to impose -- klait(ch) jchet dael baan bong kom

reluctantly adv. dow'ee teuh twal; dow'ee steh steu: do reluctantly -- tveu... dow'ee teuh twal; He did it very reluctantly. -- Gwat tveu veea dow'ee teuh twal nah.

rely on v. thi pung leuh; pung leuh; sum'ang leuh; rely on for help or favor -- pung piak

remain v. continue to be in a conditiin -- kuung noeh: The seeds remain in good condition. -- Kro'up puuch kuung noeh la'aw.; noeh tai: He remains opposed to it. -- Gwat noeh tai praw'chang veea.; continue to exist, be "left" -- miun... noeh sahl(t): [Only] the seeds remain. -- Miun [tai] kroo'up puuch [pun'noh] dael noeh sahl(t).; stay in place -- snak noeh: The troops remained at Moong. -- Tee'hee'an snak noeh Moong.

remaining adj. continuing to be -- noeh owi: Remaining silent is not the answer. -- Noeh owi scnee'um scn'ut mun maan jchum'la'wee.; still, yet (to go, to do, in existence, available, etc.) -- noeh sahl(t): There are ten more kilometers remaining to go. -- Miun noeh sahl(t) dop kilomet tee'it tro teuh.; the remaining troops -- tee'hee'an dael noeh sahl(t)

remark n. kaa sum'kwaal; kaa sum'kwaal keunyh

remark (that) v. kaat sum'kwaal (tha)

remarkable adj. daw awh'jcha

remedy n. t'nam sung'koeuv

remember v. jcham; jchong jcham: Remember that word! -- Jchong jcham peea!

remind v. ruhm leuk: Remind me to go. -- Ruhm leuk kyom k'nong (or jchum'poo'h) kaa teuh.; remind repeatedly -- teuu'un

reminder n. kaa ruhm luk; kaa dah(k) teuu'an

reminisce v. nuhk keunyh

remodel v. gkye gkun

remote adj. chng'eye; dach sraw yaaa'll; chng'eye dach song venyh; remote area -- cheu'na'bot dach sraw yaa'll; remote village -- phum chng'eye dach song venyh

removable adj. adje dawh jchenyh baan: The top of the Kamanka was removable. -- Dum'bole Ka'man'ka adje dawh jchenyh baan. (NB: A "Kamanka" is a Soviet "jeep" extensively used by the Cambodian armed forces in the 1980s and early 90s.)

remove v. s. thing from a place -- yok... jchenyh: remove garbage -- yok sum'raahm jchenyh; s. o. [from] office -- dawh yok jchenyh [om'pee/pi] mok dum'nyne; a stain -- tveu owi ch'reh ka'isle; eliminate -- mom'butt: remove suspicion -- mom'butt kaa song'sye

renaissance n. dum'narr miun; chia t'maee; kaa kaut laung miun chia t'maee

rendezvous n. kaa not choop ka'neea; cunlye'ng choop; have a rendezvous -- miun kaa not choop ka'neea

rendezvous v. not choop ka'neea

renegade n. ma'nooh dael praw'preut teuh taam tai jchet ro'bah kloo'an

renew v. extend -- bun'taw noeh: renew a lease -- bun'taw noeh kaa ch'nool; renew diplomatic relations -- bun'taw chia t'maee kaa toot; renew efforts -- kum'prung chia t'maee; do again -- tveu dow'ee chia t'maee

rent n. in general -- tlai ch'nool: rent for a house -- tlai ch'nool ptay'a; What's the rent for this moto? -- Tlai ch'nool moto ni pu'man?

rent v. ch'ool

repair adj. choo'ah chul: We took it to the (bicycle) repair shop. -- Yeung yok veea teuh hawng choo'ah chul (kong).

repair n. kaa choo'ah chul; kaa kye'kawn

repair v. choo'ah chul; fix up, remodel -- gkye gkun

repatriate v. bun'choon... venyh: The Khmer Rouge want to repatriate [all (their) people] from Thailand to Cambodia. -- Khmei Kra'hom jchong bun choon [pra'chee'chuun te'ang awh] pi sruk See'um teuh Kampuchea venyh.

repay v. song venyh

repayment n. kaa song venyh; sum'nong venyh

repeal v. kum'chat; leuk... jchowl: repeal a law -- leuk ch'bop jchowl

repeat v. say s. th. again -- taa taam; do s. th. again -- tveu m'dong tee'it (less frequently: tveu d'dael)

repeatedly adv. ny'uk n'yoo'up

repel v. bun chope; vye ch'raan... teuh venyh; repel the enemy -- vye ch'raan sa'tro teuh venyh

replace v. chuum'nooh(s); plas t'maee

reply v. jchum'la'wee (AP: ch'la'wee); tawp; jchum'la'wee tawp

replacement n. mechanical -- kaa pdo; kaa dah(k) choo'ah t'maee: This part is a replacement. -- P'nyke ni keuh chia kaa dah(k) choo'ah t'maee.; human -- ma'nooh chuum'nooh(s): He is my replacement. -- Gwat chia ma'nooh chuum'nooh(s) kyom.; replacement part -- plas kreung k'chow

report n. ro'bye'kaa: make a report -- tveu ro'bye'kaa; s'kd'eye ri'yaye kaa; or, kaa ri'yaye kaa: [send] a report -- [p'nya(r)] kaa ri'yaye kaa

report v. p'dung; ri'yaye'kaa; I will report it to the police. -- Kyom nung p'dung veea teuh dum'roo'it.; ri'yaye owi/teuh police; report for a newspaper -- yok kaa owi neh ka'ssett; report [a crime] -- ri'yaye kaa (or, p'dung pi) [bot ok'krut]

repossess v. oh yok venyh

represent v. dum'nahng

representative n. neh dum'nahng ree'eh (NB: ree'eh = people): Who is the representative from Tnal Byke? -- No na chia neh dum'nahng ree'eh pi Tnal Byke?

repress v. tooo'b

repression n. kaa tooo'b

reprimand n. kaa s'kd'eye bun'toh

reprimand v. s'kd'eye bun'toh

reprint v. bawh pum laung venyh m'dong tee'it

reprisal n. kaa p'chaal thaawp

reproduce v. a picture or other object -- tveu sah chia t'maee; procreate -- bung kaut

reproduction n. vuh'to jchum'long taam: That [painting] is a reproduction. -- [Kum'noo lee'ab pwa] nung keuh chia vuh'to jchum'long taam.

republic n. sa'teea'ra'na ratt (APs: sa'teea'raw'na; rawt): The United States is a republic. -- Sruk Am'rik keuh chia sa'teea'ra'na ratt.

republican adj. sa'teea'ra'na ratt

Republican n. sa'ma'chik [member of] ka'na'pac [party] sa'teea'ra'na ratt [Republican]

reputable adj. sm'oh trong; dael miun ch'moo'h la'aw

reputation n. gkay ch'moo'h

request n. sum'nom'po'; kaa snaal sum

request v. sum; snaal sum; (NB: although it does not translate as "request" per se, the Khmer word "sun" may be used in making requests which may verge on being polite orders, viz: Wait! -- Choop sun.; Don't go [yet]. -- Kum ['aal] teuh sun.; Try some. -- Lo'meuhl sun teuh.)

require v. need from s.o. else -- tro kaa: [Because of the floods], Cambodia will require an [extra] 10 million tons of rice. -- [Dow'ee sa tuk chuum'nuun], Kampuchea yeung nung tro kaa ung'kaw dop lee'en town [bun'tyme].; compel provision from s.o. else -- dum'ro(v). They required this from us. -- Pooh'gkay dum'ro(v) ni pi yeung.; be required to do s. th. -- dum'ro(v) k'nong: We are required to [check in] one hour before the flight leaves. -- Yeung dum'ro(v) k'nong [kaa ch'eye ch'aae jchole k'nong] moi mao muun peyr yun'hawh jchaak jchenyh.; be required to do s. th. -- tro baan dum'ro(v) owi: I am required to work late. -- Kyom tro baan dum'ro(v) owi tveu kaa yeut.

requirement n. kaa dum'ro(v); meet the requirement -- penyh leh ka'nak teuh: He does not meet the requirements for being a pilot. -- Gwat ot penyh leh ka'nak tveu chia neh baahk baw yun hawh tay.; kum'nauwt

rescue n. kaa choo'ay yok a'saa

rescue v. yok a'saa; choo'ay; srow'eet srong

research n. srauw ch'ree'oo

research v. tveu srauw ch'ree'oo

resemble v. doj

reservation n. restaurant table, room, etc. -- kaa bum'rong tooo'k; kaa tveu tooo'k muun (both = lit. s.th. done in advance); make a reservation for... -- chool... tooo'k sum'rap... : I want to make a reservation for a room tomorrow. -- Kyom jchong chool ban'tope moi tooo'k sum'rap t'ngai's'eye'd.; (NB: chool = v., to rent; ch'nool = n., the amount of the rent to be paid); have a reservation about [that plan] -- miun kaa song'sye klaah klaah om'pee [pyne'kaa nu]: [I agree with] your idea but I have reservations [about it]. -- [Kyom yul'prome chi'moi] kum'nut neh, pun'ta'aae kyom miun kaa song'sye klaah klaah om'pee veea.

reserve v. generally -- tooo'k bum'rong; bum'rong tooo'k; reserve a room -- tooo'k bum'rong ban'tope; reserve a seat or place -- bum'rong cunlye'ng tooo'k; reserve the right to -- re'eh'sa sutt (AP: suh'ti) noeh: I reserve the right to do s. th. -- Kyom re'eh'sa noeh sutt tveu kek kaa p'sayng p'sayng.

reserve adj. bum rong; bum rong tooo'k: use the reserves -- pra tee'hee'an bum rong tooo'k; in reserve -- dael bum'rong tooo'k; or, k'nong kaa bum'rong tooo'k

reserved adj. taken -- dael tooo'k owi gkay owi; reserved seat -- cunlye'ng dael tooo'k owi gkay owi; reserved person -- ma'nooh sraw'kut sraw'kum; ma'nooh mun seu baan mwot kaw

reservoir n. anhg tuk; tuum

reside v. has a residence -- miun ti luum'noeh; lives, generally -- noeh; resides on temporary basis -- snak noeh

residence n. ti luum'noeh: Where is his residence? -- Tau(v) gwat miun ti luum'noeh noeh ti na?; during his residence -- ro'yeht peyr noeh; in residence -- dael noeh k'nong

resident (of) n. neh sruk (ney)

residential adj. sum'rap ti luum noeh eyke'a'chuun

resign v. sum chope pi dum'nye'nyh; leea'leng pi dum'nye'nyh

resignation n. from s. th. -- kaa sum chope: resignation [from a position] -- kaa sum chope [pi dum'nye'ng]; or, kaa leea'leng chope [pi dum'nye'ng]; acceptance, willingness to endure -- pheap (or, aae'ree'a'but (lit: attitude of)) to'tool tro'am teuh

resigned adj. dael to'tool ot tro'am (NB: ot tro'am and tro'am both mean patience or willingness to endure)

resist v. generally -- tooo'b t'ool: resist [the enemy] -- tooo'b t'ool [sa'tro]; kawm ot tro'am: resist the temptation to eat peanuts -- kawm ot tro'am mun nyam sun dyke daiy.; resist [arrest] -- rung to'tung mun prome owi police [jchaap kloo'an]; resist my [suggestion] -- mun yul'prome kaam [kaa owi yo'baal] ro'bah kyom

resistance n. kaa tooo'b t'oool; krum ney taw'soo: join the resistance -- jchole ruum krum ney taw'soo (taw'soo lit. = relentless)

resolution n. personal -- kaa tang jchet; governmental -- s'kd'eye sum'rach jchet; outcome, settlement -- kaa dawh sr'eye: resolution of the conflict -- kaa dawh sr'eye noeh chuum'loo'h

resolve v.   dawh sr'eye: resolve a problem -- dawh sr'eye pun'ha; mediate and resolve -- p'sahs p'sah; kum'chat: resolve doubts -- kum'chat kaa song'sye

resort n.   summer resort -- cunlye'ng kum'sonn; last resort -- mach'eeo'bye krow'ee bum'pot; kreung daw twal (AP: to'al); (NB: twal = to be lacking; Kum'nut twal -- "No idea"; kreung twal -- no tricks left)

resort v.   resort to -- tro baan bung kum jchet: She resorted to [changing her name]. -- Nee'eng tro baan bung kum jchet [pdo chamoo'h].

resourceful adj.   praw'sawb

resources n.   tuun tee'an: natural [lit: primary] resources -- tuun tee'an [daum]; [natural] resources -- tuun tee'an [twaum'a chee'it]; financial resources -- praa(k): Funcinpec had more resources than the CPP. -- Fun'cin'pec miun praa(k) ch'raan chiang CPP.

respect n.   admiration -- s'kd'eye ko'rup; aspect -- praw'kaa: in some respects -- chia praw'kaa klaah; with respect to -- jchum'poo'h: with respect to the weather -- jchum'poo'h a'kas'tee'ut

respect v.   ko'rop (AP: ku'roop) jchum'poo'h: They respect doctors more than police. -- Gkay ku'rop jchum'poo'h kruu peyt ch'raan chiang dum'roo'it.

respectable adj.   trum tro; (NB: not respectable -- sma'h); la'aw; respectable neighborhood -- cunlye'ng rooh noeh la'aw

respective adj.   tee'tay; ree'eng kloo'an: They do well in their respective positions. -- Pooh'gkay tveu baan la'aw noeh k'nong chuum'ho ree'eng ree'eng kloo'an.

respectively adv.   tee'tay pi ka'neea; (less frequently: tai ree'eng kloo'an; tee'tay ree'eng ree'eng kloo'an): [The two groups of observers] went to Po'sat and Samroang, respectively. -- [Krum neh song'khet'kaa pi krum] baan teuh Po'sat howi nung Samroang tee'tay pi ka'neea.

respiratory adj.   dael praw'dop dawk dung'hauwm (lit: re the system for breathing); respiratory disease -- chuum'ngeu ney kreung dawk dung'hauwm

respond v.   ch'l'eye tawb

response n.   to a question -- jchum'la'wee (AP: ch'la'wee); to a letter -- kaa tawb sum'buht

responsibility n.   kaa to'tool kaa tro; take responsibility -- to'tool kaa tro: The child is his responsibility. -- Gkon keuh to'tool chia bun'tooo'k ro'bah gwat.; function, job responsibility -- leh kan'taae'kah

responsible for adj.   to'tool kaa tro jchum'poo'h: responsible for that accident -- to'tool kaa tro jchum'poo'h kroo'ti'nak nu; chia daum'hyte sum'rap: [Inflation] is responsible for the decline in [sales]. -- [Kaa laung tlai] chia daum'hyte sum'rap bun'toi noeh [kaa looh].

rest n.   repose -- kaa sum'rach: take a rest -- yok kaa sum'ra(ch); at rest, tranquil -- s'kd'eye snawp; remainder -- noeh sawl; aae tee'it; the rest of the money -- jchum'nye dael noeh sawl; the rest of you -- neh aae tee'it

rest v.   rest arms on the table -- dai noeh leuh toh; rest oneself -- sum'rach; rest the horses -- owi seh sum'rach

restaurant n.   haang bye; haang nyam bye; poch'ni'tan (AP: po'nee'ton, poch'a'neea'ton)

restless adj.   raw'sap raw'saw

restore v.   choo'ah chul; owi.... doj daum venyh: restore a building -- choo'ah chul a'keea; owi a'keea doj daum venyh; song venyh; restore lost property -- kaa pro'kul song venyh

restrain v.   generally -- tooo'b; s.o. or oneself emotionally or psychologically (rather than physically) -- tooo'b jchet; restrain s.o. or oneself -- cong'tron (fr. Fr. verb "controller"): They had to restrain the prisoner. -- Pooh'gkay tro tai cong'tron neh cho'op cooo'k.; be restrained from -- tooo'b... kum owi; or, tooo'b om'pee kaa: He [had to be] restrained from hitting the guard. -- Gwat [tro baan] tooo'b kum owi vye neh yee'im la'bot.; or, Gwat [tro baan] tooo'b om'pee kaa vye neh gyhee'um la'bot.; restrain a horse [from bucking] -- tooo'b seh kum owi [kun'chreul]

restraint n.   s'kd'eye tooo'b

restrict v.   tveu owi teuh teng; dah(k) kum'rut (lit: put rules or regulations); dah(k) prum'dyne: restrict [international] trade -- dah(k) prum dyne chuum'noo'inyh [un'ta'ra'chee'it]

restriction n.   kaa tveu owi teuh teng, kaa dah(k) kum'rut. restrictions on freedom of the press -- kaa dah(k) kum'rut noeh leuh kaa p'sye

restrictive adj.   dael teuh teng

restroom n.   bang kuhn; ban'tope tuk

result n.   leh'ta'p'auwl: What was the result? -- A'veye chia leh'ta'p'auwl?; final result -- leh'ta'p'auwl jchong krow'ee; or, leh'ta'p'auwl jchong bun chope; get results -- baan kaa; results in -- chia leh'ta'p'auwl; results from -- kaut miun laung dow'ee sa

resultant adj.   chia leh'ta'p'auwl

resume v.   song kye'b

resume n.   bun'taw

resurgence n.   kaa miun laung venyh

resurgent adj.   dael miun laung venyh

retail adj.   loo'a ree'aae; (n: wholesale = loo'a duhm; "ree'aae" = "piece by piece"; "duhm" = "by lot")

retail n.   kaa loo'a ree'aae

retail v.   loo'a ree'aae

retain v.   tooo'k; retain for himself -- tooo'k sum'rap kloo'an gwat p'twal; retain its color -- jcham pwa; tooo'k owi bun taw: retain in office -- tooo'k owi bun taw noeh k'nong mok dum'nye'nyh; retain facts -- jcham; retain s.o. to do s.th., i. e., hire -- ch'ool: They retained a new [attorney]. -- Gkay ch'ool [may teea'vi] t'maee.

retaliate v.   song'suk; retaliate in kind -- tveu teuh owi doj venyh

retaliation n.   kaa tveu tawb

retinue n.   neh hye'hom; bo'ri'va

retire v.   from a job -- jchole ni vwot: The Minister retired [last year]. -- Mun'trei baan jchole ni vwot pi [chh'nam muun or, chh'nam teuh].; go to bed -- jchole daeyk; jchole geyng; [from battle] -- dah jchenyh [pi sa'mau'ra'phum]; toi jchenyh [pi sa'mau'ra'phum]

retiring adj.   nung ni'vwut; dael nung jchole nung ni'vwut

retract v.   s. th. material -- puun lup jchole: retract [an antenna] -- puun lup jchole [ong-tyne]; retract [a statement] -- dawk [sum'num ru'ung]

retraction n.   kaa dawk

retreat n.   kaa dawk toi

retreat v.   dawk toi; toi krow'ee

retrench v.   bun'toi (liy: reduce, decline, become smaller in quantity, etc.)

retribution n.   pee'a; kaa song'suk; (NB: pee'a = revenge or retribution by anyone; kaa song'suk = revenge or retribution by the person wronged or injured himself, or herself)

retrieve v.   teuh yok mok owi

retroactive adj.   pra'ti'sa'kaam

retrospect n.   in retrospect -- krau leh meuhl teuh kang krow'ee

return n.   to a place -- kaa tra'laawp mok doll: await his return -- rong cham kaa tra'laawp mok doll ro'bah gwat; profit -- jchum'nye; in return -- chia sum'nong

return v.   to a place, generally -- tra'laawp (AP: traw'lap); tra'laawp venyh (frequent AP: veng); tra'laawp mok venyh; return from there to here -- mok venyh; return from here to there -- teuh venyh; return a favor -- tveu tawp venyh; return s. th. borrowed, lost, etc. -- song venyh; return a profit -- owi praw'rawk baan teuh venyh; return fire -- banyh teuh venyh

returnee n.   a'ni'ka'chuun

reunion n.   kaa choop ka'neea

reunite v.   choop chuum ka'neea laung venyh

reveal v. s. th. knowable, such as a secret -- bun jchenyh owi dung; s. th. visible, such as a thigh -- bun jchenyh owi keunyh

revelation n. kaa bun jchenyh owi dung; kaa bun jchenyh owi keunyh

revenge n. retribution sought by the person wronged or injured him-, or her-, self -- kaa song suk; revenge sought (generally) -- pee'a

revenue n. praa(k) jchum'nole

reversal n. of direction -- kaa tra'laawp teuh krow'ee venyh; of a decision -- kaa pr'eye tra'laawp

reverse adj. banyh'chi'rah: Count in reverse. -- Jchole rawp banyh'chi'rah.; opposite -- p'toi: the reverse/opposite of his [intention] -- p'toi nung [kaa pun pong] ro'bah gwat; reverse side of -- kang m'kang tee'it; reverse gear -- raw'y'eye; put a car in reverse -- raw'y'eye laan; or, toi laan; or, dah(k) laek toi krow'ee (layke toi krow'ee = reverse gear)

reverse v. reverse the order -- dah(k) bun ch'rah ney ro'bee'up; reverse a decision -- pdo bun ch'rah teuh venyh noeh kaa sum'rach jchet; pr'eye tra'laawp sum'rach jchet

review n. of a situation -- kaa pee'nut laung venyh noeh s'ta'na'pheap; of a book -- vee'vay chuh na ney s'po; of a lesson -- kaa ree'en sa laung venyh

review v. pee'nut laung venyh noeh; review alternatives -- pee'nut laung venyh noeh kaa prye proo'ul; tveu vee'vay chuh na; review a book -- tveu vee'vay chuh na ney s'po; review a lesson -- ree'en sa laung venyh

revile v. jcheyr praw mwot

revise v. make revisions to -- meuhl kye saa laung vengy (lit: look and correct again): We have to revise our report. -- Yeung tro kaa meuhl kye saa laung venyh ro'bye'kaa yeung.; revise an article -- meuhl kye a'ta'baht saa laung venyh; change -- plas pdo: change one's opinion -- plas pdo jchet kum'nut

revision n. kaa kaa'aae; latest revision -- kaa kaa'aae jchong krow'ee; kaa bun tyme bun toi

revival n. kaa nee'jyum laung venyh

revive v. nee jyum laung venyh

revoke v. dawk hote mok venyh

revolt n. kaa baah bauw; pa'ti'vwut

revolt (against) v. baah bauw (praw'chang)

revulsion n. s'kd'eye chin cha'on

revolution n. political -- pa'ti'vwut; (NB: pa'ti'kaam = strike or demonstration); upheaval -- jcheh'la'jchal; rotation, as earth around sun -- kaa vull chuum'venyh

revolutionary adj. re physical rebellion -- pa'ti'vwut: revolutionary war -- song'kree'um pa'ti'vwut; new, unusual -- kaa plyte ch'raan pi twa'ma'da: [Letting women vote] is a revolutionary idea. -- [Kaa a'noo'naaht owi sraae bawh ch'naut teuh] chia kum'nut dael kawh plyte ch'raan pi twa'ma'da.

revolutionary n. neh pa'ti'vwut

revolutionize v. plas pdo yang klang

revolver n. kum'pleung dai; ree'vol'vayre

revulsion n. kaa sa'ob yang klang

reward n. kaa owi rung vwun; rung vwun; reward for capturing a criminal -- rung vwun sum'rap jchaap jchaao

rhetoric n. vo'ha'sa

rhetorical adj. kang vo'ha'sa; rhetorical question -- sum'noo'a dael ot bum'rong nung owi mium jchum'la'wee (lit: question for which no answer is prepared)

rhinoceros n. ro'mee'a

rhyme(s) n. similar sounds ("bat", "cat", "rat") -- peea jchong chuon; or, peea jchaap jchong chuon: I like rhymes. -- Kyom jchole jchet peea jchong chuon.; poems -- kum'nap; make up rhymes or poems -- saw say kum'nap

rhyme v. chu'on ka'neea; make rhymes -- tveu owi chu'on

rhythm n. jchong'vaa(k)

rib n. cha'ung chuum'nee

ribbon n. hair ribbon -- bo; typewriter ribbon -- loo'bong (fr. Fr. pronun. of ribbon: "li'bon")

rice n. stalks -- daum sro; harvested but unmilled with stalk still attached -- sro; milled but not yet cooked -- ung'kaw; cooked -- bye; specifically, boiled -- bye saw; specifically, fried -- bye chaa; boiled rice cooked with chicken -- bye muon; (NB: sro is rice growing in a paddy; sr'eye is the paddy itself)

rice cooker (electric) n. chhn'aang pleung dom bye (lit: electric rice boiling pot)

rice paddy n. veal sr'eye

rice soup n. thick, with shrimp, chicken, etc.; usually available only for breakfast -- baa'baw; baa'baw kreun

rich adj. miun: rich person -- neh miun; rich food -- ma'hope dael kreung ch'raan; dutt: rich color -- pwa dutt; tun tee'im; rich source -- sum bo' tun tee'im; chee chee'it la'aw; rich soil -- daiy chee chee'it la'aw

riches n. po'kaa tro'up; riches of a nation -- tun tee'in twa'ma chee'it

rickety adj. rok tai ba(k); (lit: looks like it must break)

ricochet n. dum'narr pla'ht

ricochet v. pla'ht

rid v. kum'chut: rid the country of criminals (lit: expel criminals from the country) -- kum'chut om'peuh o'krut jchenyh pi praw'tet; rid the mind of worries -- bum'bot kum'nut proo'i ba'rum; or, kum'nut proo'i ba'rum jchenyh; get rid of -- kum'chut: get rid of evidence -- kum'chut mum'but noch pwah'taang; get rid of that guy -- kum'chut gwat jchenyh teuh; Get rid of it. -- Luup veea jchowl.

riddance n. but teuh kaa m'yang da'aae; awh teuh kaa m'yang da'aae: Good riddance to bad garbage! -- But teuh kaa m'yang da'aae sum'rap sum'rahm a'krah!

riddle n. pee'a praw'dow; kaa dael koo'a owi pi'bah yul

ride v. a bike -- jchi kong; ride a horse/ride a buffalo -- jchi seh/chi kraw'bye; ride double on a bike -- kong doop; ride double on a moto -- moto doop

rifle n. kum'pleung: hunting rifle -- kum'pleung banyh saat

right n. suut (AP: suh'ti): have the right to -- miun suut: have no right to sell the car -- ot miun suut looh laan; the right to work the land -- suut tveu kaa tuk daiy

right adv. opp. of left -- s'dam

right here adv. cunlye'ng ni

right there adv. cunlye'ng nu

Right, right! xcl. Baa, baa!; Tro howi!

Right? xcl. in sense of, "You've got it, right?; i. e., "You understand and you're going to do it, right?" -- most common: Nung, eh? or, Nung aae?; also: Leu, eh?

ring n. for a finger -- n'chee'un; ring of thieves -- krum jchaao; a ring of trees around the village -- daum cheu pwot chuum'venyh phum; sound made by bell -- kun'dung; sum'leng kun'dung; sound made by telephone -- loo' tele'phone ro'

ring v. by hitting -- vye: ring a bell -- vye joo'ung; by pushing buttton, as doorbell -- chuch (lit: push)

ring-worm n. dum'bow kla'ee

rinse v. lee'ung (also means, to wash)

rim n. gkaem: rim of the tire -- gkaem kong

rip v. lo'hyte; rip up -- tee'enyh owi lo'hyte

ripe adj. tuum; over-ripe -- jcho; un-ripe -- k'chey

rise v. generally -- laung: rising prices -- tlai laung; The water is rising. -- Tuk laung.; re the sun -- reh

river, lake n. tun'lay

river bank n. mwa tunlay; ch'raae'ung

riverside landing n. kom'puung (same word as in provincial names such as "Kom'puung Cham" (usually Romanized on maps as "Kompong", viz., "Kompong Cham", "Kompong Speu", etc.); also, same as verb marker for "ing")

road n. ploe; t'nawl (AP:tha'nol, th'non, t'nal; NB: t'nawl is applied more to paved roads than to unpaved.)

roast v. ang

rob v. jchun: Last night I was robbed in the street. -- Yoop munyh gkay jchun kyom taam ploe.

robber n. jchaao

rock(s) n. t'maw

role n. in a play -- dal too'a; political/historical role -- Kum'roo: Sihanouk played an important role in the histrioy of his contry. -- Si'ha'nou miun kum'roo neh snai'ha tee'it noeh pra'wa'ti'saa sruk gwat.

roll n. piece of bread -- num pahng; roll of film -- dum'role svil; roll of paper -- dum kra'dah; "on a roll!" -- ch'neh cho'op howi!

roll v. roll over -- ta'lawp; roll down a hill -- ta'lawp jchoh phnom; roll up [a carpet] -- moool laung [pruhm]

roof n. k'nong; dum'bole

room n. element of a house -- ban'tope: bathroom -- ban'tope tuk; living room -- ban'tope to'tool p'nee'oo (lit: room to receive guests); bedroom -- ban'tope geyng; single room -- ban'tope sum'rup ma'neh; double room -- ban'tope sum'rup pi neh; space, area -- cunlye'ng: Do you have room for another [passenger]? -- Tau(v) neh miun cunlye'ng sum'rap [neh dum'narr] moi tee'it tay?; Is there room [to store] these boxes here? -- Tau(v) miun cunlye'ng [sum'rap tooo'k] praw'op ni?

rooming house n. ptay'a miun ban'tope sum'rap ch'ool (lit: house that has rooms for rent); (house for rent = ptay'a ch'ool)

root n. roos

rope n. k'sye poo'a

rose n. gu'lab

rosewood n. ku'ring

rotten adj. bot syke: rotten meat -- sat(ch) bot syke

rough adj. uneven -- ro'laae'eh: a rough road -- ploe ro'laae'eh; coarse, scratchy -- ko'kree'it; or kaw'kreuum: rough wood -- cheu ko'kree'it; difficult -- pi'bah; or ko'kree'it: a rough day -- t'ngai pi'bah; a rough time -- peyr pi'bah; t'ngai ko'kree'it; ot peyr ko'kree'it; rough talk or manners or personality -- kahtch

round adj. mool

round-trip adj. and n. teuh mok venyh (common AP: to' mow venyh)

rout n. kaa para'chey

route n. means of getting to a place or atttaining an objective -- ploe; highway -- ploe; street -- ploe t'nawl

row n. a line of s. th. -- choo'a: a row of ducks -- choo'a tee'a; get one's ducks in a row (get organized) -- ree'up jchum kloo'an eiyne owi sroul boul

row v. um: row a boat -- um toook

royal adj. ney s'dach; ree'ech chia

rubber n. kaow'soo

rubber boots n. kaow'soo (lit: rubbers); (APs: ba'loo; bal'soo)

ruby n. t'bong kun'tum; (PS: t'bong kra-hOm -- lit: red gem); (sapphire -- t'bong kan'dee'um)

rude adj. ch'leu'ee; kahtch

rudder n. chung'kauwt cun'toi toook

rug n. pruhm

rule n. regime -- ro'bab; regulations collectively -- praw'kaa: an individual rule -- praw'kaa na moi; "the rule of law" -- ch'bop tuum'lawp

rule v. kroop krong

rum n. sra rum; palm rum -- tuk snau chooo

rumor n. peea jcham a'ram

rumpled adj. ktoo'a k'tee

run v. sprint -- rut; run after s. th., literally -- rut denyh; or, rut taam; run after figuratively, court, pursue emotionally -- rut teuh taam; rut roo'it teuh taam; run away -- rut teuh: Srei Peau ran away to Vietnam. -- Srei Peau rut teuh sruk Yu'en., run away from, abandon -- rut johowl; function -- chheh: [The cassette player] was fixed so it would run. -- [Mun'yaye] tro baan choo'ah chul teup adje chheh loo.; (NB: "run" for different machines is expressed with different words, viz: The car was fixed so that it [would run]. -- Laan tro baan choo'ah chul teup adje [baahk baan].; The watch was fixed so that it [would run]. -- Nee'a'li'ka tro baan choo'ah chul teup adje [pra'kaa kaut]. (lit: so that it [could be used])); doesn't run -- (s.th. that moves directionally) ot chheh; (s.th. that moves directionally or is stationery but has moving parts) -- ko'ich; (s.th. that can be driven, flown, etc.) -- baahk ot baan: The tractors aren't running. -- Trac'taw mun chheh; or, trac'taw ko'ich; or, trac'taw baahk mun baan.; also, dah (lit: walk): The "air con" doesn't run. -- "Air con" ot dah.; control, administer -- kaan kaab: run a business -- kaan kaab chuum'noo'inyh

rural adj. sruk sr'eye; ney sruk sr'eye; cheu'na'boht; ney cheu'na'boht

ruse n. kaa bauwk; trick to get money -- kaa bauwk praa(k)

rush v. teuh praw'nyab

Russia n. Roo'si'a; sruk So'vyeh'tique

Russian adj. So'vyeh'tique

rust n. ch'reh

rust v. ch'reh jchaap

rut n. snaam kong laan

ruthless adj. k'miun may'daa

S

sabotage n. kaa bum plynyh (lit: destruction)

sabotage v. teuh bum plynyh: The Khmer Rouge sabotaged the bridges around Moun all the time. -- Khmei Kra'hom teuh bum plynyh spee'un chit Moun kroop kroop peyr.

sack n. generally -- s'bowng; large enough for approx. 30 kilos -- kaa rong; large enough for approx. 100 kilos of rice -- ba'oo; a large rice sack -- ba'oo ung'kaw (contracts in speech to "ba'ang kaw")

sacred adj. sak'sit

sacrifice n. peh'li'kaam; kaa bo'chia

sacrifice v. bo'chia: He sacrificed his life out of friendship. -- Gwat bo'chia chi'vut dum'bye mi'ta'pheap.; sok jchet pdo: She sacrificed her happiness for her children. -- Nee'eng sok jchet pdo kaa sok sam'rup gkon rob'ah nee'eng.; I would sacrifice my life for you. -- Kym sok jchet slop roo'h pdo chi'vut chi'moi neh. (liy: I will happliy die to give (exchange) my life to you.); (formal, principally written, term: tveu peh'li kaam);

sad adj. kum'sot: That person is sad. -- Ma'nooh nu kum'sot.; sad music -- plaeng kum'sot; pi'bah jchet: Why are you sad? -- Hyte eye neh pi'bah jchet?; proo'i jchet: He looks sad. -- Gwat meuhl teuh doj proo'i jchet.; kaut tuk

safe adj. kung vung; sohk: It is no longer safe in Prea Vihear. -- Veea ot baan sohk tee'it tay noeh Prea Vi'hear.

safety n. kaa sohk

saffron adj. color of monks' robes -- pwa sla'tuum

Saigon n. HCM; HCMC; Ho Chi Minh; Saigon; Preah'noo'ko

sail v. bauw (tooo'k ka'daouwm)

sailboat n. tooo'k ka'daouwm

sailor n. tee'hee'an jcheung tuk

salad n. salad with meat -- plee'a: Khmer style with meat: beef salad -- plee'a gko; fish salad -- plee'a trei; chicken salad -- ny'aum muon; salad without meat -- salat ("salat" also translates as "lettuce")

salary n. praw'kye; bee'vwut

sales n. volume of business -- looh: Sales were down. -- Looh mun da(tch).; on sale -- jchoh tlai (lit: price cut!)

salt n. um'bul

salvation n. national or group salavation -- srau'ich srong: Ratt'a'pi'bal Srau'ich Srong Chee'it -- Government of National Salvation (name used by administration of Lon Nol in early 1970s); individual -- srong chi'vut: srong chi'vut kyom -- my salvation; rescue -- kaa sung'kroo'ah; re "rum'doh" as translation for "salvation", see definition of "liberation"

same adj. doj; doj ka'neea; d'dael: Always the same food! -- Nyam d'dael d'dael; always the same story! -- ni'yaye d'dael d'dael; equal to -- pun ka'neea; Those men are the same size. -- Mee'ut gwat pun ka'neea.; almost the same as -- pra'heil ka'neea nung: Cambodia is almost the same [size] as Burma. -- [Mee'ut] Kampuchea pra'heil ka'neea nung [mee'ut] Poo'mia.; twa'ma'da: Same time tomorrow. -- S'eye'd peyr mao twa'ma'da.; corresponding, similar -- haow sum ka'neea

sampan n. tooo'k

sample n. free sample [of food] -- [ma'hope] 'sahk; or [ma'hope] sum'rap ploo'ah; dum'nahng: I need to see a sample [of his work]. -- Tro kaa meulh dum'nahng [ney kej kaa ro'bah gwat].; kum'roo: Send them a sample of the fabric. -- P'nya(r) owi gkay noeh kum'roo ney kraw'not.; pattern -- kum'noo: Send me the pattern. -- P'nya(r) kum'noo owi kyom.

sanction n. penalty -- kaa bun to'h; kaa pee'ney; trade sanction -- kaa tveu twun na kaam; approval -- kaa yul' prome (lit: approval)

sanctlon v. approve -- yul'prome; (written form: a'noo'mu'tay)

sanctuary n. choom'rok: The Khmer Rouge use Thai territory as sanctuary. -- Khmei Kra'hom pra daiy see'um chia choom'rok.

sand n. k'suj; daiy k'suj

sandals n. s'bye'k cheung sung reik

sandwich n. pan'sock (compression of "num pahng dah(k) sat(ch)", lit: bread with meat)

sapper team n. kawng ch'lope (lit: hidden force; term may also convey reconnaisance, scout, advance or guerrilla force)

sapphire n. generally -- t'bong kan'dee'um; black sapphire -- t'bong neul; green sapphire -- t'bong kee'oo

sarong n. sa'rong; sum'pot (lit: skirt)

satelite n. orbiting facility -- sat'leet; bo'ri'va; da'ra run'awh; political dependency -- sat'leet: [East Germany] was a satelite of Russia. -- [Sruk A'la'man Kang Kaut] keuh sat'leet Sruk Roo'see.; (NB: colony = praw'tet ru'nawt)

satisfactory adj. penyh jchet: His work was satisfactory. -- Kej kaa (or kaa tveu) ro'bah gwat koo'a owi penyh jchet.

satisfied adj. tro jchet; penyh jchet: satisfied with -- penyh jchet jchum'poo'h; He was not satisfied with the prisoner's answer. -- Gwat ot penyh jchet jchum'poo'h jchum'lye neh choop cooo'k.

satisfy v. tro jchet; bum penyh jchet: The government cannot satisfy the people with [promises alone]. -- Ratt'a'pi'bal mun adje bum penyh jchet pra'chee'chuun chi'moi [kaa sun'nyaa tai m'yang].

Saturday n. saow; t'ngai saow (AP: sa'oo)

sauce n. tuk + noun; soy sauce -- tuk si'ee'oo; fish sauce -- tuk trei; tomato sauce (catsup) -- tuk paeng pawh

sausage n. sat(ch) kraw(k)

savage adj. ko'ko'oo

save v. conserve -- sun'sum: save money -- sun'sum loi; save a life -- sung'kroo'ah chi'vut: The doctors saved his life. -- Kruu pet sung kroo'ah chi'vut ro'bah gwat.

saw n. a'naa (written and sometimes spoken form, ro'naa)

sawmill n. ro'ng jcha cheu

say v. taa: He said, where did you go? -- Gwat taa, neh teuh ti na?; ni'yaye tha: He says that it is too expensive. -- Gwat ni'yaye tha veea tlai nah.; bol: He said that she said that we are no good. -- Gwat bol tha nee'eng ni ni'yaye tha yeung ot la'aw.; (NB: "He said that... " may be expressed either by "gwat taa" or "gwat ni'yaye tha" or "gwat bol tha"; the construction "gwat taa tha..." is generally not used); What did he/you/they/etc. say? -- Taa mutch?; tell -- prap; say good-bye -- lee'a; referring to speaking done by person worthy of respect (older person, teacher, etc.) -- miun praw'saa; My father said that... -- Pa miun praw'saa tha...; The teacher said that... -- Neh Kruu miun praw'saa tha...

saying n. proverb -- so'pheap'sut

scale n. for weighing -- chuhn ching; "on a [scale] of one to ten" -- "noeh leuh [kaa vi'ni'chai] pi moi teuh dop"

scallions n. sluk k'tum

scandal n. ru'ung a'sro (lit: bad stories); kaa a'sro

scanty adj. doo'itch s'd'auwng

scar n. sn'aam (also means mark or spot, e. g., as on clothes, furniture, walls, etc.)

scarce adj. k'sot: Food is scarce. -- Ma'hope k'sot.; mun scou miun (lit: not much available).

scare v. scare mildly, make nervous -- bum laa(tch): [Ghosts] scare people at night. -- [K'mau'it] bum laa(tch) ma'nooh peyr yoop.; scare seriously -- bum'pay: Lightning scares many people. -- Run'tay'h bum'pay ma'nooh chia ch'raan.

scared adj. klait(ch) (AP: kl'eye't, klaat; written kla(ch)): I'm not scared of ghosts. -- Kyom ot klait(ch) k'mau'it tay.; He's not scared of you. -- Veea mun klait(ch) neh eiyne tay; preu: I'm not scared (of that). -- Ot preu tay.; pay klait(ch): She's scared of deep water. -- Nee'eng pay klait(ch) tuk chro'.; pay: I was scared to death. -- Kyom pay [loo'ah pro'lung] sung slap. (lit: I was scared almost to death [I would lose my soul].)

scattered pp. tro baan pong ri'yaye: The members of my family are scattered [all over] the world. -- Sa'ma'chik ney kroo'e'sa kyom tro baan pong ri'yaye [kroop ti cunlye'ng ney pi (or kroop ti cunlye'ng k'nong pi)] pope'lok.

scatter v. ri'yaye ka'neea: When [the attack] came, the soldiers scattered. -- Noeh peyr [kaa praw'yoot (or vye, or vi'yaye)] mok dull, tee'hee'an ri'yaye ka'neea.; throw, or spread, seeds -- proo'a: scatter rice seed -- proo'a sro

scenery n. teh'so'pheap

schedule n. kam'vi'ti

schedule v. tveu kam'vi'ti sum'rap (lit: make a schedule for): We must schedule the meeting. -- Yeung tro tai tveu kam'vi'tee sum'rap pra'choom.; (NB: While it is fairly clear that the English original means that a time must be selected at which to hold the meeting, the Khmer translation, while accurate, is ambiguous: it can be understood to mean either "make a schedule for (what will happen at) the meeting" or "make a schedule of when the meeting will take place". If it is the latter meaning that is intended, and if there is some idea when it is desired that the meeting be held, that can be made explicit by changing the English to, for example, "We must schedule the meeting for sometime next week." which would translate as, "Yeung tro tai tveu kam'vi'ti pra'choom sum'rap a'tthit krow'ee peyr klaah." If it is not possible to add in an indication of meeting time, the sentence must remain as given at the beginning of the definition to be clarified if necessary by additional questions.)

school n. sa'la; sa'la rin

science n. vi'chi'a'sa

scientist n. neh vi'chee'a'sa

scissors n. kun'trei

scrape v. khow(s)

scratch v. khows; by chicken -- kaw kye; by cat -- gkrun yauw; if done by human -- eh': I need to scratch my leg. -- Kyom tro tai eh' cheung.

scream n. sum rye; kaa sr'eye'k

scream v. sr'eye'k: I [heard] someone scream. -- Kyom [loo] gkay sr'eye'k.

screens n. ru'nay'ung

screw n. k'chow

screw v. koo'ung

screwdriver n. tuur'na'veese

scrub v. with nouns where the cleaning is typically vigorous -- dos: scrub teeth -- dos t'ming; scrub pots -- dos chn'aang; scrub clothes -- dos kow-aow; less vigorous cleaning -- lee'ung: scrub plates -- lee'ung jchaan

sculpture n. roob jchum'lak

sea n. sa'mut (AP: samud)

seashore n. mwot sa'mut

seafood n. ma'hope sa'mut

seal v. close -- butt; butt kan'chawb: seal a letter (i.e., close an envelope) -- butt sum'buht; stamp with a seal -- bawh tra: seal a document -- bawh tra leuh sum'buht; bawh tra eyke'a'saa

search v. ro'k: We searched for the child. -- Yeung ro'k gkon.; sveye ro'k: They are looking for a place to stay. -- Gkay kom'puung sveye ro'k cunlye'ng snak noeh.; ree'oo ro'k: We searched for a solution. -- Yeung ree'oo ro'k dum'naugh sr'eye. (NB: find = ro'k keunyh)

season n. ro'doe: Cambodia has three principal seasons: 1) March to May, hot season -- ro'doe k'dau; also referred to as "dry season" -- ro'doe prah'ng; 2) May to October, rainy season -- ro'doe plee'eng; also referred to as "wet season" -- ro'doe voh'sa, and, in some parts of Cambodia, as "flood season" -- ro'doe tuk choom'nuhn, or ro'doe tuk laung (lit: water rising); and 3) October to February, windy season -- ro'doe ruhm howi; or, ro'doe t'leh kshaal

seat n. on a plane, bus, etc. -- cunlye'ng (lit: place)

second adj. next after "first" -- ti'pi

second n. sixtieth of a minute -- vit'na'ti; a moment, a short time, an instant -- plet: Wait a second. -- Jcham moi plet.

second-class adj. t'nak ti'pi

second-hand adj. chuum'nuuhm; jchaah (lit: old)

secret adj. sum'ngut

secret n. kaa sum'ngut

secretly adv. chia sum'ngut; dow'ee loo'it leh (lit: by means of stealing [and] hiding)

secretary n. person in charge of office, generally -- leh'ka'ti'kaa; typist (whether m. or f.) -- neh vi'yaye ong'glee'laek; secretary general -- a'kaae'a leh'kaa'ti'kaa

sect n. kaa ni'kai: They belong to a Buddhist sect. -- Pooh'gkay pra'kan kaa ni'kai put'eh'se'sna; ka'na (also means "party" or "group").

section n. portion or part of s. th., generally -- jchum'nyke; p'nyke: section of a book -- p'nyke s'po; department of an organization -- p'nyke kang: visa section -- p'nyke kang tveu vee'za; p'nyke kang tveu tee'teh'kaa; section of town -- dum'bun; cross-section -- muk kaat

sector n. p'nyke: of the economy -- p'nyke set'a'kej; administrative sector -- p'nyke kang kaa chat'kaa; sector of society -- p'nyke sung'kuum'atek

secure adj. usually translated as sohk, sohk sann or san'tek'sohk all of which also mean "peaceful" or "peace"; viz, "The village was [secure] but not peaceful." could be rendered as "Phum keuh chia [sohk] pun'ta'aae mun miun pheap sohk sann."; differentiation between "secure" and "peaceful" is best achieved by using for "secure", "ot kroo'ti'nak" -- not dangeous -- or "mun seou kroo'ti'nak" -- not very dangerous -- and for "peaceful" sohk, sohk sann, or san'tek'sohk.

security n. pheap sohk sann; san'tek'sohk (NB: terms for peace and security are essentially the same; see discussion under "secure", above); Security at [the airport] is tight. -- San'tek'sohk noeh [chuum'naut yun'hawh] tung tyne.; (NB: tung tyne lit. = strict); in written form, pheap pot'pee kroo'ti'nak (lit: condition [pheap] of no [pot'pee] danger [kroo'ti'nak])

see v. look at -- keunyh; meuhl: I have seen that, too. -- Kyom kaw baan keunyh da'aae.; I want to go see. -- Kyom jchong teuh meuhl.; meuhl keunyh: We could see the rockets. -- Yeung meuhl keunyh ro'kit.; understand -- keunyh: Ah, I see. -- Aw, keunyh howi.; meet -- choop: See you later. -- Choop ka'neea peyr krow'ee.; Nice to see you. -- S'bai dow'ee baan choop neh.; visit -- tooo's na: The journalists wanted to see Chom Kho'san. -- Neh ka'ssett jchong tooo's na Chom Kho'san.

see a doctor v. teuh choop doc'teur

seed n. kro'up (NB: candy is "sugar seeds" or "kro'up sc'aaw")

seed-throwing game n. angh cuuh'nyh (children's game similar to Italian "bocci" in which object is to throw one large seed or fruit pit so that it lands as close as possible to a previously-thrown seed or pit.)

seem v. hahk doj chia: It seems OK. -- Veea hahk doj chia tro.

seize v. ree'up oh (AP: rup'oh); take over s. th. -- ree'up oh yok

select v. jchreu'reu'

selection n. kaa jchreu'reu'

-self prn. by oneself, i. e., just one person -- ma'neh eiyne: I'll go by myself (i.e., without you, without them, etc.). -- Kyom teuh ma'neh eiyne.; She can go by herself. -- Nee'eng adje teuh ma'neh eiyne.; by oneself, i. e., without assistance -- kloo'an eiyne: You can do it by yourself. -- Neh adje tveu veea kloo'an eiyne.; We can fix it ourselves. -- Yeung adje choo'ah chul veea kloo'an eiyne. (NB: a third construction (using "neh" as the example) is neh eiyne, as in, You can go by yourself. -- Neh adje teuh neh eiyne.; this, however, is considered somewhat abrupt and the preferred (courteous) phrasing is "kloo'an eiyne": Neh adje teuh kloo'an eiyne.)

self-centered adj. kut tai kloo'an

self-confidence n. tooo'k jchet kloo'an eiyne (lit: trust oneself)

selfish adj. greedy -- kum'nenyh; kut tai kloo'an ni'yuum; meuhl keunyh tai kloo'an eiyne; extreme slang, vulgar -- a'ko dop **sell** v. looh: food store (lit: store selling food) -- haang looh ma'hope

sell out v. go against one's principles, support s. o. or s. th. while ignoring its faults/flaws -- troh peyk: Don't sell (yourself) out. -- Kum troh kaw peyk.

send v. [a letter] -- p'nya(r) [sum'buht]; [a telegram] -- p'nya(r) [tel'gram]; vye [too'ra'layke], etc. (see other phrases under "telegram"); s. o. on an errand: if sending a young person, pra (lit: use); if sending an older person, ro'k: I sent [the boy] to the market. -- Kyom pra [own proh] teuh psa.

sentence n. written words -- khlia; of a court -- to'h; kaa vi'ni'jchay

separate adj. p'sayng ka'neea: separate checks -- check p'sayng ka'neea; p'sayng tee'it: That is a separate issue. -- Nu keuh chia ru'ung moi p'sayng tee'it.

separate v. go off in different directions -- jchaiyk mok; jchaiyk mok ka'neea: They separated so he could go earn money for the restaurant. -- Gkay jchaiyk mok ka'neea dum'bye gwat adje teuh ro'k loi sum'rap poch'ni'tan.; separate from -- byke jchenyh pi: Hun Sen separated from the KR in 1977. -- Hun Sen byke jchenyh pi KR noeh 1977.; to be separated from -- tro baan bum byke jchenyh pi: He was separated from Srei Peau in 1990. -- Nee'eng tro baan bum byke jchenyh pi Srei Peau noeh 1990.

September n. Ken'yaa

sergeant n. pul; pul'la'boh; or, pul'la'boh toe; (NB: "NCO" ranks in the Khmer system run approximately as follows (with words trei, toe and eyke meaning third-, second- and first-class, respectively): lance corporal -- pul'la'boh trei; regular sergeant -- pul'la'boh toe; 1st, or top, sergeant -- pul'la'boh eyke)

serious adj. not joking/not to be joked about -- mutt jchawt: serious student -- gkon'sa mutt jchawt; serious work --- kej kaa mutt jchawt; important -- tung tyne; to'ang tung: a serious problem -- pun'ha tung tyne; pun'ha to'ang tung; never smiles -- mung mutt; ch'bah lo'a; yok jchawt tok dot

seriously adv. chia trum trau; chia mun cum'plyne

Seriously! interjctn. Trum trau!; Mun ko'hawk! (lit: No lie!)

serpent n. snake -- poo'ah; mythical serpent portrayed, e. g., at Angkor Wat -- Neak Poan (lit: dragon (that) winds; AP: Ne' pwun)

servant n. common expressions for butler, maid, cook. etc. -- neh ch'nool; or, neh bum raahl; also: k'mayng bum raahl; bauw'ee prio; bauw'ee; (derogatory = kyom (same word as for "I"; lit means "slave")

serve v. assist -- choo'ay; give service -- bum raahl: food served by [a waiter] -- ma'hope bum raahl dow'ee [neh to'tool pnee'oo]; serve food with a spoon, ladle, etc. -- doo'h; serve rice -- doo'h bye; miun: This restaurant serves good food. -- Poch'ni'tan ni mium ma'hope chng'anyh.; serve in the army -- tveu chia tee'hee'an

service n. generally -- kaa bum raahl; civil service -- ratt'a'kaa; saw'teea'ra'na; good service [in a restaurant] -- kaa bum raahl la'aw [noeh poch'ni'tan]; service to one's country -- kaa bum raahl chee'it

sesame n. lung'go

session n. sa'mye pra'choom: The council is in session. -- Krum'pruk'sa noeh k'nong sa'mye pra'choom.; or, Krum'pruk'sa kom'puung pra'choom.

set n. have a set of dishes -- miun jchaan moi cum'play (fr. Fr. "complet" meaning "complete"; (NB: pair = koo: a pair of earrings -- kro'vull (AP: ka'bal) moi koo)

set v. set up, arrange -- ree'up (AP: reep) jchum: He set the table. -- Gwat ree'up jchum tohk.; set on fire -- dop: Do you know who set the building on fire? -- Tau(v) neh dung tay tha neh na dop a'keea?; go down -- lic: The sun has set. -- Preah a'tthit lic howi.

settle v. sum'raah sum'rool; settle an account -- too t'wut; establish residence -- ch'raw(k): The Vietnamese settled along the Tunlay Sap. -- Pooh yuen ch'raw(k) noeh taam mun dow'ee Tunlay Sap.

settlement n. conceptual resolution of a dispute -- dum'naugh sr'eye; payment terminating a dispute -- dawh sr'eye: We received a good settlement from the company. -- Yeung to'tool kaa dawh sr'eye pi kum'huun baan la'aw.; meeting at which property title is transferred -- kaat chamoo'h (lit: cut, or change, name; i. e., changing the name in which the property is held); place where people have settled -- ch'raw(k), or cunlye'ng ch'raw(k): Khmer settlements in Thailand... -- cunlye'ng ch'raw(k) ro'bah Khmei noeh Sruk See'um...

seven n. prum'pi (PS: prum'pul)

seventy adj. jchet'sup

sew v. day; day kow-aow

sewing machine n. ma'seen day

sex n. gender -- payt; intercourse (to have sex) -- ruhm dum'neyk

sexy adj. sraep srahl; a sexy shape -- ree'ung ree'o (lit: thin and flowing)

shabby adj. jchaah (same as word for "dark" and "old"); troohk tro'um

shackle n. knawh: prisoner -- neh cho'op knawh

shade n. m'lope

shadow n. m'lope

shake v. to be shaking -- ruhm choo'ay,: The house is shaking. -- Ptay'a ruhm choo'ay.; ruhm keuh; shake hands -- jchaap dai; shake s. th. -- kraaw'leuk

shaken up adj. emotionally -- ruhm choo'ay jchet: He was shaken up by the news. -- Gwat ruhm choo'ay jchet dow'ee por'da'mee'an.

shakey adj. physically or emotionally -- n'yaw (AP: n'yoa)

shall v. nung (AP: nuung): We shall see. -- Yeung nung meuhl.; mok chia: I shall go tomorrow. -- Kyom mok chia teuh s'eye'd.

Shall we go? q. Teuh, ehh?

shallow adj. reh: Tunlay Sap gets shallower and shallower every year. -- Ree'ung rawl chh'nam Tun'lay Sap reh teuh reh teuh.

shame n. k'mah: Shame, shame! -- K'mah, k'mah!

shameless adj. mok 'kraa' (contraction of "a'krah"): Don't be so shameless! -- Kum mok 'kraa' peyk!

shape n. ree'ung: sexy -- ree'ung ree'o (lit: flowing shape)

share v. ru'um layke: They do not want to share their [food]. -- Pooh'gkay ot jchong ru'um layke [ma'hope jchum'nyke (lit: food food)] tay.

sharp adj. muuht: decisive -- muuht mo'um; a sharp mind -- vee'ung vaye; ch'lee'uh vaye: She has a sharp mind. -- Nee'eng miun ch'lee'uh vaye.

sharpen v. sum'lee'eng: sharpen a knife -- sum'lee'eng kum'but

shatter v. kum'tic; bum byke

shave v. gkhao: He needs to shave and take a shower first. -- Gwat tro kaa gkhao nung moiy tuk muun.; to shave one's head -- gkhao saahk k'bal

she pr. nee'eng (generally means "she" but can mean "he" with ref. to pre-teen-age boy (term in this case is "a' nee'eng", close to "kid"); used primarily re younger women; can be used whether or not woman is married; if married and older, is more appropriate to use gwat or lok srei (formal)); gwat (generally used re men and so to mean "he" but can also be used re women to mean "she"; used primarily re older women): She's a good person. -- Nee'eng la'aw.; nee'eng ken'yaa or, ken'yaa -- used only for unmarried (equivalent to "miss"; see discussion under "Miss"); lok srei -- formal term, equivalent to "ma'am"; veea -- familiar term to be used only re close friends or younger family members, else derogatory/disrespectful.

sheep n. chee'm

sheet n. poo'it; k'mraal poo'it

shelf n. t'neuuh

shell n. of crustacean -- sum'bahw; spent cartridge -- sum'bahw kum'pleung; coconut shell -- lo'leea do'hng

shelling n.   banyh p'tuck (lit: firing on an arc, i. e., with a trajectory); small arms fire -- banyh trung (lit: shooting straight, without arc); harrassing fire -- harcelement (fr. Fr.)

shelter n.   choom'rok: shelter from the storm -- choom' rok pi k'shaal p'chooh; ro'ng

shield n.   k'eye'l

shift v.   pr'eye prool; pdo: Last week they shifted [some employees] from the Foreign Ministry to the Ministry of Education. -- A'tthit muun pooh'gkay pdo [neh tveu kaa klaah] pi Kra'soo'ung Kaa Bor'tay teuh Kra'soo'ung Op'ruhm.

shine v.   sum jchang; sum bun jchang: Shine your [flashlight on] the road a second. -- Sum jchang [pleung pul teuh] ploe moi plet.

ship n.   ka'pal; neea'veea

shirt n.   aow

shock v.   p'nyeh

shocked adj.   electrically -- chawh(k): I was shocked by [the electricty]. -- Plueng chawh(k) kyom.; amazed -- t'leh tlauwm ka'dook: I was shocked by the news. -- Kyom t'lch tlauwm ka'dook dow'ee sa por'da'mee'an.; startled (milder than t'leh tlaum ka'dook) -- loo'ah pro'lung (lit: lose one's soul)

shoe n.   s'bye'k cheung

shoe laces n.   k'sye s'bye'k cheung

shoot v.   banyh

shop, store n.   haang; small store or shop -- haang looh aye'von; haang looh do (lit: sell (looh) and exchange (do))

shopping n.   teuh p'sa

shopping mall n.   p'sa thum

shore n.   of the ocean -- ch'naae; ch'naae sa'mut; bank of a river -- ch'raae'ung

short adj.   re people -- k'tee'up; tee'up: [Only] short people can sit in those bus seats comfortably. -- Miun [tai] ma'nooh tee'up [pun'noh] adje ung'koi noeh k'nong kaeo'eye bus ngi'yaye sroul.; re things -- to'ich (lit: small): She likes short dresses. -- Nee'eng jchole jchet kow-aow to'ich to'ich.; klai: She likes short dresses. -- Nee'eng jchole jchet kow-aow klai klai.; That's a short pen. -- Bic nu klai.; a short distance -- praw'veye'ing klai; chit: a short distance to that table -- jchum'ngai chit teuh tohk nu; not lengthy -- klai: a short book -- ru'ung klai; a short movie -- ru'ung gkun klai; a stort time -- peyr klai (or klai klai); short-sleeved shirt -- aow dai klai; in short -- sa'rup teuh

short change s. o. v.   bung ot

short cut n.   ploe kaat; ploe vee'ung

short of adj.   lacking, deficient in -- k'vah (AP: k'wah): The farther they get (i.e., come in) from the border, {the more} they are short of [supplies]. -- Jchum'ngai chng'eye dael pooh'gkay mok pi tul'dyne, pooh'gkay nung k'vah [sabee'ung] {rut tai ch'raan}.; k'vah... um'va: We could be one or two, or zero, men "short." -- Yeung adje k'vah moi roo pi, roo ot um'va.

shortage n.   k'vah (AP: k'wah): In this province there is a shortage of good doctors. -- Kyte ni k'vah kruu'peyt daw poo'k'eye.; There is a shortage of good teachers. -- Miun k'vah kruu'bung'rian daw jchum'nan.; k'vah kaat: food shortage -- k'vah kaat ma'hope

shortcut n.   ploe kaat

shot pp./adj.   He was shot with his own gun.-- Gwat tro kro'up dow'ee kum'pleung p'twal kloo'an.; big shot -- neh thum: He thinks he's a big shot. -- Gwat kut tha gwat chia neh thum.

should v.   should, have to, with connotation of optional act, ought to -- koo'a tai; or, tro: The government should fix the roads. -- Ratt'a'pi'bal koo'a tai chooh chul ploe.; Should we (do we have to) give them money? -- Tau(v) yeung tro owi loi teuh neh nung, tay?; (NB: English have to, need to or must with connotation of mandatory act would in Khmer be "tro tai"); judgmentally should or ought -- koo'a: You should not go. -- Neh mun koo'a teuh.

shoulder n. smaa

shout n. kaa sr'eye'k

shout v. sr'eye'k

shovel n. peye'l; jchawb; jchawb ti

show n. kaa bung hanyh: a dance show -- kaa bung hanyh ro'bohm; manifestation of s. th., as in "a show of force", a "show of affection" -- kaa sum dye'ng

show v. bung hanyh: Please show me the way (the road). -- Sum bung hanyh ploe kyom.; prap (lit: tell): Please show me how to do it. -- Sum prap kyom tha tveu yang na.

shower n. s. th. to get clean -- ngoo' tuk; moi (written moi(ch)) tuk; short rainfall -- plee'eng srec srec

shower v. take a shower -- moi tuk

showy adj. h'uu haa: I think clothes like that are a little showy. -- Kyom kut tha kow-aow doj chia nu (AP: ch'nu) h'uu haa baan tic hi'. (NB: hi' is AP for howi)

shrapnel n. kum'tic kraw: He was hit by a piece of shrapnel. -- Gwat tro baan veea dow'ee kum'tic kraw.; (NB: "tro" in this use indicates the passive voice; see, similarly, under "shot": "He was shot..." = "Gwat tro kro'up...")

shrimp n. fresh water shrimp (small in size) -- kraw'peu(s); salt water shrimp (larger in size) -- bung keea; prawns (large, with tail) -- bung kaaw (also means lobster); dried shrimp (large) -- bung keea kree'um

shy adj. ee'en; embarrassed -- k'mah

shut adj. baan butt

shut v. butt: Shut the door. -- Butt t'veea.

Shut up! excl. Butt mwot!

sick adj. chh'ooh: stomach ache -- chh'ooh poo'ah; get sick -- t'lch kloo'an chh'ooh

sick and tired (of) adj. tunyh tro'ang (nung)

side n. directional location -- pyke kang; kang; or, pyke: Stay on this side of the road. -- Noeh pyke kang ni ney ploe.; on that side of the house -- noeh kang nu ptay'a; over there, on that side of the village -- pyke nu ney phum; face or exposed surface of an object -- ch'rung lok: A Cube has six sides. -- Duhm miun prum'moi ch'rung.; team, position, faction etc. -- krum; or kang: I hope that side wins. -- Kyom sung'khum tha krum nu nung ch'neh.; [Whose] side are you on? -- Tau(v) kang [neh na] neh eiyne jchole jchet?

sign n. display, advertisement, etc. -- generally -- plaa (fr. Fr. "placard") or sen'ya; poster -- roob'peap bung hanyh; notice -- bun praw'kas; indication, signal -- sen'ya

sign v. seen'yaye (fr. the Fr. "signer"); jchoh hah'tah'lay'kaa

signal n. se'no (fr. Fr.); turn signal -- se'no bawt

silent adj. sngyee'im sng'at

silver adj. or n. praa(k); spo'an saw

sin n. om'peuh baap: You have to [pay for] your sins. -- Tro tai [song noeh] om'peuh baap.

since adv. time -- jchaap tang pi; tang tai pi: I have not been to Po'sat since a year ago April. -- Kyom ot baan teuh Po'sat tang tai pi kye Me'sa chh'nam teuh.; because of the fact that -- bee'proo'a; tang tai pi: ... because you did not come on time... -- ... tang tai pi neh ot mok twon peyr...

sincere adj. sm'oh; tro(ng)

sing v. jch'ree'ung;(NB: song = jchum'rec'ung; or, bawd; hence: I would like her to sing this song. -- Kyom sum owi nee'eng jch'ree'ung jch'um'ree'ung ni.; or, Kyom sum owi nee'eng jch'ree'ung bawd ni.)

singer n. neh jchum'ree'ung (APs: neh jchum'rec'eng)

singing n. kaa jchree'ung

single adj. unmarried -- noeh liv: Is she single? -- Tau(v) nee'eng noeh liv tay?; never married -- kra'mom (also connotes "virgin"; explicitly virgin = kra'mom prum'ja'rye); one only -- tai moi kut; tai moi: We have a single telephone. -- Yeung miun to'ra'sap tai moi.

sink n. kitchen or bathroom sink -- basin tuk

sink v. lic; (NB: same word as in "kang lic", "west", i.e., the direction where the sun "sinks")

sinner n. neh miun baap

sir n. lok; (also, if addressed to a man, is respectful form of "you")

sister n. bong own sraae: How many sisters do you have? -- Bong own sraae pu'man neh?; older sister -- bong sraae; younger sister -- p'own sraae; sister-in-law -- bong tl'eye sraae

sit, sit down v. ung'koi: Please sit down. -- Un'cheunyh ung'koi.; to sit in or on s. th. -- koi leuh s. th.: Please sit in that chair. -- Cheunyh koi leuh kaeo'eye nu.; We told him to sit on a rice sack. -- Yeung pra veea koi leuh bauw ung'kaw.; stay in a place -- thuum: The animal sat (stayed) in the tree. -- Saat thuum leuh daum cheu.

situation n. s'tan'kaa: a difficult situation -- s'tan'kaa lum'bah; s'ta'na'pheap (AP: tana'pheap); in sense of problem or case -- ru'ung (same word as "story"); pheap; sak'pheap: Sak'pheap ni mun la'aw tay. -- This is not a good situation.

six adj. prum'moi; (condensed AP: pra'moi)

sixty n. hok'sup; sixty-eight -- hok'sup prum'bye

size n. generally -- toom huum: What size is your office? -- Kaa'ri'lye neh toom huum pu'man?; re people or things being compared -- mee'ut: Those men are the same size. -- Mee'ut gwat pun ka'neea. (NB: pun ka'neea lit. = equal); Cambodia is almost the same size as Burma. -- Mee'ut Kampuchea praw'heil ka'neea nung mee'ut Poo'mia. (NB: ka'neea nung = equal); re items whose sizes can be expressed by a number -- layke (AP: lay, lit: number): What size shoes do you wear? -- Neh peh s'bye'k cheung layke pu'man?

sketch n. s'kd'eye pri'ieng

sketch v. pri'ieng; kooh: draw or sketch a picture -- kooh kum'noo

skill n. kaa pun praw'sawb

skilled, skillful adj. generally -- pun praw'sawb; good at s. th. -- poo'k'eye; specialized in s. th. -- jchum'nan; or, chuum'nee'inyh; a skilled worker or specialist -- chee'ung... jchum'nan: a Porsche specialist -- chee'ung Porsche jchum'nan

skin n. s'bye'k

skinny adj. scoe'm

skip v. jump over -- ruhm'long (AP: mu'long): skip or jump over a ditch -- ruhm'long pro'lye; omit, not do -- ruhm long; or, jchun'lawh: I skipped some pages. -- Kyom ruhm'long tum'poa klaah klaah.; or, Kyom meuhl s'po jchun'lawh jchun'lawh.; miss an appointment -- baan chia... ot: Why did you skip the meeting yesterday? -- Hyte eye baan chia neh ot pra'choom musl'munyh?

skirt n. sum'pot

skull n. lo lee'a; k'bal

sky n. meyk: cloudy sky -- meyk ngo ngut; clear sky -- meyk sraw'la; in the sky -- noeh leuh meyk

slam v. hit hard against -- buhk: The car slammed into the wall. -- Laan buhk chuun chee'ung.; The cars slammed into each other. -- Laan buhk ka'neea.; slam s. o. or s. th. with a fist -- dawl; or thwaap: He slammed the wall (with his fist). -- Gwat thwaap chuun chee'ung.

slander v. ni'yaye bung ko'itch; ni'yaye daum

slang adj. jchum awh; tee'uo tauk; ch'leu'ee: a slang word -- peea jchum awh

slang n. the body of "slang" words as a group -- pee'esa jchum awh; pee'esa tee'up tauk; or, pee'esa ch'leu'ee; particularly crude slang -- pee'a bot p'sa (lit: bottom of the market, i. e., talk like the lowest people in the market): Don't (talk like those) low (people in the) market. -- Kum ni'yaye bot p'sa peyk.

slap v. vye; teh; slap in the face -- teh cum'plec'an

slave n. k'yon kum'dawh; k'yom kun chee'eh; tee's'kaw

slavery n. tee s'pheap

sleazy adj. kum'rooh: a sleazy person -- ma'nooh kum'rooh

sleep n. most common -- geyng; or kaa geyng: I need sleep. -- Kyom tra kaa geyng.; or, Kyom tro teuh geyng.; more casual -- daeyk; or kaa daeyk: I had only five hours of sleep. -- Kyom miun daeyk tai prum mao kut.; respectful, to be used to elders, etc. -- sum'raan: Did you have enough sleep? -- Lok sum'raan ch'eyte tay?

sleep v.   geyng; or daeyk: She is sleeping. or, She is [already] sleeping. -- Veea geyng [looh howi].; go to sleep -- teuh geyng; or, teuh daeyk; They went to sleep early. -- Pooh'gkay teuh geyng pi pro'lup; Go to sleep! -- Daeyk teuh!; They've already gone to sleep. -- Gkay teuh daeyk howi. (NB: wake up = pn'yoh pi goyng; get up = krau pi geyng; early a. m. = pro'lum; early p. m. = pro'lup; late = yeut: Early to bed, early to rise... -- Teuh daeyk pro'lup, krau pi geyng pro'lum...); sum'raan: Did you sleep well? -- Lok sum'raan sroul tay?

sleep with s.o. v.   sexual connotaion -- teuh daeyk chi'moi + appropriate context

sleeping adj.   daeyk looh

sleepy adj.   ngoi geyng; ngoi daeyk; ngaw ngoi: Are you sleepy? -- Neah ngaw ngoi geyng tay? or, Tau(v) ngoi daeyk noeh?; I'm sleepy. -- Kyom ngo ngoi daeyk.; or Kyom ngo ngoi geyng.

sleeve n.   dai (lit.: arm); short sleeves -- dai klai

slender adj.   scoe'm

slice n.   for baked goods or fruit -- chuum'nut; a slice of bread -- num pahng moi chuum'nut; a slice of pineapple -- mu'noo'a(s) moi chuum'nut; for meat -- bun taae'a; a slice of ham -- sat(ch) ch'roook moi bun taae'a; (NB: bun taae'a can also be used re bread)

slice v.   chut; hahn chum'nut (lit: to cut into slices)

slide v.   ro'ul: The truck went off the road and slid down the mountain. -- Rot yun jchenyh pi ploe howi ro'ul jchoh pi phnom.; ruum'ul: slide on the ice -- ruum'ul leuh t'kaw; slide in the snow -- ruum'ul leuh preu(l); luhm'ul; (NB: ro'ul, ruum'ul, and luhm 'ul and all close in meaning and usage.); slide downhill, get worse -- t'leh jchoh: The economy of the country is sliding downhill. -- Set'a'kej praw'tet t'leh jchoh.

slightly adv.   baan tic

slime n.   sl'eye (algae material found in ponds ("bung"), rivers ("tun'lay"), etc.)

sling-shot n.   colloquial -- pee'um; (full term = chum'pee'um kaow'soo)

slink v.   walk seductively -- dah kach rian

slip v.   ro'ul

slip of the tounge n.   ro'bo(t) mwot (lit: mistake of mouth): Excuse me, that was a just a slip of the tounge! -- Sum to kyom ro'bo(t) mwot.

slippery adj.   paaw pet paaw peut(ch): In rainy season parts of [Highway 69] are muddy and very slippery. -- Noeh ro'doe plee'eng pich klaah ney [ploe layke hok'sup prum'buon] miun phoo'(a) ch'raan howi nung paaw pet paaw peut(ch) nah!

sliver n.   chum'ngut

slope n.   jchum'nowt

sloppy adj.   lawt

slow adj.   not fast -- yeut (AP: yoo'): a slow train -- ro'teh pleung yeut; not fast -- sum'puk: Don't be so slow! [Hurry up!] -- Kum sum'puk peyk! [Roh roo'an laung!]; colloquialism: (You're so slow) You seem like you're [counting grass]! -- (   ) Neh ciyne dael doj [ro'up smauu]!; not intelligent -- l'ngo'ng

slowly adv.   yang yeut yeut; yeut yeut; muiy muiy; meuuk meuuk

Slow down v.   bong ong or bong toi; reduce speed -- bong ong la'beu'an; bong toi la'beu'an

sly adj.   leh lee'em; loo'it(ch) leh

small adj.   to'ich (AP: tow'ich, ta'wich, to'wee, tuuw(ch), toe'ch, etc.); la'ut la'ut: small pieces -- kum'tic la'ut la'ut; insect -- saat la'ut; klai

smart adj.   ch'laat; praw'ngya

smash v.   destroy -- bum byke: smash the window -- bum byke bung'oo'it; smash the enemy -- bum byke sa'tro; throw down and smash -- bauwk; (colloquial expression/threat) smash s. o. like a frog -- bauwk doj kong'kype; (NB the difference between "smash" and "break": He smashed it on the ground and it broke. -- Gwat bauwk veea nung daiy howi veea bahk.)

smell n.   klen: bad smell -- klen sa'oi; or, klen a'krah

smell v. smell s. th. -- thum klen: I can smell the food they are cooking. -- Kyom thum klen ma'hope dael pooh'gkay kom'puung chum'un.; klen... sye mok doll: I could smell your [perfume]. -- Klen [tuk op] neh sye mok doll kyom.; have a smell, smell like -- klen: The food smells delicious. -- Ma'hope klen chng'anyh.; thum klen: It smelled like oil. -- A nung thum klen doj praeng.

smelt n. trei jchong'vaa

smile n. kaa nyo nyim

smile v. nyim; nyo nyim

smoke n. ps'eye'n

smoke v. choohk; smoke a cigarette -- choohk ba'r'eye

smoking n. kaa choohk ba'r'eye

smooth adj. raw'leeng

smuggle v. rut puun; rut gkoi

snack n. jchum'naee jchum'nuk

snail n. k'chong

snake n. poo'ah

snare n. un'tay'k

snare v. tay'k: snare an elephant -- tay'k dum'rei

snatch v. jchaap gkun chaaw: He snatched money from that [old woman]. -- Gwat jchaap gkun chaaw loi pi [sa'trei jchaah] nu.

sneak v. loo'it: sneak in -- loo'it jchole; sneak out -- loo'it jchenyh

sneakily adv. lope lope

sneaky adj. miun poo't

sneeze v. kun'dah

sniff v. k'seuht: to sniff glue -- k'seuht kaow

snipe v. ch'mawh

sniper n. neh loo'ich banyh

snore v. sraw'muk

snotty adj. "stuck up" -- kahtch rian

snow n. preu(l)

so adv. to such an extent -- peyk (AP: pay'): Because he drove so slowly, [we arrived late]. -- Mok pi gwat baahk yeut peyk, [baan chia yeung teuh mun twon peyr] (lit: not on time).; He drives so slowly. -- Gwat baahk yeut peyk.; Don't be so bad! -- Kum mok kaa peyk!; Don't be so weird! -- Kum pleuh pleuh peyk!; Don't be so angry! -- Kum khung peyk!; therefore, consequently -- doj cha'neh (AP: doj ch'nye); He wanted to get to France quickly, so he had to take a plane. -- Gwat jchong teuh sruk Ba'raang chhop ro'has, doj cha'neh gwat tro jchi yun'hawh.; similarly, "likewise", "egualmente", "same with me" -- kaw un'cheunyh da'aae: Mr. A.: I have a head ache. Mr. B.: So do I. -- Mr. A.: Kyom chh'ooh k'bal nah. Mr. B.: Kyom kaw un'cheunyh da'aae.; to such an extent -- ma'leh (AP: m'eh); Why are you so crazy? -- Mutch kaw ch'coo'it ma'leh?; Why are you so grumpy? -- Mek (AP for mutch) baan mok 'chooo ma'leh?; Why was he so careless? -- Hyte eye baan chia gwat praw'heh ma'leh?; tha un'cheunyh: Someone told me so. -- Miun gkay pra kyom tha un'cheunyh.

So long! xcl. good bye -- Lee'a hi!; or, Lee'a sun hi!

so many (that) adv. ch'raan doj ch'neh: They have so many weapons that... -- Pooh'gkay miun a'vwut ch'raan doj ch'neh...; chia ch'raan dael: They have cut so many trees that now there are no more. -- Kaat daum cheu chia ch'raan dael eye'leaou ot miun tee'it.

so much adv. peyk howi: We miss them so much. -- Yeung nukh gkay peyk howi.

so, so adv. more or less OK (re a person) -- sok s'bai tic tic; as usual, same as always -- twa'ma'da; not good, not bad (re a thing) -- mut s'yum; "fifty/fifty" -- ha'sup, ha'sup

so that adv. baan chia: The car was fixed so that it would run well. -- Laan chooh chul roo'it baan chia veea rut la'aw.; teup adje: We fixed it so that it would work. -- Yeung chooh chul veea teup adje pra kaa kaut.

So what? (or !) adj. Mutch chaw?

soak v. traahm: soak clothes -- traahm kow-aow

soap n. sa'boo

soar v. plong; rockets soared -- rocket plong; (NB, also: birds fly -- saat haah; airplanes fly -- yun hawh hawh; note difference in pronunciation between "haah" and "hawh.")

sob v. cry -- yuum; sob noisily -- yuum law'uk; shed tears quietly -- k'suk sup

soccer n. bal toat; to play soccer -- toat bal (toat = kick)

sociable adj. jchole jchet jchole ru'um nung sum'kuum; jchole jchet jchole ro'bee'up (lit: likes to join in)

social affairs n. sung'kuum kej

socialism n. sung'kuum ni'yuum

socialist adj. sung'kuum ni'yuum

socialist n. neh sung'kuum ni'yuum (lit: sympathetic to society); socialist regime -- lok'bit sung'kuum ni'yuum

society n. sung'kuum

sociologist n. sung'kuum vi'too; neh sung'kuum

socks n. sr'auwm cheung

sod n. baeou

sofa n. salon

soft adj. tuun (expresses both "not hard" and "weak"): a soft pillow -- knauwi tuun; a soft voice -- sum laeng tuun; re sound -- tic; tuun pluhn; soft-hearted -- jchet tuun; jchet mun dach: He who is soft-hearted will never be king. -- Jchet mun dach tveu s'dach mun baan. (proverb)

soften v. bun tuun

softly adv. tic; tic tic; She speaks softly. -- Gwat ni'yaye tic.; tuun pluhn: Speak softly but carry a big stick. -- Ni'yaye tuun pluhn kaw pun'ta'aae kaan dum'bawng thum.

soil n. dirt -- daiy; mud -- daiy phoo'a

Sokhalay Hotel n. O'tyle 'Ka'lye (Pec'esa Sa'muun name alteration; with Monorom and Samaki, Sokhalay was among the most popular hotels in pre-UNTAC Phnom Penh)

soldier n. tee'hee'an; tee'hee'an cheung ko'k (lit.: soldier with dry feet); G.I., foot soldier, "grunt" -- pul toe tee'hee'an

sole n. of foot -- bot cheung

solid adj. taan: a solid object (not hollow) -- ro'bah taan; hard, i.e., not soft -- rung

solidarity n. sa'ma'ki'pheap; jchum'nong sa'ma'ki'pheap: There should be solidarity between the farmers and the army. -- Koo'a miun sa'ma'ki'pheap ro'vieng kah'se'ko nung yo'tee'a.

solution n. dum'naugh sr'eye; ma'choe'bye dawh sr'eye: I have the solution. -- Kyom miun ma'cho'bye dawh sr'eye.; I have the answer. -- Kyom miun jchum'la'wee.

solve v. dawh sr'eye; unravel, sort out -- dum'naugh sr'eye; solve a problem -- dawh sr'eye pun'ha

some adv. klaah: I need some paper. -- Kyom tro kaa kra'dot klaah.; klaah klaah

some day n. t'ngai na moi; Someday there will be peace. -- T'ngai na moi nung miun san'ti'pheap.

some more adv. tee'it (also means "any more"): Do you want some more rice? -- Neh jchole jchet bye tee'it tay?

someone n. neh na ma'neh: I want someone (one person, one of you, one of them) to go with me. -- Kyon jchong baan neh na ma'neh mok chi'moi kyom.; neh na: Is there someone at the door? -- Tau(v) miun neh na noeh eye t'veea tay?; ma'nooh klaah: I want someone to go with me. -- Kyom jchong baan ma'nooh klaah mok chi'moi kyom.; miun gkay: Someone said that... -- Miun gkay ni'yaye tha...

some place n. We need to find some place [private] to go. -- Yeung tro kaa sveye ro'k cunlye'ng eyke'a'chuun dum'bye teuh.

something n. kaa: I have something to do. -- Kyom miun kaa.; or, Kyom miun kaa nung tveu.; kaa klaah: Kyom miun kaa klaah nung tveu.; kej kaa klaah: They want something else. -- Gkay jchong kej kaa klaah p'sayng tee'it.; sum'dai klaah: Something he said bothered me. -- Peea sum'dai klaah gwat ni'yaye baan ruhm kaan kyom.; roo'un klaah: There's something I want to tell you. -- Miun roo'un klaah kyom jchong ni'yaye prap neh.; ro'bah klaah: ...something he ate... -- ...ro'bah klaah dael gwat nyam...; something different -- p'sayng: That means something different. -- Veea miun ney p'sayng.; aae moi: They want something [else]. -- Gkay jchong baan a'veye moi [tee'it].

sometimes adv. choo'un kaal; peyr klaah; m'dong m'dong

somewhere adv. cunlye'ng (AP: kunlyne, kunlie, ka'lye) na moi: He went somewhere [I don't know where]. -- Gwat teuh cunlye'ng na moi [dael kyom ot dung].; krau (lit: "out"): He went somewhere. -- Gwat jchenyh teuh krau. (lit: He went out.); noeh cunlye'ng p'sayng: Maybe we can't get (lit: find) this book in Phnom Penh but we can get it somewhere. -- Praw'heil chia yeung mun adje ro'k s'po ni noeh Phnom Penh, pun'ta'aae yeung adje ro'k veea noeh cunlye'ng p'sayng.; (NB: the word-for-word translation of "somewhere" would be "cunlye'ng klaah"; this, however, means "a lot of" or "a number of", different places, as: I used to go to (a lot of) different places in Cambodia. -- Kyom tra'laawp teuh leng cunlye'ng klaah noeh sruk Khmei.)

son n. gkon proh

son-in-law n. gkon praw'sa proh

song n. jchum'ree'ung; (singer = neh jch'ree'ung (APs: neh jchum'ree'ung, neh jchum'ree'eng))

soon adv. quickly -- chhop chhop; within a short time -- k'nong peyr chhop chhop ni (lit: "in a short time"); plee'um plee'um ni; as soon as possible -- chhop bom'pot

soothsay v. tee'aae

soothsayer n. kruu tee'aae

sorcerer n. kruu khmei

sore adj. chh'ooh: sore throat -- chh'ooh khaw

sorry adj. feeling apologetic -- sum to'h: I am sorry. -- Kyom sum to'h.; or, Ot to'h owi kyom pong. ("ot" = "no"; "to'h" = "punishment"; "pong" = please"; hence, literally, "Do not give me punishment, please."); pity, feel sorry for -- a'nuhk; He doesn't feel sorry for them. -- Gwat ot a'nuhk pooh'gkay tay.; We should feel sorry for them. -- Yeung koo'a tai a'nuhk pooh'gkay.; feel regret for one's own situation -- sowk s'daye

Sorry about that! xcl. Ot to'h kum praw'kaan!

sort out v. dum'naugh sr'eye

sorrow n. kaa thuk; the sorrow of separation, of being apart -- kaa thuk ney kaw pra'h praauwt

soul n. metaphysically -- pro'lung (used to refer only to persons decreased) or vig'nyee'an (may refer to persons living or dead): May his soul go [to a peaceful world]. (funeral invocation) -- Sum owi vig'nyee'an na'kan ro'bah gwat [teuh kaan soh'a'tey pope].; romantic term of address -- pro'lung (connotes "sweetheart")

sound n. sum'leng (also means "noise" and "voice"): What's that sound? -- Tau(v) chia sum'leng a'veye?; so: I [heard] the sound of the music. -- Kyom [loo] so sum'leng plaeng.; I like the sound of running water. -- Kyom jchole jchet so tuk ho.; the sound of fighting ["boom-bang!"] -- so banyh ka'neea [ka'doom ka'dung]

sound v. seem -- doj chia: His plan sounds (seems) good. -- Pyne'kaa ro'bah gwat doj chia la'aw.; or, hahk doj chia: It sounds like a bad idea. -- Hahk doj chia kum'nut mun la'aw.; strike the ear as -- sum'leng.... (adjective): That music sounds [sad]. -- Sum'leng plaeng nu [kum'sot].; He sounds angry. -- Sum'leng gwat khung.

soup n. generally, any soup with vegetables and meat (i. e., but not rice only, or curry) -- sam'law; or, sa'law (very common AP for sam'law): curry soup with chicken -- sa'law meh chooo kreung muon; non-spicy, non-salty clear soup -- tuk sam'law tlaa'; vegetable soup -- sam'law bun'lye; rice soup -- baa' baw; rice soup with shrimp or chicken -- baa' baw kreung (lit: rice soup with other "things" or "ingredients"); lemon grass soup with chicken -- scgn'au ch'roo'hk muon (AP for scgn'au = scngahw; lit: "boiled"); thin noodles with curry (usually chicken) soup, bean spouts, etc., in bowl -- excellent and widely consumed Khmer market and village-food-stall cuisine -- num bun chawk; noodle soup -- k'tio: k'tio Phnom Penh -- noodles with pork and shrimp; k'tio sa'mut -- noodles with shrimp, squid and crab; etc.; to make soup -- tveu sam'law; slaw sam'law

soup cooker n. chan'am pleung, soup made in soup cooker -- sam'law chan'am pleung

sour adj. chooo: too sour -- chooo chooo; chooo haang; sour ingredient -- meh'chooo: Don't be so sour (i. e., glum, bad-natured)! -- Kum muk chooo peyk!; Why are you so grumpy? -- Hyte a'veye baan neh muk chooo ma'leh?; Why is your face so sour? (fast colloquial) -- Mek baan muk chooo m'eh?; sour, as part of description of food -- meh'chooo; pickled -- ch'roo'hk

source n. praw'pope; reliable source -- praw'pope ch'bah kaa

south n. kang t'bong; pyke te'ak'sen

south-east adj. kang t'bong chiang kang kaut; (or) kang kaut chiang kang t'bong; (written system: pyke a'k'neea)

Southeast Asia n. Asie pyke' a'k'neea

south-west adj. kang lic chiang kang t'bong; or, kang t'bong chiang kang lic; (written system: pyke neea ruh'dye)

souvenir n. a'noo'sow'ree (AP: a'nuuk sa'va'ree); (also means memory, remembrance, and memorial)

sovereignty n. a'tep'a'dye'pheap

Soviet adj. So'vee'e'tique

Soviet Union n. Sa'ha'pheap So'vee'e'tique

sow v. sow [rice] seeds -- bawh; proo'a; sap + [sro]; sow [corn] seed; plant [corn] -- dam [po't]

soy bean n. sun dyke siang; saw'yaa; (NB: sun dyke = bean or pea; sun dyke saw = black eyed pea; sun dyke bye or kee'oo = green beans; drink made from powdered soy beans -- tuk sun dyke; bean sprouts from sun dyke kee'oo = sun dyke bun'doh)

soy sauce n. tuk si'ee'oo

space n. outer space -- a'kas; luhm hawh; space to work, to play, etc. -- cunlye'ng; space between letters, e. g., when writing or typing -- klia; Space! or, Leave a space! (said in course of dictation) -- Dah(k) klia.; [Leave] me a space (on the page), not too big . -- [Tooo'k] jchun lawh owi, thum baan tic.

space v. space a number of lines, inches, feet, etc., long -- jchum'lahw

spacecraft n. j'yee'in ow'va'ka; (j'yee'in = transportation)

spacious adj. too'lee'aae

spade n. pyle

Spanish adj. espan'; espan'yol

spareribs n. chh'ung chuum ni (ribs = chuum'ni) ch'roo'k

spare time n. peyr tum'naae

spark n. electrical or from fire -- p'kaa pleung

sparrow n. jchahb; fried sparrow -- jchahb jchian

speak v. ni'yaye; speak with -- ni'yaye chi'moi; speak with an accent -- ni'yaye ro'deun ; speak ill of s. o. -- baw(k): Why did you insult me? -- Hyte eye baw(k) kyom?; speak badly of s.o. behind his/her/etc. back, gossip -- ni'yaye daum

Speak of the devil! xcl. Nuhk daum doll!

spear n. num peyng; snaw

special adj. pi'seh (AP: pi'set): special forces -- tee'hee'an pi'seh: special guest -- pnyee'oo pi'seh; important -- sum'kahn

special action group n. kawng ch'lope (also used to refer to scouts and sappers)

specialist n. neh pah'jchaiyk'a'tay; intellectual, expert -- neh pra(ch); worker specialized in s. th. -- chee'ung... jchum'nan

species n. poo(ch); seeds (i. e., of different species) to plant next year -- kru'op poo(ch) sum'rap dam chh'nam krow'ee; animals perpetuate their species -- sat(ch) bun thaw poo(ch)

specifically adv. noeh trong

spectator n. neh meuhl; tooo's na kaa chuun (;it: person who watches s.th.)

speculate v. kayng; pro'van'g

spectre n. mirage, hallucination -- k'mau'it laung

speech n. an address -- sung'kaa'taa: interesting speech -- sung'kaa'taa yang jchaap a'ro'um; sum'lng; give a speech -- thlaeng kaa: Yesterday the minister gave a long speech. -- Musl'munyh rawt'mun'trei thlaeng kaa chia yeut.; speech as a human facility -- sum'dai; or, sum'leng

speechless adj. t'wal kum'nut (lit: without an idea)

speed n. la'beu'an

speed v. teuh leau'an

spell n. magic spell -- moun vi'chi'a; dizzy spell -- san'lop; put a spell on s. o. -- tveu um'peuh

spell v. sor'se: How do you spell it? -- Sor'se yang na?

spelling n. a'ka'ra'vi'rut

spend v. jch'eye: spend money for nothing -- jch'eye loi jchowl; jchum'nye

spices n. kreung

spicy adj. kreung; "hot" with chilies -- huhl (AP: hahl)

spider n. ping pee'ung

spike n. dyke gol

spill v. tveu owi... lee'a: He spilled the water. -- Gwat tveu owi tuk lee'a.

spin v. bong vull: spin the coin -- bung vull kaa(k); ro'vieng; cut'vull: [He had an accident] when his car spun. -- [Gwat miun kroo'ti'nak] noeh k'nong rot'yun dow'ee sa laan cut'vull.

spinach n. p'tee ba'raang

spine n. cha'ung knawng

spiral v. spiral upwards -- koo'it(ch)

spirit n. soul or spirit of deceased person, in non-threatening sense -- vi'gnyee'an leh kan: the spirit of my dead uncle -- vi'gnyee'an leh kan ro'bah poo kyom; ghost, generally used with somewhat threatening or frightening connotation -- k'mau'it (also means corpse); soul (generally used re person deceased or in imminent danger of being so) -- pro'lung; spirit medium -- roop ara' (NB: ara' = similar to "genie in a bottle'" i. e., a spirit that can be called forth at the will of the "roop ara.")

spit v. s'dawh; spit on -- s'dawh dah(k): People spat in Khicu Samphan's face when he came to Phnom Penh. -- Pra'chee'chuun mok chia s'dawh tuk mwot dah(k) muk Khieu Samphan peyr gwat baan mok Phnom Penh.

spite prp. in spite of -- too'a chia... yang na kaw dow'ee; They went to the village yesterday in spite of the danger. -- Pi musl'munyh pooh'gkay teuh phum too'a chia miun kroo'ti'nak yang na kaw dow'ee.; We want to go to Siem Riep [by car on Route 6] in spite of [the hazards]. -- Yeung jchong teuh Siem Riep [dow'ee laan taam ploe chia layke prum'moi] too'a chia [aw'pa'sa] yang na kaw dow'ee.

splash v. tveu owi... k'chai: The children splashed water. -- Gkon k'mayng tveu owi tuk k'chai.

split v. split wood -- poo'h cheu; (NB: to cut trees = kaat daum cheu, to "part" trees to clear the way = n'yaek daum cheu); split up, divide -- jchaiyk: The family was split up. -- Kroo'e'sa jchaiyk ru'um layke.; split up money -- jchaiyk loi; split up, i. e., take different roads/paths from one another -- jchaiyk ploe ka'neea; divide into categories, sections, conceptual parts -- bye'ng; bye'ng jchaiyk; split up, end a relationship -- byke ka'neea

spoil v. spoil s. o. -- tum reuh: You shouldn't spoil your [niece] [like that]. -- Neh mun tro tum'reuh [ka'moo'i sraae] neh [un'cheunyh] tay.

spoiled adj. re crops, produce, etc. -- ro'loo'ee; spoiled food -- ma'hope ro'loo'ee; spoiled vegetables -- bun'lye ro'loo'ee; spoiled fruit -- plai'cheu ro'loo'ee; re prepared (i.e., cooked) food -- p'o'm; (NB: ko'itch, sometimes given as a translation of "spoiled," generally means "evil/bad," as in "ma'nooh ko'itch," "a bad man," or "dead," as in "Yaye kut ko'itch howi," "The old woman is dead" or "ma'nooh ko'itch" which can also mean "a dead man."); re people -- baan jchet or baan dye; The child is very spoiled. -- Gkon k'mayng baan jchet nah.

spokesman n. ka'na'ta ma'ti'ka (lit: one who speaks from a platform)

sponsor v. tee'a'nee'a. The Catholic Church sponsored many families [to come (and stay)] in America. -- Sa'sna Ca'to'lic tee'a'nee'a kroo'esa ch'raan [mok noeh chi'moi ay] sruk Am'rik.

sports n. kay'la

spot n. praw'la: spots on my shirt -- praw'la noeh leuh aow; My shirt has a spot on it. -- Aow kyom praw'la.; many small spots -- a'rroy (lit: fly feces, fly specks); larger spot -- praw' ch'rroy; spot, mark or scar -- sn'aam: My shirt has a spot (mark) on it. -- Aow kyom sn'aam.

sponsor n. neh tum nuuk bum raung

spoon n. preea; slop preea

sprain v. krae'k: sprained leg, neck, arm -- kraek cheung; kraek khaw; kraek dai: He has a sprained leg. -- Gwat kraek cheung.

spray v. banyh; spray water -- banyh tuk; (also means "fire" or "shooting" as in "banyh kum pleung" -- "gunfire" or "fire a gun" -- and "banyh kum chroo'ik" -- "[shooting off] fire- works."); spray water from one's mouth (techinique used in ironing clothes if no spray bottle is available) -- proo'a

spread v. disseminate itself to, go to -- miun p'sup p'sye: The English language has spread to all parts of the world. -- Pee'esa Anglais miun p'sup p'sye penyh k'nong pi pope'lok.; The rumor spread. -- Peea jcham a'ram ri'yaye doll.; p'sye: The [smell of the] perfume spread [throughout] the room. -- Tuk op p'sye [penyh k'nong] ban'tope.; disseminate, broadcast, issue s. th. -- p'sye saa: Radio and television spread the news. -- Vi'choo nung too'ra'too'ah p'sye saa por'da'mee'an.; scatter -- proo'a: spread rice seed -- proo'a sro; scatter -- ri'yaye; spread s. th. on s. th. -- vay't

spreading adj. ree'up daal: The war is spreading. -- Song'kree'um ree'up daal.

spring n. months in Cambodia with not-yet-too-hot weather comparable to "spring" climate in United States and Europe are those which follow the monsoon months of June-September; they include October through January and are called collectively ro'doe ruhm howi; spring in cushion, car, etc. -- ruh'saw (or) dyke loo'a lau'ght (dyke = metal, lau'ght = to jump); spring that produces water -- ch'roo'h: ... the spring at Bo'ko... -- ... ch'roo'h noeh Bo'ko... ; (NB: The village of Phum Bo'ko in Kom'puung Speu is the site of one of the better-known springs in Cambodia.); spring water -- tuk ch'roo'h

spring v. lote: the tiger sprang -- satch klaa lote

sprinkle v. s'row'eet; We need to sprinkle water on the flowers today. -- T'ngai ni yeung tro kaa s'row'eet tuk leuh p'ka.

sprout v. baan'dos; The seeds have sprouted. -- Kro'up baan'dos howi.; bean sprouts -- sun'dyke baan'dos (lit: sprouted beans)

spy n. neh seup kaa (seup = find out s. th. secretly); neh ch'lawb; neh yok kaa sum'ngut: He is a spy. -- Gwat ch'lawb.

spy v. generally -- ch'lawb meuhl; ch'lawb: He spies on me. -- Gwat ch'lawb meuhl kyom.; He spies [for] the government of Thailand. -- Gwat ch'lawb [owi] ratti'pi'bal See'um.; yok kaa; seup on'khet (seup = secretly try to find s. th.; on'khet = inspect)

spyglasses n. kaae'ooo yeut

squander v. k'chee'a k'ch'aae; (AP: k'cheh k'chee'a): He squandered his money on Khmer food! -- Gwat chai loi k'cheh k'chee'a noeh leuh ma'hope Khmei.

square n. kraw'la (buon ch'rung sm'auu) (lit: square with four [buon] equal [sm'auu] sides [ch'rung])

square adj. buon ch'rung sm'auu: a square sign -- [sun'ya] buon ch'rung smauu; ri'ung buon ch'rung: These mirrors are square-shaped. -- Kun'chuhh(k) ni ri'ung buon ch'rung sm'auu.; a square table -- tohk buon ch'rung sm'auu; square meter -- met' ca'raae (fr. the Fr. "carre")

squash n. vegetable: long, ridge-skinned variety -- ruu no'ng; smooth-skinned variety -- ta'ka(ch)

squash v. song'kat

squeeze v. with hands -- cha'ra' batch; squeeze lemons -- cha'ra' batch krau'itch ch'mah; (also "cha'ra' batch" are oranges -- krau'itch po'sat -- and grapefruit -- krau'itch t'long); between two pieces of s. th. -- kee'up; We have to squeeze the sugar cane today. -- Yeung tro kaa kee'up am'peau t'ngai ni.; squeeze together -- praw cha'ree'ot ka'neea; squeeze very hard -- kee'up song'kat; squeeze s. th. into a space -- praw'chree'ut; squeeze politically or financially -- kee'up

squid n. meuk

squint-eyed adj. pn'aae'k prium prium

stab v. jchak: stab with a knife -- jchak chi'moi kum'but: Don't stab him! -- Kum jchak veea!

stable n. krow'r

stable adj. nung noeh; reung pung; mun plas pdo; The government is stable. -- Ratt'a'pi'bal nung noeh.

stack n. choo'ung; a stack of dishes -- jchaan choo'ung; ro'bach

stadium n. cunlye'ng leng kay'la; stahd; the Olympic Stadium in Phnom Penh -- Stahd Olympic noeh k'nong Phnom Penh

staff n. private staff -- neh chuum n'ehtt; staff of an establishment -- neh tveu kaa; the staff of the Foreign Ministry -- neh tveu kaa Kra'soo'ung Kaa Bor'tay

stage n. phase -- chuum'no'un; t'nak; at this stage... -- dom'nak ni... ; stage in or of a process -- ta'la'tay'saak: This plan has three stages. -- Pyne'kaa ni miun ta'la'tay'saak bye.; of theatre -- chaa(k): on stage -- leuh chaa(k); theatrical stage, formal term -- ve'ti'kaa

stagger v. dah trei(t) tro(t) (lit: walk unevenly); [drunks] stagger -- [ma'nooh sro'vung] dah trei(t) tro(t); or, [neh praw'muk] dah trei(t) tro(t)

stagnant adj. dirty -- kra'kwah; smelly -- sa'oi: Stagnant water causes mosquitoes. -- Tuk kra'kwah bun doll owi miun moo'. **stain** n. praw'lak; a stain on clothes -- praw'lak noeh leuh kow-aow

stain v. praw'lak cho'up; praw'lak: If you [knock over] your coffee, you will stain [your skirt]. -- Baa neh [tveu owi kraw'puub] cafe neh, neh nung tveu owi praw'lak [sum'put neh].;

stair, staircase, stairway n. chan'dal; step of a stair -- kam chan'dal

stale adj. pa'ome; stale bread -- num pahng pa'ome: Some restaurants serve stale food. -- Poch'ni'tan klaah tveu ma'hope pa'ome owi.

stalk n. daum (APs: dow'm, dam, dum, dome; also means "trunk" in "daum cheu", tree trunk, and "stem" in "daum p'ka", stem of a flower); stalk of suger cane -- daum am'peau

stall v. bun yee'a peyr: They were just stalling us. -- Gkay kron tai bun'yee'a peyr yeung.

stalled adj. (re bus, car, etc.) ro'luht;

stamp n. for a letter -- pry'su'naae; or, tim(bre) or 'ta'em (both fr. Fr.); for a document -- bawh tra

stamp v. stamp one's foot -- sun trum cheung; stamp or mark s. th. -- vi'yaye tra: stamp a log or tree (i.e., with metal plaque, a step in the logging process in Cambodia by which trees eligible for cutting and logs eligible for removal from the cut area (or "coupe") can be identified; routinely flauted by both foreign and domestic logging companies) -- vi'yaye tra cheu

stand v. choh: stand in line -- choh bun taiw ka'neea; stand in the way -- pe'ang ploe: The women stood in the way and would not let them pass. -- Sraae pe'ang ploe' mun owi gkay teuh roo'it.; stand up -- krau choh: Please stand up. -- Sum krau choh.; have -- miun: You stand [a better chance than] I. -- Neh miun [pree'up chiang] kyom.; abide, accept, tolerate -- tro'um chi'moi: I can't stand ["Heavy Metal"]! -- Kyom mun adje tro'um chi'moi sum'leng plaeng [heh'vi me'tull]!

standard n. (i. e., units of measurement) kum rut; standard of living -- kum rut chi'vu'pheap

standing n. class, social standing -- t'nak

star n. in the sky -- da'ra; p'k'eye; movie star -- da'ra pheap'yun; leading characters in a film -- too'a eyke gkun

stare at v. sum'lung (AP: sum'laah); Why does he stare at her? -- Gwat hyte eye sum'lung nee'eng?

start v. jchaap p'daum: I started studying [one month ago]. -- Kyom jchaap p'daum rian [moi kye kum'lung howi].; The rain started [last month]. -- Plee'eng jchaap p'daum [pi kye muun].; start a business -- jchaap p'daum raw'see; start a fight -- ro'k ru'ung (lit: look for trouble); start a fire -- dut (or, baan kat) pleung; start an engine -- banyh chheh: Hurry up and start the car! -- Leu'an laung (or chhop laung) banyh chheh ma'cheen!; start school -- jchole rian; jchaap p'daum rian

startle v. pn'yeh

startled adj. p'auwl; pn'yeh p'auwl

starvation n. kaa ot bye

starve v. ot bye; People are starving in Po'sat. -- Pra'chee'chuun kom'puung tai ot bye noeh Po'sat.

state n. praw'tet; ratt (AP: rawt): The state of Cambodia -- Praw'tet Khmei; Ratt Khmei; in sense of "country" -- sruk; Cambodia and Laos -- sruk Khmei howi nung sruk Lao'; in sense of nation -- n'ko: We must protect the Khmer state/nation. -- Yeung tro tai kaa'pee'a n'ko Khmei.

state v. say -- taa: He stated that... -- Gwat taa... ; prap (lit: tell): Please state your name. -- Jcho(r) prap chamoo'h neh.; formally state -- tlye'ng: The minister stated that [all the other members of the government] had stolen money but not him. -- Ratt'mun'trei tlye'ng tha [kroop sa'ma'chik ratt'a'pi'bal daw tay] pu'ka'ra loi pun'ta'aae ot gwat.

state of affairs n. s'ta'na'pheap

statement n. official declaration -- kaa tlye'ng

static adj. not moving -- nung

static n. on a phone line or radio -- so mun ch'bah (lit: unclear sound)

station n. generally -- s'ta'nee (PS: 'ta'ni); railroad -- s'ta'nee rot pleung; jchum'naut: bus station -- jchum'naut rot'yun; jchum'naut bus; jchum'naut laan ch'nool; cyclo stand -- jchum'naut cyclo; beyn: taxi stand -- beyn taxi; beyn laan; radio station: transmitter/ office location -- s'ta'nee vi'choo; frequency on dial -- pahw; electric power station -- may pleung

station v. to station s. o. -- praw'jcham kaa: We will station them in Po'sat. -- Yeung nung praw'cham kaa gkay noeh Po'sat.; to be stationed -- tro dah(k)... praw'jcham kaa: He was stationed in Po'sat. -- Gwat tro baan dah(k) praw'jcham kaa noeh Po'sat.

stationary adj. noeh nung

statistics n. sa'tay'tek (AP: sa'te(k)'tch')

statue n. roob jchum'lak; statue of Buddha -- preah poot'te' roob

status n. t'nak (AP: t'nok, ta'nak); to have the status of s. th. -- miun t'nak chia; good social status, status in society -- ka'boo'an muk: To have status in society, one must be honest (lit: do honestly). -- Dum'bye owi ka'boo'an muk, tro tveu trung tro.; status, prestige -- t'nak ka'boo'an: Does he have (much) status in the government? -- Tau(v) gwat miun t'nak ka'boo'an k'nong ratt'a'pi'bal?

stay v. generally -- noeh: Stay [on this side] of the road. -- Noeh [pyke kang ni] ney ploe.; rooh noeh (usage essentially same as "noeh"); stay the same -- noeh d'dael: Some people want [Khmer society] to stay as it is. -- Pra'chee'chuun klaah jchole jchet tooo'k [sung'kuum Khmei] noeh d'dael.; stay on a temporary basis, as would tourists, visitors, encamped troops, etc. -- snak... noeh: [Those tourists] will stay at the Monorom (Hotel). -- [Neh too'snak nu] nung snak noeh Mo'no'ram.; take a break, rest -- sum'raak: She stayed under a tree [during the storm]. -- Nee'eng sum'raak noeh krowm m'lok cheu [noeh peyr k'shaal p'chooh].

steadily adv. ro'hote; work steadily -- tveu kaa ro'hote

steak n. sat(ch) gko

steal v. loo'ich: Someone stole my bike. -- Gkay loo'ich kong kyom.; grab and run -- jchak: steal money -- jchak loi; steal a glance at, peek at -- loo'ich meuhl

steam n. jchuum hoi

steel n. dyke; dyke type

steer v. bawt jchung ko't

steering wheel n. jchung ko't

stem n. daum; stem of a flower -- daum p'ka; (NB: also means "trunk" in "daum cheu", tree trunk, and "stalk" in "daum am'peau", stalk of suger cane)

step n. a step with the feet -- chuum'hee'an: Take two steps backward. -- Bawh pi chuum'hee'an teuh krowee; of a stair, ladder, etc. -- kam chan'dal; (NB: see, also, "steps")

step v. take a step -- bawh chuum'hee'ang: Step outside. -- Bawh chuum'hee'ang teuh krau.; step on, put one's foot onto -- cho'un leuh: step on a snake -- cho'un leuh poo'ah; step on, trample, abuse -- bum pee'a bum pee'an: The rich step on the poor. -- Neh miun bum pee'a bum pee'an neh kraw.; Step aside. -- Teuh moi chuum'hee'an.

step-mother n. m'dye jchong

steps n. taken together as a stair -- chan'dal; an individual step -- kam chan'dal; measures, action -- vi'te'an'akar; take steps to (accomplish s. th.) -- chaht vi'te'an'akar dum'bye

sterilization n. vi'ti sum'lap may'rohk (lit: way to/ kill/ germs)

stick n. club, stick to hit with -- dum'bawng; praw'nung

stick v. glue, attach -- butt: stick the paper on the wall -- butt kra'dah noeh leuh chuun'chee'ung

stick out v. dah(k): stick, put, extend a hand out -- dah(k) dai jchenyh krau

sticky adj. su'utt

stiff adj. rung pung

stiffen v. tveu owi rung

still adv. noeh: We still have [ten kilometers] to go. -- Yeung noeh [dop 'lo] tee'it dael tro teuh.; noeh tai (AP: ta'ee): This is still Kandal. -- A ni noeh tai Kan'dal.; noeh low'ee (AP: laaw'ee): There is still 70% to go. -- Miun jchet'sup pi roi tro tveu noeh low'ee.; We still have ten days to go. -- Yung miun dap t'ngai tee'it noeh low'ee.; He's still here. -- Gwat noeh ti ni noeh lowee.; noeh miun... d'dael: The Khmer Rouge are still in power. -- Khmei Kra'hom noeh miun um'natch d'dael.; rooh riun: He's still alive. -- Rooh riun miun chi'vut.; still not (done s. th.) -- howi noeh... mun... tee'it: [Even now] he has still not come. -- [Sm'auu ni] howi noeh gwat mun mok tee'it.

still adj. not moving -- nung; still water -- tuk nung t'kawl; sngee'im; quiet -- sng'aat: remain still (not moving or talking) -- noeh owi sngee'im sng'aat

still n. for making alcohol -- cunlye'ng butt sra

sting v. ti(ch)

stingy adj. kum'nenyh

stink v. tuum klen sa'oi (lit. smell bad): Most of the alleys stink [of garbage]. -- Ploe ch'raw pieh ch'raan tuum klen sa'oi [sum'raam]. (NB... that the "of" in "of garbage" is unstated)

stinky adj. sa'oi

stir v. gko: stir the soup -- gko sam'law

stir up trouble betw. v. tveu owi kaut pun'ha

stir-fried adj. chaa: vegetables and beef, stir-fried -- chaa bunl'eye chi'moi sat(ch) gko; stir-fried beef over salad -- lok'lak chi'moi sa'lat

stitch v. sew -- day

stocking n. sr'auwm cheung s'tray

stoic adj. a'char; a stoic -- ma'nooh a'char; stolid -- nung (same as word for "still")

stomach n. poo'ah (NB: same pronunciation as word for "snake"): stomach ache -- chh'ooh poo'ah; I'm hungry! (lit: My stomach is turning over!) -- Kyom ro'mool poo'ah.; empty stomach -- to'tay poo'ah

stomp v. tun tro'um cheung (lit: step hard with foot)

stone n. t'maw; set'la: The house was built of stone. -- Ptay'a song pi t'maw.

stooge n. bo'ri'va dai cheung (lit: flunkey hand and foot): The military of that country are just stooges of China. -- Tee'hee'an sruk nu keuh chia kuut bo'ri'va dai cheung sruk jchun.

stool n. cheung ma

stool pidgeon n. neh koh'bot (AP: k'bawt) owi kaa: He was a well-known stool pidgeon. -- Gwat chia neh koh'bot owi kaa l'bye chamoo'h.

stop n. chope (AP: choop): a stop on a trip -- chope moi dum'nak: We have to make two stops [on the way to] Battambong. -- Yeung tro chope pi dum'nak [k'nong kaa tveu dum'narr] teuh Battambong.; The plane made only one stop. -- Yun hawh chope tai moi dum'nak tay.; She stopped the car. -- Nee'eng bun chope laan.; (NB: "end " or "finish" = banyh jchawb: They ended the war. -- Gkay banyh jchawp sung'kree'um.; I finished the exam. -- Kyom banyh jchawp praw'long.)

stop v. chope (AP: choop): Stop! -- Chope!; Stop working, rest, for a while -- Chope sun.; jchawt: I want to stop here. -- Kyom jchong jchawt noeh ti ni.; The car stopped at the market. -- Laan jchawt noeh ti p'sa.

stop up v. jchawk: I need [a plug] to stop up the sink. -- Kyom tro kaa [ch'nawk] sum'rap jchawk basin tuk.; "cork", or stop up, a bottle -- dah(k) (or, jchawk) ch'nawk dop

storage, storage area n. either open or inside a building -- klay'ung: The embassy will need storage space. -- S'tahn'toot nung tro kaa klay'ung.; cunlye'ng dah(k) aye'von; cunlye'ng tooo'k aye'von: We need more storage space than we have now. -- Yeung tro kaa klay'ung ch'raan chiang yeung miun eye leaou ni.

store v. tooo'k; dah(k): I need to store my books someplace. -- Kyom tro kaa tooo'k s'po noeh cunlye'ng na moi.; store in hidden place, hide -- leh: The KR will store their weapons underground. -- Khmei Kra'hom nung leh a'vwut gkay noeh krowm daiy.

store n. place that sells things -- haang (AP: hawng): pharmacy -- haang looh tnam peyt; shop, small store -- haang looh do; haang to'ich; supply, stockpile -- chuung ruhk: a store of rice -- chuung ruhk sro; store of corn -- chuung ruhk po't

storehouse n. klay'ung

store-room n. ban'tope dah(k) aye'von

storm n. k'shaal p'chooh

story n. ru'ung (AP: reu-ung, ri'ung): What's the story? What's happening? -- Ru'ung eye?; old story, folk story, myth -- ru'ung praeng; to make a long story short -- tveu ru'ung veng owi klai; make up a story -- tye'ng ru'ung; floors in a building -- cho'un: That building has four stories. -- A'keea nu miun buon cho'un.

stove n. jchong kran; gas stove -- jchong kran gaz

strafe v. banyh r'a'eh mok leuh: The Thais claimed the Vietnamese planes strafed them. -- Thai praw'kas tha yun hawh Yuen banyh r'a'eh mok leuh pooh'gkay.

straight adv. ahead -- trong (AP: trung); tee'ung trong: Go straight ahead. -- Teuh trong.

straight-forward adj. honest, open -- slote trong: He is straight-forward type. -- Gwat chia ma'nooh slote trong.

straighten v. tveu dum'rong

straighten out v. solve -- dum'naugh sr'eye; resolve, mediate -- p'sahs p'sah noeh: The [(1) UN] straightened out [(2) the problem] between [(3) the volunteers] and [(4) the camp "admin."] -- [(1) Ong'kah Saha'praw'chia'chec'it] p'sahs p'sah noeh [(2) kaa cho chaae'k] ro'vieng [(3) neh chum'noo'ee] nung [(4) ratt'ta'bal chuum'ruhm.]

straighten up v. clean up, neaten -- bauhh sum'aat (bauhh = sweep)

strain v. strain out water, etc. -- trawng; make a difficult effort -- kum'prung: The government had to strain to find [housing (e.g., shelter)] for all the displaced persons. -- Ratt'a'pi'bal tro tai kum'prung sveye ro'k [choom'rok] sum'rap chuun pieh kloo'an te'ang awh.

strainer n. k'twong; (AP: k'trong)

strand n. saw'sye: strand of hair -- saw'sye saw(k)

strange adj. difficult to believe -- pi'bah cheu'a; unusual, odd, different -- jchum'lyke; or ply'ke; strange food -- ma'hope jchum'lyke; a strange person -- ma'nooh pl'yke (or jchum'lye); weird (in non-humorous, derogatory sense) -- kat(ch)

stranger n. ma'nooh jchum'lyke; ma'nooh pl'yke

stratagem n. trick -- l'but(ch); l'but(ch) kawl; plan -- pyne'kaa

strategy n. [military] strategy -- kaa boo'un [suk]; [business] strategy -- vi'ti sa [chuum'noo'inyh]

straw n. dry grass -- sm'au kree'um; hay -- jchum balng; for drinking -- um'peung beuwt; or, praw'dob beuwt [tuk t'krau'itch] (lit: s. th. to suck [orange juice])

stream n. prayk; (NB: "forest" is "prey"); small tributary stream -- dai prayk; small stream (smaller than a prayk) -- O: commonly used in village names such as those of Khmer Rouge base "villes" O Bawk, O Smach and O Trau.

street n. ploe: in the street -- taam ploe; street talk, slang -- pee'a sa'muun; (NB: formal word for street = vi'teye, as used in "boulevard," -- ma'ha vi'teye (lit: big street); t'nawl (AP: th'non); ploe t'nawl

strength n. kum'lung; pul'laeng ("pul" here is same word as that used in term "kawng'pul" -- army division -- literally, "strong force"); full strength -- kum'lung penyh lung; physical strength -- kum'lung gkai

strengthen v. puung rung

strenuous adj. klang klaah: This is strenuous work. -- Ni chia kej kaa daw klang klaah.

stretch v. expand/contract -- tveu a'yoot; stretch rubber -- tveu a'yoot kaow'soo; reach, be long/large enough -- bun lye: Can this rope stretch across the river? -- Tau(v) k'sye poo'an ni adje bun lye kat stung ni baan tay?; extend -- lee'it sun tung: The Cambodian border stretches from the Gulf of Thailand to Vietnam. -- Tul dyne Kampuchea lee'it sun tung pi choong sa'mut see'um teuh doll sruk yuen.

stretched adj. tung

strict adj. mildly -- tung rung; seriously, as in army training -- mung mutt

strike n. pa'ti'kaam: There will be a strike in Phnom Penh. -- Nung miun pa'ti'kaam noeh Phnom Penh.; (also, sometimes, kaa baah bauw)

strike v. cease work -- tveu pa'ti'kaam: The factory workers will strike tomorrow. -- Neh tveu kaa ro'ng jcha nung tveu pa'ti'kaam noeh t'ngai s'eye'd.; hit, attack -- vye: sum'pong; beat a drum -- tooo'ng sco; hit -- vye; vi'yaye; strike (a match) -- kooh (   )

string n. k'sye (also used in phrases for "rope" (k'sye pooa, or k'sye)) and "wire" (k'sye)); thin string -- k'sye um'bauw; string used to sew up bags -- saw'sye um'bauw (lit: strands of thread)

strip v. take off (e.g., paint) -- kowh jchenyh; or, baw(k) jchenyh; strip of rank or office -- dawk jchenyh; or, dawk yok jchenyh; take clothes off (either oneself or s. o. else) -- dawh kow-aow; dawh kow-aow jchenyh; dawh yok jchenyh; sraat; sraat kow-aow; (NB difference in usage between dawk and dawh); disassemble a weapon or machine -- bum byke jchenyh chia p'nyke (chia p'nyke = apart, into pieces)

stripe n. ch'note; as sign of rank -- saak

strive v. works hard -- kut kum: We must strive to build up the country. -- Yeung tro kaa kut kum jchum raan praw'tet.; struggle -- taw'soo; attempt to do s. th., try -- prung pryne

stroll v. dah'leng

strong adj. generally -- klang: He's a strong guy. -- Gwat chia ma'nooh klang; m'wom twom; m'wom moo'un: He's strong. -- Gwat m'wom t'wom.; or, Gwat m'wom moo'un.; a strong (alcoholic) drink -- sra klang; sra chit thum; strong chance or possibility -- o'kaa la'aw: There's a strong chance I will sell my house. -- Miun o'kaa la'aw dum'bye loo'a ptay'a kyom.; strong, healthy, in good condition -- rung'mo'an: For the economy to be strong, the people must [work together]. -- Dum'bye set'a'kej rung'mo'an, pra'chee'chuun tro tai [sr'aaw ka'neea].

struggle n. chia kaa taw'soo: Life is a struggle. -- Chi'vut keuh chia kaa taw'soo.; taw yoot

struggle v. work to achive s. th. -- pooh'peea; taw'soo; struggle against -- taw'soo praw'chang

stubborn adj. most common -- k'bal rung; rung k'bal: stubborn person -- ma'nooh rung k'bal; also -- rung roo(s); jchaw traw'jcheh; mee'a naae'ch

stuck, to get v. cho'up: The car got stuck in the mud. -- Laan cho'up k'nong daiy phoo'a.; stuck in throat -- cho'up noeh bum'pung khaw

stuck up adj. cha'ma'ng: The minister's wife was stuck-up because of her husband's [position]. -- Pra'pun ratt'mun'trei cha'ma'ng bee'proo'a [bun'saak] p'dye.; kach rian

stud n. male animal used for breeding -- baah: a stud pig -- ch'roook baah

student n. generally, as well as specifically re elementary and secondary school students -- gkon suh(t); specifically university -- nee'suh(t)

study n. [research] paper -- kaa [srauw'chree'oo]; continuing investigation or scrutiny -- suk'sah srauw'chree'oo: Cambodia Study Group -- Krum Suk'sah Srauw'chree'oo Kampuchea; the concept of studying -- kaa suk'sah

study v. do an academic/intellectual report or analysis -- rian; or, rian om'pee: [Few] Americans study Khmer. -- Americang [chuum'noo'an tic to'ich] rian om'pee pee'esa Khmei.; conduct research, expert analysis -- suk'sah; or, suk'sah om'pee

stuff n. kreung; aye'von

stuff v. ch'raaaw; n'yo'at: Just stuff the clothes in the bag. -- N'yo'at kow-aow k'nong va'leez.; praw'chree'ut

stuffed adj. jammed into a space -- penyh; n'nyne: The books were stuffed in the box. -- S'po penyh noeh k'nong praw'op.; people and animals -- ch'eyte: The cow ate grass (until it was) stuffed. -- Gko see sm'auu ch'eyte.; possible response if offered more food at a meal -- No, thanks, I'm full (stuffed). -- Aw'kuun, ch'eyte howi.; n'yo'at: stuffed (with frog or minced pork) chicken wings (traditional Khmer cuisine) -- slaab muon n'yo'at

stuffy nose n. tung ch'raw muk

stumble v. chit duel (lit: almost fall); p'lawt cheung

stump n. kaat kuhl cheu (NB: "kuhl" is portion of tree trunk closest to ground.)

stump v. t'wal (lit: blocked); I'm stumped. -- Kyom t'wal howi.

stun v. render unconscious -- tveu owi sun'lop; (NB: to kill is sum'lap); render surprised -- tveu owi pn'yeh preut: This development will stun everyone! -- Kaa ni nung tveu owi pn'yeh preut te'ang awh ka'neea.

stunned adj. very surprised -- pn'yeh (AP: pee'nyeh) preut pro: He was stunned by the news. -- Gwat pn'yeh preut pro dow'ee sa por'da'mee'an.; or, He was stunned by (i. e., on hearing) the news. -- Gwat pn'yeh preut pro noeh peyr loo por'da'mee'an.; rendered physically dizzy -- ngee ngeuuh: He was stunned by the explosion. -- Gwat ngee ngeuuh dow'ee sa kro'up p'tooh.

stupa n. jch'eye't daiy

stupefy v. tveu owi pn'yeh preut

stupid adj. l'ng'ong; pleuh pleuh; pleuh: Don't be stupid. -- Kum pleuh pay'k!; less harsh than "pleuh pleuh," closer to "dumb," is "plee pleuh" or "bo' plee bo' pleuh"; naive -- chhaut

style n. baep: What style of clothes do you like? -- Neh jchole jchet kow-aow baep na?; ro'bee'up: a style of writing -- ro'bee'up saw say; way of acting -- ro'bee'up... tveu:I don't like his style. -- Kyom ot jchole jchet ro'bee'up gwat tveu tay.; style of building -- ro'bee'up sang song: That is French [colonial] style. -- Ni chia ro'bee'up sang song [ro'bah a'naa'ni'kuum] Ba'raang.; or, A ni ro'bee'up a'naa'ni'kum Ba'raang.; vi'ti; style of decoration -- vi'ti ree'up jchum; style of carving -- vi'ti ch'laak

suave adj. lo'ee sung ha; charming -- miun sum'po'ah

sub-category n. kaw: You are making (lit: dividing into) too many sub-categories. -- Neh bye'ng jchaiyk ch'raan kaw nah.

sub-continent n. uh'pa'twib

subject n. of study -- muk vi'chee'a; subject of discussion -- kaam vuh'to: The subject [of discussion] was the Vietnamese economy. -- Kaam vuh'to [ney kaa pee'pee'a(k) sa] keuh set'a'kej Yuen.; of a sentence -- praw'tee'un; of an examination -- vi'gnyee'a sa

subject to adv. noeh k'nong kaa ru'nye: Hun Sen agreed to meet Sihanouk subject to (getting) [the approval] of the Assembly. -- Hun Sen sohk jchet choop Sihanoo' noeh k'nong kaa ru'nye [ney kaa yul'prome] ro'bah su'pheea.

submarine n. neea'veea moi tuk

submerge v. lic (NB: also means sink)

submit v. give up -- leh bong; hand in, tender -- pdull owi noeh: Please submit your [resignation] immediately. -- Jcho(r) pdull owi noeh kaa lee'aae chope pee'dum'nyne ro'bah neh chia bun twon.

subordinate n. gkon jchao

subpoena n. kaa kaw(ss)

subpoena v. kaw(ss)

subscribe to v. [subscribe to] a magazine -- [chee'oo] too'a'su'na'va'dye; [subscribe to] a theory -- [yul'prome nung] treuus'dye

subscript n. footnote -- layke yong (lit: reference number)

subscription n. kaa ch'eeo: a year's subscription -- kaa chee'oo praw'cham chh'nam

subservient adj. ruh'naup; bo'ri'va (as noun means, sycophant, boot-licker, "yes man," lackey, follower, supporter, backer, etc.)

subsidiary n. kruum'huun sa'ka (lit: company branch)

subsidy n. kaa chuum'noo'ee loi

subsidize v. tooo'b tul chuum'noo'ee loi

subsistence adj. just enough -- chi'vut pheap kroop kro'un: subsistence economy -- set'a'kej dael kro'un tai kroop kro'un (lit: an economy which is just enough); in sense of not enough because unstable, dependant on "whatever may come" -- a'chi'vut'kaam

subsistence n. pheap kro'up kro'un tai jchenyh chum chi'vut; phcap a'chi'vut'kaam

substance n. matter, chemical, ingredient, etc. -- tnam; vu'to; "bottom line," essence -- sa'rob s'kd'eye: The substance was, we could not go. -- Sa'rob s'kd'eye, yeung mun adje teuh.; (NB sa'rob s'kd'eye can also mean "in summary")

substitute for v. chuum'nooh(s): He will substitute for me at the meeting. -- Gwat nung chuum'nooh(s) kyom noeh peyr pra'choom.

substitute n. neh chuum'nooh(s)

subtle adj. pun praw'sah: This is a subtle joke. -- Ni chia kaa cum'plyne pun praw'sah.; That guy is a subtle politician. -- Gwat nu neh na'yo'bye pun praw'sah.

subtract v. dawk; dawk jchum'noo'an: I want you to subtract 2 [from 4]. -- Jchong owi neh dawk jchum'noo'an pi [pi buon].

subtraction n. layke saw; layke dawk; kaa dawk

suburb n. chee'aae ti'krong (lit: side or edge of (a) town)

subversion n. vi'toom'sa'na

subway train n. rot pleung krowm daiy (lit: train underground)

succeed v. miun choke chey: I hope you will succeed in your studies. -- Kyom sung'khum tha neh nung miun choke chey noeh kaa suk'sah.; complete or accomplish s. th. -- baan sum'ra(ch)

success n. kaa chuum raan; choke chey: May you have success. -- Sum owi baan choke chey.; accomplishment -- kaa sum ra(ch);

successful adj. baan sum ra(ch): That business has been successful. -- Chuum'noo'inyh nu baan sum ra(ch) howi.; ch'neh: a successful attack -- vye ch'neh; famous -- l'bye l'banyh

successfully adv. ch'neh: We successfully defended the village. -- Yeung kaa'pee'a phum ch'neh.

such prp. nung (AP: nong): I don't like such people. -- Kyom ot jchole jchet pooh nung tay.; (unstated): [He gave me] such trouble [that] I had to fire him. -- [Gwat p'dull owi kyom] kaa lum'bah [doll] kyom tro tai denyh veea jchowl.; ot miun: no such thing -- veea ot miun;

such as adj. doj chia; doj: such as him -- doj gwat; Such as?? -- Doj aae klaah?? or, Tau(v) chia a'veye teuh??

suck v. cho'chua; beuwt; place s.th. in mouth -- bee'um

suckle v. ba(ll): The child suckles at the breast of its mother. -- K'mayng ba(ll) dawh m'dye.

suddenly adv.   moi ruhm pech: He appeared suddenly.   --   Veea kaut laung moi ruhm pech.; sro'p tai: He [appeared] suddenly.   --   Gwat [lik laung] sro'p tai.

sue v.   pa'dung: They may sue the airline company [about the] lost luggage   --   Gkay pra'heil chia pa'dung krum'huun yun hawh [om'pee kaa] bot aye'von.

suffer v.   rong tooo'k: The people suffered greatly [under the regime of] the Khmer Rouge.   --   Pra'chee'chuun rong tooo'k yang klang [noeh kraum ro'bab] Khmei Kra'hom.; rong krooh

suffering n.   kaa vaye'ta'neea; tooo'k vaye'ta'neea: [Even today] the KR cause much suffering.   --   Mok doll t'ngai ni Khmei Kra'hom noeh tai bong'kaut tooo'k vaye'ta'neea chia ch'raan.

suffocated adj.   to'p dung howm

sugar n.   generally -- sc'aaw; raw, brown colored sugar, as pressed from cane -- sc'aaw tnaut; white table sugar -- sc'aaw saw

sugar cane n.   the plant in the field -- am'peau; a piece of cane, cut -- daum am'peau saang

suggest v.   owi yo'ball: Can you suggest a good [restaurant]?   --   Tau(v) neh adje owi yo'ball tha [haang bye] na la'aw?; sna'rr tha: Please suggest a good [restaurant] (lit: what restaurant is good).   --   Sum sna'rr tha [poch'ni'tan] na la'aw.; I suggest that you think again.   --   Kyom sn'aar sum owi neh kut chia t'maee.

suggestion n.   yo'ball: Please give me a suggestion about what food is good (here).   --   Jcho(r) neh owi yo'ball kyom tha ma'hope a'veye chng'anyh.; Please give me some suggestions about business.   --   Jcho(r) neh owi yo'ball kyom om'pee chuum'noo'inyh.; s'kd'eye sna'rr

suicide n.   kaa sum'lap kloo'an; commit suicide -- sum'lap kloo'an eiyne

suit n.   legal action -- k'dye; bring a lawsuit -- tveu k'dye; sue each other -- k'dye ka'neea; clothing -- moi praw'dop; moi sam'rap (lit: a pair or set, i.e., of jacket and pants)

suitable adj.   koo'a sum (NB: sum = pleasing): These waitresses are not suitable.   --   Neh bum raahl ni k'miun kaa koo'a sum tay.

suitcase n.   leather case -- va'leez; wooden, trunk-like case -- hopp (AP: hepp)

sullen adj.   sawh'ka'krah

summarize v.   sang khep; sa ro'p: Please summarize your story.   --   Jchole sa ro'p ru'ung neh.

summary n.   s'kd'eye song khaiyp: Please give me a summary.   --   Jchole owi kaa song khaiyp mok.

summer n.   literally, "hot season" -- ro'doe k'dau; (NB: in Cambodia refers to March-through-May; term in written Khmer is "kern mahan ro'doe"); March-May in Cambodia is also referred to as "dry season" -- ro'doe prah'ng

summit n.   kum'pool phnom

summon v.   mandatory, as if done by court -- kaw(ss); urgently invite -- un'cheunyh: The Minister summoned him.   --   Ratt'mun'trei un'cheunyh gwat.

summons n.   kaa kaw(ss)

sun n.   preah'a'tthit

Sunday n.   t'ngai a'tthit; a'tthit

sunglasses n.   ven'taa

sunk pp.   completely submerged in water -- lic; almost completely submerged -- luup

sunken v.   srup(t)

sunrise n.   t'ngai reh (AP: ray'uh)

sunset n.   t'ngai lic: The sun has set.; or, The sun is setting. (hence, loosely, it is sunset) -- T'ngai lic howi.; or, Preah a'tthit a's'dang kaat howi.

superficial adj.   saa(rl): a superficial wound -- chh'ooh saa(rl)

superficially adv.   saa(rl) saa(rl)

super-human adj.   miun bun: God is super-human.   --   Preah neh miun bun.; (preah = god, bun = power)

superior adj.   thum; miun mo'ha'teh'ret; (mo'ha'te'ret = power)

superior n.   boss -- jchao'vye (AP: cho'vye); in a wat -- kruu cho' ak'thee'kaa

superiority n. oot'da'ma'pheap

supervise v. kroop krown; troo'ot trra; meuhl kaa koh tro: It will be difficult to supervise the elections. -- Veea nung pi'bah nah troo'it tra k'nong kaa bawh ch'nowt.

supervisor n. jchao vye (AP: cho'vye); neh yoo'up; neh meulh kaa koh tro: Who is the supervisor of this restaurant. -- Neh meuhl kaa koh tro k'nong poch'ni'tan nee no na?.

supplies; supply of s. th. n. re consumables only -- sa'bee'ung: supplies of food -- sa'bee'ung a'ha; re equipment, etc. -- sum'phea'reh(k)

supply n. kaa pdull: the supply of oil -- kaa pdull praeng

supply v. pdull owi; pdull noeh

support v. intellectually/politically -- kwam tro: That group supports the government. -- Krum nu kwam tro ratt'a'pi'bal.; financially -- tuum nup bum rong: They support their families in the camps by sending money every month. -- Pooh'gkay tuum nup bum rong kroo'e'sa gkay noeh k'nong chuum ruum dow'ee sa p'nya(r) loi ree'eng rawl kye.; physically -- tro: [It will be necessary] to support that old house. -- [Nung tro kaa] tro ptay'a jchaah nu.; support from underneath -- tul: How can we support that bridge? -- Yang na yeung adje tul spee'un nu?; physically support a person, e. g., while walking -- kree'a

support n. support for the government -- kaa kwam tro jchum'poo'h (or teuh) ratt'a'pi'bal; moral, financial, psychological, etc. support for s. o. -- kaa tuum nup bum rong jchum'poo'h (or tueh); physical support -- kaa troh; kaa tul

suppose v. sun'tahn: I suppose [you will be late] as usual. -- Kyom sun'tahn tha [neh nung mok yeut] doj twa'ma'da.; op'pa'ma: Suppose they don't agree. -- Op'pa'ma gkay ot yul prome.

suppress v. bung kraa(b)

sure adj. certain -- ch'bah: I am not sure. -- Kyom ot ch'bah.; praw'kat: for sure -- piht (AP: put) praw'kat; thee'ung

surely adv. piht (AP: put) chia: He will surely come. -- Gwat piht chia mao.; kung... chia mun kaan: He will surely come. -- Gwat kung nung mok chia mun kaan.

surface n. p'tay: a flat surface -- p'tay ri'ep

surge v. move fiorward forcefully -- bauw

surmise v. smaa'n

surpass v. pa'lut leuh; pa'lut hoo'a: They surpassed their [crop] production target. -- Gkay pa'lut leuh kum'rut kum'nauwt ney [po't p'auwl].; (NB: pa'lut = produce; pa'lut [leuh] = produce [above]; kum'rut kum'nauwt = limit, i. e., target)

surprise n. kaa pn'yeh p'auwl: I don't like surprises. -- Kyom ot jchole jchet kaa pn'yeh p'auwl.

surprise v. tveu owi pn'yeh p'auwl: We surprised the enemy. -- Yeung tveu owi pn'yeh p'auwl doll sa'tro.

surprised adj. pn'yeh p'auwl: I was surprised by the news. -- Kyom baan pn'yeh p'auwl dow'ee sa por'da'mee'an.; (PS: Amazing! -- Baah saahk (lit: makes his hair stand up!))

surrender (to) v. capitulate -- jchaw jchanyh: Iraq surrendered to the USA. -- Iraq jchaw jchanyh USA.; We will never surrender. -- Yeung nung mun jchaw jchanyh tay!; give over, hand over -- leh bong; leh bong jchowl: The Khmer Rouge did not want to give up its [equipment] and [weapons] and surrender to the UN. -- KR ot jchong leh bong jchowl [sum'phe'a'reh(k)] nung [kreung a'vwut] nung jchaw jchanyh UN.; (NB: jchanyh = to lose, and is the same word as in the term for malaria, kruun jchanyh)

surround v. chuum; huhm; po'at; huhm po'at: Their group surrounded the enemy. -- Krum gkay huhm (or, po'at; or, huhm po'at) sa'tro.; po'at chuum'venyh; to be all around s. th. (without necessarily the intent to surround) -- noeh chuum'venyh: There were hills all around the village. -- Miun phnom noeh chuum'venyh phum.

survey v. stuung: survey the people's [opinions] -- stuung [ma'teh(k)] pra'chee'chuun

suspect n. neh cho'op jchowt

suspect v. song'sye: We suspect that there will be an attack tomorrow. -- Yeung song'sye tha nung miun kaa vye ka'neea s'eye'd.; (written form -- muun'hul song sye)

suspend v.   pa'aak (lit: stall or delay); suspend a sentence -- p'shooa' to'h; or, bun yee'a; suspend a license, suspend a student from school, etc. -- bun yee'a

swagger v.   seulng, (NB. as adjective connotes arrogant.)

swallow v.   laae'b: The politicians eat money like snakes swallowing frogs. -- Neh na'yo'bye see loi doj chia poo'ah laae'b kong kype.

swap v.   do; pdo; (NB: (1) both "do" and "pdo" are derived from a word written "pdo(r)"; (2) "do" is more commonly used as a verb -- to swap, to change, to transfer, etc. -- while "pdo" more frequently appears in the noun form "kaa pdo", a swap, a move, a transfer, etc.)

swarm (around) v.   jchowm; ro'me; jchowm ro'me; chuum'venyh: The people swarmed around the UN truck. -- Pra'chee'chuun jchowm ro'me venyh laan trung Ongka Saha Praw'chee'a'chee'it.

sway v.   yo'l; klo'ng: The trees swayed in the wind. -- Daum cheu yo'l dow'ee sa k'shaal.

swear v.   curse -- jcheyr; promise (more or less) -- sun'nyaa; promise absolutely -- s'bot

sweat n.   ny'uh; sweaty body -- kloo'an byke ny'euuh

sweat v.   byte ny'euuh

Sweden n.   praw'tet Suu'edd: Swedish -- Suu'edd; That guy's a Swede. -- Gwat nu chee'it Suu'edd.

sweep v.   bauhh; to sweep or clean -- sum'aaht

sweet adj.   p'eye'm

sweet potato n.   dum'lung ch'veea

sweetheart n.   term of address -- pro'lung (lit: soul): What do you want, sweetheart? -- Jchong baan a'veye, pro'lung?; term of address -- baan doll jchet; term of reference with connotation of "lover" -- snai ha: Is she your sweetheart? -- Tau(v) nee'eng snai ha neh, tay?

sweets n.   dessert -- bong eye'm (typically compressed in speech to "b'eye'm"): Please bring me a dessert. -- Owi kyom b'eye'm moi jchaan.

swell v.   increase -- kauwn laung: If there's no [food] in the countryside, the [population] of the cities will swell. -- Praw'sun baa ot miun [ma'hope jchum'nace] noeh cheu'na'bot, [jchum'noo'an pra'chee'chuun] ti krong nung kauwn laung.; re wounds -- howm (AP: hahm); ree'k: The wound swelled more and more (lit: bigger and bigger.) -- Dum'bauw ree'k thum laung thum laung.

swim v.   hahl tuk; (AP: hyle tuk)

swimming n.   kaa hahl tuk; swimming pool -- pi'sceen; or cunlye'ng hahl tuk

swindle v.   bauwk bun chh'aut: He said [some leaders] swindle their [followers] and the Thais swindle the leaders! -- Gwat ni'yaye tha [neh duk'noo'an klaah klaah] bauwk bun chh'aut [neh krowm um'natch] howi nung neh See'um SNL bauwk bun chh'aut neh duk'noo'an.

swing v.   yo'l to'ng: children's game of swing a string around the head -- kro' vee k'sye, or, kro vee lo't un'ta'eh

swing n.   to'ng

switch n.   electrical -- kon'tac

switch v.   do; pdo; plas; (see definitions of "change", "move" and "transfer" for discussion of usages.)

Switzerland n.   praw'tet Swiss

swollen adj.   howm

swoop v.   moo(ch) jchaap; jchaap: children's game of "hawks and chickens" -- kl'eye'ng jchaap kgon muon

sword n.   daa'oo

sycophant n.   a'mye'a'towng: He has been a sycophant his whole life. -- Gwat chia a'mye'a'towng penyh moi chi'vut.; neh eye'b lawb

syllable n.   p'schee'ung

symbol n.   ni'mu'ta'roo: He is a symbol of the past. -- Gwat ni'mu'tar'oo ney a'tay'ta'ka.; emblem -- sun'ya: The eagle is the symbol of the United States. -- Un'tree keuh chia sun'ya ratt Amerique.; sign -- sun'ya

sympathetic to adj. concerned about -- proo'i om'pee; politically -- kaan cheung: [That group] is sympathetic to Vietnam. -- Pooh nu kaan cheung praw'tet Yuen.; favors -- ni'yuum: UNTAC was sympathetic to Ranariddh's faction. -- UNTAC ni'yuum p'nyke Ranariddh.

sympathize with v. ru'um layke: I sympathize with your problem. -- Kyom ru'um layke chi'moi pun'ha neh.

symptom n. ni'mut'ta'roop; sun'ya

synchronize v. p'tee'ung: Synchronize your watches! -- P'tee'ung ni'a'li'ka neh teuh!

syndicate n. corporation -- sa'ha'chuun; company -- kruum'huun; bo'ri'sat

syringe n. chul jchak t'nam; ma'chul

system n. of doing s. th. -- baep pyne (lit: "style" + "plan"); network, on large scale -- praw'po'an: the elecrical system in Phnom Penh -- praw'po'an a'ti'ce'nee noeh Phnom Penh; network, on small scale -- k'sye: My car's electrical system is broken. -- K'sye pleung la'an kyom ko'itch; praw'dop: [respiratory] system -- praw'dop [dawk dung'hauwm]

systematically adv. dow'ee baep pyne (lit: according to plan)

T

table n. tohk: set the table -- ree'up tohk

table of contents n. bun'chee ru'ung; sa'ra'ban ru'ung

tablecloth n. sum'raww tohk

tackle v. taw twul; taw thoop

tact n. kaa koo'sum; sa'pheap ruum tuum

tactics n. generally -- kul la'byke; snee'it; ma'choo'bye (also means "technique"); military tactics -- ka'boo'un suk

tail n. cun'toi

tailor n. chiang kaat kow-aow

tailor shop n. haang kaat day kow-aow (lit: shop to cut/sew clothes)

take v. generally -- yok; take from a near point to far point, or far point to far point (i. e., from here to there, or from there to there) -- choon tueh; yok teuh; or no'um teuh (generally, choon is used with people, yok with objects and no'um with either): choon: I will take you from here to [the airport]. -- Kyom nung choon neh teuh [jchum'naut yun hawh].; Take him from the house to [the hospital]. -- Choon gwat pi ptay'a teuh ['pet].; take... to... -- yok... teuh dah(k): [Pick up those packages] at the airport and take them from there to the customer's shop. -- [Yok aye'von nu] pi jchum'naut howi nung yok veea teuh dah(k) noeh haang p'nee'oo.; no'um: Take her to the hotel. -- No'um nee'eng teuh o'tyle.; take s. o. around -- no'um... doll: I took the visitors on a tour of Phnom Penh. -- Kyom no'um p'nee'oo doll kum'san leng k'nong Phnom Penh.; (NB: take from far point to near point (i.e., from there to here) is defined under "bring"; "bring" generally is expressed by choon, yok or no'um followed by "mok" instead of "teuh"; for example: They will bring her to my house. -- Gkay nung no'um gwat mok ptay'a kyom.; NB, also: pick s. o. up = to'tool mok: We will pick her up at the airport. -- Yung nung to'tool nee'eng mok pi airport.); also:

take a bath -- moi tuk

take after -- copy, follow the example of -- tveu taam: Don't take after (the examples of) bad people. -- Kum tveu taam (kum'roo) ma'nooh a'krah.

take an exam -- praw'long; go take an exam -- teuh praw'long

take as -- tooo'k chia: I took (it) as a souvenir. -- Kyom tooo'k chia a'noo'sow'ree.; (NB: no "veea" or other word for "it" is required if the item taken/referred to is already known to the speakers);

take (s. th. non-divisible) away -- yok: They took my (cup of) coffee away. -- Gkay yok cafe ro'bah kyom teuh howi.

take (s. th. divisible) away, reduce the quantity of -- bun toi yok jchenyh; bun tic teuh; dawk jchenyh; bun toi yok jchenyh: There's too much food; take some away. -- Ma'hope ch'raan nah; tro bun'toi yok jchenyh klaah.

take care of -- tai reh'sa: Children [should] take care of their parents. -- Gkon [koo'a tai] tai reh'sa ouev'puk m'dye.

take care of oneself -- t'nam kloo'an

take for -- tooo'k.... doj chia: I took him for a monk, but he was only [an actor]. -- Kyom tooo'k gwat doj chia lok sang, pun'ta'aae gwat krun tai [chia dah too'a].

Take it easy! -- T'veu taam sr'ool.

take it (endure it) -- tooo'b tool: I can't take it anymore! -- Kyom tooo'b tool mun ch'neh!

take leave of -- lee'a: Goodbye (familiar). -- Lee'a sun hi'.; or, Lee'a hi'. (NB: "hi'" is a contraction of, and in these phrases is typically used in place of, howi); Goodbye (respectful) -- Kyom sum ree'up lee'a.

take (lit: swallow) medecine -- laae'b t'nam

take off clothing -- dawh... jchenyh: Take everything off. -- Dawh sum lee'a bum pieh jchenyh.; dawh sraat; sraat... jchenyh: Take off all the clothes   (as to a child before a bath). -- Sraat kow-aow jchenyh.

take steps (to) -- jchat kaa [or, jchat vi'ti kaa]dum'bye; (jchat = expedite, vi'ti and kaa = action or activity): The government should take steps to help the people. -- Ratt'a'pi'bal koo'a tai jchat vi'ti kaa dum'bye choo'ay pra'chee'chuun.

take out on a date -- no'um dah leng

take out of a box -- dawk jchenyh pi praw'op

take over in unfriendly way; commandeer, expropriate -- ruhb yok: He took over [her job]. -- Gwat ruhb yok [kaa'ngyeea nee'eng].

take over work in sense of take responsibility for (non-hostile) -- yok kej kaa; (see, also, "take responsibility", below)

take part in, join in -- jchole ru'um: take part in theelections -- jchole ru'um baw ch'nowt

take a picture -- tawt roob

take place -- kaut laung; praw'preut laung

take responsibility -- to'tool kaa tro: If he goes away, you must take responsibility for this work. -- Ot pi gwat teuh, neh tro kaa to'tool kaa tro.

take the side of -- kaan cheung (lit. hold the feet (ofs.o.))

take s. th. out of s. th. -- yok... jchenyh pi: take the flower out of the bottle -- yok p'ka jchenyh pi dop

take time -- ch'lee'it yok peyr: It takes time to learn Khmer. -- Veea ch'lee'it yok peyr rian Khmei.

take a trip -- tveu dum'narr

take up, in sense of start learning -- jchaap p'daum rian: I took up tennis a long time ago. -- Kyom jchaap p'daum rian te'nnit chh'nam ch'raan mok howi.

talented adj. praw'sup

talk (to or with) v. ni'yaye (chi'moi); pee'pee'eh' chi'moi neh; talk back to -- thaw mwot: Don't talk back to me! -- Kum thaw mwot nung kyom!; talk loudly -- mwot klang; to talk to -- ni'yaye ro'k: I want to talk to him. -- Kyom jchong ni'yaye ro'k gwat.; talk a lot -- paw pet paw pow'it(ch): Don't talk so much. -- Kum paw pet paw pow'it(ch) ch'raan peyk.; talk too much -- ni'yaye ch'raan nah; babble on and on -- la'oo (AP: ra'oo); talk very pleasantly, smilingly -- roo'h ri'yaye; talk nonsense -- ni'yaye ot baan kaa

tall adj. k'pooh

talon n. kraw chaw(k); (also means "claw")

tamarind n. um'pil: tamarind tree -- daum um'pil

tame adj. re animals -- san'g; tame animals -- saat san'g; domestic animals -- saat sruk; for people, translated as "gentle" -- slote; to tame s. th. -- p'san'g

tan adj. pwa sraw'eyme

tangerine n. krau'itch kwit

tangled adj. kroy'ngyanyh: tangled hair -- saahk kroy'ngyanyh; praw'tehk ka'neea: tangled thread -- um'bawh praw'tehk ka'neea; chum'peh(k) ka'neea: tangled rope -- k'sye poo'a chum'peh(k) ka'neea

tank n. for holding liquids -- tuung; water tank -- tuung tuk; 'ahng; armored vehicle -- ro't kra

tape n. material for sealing packages, etc. -- scot' (from "scotch tape"); material on which to record sounds -- ka'ssett (common AP: k'syte); (NB: ka'ssett is also used to mean the "cassette" on which recording tape is wound, and the machine that plays the cassette; context usually indicates which of the three possible meanings of "ka'ssett" the speaker intends.)

tape machine (cassette player) n. mun'yaye (fr. Fr.); ka'ssett (AP: k'syte)

tape measure n. met sum'puht

tape recorder n. ma'seen tawt sum'leng; (lit: machine to copy sound: sum'leng = sound; tawt = copy (or take, as in take a picture = tawt roob))

tapering adj. sroo'it tang chung

tapeworm n. pr'ooon

target n. to shoot at -- ti dow; kaw p'tooh dow; production or other commercial target -- kum'rut kum'nauwt; conceptual target, s.th. to be attained -- dum'ro(v) teuh ro'k

tart adj. jchot: a tart green banana -- jchayk k'chey jchot

task n. assigned job -- phea'reh'kej: [Teaching] is the task of teachers, lying [is] the task of lawyers. -- [Kaa bong rian] chia phea'reh'kej ro'bah kruu, kaa ko'hawk [chia] phea'reh'kej ro'bah neh ch'bop.

taste n. flavor -- chee'it; rooh chee'it: The taste of this soup is delicious. -- Rooh chee'it sa'law ni chng'anyh.; dry or weak taste -- sawh'kaw'kra'h: This bread has no taste. -- Num ni sawh'kaw'kra'h.; bland tasting, not enough sugar, soy sauce, etc. -- plee'o: That soup is too bland. -- Sam'law noo plee'o.; "just right" -- tro mwot

taste v. ploo'(k): Do you want to taste the soup? -- Neh jchong ploo'(k) sam'law roo tay?; ploo'(k)... lo meuhl: Do you want to taste the soup and see if its good? -- Neh jchong ploo'(k) sam'law lo muehl chng'anyh roo tay?

tasty adj. chng'anyh; miun roo'a chee'it; tro mwot

tattoo n. saak: tattooed all over (phrase descriptive of appearance of some Khmer men from remote rural areas) -- saak penyh kloo'an; to tattoo s. o. -- saak

tax n. puhn: pay taxes -- bung puhn; on a tax-free basis (lit: without paying taxes) -- k'miun bung puhn tay; money to be used for paying taxes -- praa(k) puhn

taxi n. laan ch'nool; (bus = rot yun ch'nool, or bus)

T. B. n. ro'beyng

tea n. generally -- ta'aae (AP: "thigh", ta'ee); tea leaves (lit: dry tea) -- ta'aae kree'im; tea in regular, drinkable liquid form -- tuk ta'aae; tea with [milk] -- ta'aae [tuk'dawh'gko]; tea with canned milk -- ta'aae ta'd'koo kum'pong; (NB: "ta'd'koo" is typical spoken compression of "tuk'dawh'gko".); hot tea -- ta'aae k'dau; iced tea -- ta'aae t'kaw; tea pot -- pan' ta'aae

teach v. bung rian; maintain discipline in a school -- praw'dai, praw'dow

teacher n. generally -- kruu; kruu bung rian; usually refering to a specifically female teacher -- neh kruu; or, neh kruu bong rian; usually referring to a specifically male teacher -- lok kruu; or, lok kruu bong rian; teacher who is a monk -- preah ree'ech kruu; professor -- sas'tra'cha; professor, specifically female -- neh kruu sas'tra'cha; specifically male -- lok kruu sas'tra'cha; learned person who pamy or may not live in wat -- a'char

teaching n. kaa bung rian: the teaching of physics -- kaa bung rian ney ruu vi'chee'a; teachings, advice (fr. higher authority) -- dum'bol miun; or, kaa too miun: ... the teachings of Buddha -- dum'bol miun ney Preah Phut; need advice from -- tro kaa kaa too miun pi... ; kaa dum'bol miun pi neh.; (studying = kaa rian so't or kaa suk'sah)

team n. krum; pooh; vung; military team, force -- kawng: special action team -- kawng ch'lope

teapot n. pan'ta'aae

tear v. hyke; raw hyke: You will tear the book. -- Neh raw hyke s'po.; tear apart, i. e., into pieces -- hyke ro'yee ro'yaiye; tear apart, i. e., turn inside-out, upside-down -- reuh cho'choos; reuh kaw'kye: The police came in and tore the whole house apart. -- Dum'roo'it jchole mok reuh kaw'kye penyh ptay'a.

tear n. tuk pn'aae'k; tears of joy -- sow'eet te'ang tuk pn'aae'k

tease v. jchum'on; jchum'on leng; ni'yaye jchum'on; inclined to tease -- ro(r) peu(s) mwot: He's a tease, he likes to tease, he likes to kid around, etc. -- Gwat ro(r) peu(s) mwot.

technical adj. pa'chay'ka'tay

technician n. neh pa'chay'ka'tay; Soviet technicians -- pa'chay'ka'tay So'vee'e'tique

technique n. ma'choo'bye; snee'it

teenager n. k'mayng chum tung: You are acting like a teenager. -- Neh tveu ro'k doj chia k'mayng chum tung.

teeth n. t'ming: brush teeth -- dos t'ming

telecommunications n. to'ra'kej

telegram n. too'ra'layke; k'sye loo'ah; tel'gram; (NB: The phrase "send a telegram" can be expressed by at least five different phrases: vyo too'ra'layke; vye k'sye loo'ah; vye tel'gram; p'nya(r) too'ra'layke; and p'nya(r) tel'gram

telephone n. to'ra'sap (AP: too'ra'sap): Do you have a telephone here [that I can use]?. -- Tau(v) neh miun to'ra'sap noeh ti ni [dael kyom adje pra] baan tay?

telephone v. make a call -- haow; to'ra'sap: I telephoned him this morning. -- Kyom to'ra'sap gwat pruhk muun.; answer the phone -- soo'a to'ra'sap; or, leuk telephone: Why didn't you answer [when I called]? -- Neh hyte eye mun leuk telephone [peyr kyom haow]?; The line is busy -- Telephone ro'vull.; no answer -- ot miun jchum'la'wee; wrong number -- layke koh; leave a message for -- p'dum p'nya(r) sum'rap: Can I leave a message for her? -- Kyom adje p'dum p'nya(r) sum'rap nee'eng baan tay?; Please [tell him] I want him to... [do this and do that]? -- Sum prap gwat tha kyom jchong owi gwat tveu... [tveu ni, tveu nu, etc.]; I will call back. -- Kyom nung haow mok venyh.

television n. too'ra'too'a; vee'day'o; (radio = vi'choo)

tell v. prap (AP: pra'): Someone told me. -- Miun gkay prap kyom.; ni'yaye prap: Someone told me so. -- Miun gkay ni'yaye prap kyom tha un'cheunyh.; respectful, for elders, etc. -- jchuum ree'up: I will tell my father tomorrow. -- Kyom nung jchuum ree'up Paa s'eye'd..; tool: I told the monk the year of my birth (lit: my year). -- Kyom tool lok chh'nam kyom.; tell s.o. to do s.th. -- prap owi: He told me, "do this, do that." -- Gwat owi kyom, "tveu ni, tveu nu."; tell in detail, tell all about -- ree'up ro'ap: Please tell me all about your trip. -- Jchor neh ree'ap ro'ap om'pee kaa tveu dum'narr ro'bah neh.

temper v. loo'ut; (tempered steel -- dyke loo'ut)

temper n. jchet klang; or, chhop khung (lit: gets angry quickly)

temperature n. say'twun'nu'pheap: What is the temperature now? -- Say'twun'nu'pheap [pu'man ong'sa] eye leaou? (lit: The temperature is how many degrees now?); What is the temperature outside? -- Tau(v) say'twun'na'pheap kang krau pu'man ong'sa?

tempest n. k'shaal p'chooh

temple n. overall temple complex -- wat: major wat in downtown Phnom Penh -- Wat Phnom; prayer building or room -- vi'he'ar: (i) northern Cambodian province bordering Thailand and (ii) well-known wat in far north of that province for which province was named -- Preah Vi'he'ar; monks' reception and living areas -- sa'la jchung; monks' residence -- kut lok; as monument -- praw'satt: praw'satt Angkor Wat

temporary adj. bun'daah'a'sun: temporary job -- kaa bun'daa'a'sun; chen'trei; (permanent -- a chen'trei (lit: not temporary))

tempt v. tveu jchet owi; tveu owi jchong

temptation n. kaa num owi jchong; jchum'nung

ten n. dup; ten [bottles] of beer -- bee'a dup [dop]; dup + classifier: ten cows -- gko dup k'bal (lit: cows ten head); ten men -- ma'nooh dup neh (lit: people ten persons)

ten thousand adj. dup pwan; moi meun

tendency n. s'kd'eye lome'ee'un: He has a tendency to lie. -- Gwat miun lome'ee'un ko'hawk.

tender adj. tuun; paw'ee paw'ee: tender meat -- sat(ch) paw'ee paw'ee

tendon n. saw'sye (also means "strand")

tennis n. te'nnit

tense adj. tung

tent n. ten'g (fr. Fr.); k'tome (lit: hut)

tenure n. term of office -- ro'yeht kaal: His term was two years. -- Ro'yeht kaal ro'bah gwat keuh pi chh'nam.; kaan kaab mok dum'nyne; (written form = a'ni'tek'kaal); land tenure -- suut tveu kaa tuk daiy [baan ro'hote] (lit: [perpetual] right to work land)

term n. of a contract, treaty, agreement, etc. -- kaw; term of office -- ro'yeht kaal; be on good terms with -- tro ka'neea chi'moi: I hope I [will stay] on good terms with you. -- Kyom sung'khum tha kyom [nung] tro ka'neea chi'moi neh.

terminal n. i. e., bus station -- beyn laan; jchum'naut la'an; jchum'naut ro't'yun; s'ta'nee laan; train station -- s'ta'nee ro't'pleung

terminate v. banyh jchawp: They terminated the aid. -- Gkay banyh jchawp kaa choo'ay.; terminate or break off a relationship -- p'dach: You and they should terminate your relationship. -- Neh nung gkay tro kaa p'dach kaa tek tong ka'neea.

termite n. kun dee'a

terrain n. ree'ung teh'sa'pheap; alluvial terrain -- veel la'bub (lit: plain of mud/clay)

terrible adj. a'krah nah

terribly adv. sum bahm: It's terribly hot today. -- T'ngai ni k'dau sum bahn.; This restaurant is terribly expensive. -- Noeh k'nong poch'ni'tan ni ma'hope tlai sum bahm nah.

territory n. in sense of land area -- tuk daiy; in sense of administrative area -- dum'bun: They lost a lot of territory in Po'sat. -- Pooh'gkay bat bong tuk daiy ch'raan noeh dum'bun Po'sat. (NB: as in this sentence, dum'bun can also mean region, area of, etc.); dyne daiy; or, dyne; (border = tul'dyne, connoting, "across from (another) territory")

terror n. peer'veh'kaam

terrorism n. peer'veh'kaam; vi'chi'ta'kaam

terrorist n. peer'veh'chuun

test n. exam -- kaa praw'long; kaa sahk: trial run -- kaa sahk lo'bong; rocket test -- kaa sahk lo'bong ro'kit; medical test(s) -- kaa pee'nut ro'bah peyt: go get a test or check-up: teuh owi peyt pee'nut; sahk lo'bong: a test of your character -- sahk lo'bong leh ka'nak neh

test v. sahk... lo'meuhl; test the radio -- sahk radio lo'meuhl; Test it and see (if it's OK). -- Lo'meuhl sun teuh.; sahk lo'bong; experiment -- pi' sowt: We need to test the new engine. -- Yeung tro kaa pi'sowt kreung ma'seen t'maee lo meuhl.; praw'long: We will test the students tomorrow. -- Yeung nung praw'long gkon'sa s'eye'd.

testimony n. kaa sun sah'sye; saa kye'ya'pheap; deposition -- kaa jchum'la'wee bun'chee

Thai adj. Tha'ee; See'um

Thailand n. sruk See'um; sruk Tha'ee

than conj. more... than -- chiang: His car is more expensive than my house. -- Laan ro'bah gwat tlai chiang ptay'a ro'bah kyom.

thank v. aw'kuun

Thank God! xcl. Aw'kuun Preah!.

thanks n. umn'aw kuun; kaa aw'kuun

that adj. that -- nu; nung: that teacher -- lok kruu nu; lok kruu nung; that one -- moi nu; moi nung; a moi nu; a moi nung

that adv. [unstated]: It isn't that far. -- Veea mun chng'eye tay.

that prn. generally -- nu; nung: That is good. -- Nu la'aw.; colloquial -- a nu; a nung: That's no good. -- A nu mun la'aw.; that in sense of "that way" -- aae'chung: Why did you ask that? -- Mutch baan neh soo'a aae'chung?; an'chung: He shouldn't do that. -- Gwat mun koo'a tveu eye an'chung.; like that -- doj cha'neh; doj cha'nawh: Why did you say that? -- Hyte eye ni'yaye doj cha'nawh?; (NB: cha'neh = this way; cha'nawh = that way; they are compressions, respectively, of "doj chia nehh" and "doj chia nawh"); m'lung m'lung peyk: Don't do that. -- Kum tveu m'lung m'lung peyk tay.; yang ni: That's the reason why. -- Yang ni howi baan.; ru'ung nu: That is a problem, too. -- Ru'ung nu pun'ha da'aae.; dael: the car that he bought -- laan dael tinh

that conj. doll: He [gave] me such trouble [that] I had to fire him. -- Gwat [pdull] owi kyom kaa lum'bah [doll] kyom tro tai denyh veea jchowl.; tha: He says that... -- Gwat ni'yaye tha...

That's alright. xcl. Mun eye tay.

theater n. for movies -- ro'ng gkun; rong pheap yun; for classical dance -- ro'ng ma'how'srawp; (NB: two leading classical dance theatres in Phnom Penh before 1975 were the Che'ta Muk and the Tunlay Bassac)

their poss. prn. object + pooh'gkay: their houses -- ptay'a pooh'gkay; object + gkay: their books -- s'po gkay; object + ro'bah pooh'gkay: their weapons -- a'vwut ro'bah pooh'gkay; object + ro'bah gkay: their clothes -- kow-aow ro'bah gkay; colloquial -- a nu; a nung: their teacher -- lok kruu a nu; or, lok kruu a nung; (both lit: the teacher of them)

them prn. referring to a general, non-specified "them" -- pooh'gkay (APs: poo'kay, pooh'kay, por'gkay, poor'kay, pwa'gkay, poo'a gkay' poo'h gkay); also: gkay; referring to specific groups of them: them (those people over there) -- pooh'gkay nu, pooh'gkay nung (APs: pooa'nu, pooa'nung); referring to females -- pooh'nee'eng; referring in a less-than-completely respectful way, i. e., for close friends, children, those of lower social rank -- pooh'veea; referring to "those guys" -- pooh'gwat; them, all of them, in a group -- te'ang awh ka'neea; [unstated] -- Them?? (in sense of, "was it really them?") -- Maan'ch?? (lit: Really??)

then adv. next in order -- bun'to'up: First we ate, then we slept. -- Dum'bong nyam bye, ban'to'up teuh dayke.; ban'to'up mok: I have to wake up at 7 a. m., then brush my teeth. -- Tro krau pi geyng mao prum'pul, bun'to'up mok dos t'ming.; What then? -- Ban'to'up mok?; at that time -- peyr nu: It happened then. -- Kaut laung peyr nu.; howi nung: He came home, then left (again). -- Gwat mok ptay'a venyh howi nung jchenyh tee'it.; roo'it mok: They went to the market, then home. -- Gkay teuh p'sa, roo'it mok teuh ptay'a.

then conj. as a result -- an'chung: (Person A: I can't go now. Person B:) Well, then, you'll be late. -- An'chung neh nung yeut howi.; as a result, consequently -- kaw: If I go, then you go too. -- Kyon kaw teuh, neh kaw teuh.

theory n. treuus dai (AP: troos'dye): That [sounds like] a good theory, but I don't think it will work. -- A nu [hyte doj chia] treuss dai la'aw, pun'ta'aae kyom ot kut veea nung praw'ka kaut.

therapy n. vi'ti p'chia'bal rohk [vi'ti = action; p'chia'bal = to treat, rohk = disease, disbility]

Theravada adj. Tee'ra'vit

there adv. ti nu: She lives there (where I'm pointing). -- Nee'eng noeh ti nu.; ti nung (lit: that place): She lives there (in that place we were talking about). -- Nee'eng noeh ti nung.; over there -- eye nu: She lives there (over there, a bit far away). -- Nee'eng noeh eye nu.; noeh ti nu; or, noeh ti nung: (NB: In constructions such as these, "noeh" may convey "located" (express or implied) or "is located", rather than "lives", as appropriate to the context, viz: i) I see smoke (located) over there. -- Kyom keunyh ps'eye'n noeh ti nu.; ii) The house is (located) over there. -- Ptay'a noeh ti nu.)

there prn. veea: [There] will not be food [there]. -- [Veea] nung ot miun ma'hope [ti nu].; there is, there are -- miun: There is no rice. -- Bye ot miun.; There's [plenty of] soup here. -- Miun sam'law [ch'raan ho'hee'a] noeh ti ni.; noeh: There are eight days [left]. -- Noeh [sahl(t)] prum'bye t'ngai.; there is not, there is nothing -- k'miun: There is nothing I can do. -- K'miun a'veye dael kyom adje teuh baan.

thereby adv. taam ro'yeht ni; taam ro'yeht nu; taam hyte

kaa ni: The driver [refused] to bring the car, thereby making it impossible to go. -- Neh baahk baw [mun prome] no'um laan mok, taam ro'yeht nu tveu owi kyom ot miun ra'ta'pheap nung teuh.

therefore adv. doj cha'neh

thermometer n. taae'ya'mo'met

thermos, thermos bottle n. thay'r'mo's (fr. Fr.)

these adj. and prn. ni; a ni; or, a moi ni: (same words and usage as for "this"; see examples under that heading)

thesis n. concept -- kum'nut; degree paper -- ni'kype bawht

they prn. generally -- pooh'gkay: They refused. -- ; re variations, see discussion under "them".

thick adj. krah; kobb

thief n. jchaao

thigh n. ploe

thin adj. skinny, of solid objects, including the human body -- scoe'm; like paper -- s'dalng; a thin wall -- chuun chee'ung s'dalng; slender -- ree'o; of liquids, watery -- ree'o: This soup is very thin, i. e., watery. -- Sa'law ni ree'o nah.

thing(s) n. ro'bah (AP: ro'bawh, ro'ba, ra'bah): many things -- ro'bah ch'raan; these/those things -- ro'bah ni/nu; yang: many things -- yang ch'raan: This one word means two things. -- Peea moi ni mutch pi yang.; ru'ung: There were sure a lot of (bad) things that happened (e.g., while he was gone, during the war, that year, etc.) -- Kaw miun ru'ung ch'raan ma'lch.; in sense of story, case, situation -- ru'ung: I am happy about only one thing. -- Kyom jchet s'bai om'pee ru'ung moi kut.; relations between people -- tum neh tum nong: Things are getting better between them. -- Tum neh tum nong ro'vieng pooh'gkay miun pheap praw'sar laung.; relations ("things") between institutions, nations, etc. -- kaa tek tong; unfavorable developments -- ru'ung roaw: A lot of (bad) things [happened]. -- Miun ru'ung roaw pieh ch'raan [kaut laung].; conditions -- s'ta'na'pheap: Things in Phnom Penh are better [now]. -- [T'ngai ni] s'ta'na'pheap noch Phnom Penh praw'sar laung.; conditions -- yang: How are things in Po'sat? -- Tau(v) yang na da'aae noeh Po'sat?; "things" in a house, furnishings -- vuh'to; things to carry, to store, to pack, etc. -- aye'von

think v. cogitate -- kut: He doesn't think very quickly. -- Gwat kut mun ro'has tay.; Think fast! -- Kut owi ro'has teuh!; think ahead (i. e., think long-term) -- kut venyh chng'eye; think ahead (i.e., anticipate, think before doing) -- kut chia muun;

  have an opinion -- kut: What do you think of it? -- Kut yang na da'aae om'pee veea?; think so, think (that), or think s. th. -- kut tha (generally compressed in speech to "k'tha"): I think so. -- Kyom kut tha.; Kyom kut tha yang.; (NB: common contrction of kut tha' is "k'I think that we should go. -- Kyom k'tha yeung tro jchenyh.;

believe that -- kut tha: I thought I saw my friend.-- Kyom kut tha keunyh mit kyom.;

consider -- kut koo: Think about that plan. -- Kut koo om'pee pyne'kaa nu.; think hard about, analyze -- treh' ree pi ch'raan om'pee pun'ha nu;

think of (be able to recall) -- kut lic om'pee: I couldn't think of his name. -- Kyom kut mun lic om'pee ch'moo'h gwat.;

think of (think about) -- kut doll: thinking of you -- kut doll neh;

think up -- kut ro'k: I have to think up a name for my dog. -- Kyom tro kut ro'k chamoo'h sh'kye kyom.;

be not quite sure -- praw'heil, praw'heil: I think (but I am not quite sure that) I saw you [somewhere else]. -- Kyom praw'heil praw'heil keunyh neh [noeh aae na].

thinking n. kaa kut

third adj. ti bye

Third World n. praw'tet ti bye (lit: third countries)

thirst n. kaa sreyk; sreyk tuk: This animal will die of thirst. -- Saat praw'ha ni nung slop dow'ee sa sreyk tuk.

thirsty adj. sreyk tuk; I'm thirsty. -- Kyom sreyk tuk.

thirty adj. sam sup

this adj. ni: this road -- ploe ni, t'nawl ni

this prn. ni: like this -- doj ni; a ni: This is the best. -- Ni la'aw bom pot; this (one) -- a moi ni: I'll take this (one). -- Nung yok a moi ni.; this (thing, item) -- ro'bah ni: This is for you. -- Ro'bah ni sum'rap neh eiyne.; this (thing, piece of work, etc.) -- kej kaa nee

this way adv. ph. in this direction (lit: here) -- mok nchh; in this fashion or manner -- ro'bee'up ni

thorn n. bun'la

thoroughly adv. saw(p) te'ang awh

those adj. nu; or, nung (AP: nong): those men -- ma'nooh nu

those prn. a nu; or, a nung (AP: nong): Those are no good. -- A nu ot la'aw. (see, also, examples under "that"; ni, a ni, a moi ni, etc. can mean "those" as well as "that")

thought n. kum'nut

thousand adj. generally -- pwan (APs: pwun, po'an): one thousand -- moi pwan; ten thousand -- moi meun; one hundred thousand -- dop meun; moi syne

thread n. jchey(ɜɜ); um'bawh; thick thread/thin string -- saw sye um'bawh

threat n. kaa kuum ree'un; kaa bum pheut.bum pay

threaten v. kuum ree'um kuum hye'ng: The State Department [always said] that Vietnam was threatening Thailand. -- Kra'soo'ung Kaa Bor'tay [tyne tai ni'yaye chia'nik] tha praw'tet Vietnam kuum ree'um kuum hye'ng praw'tet See'um.; bum pheut bum pay: The student threatened the teacher. -- Gkon'sa bum pheut bum pay kruu.; seems/seemed likely to -- meuhl adje: It threatened to rain. -- Veea meuhl adje plee'eng.

three adj. bye

thresh v. by beating -- bauwk; beat/thresh rice -- bauwk sro; by walking on s. th. -- byne; walk/thresh rice -- byne sro; by using animals to step on s. th. -- byne cho'un

thrifty adj. tahm

throat n. bum puu'ng khaw: a dry throat -- khaw sngoo'it; a sore throat -- chh'ooh khaw; a bitter taste in the throat -- kaah khaw

throne n. the physical object -- ba'laahng; the office/ position/institution -- ree'ech ba'laahng: The king ascended the throne (i.e., became king) in 1945. -- S'dach laung to'tool ree'ech ba'laahng k'nong chh'nam 1945.

through prp. down the middle of -- kaat: We drove through [the town]. -- Yeung baahk baw kaat [ti krong].; We walked through the jungle. -- Yeung dah kaat prey la'bot.; from one side to the other, in one side out the other -- ch'long (lit: across): through the mountains -- ch'long phnom; by means of -- taam: The thieves came in through the window. -- Jchaao jchole taam bung'oo'it.; dow'ee sa: He got his job through [influence]. -- Gwat baan kej kaa tveu dow'ee sa [a'ti'pul].

throughout prp. penyh moi: Throughout his life he was an honest man. -- Penyh moi chi'vut ro'bah gwat, gwat chia ma'nooh sm'oh trong.; Throughout his career... -- Penyh moi chi'vut kaa'ngyhee'a gwat...; ch'long kaat peyr: Throughout the war it was difficult to find food. -- Ch'long kaat peyr sung'kree'um pi'bah sveye ro'k ma'hope.

throw v. throw overhand -- kuup; or (countryside, esp. Battambong) kro'vanyh; or, kro'vwat; or, jchowl; throw casually or not too hard, usually underhand, i. e, toss -- bawh: toss a ball around -- bawh balle; throw away -- bawh jchowl; kro'vanyh jchowl: He threw away your picture. -- Gwat bawh jchowl roob tawt neh.; Throw it away. (Get rid of it.) -- Kro'vanyh jchowl teuh.; throw in with, join -- jchole ru'um; throw in the towel, give up -- jchaw jchanyh

thumb n. may dai

thunder n. p'kaw lo'an

thunderbolt n. lightning -- ru'n ta'ch

Thursday n. pro'hoa; t'ngai pro'hoa

thus adv. consequently -- doj cha'neh (AP: doj ch'nawh): The government had a plan for [the budget] already; thus there was no way to get money for the school. -- Ratta'pi'bal miun pyne [kaa sum'rap taa'vi'kaa] roo'it howi; doj ch'neh ot miun ploe nung baan loi sum'rap sa'la'rin.; this way; so -- un'cheunyh: It cannot be thus. -- Veea ot un'cheunyh tay.; therefore, as in, inter alia, mathematical proof -- no'um owi: A = B, B = C, thus A = C -- A = B, B = C, no'um owi B = C

ticket n. li'kut; sum'buht: movie ticket -- sum'buht gkun; airline ticket -- sum'buht yun hawh; police ticket -- bun: I got two tickets [from the police]. -- Kyom to'tool bun pi [pi police].

ticklish adj. raw sauwp

tie n. necktie -- kro'vat; kro'vat khaw; even (score) -- sm'aar: It ended in a tie. -- Lo'bye'ng sm'aar ka'neea.

tie v. jchaawng: tie rope -- jchaawng k'sye; tie one's shoes -- jchaawng s'bye'k cheung; kree'ik; to be tied up -- cho'op knawh; cho'op jchum'nong; (knot -- jchum'nong)

tiffan n. stacked food bowl set -- seh dah(k) ma'hope

tiger n. saat kla

tight adj. of clothes -- tung: This clothing is tight. -- Kow-aow ni tung.; chung'eet; strict, rigorous -- tung tyne: tight security -- san'tek'sohk tung tyne; Tie it tightly. -- Jchaawng veea owi tung.

tighten v. rut: Please tighten the knot. -- Sum rut jchum'nong owi tung.

tile n. for roof -- k'boo'ung; for floor -- utt sum'rap kral (utt = brick; kral = covering for/over a dirt floor)

tilt v. bum bahh: Don't tilt the table. -- Kum bum bahh tohk.

tilted adj. jchum tut k'dut k'dut svaw

timber n. felled tree trunks' logs -- cheu hope; sawn timber -- cheu; house timbers -- cheu song ptay'a

time n. generally -- peyr (written peyl, pronounced closer to peyr): Do you have time now? -- Tau(v) neh miun peyr eye leaou?; instances -- peyr; or, leuk; or, dong: I've been to Siem Reap two times. -- Kyom teuh Siem Reap pi dong howi. (see, also, examples under "times (instances)", below); time on the clock -- mao (written maong, pronounced mao): What time is it? -- Mao pu'man eh? (NB: "ch" is contraction of "howi" very commonly used in this phrase.); time in sense of era or time perod -- kaal; or, ro'yeht peyr (see examples in usage list below); also:

any time at all -- peyr na kaw baan da'aae

at a time when -- peyr dael: At a time when I needed help, you were not around (lit: went far away). -- Peyr dael kyom tro kaa choo'ay, neh teuh chng'eye.; also, noeh peyr dael; kaal dael chng'eye

by the time that -- peyr dael: By the time that you telephoned me, I had already left. -- Peyr dael neh telephone owi kyom, kyom jchenyh bot howi.

during the time that -- kum'lung peyr dael: during the time Lon Nol was in control... -- Kum'lung peyr dael Lon Nol kroop krong...

(the) first time -- leuk ti moi

for the time being -- bun daw'a'sun

give a hard time to -- tveu baap teuh

good time. -- s'bai: Have a good time. -- Teuh owi baan s'bai.

It's time. -- Doll peyr howi.

long time/for a long time -- chia yoo' mok howi

lose time -- bot peyr

on time -- tee'ung mao; tee'ung twon; tee'ung peyr; twon peyr; twon mao; tro mao;

not on time -- ot twon mao; mun twon

over (the course of) time -- tic m'dong tic m'dong

same time (i. e., as before) -- mao twa'ma'da

spare time, to do s. th. during (lit: to do s. th. while waiting) -- tveu kaa baan doll baan doll

take a long time -- yok peyr yang yoo': It takes a long time to drive from Ho Chi Minh to Phnom Penh. -- Veea yok peyr yang yoo' dum'bye baahk baw pi HCM teuh Phnom Penh.

this time -- peyr ni; also: leuk ni, dong ni, m'dong ni, va'lee'a (AP:vaae'lee'a) ni;

this time tomorrow -- s'eye'd sm'auu ni

that time -- peyr nu, etc.

time/era -- chuum'no'an: In [President] Reagan's time, prices went up. -- Chuum'no'an [praw'teea'neea tep'a'dye] Reagan, tuum ninyh laung tlai.); also, sa'mye: in Lon Nol's time... -- noeh sa'mye Lon Nol...;

time [limit] -- peyr va'lee'a dael [kum'nauwt]

time in sense of an interval -- peyr va'lee'a (AP: vaae'lee'a)

time in sense of reign -- ree'ech kaal: In Sihanouk's time (i. e., during Sihanouk's reign) -- noeh ree'ech kaal See'a'noo;

Time's up! -- Doll mao howi.; or, Kum'roop peyr; or, Chope! (lit: Stop!)

waste time -- kaht peyr

times n. instances -- leuk: the first time -- leuk ti moi, dong: [The first] three times I got lost. -- Bye dong [dum'bong] kyom vehng ruung.; I have eaten fish [many] times. -- Kyom nyam trei ch'raan dong howi.; va'lee'a

(AP: vaae'lee'a): this time -- va'lee'a ni; m'dong: this time -- m'dong ni; one or two times -- m'dong pi dong howi: You have already lied one or two times (once or twice). -- M'dong pi dong howi dael neh ni'yaye ko'hawk.; a few times -- pi bye m'dong (lit: two-three times)

timid adj. toi moy

timing n. peyr va'lee'a

tin n. sum'naw pa'hahng

tin can n. kum'pong; (NB: river bank = kom'puung)

tinder n. ahws to'ich to'ich

tiny adj. la'ut la'ow'ich: This fruit is too tiny (i. e., not big enough)! -- Plai cheu ni la'ut la'ow'ich doll howi.

tip n. gratuity: generally -- kum r'eye; slang term which can refer either to a legal or an illegal tip -- tuk ta'aae (lit: tea; similar to Thai expression with same meaning, "tea money"); extreme end of s. th. -- jchung: tip of the tounge -- jchung un'dah; tip of a pen -- jchung "bic"

tip off v. owi kaa (lit: give information)

tip-toe v. dah chuum'eeu(t)

tire n. of bicycle -- kong kong: I need a tire for my bike. -- Kyom tro kaa kong sum'rap kong kyom; of car -- kong laan; of motorbike or motorcycle -- kong mo'to

tired adj. hawt: tired and hungry -- hae'uv hawt; weak -- awh kum'lung; noo'i

tired of s. th., to get v. tunyh tro'ung: I'm tired of listening to his [complaining]. -- Kyom tunyh tro'ung loo [kaa la'oo ro'too'am] ro'bah gwat nah.

title n. name of s. th. -- jchum'nong cheung: What is the title of the book you're looking for? -- A'veye chia jchum'nong cheung ney s'po dael neh sveye rok?; title to property -- sum'buht m'chah: title to a car -- sum'buht m'chah laan (me'cha = owner)

to v. as an infinitive marker, the English "to" is either a) contained in main verb word or, b) if the action of the infinitive verb was to have taken place in the future, indicated by "nung", viz: a) I want to eat. -- Kyom jchong nyam bye.; and b) It's impossible to go. -- Ot miun rat'ta'pheap nung teuh. (rat'ta'pheap = possibility, ability, capability)

to prp.

in the direction of -- teuh; jchum'poo'a; or, mok:

When the movement of the action verb is specifically or implicitly away from the speaker -- as, "This road goes (from here) to Po'sat." -- "to" is expressed by teuh, teuh kaan, or jchum'poo'h. Thus the sentence abovecould be "Ploe ni teuh jchum'poo'h   Po'sat." (with "teuh" in this sentence meaning "goes" and "jchum'poo'h" supplying the "to"). Similarly: "They walked to the market." would be "Gkay dah teuh p'sa.", with "to" translated by "teuh".

When the movement of the action verb is specifically towards the speaker "to" is expressed by "mok", as: They walked to my house last night. -- Gkay dah mok ptay'a kyom yoop munyh.

Some sentences, identical in English, will thus be expressed differently in Khmer depending on where the speaker is located. For example, "They want to drive to Ho Chi Minh." would be "Gkay jchole jchet baahk teuh HCM." if the speaker is in or near Phnom Penh and the "driving" is headed away from him/her, but "Gkay jchole jchet baahk mok HCM" if the speaker is already in or near HCM and the "driving" would be coming towards him/her.

in order to -- dum'bye: He did it to help. -- Gwat tveu veea dum'bye choo'ay.; To get there quickly, take Highway 5. -- Dum'bye teuh doll yang ro'has, yok ploe layke pram.;

with which to -- dum'bye: [tools] to fix the car (with) -- [kaa praw'dop, praw'daah] dum'bye choo'ah chul laan.;

to benefit s.o. or s. th. -- teuh or mok depending (as above) on direction of movement of action: He gives money to them. -- Gwat owi loi <u>teuh</u> neh nung.; mok: Please hand that telephone to me. -- Sum owi to'ra'sap nu <u>mok</u> kyom.;

relating to, on the part of -- jchum'poo'h: [He seems] to me to be a good person. -- Jcham'poo'h kyom [gwat doj chia] ma'nooh la'aw.;

up to, as far as -- teuh doll: up to Po'sat -- teuh doll Po'sat;

up to you -- srech tai neh eiyne

toad n. king koo'a (NB: frog = kong kype)

toady n. hanger-on -- neh aiype awhp; a'may'a'tong: Lon Nol's group of hangers-on [fell from power] because of corruption]. -- Pooh a'may'a'tong ro'bah Lon Nol [baan t'leh pi um'natch] dow'ee sa pu'ka'ra loi.

toast n. num pahng ang (lit: grilled bread)

tobacco n. tnam chooh; ba'r'eye tnam

toe n. generally -- ma'ree'um cheung: big toe -- may cheung; little toe -- gkon cheung; toe-nail -- kraw'haw cheung; (N: finger = ma'ree'um dai); (n: nail in wood = dyke kohl)

today n. t'ngai ni; (PM: t'ngai nik)

together adj. coordinated; "on the same wavelength" -- sraw ka'neea: That band is really together. -- Krum plaeng nu leng sraw ka'neea.; The team never got it together this year. -- Chh'nam ni krum ni leng mun sraw ka'neea.

together adv. chi'moi ka'neea: Let's go together. -- Tau(v) yeung teuh chi'moi ka'neea.; all together -- te'ang awh ka'neea; choop chum chi'moi: She wanted to live together with her older brother. -- Nee'eng jchong roo noeh choop chum chi'moi bong proh nee'eng.; get together with (friends) -- mool ka'neea chi'moi (mit pa'ya); put together -- p'kuum; p'chuu'op; together with -- ru'um chi'moi

toil n. kaa tveu kaa noo'i hawt (lit: tiring work)

toil v. tveu kaa noo'i hawt (lit: do s. th. tiring)

toilet n. bung kuuhn: toilet paper -- kra'dah bung kuuhn; go to the toilet -- teuh bawt cheung

told pp. prap; (AP: pra); ni'yaye prap: Someone told me... -- Gkay ni'yaye prap kyom tha...; to be told of -- tro baan prap

tolerant (of) adj. leuk to'h (jchum'poo'h); yok yul (jchum'poo'h): This government is too tolerant of [corruption]. -- Ratt'a'pi'bal ni yok yul nah jchum'poo'h [om'peuh pu'ka'ra loi].

tolerate v. tra praw'nye; ot to'h; (NB: to'h alone = to punish; ot to'h = not punish, or, forgive)

tomato n. paeng pawh: tomato sauce (catsup) -- tuk paeng pawh

tomb n. grave -- p'no; tomb in a stupa -- jch'eye't

tomorrow n. t'ngai s'eye'd; s'eye'd; day after tomorrow -- kaan s'eye'd; two days after tomorrow -- kaan s'eye'd moi

ton n. tauwn; ton-kilometer (unit of measurement of amt. of goods transported) -- tauwn'kilo'

tonight n. yoop ni

tontine n. tontine (lottery or raffle in which players contribute to a "pot" held by a "chief" and then try to win the pot by submitting supposedly sealed bids to the chief and hoping to be the highest bidder. While "chiefs" are sometimes thought to rig play in favor of friends and family, tontine remains popular.)

too adv. excessive -- nah (also connotes "very"; AP: na'): too hot -- k'dau nah; too cold (or very cold) -- traw'cheh'(k) nah; It's too loud! -- Loo nah!; too s. th. to s. th. -- nung: too tired to play -- awh kum'lung nung leng; also -- da'aae; kaw... da'aae; pong da'aae: I will tell you too. -- Kyom nung prap neh pong da'aae.

too bad xcl. s'dye nah: Too bad I can't come. -- S'dye nah kyom ot baan mok.

too many adv. ch'raan nah (AP: commonly compressed in speech to "ch'ra'na", "char'na" or "charn"): There are too many people without jobs. -- Pra'chee'chuun ch'raan nah dael ot miun kaa tveu.; too many problems -- pun'ha ch'ra'na; most emphatically "too many", not just "many, many" -- ch'raan peyk: He bought too many gifts. -- Gwat tinh om'now'ee ch'raan peyk.; not too many -- ch'raan nah tay; or mun seu ch'raan nah tay: I do need to take a lot of clothes but not too many. -- Kyom tro kaa yok kow-aow ch'raan pun'ta'aae mun ch'raan nah tay. or, This market has a lot of things for sale, but not too many. -- Psa ni miun [aye'von looh ch'raan] pun'ta'aae [mun] ch'raan nah tay.

too much adv.　ch'raan: Too much! Too many! -- Ch'raan hoo'a!; Don't think too much. -- Kum kut ch'raan.; Too much hassle! -- Ru'ung ch'raan hoo'a hyke!

tool n.　praw'dab praw'dah: I need tools to fix the car. -- Kyom tro kaa praw'dab praw'dah dum'bye choo'ah chul laan.; (NB: instruments, as medical or scientific, = pah'ri'kaa)

tooth n.　t'ming: toothbrush -- ch'a'ruh dos t'ming (lit: brush [ch'a'ruh] to scrub [dos] teeth [t'ming]; toothpaste -- t'nam dos t'ming; toothpick -- cheu jchak t'ming (lit: wood to pick teeth)

top n.　leuh: top of the table -- leuh tohk; top of the head -- leuh k'bal; kum'pool: top of the hill -- kum'pool phnom; on top of -- noeh leuh: The book is on top of the table. -- S'po noeh leuh tohk.; on top of -- noeh leuh kum'pool: on top of the hill -- noeh leuh kum'pool phnom; put on the top of -- dah(k) noeh leuh

topic n.　ru'ung: Today I have to speak on the topic of economic development. -- T'ngai ni kyom tro kaa ni'yaye pi ru'ung a'pi'vwut.; praw'tee'un: The topic of the discussion is the economy. -- Praw'tee'un ney kaa pee'pee'a(k) saa keuh set'a'kej.

torn pp.　ro'hyke: The papers were all torn. -- Kra'dah ro'hyke aw'.; (NB: to tear = hyke); to be torn -- ro'hyke (or) tro baan hyke; torn to rags -- ro'hyke ro'ya; to be torn apart -- ro'hyke ro'yee ro'y'eye: The book was torn apart. -- S'po ro'hyke ro'yee ro'y'eye.

tornado n.　k'shaal koo'itch

torture n.　teea'run'na'kaam

torture v.　tveu teea'run'na'kaam; dah(k) veea'run'na'kaam; torture s. o. -- dah(k) veea'run'na'kaam jchum'poo'h gkay (lit: give, or inflict, torture)

total adj.　sa'rup: the total cost [of my trip] -- sa'rup dum'lye [ney dum'narr kyom]; jchum'noo'an: a total of three days -- jchum'noo'an bye t'ngai

totalitarian adj.　kaan um'natch p'dach kaa: totalitarian government -- ratt'a'pi'bal dael kaan um'natch p'dach kaa; dictatorial person, person "at the pinnacle of power" -- neh ka'dop um'natch

totalitarianism n.　kaa kaan um'natch p'dach kaa

toss v.　jchowl; bawh

touch v.　pah; p'waal: Don't touch me, and don't hit me either! -- Kum pah kyom, nung howi kum vye kyom pong da'aae!; put a finger or hand on s. th. -- kaan; stroke, touch tenderly -- stee'up; or, ong'eye'l; reach -- looo'k doll: Can you touch the ceiling? -- Tau(v) neh looo'k doll pee'dan?; get in touch with -- tek tong chi'moi gkay

touching story n.　ru'ung ruhm choo'ay jchet

tough adj.　not tender -- s'vut; hardy, aggressive -- soo; tough-talking -- rung mwot; get tough with s. o. -- leng toa k'dau

tounge n.　un'dah: (proverb) "Tounges have no bones (i.e., no discipline); they're only good for talking." (i.e., "Talk is cheap.") -- Un'dah ot cha'ung, jcheh tai ni'yaye.; slip of the tounge -- ch'roul mwot; plo'ot mwot; or r'boat mwot

tour n.　tour around an area, having a good time; used more typically re tour of a country or city -- kum'san leng k'nong; strictly "go and see", more typically used re tour of house, museum, palace, i.e., one fixed site -- kaa dah meuhl: tour of the palace -- kaa dah meulh vaac'eng

tour v.　dah'leng; tool s'nah; teuh leng; dah meuhl

tourism n.　tay sa'chaw

tourist n.　neh too's'naa; neh tay sa'chaw

tourniquet n.　kraw'not jchaawng tooo'b chee'im

tow v.　sun'dauw(ng): tow a boat to the beach -- sun'dauw(ng) toook teuh sa'mut; oh: He came to tow my car. -- Gwat muk oh laan kyom.

toward, towards prp.　indicating movement: direction of movement away from speaker -- teuh; teuh kang; sum'dau teuh; direction of movement toward speaker -- mok; mok kang; mok sum'dau:

When the movement of the action verb is either 1) specifically away from the speaker -- "He left me and headed toward the station." -- or 2) indeterminant re the speaker -- "They said he was heading towards his home, but I don't know where he lives." -- "toward" or "towards" is expressed by teuh, teuh kang or sum'dau teuh. In the first sentence above, "toward the station" would be "teuh s'ta'nee", and in the second, "towards his home" could be "teuh kang ptay'a gwat". Similarly, "I'm going to walk toward my house." would be "Kyom nung dah sum'dau teuh ptay'a kyom." since the action is moving away from where the speaker is at the time he makes his statement.

When the movement of the action verb is in the direction of the speaker -- "The child walked toward me." -- "toward" or "towards" is expressed by "mok", "mok kang" or "mok sum'dau". The sentence above would be "Gkon k'mayng dah sum'dau mok kyom."

Both teuh sum'dau and mok sum'dau suggest movement toward but not arrival at a certain point, viz.:
        going towards -- This road goes towards Po'sat (but doesn't go all the way to it.) -- Ploe ni teuh sum'dau Po'sat (pun'ta'aae mun teuh doll Po'sat tay.); The last time I saw him he was walking towards the hotel. (I don't know if he got there or not.) -- Peyr krow'eebung awh kyom keunyh gwat, gwat dah teuh sum'dau o'tyle;
        coming towards -- sum'dau mok or mok sum'dau: The enemy [tank] was coming towards us. -- [Ro'tkra] baahk sum'dau mok yeung.

towel n.   kun'syne; kun'syne poo'ah gko; (kun'syne originally referred to a towel of thin cotton cloth or "kra'mah," while kun'syne poo'ah gko referred to the thicker (Western-type) towel; kun'syne is now generally understood to refer to a standard, thick towel.)

tower n.   pahm

town n.   krong; ti'krong: head, or chief, of a town -- jchao'vye ti'krong; (NB: largest town subdivision (similar to a US "ward") = "kaahn"; kaahns in turn are subdivided into "sun kaats".)

townhouse n.   ptay'a cho'up ka'neea (lit: houses joined together); ptay'a l'veng (same word as that for apartment)

township n.   kuum (effectively, sub-district, i.e., subdivision of "sruk"/"district")

toy n.   praw'dob k'mayng leng

trace n.   sn'ahm; daan

trace v.   taam sn'ahm; taam daan

track n.   railroad -- ploe dyke; animal -- sn'ahm daan: tiger track -- sn'ahm daan kla

track v.   follow -- taam sn'ahm; taam daan

tract n.   piece or parcel of land -- daiy duhm; daiy... k'bal; daiy... lo: I have four or five tracts in Kompuung Cham. -- Kyom miun daiy buon pram k'bal noeh Kom'puung Cham.; report -- ro'bye'kaa

tractor n.   tractor: My father had two tractors [for ploughing] the paddies. -- Pa miun tractor pi [sum'rap p'shoo'a] sr'eye.

trade n.   commerce in general -- kaa looh do (lit: exchange); chuum'noo'inyh: international trade -- chuum'noo'inyh un'tra'chee'it; specific business -- muk ro'bab ro'see: What is your trade? -- Muk ro'bab ro'see tveu a'veye? (lit: What occupation/business do you do?); job, area of responsibility -- muk'ngeea; job, occupation -- kaa'ngyeea

trade v.   carry on commerce, or a business -- tveu chuum'noo'inyh; exchange, give s. th. for s. th. else -- do

trade-mark n.   ma'(k): What make is that car? -- Laan nung ma'(k) aae?; business name -- yee haow: What is the name of that book store? -- Haang looh s'po miun yee haow a'veye?

trader n.   neh chuum'noo'inyh

tradition n.   pra'pay'nee; tum'lee'um tum'law

traffic n.   jcheh'ra'jchaw; traffic jam -- ste'h jch'raw'jchaw

traffic-light n.   pleung stop; pleung kra'hom

trail n.   ploe looom

trailer n.   yee'un sum'dau; wagon towed behind cyclo -- ru'man

train n. ro'teh pleung (lit.: "wagon electric").

train v. bung haht; vuck veun; haht rian

trainer n. neh bung haht

training n. kaa bung haht; practice -- a'noo'vwut; or, kaa haht rian: I'm in training. -- Kyom kom'puung haht rian.

transfer v. bun chuun; pdo; plas: I was transferred. -- Kyon tro baan pdo. or, Kyom tro baan bun chuung.; or, Kyom tro baan plas.; Tranfer this file to [the other office]. -- Bun chuun ru'ung ni teuh [kaar'ya'lye moi tee'it teuh].; transfer from one place to another -- do pi cunlye'ng moi teuh cunlye'ng moi tee'it

transform v. tveu owi... plas pdo: We need to transform the economy. -- Yeung tro kaa tveu owi set'a'kej plas pdo.; to be transformed from.... to.... -- tro baan tveu owi klai om'pee... teuh... : Phnom Penh was transformed by the Khmer Rouge from [a beautiful city] into [a ruined city]. -- Phnom Penh tro baan tveu owi klai om'pee [ti'krong daw chat'i'chai] teuh [chia ti'krong bah(k) byke] dow'ee Khmei Kra'hom.

transgress v. commit unfriendly acts against -- la'meuh(s) praw'chang nung: In aiding the KR, the Thais transgressed international law. -- Dow'ee kaa choo'ay KR, See'um la'meuh(s) praw'chang nung ch'bop un'tra'chee'it.; (NB: la'meuh(s) = act against s. th., violate, etc.: This guy [always] violates the law. -- Neh ni la'meulhs nung ch'bop [chia'nik].)

transistor n. transistor

translate v. baw(k) pr'eye

translator n. neh baw(k) pr'eye

transparent adj. tlaa: clear water -- tuk tlaa: re clothes -- s'dawng: Why is she wearing such transparent clothes? -- Aae kaw pe' kow-aow s'dawng ma'leh?

transplant v. tooong: transplant rice sprouts -- tooong sro

transport n. kej m'ngee'a kaam

transport v. jchunyh'jchuun jchenyh; or, jchunyh'jchuun: We will transport the goods to Phnom Penh by boat. -- Yueng nung jchunyh'jchuun aye'von teuh Phnom Penh dow'ee kra'no't.; duk no'um: transport goods -- duk no'um ro'bah

transportation n. anything that can carry s. th. else (i. e., bus, truck, train, car, etc.; means of transportation) -- jchum'nee; or, yee'an jchum'nee; road or transport system -- Kej Ma'nee'a'kaam: Ministry of (Roads and) Transportation -- Kra'soo'ung Kej Ma'nee'a'kaam

trap v. teh(k): They trapped snakes for food. -- Gkay teh(k) poo'ah (dum'bye) n'yaam.; dah(k) un'tay'k

trap n. generally -- un'tay'k: set a trap for -- dah(k) un'tay'k; walk into a trap -- dah jchole un'tay'k: The KR walked into the unit's trap. -- KR dah jchole un'tay'k krum gkay howi.; fall into a trap -- t'leh k'nong, or t'leh jchole, un'tay'k: The KR fell into our trap. -- KR t'leh k'nong un'tay'k yeung howi.; for mice and very small animals -- un'coob

trapped pp. tro baan teh(k): Elephants were trapped by the king. -- Dum'rei tro baan teh(k) dow'ee sa s'dach.; to be trapped by -- tro baan t'leh jchole un'tay'k (lit: made to fall into a trap): The KR were trapped by the soldiers. -- KR tro baan t'leh jchole un'tay'k dow'ee sa tee'hee'an.

trash n. sum'raam

trauma n. bad or shocking experience -- kruu'ti'nak thum (lit: major accident); effect of shocking experience -- dum'nall thuk pic yang klang; or, kaa chh'ooh jchaap om'pee thuk pic yang klang: Did many of your soldiers [suffer] trauma in the war? -- Tau(v) tee'hee'an pieh ch'raan ro'bah neh [to'tool] kaa chh'ooh jchaap om'pee thuk pic yang klang noeh peyr sung'kree'um, roo tay'?

traumatic adj. a'krah; traumatic experience -- kaa pi'sowt a'krah

travel n. kaa tveu dum'narr

travel v. tveu dum'narr

tray n. tah

treasure n. generally, connoting any precious things, wealth, etc. -- kum'naup: Parents think their kids are their [greatest] treasure. -- Oeuv'puk m'dye kut tha gkon keuh chia [ma'ha] kum'naup ro'bah gkay.; sum'baat

treasury n. generally -- klae'ang: The Treasury (institutionally, and the physical building) in Phnom Penh -- klae'ang praa(k); (praa(k) = money, wealth); sum'baat

treasurer n. high governmental position -- may klae'ang; of any organization -- neh heh'ranya'vuh'to

treat v. medically -- hye too'um: treat an illness -- hye too'um chuum'ngeu; act towards s. o. -- tveu... dah(k) gkay: treat me well -- tveu la'aw dah(k) kyom; purchase for s. o. -- pa'ooo: Will you treat me to dinner on Saturday? -- Tau(v) neh pa'ooo kyom nyam bye t'ngai sow, roo tay?

tree n. generally -- daum (APs: dahm, dome, dum, daawm) cheu; specific tree types -- daum + species name: mango tree -- daum sveye; tamarind tree -- daum um'pil; palm tree -- daum knaut; tall, oak-like tree -- daum gko (source of cotton-like pillow fill)

tree trunk n. standing -- daum; or, daum cheu; felled -- cheu hope; (limb = mek, small branch or twig = tee'an, leaf = sluk); base of tree trunk -- kuhl

trellis n. troh neung: We grow [grapes] on our trellis. -- Yeung dam [tum'paae'ang bai'choo] noeh leuh troh neung ro'bah yeung.

tremble v. ni'ooo'a; rum chul; rum choo'i

trench n. tre'nsay

trial n. judicial proceeding -- kaa vi'ni'ch'eye; test run -- sahk

tribe n. kul sum po'ang

tributary n. political -- soo'sa a'kaw; riverine -- dai tun'lay (lit: arm of river)

tribute n. puss'do'kaa; soo'sa a'kaw

tribute, to pay verbal v. ni'yaye peea om'peuh la'aw

trick n. gimmick, "twist", secret, etc. -- a'kum'bong; or, kaa sum'ngut: I have one (more) trick! -- Kyom miun a'kum'bong moi!

trick v. tveu la'buch; leng la'buch kahl; play a trick on -- leng la'buch chi'moi(lit: play a trick with): The students tricked the teacher. -- Gkon'sa leng la'buch chi'moi lok kruu.; deceive -- bun lawm; trick the enemy -- bun lawm sa'tro

tricked (by), to be v. p'jchanyh pra(ch) (lit: to be outsmarted): The teacher was tricked by the students. -- Kruu p'jchanyh pra(ch) gkon'sa.

tricky adj. untrustworthy -- ku'chik ku'cho'k

trigger n. kun'leuh

trigger v. nom owi miun; bun kaut

trim v. che'rup; dum run; trim off -- leuh jchenyh; or, dum run jchenyh

trimester n. tri'mee'eh; (sound close to that of words for "gold fish")

trip n. dum'narr; kaa tveu dum'narr; take a trip -- tveu dum'narr

trip v. trip (and) fall -- plo'at cheung doo'ul

trivial adj. to'ich ta'ch: a trivial question -- sum'noo'a to'ich ta'ch; bun to'up bun sum

troops n. kawng th'wap; kawng pul; krum tec'hee'an

tropic(s) adj. and n. tropics -- tro'pee

trouble n. generally -- pun'ha (AP: pun'iha, punyha); lum'bah; or kaa lum'bah: What's the trouble? -- Pun'ha aae? or Pun'ha a'veye?; The trouble with him is... -- Pun'ha chi'moi gwat keuh... ; or, Kaa lum'bah chi'moi gwat keuh...; (It's) too much trouble. -- Pun'ha ch'raan na.; There's trouble in that village again. -- Miun pun'ha m'dong tee'it noeh phum ni.;

in sense of disorder, chaos, confusion -- jch'raw'jch'al; chheh'la'jchal; jch'raw'jchaw; jchrool jchraw'bal; or, jchrool jchraal: There was trouble in Phnom Penh last night. -- Miun jch'raw'jchaw kaut laung noeh k'nong Phnom Penh yoop munyh.;

bad luck, difficulty -- ru'ung raow: Sam has had a lot of trouble [lately]. -- [K'nong peyr t'maee t'maee ni] miun ru'ung raow chia ch'raan kaut laung jchum'poo'h Sam.; difficulties -- kaa lum'bah: The farmers have had a lot of trouble this year. -- Neh sr'eye miun kaa lum'bah ch'raan chh'nam ni.;

also:

cause trouble -- bung kaut ru'ung; bung kaut ru'ung raow

give trouble to -- tveu thuk... teuh (or owi): They gave us a lot of trouble about that. -- Pooh'gkay tveu thuk ch'raan teuh/owi yeung om'pee nu.

(Don't) go to any trouble. -- (Kum) teuh ro'k pun'ha.

have trouble -- miun pun'ha; miun too'reh

in trouble -- noeh k'nong pun'ha; noeh k'nong pheap vuck vaw

look for trouble -- ro'k ru'ung

make trouble for -- tveu owi miun alm'pul; tveu owi miun ru'ung; tveu owi miun thuk

troubled by, with or about -- kwaahl kv'eye om'pee: troubled about his job -- kwaahl kv'eye om'pee mok'ngyeea gwat

trousers n. kow

truce n. kaa pa'aahk

truck n. laan trung; rot yun thum

true adj. piht; piht'tay: That's true. -- Piht man.; true friendship -- mit'a'pheap piht'piht

trumpet n. trumpet

trunk n. for storage -- hopp (AP: hepp); of [elephant] -- pra'ma'wee [dum'rei]; of tree -- daum

trust v. tooo'k jchet

truth n. kaa piht; set'cha; in truth -- taam piht; seek the truth -- ro'k kaa piht; ro'k koh tro (lit: seek the wrong and the right); to tell the truth -- prap kaa piht

try v. pyee'a'yee'um: I will try to leave tomorrow. -- Kyom nung pyee'a'yee'um jchaak jchenyh noeh t'ngai s'eye'd.; sa lo'bong (same word as "test"): (Before you reject it,) try it first. -- ( ), sa lo'bong sun teuh. (sun teuh = first); [Let's] try to go to Battambong. -- [Tawh] sa lo'bong teuh Battambong.; kut'cum: Please try to study hard. -- Jcho(r) kut'cum rian so't.; I'm trying to learn Khmer. -- Kyom kut'cum rian pee'esa Khmei.; prung yang klang; prung pryne: They are trying to make friends with women. -- Pooh'gkay prung pryne jchong mit'a'pheap chi'moi sraae sraae.; try hard -- kum yang klang; or, prung pryne

try on clothes v. lo' meuhl kow-aow

try out v. test -- sahk

T-shirt n. aow yoo'

tube n. for water, air, etc. -- bum pong; of a bicycle tire -- poo'ah vee'un kong kong; of a car tire -- poo'ah vee'un kong laan; of a motorbike or motorcycle -- poo'ah vee'un kong mo'to

tuber n. dum'lung

tuberculosis n. chuum'ngeu ro'beyng; ro'beyng

Tuesday n. ong'keea; t'ngai ong'keea

tuft n. pr'oiiy

tug v. tee'ingyh

tug-of-war n. tee'ingyh pr'owat

tumor n. ruuh do

tumultuous adj. kawn ruum pong

tune n. melody -- tuum nok

tune v. a guitar, piano, stringed instrument -- ruut k'sye sum leng; a radio, TV, electical instrument -- mool; stay tuned -- jcham s'dap (lit: wait (and) listen)

tune up v. car or musical instrument -- ruut; an engine -- lee'eng

tunnel n. roong

turkey n. muon ba'raang

Turkey n. praw'tet Too'kee

turmeric n. rum'mee'et

turmoil n. s'kd'eye jchrool jchraal; jchraal; s'kd'eye jchool jch'raw'bal: Since her mother died, she has been in turmoil. -- Tang pi peyr m'dye gwat slop teuh, gwat tai'ng miun s'kd'eye jchrool jchraal.

turn v. rotate s. th. -- bum ba'aae; or, ba'aae: Turn [the camera] this way. -- Ba'aae [a'ppar'aae] mok nehh.; turn around (action by a person) -- ba'aae kloo'an: Please turn around. -- Sum ba'aae kloo'an.; reverse, make opposite, turn 180 degrees -- ba'aae tra'laawp; or tra'laawp ba'aae; turn ones head or head of s. th. -- ba'aae k'bal: Turn the (front of the) car that way. -- Ba'aae k'bal laan teuh nu.; turn and look over shoulder -- ngyee'a(k) kloo'an; steer a vehicle -- bawt: turn left -- bawt chwayne; turn right -- bawt s'dam; Turn right, then turn left. -- Bawt s'dam, howi bawt chwayne.; (NB the difference between drive and turn: drive off the road = baahk jchenyh ploe; turn off the road = bawk jchenyh ploe; Drive straight then turn right. -- Baahk teuh trong, howi bawt s'dam.;

also:

turn around, go back other way -- toi

turn aside -- ngyee'a(k)

turn away from s. th,. or s. o. -- ngyee'a(k) jchenyh

turn away, not permit to enter -- ot owi jchole

turn back, reverse one's direction of movement -- tra'laawp krow'ee; toi

turn into (become) -- pr'eye chia; tveu owi pr'eye

turn off a light, engine, etc. -- butt: turn off the light -- butt pleung

turn on a light -- baahk (same word as to drive): turn on the light -- baahk pleung

turn on s. th. with an engine -- chheh

turn one's head -- ngyee'a(k) k'bal

turn one's [back] on -- ba'aae [kanong] dah(k): He turned his back on his friends. -- Gwat ba'ee knawng dah(k) owi mit'paya.

s. th. turning over by itself -- ro'lap or ploo'k: The car turned over. -- Laan ro'lap.; kraw lup: The truck turned over. -- Laan trung kraw lup.

turn s. th. over -- pr'eye: turn over fish while cooking it -- pr'eye trei; turn over a piece of paper -- tra'laawp kra'dah

turn to (look to ...for s. th.) -- mok rok: The refugees turned to the government for help. -- Chuun pieh kloo'an mok ro'k ratt'a'pi'bal owi choo'ay.

turn upside down -- tra'laawp p'kob

turn rightside up -- p'ngaa

turn n. vaeng: This is my turn. -- Ni chia vaeng kyom.; in turn -- chia vaeng; take turns -- dah(k) vaeng ka'neea; one by one -- ma'neh m'dong; or, m'dong ma'neh

turtle n. land -- un'dauk; sea -- kun'tee'aae

tusk n. plooh

twelve n. dup pi; pi tun'dup

twenty adj. ma'pay (APs: ma'pye, m'pye)

twice adv. pi dong; pi leuk

twice as much adv. t'vaye chia pi (lit: multiplied by two)

twin adj. ploo'ah: twins (children) -- gkon ploo'ah

twine n. k'sye

twist v. mool: twist a screw -- mool k'chow; twist s.o.'s arm -- mool dai gkay; change the meaning of -- pdo; bung vull; or, pdo bung vull: He twisted my words. -- Gwat pdo bung vull pee'a kyom.; twist or roll threads into string or twine -- vaeng k'sye

twisted adj. ro'mool: a twisted muscle -- sak'dum ro'mool

twitch v. ngy'ek

two adj. pi: two cats -- pi chmaa'; one, two, three -- moi, pi, bye

tycoon n. tow'kaly; neh thum

type v. tap; vye (AP: vee, vi'yaye): type words [into a computer] -- tap pee'a [teuh k'nong com'pu'teuh]; type on a typewriter -- vye dac'tee'lo; or, vye ong'glee'laek

type n. kind, variety -- jchuum'poo'h; praw'pet; baep; thuun: What type? -- Thuun na?

typhoon n. k'shaal p'chooh

typewriter n. dac'tee'lo; ong'glee'laek

typical adj. twa'ma'da

U

ubiquitous adj. jchrohng jch'rang: ... the ubiquitous Sonn San pictures in Stung after the battle... -- ... roop tawt Sonn San jchrohng jch'rang noeh Stung krow'ee vi'yaye... ; found "all around" -- noeh chuum'venyh

udder n. dawh gko

umbrella n. chaht

un- p.p. mun: unnecessary -- mun tro kaa; or, mun jcham but (necessary = tro kaa or jcham batch); ot: unhappy -- ot s'bai (happy = s'bai)

unable adj. mun adje: Sh'e unable to speak. -- Nee'eng mun adje ni'yaye.; unable to get away, busy, occupied -- cho'op dai; or, ro'vull (AP: ro'vwul); or, cho'op ro'vull; or, ro'vull nah

unadorned adj. to'tay

unambiguous adj. chia leh; ch'bah

unanimous adj. eyke'a'chuun; the unanimous choice of the community -- jchreu'reu' eyke'a'chuun ney sa'ma'kuum

unanimously adv. chia eyke'a'chuun

unattractive adj. a'krah

unaware (of) adj. mun dung kloo'an (jchum'poo'h; or, noch lcu): He was unaware of that problem. -- Gwat mun dung kloo'an jchum'poo'h pun'ha nu.

unbalanced adj. out of balance -- klo'ng; or, pak p'auk: [The boat] was out of balance. -- [Toook] klo'ng.; mentally disturbed -- lung'ee lung'euh

unbearable adj. dun'daap

unbutton v. dawh

unceasingly adv. tut'tay

uncertain adj. not decided -- steh'steuh: I'm uncertain if I will go. -- Kyom steh'steuh nung teuh.; not clear -- mun ch'bah: The future is uncertain -- Ah'na'kuut mun ch'bah.

uncle n. older than parent to whom uncle is related -- uhm; oeuv'puk uhm; younger than parent of which uncle is sibling -- pooo; mee'a; ouev'puk pooo; oeuv'puk mee'a

unclear adj. mun ch'bah; ot ch'bah

uncomfortable adj. mun sroul

unconcerned adj. rung'eeuy; kun tauw'ee

unconscious adj. bot smaa ru'da'ee (lit: lost consciousness); sun lob

uncover v. baahk (also means, "to drive")

undecided adj. tee'teuh

under prp. krowm; kang krowm; noeh krowm: ... under the (rule of the) KR... -- ... noeh krowm (ro'bab) Khmei Kra'hom...

underdog n. kang kut tha jchanyh (lit: team or side expected to lose); or, ma'nooh kut tha jchanyh (lit: person expected to lose)

undergarment n. aow k'nong (shirt) or kow k'nong (pants)

undergo v. tro: I underwent [an operation] at Calmet Hospital. -- Kyom tro baan [veh kut] k'nong Calmet.; undergo [suffering] -- tro [rong tooo'k]; to'tool: undergo treatment -- to'tool kaa p'chia bal; to undergo an experience -- miun kaa pi'sowt

underground adv. noeh krowm daiy

underline v. kuh bun'twot

271

undermine v. bun tee'up; bun tawp; praw'mat

underneath prp. kang krowm; noeh krowm; put underneath -- dah(k)... pi krowm; tro'up... pi krowm; or, dah(k) tro'op... pi krowm: put the saucer under the cup -- dah(k) jchaan tro'up pi krowm paeng

undershirt n. aow k'nong

understand v. comprehend -- yul: Do you understand? -- Yul howi, roo noeh?; I understand. -- Kyom yul howi.; I don't understand. -- Kyom mun yul tay.; hear and agree -- s'dap baan: Understand me?? -- S'dap kyom baan, 'aae?; (NB: s'dap alone means "listen"); understand someone's feeling -- dung jchet gkay

understanding n. ni'sye; kaa yul; kaa s'dap baan

undertake v. to'tool tveu; p'dach ngy'a nung tveu

underwear n. aow-k'nong, kow k'nong; kow troh'nwap

undo v. dawh: undo shoe-laces -- dawh k'sye s'bye'k cheung; sr'eye

undoubtedly adv. mok chia

undress v. sum'raht

undressed adj. ot kow-aow

undulate v. wave -- ro'lawk; put'pan: The dancer undulated her body [to the rhythm of the music]. -- Neh ro'um put'pan kloo'an pran [taam jchong'vaa(k) plaeng].

uneasy adj. ra'sap ra'sol; proo'i; mun sroul; feel uneasy -- pay b'a'rom; or, rong kloo'an

unemployed adj. k'miun kaa'ngyeea

unemployment n. k'miun kaa'ngyeea; kaa'ngyeea mun kroop krawn kwah kaan

uneven adj. kra haeng kra ho'eng

unfaithful adj. mun sm'oh trong; unfaithful dog -- sh'kye mun sm'oh trong; jchet chal'k

unfamiliar adj. jchum'lyke; be unfamiliar with -- ot dung

unfavorable adj. raow: unfavorable development(s) -- ru'ung raow

unification n. sohk'sac; national unification -- sohk'sac chee'it

unfold v. traw dang; lee'a; lee'ut

unfortunate adj. a'ka'sawl; ah'ni'cha; ah'po'up: an unfortunate thing that... -- chia a'ka'sawl tha...

unfortunately adv. a'ka'sawl; a'p'wop: Unfortunately, yes! -- A'ka'sawl, baa(t)!

ungrateful adj. lu'meuh kun; plic kun; ru'mul kun

unhappy adj. mun s'bai; proo'i; grief-stricken -- sauwk song'raeng

unhealthy adj. koh kroo'a; tuk kra'kwah; not healthy (said of a person) -- sa'ka'pheap mun la'aw (lit: health not good)

unheard adj. mun dael loo pi muun (lit: never before heard)

uniform n. eyke sun'ton

unimaginative adj. lacking new ideas, afraid to act, etc. -- sanyh: He has no new ideas. -- Gwat nu sanyh nah.

unimportant adj. ot sum'kahn; kum peyk kum pawk; bun to'up bun sum; la'ut la'o'weet; unimportant affair -- ru'ung bun to'ap bun sum

unintentional adj. a'chaye'tu'na

uninterested adj. la'veu'ee; mun jchaap'arom

union n. generally -- sa'ha'po'an; sa'ha'pheap: Soviet Union -- Sa'ha'pheap So'vee'e'tique; labor union -- ka'ma'ka sa'ha'chee'it

unit n. kawng: a (military) unit -- tee'hee'an moi kawng

unite v. ruu'ub ruu'um; to cause to unite -- bong ruu'up bong ru'um

united adj. agglomerated -- sa'ha: (see definitions of UN and US, below); politically allied -- ree'up ru'um jchet: united front -- ro'na'sey ree'up ru'um jchet

United Nations n. Ong'kah Sa'ha Pra'cheea'chee'it

United States of America/United States n. sruk Am'rik (AP: A'mer'reek); Sa'ha Ratt Am'rik

unity n. sa'ma'ki; eyke'a'pheap

universal adj. sa'kawhl: a universal problem -- pun'ha to te'ang sa'kawhl

universe n. pi'pope'lok; (NB: star -- da'ra; p'kye; planet -- pi'pope; moon -- lok'keye; world -- pope'lok; pi'pope'lok; Earth (as a planet) pyne'daiy; preah tor'ni)

university n. ma'ha'vi'ti'a'lye: medical school -- ma'ha'vi'tia'lye vi'chia'sah; school of pharmacology -- fac' medecine -- sa'la t'nam peyt

unjust adj. ayoo'tay'to'a: unjust decision -- kaa sum'rach dow'ee ayoo'tay'to'a

unless conj. daw'rap na; baa mun

unlikely adv. praw'heil chia mun: It is unlikely my house will be sold. -- Veea pra'heil chia mun adje looh ptay'a kyom.

unlock v. jchak sauw (lit: stab lock); (NB: depending on context, jchak can mean lock or unlock;' see discussion under "lock")

unlocked p.p. mun jchak sauw; kum jchak sauw: Leave the door unlocked -- But t'veea kum jchak sauw.

unlucky adj. k'miun sum'nang; ot sum'nang; a'ku'sol; a'po'up

unmarried adj. noeh liv (fr. Fr. "libre"); ot tum'nay

un-milled adj. re rice -- sro

unnecessary adj. mun jcham'batch; ot jcham'batch

unofficial adj. krau ploe' kaa

unorganized adj. ot ro'bee'up; rawt ree'aae

unpack v. reuh jchenyh: unpack (clothes from) a bag -- reuh jchenyh kow-aow pi va'leez

unpopular adj. mun seou la'bye; saab

unpredictable adj. mun tee'eng (lit: cannot be foreseen)

unpremeditated adj. k'miun tuk mok

unprocessed adj. mun twon cha'nai: unprocessed wood -- cheu mun twon cha'nai

unproductive adj. mun baan kaa; mun sum'raan; scaw(k)

unravel v. dum'naugh sr'eye; dawh sr'eye; sr'eye: Did you unravel this problem yet? -- Neh sr'eye pun'ha ni baan, roo noeh?

unrest n. kong vul

unripe n. k'chey

unroll v. lee'aae jchenyh; unrolled -- ro'lee'a

unstable adj. government -- trey't tro't; mentally -- lung'ee lung'euh; unstable person -- ma'nooh tyl' towl (lit: person with no home, no job, no friends, no relatives, etc.)

un-tie v. dawh

until prp. ro'hote doll (AP: doll): until four o'clock -- ro'hote doll mao buon; (NB: "ro'hote doll" is frequently compressed in conversation to only "doll," as: until tomorrow -- doll s'eye'd); do'rup doll; unless -- looh tra tai: I won't go until I have the money. -- Kyom mun teuh looh tra tai miun loi.; not until; when -- baan... teuh: When I get the money, I go. -- Baan loi teuh, kyom teuh.

untrustworthy adj. ro'puhl ro'po'ich

unveil v. baahk

up prp. teuh leuh (AP: leu, loeh): He pointed up. -- Gwat chum'all teuh leuh.; laung: Prices went up. -- Laung tlai.; We need to go [further] up [the hill]. -- Yeung tro ka laung [tuu'ul] [bun taa tee'ut].; leuh laung: [Lift] it up. -- Leuk laung leuh.; k'pooh laung: [Starting in Skoon,] Highway 7 goes up (rises). -- [Jchaap p'daum pi Skoon teuh], ploe layke prum'pul k'pooh laung.; noeh pyke kang leuh: Up in Stung Trang... -- Noeh pyke kang leuh Stung Trang....; also:

Up to you! -- Srech tai neh eiyne! or, Srech tai leuh neh!

up to date -- twon peyr; twon sa'mye

up to now -- mok doll eye leaou ni

upheaval n. disorder, disturbance -- chheh'la'jchal; revolution -- pa'ti'vwut (NB: pa'ti'kaam = strike)

upper adj. k'pooh: upper floors -- cho'on k'pooh; leuh: the upper part or area of s. th.; "upstairs" -- kang leuh

uproot v. ruhm leung

upset adj. on jchet; mua moaw

upset v. tveu owi on jchet: He upset you. -- Veea tveu owi neh on jchet.; bother -- ruhm kahn

upstairs n. kang leuh; the next [floor/story] up -- [cho'an] kang leuh; go up -- teuh leuh; go upstairs -- teuh kang leuh

urge n. jchum'nung jchong; have an urge to -- miun jchum'nung jchong: I have the urge [to eat "song k'sha'a l'peau"]. -- Kyom miun jchum'nung jchong nyam song k'sha'a la'peau.; (song k'sha'a l'peau = dessert made by pouring a mixture of egg, sugar, coconut milk and spices inside a small pumpkin and steaming it to produce pumpkin with sweet cake inside).

urge v. teu'en; or, teu'en owi: I urge you to go to computer school. -- Kyom teu'en owi neh teuh sa'la'rin com'pu'teuh.; jchum'runyh owi

urgent adj. pra'nyab pra'nyal; chia bun to'an: urgent affair -- kaa bun to'an; very urgent -- yang praw'nyab

urgently adv. mo miun nyuk

urinate v. bot cheung to'ich

urine n. tuk no'm

us prn. yeung (AP: yung)

use v. generally -- pra; use in cooking -- psawlm (lit: spoon in); to be of use -- praw'yow'it (written praw'yow'itch); no use -- mun baan kaa; ot baan kaa; k'miun baan kaa; ot mium praw'yow'it: It is no use [to complain]. -- K'miun baan kaa aae tay la'ooo. [NB: complain = written ra'oo, pronounced, la'oo]; or, La'oo kaw k'miun baan kaa a'veye da'aae.; use against s. o. -- yok muk praw'pra

used for adj. pra sum'rap

used to adj. comfortable with, tolerant of -- so'um k'nong: Are you used to driving in the rain? -- Tau(v) neh so'um k'nong baahk baw noeh k'nong peyr plee'eng tay?; to be in the habit of s.th. -- ruhm lawp: I'm used to eating at 6 (a.m. or p.m.) every day. -- Kyom ruhm lawp nyam bye peyr mao prum moi rawl t'ngai.

used to v. did/was in past -- tlo'up: He used to be a soldier. -- Gwat tlo'up tveu tee'hee'an.; Did you used to play tennis? -- Neh eiyne tlo'up dah leng te'nnit tay?

used up adj. praw'awh: used up little by little -- praw'awh baan tic m'dong baan tic m'dong; also, [are used up] little by little -- [tro ko'ich laung ko'ich laung] chia loom'dap

useful adj. miun praw'yow'eet

useless adj. ot miun praw'yow'eet; ot praw'yow'eet; jchowl ma'see'it (jchowl = throw out)

usual adj. twa'ma'da: as usual -- chia twa'ma'da; chia pra kraw da'aae

usually adv. twa'ma'da; chia twa'ma'da

utensil n. jchaan cha'nang; praw'dab praw'dah

uterus n. s'bo'ne

utility n. public utility -- krum huun tuk, krum huun pleung, krum huun telephone, etc. (water company, electric company, telephone company, etc.)

utterance n. praw'sah; pec'a

V

vacant adj. tum'nay

vacation n. vi'sa'mak'kaal; vaa'kawng (fr. Fr.); holiday -- t'ngai bun; take a vacation -- vaa'kawng; Next week I'm taking my vacation. -- A'tthit krow'ee kyom vaa'kawng.

vagabond n. tyle'towl

vaguely adj. pree'ung; raw'hah raw'hee'eng

validation n. suh'pul'la'kaam

valley n. ch'roo'eh

value n. dum'lye; kuun sum'baat; kaa miun dum'lye

valuable adj. tlai t'noeh; tlai

vanish v. bot; bot plee'um; bot moi ruhm pech (lit: disappear in an instant): She vanished at the end of the road. -- Nee'ung bot moi ruhm pech noeh aae jchong t'nawl.

vanished p.p. bot; bot plee'um plee'um

variety n. mok p'sayng p'sayng

various adj. p'sayng p'sayng; ni'moi ni'moi

vase n. small, for table -- to': a small vase on a table -- to' moi noeh leuh tohk; large, on floor -- paa'ng

V. D. n. kaam rohk (lit: sperm disease)

veal n. sat(ch) gkon gko

vegetable n. bun'lye: vegetable garden -- suon bun'lye; ch'baa dum'nam

vegetation n. prey (same word as for forest and jungle); daum cheu (lit: "the woods"); (written or formal terms: pruk'sa; prey pruk'sa; or, ro'ka chee'it)

vehicle n. rot yun (lit: runs by engine)

vein n. saw sye; saw sye vein (NB: artery = a'tay'a)

velocity n. la'buu'un

venom n. peuuhs

verb n. kej ree'ya'sab

verdict n. sal krum; s'kd'eye sum'rap

verify v. banyh'che'ehk

vertical adj. trong

very adv. nah (AP: na'): very smart -- ch'laat nah; very expensive -- tlai nah; very, very (somewhat stronger than "nah" alone) -- klang nah: very, very expensive -- tlai klang nah; very, very hot -- k'dau klang nah; not very -- mun.... nah naa: It's not very hot. -- Veea mun k'dau nah naa tay.; not very -- mun... pu'man: seems not very interesting... -- mun koo'a owi jchaap'arom pu'man tay...

very much adv. phrase. yang puun; yang puun pra'man.; (slang) -- chia a'nyke: I thank you very much. -- Kyom sum aw'kuun neh chia a'nyke.

vibrate v. rung keuh

vice n. gambling, prostitution, etc. -- um'peuh a'bye'a'mok

vice adj. a'noo: vice president -- a'noo' praw'tee'a nee'a tep'a'dye; vice premier -- a'pah nee'a'yoo ratt'mun'trei;

vicinity n. p'dum; dum'bun

victim n. neh rong kruu'h; be a victim of or fall victim to -- rong kruu'h ney

victory n. choke chey; chey chuum'nay'eh

Vietnam n. sruk Vuetnam; praw'tet Vietnam; (PS: basically degrogatory implying "country of the barbarians" -- sruk (or, praw'tet) yu'en)

Vietnamese adj. yu'en

Vietnamization n. Vietnam moo'put'naya'kaam

view n. teh'sa'pheap; tut'ta'pheap

villa n. vee'lla

village v. phum

villager n. neh phum (lit: person of a village); neh sruk (lit: person (from the) district)

vindictive adj. kuum kooun; ching peea'; song'suk

vine n. vwul; leh'taa

vinegar n. tuk k'meh

violation n. kaa ch'lee'an pee'n; kaa ruum lo'b bum pec'un

VIP n. neh thum; e'sra'chuun; vorak'chuun

virgin n. kraw'mom prum'ja'rye

virginity n. prum'cha'rye; lose ones virginity -- ko'ich kloo'an

violate v. ch'lee'an pee'n; praw'chang

violin n. vee'o'lon

virtue n. t'wa

visa n. vee'za; (formal term = tee'teh'kaa): issue a visa -- jchenyh vee'za; or, owi vee'za; get a visa -- yok vee'za **vision** n. kaa meulh keunyh

visit v. tooo's na: They visted the Sneng-S'dao frontline. -- Gkay tooo's na sa'mau'ra'phum tee Sneng nung S'dao; visit for fun, vacation, etc. -- teuh leng: to visit Mundolkiri -- teuh leng Mun'dol'ki'ri; make family or social visit -- teuh leng: She visited her family in Kam'pot. -- Nee'eng teuh leng kroo'e'sa gwat noeh Kam'pot.

visitor n. at a house -- p'nee'oo; to another town, country, etc. -- te's'jchaw; tourist -- neh too'sna

visualize v. nuhk sra'mye: Try to visualize it. -- Nuhk sra'mye veea lo meuhl.

vitamin n. chii'va'chee'ut

viva xcl. ch'ey yo': Viva Hun Sen! -- Ch'ey yo' Hun Sen!

voice n. sum'leng: Voice of America -- Sum'leng Sa'ha Ratt Am'rik

volume n. of sound -- sum'leng; turn down -- bun toi sum'leng; or, butt sum'leng baan tic teuh; of business -- pah'ree'man; chuum'noo'inyh

volunteers n. chum'noo'yh; neh chum'noo'yh: She needs three volunteers. -- Nee'eng tro kaa chum'noo'yh bye neh.

vomit v. ka'oo'it

voodoo n. magic generally; in Cambodian context, often referring to magic practiced by Chams (Khmer Muslims) -- kaa tveu um'peuh; to make magic against (someone) -- tveu um'peuh dah(k) ( )

vote n. ch'nowt; sum'leng: How many votes did you get? -- Tha neh baan to' tool sum'leng pu'man neh?

vote v. bawh ch'nowt

voter n. neh bawh ch'nowt

voting n. kaa bawh ch'nowt

vow n. p'dach ngya

vowel n. sra'(k)

wacky adj. (analogous to "not playng with a full deck") -- mun kroop tuk

wager v.   p'nawl

wages n.   bee(r)'vwut; praa(k) (lit: money): monthly pay -- praa(k)'kye

waist n.   chun'keh

wait v. jcham: wait here -- jcham nung howi; many people waiting for him -- ma'nooh pieh ch'raan rong jcham gwat; Wait a minute -- Jcham moi plet; Wait a bit -- Jcham baan tic.; or, Jcham tic tee'it.; Wait, wait! (lit: "Stop a bit") -- Chope sun, chope sun!; or, Chope, chope!; Wait till your next life! (PM meaning "you'll never get it") -- Jcham chi'vut krow'ee teuh!; wait for -- rong jcham; wait on -- bum raahl; jcham bum raahl; jcham to'tool

waiter n. neh bum raahl; (NB: occassionally given as Khmer for "waiter" is "bau'wee bum raahl"; this term is somewhat out-dated, and in past referred to a man or woman servant in an almost indentured-servant position, rather than one functioning as waiter or waitress to the public)

waitress n. neh bum raahl sraae; bau'wee; bau'wee bum raahl

waiting n. kaa rong jcham

wake s. o. up v. tveu owi pn'yeh; dahs ... owi pn'yeh laung; dahs laung: Go wake him up! -- Teuh dahs gwat laung!

wake up v. pn'yeh; pn'yeh geyng; pn'yeh daeyk; (NB: krau pi geyng lit. = "get up" although (as with "wake up" and "get up" in English) pn'yeh and krau pi are used essentially inter-changeably); wake up early -- pn'yeh pi pro'lum

walk v. dah (written dah(r)): to walk fast -- dah leu'an; go out, go out for a walk, go out to have some fun -- dah leng

walk n. kaa dah; go for a walk -- dah'leu'an; take a walk -- teuh dah'leu'an

wall n. chuun' chee'ung

wallet n. kaa bo'b

want v. generally -- jchong: She wants to get her umbrella before it rains. -- Nee'eng jchong yok chaht krow'ee veea plee'eng.; They want more rice. -- Pooh'gkay jchong bye tee'it.; I want to eat. -- Kyom jchong ni'yaam.; As soon as you... you want to... -- Doll..., jchong...: As soon as you learn a little, you want to go too fast. -- Doll jcheh, jchong leu'an hoo'a.; jchong baan: I want more pay! -- Kyom jchong baan praa(k) 'kye tyme tee'it.; (NB: when expressing "want s.o. else to do s.th." the polite form is "jchong owi", as in, "Kyon jchong owi neh teuh psa." -- I want you to go to the market"; omitting "owi" -- "Kyom jchong neh teuh..." -- is less polite, and more generally used for younger persons, or those otherwise of less social standing than the speaker; when owi is used, it is often contracted to "a", as , "Kyom jchong a neh teuh..."); "want" in sense of "like to" -- jchole jchet: Do you want to (would you like to) stay? -- Tau(v) neh jchole jchet noeh tay?; Do you want to talk to him or not? -- Jchole jchet ni'yaye chi'moi gwat roo ot?; [unstated + 'ch or aae? as question marker]: Do you want to) eat this? -- Nyam, 'eh?; Do you want to go?/Shall we go? -- Teuh, 'aae?; either i) tolerate or ii) want avidly -- see (lit: eat): i) I do not want flattery. -- Kyom ot see jcho(r) tay.; ii) They really (avidly) want money. -- Gkay see loi ch'raan. (lit: They "eat up" lots of money.)

war n. sung'kree'um

ward n. municipal sub-division -- kaahn; (NB: sub-ward = song'kaat)

ward off v. bong vaeng

warehouse n. kla'ang

warfare n. war, generally -- sung'kree'um; psychological warfare -- sung'kree'um jchet tasa(s)

warm adj.   k'dau; kuum; kaw k'dau

warn v.   haahm

warrant n.   dyc kaa; issue a warrant -- jchenyh dyc kaa

wash v.   [clothes] -- bauwk [kow-aow]; [face] -- lee'eng [muk]; luk [muk]; wash [hair] -- kaah(k) [saahk]; wash in the shower -- ngoi'eet (AP: nguu't); wash up, clean up, take a bath or shower -- moi tuk: I have to wash up/wash my face/clean up/take a shower/etc. first/. -- Muun (kyom) tro moi tuk.; wash [one's hands] of -- ro'lawh dai; dawh dai jchenyh pi: I wash my hands of this problem. -- Kyom dawh dai jchenyh pi pun'ha ni.;

wasp n.   auw'mall

waste v.   kaht: They wasted too much time. -- Yeung bung kaht peyr ch'raan.; k'cheh' k'chee'aae: Don't waste food! -- Kum k'cheh' k'chhe'aae ma'hope jchum'naee!; lay waste to -- bum plyne; kum'tic

wasted adj.   kaht: One more week wasted. -- Kaht moi a'tthit.

wat n.   wat

watch n.   ni'a'li'ka (APs: na'li'ka, lee'li'ka, mee'li'ka); alarm clock -- ni'a'li'ka ro'; wall clock (with pendulum) -- ni'a'li'ka p'auwl

watch v.   meuhl; klo'um: Watch carefully. -- Meulh dow'ee prong praw'yaat.; watch from hiding -- klo'um meuhl; watch a movie -- meuhl gkun; Watch it! (Be careful!) -- Praw'yaat!; watch over -- krook krong

water n.   tuk: running water -- tuk ho; salt water -- tuk pr'eye; fresh water -- tuk sap; (NB "tuk" commonly appears in names of various liquids, viz: fruit juice -- tuk + name of fruit; milk -- tuk'dawh'gko (lit.: "water of cow's breast"); soy sauce -- tuk si'ee'oo)

water v.   srau'ich: water the vegetables/crops -- srau'ich dum'nam

waterfall n.   tuk chr'oo'a (Phnom Penh term); tuk t'leh (country term)

water jar n.   large, to hold household water supply -- pee'ung

watermelon n.   ow'luk

waterway n.   bun'lye tuk; ploe tuk

waterwheel n.   ro'ha tuk

watery adj.   re food -- ree'oo

wave n.   in water -- ro' lo'

wave v.   bau'wee dai

way n.   means of doing s. th. -- ploe: There was no way to get the money. -- Ot miun ploe baan loi tay.; method of doing s. th. -- vi'ti'sah; or, ro'bee'up: the Khmer way -- ro'bee'up Khmei; There are three ways to say it -- Miun bye ploe dum'bye ni'yaye.; or, Ni'yaye baan bye yang.; also:

way of doing -- dum'narr

way of life -- ro'bee'up rooh noeh

No way! -- Ot ploe!; or, Ot ploe tay!

there's no way -- Ot miun ploe.

have one's own way -- baah bauw: [The minority] wants to have its own way. -- [Chuun pieh tic] jchong
        baah bauw.

be in the way -- teuh ploe

get out of the way -- toi; chi(ss) jchenyh

a way, one way -- ploe moi; moi yang

all the way -- ro'hote: We need to go all the way to Battambong. -- Yeung tro kaa teuh ro'hote
        Battambong.

there is a way -- miun ploe

That way is OK, too. -- An'chung kaw m'yang da'aae.

this way (this direction) -- mok nehh

waylay v.   scutt ploe (NB: essentially "intercept"; hence, can also mean simply meet up with s. o. with no hostile intent); They [plan] to waylay him on his way home. -- Pooh'gkay [miun kum'rong] scutt ploe gwat [peyr gwat jchenyh teuh].; ... waylay him in the middle of the village. -- ... teuh howi scutt ploe gwat noeh pi'eh kan'dal phum.

wax n.   kruh'muu'on

we pnn.   yeung

we, all together... pnn.   yeung, te'ang ahw ka'neea...

weak adj.   k'sow'ee; jchet tuun; tuun k'sow'ee; tuu run tuun ree'a

weak-kneed adj.   tuun cheung'kung

weakling n.   wimp -- ma'nooh kum'ruuh: He's a real weakling. -- Gwat chia manooh kum' ruuh'a jchowl m'see'it.

weakness n.   kaa tuun k'sowee; pheap tuun k'sowee

wealth n.   sum'baat; hidden wealth -- kum'naup; tun tee'eng: That familiy has much wealth. -- Kroo'e'sa nuu miun tun tee'en ch'raan.

wealthy adj.   s'dawk s'dum; miun

weapon n.   a'vwut; kreung a'vwut: all kinds of weapons -- sap'peea a'vwut

weaponry n.   a'vwut juh'teh-po'an

wear v.   peh; slee'uh peh; re monks -- krong: Monks do not [wear regular clothes], they wear (robes called) "s'bong chi po". -- Lok'sung ot [slee'uh peh kow-aow twa'ma'da] tay; lok krong (   ) "s'bong chi'po".

weather n.   tee'ut a'kas; a'kas tee'ut: What does the weather look like outside? -- Tau(v) tee'ut a'kas kang krau yang mutch?; What's the weather going to be? -- Tau(v) tee'ut a'kas yang mutch teuh?; The weather is not so good. -- Tee'ut a'kas mun seou la'aw.

weave v.   ta'bonn

wed v.   ree'up kaa

wedding n.   marriage -- ree'up kaa; wedding ceremony -- mun'kul kaa; (formal term -- a'pee'a pee'pee'a)

Wednesday n.   puut; t'ngai puut

weed n.   yuum

week n.   su'pa'da; a'tthit; last week -- a'tthit muun; next week -- a'tthit krow'ee; weekday -- t'ngai tveu kaa; weekend -- jchong a'tthit: We will find them next weekend. -- Yeung nung sveye ro'k gkay noeh jchong a'tthit krow'ee.; (NB: "next weekend" is sometimes also expressed by reference to one of the specific weekend days, as: "t'ngai saow krow'ee" (lit: next Saturday)

weep v.   yuum

weevil n.   k'mo't

weigh v.   to weigh s. th. -- t'lung; to be of a certain weight -- miun tuum ng'uuun: How much do you weigh? -- Neh eiyne miun tuum ng'uun pu'man?

weight n.   tuum ng'uun; gain weight -- twot; miun sat(ch); lose weight -- sraw sat(ch); sell by weight -- looh dow'ee t'lung

welcome v.   receive -- to'tool: Please go and welcome (i. e., pick up, receive) my friends. -- Teuh choo'ay to'tool p'nee'oo kyom.; greet with words of welcome -- svaa'kum; to'tool svaa'kum; re(k)'taae'a(k); to'tool re(k)'taae'a(k): We will welcome them at Pochentong. -- Yeung nung to'tool re(k)'taae'a(k) pooh'gkay noeh Po'chen'tong

welcome n.   svaa'kum; kaa reh'taae'a: You are welcome to my home.   -- Neh svaa'kum nung mok ptay'a kyom.

Welcome! excl.   Svaa'kum, svaa'kum!

weld v.   p'saa

welfare n.   e.g., of the community, society -- sa'ma'kuum a'kej

well adj.   healthy -- sohk; sroul kloo'an; chia: Is he well? -- Gwat chia tay?; healthy or happy/content -- s'bai: Is he well now? -- Eye leaou gwat s'bai tay?; successfully -- la'aw: He did the job well. -- Gwat tveu kaa la'aw.

well (for water) n.   an'do'ng; well with hand pump -- an'do'ng sap'dai

well-being n.   sohk s'bai

well-behaved adj. nung noo'an; nung tung

Well! intr. Nay!; Eh!; An'chung!; Mutch!

well-known adj. l'bye, l'bye chamoo'h, l'bye l'banyh

well-wishing ceremony n. jchaawng dai (lit: tying hands; part of marriage ceremony)

west n. kang lic; pyke paa'jchum

wet adj. to be wet -- to'tuk; slightly wet -- saalm; soaking wet -- to' tuk cho'ke; get wet -- to' tuk

wharf n. pa'aae; cunlye'ng jchawt ka'pal

what adj. na: What temple? -- Wat na?; What village do you live in? -- Neh noeh phum na?

what prn. generally -- a'veye (often compressed in speech to "eye"; other APs: a'vaae, compressed to 'aae);
(NB: In the examples that follow, "a'veye" and "a'vaae" can be considered standard, proper speech forms, and "eye" and "aae" rapid or casual conversational forms. The practical differce in the usage between the two pairs is that the shorter forms -- "aae" and "eye" -- would not be appropriate for formal, or respectful conversations (for example, business talks, meetings with government officials, speaking to elders, etc.), but are perfectly acceptable among friends, family, work colleagues, and social equals in general; viz:
What work do you do? -- Miun mok'gnyeea chia a'veye?; What are they doing? -- Pooh'gkay tveu aae nung?; What is [the purpose of] this? -- A'veye [chia kohl bum nong] nay kaa ni?; also, for what is, what are -- s'eye (AP: s'aae): What's that? -- S'eye nu?; What's he doing? -- Gwat tveu kaa s'eye?; what in sense of that which -- a'veye dael: ...what he did.... -- a'veye dael gwat tveu; ...what you want... -- a'veye dael neh jchong; re purpose: What for? or, To do what? -- Yok tveu eye?; also:

What do you think? -- Kut yang na da'aae?

What else -- aae (AP: eye)... tee'it: What else do you want to study? -- Tro kaa aae rian tee'it?

What time is it? -- Mao aae?; or, Mao pu'man howi?

What did you/he/she/etc. say? -- Taa mutch?

What's up? -- Miun ru'ung a'veye?; Miun ru'ung eye?; Miun ru'ung a'veye nung?; or, Miun ru'ung eye nung?

What's happening? -- Miun kaa aae?; Miun kaa eye?

What's the matter?   )

What is it?   ) -- Miun kaa aae? or, Hyte aae?

What's the problem?)

What is that? --
(S'eye nu?
(S'eye nung?
(A'veye nu?
(A'vaae nung?
(Nu chia a'veye?
(S'eye ni?

What is this? --   (A'veye ni?
                    (Ni chia a'veye?

what kind of adj. phrase   baep na dael: What kind of books do you read? -- S'po baep na dael neh an? (NB: "S'po na dael neh an?" would be "Which (or what) books do you read?"); jchum'poo'h na dael: What kind of people do you like? -- Ma'nooh jchum'poo'h na dael neh jchole jchet?; praw'pet na dael: What kind of food do they have here? -- Ma'hope praw'pet na dael miun noeh ti ni?

whatever prn. a'veye dael: Whatever you want, we can get. -- A'veye dael neh jchong baan, yeung nung yok baan.; Whatever will be will be. -- A'veye dael nung kaut laung, nung kaut laung.; Whatever.; or, Oh, whatever. (off-hand response, as to questions requesting a judgement, like "Shall we go now?" or "What do you want to order?", etc.) -- Eye kaw baan da'aae [and/or] S'eye kaw dow'ee: (Q: What do you want to order? A:) Oh, whatever. -- Eye kaw baan da'aae.; or, S'eye kaw dow'ee.; Whatever's good. -- Eye kaw baan da'aae owi tai chng'anyh.; or, S'eye kaw dow'ee.

whatsoever adv. t-o'al tai sahl(t): [There should be no] food whatsoever in the classroom. -- Noeh k'nong t'nak [koo'a tai mun miun] jchum'naee tual tai sahl(t).

wheat n. sro'sa'lye

wheel n. kong

wheelbarrow n. a'teea roo'inyh (lit: push-cart)

when adv. peyr na: When can we go there? -- Peyr na teuh cunlye'ng nu?; When are they arriving? -- Gkay nung mok peyr na?; When do I have to time for that? -- Peyr na kyom miun peyr sum'rap nu?; specifically re future events -- an'kaal: When will he arrive? -- An'kaal na gwat mok doll?; specifically re past events -- pi an'kaal: When did he arrive? -- Pi an'kaal na gwat mok doll?

when conj. peyr noeh: When the attack came, the soldiers scattered. -- Noeh peyr vye mok doll, tee'hee'an ri'yaye ka'neea.; peyr: When I was [still] young... -- Peyr kyom [noeh] to'ich...; kaal na: The Thai's aren't happy when Khmer call them "see'um." -- Thai ot s'bai kaal na saah khmei ni'yaye prap gkay see'um.; in sense of if, or after, s. th. occurs -- ot pi: When he goes, I will be happy. -- Ot pi gwat teuh, kyom keuh chia s'bai.

whenever conj. kaal na; rawl peyr dael: Whenever he went to Cambodia, he took [medecine] for Calmet Hospital. -- Rawl peyr dael gwat teuh Kampuchea, gwat yok [t'nam peyt klaah] sum'rap Mun'ti'peyt Cal'met.

where? adv. noeh aae na?: Where is your house? -- Ptay'a neh noeh aae na?; (NB: In conversation the phrase "noeh aae na?" is invariably compressed either to "n'oi na" (two syllables) or (by dropping "aae" altogether) to "noeh na". Thus, with the first compression, "Where is my bed?" would be "Krey kyom n'oi na?. With the second, "Where did you go?" would be "Teuh noeh na?"); ti na?: Where are you going? -- Teuh ti na?; eye na: Where are you going? -- Teuh eye na?; cunlye'ng na? (lit: what place?): Where are you going? -- Neh teuh cunlye'ng na? or, Teuh 'na? or, Teuh na nung?; (PS for teuh = toe': Hey, where you goin'? -- 'Eh, veea, toe' na?)

where conj. Is this the village where you were born? -- Ni chia phum dael neh kaut, roo?

whereas conj. but -- jchum'nyke eye; ree'eye: They are rich, whereas most Cambodians are poor. -- Pooh'gkay miun, ree'eye Kampuchea pieh ch'raan mom bot kraw.; in that, in view of the fact that -- kaw pun'ta'aee

whether conj. tha tau(v): I do not know whether you want to go or not. -- Kyom ot dung tha tau(v) neh jchong tueh roo ot.; whether or not -- tau(v)... roo ot: Whether or not they agree, we are going. -- Tau(v) pooh'gkay yul'prome roo ot, dael yeung teuh.

which adj. in sense of what -- na: Which car is first? -- Laan na muun?; Which books do you read? -- Miun si'po na dael neh an?; which in sense of which number -- ti pu'man: Which page? -- Tum'poa ti pu'man?; in which -- dael: the bus in which we came... -- laan bus dael duk no'um yeung mok...

which (e.g., which one) prn. moi na: Which (one) is my bed? -- Krey kyom moi na?; The question is, which ( ) to choose (i.e., take). -- Sum'noo'a keuh, moi na tro yok.

whichever (one) prn. moi na: Whichever (one) you like, choose (i.e., mark) that one. -- Sra'laanyh moi na, kooh moi nung.; whichever way you go... -- ploe moi na neh teuh....

while adv. noeh peyr dael: Let's eat while we're waiting. -- Tawh yeung nyam noeh peyr dael yeung rong jcham.; once in a while -- yeut yeut m'dong

while n. sun'too: a little while -- sun'too to'ich; I-waited for you [quite a] while. -- Kyom jcham neh [moi] sun'too [thum] howi.

whine v. la'oo ro'to'um

whip n. ruhm po'at; moa'ng

whip v. vee'aae; vwot

whirlpool n. eddy -- tuk koo'ich (lit: twisting water)

whiskey n. whiskey; sra' whiskey

whisper n. kaa k'sup; to whisper -- k'sup; k'sup k'sup

whistle n. kun'ch'eye

whistle v. plum

white adj. pwa saw

who prn. interrogatory:

neh na? (lit: what person). Who is speaking? -- Neh na ni'yaye?; Who are they?   Noh na nung?; Who is [that]? -- Neh na [nu]?; Who is this? -- Neh na ni?;

no na? ("neh na" is the term most common in urban areas, while "no na" is primarily rural, although widely heard in Phnom Penh as well): Who are they? -- Gkay chia no na?; Who are those people? -- Pooh'gkay chia no na?; Who is he? -- Gwat chia no na?; Who is [that]? -- No na [nung]?;

pi na? -- generally used as first word in short interrogatory sentences, viz.: Pi na nu? -- Who's there; Pi na mok ni? -- Who's coming? or Who's that (there)?

in relative clauses (i.e., in sense of that) -- dael: ...a person who thinks he's important... -- Neh dael kut taa gwat sum'kahn...; people who stay in this hotel -- ma'nooh dael rooh noeh o'tyle ni; Many foreigners who [come here have moustaches]. -- Chuun bor'tay ch'raan dael [mok ti ni miun pu'mwot].; the people who -- neh + [unstated]: the people [who] train them -- neh [   ] bung haht pooh'gkay

whole adj. penyh: Long ago, [Cambodian men] tattooed their whole [bodies]. -- Pi daum, [saah Khmei ma'nooh pro] saak penyh [kloo'an].; the whole day -- penyh moi tngai; te'ang mool: the whole country -- praw'tet te'ang mool; te'ang awh: the whole time -- peyr te'ang awh

wholesale adj. looh daum

whorehouse n. bun sum'pung

why? adv. hyte aae; (common APs for hyte include hat, hutt and hot; aae is often pronounced closer to eye; hence, in conversation, "hyte aae" may sound more like "hot eye"); hyte a'vaae; hyte a'veye; hyte aae: Why did I ever have to meet you? -- Hyte aae kyom keunyh neh.; hyte eye: Why did you cry? -- Hyte eye baan chia own yoom?; yang mutch (AP: mut, met); Why did that happen? -- Yang mutch baan chia ru'ung kaut laung?; yang doj ma dek; or, hyte doj ma dek: Why did that happen? -- Yang doj ma'dek baan chia kaut laung?; Why is he unhappy? -- Hyte doj ma'dek gwat mun s'bai?; mutch: Why is it that... -- Mutch baan chia...; Why are you lazy? -- Mutch baan chia neh k'chill?; bee'proo'a a'veye; 'proo a'veye: Why are you late? -- Proo'a'veye baan chia neh yeut?; mutch an'chung: You're late! Why?? -- Neh einye yeut! Mutch an'chung!

Why not? xcl. Hyte eye mun baan? Hyte a'veye kaa mun baan? Hyte eye kaw ot?

wide adj. too'lee'aae; thum

widow n. may mye

widower n. pooh mye

width n. taw'tung: width of the bridge -- taw'tung spec'un; (NB: length = praw'veng; long = veng; size = tuum huum; taw'tung can also be used to mean the shorter of two sides of a rectangle, whether that side in English would be a width or a length. The longer side would be called "bun'dow'ee", also regardless of width or length.)

wierd adj. humorous term, not seriously derogatory -- plaak plaak; serious, derogatory -- kaat(ch)

wife n. generally -- pra'pun: Do you have a wife [yet]? -- Tau(v) neh einy miun pra'pun howi [roo noeh]?; first wife -- praa'pun ti moi; or, pra'pun daum; minor wife -- pra'pun jchong; formal, or polite, term -- peh'ri'yee'a

wild adj. undomesticated, savage, dangerous -- sa'haow: wild animal -- saat sa'haow

will v. future tense marker -- nung: I will eat. -- Kyom nung ni'yam bye.; I will (go to) sleep. -- Kyom nung teuh geyng.; mok chia: I will go soon. -- Kyom mok chia teuh yang ro'has.; is going to -- nung: I'm going to see him next week. -- Kyom nung teuh choop gwat noeh a'tthit krow'ee.

will power n. chun'tehh: It takes will-power to stop smoking. -- Tro kaa miun chun tehh dum'bye chope chooo'k ba'r'eye.

win v. ch'neh: I won [the bet]. -- Kyom [p'noo'ul] ch'neh.; Who won? -- No na ch'neh?

wind n. k'shaal

wind v. to wind s. th. -- mool: wind a watch -- mool ni'a'li'ka; s. th. winding by itself -- bawt byne: the road winds [through the mountains] -- ploc bawt byne [neoh leuh phnom]

windbag n.   baan tai mwot

window n.   bung'oo'it (AP: bung-oy't(ch))

wine n.   sra' [tum'paae'ang bai'choo] (lit: [grape] liquor)

wing n.   slaa'b (AP: slob)

wink v.   ny'eh pn'aae'k; prik pn'aae'k (also means "blink")

wipe v.   choo't

wipe out v.   bot kum'chaat; bot kum'chaat awh howi: If they wipe out the enemy in that village, they will win the war. -- Baa gkay nung bawh bong sa'tro jchowl noeh phum nu, gkay nung tveu owi vit'ni'eh.; baan awh daum tuun: His [business/ property/assets] was/were wiped out [in the war]. -- Kruum'huun gwat baan awh daum tuun [kaal pi sung'kree'um].

wire n.   loosely -- k'sye; barbed wire -- k'sye loo'ah bun'la; electric wire -- k'sye pleung; telephone wire -- k'sye tel'phone

wire v.   send by wire -- vee'aae k'sye'loo'as (see, also other phrases under "telegram"); instal wiring -- dah(k) k'sye

wisdom n.   keh'tay'bun'dut

wise adj.   ch'laat; praw'ngya

wish n.   kaa bun srun; make a wish -- tveu kaa bun srun: Whenever I go to the wat, I [burn incense and] make a wish. -- Rawl peyr dael kyom teuh wat, kyom [dut toook howi] tveu kaa bun srun moi.; pawh (written: pawh(r)): Make a wish! -- Sum pawh moi!

wish v.   prat'na: I wish it were clear but it is not. -- Kyom prat'na owi baan ch'bah pun'ta'aae veea ot.

witch n.   pree'aae

with prp.   chi'moi: I will go with you. -- Kyon nung teuh chi'moi neh.; meet with s. o. -- pra'choom chi'moi gkay; jchum'poo'h: with promises alone -- jchum'poo'h kaa sun'nyaa tai m'yang; nung: connected with [construction] -- tek tong nung [som nong; or, kaa song]; [unstated]: village [with] ten rooves -- phum [ ] dab k'nong; a well [with] a hand pump -- an'do'ng [ ] sap dai

withdraw v.   dawk; toi (lit: back up: back a car up -- toi laan)

within prp.   jchum'gnai; noeh k'nong... pi jchum'nutch na moi: There are two hospitals within about a kilometers (of here). -- Miun pi munti'peyt jchum'ngai pra'heil moi ki'lo'met.

without prp.   k'miun (opp. of miun (to have, having, being, etc.)); without friends -- k'miun rop'an; dow'ee mun but(ch): I can remember without looking at the paper. -- Kyom jcham dow'ee mun but(ch) meuhl kra'dah.

witness n.   sah sye

witty adj.   pra'ngya

wobble v.   klee'ung kloung

wolf n.   sh'kye jchaw jchahk

woman n.   sraae: (NB: sraae used unmodifies, as in "Meuhl sraae nu." ("Look at that woman."), suggests woman is not known to speaker or if known, may connote some disapproval. Sraae modified connotes no disrespect and is a standard form of reference to females, viz: Khmer woman -- sraae Khmei; young woman -- sraae k'mayng; also respectful and standard forms of reference are: lok sraae; sa'trei (AP: sch'tray); nee'ree (AP: naae'ree); pooh nee'ree; and ma'nooh sraae: older woman -- ma'nooh sraae jchaah; also, sa'treye jchaah

(Khmer) Women's Association n.   Sa'ma'kuum Sa'trei Khmei

womanizer n.   prian nee'ree (lit: hunter of women)

women n.   sraae; that group of women, those women -- pooh sraae sraae nu); [Most of] the voters were women. -- [Pieh ch'raan ney] neh baw ch'nowt keuh chia sa'trei (or, nee'ree, or ma'nooh sraae).; Khmer women -- sraae Khmei

wonder v.   chng'all: wonder about s. th. -- ngu'i chng'all

wonderful adj.   la'aw na; awh jchaa; a wonderful life -- chi'vut awh jchaa; have a wonderful time -- miun peyr daw praw'sal

wood n.   generally -- cheu; wood for building s. th. -- cheu; firewood -- awhs; made of wood -- tveu pi cheu
wooden adj.   cheu

wool n.   lyne

word n.   element of grammar -- pee'a (written pee'ak); two words -- peea pi; have the last word -- miun peea jchong krow'ee; undertaking, promise -- kaa sun'nyaa; break one's word -- ot tveu taam kaa sun'nyaa; give one's word -- sun'nyaa; He gave us his word. -- Gwat dah(k) kaa sun'nyaa chin'moi yeung.; in other words -- sa'rup mao; hear by word of mouth -- loo taam kaa ni'yaye

work n.   occupation, job description or category -- mok'ngyeea: What work do you do? -- Mok'ngyeea neh a'veye?; occupation, area of responsibility -- kaa'ngyeea; physical work -- kej kaa; kej kaa tveu; tveu: What is your work? -- Tveu neh eye klaah?; work product -- kej kaa: Her work is always on time. -- Kej kaa nee'eng tyne tai tee'eng to'at.; This work must be done today. -- Kej kaa ni tro tai bun jchawp tngai ni.; kaa tveu: He can't find work. -- Gwat sveye ro'k kaa tveu ot baan.

work v.   tveu: I work in [construction]. -- Kyom tveu kang p'nyke [kaa song].; They work at the Ministry. -- Pooh'gkay tveu noeh Kra'soo'ung.; do things -- tveu kaa: She works well. -- Nee'eng tveu kaa la'aw.; work hard, strive, struggle -- sraaw ka'neea: For the country and the economy to be strong, the people must work together. -- Dum'bye praw'tet nung set'a'kej rung moam, tro kaa pra'chee'chuun sraaw ka'neea.; to work against s. th. -- sraaw ka'neea praw'chang a'veye klaah; function properly, run (for immovable likes watches, copying machines, etc.) -- dah: Does your watch work OK? -- Tau(v) nee'a'li'ka neh dah sroul tay?; function properly, run (for movables like cars, trains, etc.) -- rut; or, chheh: Does your car work OK ? -- Tau(v) laan neh rut sroul tay? or, Tau(v) laan neh chheh sroul tay?; be successful -- pra ka kaut: I don't think this plan will work. -- Kyom mun kut tha pyne'kaa ni nung pra kaa kaut. or, Kyom kut tha pyne'kaa ni pra kaa mun kaut.; not work, not function -- ot chheh: The light doesn't work. -- Pleung ot chheh.; stop working, go out -- ro'luht: The light stopped working/went out. -- Pleung ro'luht.

work on v.   tveu kaa: I will work on [changing] his mind -- Kyom nung tveu kaa [kye prye] kum'nut ro'bah gwat.; tveu kaa noeh leuh: We will work on this problem. -- Yeung nung tveu kaa noeh leuh pun'ha ni.; work on a book -- jchaawng krong s'po (lit: put together, assemble); or, saw'say s'po (lit: write a book); work on a car -- choo'ah chul laan; work on a house -- san song ptay'a; work on a report -- saw say ro'bye'kaa

work together v.   cooperate -- sraaw ka'neea

worker n.   neh tveu kaa

world n.   Earth, this Earth, the globe -- lok; or, pope'lok; or, pi'pope'lok: ... every country in the world... -- praw'tet noeh k'nong pi'pope'lok te'ang mool...; around the world -- chuum'venyh pi'pope'lok; people all over the world -- ma'nooh te'ang awh noeh k'nong pi'pope'lok; this earth, this life (only used in speech in stage-dramas or for melodramatic or humorous effect) -- lok'k'eye: Ah, this world is no good for me! -- Aiee, lok'k'eye ni a'krah nah sum'rap kyom!; spiritual world -- pope: May his soul go to a peaceful world. -- Sum owi pro'lung ro'bah gwat teuh kaan sok'a'tey pope.; milieu, arena -- kaa kang; p'nyke kang; p'nyke: She likes the world of banking. -- Nee'eng jchole jchet kaa kang banque.; the world of tennis -- p'nyke te'nnit

worried adj.   proo'i: worried about Cambodia -- proo'i om'pee Kampuchea

worry v.   proo'i

worse adj.   a'krah chiang

Worse and worse! xcl.   ko'itch laung ko'itch laung!

worth prep./n.   dum'lye: How much is it worth? -- Tau(v) veea miun dum'lye pu'man?; It's not worth it. -- Veea ot dum'lye.; Its worth it. -- Veea miun dum'lye praw'sar chiang.

worthless adj.   (S) tung'yne: worthelss person -- ma'nooh tung'yne

would like to v.   jchole jchet

wound n.   dum'bauw

wounded adj.   ro'booh

wrap v.   ruhm; wrap around -- ruhm chuum'venyh

284

wrist n. khaw dai (lit: neck of arm or hand)

wrist-watch n. ni'a'li'ka (Aps: mee'a'li'ka, mee'a'ri'ka, lee'la'ka)

write v. saw say (AP: s'day); write fiction -- tye'ng: write a novel (or other story) -- tye'ng ru'ung; write a script -- tye'ng gkun

wrong adj. ko'h: the wrong street -- ko'h ploe'; I'm wrong -- Kyom ko'h.

X

x-ray n. ray'ong-X
xenophobia n. kaa sa'op chuun bor'tay
xylophone n. raw'nee'it

X

Y

yard n. land near house -- tee'klee'a; 36-inch unit of measurement -- ya'hd Americang

yarn n. um'bawh jchak (lit: thread for knitting needle); um'bawh d'baanyh; (sewing thread = um'bawh day)

yawn v. sngaa'p

year n. chh'nam: this year -- chh'nam ni; last year - chh'nam muun; or, chh'nam teuh; next year chh'nam krow'ee; three years ago -- bye chh'nam mok howi; years and years -- chh'nam chh'nam howi; or, ro'up chh'nam howi; in years past -- k'nong a'tay'ta (lit: in the past); year after year -- chh'nam howi moi chh'nam tee'it: It happened year after year. -- Veea kaut laung chh'nam howi moi chh'nam tee'it.; What year (i.e., numerically, 1943, 1951, etc.) were you born? -- Kaut noch chh'nam na?; What year (i.e., of which animal) were you born in? -- Kaut noch chh'nam a'veye?; year of the: rat = choo't; cow = cha'lo; tiger = kal; rabbit = tawh; dragon = ro'ng; snake = m'sunn; horse = mo'mee; goat = mo'may; monkey = vo'ke; chicken = ro' ka; dog = jch'aw; pig = kaw'l: Year of the monkey -- chh'nam vo'ke

yell v. sr'eye'k: Stop yelling! -- Chope sr'eye'k teuh!

yellow adj. and n. leu'ung: a yellow coat -- aow leu'ung; I like (the color) yellow. -- Kyom jchole jchet pwa leu'ung (lit: the color yellow).; deep browish yellow, saffron -- pwa sla'tuum

yes adv. used by M. speakers -- baa(t); used by F. speakers -- chaa; slang -- eu'h ; spoken by monk -- chum rann po; to monk -- kaa'ruu'naa

yes-man n. a'ma'ya'taung; neh aiype'op

yesterday n. musl'munyh; day before yesterday -- musl'mu' ngai; yesterday morning -- pruhk musl'munyh

yet adv. howi roo noch: Have you eaten yet? -- Neh nyam bye howi roo noch?; twon: not ready yet -- ot twon howi; don't yet have -- ot twon miun; Not yet! -- Ot twon howi!; twon... noch low'ee: He is not yet ready. -- Gwat mun twon roo'it ro'al noch low'ee.; noch low'ee: not yet -- noch low'ee; not yet dead (mildily humorous response to question, How are you?) -- Mun twon slop.; aal: Don't eat yet. -- Kum aal nyam sun.

yield v. produce crops -- pdull p'auwl; give up, give way -- tveu taam; agree to s. th. wanted by another -- owi p'auwl

yogurt n. m'sang gko

yoke n. n'um

yoke v. t'um

you prn. respectful, non-familiar forms used to address people other than friends, relatives, children, etc.: addressed to a man -- lok; addressed to a woman -- lok sraae; more familiar forms: addressed to a man -- neh; addressed to a woman -- neh sraae; (NB: neh (AP: nee'ch) is written "nea(k)", and can also mean person or people) also: bo'ng and own: for usage, see "Prepositions" in List section.

young adj. k'mayng: young woman -- k'mayng sraae; young leaves -- sluk k'chey (NB: old = jchaah)); young lady -- nee'eng ken'yaa; or, neh sraae k'mayng; young man -- lo'k; or, k'mayng proh; that young man -- lok nu; or, nee'eng nu; young people -- [yoo'veh chuun] nung [yoo'veh nee'ree] (lit: [boys] and [girls]); young re animals -- gkon: young chickens -- gkon muon; young horse -- gkon seh

younger brother n. own proh

younger sister n. own sraae

youngest adj. gkon peau

your prn. ro'bah neh; ro'bah lok; ( ) neh; or, ( ) lok; your house -- ptay'a ro'bah neh; ptay'a neh; ptay'a ro'bah lok; or, ptay'a lok; your books -- s'po lok; your fault -- kum'hawh ro'bah neh

youth n. yoo'veh; yoo'veh'v'eye

Z

zero n. so'ne
zipper n. sai hoot
zombie n. k'mau'it chau(v)
zone n. dum'bun; mil zone -- dum'bun tee'hee'an
zoo n. suan saat